The Computer Animator's Technical Handbook

The Morgan Kaufmann Series in Computer Graphics and Geometric Modeling

Series Editor: Brian A. Barsky, University of California, Berkeley

The Computer Animator's Technical Handbook
Lynn Pocock and Judson Rosebush

Computer Animation: Algorithms and Techniques
Rick Parent

Advanced RenderMan: Creating CGI for Motion Pictures
Anthony A. Apodaca and Larry Gritz

Curves and Surfaces in Geometric Modeling: Theory and Algorithms
Jean Gallier

Andrew Glassner's Notebook: Recreational Computer Graphics
Andrew S. Glassner

Warping and Morphing of Graphical Objects
Jonas Gomes, Lucia Darsa, Bruno Costa, and Luis Velho

Jim Blinn's Corner: Dirty Pixels
Jim Blinn

Rendering with Radiance: The Art and Science of Lighting Visualization
Greg Ward Larson and Rob Shakespeare

Introduction to Implicit Surfaces
Edited by Jules Bloomenthal

Jim Blinn's Corner: A Trip Down the Graphics Pipeline
Jim Blinn

Interactive Curves and Surfaces: A Multimedia Tutorial on CAGD
Alyn Rockwood and Peter Chambers

Wavelets for Computer Graphics: Theory and Applications
Eric J. Stollnitz, Tony D. DeRose, and David H. Salesin

Principles of Digital Image Synthesis
Andrew S. Glassner

Radiosity & Global Illumination
François X. Sillion and Claude Puech

Knotty: A B-Spline Visualization Program
Jonathan Yen

User Interface Management Systems: Models and Algorithms
Dan R. Olsen, Jr.

Making Them Move: Mechanics, Control, and Animation of Articulated Figures
Edited by Norman I. Badler, Brian A. Barsky, and David Zeltzer

Geometric and Solid Modeling: An Introduction
Christoph M. Hoffmann

An Introduction to Splines for Use in Computer Graphics & Geometric Modeling
Richard H. Bartels, John C. Beatty, and Brian A. Barsky

The Computer Animator's Technical Handbook

Lynn Pocock
New York Institute of Technology

Judson Rosebush
The Judson Rosebush Company

MORGAN KAUFMANN PUBLISHERS

AN IMPRINT OF ACADEMIC PRESS
A Harcourt Science and Technology Company
SAN FRANCISCO SAN DIEGO NEW YORK BOSTON
LONDON SYDNEY TOKYO

Executive Editor	Diane D. Cerra
Publishing Services Manager	Scott Norton
Assistant Publishing Services Manager	Edward Wade
Assistant Editor	Belinda Breyer
Editorial Assistant	Mona Buehler
Cover Design, Interior Design, and Composition	Frances Baca Design
Technical and Editorial Illustration	Dartmouth Publishing, Inc.
Color Art Preparation	Side By Side Studios/Mark Ong
Copyeditor	Jennifer McClain
Proofreader	Ken DellaPenta
Indexer	Steve Rath
Printer	Courier Corporation

Far left and far right cover images copyright 2001 by Frank Vitale, *www.vitalef.com.* Second cover image from left courtesy of Arnold Sakowski, *www.digitalsolution.de.* Third cover image from left courtesy of Robert Kuczera, *www.3dcharacters.de.* Spine image copyright 2000, 2001 by Rockford Corp., courtesy of Frank Vitale.

Morgan Kaufmann Publishers
340 Pine Street, Sixth Floor
San Francisco, CA 94104-3205, USA
http://www.mkp.com

ACADEMIC PRESS
A Harcourt Science and Technology Company
525 B Street, Suite 1900
San Diego, CA 92101-4495, USA
http://www.academicpress.com

Academic Press
Harcourt Place, 32 Jamestown Road, London, NW1 7BY, United Kingdom
http://www.academicpress.com

Printed in the United States of America

06 05 04 03 02 5 4 3 2 1

Library of Congress Control Number: 2001092380
ISBN: 0-12-558821-6

This book is printed on acid-free paper.

A Note from the Series Editor

Brian A. Barsky, University of California, Berkeley

Computer animation has captured the public's attention in recent years with the success of such releases as *Toy Story*, the first fully computer animated feature-length film. But this endeavor did not just commence recently; rather, the techniques have been evolving over the course of several decades. Historically, one of the important films was Disney's *Tron*, which, in 1982, was the first feature film to include computer-generated shots (continuous camera recordings) that comprised completely synthetic images of a 3D world. The computer animation was produced by four now-defunct companies: Information International, Inc. (III) and Robert Abel & Associates, both of which were Los Angeles based, and the Mathematical Applications Group, Inc. (MAGI) and Digital Effects Inc., which were both located in New York. Digital Effects Inc., which existed from 1978 through 1985, is of particular interest because it was founded by Judson Rosebush, one of this book's coauthors.

Computer animation is an eclectic subject, drawing on a panoply of diverse fields such as storytelling, illustration, cinematography, photography, mathematics, design of computer algorithms and software, anatomy, kinematics, dynamics, video electronics, and so forth. Defying our age of specialization, here is a synergistic discipline that benefits greatly from the breadth of this gamut of fields.

In *The Computer Animator's Technical Handbook*, Lynn Pocock and Judson Rosebush present a comprehensive yet accessible exposition of computer animation. The hallmark of this book is its success in tackling a broad range of topics, providing significant depth in a very readable style.

"The Handbook" begins by explaining the underlying mathematics of digital images. Computer algorithms for the creation and manipulation of digital images are covered in Chapters 2 and 7. Relevant principles of photography, cinematography, and film are discussed in Chapters 4 and 5, and then analogue and digital video electronics are presented in Chapter 6.

"The Handbook" goes on to present animation methods and cel animation. Then motion, including physics-based simulations and behavioral modeling, is covered in Chapters 11, 12, and 13. Digital special effects are treated next, followed by a discussion of computer languages for animation. Finally, the production process is presented with an explanation of the concepts of storyboard, script, soundtrack, exposure sheet, animatic, motion study, pencil test, lighting, and rendering.

This book complements the other animation books in Morgan Kaufmann's Computer Graphics and Geometric Modeling Series: *Computer Animation: Algorithms and Techniques* by Rick Parent, *Advanced RenderMan: Creating CGI for Motion Pictures* by Anthony A. Apodaca and Larry Gritz, and *Making Them Move: Mechanics, Control, and Animation of Articulated Figures* by Norman I. Badler, Brian A. Barsky, and David Zeltzer. "The Handbook" differs from these books in that it relaxes the technical exigencies that are imposed on the reader by our more technical books, while still maintaining our high standards in technical accuracy and rigor. I hope that the publication of the more accessible *Computer Animator's Technical Handbook* will enable the Computer Graphics and Geometric Modeling Series to reach out to a wider audience.

Foreword

Glenn Entis, Electronic Arts

Clear understanding requires clear language. If we hope to comprehend anything, analyze it in depth, and communicate it with precision and in rich detail, then we must command a vocabulary that is equal to the task.

If you lived your entire life in the tropics, you might have a single word for snow. But if you are a native of the Artic or an avid skier, you will have dozens of words for snow—each precisely communicating something slightly different about its consistency, depth, freshness, whether anyone else has skied on it yet, and so on. You will have a rich vocabulary because you care about the details, and distinctions that might seem "subtle" to an outside observer are vitally important to you. This book is for people who want to be able to explore and express their ideas about animation with the precision and richness of a native.

When I first met Judson Rosebush in 1982, he was running a New York–based computer animation studio called Digital Effects, Inc., and I was one of three guys who had just figured out how to make images move at our new company Pacific Data Images (PDI) (we briefly toyed with calling the company "3 Guys with a VAX"). Many of the terms and ideas in this book weren't used then, either because they didn't exist yet or because they represented ideas that were beyond our reach and thus wouldn't have made any practical difference. Just as our grandparents would tell us of the "miles they walked to school," we tell our children of the "hours we took to render a few thousand polygons." But what was impossible almost 20 years ago can today be rendered in 1/30 second on a consumer videogame console, and Judson has been there from the beginning to watch the field grow up.

As an educator and artist, Lynn Pocock makes these ideas fresh, lively, and clear to wave after wave of new students. Lynn is a practicing artist with an impressive body of work. She has been both a role model to students and an inspiration to fellow artists, and she understands how the computer changes everything.

Together, this team of computer animation pioneer and educator/artist makes a great match for creating a comprehensive, readable overview of the language of the art.

This book is a valuable and important contribution that belongs on the shelf of anyone interested in animation of any kind. Hopefully this is the first of many editions, a work that will be updated regularly as the field and its language continue to grow. What is state of the art today will be quaint tomorrow, and what is invisible and unknown today will someday be the next chapter of this book.

Contents

Preface

This technical handbook on computer animation and digital media is written for technical directors, computer animators, game developers, production managers, and students in the fine arts and computer science. It is unique in that it focuses extensively on time and motion. These topics are explored in detail as they apply to animation and the creation of synthetic imagery. Issues of action are the subject here—it is assumed that the reader has a knowledge of issues related to the creation of static images. Toward this goal, the book devotes entire chapters to the vocabulary of time, to methods for easing and motion pathways, to acceleration and rates of change, and to animation languages.

This book also presents a close look at how moving picture media, including traditional film and video as well as the established and emerging digital recording technologies, represent action that occurs over time. This is of particular importance to the computer animator and the technical director because they work with time on a frame-by-frame basis and the subtle granularity of media is relevant to their work.

Finally, this book includes a rich inventory of animation techniques, both traditional as well as computational. Because we are at a unique point in history—in a transition between older traditional methods and newer computer-age techniques—both approaches are covered in this single book. Animation has always been a notational graphic science and art, but many of its best classic artists are unfamiliar with how classic production translates into a notational computer system, and conversely, many computer animators are often unfamiliar with classic techniques. This book inventories both, ranging from the cel system to key frame interpolation. It also relates elementary physics of motion and kinematics to issues of easing and motion pathways. It includes chapters on dynamic and behavioral simulation and digital special effects, as well as studio organization and production flow.

Because it focuses on the technical, this handbook is not intended as a generic book on computer graphics or, for that matter, computer animation. It consciously omits issues of aesthetics and is not a primer on how to model a virtual world or to light and render it. Nor does it explain how to tell stories, create characters, convey emotions, or change public opinion. It is not a primer on how to create character animation, design characters, imbue personality, or make characters think or be motivated. And it is not a software manual for any particular kind of animation system. Rather, this book is offered as a guide to animation and media technology, and to the physics of time and motion.

Throughout the text, old and new are woven together, since many strategies and techniques have both classic and computerized counterparts. Thus, for the most part, the organization is according to method. Since computer animation is becoming increasingly sophisticated and complex, the intent here is to be a tool guide of animation processes, techniques, and technologies that will present choices for the artists, designers, and engineers who need to express ideas as a sequence of images presented in time.

Acknowledgments

Books evolve, and this particular volume has been in the making for over ten years. Many people and institutions have aided in its development, and, at the risk of overlooking someone important, we would like to express thanks to a list of impressive people. The book began with the encouragement of Dorothy Spencer, then editor at Van Nostrand Reinhold, who helped assemble *Computer Graphics for Designers and Artists,* coauthored by Judson Rosebush and Isaac Kerlow. Many of the ideas, and some of the structure and illustration from that book, are reused in this volume. We would also like to thank everyone at Morgan Kaufmann Publishers, especially Mona Buehler, Diane Cerra, and Edward Wade, for their extraordinary efforts and patience.

One of our primary sources of information and inspiration is ACM SIGGRAPH—the Special Interest Group on Computer Graphics and Interactive Techniques. SIGGRAPH's contributors include an able, experienced, and adventuresome group of artists and scientists who cherish the craft of all things computer graphic, and relish in the sharing of enthusiasm and wisdom. Both of us have benefited from these blessings. SIGGRAPH has given us the opportunity to get hands-on tutoring on a host of issues from mentors such as Bill Kovacs, Craig Reynolds, Mark Voelpel, Bob Hoffman, Gene Miller, Pierre Jasmine and others. SIGGRAPH has also been gracious in providing funding for research in the field. Certainly special consideration goes to Tom Defanti and the crowd in Chicago, including Dan Sandin, Maxine Brown, and Dana Plepys, whose stewardship of the SIGGRAPH Video Review has included efforts at garnering filmographies of film and tapes from the 1960–1980 period (as well as right up to the present), and the construction of important chronologies. The ACM's lectureship program and the support of Hal Burgel, Lynn Shaw, and Fran Sinhart have helped draw material into focus. Special thanks are also due to Lauren Herr and the erstwhile Natalie Van Osdol, who produced a number of television programs on the state of the industry, HDTV, and virtual reality, and enabled us to stay aware of what was going on and what ideas were hot. We would also like to thank all of the ACM SIGGRAPH volunteers, Executive Committee members and Conference Chairs, especially Dino Schweitzer, John Fujii, Scott Owen, Walt Bransford, Warren Waggenspack, Jackie White, Tom Appolloni and Alyn Rockwood, for all their dedication and support of SIGGRAPH.

A goodly part of this book got its first public exposure in *The Pixel Handbook*, a sixteen page serialized center supplement to *Pixel Vision* magazine—the creation of Joel LaRoche, also the creator and publisher of *Zoom*. Joel is a man who has never let organization get in the way of a quest for quality, and provided an unparalleled artistic freedom in bringing "The Handbook" to life.

In more recent years a collaboration with Steve Cunningham produced the book *Electronic Publishing on CD-ROM* and provided another source for this material. Steve is by now an old SIGGRAPH hand and the fact that he and many of the other elite of the community still make us welcome is a relief in and of itself, and an encouragement.

The academic community has been supportive of our art and scholarship. We would like to thank New York Institute of Technology, Edward Guiliano, Robert Vogt, Peter Voci, Jane Grundy,

Robert Michael Smith, Daniel Durning, Michael Rees, Pratt Institute, Rick Barry, Don Ritter, Dena Slothower, Peter Mackey, Michael O'Rourke, Tim Binkley, Bruce Wands, Karen Sullivan, Scott Lang, Frank Marchese, Jean Coppola, Terry Blum, Jeff Handler, Trilby Schreiber, Debbie Deas, Maureen Nappi, Sonya Shannon, and many others colleagues. So too are a long list of professionals. Much of what is in this book comes from oral tradition. Stanley Beck, Moses Weitzman, Janos Pilenyi, Balazs Nyari, Dick Rauh, Dick Swanek, Eugene Mamut, John Alagna, Richard Taylor, and many others comprise a quiet sharing of techniques and trade secrets. Our mentors have also played a key role; Clark Dodsworth, Copper Giloth, Ray Lauzzana, Robert Mallary, Stan Vanderbeek, Ken Knowlton, Carl Machover, and John Roy have guided and inspired us.

Over the years we have also learned from our competitors, employees, students, and people younger than ourselves. We have vetted questions with Steve Rutt, Dean Winkler, Mike Sas, Eric Person, Don Leach, Jan Prins, Bill Lewis, Christine Shostack, Caleb Weissberg, Joe Pasquali, Sandy Streim, Harold Friedman, Gail Goldstein, Alan Green, Matt Schlanger, Frank Kubin, Wendy Arnone, Richard Sanders, Michael Smethurst, Amy Morawa, Dean and Kathy Hammond, Gwen Sylvan, and many others.

The many line illustrations in this book were inspired by a small army of illustrators who have contributed ideas, goodwill, and care, and who have shepherded these drawings through multiple incarnations. This group includes Matt Alexander, Sherwood Anderson, Helen Bayona, Luis A. Camargo, William Costello, David Anderson Deane, Suzanne Dimant, Brenda Garcia, David Hicock, Andrew Holdun, Suk-Il Hong, Pierre Jasmine, Isaac Victor Kerlow, Kathy Konkle, Khalida Lockheed, Wei-Yi Lin, Felipe Morales, Joanna Morrison, Dick Rauh, Dena Slothower, Raymond Stivala, Gwen Sylvan, and Lina Yamaguchi. Most of the color art is appropriated and its creators have graciously given us permission to reproduce it here. That impressive list of credits can be found elsewhere in the book.

Finally, a word of love and affection to those close to us who suffer neglect and rejection when we turn our attention to writing books instead of their needs, wants, and desires. We thank our parents, families, and closest friends for their love and affection and for always being there.

Introduction

Animation has existed for well over 100 years and was invented before the live action camera. Early animators bypassed the recording process, either by drawing each image by hand directly onto the viewing medium or by synthesizing the image via a formal procedure (see Figure I.1). While the techniques have changed and evolved over time, animation remains a viable expressive and narrative tool because it allows the mind of the creator to connect directly to the medium, and thus visualize beyond the domain of the real world and into the realm of dreams, imagination, trips, fantasy, caricature, and vast changes of scale and rates of time. As such, animation is a way to give visual form to time-based ideas, and conversely, it is a tool of analysis, a way to study variance or change (see Figure I.2).

Given the wide range of venues in which we find animation today—cinema, video games, CD-ROMS, the Internet, and electronic signs, to name a few—it makes sense to limit the topic and decide, at the onset, just what is animation. In the broad sense, all life is animation. But this, of course, does not help to narrow the definition. The Latin and Greek root words are equally open-ended. *Animare*, the Latin root, means "to give life to," and is closely related to the Greek *anemos*, which means "the wind," or "that which we breathe." Meanings such as these help to define the term, but in practice the animation that we are able to fabricate is much more constrained than in nature.

Perhaps our most global constraint is that animation involves a medium—an information carrier with some data and rule definitions. This context narrows our scope and focus. Animation involves time and it employs graphics. Animation is the result of the construction, recording, and sequential display of graphic images that change over time. Typically, these images are synthetic, either drawn by hand or calculated by a machine, but they may also be images derived from life that are manipulated on a frame-by-frame basis. Animation is a graphic art that involves a 2D field of view, but it is especially a temporal art because it involves time, the fourth dimension. In a practical

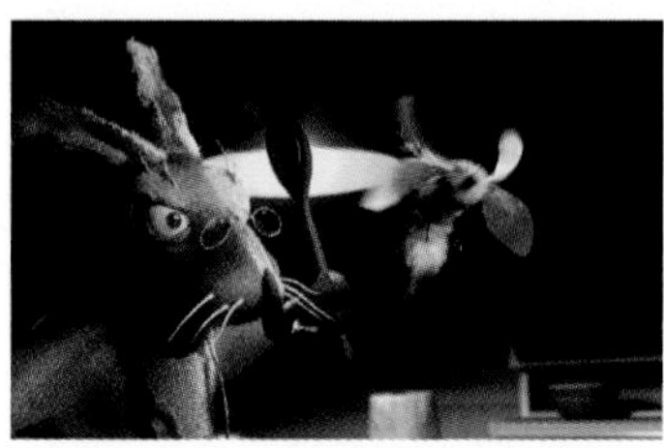

Above: From *Bunny*, a short animated film by Chris Wedge.

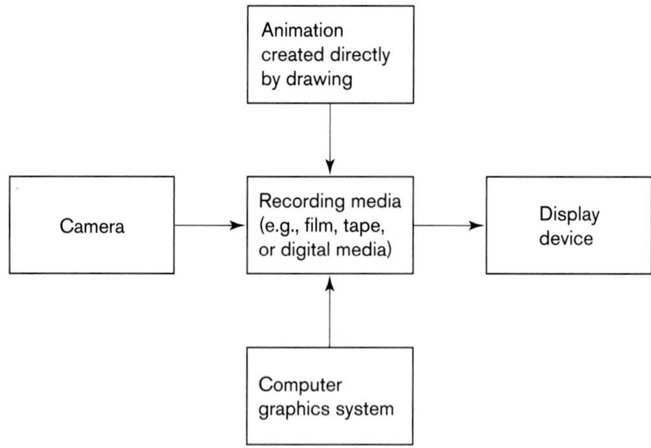

Figure I.1 Right: Animation can short-circuit the moving picture creation process because it allows images to be fabricated without a camera. One can draw on film, use a computer to fabricate the image, or draw on paper and scan the artwork.

(a)

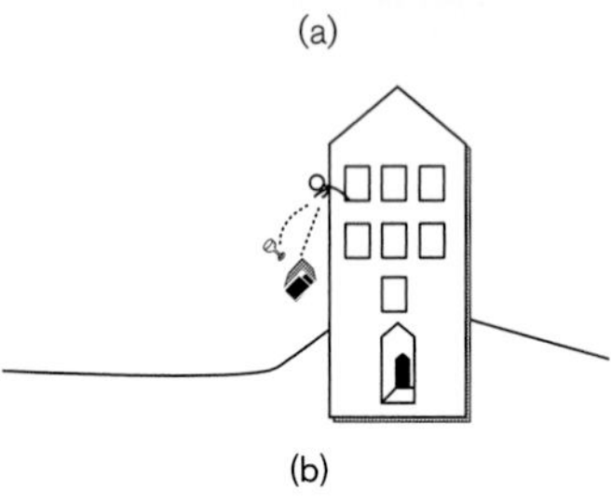

(b)

Figure I.2 Above: Animation can be used to give visual form to time-based ideas such as stories; conversely it can also be used as a tool for analysis. Animation is valuable to computer graphics because it is a way to add variance to an otherwise static picture (a). On the other hand, it enables situations that contain variance to be visualized so we may better perceive and understand our world (b). Do objects gain speed when they fall? Do heavier objects fall faster?

sense, animation is the manipulation of parameters over time, the evaluation of the parameters at a sequence of instants in time, and the recording of the results as a sequence of visual, graphic images. Inversely stated, animation is a sequence of pictures in which one or more parameters are changed over a sequence of frames. These parameters might be a lip position of a cartoon character or the position of a planet in orbit (see Figure I.3).

It is worth noting that moving picture media do not inherently record 3D information. Animation, especially computer animation, may allude to the third dimension—indeed, the ability to realistically represent 3D environments is one of the breakthroughs of this new tool, and in some respects it relates closely to live action cinema. However, as with live action, it is always the case that the third dimension is squeezed out of existence and reduced to a flat 2D pictorial representation. But note that unlike volume and depth, time has the capability of being recorded and played back at a scale identical to the original.

While it is relatively straightforward to define in words what is or is not animation, moving imagery has become increasingly difficult to classify. For example, moving images recorded from real life in real time are clearly not animation. However, if the same moving imagery were recorded with a stop-motion camera and then played back at a standard speed, would the result be animation? And what if special effects or compositing were introduced to the scene? What about video games such as Doom, where a player can freely navigate a synthetic 3D world—are they animation? Clearly, there are

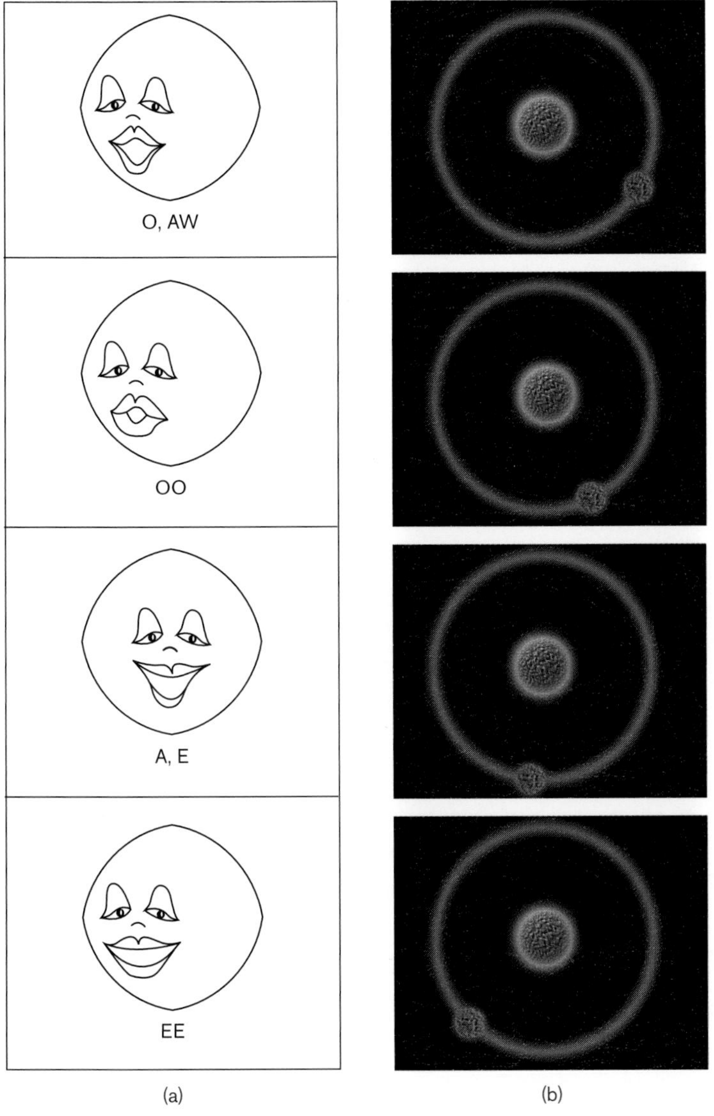

Figure I.3 Animation is the result of a sequence of pictures in which one or more parameters change in each frame. These parameters might be a lip position of a cartoon character or the position of a planet in orbit. Note that animation parameters can be hand drawn or computed. In (a), a finite set of discrete lip positions, which correspond to basic sounds, cut from one to another in sequence, whereas in (b), the position of a planet around a star is computed at a moment in time according to laws of physics and displayed, quite a different approach.

blurry areas where the results become difficult to classify; hence, defining animation in a practical sense is not a simple task.

So just how is an animation created? All animation, even classic cel animation, has an intrinsically computational aspect; illusions of change and motion are either "calculated" by hand, as with classic cel animation, or calculated by computer, as with computer animation. With all animation methods, the animator is a craftsperson whose building blocks are frames. In this regard, an animator shares an

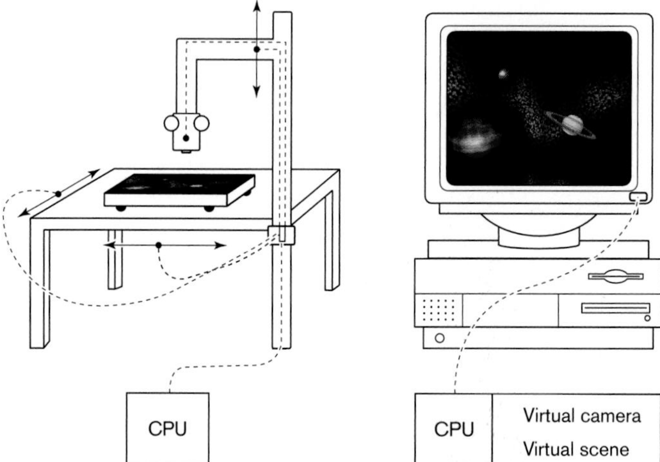

Figure I.4 Two approaches to computer animation are shown here. To the left, a computer is used to manipulate (control) a real-world camera and objects, such as 2D artwork and 3D props. To the right, the computer is also used for these manipulations, but the camera and objects themselves are stored in the computer and do not reside in the real world.

affinity with the editor or the compositor, but unlike either, the animator literally crafts and builds shots. The animator is charged with the task of forging synthetic images, either with pencil and paper or mouse and monitor, and then sequencing them to be viewed over time.

And what role does the computer play in the production process? With respect to film or television, computer animation loosely embodies a range of applications where computers are employed in the generation and manipulation of moving pictures. These include motion graphics, motion control, video synthesizers, image processing, computer-assisted cartoon animation, paint systems, special effects, 3D image synthesis simulation, and robotics. In some of these applications, computers are used to control cameras, which take pictures; in other applications, computers are used to create the pictures themselves (see Figure I.4). However it is used, the computer assists the animator in the computational aspects inherent in the animation process.

1 Digital Pictures

This chapter presents a quick and basic overview of computer graphics. The topics touched upon include an inventory of fundamental 2D graphics such as points and pixels; 3D computer graphics that include models, lights, and cameras; as well as methods to render a scene. A limited amount of information is presented on various techniques of modeling, lighting, and representation. Because the intent of this book is to focus almost entirely on issues of motion, the material in this chapter is presented in a fundamental way, and it is not our intent to explore these issues in depth, since much literature already exists. See the Further Reading section at the end of this book. Some readers, especially those with extensive experience in computer graphics, will find this chapter unnecessary. However, for the sake of completeness, the material is presented here in a compact form.

Progression of Dimensions and Coordinate Systems

Spatial dimensions must be understood before a 2D image can be made or a 3D model can be constructed. Spatial dimensions progress from the most primitive element, the *point*, a dimensionless or 0D entity. A point extended in one direction becomes a 1D entity, a *line*. A line extended along a second axis forms a 2D surface, a *plane*. A plane extended along an axis (other than the one that the plane lies on) forms a *volume*, which has three dimensions. A volume extended along another axis, for example the time axis, forms

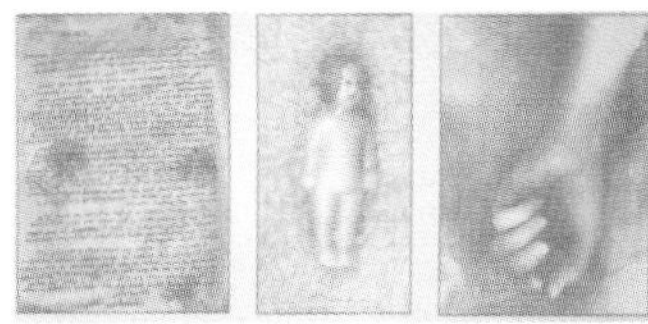

Above: *Pages from a Diary: Leaving.*

Figure 1.1 Right: The progression of dimensions. A point extended becomes a line, a plane, a volume, and space-time.

Graphical depiction					
Name	Point	Line	Plane	Volume	Space-time
Number of dimensions	0D	1D	2D	3D	4D
Discrete quantum unit	None	Unit vector	Pixel	Voxel	Timel
Continuous entity name	Point	Line	Polygon	Polyhedron	Hyperobject
Axis symbol	None	*x*	*y*	*z*	*t*

space-time, a 4D ***hyperobject***. A volume can be represented by the commonly used *x, y,* and *z* spatial coordinates (see Figure 1.1).

The model for the working area in 2D computer graphics is the ***Cartesian coordinate system***. Cartesian coordinates represent a 2D plane (such as a piece of paper) with two mutually perpendicular axes. The ***origin*** is the point at which the axes cross and has a value of 0; each axis may extend in both directions with positive and negative numbers (see Figure 1.2). The horizontal axis is called the ***x-axis***, and the vertical axis is called the ***y-axis***. The axes divide the plane into four ***quadrants***, often numbered in a counterclockwise direction. Points on the plane can be identified by an *x* and *y* coordinate pair, for example, (5.0, 4.0).

A ***3D coordinate system*** is represented by three mutually perpendicular axes intersecting at the origin. The axis that projects into the third dimension is labeled the ***z-axis***. Because paper only has two dimensions, it is not possible to actually draw the *z*-axis. Hence, it is drawn at an oblique angle as if it were projected onto the plane (see Figure 1.3). The axes have scales, and a location in 3D space is defined by an *xyz* triplet of coordinates. In the figure, the positive *x*-axis points right, the *y*-axis up, and the *z*-axis toward the viewer. It is also possible to have a coordinate system in which the positive *z*-axis points away from the viewer, the positive *x*-axis points left, or the positive *y*-axis points down. Indeed, it is possible to configure eight different axis orientations (see Figure 1.4). It is imperative to know the orientation of a coordinate system in order to navigate it successfully.

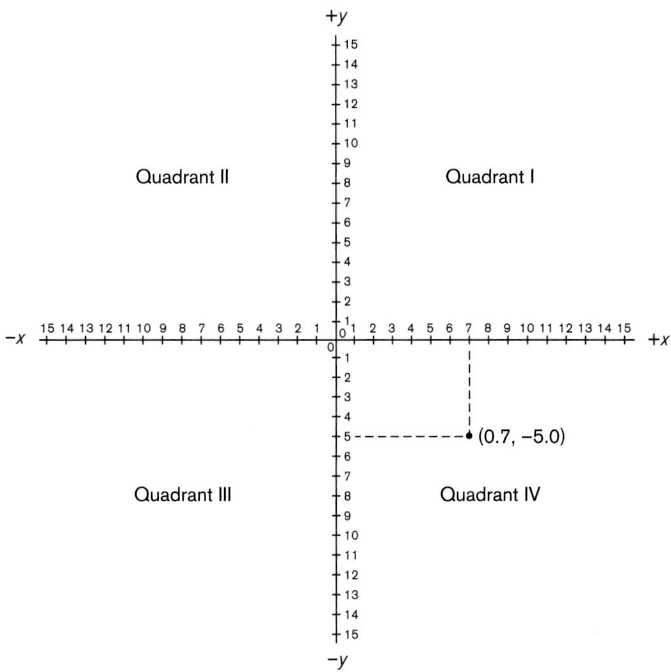

Figure 1.2 Left: Two-dimensional Cartesian coordinate system. The *x* and *y* axes are at right angles to each other and intersect at the origin, twice bisecting the plane, into four quadrants. Scales may extend in both the positive and negative directions.

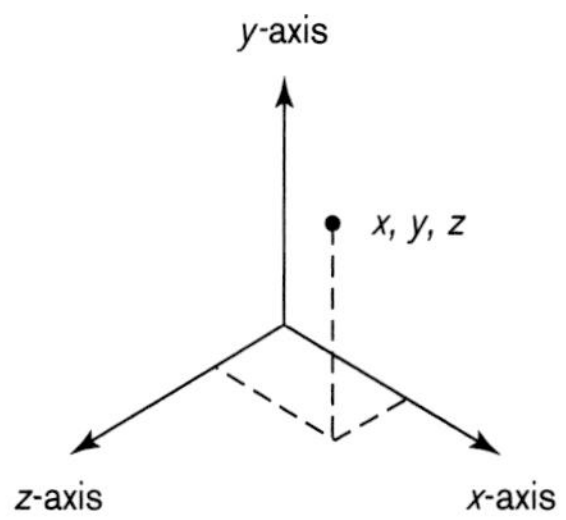

Figure 1.3 Above: A 3D Cartesian coordinate system, with *x*, *y*, and *z* axes that lie at right angles to each other and intersect at the origin. The axes may have positive and negative values and divide the volume up into eight sectors of space. A location in 3D space is defined by three numbers, *x*, *y*, and *z*. The *x* value is the distance of the point from the *zy* plane. The *y* value is the distance of the point from the *xz* plane. And the *z* value is the distance of the point from the *xy* plane.

It is worth noting that there are coordinate systems other than the Cartesian coordinate system. *Triangular coordinate systems*, in which three axes meet at a 60-degree angle (see Figure 1.5), are sometimes used for plotting functions of three variables, including perspective drawings.

Polar coordinates define 2D areas with an origin, or *pole*, at the center, and a single axis, called the *polar axis*. In Figure 1.6, the polar axis lies pointing to the right, or east, and the angular distances increase in a counterclockwise direction. This is common in most geometry but again, note that the polar axis can be located at any angle, and that angular distances may instead increase in a clockwise direction. Locations, that is point coordinates, are specified in terms of the magnitude (or radius distance) from the pole, and the angle between the polar axis and the point. Polar coordinates are often used in navigation and are relative to the navigator, located in the center.

Spherical coordinates are the corresponding 3D analogy to polar coordinates and specify a point either in terms of two magnitudes and one angle, or one magnitude and two angles (see Figure 1.7). If all the points lie on the same radius, then only the two angles are necessary, for example, when describing a location on the surface of

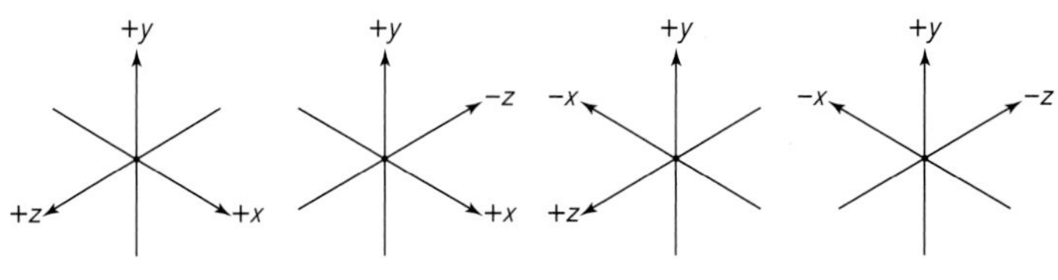

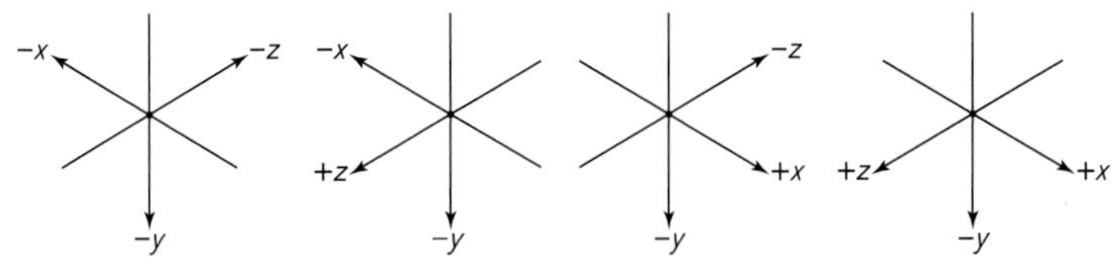

Figure 1.4 Right: There are eight different ways to orient the axes of a 3D Cartesian coordinate system. It is imperative to know which orientation is being used in order to navigate successfully.

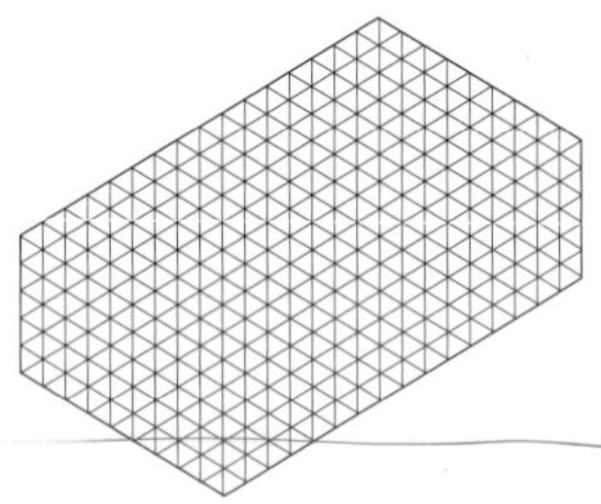

Figure 1.5 Above: Triangular coordinate system.

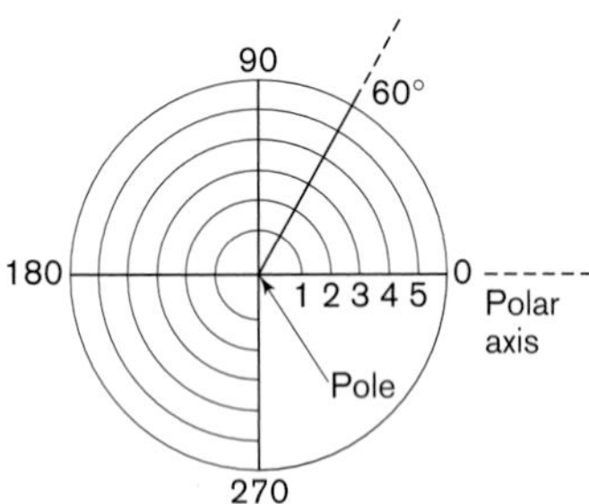

Figure 1.6 Above: Polar coordinates consist of two values: an angle and a radius. The angle is measured from the polar axis in either a clockwise or counterclockwise direction. Here the polar axis points right (east) and angles increment counterclockwise. The location of the point has an angle of 60 degrees and a radius of five units.

the Earth. As with polar coordinates, it is necessary to establish a center origin and two orthogonal reference planes. On Earth, these are usually the equator (0 degrees latitude) and the plane that intersects Greenwich, England (0 degrees longitude). Latitudes are measured north and south of the equator, reaching 90 degrees at the poles, and longitudes are measured east and west from Greenwich. In the figure, the coordinate is located at a 45-degree angle around the vertical y-axis, 65 degrees around the z-axis, and has a radius magnitude of 0.7 (assuming the radius of the sphere is 1).

Spherical coordinates are often preferred over 3D Cartesian coordinates when one wants to describe a location from the standpoint of an observer. One variation, called ***altazimuth coordinates***, provides a way to specify the location of objects relative to a viewer or camera. Altazimuth coordinates are used in surveying to measure the position and elevation of objects at a distance, and in astronomy to measure the location of a star in the sky. As a way of explaining altazimuth coordinates, consider the stars. Because the distance to a star is effectively infinity, all stars may be assumed to lie on a celestial sphere, and the ***horizon*** forms a 360-degree circle that bisects the celestial sphere. Thus, the location of a star may be defined in terms of only two angles—the altitude and the azimuth (see Figure 1.8). The ***altitude***, also known as ***elevation***, is the angle formed by the plane of the horizon with the star or reference object. A star on the horizon has an altitude of zero degrees, and a point directly overhead—called the ***zenith***—has an altitude of 90 degrees. The ***azimuth*** is the angle around the circle of the horizon. The origin (0 degrees) of the azimuth scale is a circle that passes through the zenith and the North Star—in simple terms, the origin of the scale is north. The scale increases in a clockwise direction. The azimuth is the angle from north to the circle that passes through the zenith and the star or reference object. When the angle of the azimuth is thought of as a direction of travel, it is usually referred to as a *bearing.*

Digital Images

There are a variety of ways to represent digital images. Computer graphics employs either integer or floating-point numbers, depending on whether the data being represented is discrete or continuous. *Discrete data* is data that occurs in discrete units. Individuals, playing cards, and letters of the alphabet must all be represented by discrete data, as they cannot be divided and still retain their identity. Data is said to be *continuous* if the axis or dimension along which it is being measured has no apparent indivisible unit from which it is composed. Examples abound in the space-time-matter environment and include properties such as weight, length, and temperature; no matter how precise the scale of measurement, a finer resolution always exists.

The continuous/discrete dichotomy applies to graphics as well as to Cartesian space. Both incorporate an origin, axes, and equal-interval scales. If the Cartesian space is floating point and continuous, then a location is expressed as a decimal number and called a *point.* If the Cartesian space is discrete, a location is expressed using a pair of integers and is called a *pixel* and is indivisible.

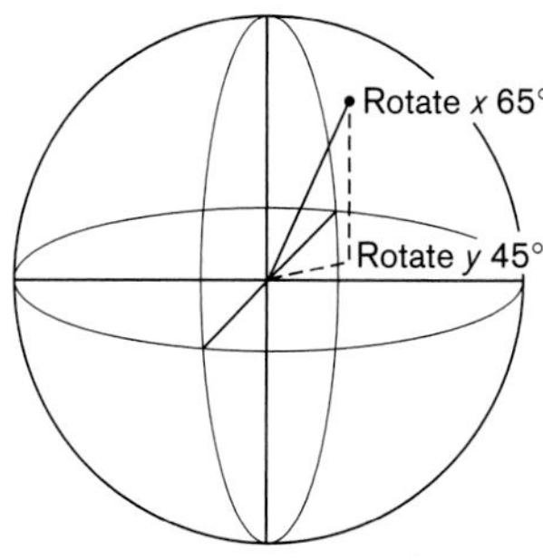

Figure 1.7 Above: The spherical coordinates of the point relocated at an angle of 45 degrees around the vertical axis, 65 degrees around the *z*-axis, with a radius of 7⁄10.

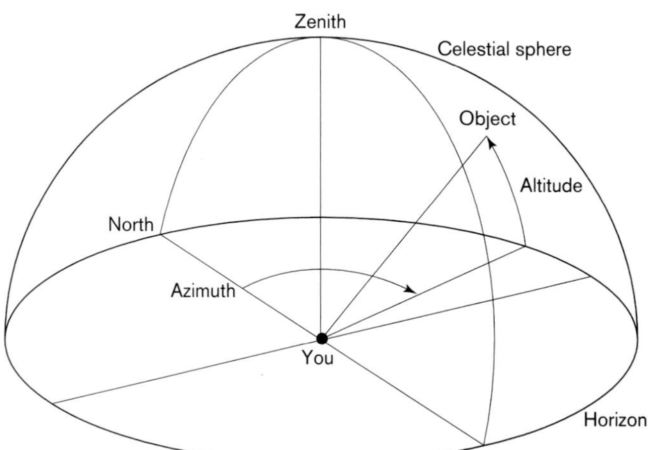

Figure 1.8 Below: Altazimuth coordinates consist of three values: the azimuth angle around the horizon, the altitude angle above the horizon, and the distance to the object (the radius of the sphere the object lies on). The zenith is a point directly overhead and has an altitude of 90 degrees. The measurement of the azimuth is accomplished with the aid of a compass; the measurement of the altitude is accomplished with the aid of a sextant.

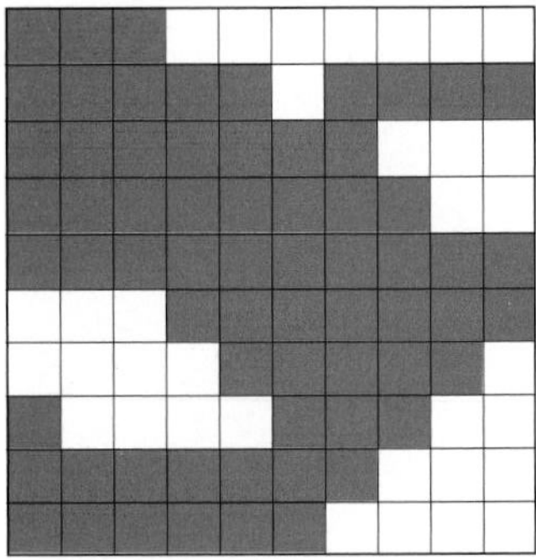

1	1	1	0	0	0	0	0	0	0
1	1	1	1	1	0	1	1	1	1
1	1	1	1	1	1	1	0	0	0
1	1	1	1	1	1	1	1	0	0
1	1	1	1	1	1	1	1	1	1
0	0	0	1	1	1	1	1	1	1
0	0	0	0	1	1	1	1	1	0
1	0	0	0	0	1	1	1	0	0
1	1	1	1	1	1	1	0	0	0
1	1	1	1	1	1	0	0	0	0

Figure 1.9 Above: An enlarged section of a digitized image shows the grid of pixels (top) with its corresponding numeric values (bottom). An individual pixel is the quantum unit of an image.

Figure 1.10 Below: A slope. The figure shows the cross section of a river valley. The slope of the valley ranges from being very flat near the river to very steep farther away from the river. The slope may be expressed as a scalar number from zero to infinity. Flat regions have a slope of zero. Cliffs have a very large slope. The slope of the line formed between any two points in the valley is equal to their difference in height divided by their difference in horizontal position.

Pixels: 2D Discrete Images

A *pixel* is the basic quantum unit of an image (see Figure 1.9). Pixels are discrete, modular units organized in a rectangular matrix, akin to a piece of graph paper. Each pixel corresponds to one square on the graph paper and is addressed with an integer *x* and *y* value. The value of each pixel in an image represents the color, or *intensity,* of the corresponding image area. The entire matrix of pixels is called a *bitmap*. The *spatial* resolution of a bitmap is the number of pixels used to represent the image from top to bottom and from right to left. The *aspect ratio* of a bitmap image is equal to the number of horizontal pixels divided by the number of vertical pixels.

A simple bitmap, or *bitplane,* is only one bit deep and stores either a 0 or a 1 in each pixel location, which can represent any two colors. The number of bits per pixel—that is, the number of bitplanes in the bitmap—is the *intensity resolution,* or *color resolution*; the number of possible intensities is equal to two raised to the power of the number of bitplanes. For example, if there are eight bits per pixel, then the number of possible intensities is 256.

Points, Lines, Planes: 2D Continuous Graphics

The differences between points and pixels stem from their continuous and discrete origins. Whereas a pixel represents an area, a point represents a location in Cartesian space.

On a plane, a point has two addresses, *x* and *y*. Two points are used to define a straight line, also called a *vector*. The orientation of a line on a plane is called the *slope* and is determined by the change in *y* divided by the change in *x* (see Figure 1.10): $(y_2 - y_1) / (x_2 - x_1)$. A horizontal line has a slope of 0; a line at an angle of 45 degrees

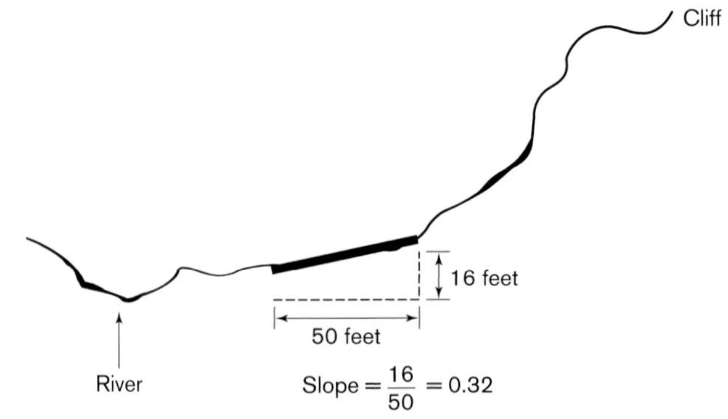

has a slope of 1; a vertical line has a slope of infinity. A complex line can be described with several points (see Figure 1.11). A *polygon* is a closed shape formed by lines. The shape may be simple—a square or the representation of a circle—or more complicated, such as the letter S or the contour of a country (see Figure 1.12). The simplest polygon is made with three points—a triangle—but the number of sides that a polygon can have is unlimited. The points of a polygon are called *vertices*, and the sides are called *edges*.

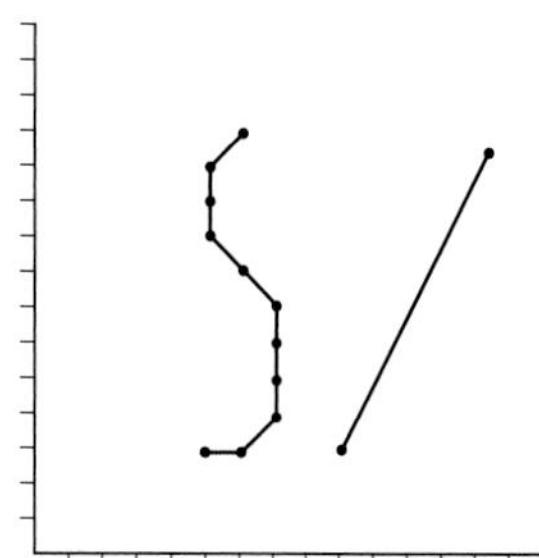

Figure 1.11 Above: A vector is defined by two points. Many short vectors are needed to make smooth curves. The individual points, or vertices, that make up an object are often listed in sequence, with the assumption that a connecting line will be drawn between them. The list for the line is 9, 3; 13, 12, and for the curve, 5, 3; 6, 8; 5, 9; 5, 10; 5, 11; 6, 12.

Voxels: 3D Discrete Volumes

Three-dimensional graphics can employ both discrete and continuous methods. The 3D analogy of a pixel is a *voxel*, a discrete quantum unit of volume in a 3D lattice of space (see Figure 1.13). Voxels do not represent a square area or a grid of reflected light values; rather, they represent a matrix of volumes. For example, a matrix of voxels is 3D and represents the pressure or densities of matter that occupy space. Objects may be constructed of voxels by specifying whether or not the object occupies the volume at a particular location.

Figure 1.12 Above: Polygons are closed shapes defined by lines.

Voxels can be digitized using density scanners, such as a computerized axial tomography (CAT) scan. The scan is made as a series of discrete sections or contours, and although individual CAT scan sections might look like images, their source is not reflected light values but tissue densities (see Figure 1.14).

A *sampling probe* is a virtual tool used to reach into a 3D interior (see Figure 1.15). It is used primarily with voxel data, when one would

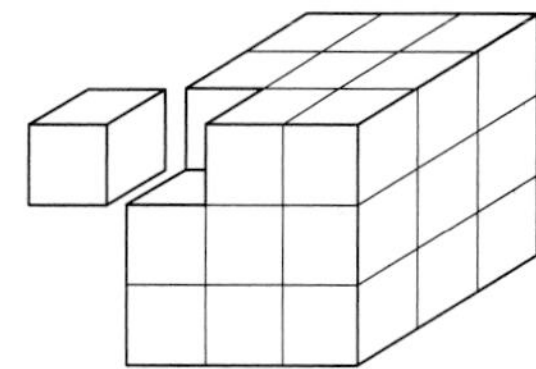

Figure 1.13 Above: Voxels are discrete quantum units of volume.

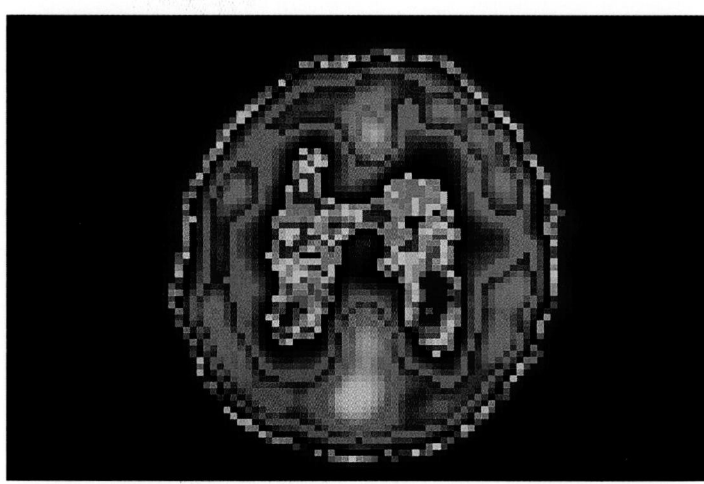

Figure 1.14 Left: A CAT scan cross section of the brain. The picture is pseudocolored so that different densities become different colors. It thus looks photographic, though it is not.

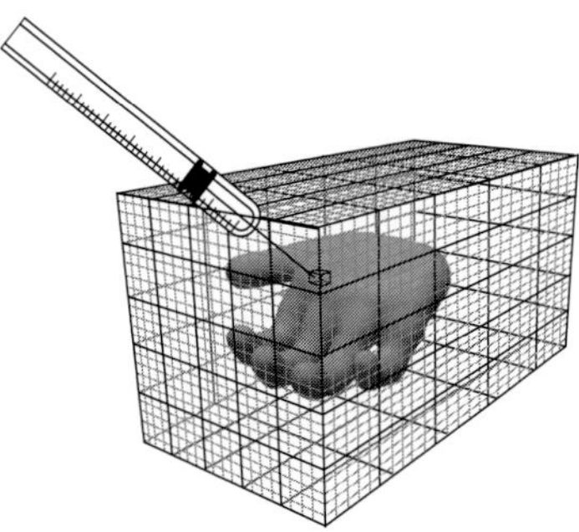

Figure 1.15 Above: Sampling probe. The user manipulates the end of the virtual measuring tool in order to access the value of a voxel within the shape.

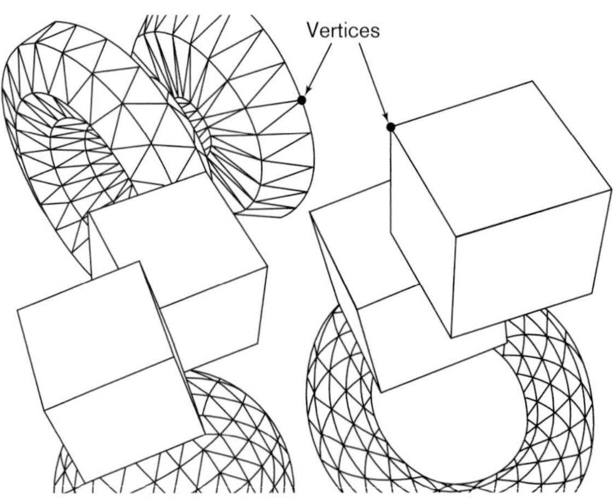

Figure 1.16 Right: Vertices are the corners where the sides of 3D objects meet. In computer graphics, vertices are used to define objects.

like to see the value, or property, of a piece of data that lies within a voxel array, but it can also be used with traditional 3D data, for which it might return data about the object touched. As such, a sampling probe is not a data manipulation tool, but rather, a data analysis tool.

Polyhedra: 3D Continuous Solids

A point in three dimensions is still called a point. Points, lines, planes, and polygons can all exist in 3D space. Three-dimensional space can also contain *polyhedra*—volumetric solid objects such as a cube, a faceted sphere, or a ship (see Figure 1.16). As in polygons, the points in a polyhedra are called vertices, they have edges, and each face of the polyhedra is called a *facet*. The simplest polyhedron, composed of four sides, is called a *tetrahedron*.

A point, line, or polygon in 3D space has three spatial coordinates, and it is important to note that the points of a polygon must lie flat on a 2D plane, even when they reside in 3D space. If they do not, then the "polygon" is called a *non-planar polygon*, and its presence will violate the rules for many 3D rendering programs, creating flaws. The 3D analogy to the slope is the *normal*, which is the orientation of a surface—that is, the direction in which the surface is facing. A normal is specified by three numbers that indicate a line drawn perpendicular from the face of the surface (see Figure 1.17). Note that all locations on a plane have the same normal. A normal is not a coordinate or a position but a direction, or orientation, and it is used especially in lighting calculations.

Three-dimensional solid objects are defined several ways in a computer. Polyhedra may be constructed as surfaces, where a network of polygons describe an object, such as a sphere constructed as a mesh of polygons. Solid objects may also be mathematically defined, so that the surface of the object is defined by a mathematical equation and not as a series of facets. This is especially useful in constructing curved objects that must be scaled orders of magnitude. In this book, the term ***solid models*** refers to 3D solid objects in general, regardless of how they are constructed.

Conversions and Hybrid Forms

A graphic cross-reference table (see Figure 1.18) summarizes the 2D/3D and discrete/continuous distinctions discussed thus far. In practice the distinctions are not always clear-cut and hybrid forms can also be used. Conversions between the different representations are all possible, although the results are often unsatisfactory. For example, a point can be approximated by a pixel, and a pixel by a point. A line can be approximated by a collection of pixels, and a collection of pixels can be converted into a line. Polygons can be approximated by areas of pixels, and areas of pixels can be converted to polygon outlines. Three-dimensional objects can be approximated two-dimensionally, but 2D images may not necessarily be interpreted three-dimensionally.

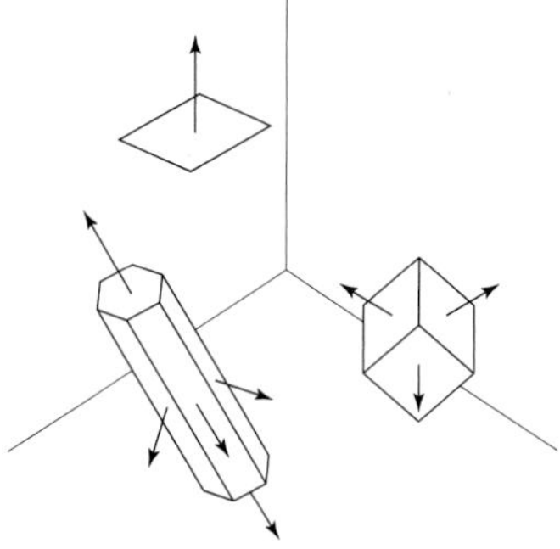

Figure 1.17 Above: Normals indicate how a polygon is angled in space and can be thought of as rays perpendicular to the surface.

Fundamental Curve Tools

Smooth curves are used to make many things; thus there are several good ways to create them. B-splines, NURBS, and Bezier curves are the three most common curves, and they can be created quickly and simply.

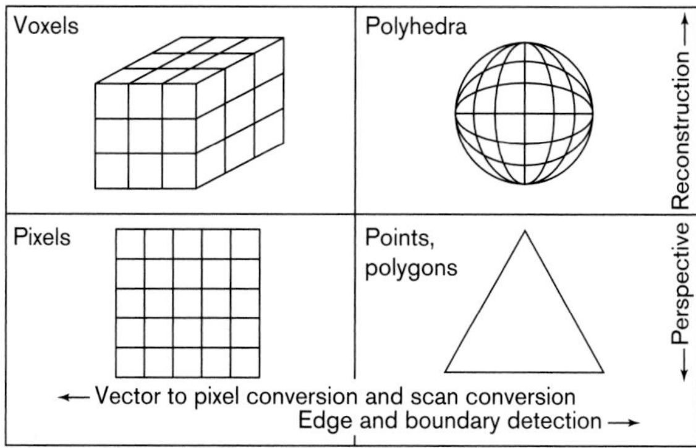

Figure 1.18 Below: Cross-reference table of 2D/3D and discrete/continuous. *Rasterization* is a technique that converts lines to pixels. Techniques that convert contours of pixels into lines are *edge detectors.* Procedures that convert polygon representations into pixel area representations are *scan conversions.* And techniques that identify areas of pixels that have a uniform value and convert them to polygons are *boundary detectors.*

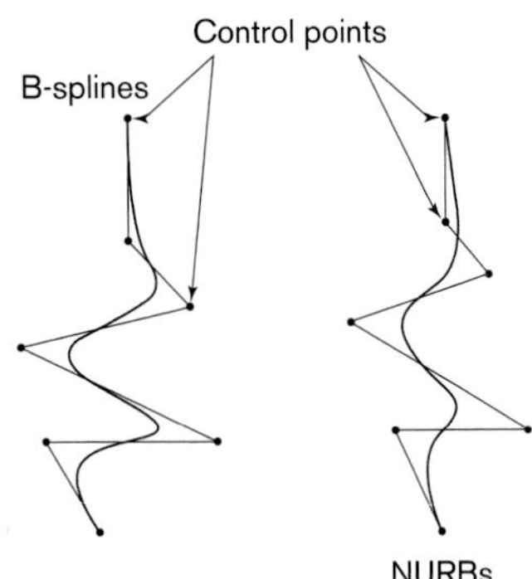

Figure 1.19 Above: B-splines are smooth curves defined by a series of equations, each of which represents a curve. A NURB is a type of B-spline but can be used to create curves of greater complexity. When using them to create models, it is often the case that fewer restrictions are placed on NURB models as compared to standard B-spline models.

B-Spline Curves *B-splines* are smooth curves that are geometrically defined by control points and whose curves are defined by a series of equations, so that they are smooth along their entire length (see Figure 1.19). Only certain types of equations may be used to define B-splines. In particular, equations must match precisely at the joint points if they are to be used to create smooth curves; in fact, the two equations must both be defined at a joint so that their locations and their slopes (or tangents) are equal. For the mathematically inclined, an additional requirement is second derivative continuity—that is, continuous rate of curvature.

In practice, B-splines are defined by control points; a B-spline passes through its end control points, but does not pass through its interior control points. The control points for B-splines are usually placed with the use of interactive software and are very simple to use. Control points are easily moved if need be.

B-splines can be used to produce many things, including the curved edge of an object, or the pathway of a moving object, including a camera. The movement of the camera through space is an integral part of storytelling, and the spline can be a sophisticated way of achieving this motion. When splines are used to produce pathways, the pathways can be used to produce camera motions that are extremely elegant. A B-spline or a collection of B-splines can be used to define surfaces.

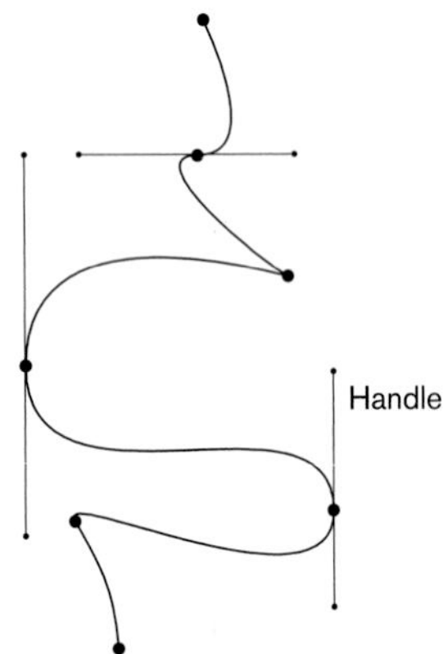

Figure 1.20 Above: A Bezier curve is defined by a series of control points; a best-fit curve is drawn through all of the control points, including the endpoints.

NURB Curves One of the most useful curves is a variation of the B-spline called a ***non-uniform rational B-spline*** (NURB). NURBs can be used to create complex curves that include creases and corners. As with B-splines, NURBs can be used to create surfaces. One of the advantages of using NURBs is that they often allow for greater flexibility when creating surfaces, depending on the software being used.

Bezier Curves A Bezier curve is also defined by a series of equations, each of which represents a curve, and is created by placing a series of control points with the use of software. By manipulating the placement of the control points, the curve can be modified. The computer draws a best-fit curve through all of the control points, including the endpoints (see Figure 1.20).

Bezier curves are widely available in graphics programs because they are easy to use to define curves. However, it is worth noting that while Bezier curves have first derivative continuity at the points, they do not have second derivative continuity at those points. Hence, Bezier curves can produce curves that have kinks at the joints.

2D Computer Imaging

Two-dimensional computer imaging systems have become increasingly important in the animation process. Images used to create animation, even 3D animation, often involve a 2D imaging system. For example, to animate a moving reflection in a window in 3D space, a 2D texture map might be applied to the window and moved to create the motion. Animated texture maps, image maps, glow maps, and reflection maps can all begin in a 2D imaging system.

Two-dimensional imaging systems allow color mixing, freehand drawing, and sizing and positioning of shapes. Many include font display and image digitizing capabilities. In general, there are two primary approaches to 2D imaging: polygon-based imaging, also known as *vector graphics*, and pixel-based imaging, also known as *pixel graphics, bitmap graphics,* and (not entirely correctly) *raster graphics.*

Vector Graphics

The term *vector graphics* has come to mean computer graphics defined by lines; it applies to both 2D and 3D graphics. Vector graphics consist of polygons and are represented inside the computer as a list of mathematical data called a *display list.* An example of the data is (0.5, 0.1) (-0.1, 0.2), which would represent a line segment with endpoints at (0.5, 0.1) and (-0.1, 0.2) (see Figure 1.21). The advantage of vector graphics is that because shapes are described mathematically, they can be manipulated mathematically—for example, they are infinitely scalable. Thus, when a polygon gets bigger, there are no corresponding pixels that get bigger; instead, the polygon is enlarged before it is converted to pixels.

Vector graphics are well suited for the makeup of linear graphics such as charts because the graphic elements can be manipulated and positioned either individually or in groups. Other types of vector graphics include letterforms, logos, cartoon characters, and anything else that can be described as an outline. Vector graphics cannot, however, be used to describe continuous tone images; such images would need to be represented as pixels.

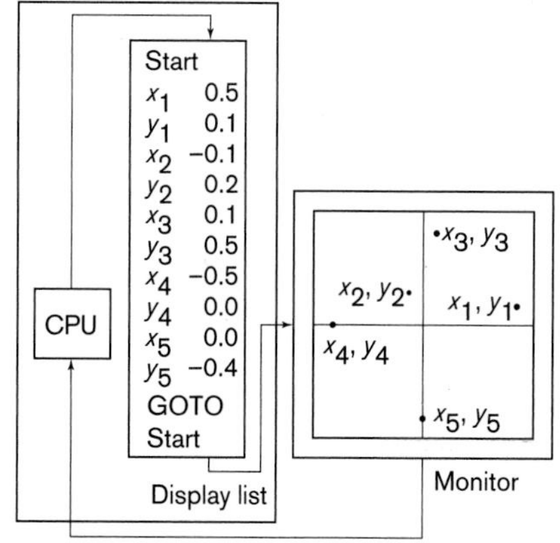

Figure 1.21 Display list memories consist of an input port, the memory itself, and an output port. The user directs the CPU to move points using an input peripheral. When the CPU changes a value in display-list memory—for example, makes the value of -0.4 equal to -0.8—the object on the screen changes.

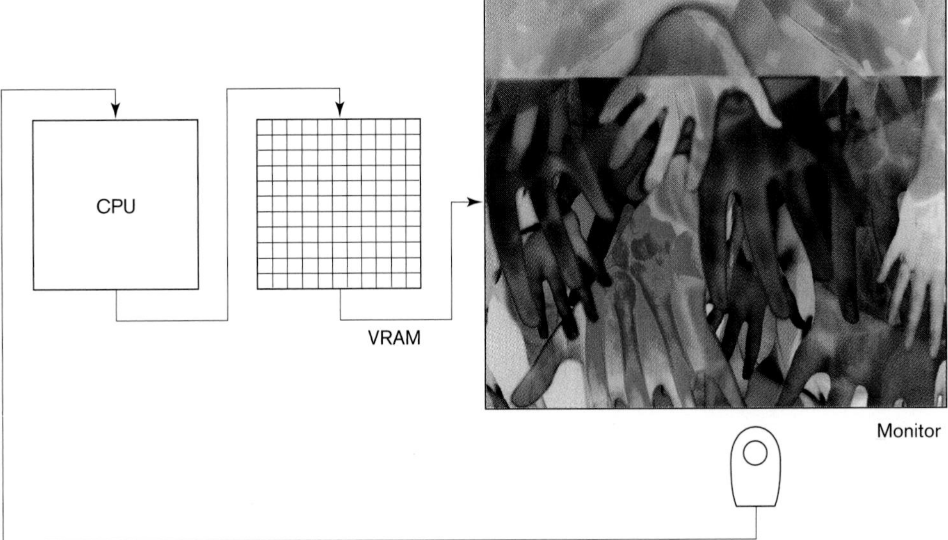

Figure 1.22 Pixel graphics require the use of video random-access memory, or VRAM, which stores the intensity value for each pixel. The user directs the CPU to modify pixel intensities using an input peripheral. When the CPU changes a value in VRAM, the pixel intensity on the screen changes.

Pixel Graphics and Paint Programs

Not all 2D imaging is done using lines or hard-edged shapes. Pixel graphics provide a way to represent photographs and continuous-tone images (see Figure 1.22), and are often manipulated with *paint programs*, which allow for images to be "painted." Paint programs can simulate the effects of an airbrush, charcoal, drawing on a roughened surface, or rubbing colors together. They can be used to cut out a block of pixels from an image, reposition it, and then use it as a rubber stamp. And they are also used to retouch and color-correct digitized photographs.

Paint programs are very versatile, and the better ones are able to place different collections of pixels on different image layers. They cannot, however, be used to create geometric objects. This is because the image is represented as a matrix of pixels, as opposed to a geometric description. Also, because an image is represented as a matrix of pixels, with a defined resolution, the scaling of raster images is problematic: scaling an image very large will typically result in undesired enlarged pixels.

3D Computer Modeling

Three-dimensional graphics is considerably different from 2D graphics. In many respects, 3D solid modeling is a lot like constructing theater props. Positioning models in the imaginary computer space

Figure 1.23 Summary of modeling techniques shows several basic primitive objects at the top, and multidimensional construction techniques at the bottom.

is analogous to classic set design. Action, characterization, and lighting are all comparable, but rendering and visualization apply only to computer graphics.

In a sense, 3D computer graphics encompass five dimensions: three from the 3D world and two from the 2D plane on which the world is being projected, that is, the dimensions of the end product. In practice, the resulting 2D plane is often brought into 2D imaging programs for final touch-ups. This section briefly reviews pertinent issues related to 3D computer graphics. Interested readers are encouraged to learn more about modeling in the current computer graphics literature. See the Further Reading section at the end of this book for selected titles.

Model Defined

A *model* is defined as a representation of a process or thing, and here the term is used specifically to mean a 3D computer object (see Figure 1.23). A *modeler* is a program used to create models. Models can consist of a singular object, such as a sphere, or can be thought of as a collection of single models, such as a sphere, two long cylinders, two short cylinders, and one short fat cylinder—which together represent a figure. Models have their own coordinate systems about which transformations take place. Models are created by a variety of techniques, some of which are inventoried below.

Modeling Methods

Computer graphics employ a variety of 2D input peripherals, including the light pen, the tablet, and the mouse, as well as some 3D input devices, such as the space wand, to assist in reading real-world information into the computer. This process, called ***digitizing***, is one way to create a 3D computer model (see Figure 1.24). The information that describes the 3D computer model is obtained via the input devices; the corresponding 3D real-world data is read into the computer and used to create a model. The other main method of creating models is to enter the data explicitly by typing it in as numbers, or by calculating it using procedures, a technique described in more detail below.

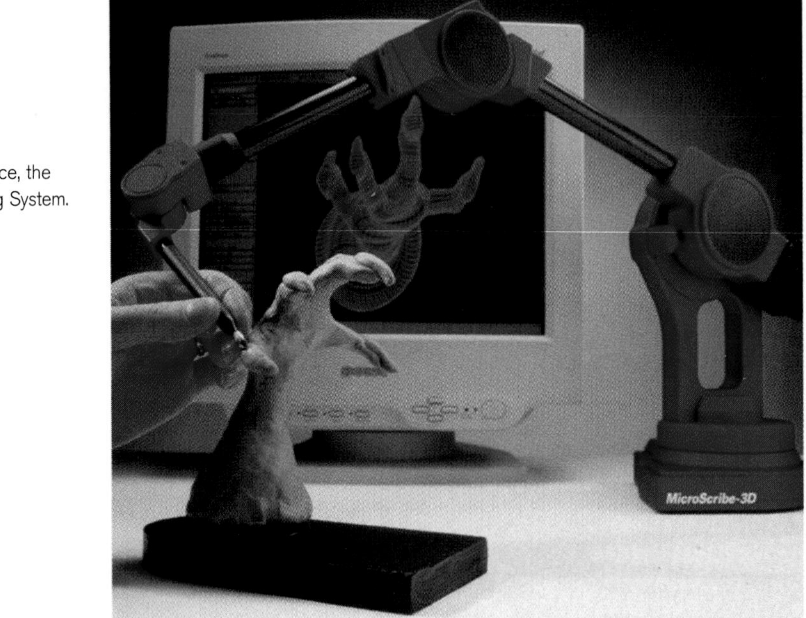

Figure 1.24 The sculpted hand is digitized using a 3D input device, the MicroScribe-3D Desktop Digitizing System.

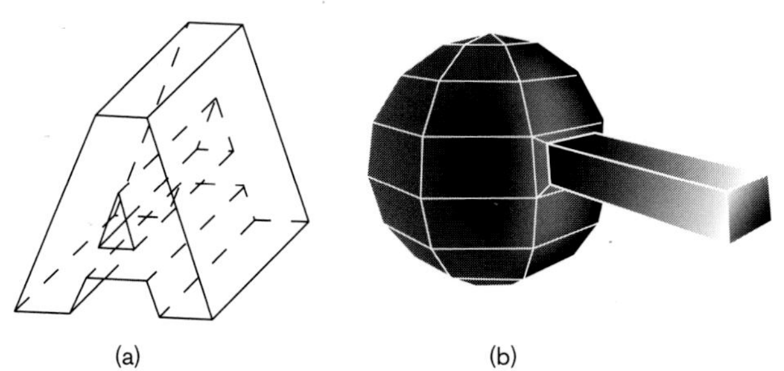

Figure 1.25 Left: Extrusion of an alphanumeric letter into a 3D volumetric representation (a). Extrusions can also be applied to polygonal models (b). Here one of the faces of the model is extruded from the sphere's surface. Complex models can be created by selectively using extrusion in this fashion.

Modeling incorporates a number of techniques to expand data computationally. Several of them are listed below:

Extrusion *Extrusion* is a technique to convert a 2D outline into a 3D object or to extract a facet of a 3D model and pull it in space (see Figure 1.25). The outline can be linear or it can be any one of the curves discussed earlier. For example, extrusion may be used to translate a surface (eventually to become the front surface of an object) back into *z* space (to a position reflecting where the back of the desired object would be); the sides between the front and back edges are then automatically connected, creating a 3D shape. Extrusion may also be used to extrude one or more facets of a polygon object in order to sculpt a model. The extrusion can be pulled into or away from the object, and the extruded piece can be scaled or rotated to add variation to the design.

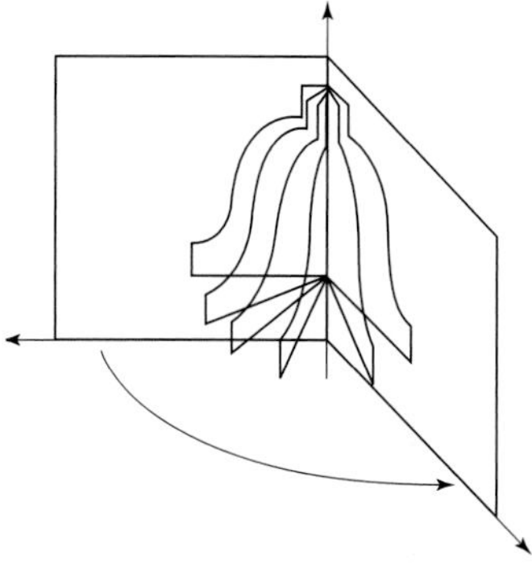

Figure 1.26 Above: Surfaces of revolution are created by spinning a curved line about an axis.

Objects of Revolution Another model-constructing technique, called *objects of revolution*, can be used to make symmetrical surfaces of revolution, such as a bell (see Figure 1.26). Objects of revolution begin with the cross section of an object, where the cross section can be linear or one of the curve types. The cross section consists of only *x* and *y* data and is centered around the *y*-axis. A computer program then spins, or rotates, this cross section around the central axis to make a solid object. Objects of revolution need very little data to construct complicated objects.

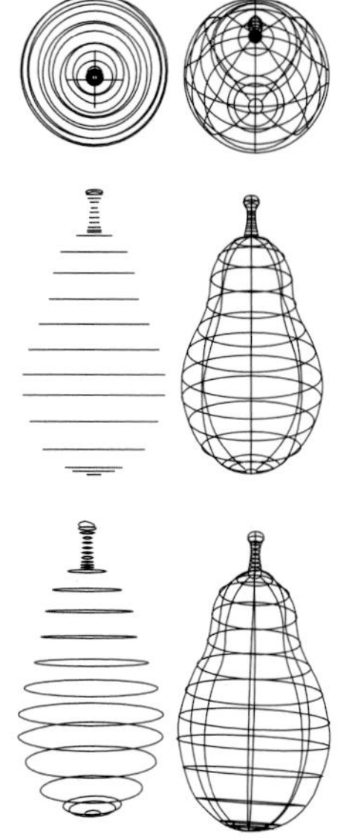

Figure 1.27 Above: Contours in 3D space define an object.

Lofting *Lofting*, or *skinning*, is another way to build 3D objects with a computer. Lofting takes a series of cross sections (again, linear or curved) and creates a surface from them (see Figure 1.27). Contour perimeters of the cross sections must first be created (drawn) and translated into their corresponding position. Then, a computer program automatically constructs a surface mesh that connects each contour to the contour above and below it (see Figure 1.28).

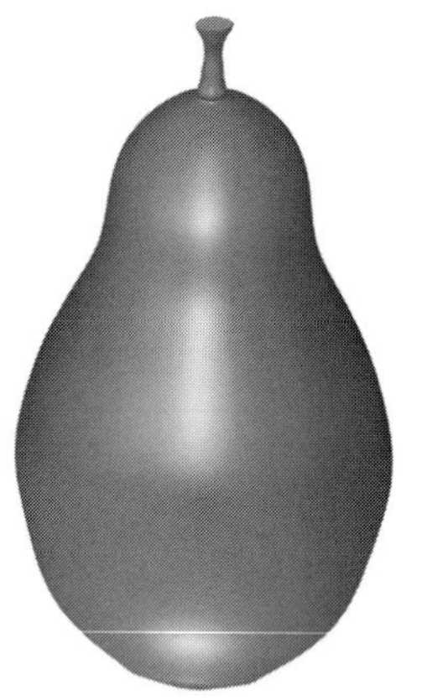

Figure 1.28 Above: A model is formed by connecting points in adjacent contours and rendering the surface.

Note that all of the techniques above can also be deployed with subtle variations—for example, sections can be rotated when they are lofted, or an extruded object can be tilted.

Coplanar Technique The *coplanar technique* of building models is used to create 3D objects from blueprints. *Coplanar* signifies two planar views, a plan and an elevation, both 2D (see Figure 1.29). The elevation, or front view, contains *x* and *y* data. The plan, or top view, contains *x* and *z* data. Thus, each data point appears in both views and is assigned a point number. The two drawings are digitized, and a computer program merges the *x* and *y* values digitized from the first view with the *z* value digitized from the second view into a single 3D point stored in computer memory. (The second *y* value is discarded.)

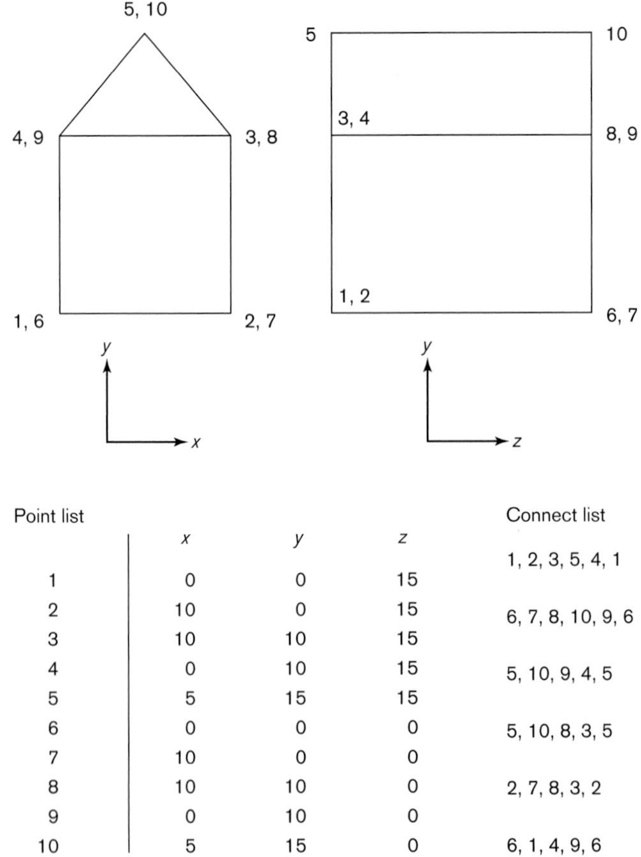

Point list

	x	y	z
1	0	0	15
2	10	0	15
3	10	10	15
4	0	10	15
5	5	15	15
6	0	0	0
7	10	0	0
8	10	10	0
9	0	10	0
10	5	15	0

Connect list

1, 2, 3, 5, 4, 1

6, 7, 8, 10, 9, 6

5, 10, 9, 4, 5

5, 10, 8, 3, 5

2, 7, 8, 3, 2

6, 1, 4, 9, 6

Figure 1.29 Right: This drawing depicts the side and front views of a house. Each point is assigned a number common to both views; this number is not a spatial coordinate but an identifying number. Many points in each elevation actually represent two points (one in front and one behind) and therefore have two identification numbers associated with them. The 3D coordinate of each point is determined by merging an *x*, *y* coordinate from the drawing on the left and a *y*, *z* coordinate from the drawing on the right. The list of points and the spatial coordinates are shown in the point list, and a separate connect list defines the boundaries of each polygon in the structure.

Photogrammetry Objects can also be created using *photogrammetry*. With this technique, a grid projected onto an actor or scene is photographed and digitized using two different cameras (see Figure 1.30). Single points appearing in both views are merged into 3D points using a special reconstruction technique. Photogrammetry is useful for objects that cannot be sectioned, are not physically accessible, or are in motion.

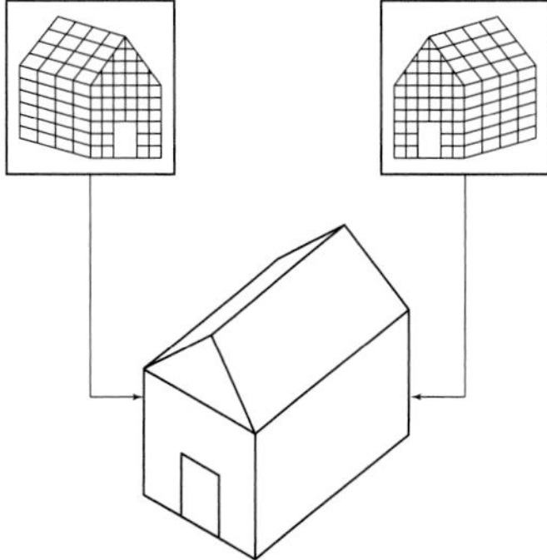

Figure 1.30 Three-dimensional reconstruction using two-view photogrammetry. A grid is drawn or projected onto a 3D object, which is in turn photographed using two cameras. The camera positions and focal lengths are known. Each point in both photographed grids is assigned a number and then digitized separately. The two sets of points are mathematically merged, creating a 3D database.

Zels Another digitizing technique represents an object or a surface as a matrix of depth values called *zels*. The depth matrix may be orthogonal or cylindrical (see Figure 1.31). The matrices of zels can be converted from polar to Cartesian coordinates; they can also be converted to mesh-surface representations as well as to contours.

The zel method is a hybrid method that stores 3D information in 2D bitplanes—the bitplanes store depth values—*z* distances from the image plane to the 3D surface or object located in space behind the image plane. Zels are similar to pixels in that they are discrete representations, but are different from them in that pixels represent the intensity at each point in an image, whereas zels represent depth.

Voxels As previously mentioned, voxels are volume elements that provide a discrete approximation of densities of space (see Figure 1.32). They have special value in situations where it may be necessary to model the interior of an object—for example, tissue, fluid, or smoke. Their use presents all the problems of discrete representations (aliasing), and in many applications, the sheer number of voxels required to model something precludes computation—for example, a volume of 1000 voxels on a side, where each voxel is represented by only one bit, contains one billion bits, or 166MB of data.

Procedural Modeling Three-dimensional computer graphics can also be created using predefined computer programs or procedures; the process of creating such graphics is called *procedural modeling*. Procedures can be used to create geometric objects such as boxes, cylinders, and doughnuts, as well as irregular forms, such as landscapes (see Figure 1.33). The procedures control the position, size, and shape of these images. In procedural modeling, the computer calculates the sequence of points that defines the object rather than directly digitizing the object. A sphere, for example, is best defined using a procedure, or formula, that determines the *x, y,* and *z* positions on its surface. This method can calculate extremely accurate spheres with an arbitrary number of sides or curved surfaces. This approach is quicker than digitizing the sphere, and the result is more uniformly round. Most 3D computer graphics systems come with a set of procedures to create simple objects; the objects, referred to as ***primitives***, typically include a sphere, cylinder, doughnut (or torus), prism, and other basic geometric figures.

Procedurally defined objects do not have to be regular; they can include irregular bloblike volumes and treelike shapes. ***Fractals***, for example, are procedurally generated objects that have irregular yet self-similar properties (see Figure 1.34). Because many natural and organic objects are better described with fractals than with primitive geometric shapes, they are often used to model objects such as mountains, rivers, and coastlines.

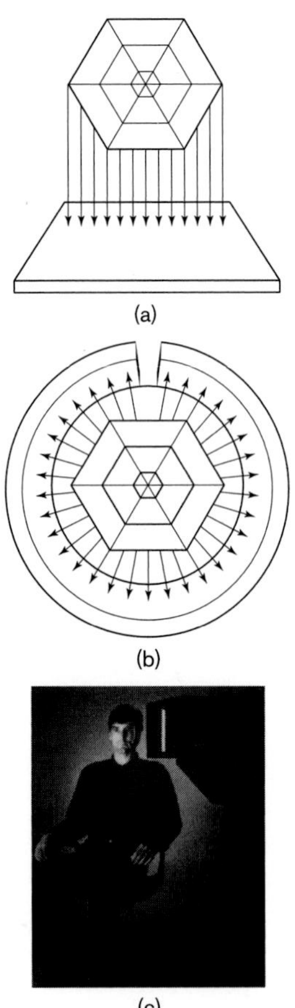

Figure 1.31 Orthogonal and polar zels are matrices of depth values. Orthogonal zels (a) are the distances from a plane in space to the surface of a reference plane; the illustration shows one row. Polar zels (b) are the radial distances from an object to a surrounding cylinder; again one row is shown. The photograph (c) shows a machine that measures polar zels of human-sized subjects. The mechanical assembly at the right rotates around the subject. The measurement is done by shining a laser beam, which can be seen on the left cheek of the subject.

Metaballs *Metaballs,* or *metaclay,* are used to model non-rigid organic shapes (see Figure 1.35). Metaballs often have properties that define the way two metaballs will interact upon an encounter. For example, they might attract and become one, which can be broken back into two, if need be. Metaballs are typically defined with a field of attraction—two metaballs within the field will attract and unite, forming one larger blobby object. Complex models can be created by adding and positioning multiple metaballs together until a model is created. Individual metaballs can also be scaled, allowing for greater flexibility when creating shapes.

Parametric Surface Patches *Parametric surface patches* describe 3D objects in terms of ***patches***, where a patch is just a section of the object's surface. A patch is represented by equations that define the four edges of the patch. Often the equations are expressed as control points at the four corners of the patch; these control points, or parameters, may be thought of as a normal with a magnitude. Given these four control points, an algorithm is used to calculate an *xyz* coordinate anywhere within the patch (see Figure 1.36). A subtle factor of this technique is that it enables the modeler to create surfaces that are continuous and to calculate as much (or as little) detail as needed. Further, these large, continuously curving surfaces can be defined and easily manipulated with very few points. Patches are widely used in applications where free-form surfaces are required.

Hierarchical Models

Hierarchical models are models that are created when several models—also called *nodes*—are joined together into a hierarchical structure (see Figure 1.37). This is usually done to facilitate manipulation or to share materials. A node in the hierarchy is said to be a *parent* if there is a model or structure of models below it in the hierarchy. The topmost parent in a hierarchy is called the *root*. Similarly, a node is said to be the *child* of the model just above itself in the hierarchy. The diagram is referred to as a *schematic representation*. The entire hierarchy is referred to as a *hierarchical tree*, and the line representing their connection is call a *branch*.

Transformations applied to a parent—either during model creation or during the animation process—propagate down the tree. Each *level* of the hierarchy has its own coordinate system and its own *local origin,* typically referred to as the object's *center*. This local origin is different from the *global origin*, which is the origin of the virtual world. The animator has the choice of performing transformation relative to either origin.

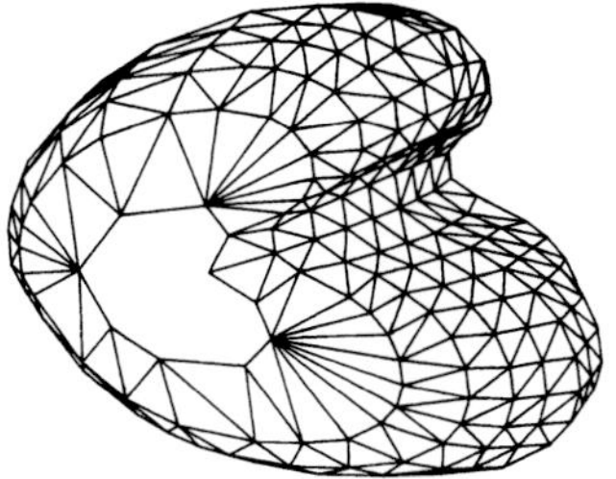

Polyhedron

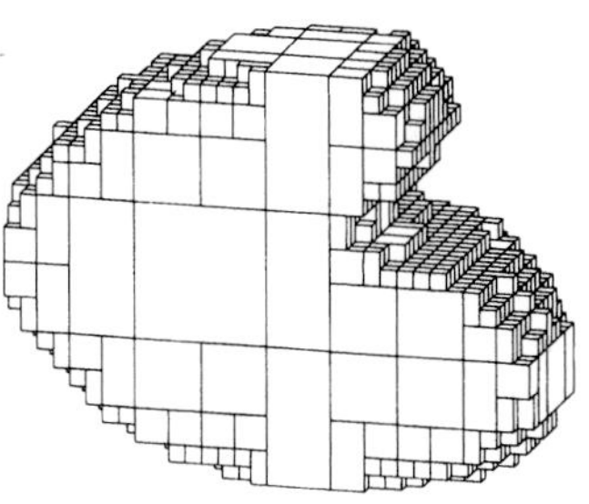

Voxel model

Figure 1.32 Above: Voxels are volumetric, not surface, representations.

Figure 1.33 Below: A procedural landscape image: *Carolina*.

Combinatorial Methods

The modeler also has a few tools useful for shaping data. *Clipping* is a process that slices an object into two parts as if cut with a knife. A fundamental tool for objects in 3D space, clipping is used to slice off pieces of objects, eliminate objects that are outside the field of view, and chop objects into pieces (see Figure 1.38). Clipping defines a plane

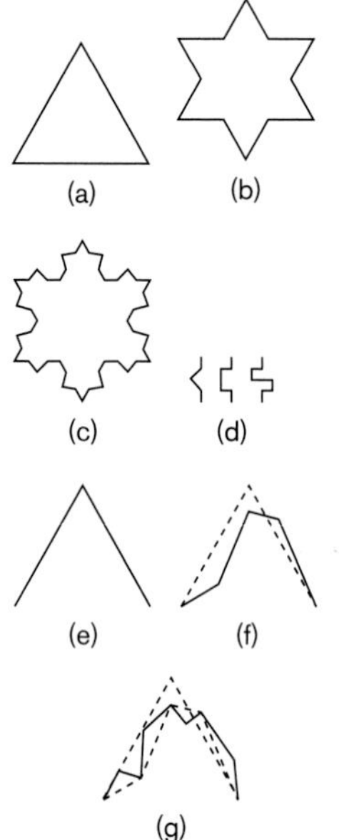

Figure 1.34 This simple 2D fractal, called a *snowflake curve*, illustrates the principle of recursive subdivision. The basic shape is a triangle (a). The Snowflake algorithm divides each side into thirds and constructs a triangle in lieu of the middle third section (b). The process repeated a second time produces (c), and the process can be continued again and again. Note that with each successive generation, the boundary line tends to get longer while the area remains relatively fixed. Note that the fractal could start out with any shape and that the subdivision rule could be anything. For example, consider subdividing the initial triangle with the various shapes of (d). A slightly different strategy used to make irregular mountains begins with a triangle (e), but picks a random point along each line and a random *y* offset to make a new shape (f). Repeating the procedure makes finer detail (g), and this too can be indefinitely repeated.

in space (essentially a giant rectangle), then divides objects between the two sides of the plane. Where a line or edge crosses the clipped plane, the procedure calculates a new point at that location, and uses the new point to define the end of the object (see Figure 1.39).

Capping is a process that defines new surfaces formed where a clipping plane truncates an object (see Figure 1.40). This prevents an object from appearing hollow; capping constructs a new side so the polyhedron looks opaque or solid. *Boolean operators* such as *AND* or *OR* may be used on 3D solid models to add two shapes together or subtract one shape from another (see Figure 1.41).

Geometric Transformations

Geometric transformations are operations that move and change objects in either 2D or 3D space. Translate, size, rotate, and shear are the four primitive transformations. Transformations can be applied to models during construction to affect the way a model looks, or during the animation process to affect the way an object moves.

Transformations describe position and motion independently of any object that is being positioned or moved. In other words, a series of rotations and translations that position an object is data in its own right and is distinct from the data that describes the object. This is a critical concept in computer graphics because it enables an animator to think about a motion pathway as a separate entity. Once a transformation is determined, it can then be applied to an object. The same transformation can also be applied to many different objects, causing them all to move in the same manner.

Translation *Translation*, or *offsetting*, is a transformation that moves an object left or right, up or down, or in or out in 3D space. A translation of some combination of *x*, *y*, and *z* repositions an object anywhere in space by adding the amount of the displacement to each point in the object to be transformed (see Figure 1.42). An *identity translation*, a translation of 0, describes a situation in which an object is not to be moved. Positive number translations displace objects along the corresponding positive axis; in other words, right, up, or toward the viewer. Negative values move the object left, down, or away from the viewer.

Sizing *Sizing* transformations either reduce or enlarge objects, multiplying their coordinates by the scaling factor(s) (see Figure

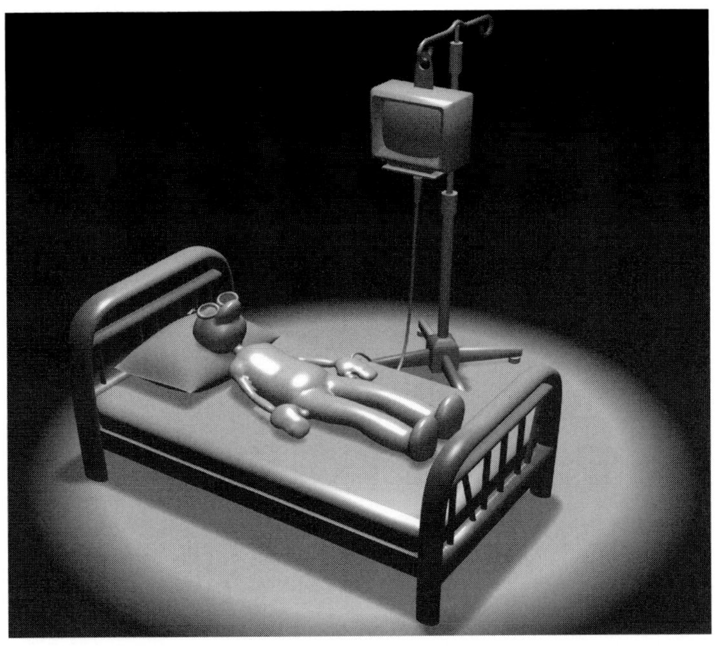

Figure 1.35 Left: The character in the illustration was created using metaballs, which give it a claylike appearance.

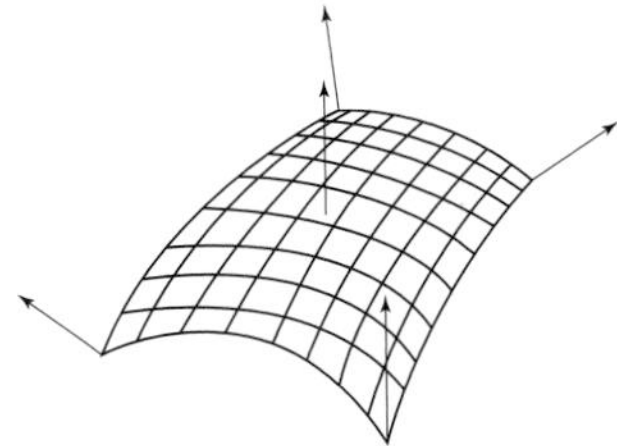

Figure 1.36 Above: The key idea behind parametric surfaces is that they are defined by only the control points at the corners of the patch, here indicated by the normals. The surface of the patch is calculated by interpolating the curves that the control points define.

1.43). By default, sizing usually occurs around their origin, which is one reason why objects tend to be defined with the origin at their center. As in translation, there are three sizing transformations, one each for *x, y,* and *z,* and it is not necessary to size an object equally in all three dimensions. Sizing a sphere in *x* and *y,* but not *z,* will create an ellipsoidal shape, for example. Sizing a letter in *x* but not *y* will condense or expand it. An ***identity sizing*** (leaving the size of an object unchanged) is a sizing of 1.0. Scaling factors greater than 1.0 enlarge the object; scaling factors between 0.0 and 1.0 reduce it. A sizing of 0.0 reduces the entire object to a point, and negative numbers flip the object into mirror-image positions or turn the object inside out.

Rotation A *rotation* specifies a pivoting, or angular, displacement about an axis (see Figure 1.44). In 3D graphics, there are three primitive rotations, one each around the *x, y,* and *z* axes (Figure 1.45). Objects are rotated by specifying an angle of rotation and an axis, and trigonometric functions are used to determine the new position. Rotation angles are usually expressed in degrees, but they can also be expressed in other rotary measures, such as radians. These angles can be positive or negative; the identity rotation is 0 degrees

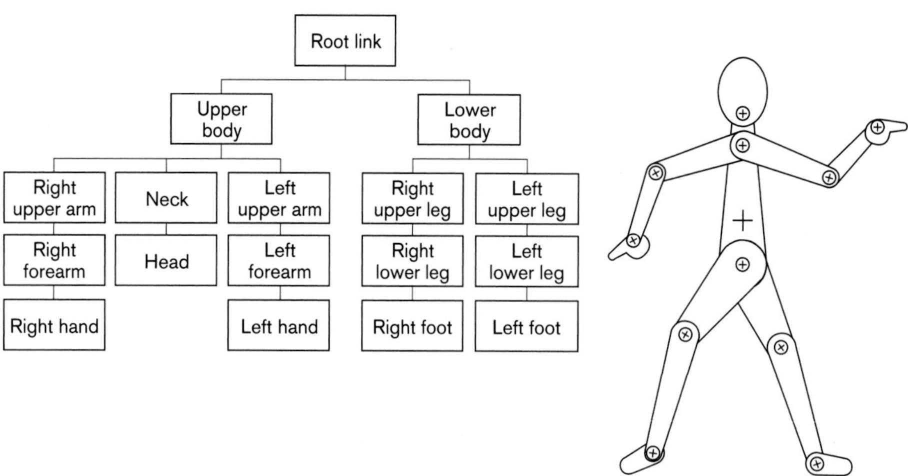

Figure 1.37 Hierarchical models are joined together into a hierarchical structure, which helps to facilitate animation. The entire model can be transformed, or just the individual nodes.

(or any multiple of 360 degrees). Rotations are said to be either *left-handed* or *right-handed*, specifying whether a positive angle rotates clockwise or counterclockwise.

Shearing The *shear transformation* displaces points relative to the origin of an object. Shearing is similar to italicization and can work forward or backward (see Figure 1.46). A shear involves the displacement of two axes against a third, and although there is only one way to shear in 2D graphics, there are six different ways to shear in 3D space.

Inversion All primitive transformations can be inverted using an *inverse transformation*—for example, the inverse of a 10-degree positive rotation is a 10-degree negative rotation—and inversion is a common command in 3D systems (see Figure 1.47). Inverting a transformation is simple, as it is not necessary to know how the transformation was made, but only to have the transformation data in order to invert it.

Concatenation The four primitive, singular transformations—position, size, rotate, and shear—are not only methods for representing single positions, but can also be combined, or *concatenated*, to specify a position that incorporates a sequence of two or more individual, primitive transformations (see Figure 1.48). The order of a sequence of transformations is critical to the result. Rotations and sizings are especially sensitive to ordering, because they occur

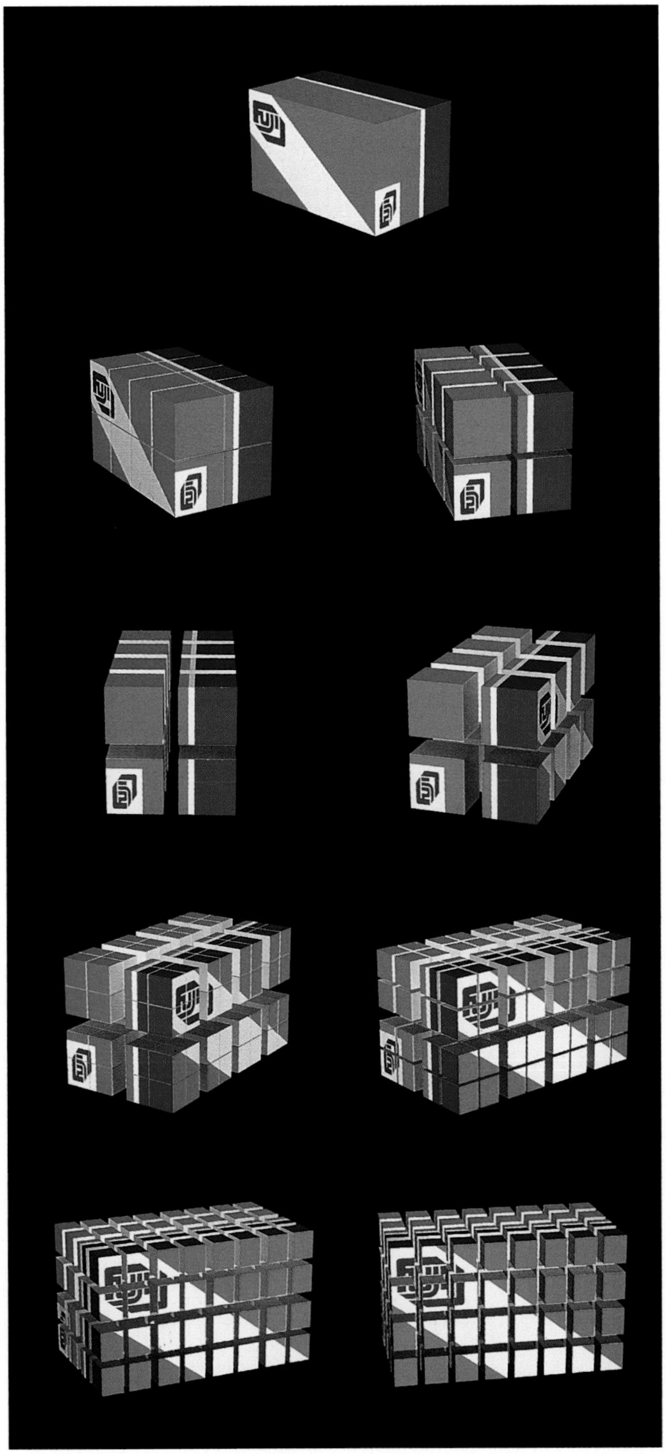

Figure 1.38 Left: The object has been clipped in *x*, *y*, and *z* to create smaller pieces (from left to right).

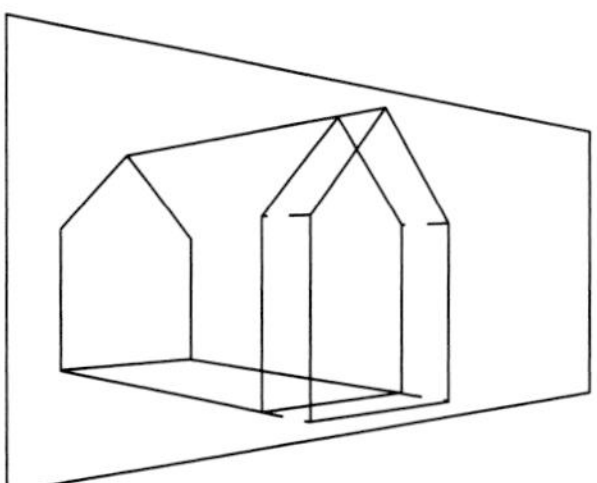

Figure 1.39 Above: This clipping diagram shows how a single clipping plane intersects a 3D house. The part of the house outside the field of vision is eliminated.

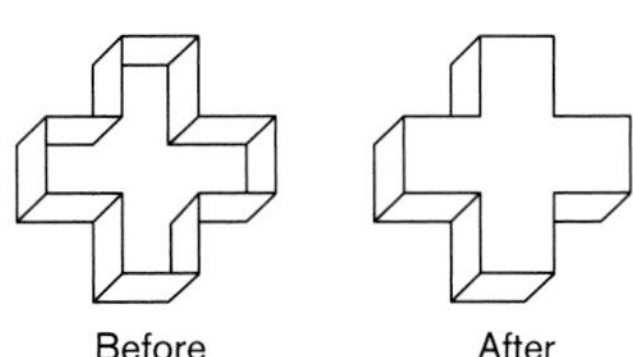

Figure 1.40 Above: An extruded cross before and after capping.

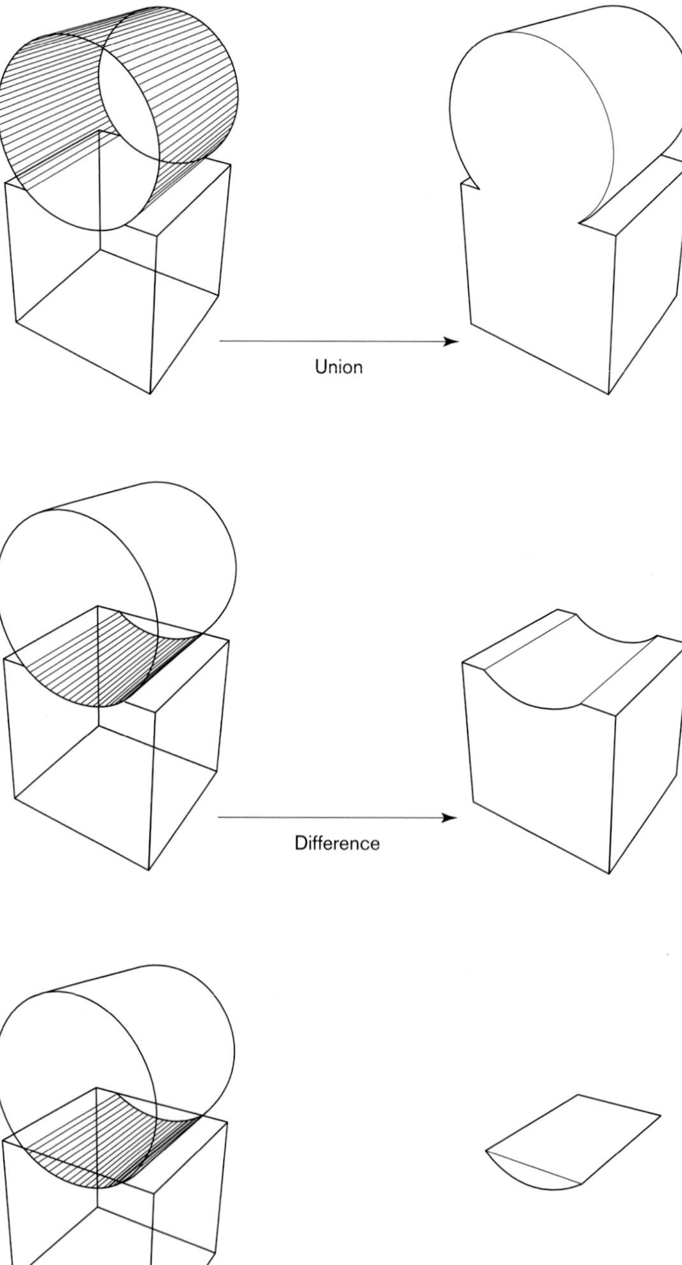

Figure 1.41 The OR, or *union*, operator produces a volume that is common to both the cube and the cylinder. The cube MINUS, or *difference*, the cylinder results in a cube with a depression. The AND, or *intersection*, operation results in a volume that contains the area common to the cube and the cylinder.

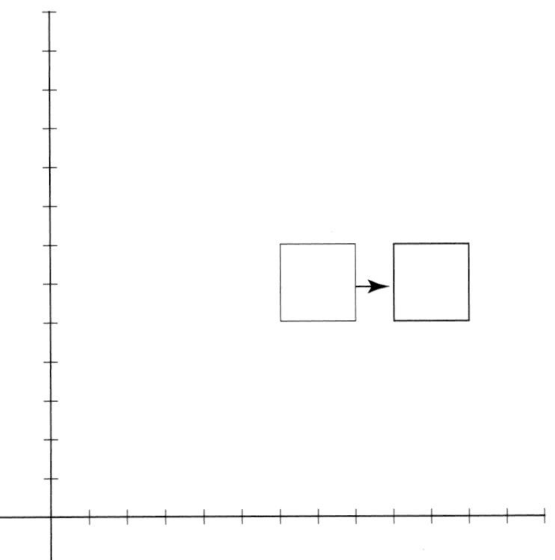

Figure 1.42 Left: Adding 3 horizontal units to a point located at 6, 5, 1 will translate that point to location 9, 5, 1. The displacement must be added to each and every point that describes a shape in order to translate a shape or group of shapes.

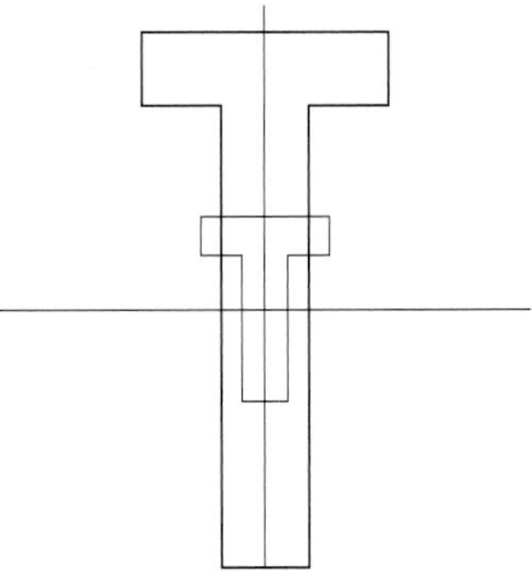

Figure 1.43 Above: A letter T sized by a factor of two would become twice as large. But the same letter sized by two in the *x* dimension, and three in the *y* dimension, will result in a larger letter with different proportions. In either case, each of the eight coordinates that describe the letter are multiplied by the scaling factor and result in a new set of coordinates.

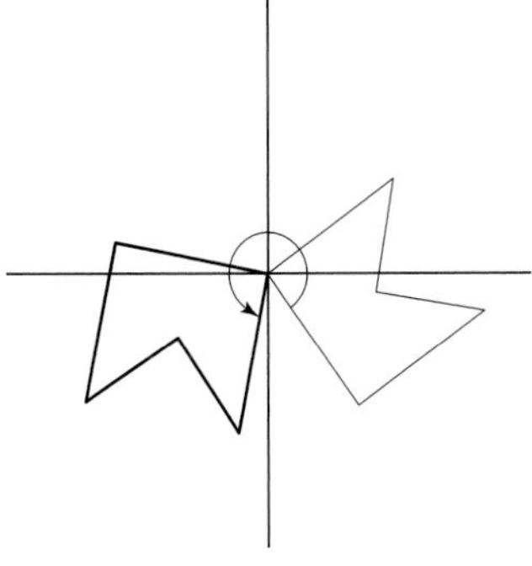

Figure 1.44 Above: Two-dimensional rotation of 310 degrees about the origin.

around an axis. Transformations can be concatenated ad infinitum and result in a single transformation, which may also be inverted.

Instancing Many applications require that a single object be repeated in many positions. This is accomplished with a technique called *instancing*, which uses only one model and defines a series of transformations that represent all the positions. Examples of instancing include multiple columns on a building (see Figure 1.49), multiple houses in a subdivision, and many trees in a forest.

Surface Attributes

Once a model is created and given visual form, it may be assigned different kinds of ***surface attributes***. These are properties of the surface, such as color and texture. In computer graphics, there are several surface attributes, which are commonly represented numerically inside the computer and associated with the geometric object data.

Color The *color* of a surface is usually represented with additive primaries as a red, green, and blue triplet (RGB), but it can also be described with subtractive primaries cyan, yellow, and magenta (CMY). Colors are represented either as real numbers between 0 and 1, or as integers, usually with a range of intensities.

Luminescence *Luminescence* is the amount of light a surface emits without reflecting light from an outside source. In other words, if one were to look at a surface in a totally dark room, the luminescence

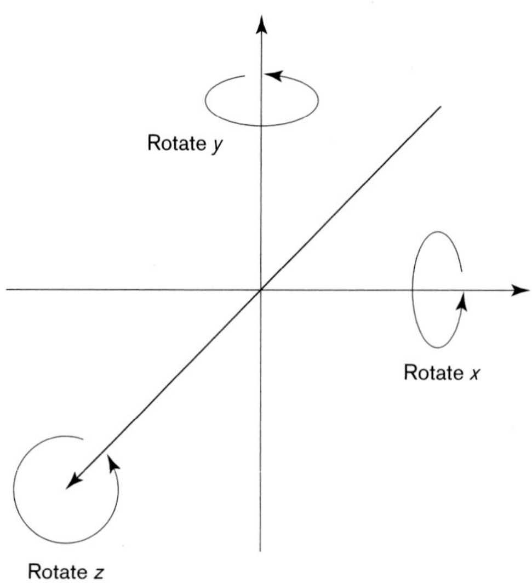

Figure 1.45 Right: Right-handed rotations in 3D graphics.

Figure 1.46 Above: Identity shears have a value of 1. Positive-number shears make objects lean forward, in the positive direction. Negative-number shears make objects lean backward, like backward-slanting letters. Shears are sometimes used in animation to "race" type into a scene horizontally, and as the type comes to a rest it relaxes, shears backward, and then returns to normal.

would be the light, if any, that comes from that surface. The luminescence property of a surface is usually not considered a light source, although it is; it is used with lighting to ensure that certain surfaces of objects will not be too dark. In situations where lighting is not used, luminescence is the same as color. Like color, luminescence is usually represented as an RGB triplet.

Transparency *Transparency* describes the amount of light that passes through a surface. A transparent surface transmits light without appreciable scattering, so that surfaces behind it are partially visible (see Figure 1.50); a fully transparent surface is invisible.

Transparency is sometimes represented as an RGB triplet so that different colors can have different degrees of transparency, permitting the implementation of colored filters. Note: Transparent surfaces also have color, and the two attributes should not be confused!

Luster Two properties control the *luster*, that is, how shiny a surface is. The ***diffuse reflective coefficient*** controls how much diffuse light the surface reflects. A *diffuse*, or matte, surface is one that reflects light randomly and evenly in all directions; the surface appears as a dull, flat color, like the felt on a pool table (see Figure 1.51). The ***specular coefficient*** controls how much specular light the surface reflects. Specular reflection is the kind of light reflected from a shiny object: a pool ball, a metal trophy, and in the extreme case, a mirror. Both diffuse and specular reflection are represented by RGB triplets.

Surfaces can also be represented with a wide variety of ***maps***, 2D arrays which represent various information. This brings the discussion to a class of surface techniques that all involve mapping. *Mapping* takes a 2D image and treats it as if it were a surface on a 3D shape. The surface can be planar or curved. Thus, in practice, a 2D pixel image can be mapped onto a rectangle, the sides of a cube, the curved surface of a sphere, or even an animated curving object, such as a flag. Images and patterns can be mapped onto surfaces with color, or onto transparent or reflective surfaces. At its simplest, mapping places a flat image in perspective (see Figure 1.52). More sophisticated methods wrap an image onto curved surfaces (see Figure 1.53). In this case, the image is slightly distorted, but an image mapped onto a sphere needs to be stretched to fit—much like a map of the Earth, which needs to be distorted at the poles—and there are a number of methods for doing this.

Mapping provides a way to incorporate photographic detail, such as a brick wall or water, into a 3D world without resorting to modeling geometric objects. Rather than creating a model of a brick wall, the graphic artist need only create an image of a brick wall and then map it onto a polygon.

Pixel images are not the only kinds of data that can be mapped. *Texture* is represented using a 2D bitmap matrix of surface normals. The normals have subtle deviations that are either patterned or random, and can be used to represent the way light is reflected, causing an object to look smooth or rough. In a manner akin to image mapping, *bump mapping* wraps the 2D texture around a virtual 3D surface, so that complicated surface textures can be created without resorting

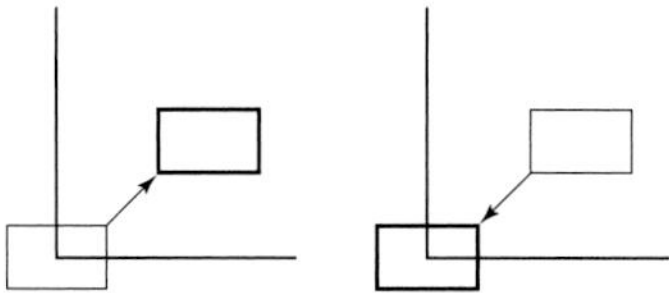

Figure 1.47 Above: The drawing on the left shows the translation of a rectangle from its initial position at the origin to a new location. The second drawing shows an inverse transformation, the translation of a new rectangle located at 4, 3, 0 back to the origin.

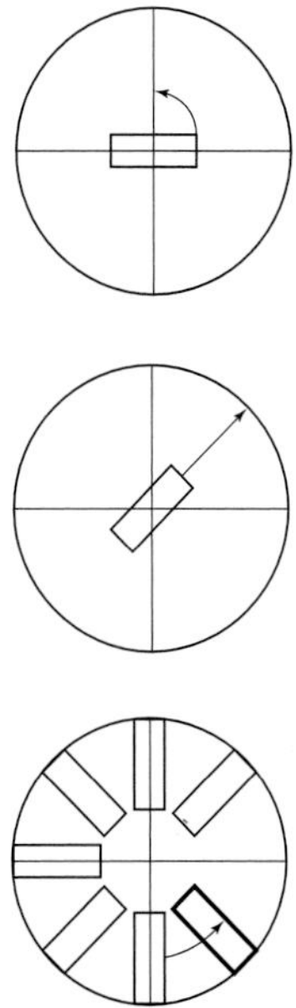

Figure 1.48 Above: Concatenated transformations involve a sequence of transformations; a paddle on a waterwheel is positioned using two successive transformations, one that rotates the paddle, and a second that translates the paddle onto the circumference of the wheel.

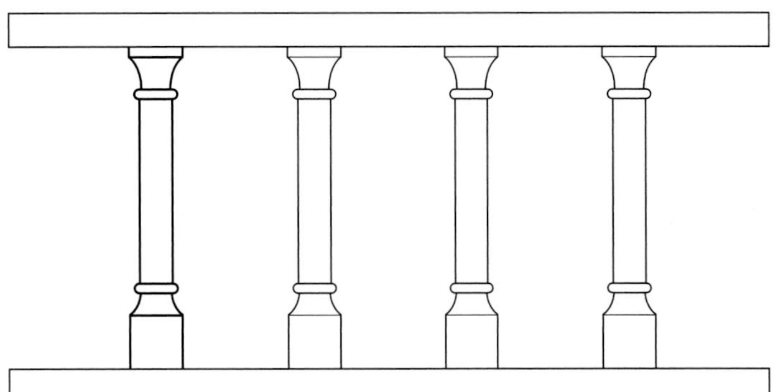

Figure 1.49 Left: Instancing a single object, in this case a column, repeatedly translates it to create a pattern.

Figure 1.50 The extent to which an object is transparent depends on how much light can pass through it. Fully transparent objects transmit light, so bodies lying beyond them are visible.

to large numbers of polygons. Texture mapping, like image mapping, does not alter the actual geometry of a surface. Surfaces with texture, or bump maps, are calculated in a similar way to surfaces with properties of diffuse and specular reflection. The reflection properties do not change, but the calculation uses the mapped normals instead of a single normal when calculating lighting, which gives the surface more life. Other kinds of maps include a reflection map, which is a spherical projection of an environment around a point, used to make objects seem reflective; a transparency map, used to control the degree of transparency of a surface; and a deformation map, which can modify the height of a surface.

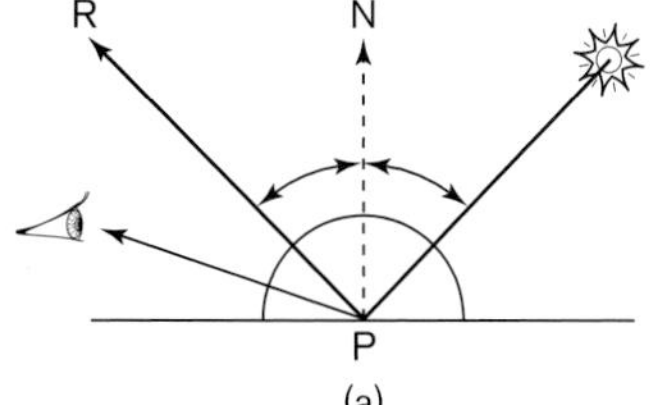

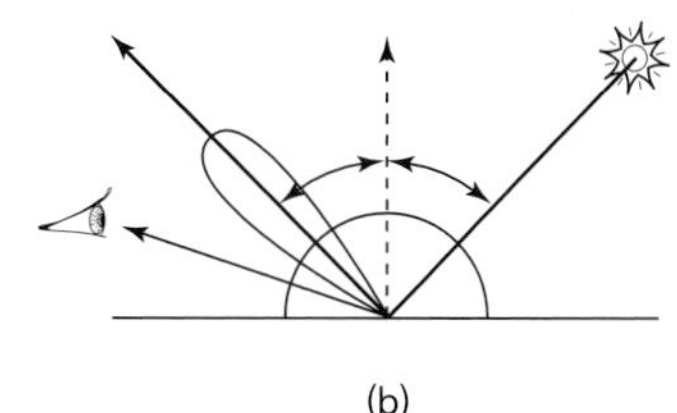

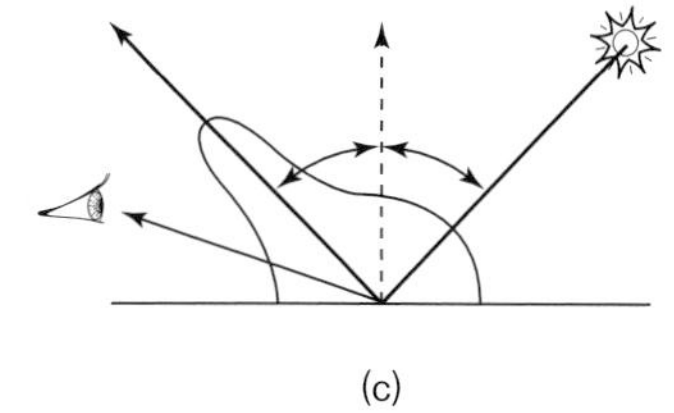

Figure 1.51 A matte, or diffuse, surface reflects light in all directions, signified by the hemisphere in the diagram (a). The amount of light reflected to an eye or camera is a function of the angle of incidence and has nothing to do with the location of the eye, since light is reflected equally in all directions. The amount of diffuse reflection is also called the *coefficient of diffuse reflection* and is essentially the radius of the hemisphere. Specular reflection (b) is the tendency of some surfaces to reflect light only in the direction of the angle of reflection. The specular light reflected to the eye is a function of both the angle of incidence and the location of the eye. With a perfectly reflecting surface, one with very high luster, the reflected light is concentrated only on the angle of reflection, and the surface becomes a mirror. But surfaces with lower luster cause some spreading of light, as in this diagram with its teardroplike reflection. Luster adjusts the width of the teardrop, and the magnitude of the teardrop along the angle of reflection is controlled by the quantity of specular reflection, also called the *coefficient of specular reflection*. When diffuse and specular reflection are combined (c), the result is a composite curve. Changing the two coefficients alters the ratios between the hemisphere and teardrop shape and provides a way to mix varying amounts of diffuse and specular components. The relation between diffuse and specular reflection, the luster, and the amount of light reflected in red, green, and blue for each, provide important visual clues about the composition of objects.

Lights and Lighting

Just as the 3D computer animation world contains objects, it also contains lights; like objects, lights have properties. After identifying some of these properties, a discussion of how light, cameras, and objects all come together will be presented.

Lighting is a subtle art and requires perception, technical skill, and sensitivity. Lighting in computer graphics is in many ways analogous to lighting for theater or film, and, like model building or action, is responsive to the touch of a creative artist. Computer graphics can simulate the physics of light itself and generate artificial perspective views of artificial realities in artificial motion. The simulation of light in 3D graphics parallels our knowledge of the physics of light. Most 3D computer graphics programs have tools for lighting a scene and modifying the lighting. Obviously, in these programs, the lights are virtual lights.

A light is, fundamentally, a source of illumination. Lights interact with a surface and determine the *chiaroscuro*, or shading, the amount of light that a surface reflects, with a range of dark to light values. Chiaroscuro is determined by surface orientation, color, and luster, as well as the light color, position, and brightness.

Lights also cast *shadows*, which are volumes in an environment that are blocked from light by other objects. Shadows provide important depth cues and heighten realism and are automatically calculated by programs in most computer systems. Multiple lights, of course, produce multiple shadows, which can be particularly interesting if the lights are colored. Shadows in computer graphics may be hard-edged, or they may have a penumbra to them (see Figure 1.54). Transparent surfaces cast shadows that are not completely black, and when superimposed upon other shadows, the shadows combine and become brighter. Images can be drawn with or without

Figure 1.52 Right: Planar mapping pivots a bitmap image in 3D space.

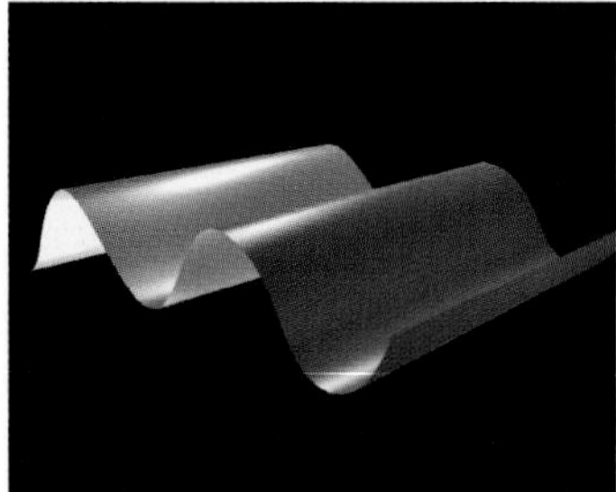

(a)

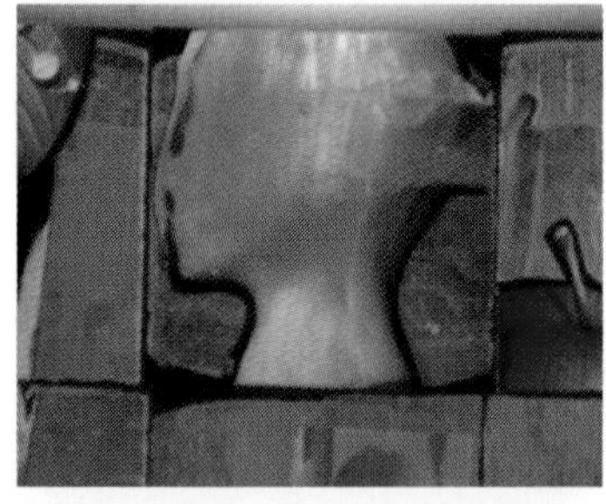

(b)

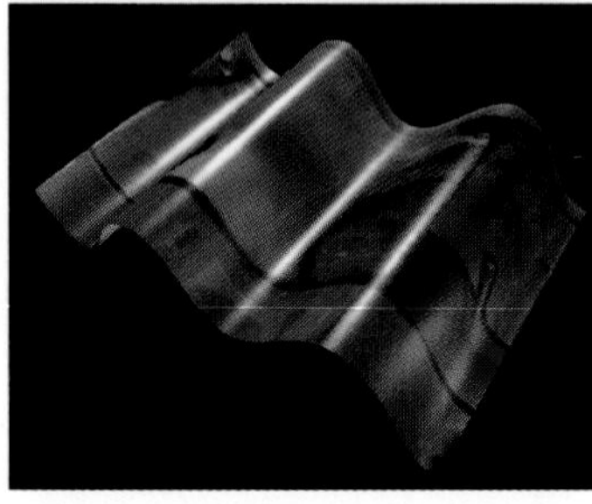

(c)

Figure 1.53 Above: Images and patterns can be mapped onto surfaces. In this case, the image is slightly distorted. In the figure, (a) shows the surface, (b) shows the image being mapped, and (c) shows the final result of the image mapped onto the surface.

shadows. Specific lights in a scene may be designated to cast shadows just as some objects can be designated to cast shadows, depending on whether or not the goal in a particular application is realistic simulation. The designer creatively and imaginatively tells stories and communicates ideas either by simulating reality or by mixing reality and imagination to create visually striking effects.

Lights have a number of properties. First, like objects, they have *position*, an *xyz* location in space. Lights may be located at infinity (like the sun) and behave like point sources; they may be located outside or within the field of view. Second, the ***brightness***, or quantity of light emitted, is expressed as an RGB triplet, usually on a scale of zero to one or zero to infinity, which determines the color of light. An ***omni-directional light*** radiates equally in all directions. A ***spotlight*** radiates in a single direction, which may be expressed as a normal (see Figure 1.55). Spotlights may have a *fall-off*, which controls the brightness of light relative to the axis of directionality. ***Barn doors*** may be used to control where light falls, and ***cookies*** cause the light to fall in patterns.

Reflection is the bouncing of light from a surface back to the environment and the point of view. Light is not always modeled in computer graphics; when lighting is employed, the reflective properties of the surface as well as the color of the lights together determine the imaged surface color. Reflection calculations involve surface normals because the normal specifies the directionality of a surface. The amount of reflected light varies according to the rela-

Figure 1.54 Shadows are cast by light sources onto objects in the scene; multiple lights cast multiple shadows.

tionship between the ***angle of incidence***, the angle between the light source and the normal, and the ***angle of view***, the angle between the normal and a camera or eye (see Figure 1.56).

There are two kinds of reflection. ***Diffuse reflection*** scatters light equally in all directions and depends solely on the angle of incidence: The smaller this angle, that is, the more directly above the surface the light is, the more light is reflected. Different surfaces reflect different percentages of light, but the diffuse reflection remains unaffected by the viewing angle. ***Specular reflections*** are not uniformly distributed; they are concentrated around the ***angle of reflection***—the angle between the surface normal and a perfectly reflected light ray. In the shiniest case, the surface functions like a mirror. Specular reflections create highlights on an object; the concentration of the highlight depends on the luster of the object. Objects with high luster reflect pinpoint highlights; objects with lower luster create more softened highlights. Specular reflections tend to be the color of the lights; diffuse reflections are the color of the surface. Different surfaces have different amounts of specular reflection.

A lighting calculation involving both diffuse and specular reflection requires information about the color, luster, and position of the surface; the proportions of diffuse and specular reflection; a point of view; and the position, color, and brightness of the light(s). These are then manipulated to simulate surfaces ranging from metals such as gold and aluminum to plastics, glass, paper, and paint.

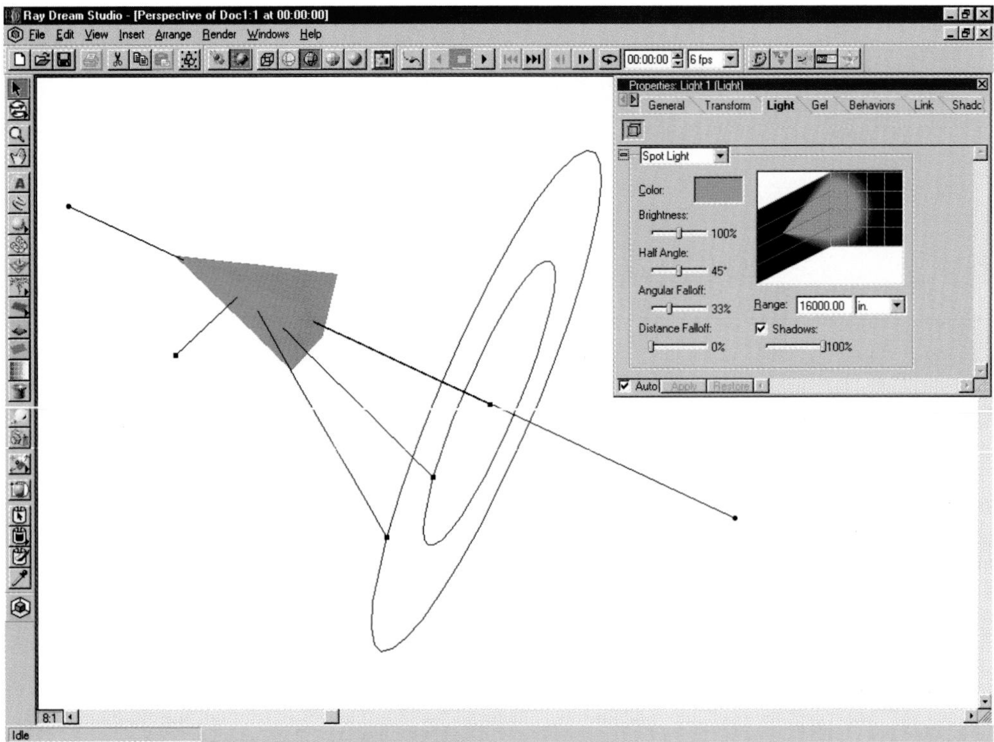

Figure 1.55 Above: A spotlight radiates in a single direction, which may be expressed as a normal.

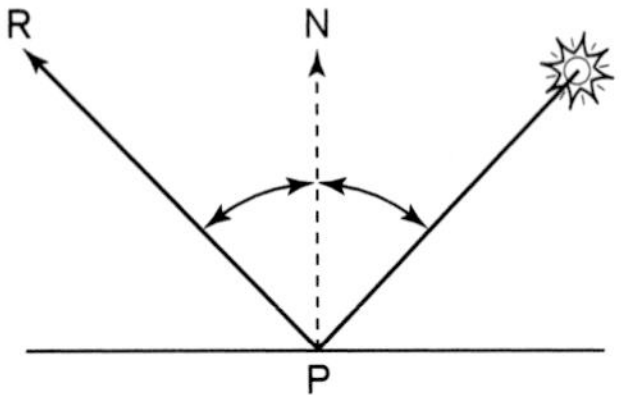

Figure 1.56 Above: The angle of incidence (LPN) is the angle between a light source (L) and the surface normal (PN). The angle of reflection (NPR) is the angle between the normal and a perfectly reflected ray (R) and is equal to the angle of incidence.

Light not only interacts with surfaces but with volumes as well. One volumetric light property is *refraction*, which causes light to bend or change direction whenever it travels from one medium to another—for example, from air into glass into water. Refraction can be modeled in computer graphics as a single constant, the refractivity of the material (see Figure 1.57), and is used to model curved surfaces such as lenses, crystal balls, and cut gems. Typically in computer graphics, Snell's laws are used to simulate refraction.

Light is affected when it passes through volumes that contain air, glass, fog, and water; the changes it undergoes are sometimes called *atmospherics*, similar to what Leonardo da Vinci called "aerial perspective." The atmospheric effects that can be created in a computer include haze, fog, rain, clouds, and translucent substances that are not appropriately represented as opaque surfaces. Atmospherics often involve an uneven absorption of light and a softening of edges, and produce effects such as depth in a landscape. They may be achieved in a variety of ways, including filtering faraway objects by the color of the atmosphere, and desaturating the colors of the objects that are farther away, which makes them appear more gray.

Figure 1.57 The refraction in this image was computed using *ray tracing*.

The Virtual Camera

Just as the data in the 3D computer world is virtual and numeric, so too is the representation of the camera itself. The ***virtual camera*** is a computer model that converts data in the 3D virtual world into 2D images (see Figure 1.58). Like the real camera, the virtual camera has a lens, shutter, and recording medium and can be moved in space. The details are covered in subsequent chapters.

Rendering

Rendering refers to the way objects are actually represented or drawn on a screen: Is a cube drawn as a wire-frame skeleton or as a solid object? Do lights cast shadow? By what rules do lights and surfaces interact? Rendering, or viewing, algorithms are fundamentally concerned not with what objects are but with how they are drawn (see Figure 1.59). Rendering is a tool of the graphic artist, and,

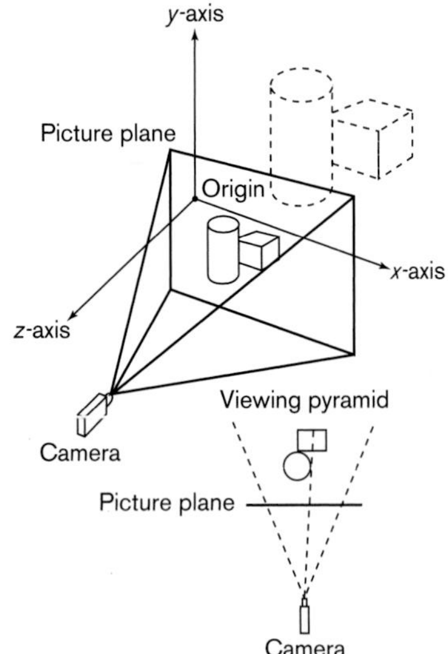

Figure 1.58 Above: A 3D environment can be viewed from a point of view, located anywhere in space, through a window connected to the point of view by a viewing pyramid (the pyramid of vision), which defines an expanding field of view. Rays drawn between a point in the environment and the point of view intersect the window, or image plane, and form a perspective projection of the environment.

Figure 1.59 Opposite: Various surface and rendering attributes applied to a single sphere. The top row shows the sphere rendered as points (left) and as a wire frame, with depth cueing (right). The second row shows the sphere rendered as a wire frame with hidden line removal (left) and with flat shading (right). The third row shows the sphere rendered with continuous (Gouraud) shading (left) and with specular (Phong) shading (right). The bottom row shows the sphere with texture mapping (left) and with ray tracing (right); the ray-traced sphere reflects a plaid surface that rests below the sphere.

though renderings sometimes model our physical world, they often involve ad hoc procedures. In many software packages it is possible to apply a specific rendering technique to a specific object; in these cases, the specific renders are called *shaders.*

The most basic rendering technique involves drawing points, which can be used to describe things that are inherently pointlike, such as atoms or stars, as well as surfaces, such as a rippling flag. In addition to having alterable spatial positions, points can also have a variety of intensities, colors, and sizes. Often, because of their small size and tendency to get lost in transmission, points are drawn with a surrounding glow that makes them seem larger.

The simplest way to represent an object is with lines. This representation, called a *wire frame*, or vector graphic, is the most economical way to display data. Wire-frame renderings may be monochromatic, colored, or even shaded. In addition to intensity and color, lines may have variable width and patterns. Because they show the backs as well as the fronts of objects, wire-frame renderings are often difficult to read and make it hard to distinguish between objects that are closer and those that are farther away. One technique to improve visibility is *depth cueing*, which, with a simple calculation, draws lines that are farther away with a dot pattern, a darker value, or a narrower width. Depth cueing is also used to color elevations, such as those found in contour maps.

In a wire-frame rendering, it is often desirable to draw only the lines that would be visible to a viewer and to omit those that would be obscured by solid objects. *Occultation* is the determination of the edges and surfaces that would be visible from the observer's point of view. Only visible surfaces are drawn, and all occulted, or hidden, ones are removed. This technique is also called *hidden line* or *hidden surface removal.*

Surfaces can be represented not only by their outlines or edges, but also as solid *opaque* areas of color. Renderings with occulted opaque surfaces are often called *solid renderings. Scan conversion*, one method of creating an opaque area of color, draws many touching parallel lines inside the surface. Another method involves *crosshatching*, drawing diagonal lines or a pattern on the surface. Like scan conversion, crosshatching is done at screen, not data, resolution. *Close-packed vectors* (CPV) draw a series of parallel lines

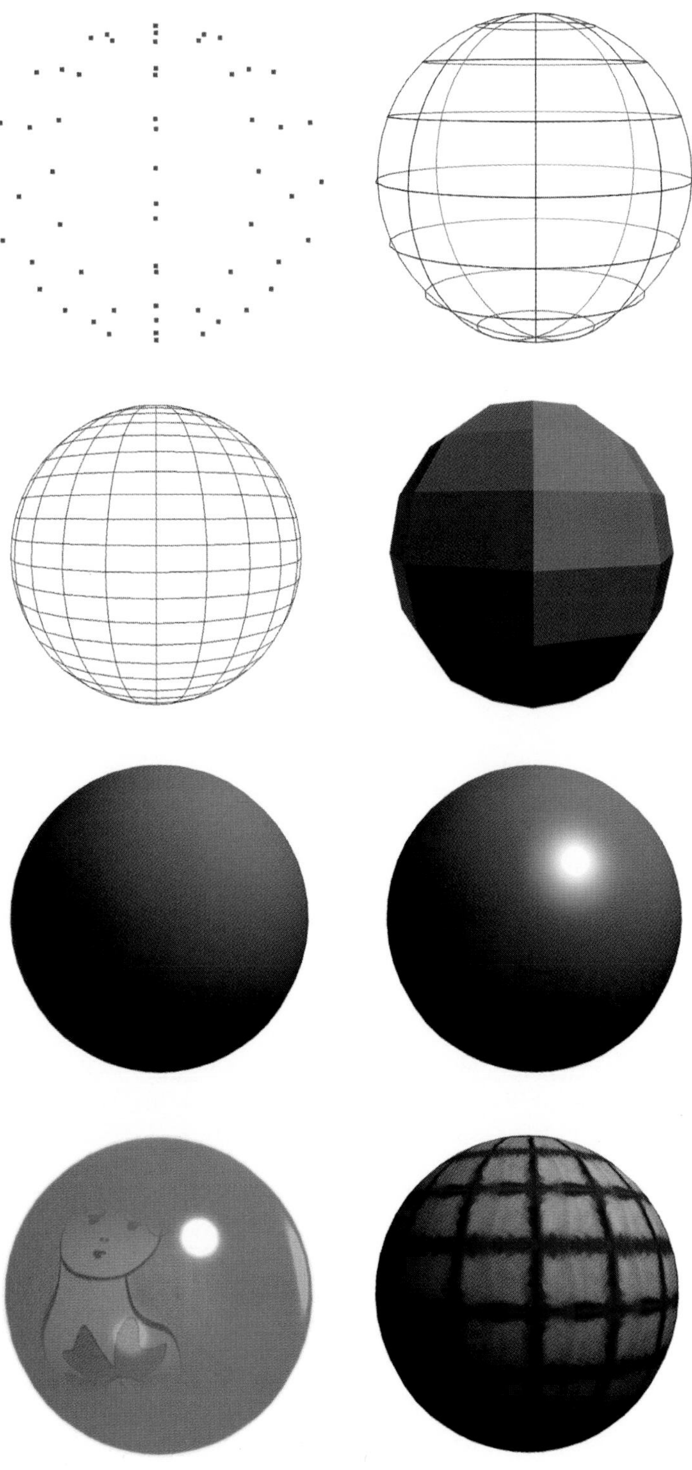

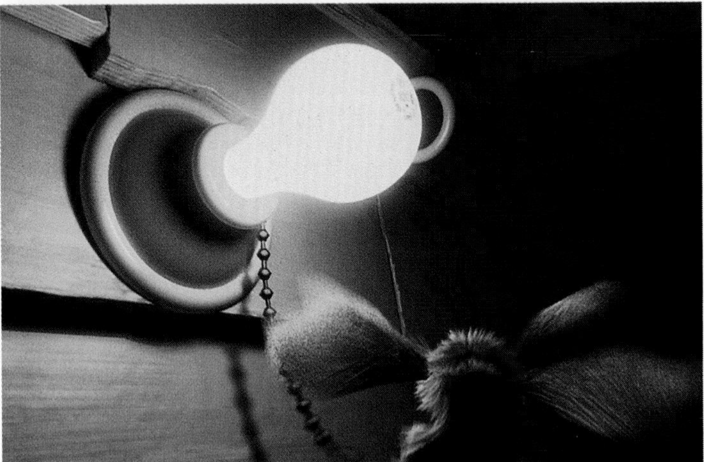

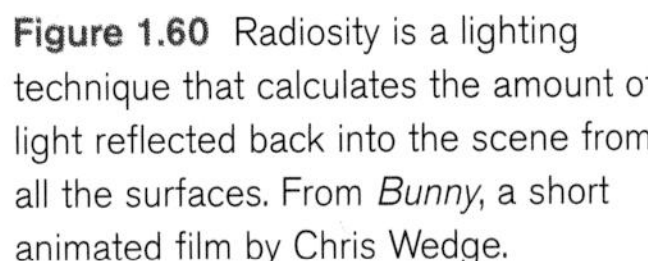
Figure 1.60 Radiosity is a lighting technique that calculates the amount of light reflected back into the scene from all the surfaces. From *Bunny*, a short animated film by Chris Wedge.

from one side of a polygon to the other; they are part of the object and scale with it.

More sophisticated renderings involve a variety of methods to incorporate a calculation of light. The simplest shading technique is called *constant-value face shading*, also known as *polygonal shading* or *flat shading*. A polygonal shader performs a single calculation for each polygonal surface of a polygonal object and renders the entire surface of each polygon with the same intensity of light. Polygonal shading makes each polygon easily distinguishable from the others, causing objects such as spheres to look faceted. If a smoother figure is required, one solution is to add more facets. This is not the best approach, however, because a very large number of facets may be needed to make the object appear smooth.

A better solution is to employ ***continuous shading***, also known as *Gouraud shading*. Continuous shading creates surfaces with continuous-tone shading, that is, shading that varies the brightness within the single polygons. Continuous shading usually has a dull overall appearance with lighting represented as varied brightness. This continuous-shading scheme eliminates the discrete brightness jumps between adjacent polygons and increases realism. Continuous shading produces a more realistic result than polygonal shading but takes longer to compute. *Phong shading* is a term often used to imply that the rendering calculations incorporate specular highlights, as well as diffuse surface reflections. Mapping can also be used to facilitate the simulation of surface effects that involve the texture of the surface itself.

A still better but even more computationally intensive approach is *ray tracing*, in which a virtual ray of light is traced from the point of view through each pixel on the screen to whatever object it intersects. One advantage of ray tracing is that if the object is transparent, refractive, or reflective, the new direction of the ray can be computed and further traced until it intersects with another object. This provides a way to create very realistic images and incorporate objects such as reflective spheres into a scene.

Illumination of a scene sometimes utilizes *radiosity*, that is, an approach where the light reflecting off each object in the scene is added back into the scene, impacting all of the other objects. This provides a calculation of ambient light that is closer to the natural laws of physics (see Figure 1.60).

But not all techniques for rendering are so complicated. A surface may also be created with a gradation of color that is not determined by lighting sources. The simplest way to do this is with *color-graduated,* or *color-ramp,* surfaces in which each corner of a polygon is assigned a color. The software then interpolates a color for each intermediate pixel of the resultant image. This is a common technique for graphically creating a sky or background in which color must vary from one hue to another.

2 The Anatomy of Time

This chapter explores the essence of time. At first glance it may seem like an unnecessary foundation, and indeed, many motion picture artists have survived with only an intuitive understanding of the concepts of time. However, while a large body of literature exists on the nature of the 2D image plane, the representation of solid objects, color, surface descriptions, lighting and chiaroscuro, and other topics, the key factor that is unique to the motion picture artist and distinguishes moving pictures from static graphics is time!

With an understanding of the formal, theoretical, and practical issues related to time, motion picture artists have a better command of their tools and the environment in which they work. This understanding helps to eliminate day-to-day production errors, as well as to broaden the possibilities during the creative process. It is time that determines the length of television shows, commercials, and movies. It is the seconds before the final buzzer that determine the last shot. It is the timing of a comedy skit that prompts one actor to lean over so that the swinging piece of lumber, blithely swung by the second character, narrowly misses his head. Timing provides rhythm to a flow of events and enables the premeditation of future actions. Without time, there is no narrative media.

Time is so ingrained that we take it for granted, but its representation in media presents us with a host of opportunities and problems. This chapter focuses on *temporal geometry*—the properties and manipulation of the time axis. The goal in studying temporal geometry is to understand time in a formal sense comparable to the

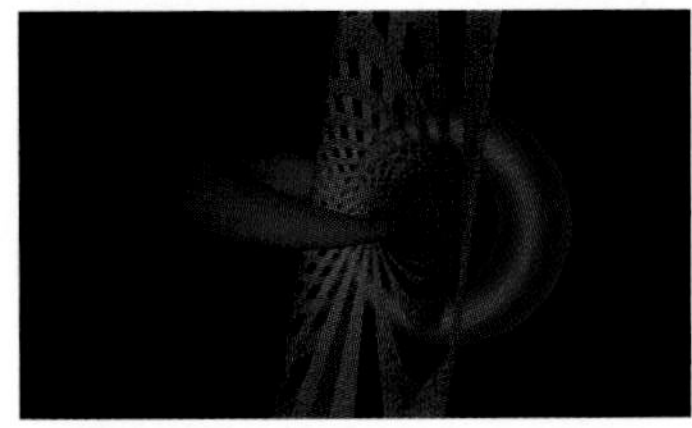

The computer allows us to manipulate time beyond ways possible with traditional media. Cyclides of Dupin shows two solid torus surfaces separated by a banded torus stretching to infinity. These algebraic surfaces are all stereographic projections from the 3D hypersphere in four-space.

understanding of plane and solid geometry. The discussion begins with a review of how we think about time as expressed in ordinary language, and quickly moves to how we represent it in media and the computerized world, and to how we confront the issues created by its representation as a series of discrete frames. The chapter concludes with some formal approaches for managing temporal events in the animation environment.

Time

Most of us take time for granted, but it is is not a trivial subject. Animation—indeed all motion picture media—involves the representation of events over time. Time involves a continuum that progresses from the past through the present into the future and can be represented on a variable axis. Time is a phenomenon with a single dimension that augments the three dimensions of space; together these form a significant part of the environment in which we subsist.

Time is required in order to effect changes in the real world. Time involves concepts about duration, such as an era, epoch, age, or for that matter a minute or a nanosecond. It also involves specific points or moments, such as a departure at 4:32 PM. We think about time as periodic, synchronous, or rhythmic. *Real time* connotes the flow of time in our real, tangible environment—the real world—as opposed to the flow of time depicted in media environments such as film and television. The term has also been used to describe the response time of processes—for example, the response of a computer program. When a program's response appears to be instantaneous, then the program is said to process "in real time." *Non-real time* often connotes a situation, related to media, where the time taken to fabricate and record something is longer or shorter than the time to view it, or where media is replayed at varying speeds, faster or slower, or forward or backward.

Time is a fundamental compositional element of any kinetic art form, be it music, theater, or any of the moving picture arts. Time has always been part of the moving picture and animation process, and the management, or *scripting*, of time has always been one of the key activities of the animator, whether or not a computer is used. Understanding time is essential to any person who makes moving pictures, be they a director, camera operator, editor, compositor, or animator. Working with time is a general art that applies across all moving picture media, be it film or videotape. The integration of computers and animation heightens our understanding of the ways we measure and control time, and relate real time to time in media. Media makes possible juxtapositions in time, such as the flashback, the flash-forward, and parallel actions. Moreover, the computer lets us scale, translate, organize, and interrelate temporal processes at a more abstract level than ever before and with greater precision and speed.

Representing Time in Words

Expressions of time are an integral part of language. Spoken and written language can be used to communicate temporal information with a battery of words, including verbs, adverbs, prefixes, conditionals, and nouns. While animation is a nonverbal, universal language, it is often directed verbally, and with computers especially, there is a one-to-one correspondence between a command and a result on the screen. In this section, everyday language is briefly examined, with an emphasis on aspects that may be adapted into animation language.

A *verb* is a word that indicates an action, condition, or process and hence is an integral part of an animator's vocabulary. One wants to direct characters in terms of verbal commands: "walk into the house," "drop the safe from the window," "jump into the rabbit hole." In fact, animate objects must be directed much like characters, and many of the actions we convey are intrinsically temporal—for example, "wait," "move," "stay." A verb's *tense* indicates the time of the event. The most obvious tenses are past, present, and future, but modern English actually employs six discrete time distinctions. Tense can take the form of a time period—such as a period piece or futuristic science fiction—or it can refer to events that lead up to the present. In a good story, the audience often figures out the actions that the character must take before the character does. Anticipating the future is a key element in drama.

Adverbs also express temporal information and can do so in three different ways: they can indicate at what point in time events occur, can specify the duration of events, and can order the succession of events. Something may happen now, or soon, or later, or may have already happened. Much of our time-oriented vocabulary relates to the clock and calendar: things happened yesterday, or are happening today, or they will happen tonight or tomorrow. Given two temporal events, one can occur before or after the other, or both can coincide. A common characteristic of many of these words is that they express relative time; today's tomorrow is tomorrow's today. Few animation languages provide this richness of language, and animators must usually resort to extremely tactile commands to express these ideas. Closely related to adverbs are ***temporal prefixes***—special prefix syllables used on the beginning of a word to place actions temporally.

Conditionals in language also show time relationships. These include *when, while, whenever, before, after, since, as, as long as, as often as, as soon as, until,* and *then.* Conditionals are part of natural language logic and are included in most computer programming languages. They play a role in animation language because they provide an easy way to synchronize events, specify durations, and enable one event to trigger the start of another. To some degree, they free animators from a world of precise frame counts and allow them to compose more freely. *"If condition 1 is true, then do event 1"* can be used to express a condition by which a certain activity might unfold. For example, if a specific object is still in the frame, then continue to shoot the scene. This type of communication is an integral part of how animation is directed.

Animators must also be aware that temporal ideas are embodied in many *nouns.* For example, *punctuality* implies a condition of being at the right place at the right time, whereas a temporal event that occurs later than expected creates a *delay,* a duration of time equal to the difference between the predicted time and the actual event time. We wait for the *future,* and *age* while we do so. Finally, animators must also be aware of special words that relate time to distance. For time is an integral part of motion, and concepts such as ***speed, velocity***, and ***acceleration*** all incorporate time; these are focal points in two subsequent chapters on easing and kinematics.

Continuous and Discrete Time

A *time axis* is a 1D vector connecting the past to the future and passing through the present. By and large, the time axis has many of the same properties and problems as the space axes. Time, like area or volume, can be measured with either continuous or discrete scales. As with graphics, the representation of continuous, temporal events as discrete units creates problems. As with two and three dimensions, time can be translated, scaled, and rotated. And, just as there exist operators in two and three dimensions for compositing elementary units, so are there functions for combining temporal actions. Finally, like graphic or volumetric data, temporal events may be organized and scripted as digital data.

The decision of whether or not to work in a continuous or discrete time domain is a paramount decision for an animator. The different modes have different quantum units, different meanings for intervals of time, and sometimes different procedures. And unfortunately, conversion between the two domains is problematic and requires special skills.

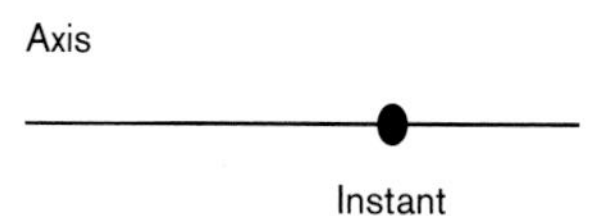

Figure 2.1 Above: A time axis and an instant, or point in time. The instant is in a continuous domain and is represented in a computer as a floating-point number.

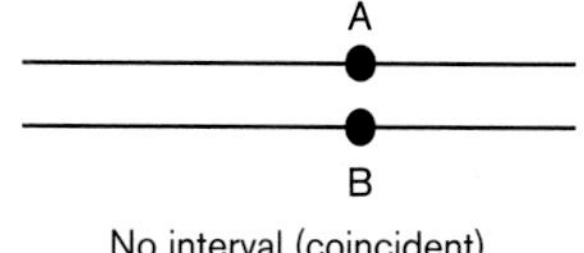

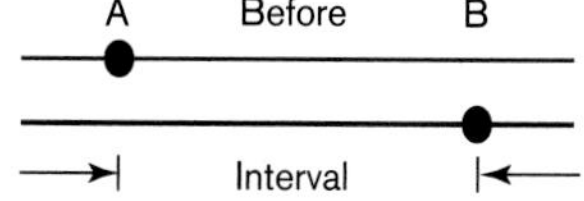

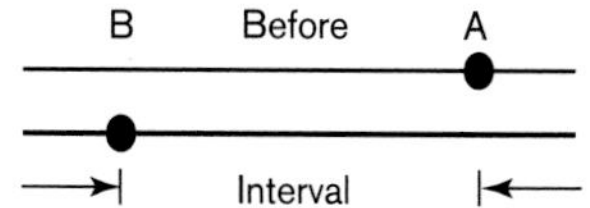

Figure 2.2 Above: Three relationships between two instants: coincident, an interval where A occurs before B, and an interval where B occurs before A. A well-ordered time continuum is that for any interval from A to B, such that A is before B, it is always possible to "split the difference" and find another instant, Q, that is between A and B such that A is before Q and Q is before B. This action may be repeated on the new interval recursively ad infinitum.

Continuous Time

Continuous time is time that is conceptualized as being infinitely divisible into smaller and smaller units. The concept of continuous time can best be illustrated by an analog clock. As the hands sweep around its face, the analog clock keeps continuous time. The minute hand does not jump from minute to minute; rather, it travels in a continuous fashion.

An *instant* is a point in continuous time (see Figure 2.1). Two instants (see Figure 2.2) are either coincident or occur at different times. Thus there are three relations between two instants: A coincident with B, A before B, or B before A. An *interval* is the segment of time between two instants.

It is worth noting that many media record data over continuous time. For example, a vinyl phonographic record, in which sound is represented as a continuously wiggling groove on a vinyl disc, is recorded when real-time air pressure analogically modulates the vinyl. The representation of the time dimension of the sound is continuous and bears a one-to-one relation with the original time.

Duration

The *duration* of an interval is the length of time of the interval. This can be specified in many ways. Spoken language employs numerous

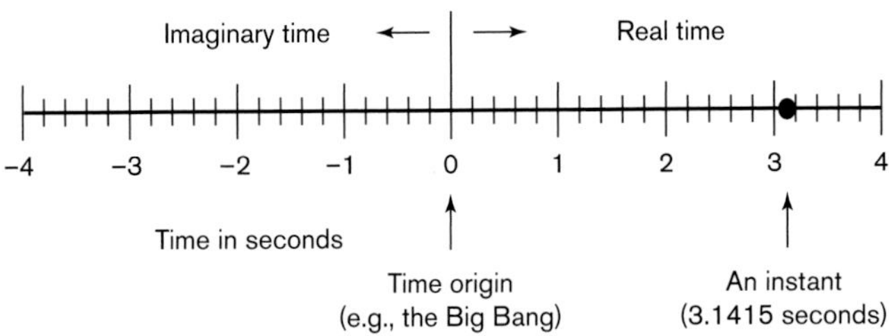

Figure 2.3 The continuous time axis is a 1D time scale with an interval, or ratio, scale. The numbers on the single axis represent relationships in time as arithmetic relationships of magnitude and make it possible to correspond a point in real time to a specific point on the time axis. Only after such a scale has been created can one count the pulses, be they natural events such as days or years, or artificial time bases such as the vibrations of a crystal oscillator. Instants are represented by floating-point numbers that may have apparent infinite precision. The instant indicated here is an event π seconds after the Big Bang. Normally, time is represented as a positive number, and an origin is chosen to be before times of particular interest. Negative time may be used for events that occur before the origin. Whether or not time existed before the Big Bang is still an open question. Hence, the portion of the time axis to the left of the Big Bang is referred to as imaginary.

words to describe a variety of time durations, from the instantaneous to the ongoing, which are ordered into eight or nine differentiations of temporal duration—for example, slow, leisurely, rapid, swift, quick. It is worth noting that quantitative measurement of duration requires an interval scale. This is done by declaring one instant to be zero, which is considered to be the origin of the time scale, and then marking out a succession of equally spaced temporal intervals. This is the function of a *clock*, an instrument that generates evenly spaced intervals, or periods, of time. In this respect a clock is the same as a *frequency generator, metronome,* or *oscillator* (see Figure 2.3). Once values are assigned to instants, it is possible to calculate the duration of an interval, which is equal to the distance between two instants—a number derived by subtracting the first instant from the second. For example, if you work from one o'clock to four o'clock, the duration of your work is three hours.

Discrete Time

Discrete time is time that is represented by discrete scales. In discrete time there are no instants, and it is not possible to "split the difference." A *pulse* is defined as a discrete quantum of time. Discrete time can be represented as a series of pulses sampled at a fixed frequency, or rate (see Figure 2.4). For example, a digital clock that counts seconds displays each second for a one-second duration, and then displays the next. When recording discrete data over time, the number of individual samples recorded per second is referred to as the *sampling frequency*. For example, the sampling frequency for conventional film is 24 individual frames/second. The inverse of the sampling frequency is the *cycle time*, the duration of time that each sampled unit represents—which typically takes into account the time needed to accomplish the sampling process. For example, in film each frame represents 1/24 th of a second—this represents the exposure time and the time needed to advance the film.

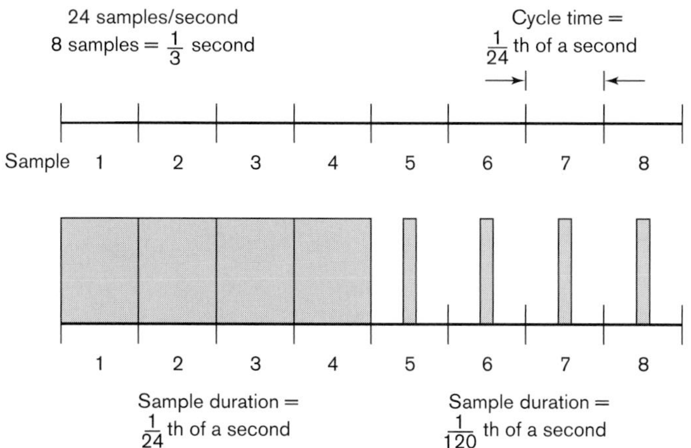

Figure 2.4 The discrete time axis. The top portion of the figure presents a discrete time axis with eight individual divisions, or samples. Each sample is represented by a whole number, with the samples incrementing to the right. There are 24 samples/second; hence the cycle time is 1/24 th of a second. At the bottom of the figure, a second axis is presented. Here, the cycle time is still 1/24 th of a second, but two different sample duration times are illustrated. On samples 1 to 4, the sample duration time equals the cycle time and each sample represents 1/24 th of a second. On samples 4 to 8, the sample duration time is less than the cycle time, and in this example, each sample represents only 1/120 th of a second.

Closely related to cycle time is *sample duration time*, the actual duration of time that each sampled unit represents. In film, the cycle time is roughly equal to the sample duration time plus the time needed to advance the shuttle mechanism of the camera.

Discrete scales typically start counting at zero or one, depending on the context (see Figure 2.5). In America, a scale with an origin of one is used for numbering the floors of a building—the ground floor is one—but in Europe the first floor is one floor up and the lobby is considered to be floor zero. Film and video likewise can begin counting with the first frame being either frame zero or frame one. What the origin is called differs from one production studio to the next.

Once unit zero has been designated, negative numbers can also exist in discrete scales. For example, negative time may be expressed using negative numbers or conventions such as BC, or with a system called *nines complement notation*, often found where there are displays that have no minus sign or where there are mechanical counters such as an odometer (see Figure 2.6).

Finally, a *timel* is defined as a discrete quantum unit of spacetime. Note that timels define indivisible durations of time, just as pixels define indivisible areas on the plane or voxels define indivisible cubes of space.

Discrete versus Continuous Time

Since discrete and continuous time scales are inherently different, there are several issues that must be addressed when comparing the two (see Figure 2.7). Because discrete scales may start at zero or one, there are two ways to align a discrete scale to an analog

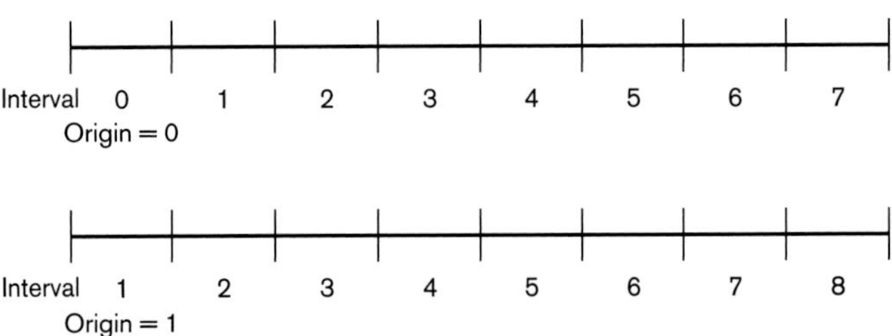

Figure 2.5 Right: Origin 0 and origin 1 scales. A discrete system that starts with the first interval considered interval 0 is called an *origin 0 system.* A discrete system that starts with the first interval being considered interval 1 is called an *origin 1 system.* Typically, discrete time scales incorporate either origin 0 or origin 1 scales. Note that in discrete systems, there are no instants, only intervals.

Numbers (+/–)	Nines complement
3	00003
2	00002
1	00001
0	00000
–1	99999
–2	99998
–3	99997
–4	99996
–5	99995

Figure 2.6 Above: Nines complement notation is typically used in digital counters, be they electronic or mechanical. An odometer clearly illustrates this concept. For instance, incrementing an odometer—sequentially counting by integers—will eventually result in the odometer reaching its maximum, a number consisting only of nines—for example, 99999. Once the odometer is at its maximum representation, incrementing the odometer one more time will turn all the digits back to 0. Running the counter backward is the equivalent of counting backward. For example, –1 is represented by 99999.

scale (see Figure 2.8). Another issue is that it is uncertain just how instants get interpreted as frames, an issue further complicated by the fact that although a frame represents a duration 1/24 th of a second, it may not actually record 1/24 th of a second of real time. A third issue pertains to the calculation of durations in discrete and continuous scales, which are performed differently (see Figure 2.9). For example, in continuous scales, you will recall, the duration is equal to instant B minus instant A, where A precedes B (duration = B – A). But with discrete scales, the frames themselves have durations, so just subtracting the frame numbers may not provide a correct duration. For example, consider how to calculate the duration of a shot that is three frames long. One approach is to subtract the first frame from the last (3 – 1), which equals two frames—the wrong answer; one more frame needs to be added to the result.

Animators are cautioned that both continuous and discrete temporal scales need to be understood and that each domain has certain advantages and disadvantages. Certain types of animation can really only be done discretely—for example, an animation in which an object is to alternate between two given colors every other frame, creating a stroboscopic effect. Conversely, continuous time is much more easily manipulated in the planning and execution of shots. The animator must also remember that even in continuous-time models, it is ultimately necessary to be able to determine a corresponding integer frame number since the animation medium is ultimately discrete. This task is not always trivial and is subject to *motion artifacts* (discussed in more detail in later chapters).

Relationships Between Temporal Intervals

Recall that Figure 2.2 identified 3 relationships between two instants in time: A coincident with B, A before B, and B before A. Here we explore the 16 relationships between two temporal intervals (see

Property of time scale	Time scale: Continuous	Discrete
Number type	Floating point	Integer
Domain	Infinite resolution	Fixed resolution
Quantum unit	Instant	Frame
Duration of interval	DURATION = ENDINSTANT – STARTINSTANT	DURATION = ENDFRAME – STARTFRAME
Origin	0.0	0 or 1
Negative time	−6.8	−6 or 9994
Translation	Addition and subtraction of numbers	Addition or subtraction of numbers; no fractions
Scaling	Multiplication and division of numbers; numbers may be whole numbers or fractions	Even integer scaling is easily accomplished; other scaling can be problematic
Rotation	Use a system of 5x5 transformation matrices	Use timels and discrete *n*-dimensional fuctions

Figure 2.7 Comparison of continuous and discrete time scales.

Figure 2.10). These relationships are important because they provide a precise language to relate intervals to each other. A situation that involves many apparently overlapping intervals may always be analyzed in terms of *interval pairs*. Hence, in this context, the 16 relationships define a finite set of temporal relationships that can exist between any set of intervals.

Temporal interval relationships provide us with a useful grammar for directing moving picture media. They provide a formalization of the adverbs and conditionals found in ordinary language and therefore enable an elementary syntax for editing, compositing, animation, and event triggering. For example, A abuts B is a meaningful description of two shots in a movie: A precedes B with no gap between. And A during B can be used to describe concurrent events, such as a newscaster with an over-the-shoulder insert window of news footage (see Figure 2.11).

Media: Recording Time-Based Events

How do instants and intervals relate to the recording and viewing of moving pictures? This issue is looked at from the point of view of various media, because they are the vehicles that record time-based events into a physical embodiment, be it celluloid coated with silver halide crystals, acetate with magnetized metals, or electrons moving in wire.

In classic moving picture recording, the dominant media have been film and tape, and as such there is a one-to-one correspondence

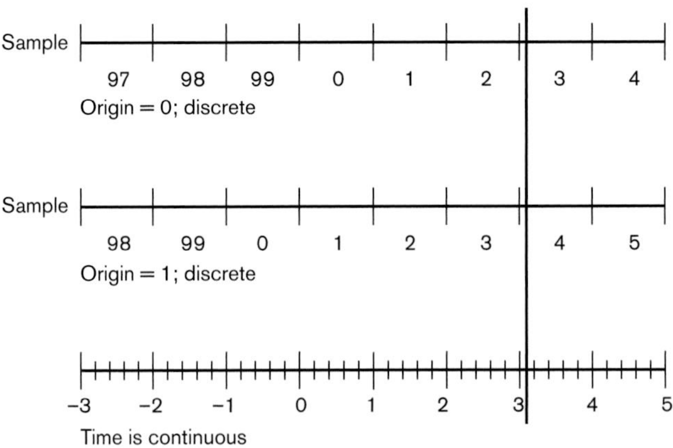

Figure 2.8 Right: Continuous instants versus discrete intervals. Two discrete time scales are above a continuous scale. In a continuous system, the origin is an instant at time 0. In discrete systems, there are no instants, only intervals, so counting starts with the first interval being either frame 0 or frame 1. The value of T = 3.1415 seconds lies within the third interval of a discrete scale with 0 origin, or within the fourth interval of a discrete scale with 1 origin.

Figure 2.9 Below: Continuous versus discrete duration calculations. On the continuous scale, the duration from 1 to 3 is 2, but on the discrete scale, the duration from 1 to 3 is 3.

between the length of the physical media and a duration of time. As a result, the nomenclature includes phrases such as "30 inches per second" for videotape, "90 feet per minute" for 35mm film, or "36 feet per minute" for 16mm film. In fact, early animators were paid by the foot, not by the second, and even today terminology still references the length of the physical medium, for example, "fade it out for 2 feet."

At the most elementary level, a single image frame is a matrix of data that can be represented digitally, as in computer graphics; electronically, as in video; or as analog data, as in film. The matrix has at least two dimensions—*x* in the horizontal direction and *y* in the vertical direction—and these dimensions together define the image plane. If a dimension is added onto this system, a 3D, or more correctly, rank three matrix is created. This new dimension is called the *component*. The components are parallel planes of *xy* information for each frame (see Figure 2.12). By implication, they are in synchronization, that is, they share the same time. For example, there may be separate red, green, and blue color components for each frame. In practice, components may record many things beside luminance and color, including ultraviolet, infrared, ultrahigh frequency imaging, ultrasound, and X-rays.

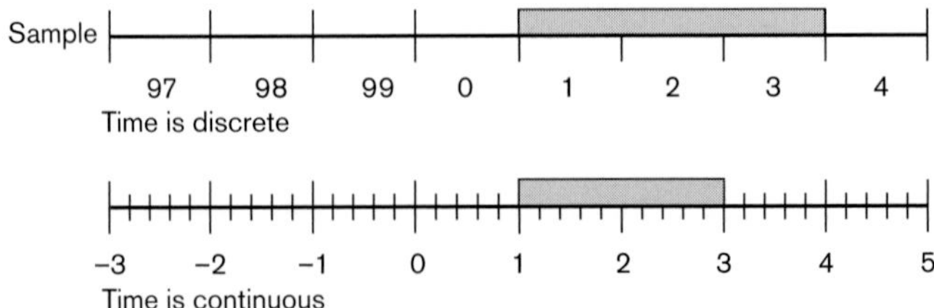

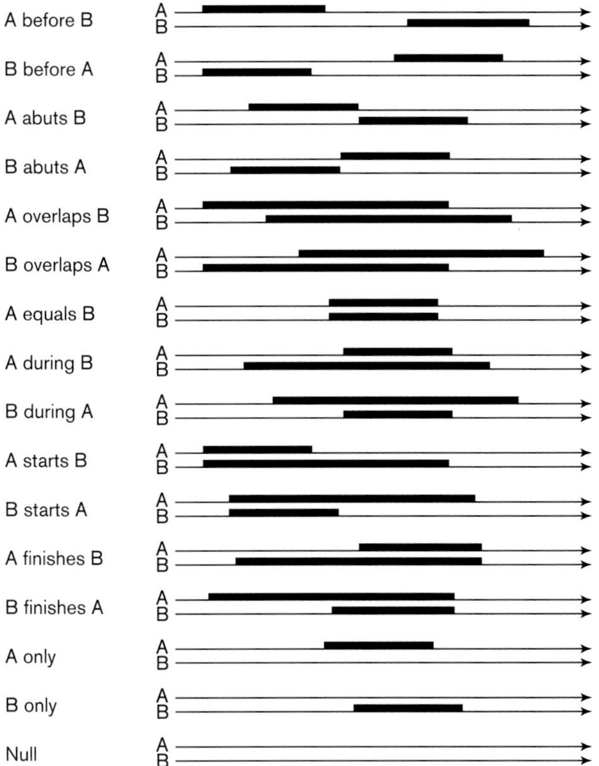

Figure 2.10 Left: Sixteen temporal relationships between two intervals. The time line flows from left to right. Intervals A and B are depicted along the time line by a thick line. Interval relationships may be organized into five groups. Intervals are sequential *disjoint* in two cases: A before B, and B before A. This may also be expressed as B after A, or A after B. Intervals are sequential *abutting* in two cases: A abuts B, and B abuts A; the second interval begins before the first one ends and continues after the first interval ends. Intervals are *overlapping* in two cases: A overlaps B, and B overlaps A. *Nested* intervals occur in seven ways: A equals B, A during B, B during A, A starts B, B starts A, A finishes B, and B finishes A. Note that the last four of these involve a synchronized start or end time and are useful when events trigger or terminate each other. A equals B and B equals A involve synchronized start and end times. Finally there are three singleton cases: A only, B only, and null—neither A or B.

Figure 2.11 Above: Example of one temporal interval nested inside another temporal interval. The insert shot (top line) might occur during the full-screen shot (bottom line) with the insert starting after the full-screen shot and ending before it.

A *shot* is an uninterrupted sequence of frames, which themselves consist of one or more components. A shot implies going from time A to time B with no discontinuities in time or point of view; colloquially, no break in action. In the computer, a shot can be represented as a sequence of digital frame matrices (see Figure 2.13).

In a practical sense, a shot represents a duration of time, plus some miscellaneous data typically associated with the shot as a whole, including the recording speed expressed in number of frames per second, the shot creation date, the manufacturer of the equipment, personnel, and a brief verbal description of content. Shots can be assembled together into larger assemblies such as commercials, news stories, television programs, or films. This also involves a temporal language, which is detailed in Chapter 14.

Normalized and Center-Unity Time

When working with time, it is often useful to have a system where the duration of shots can be represented not with actual time, but in a more abstract manner. This is particularly useful when the actual duration of the shot is unknown, but the action must be designed anyway. Two methods of assigning numeric values to an interval help the animator think more abstractly. An interval of *unit duration* is an interval with a numeric domain from 0.0 to 1.0 Thus, the beginning of the interval is 0.0, the end of the interval is 1.0, and the middle point of the interval is 0.5; thus the value 0.25 represents a time that is one quarter of the unit duration. This system is referred to as *normalized time*, and a unit duration is analogous to normalized vectors.

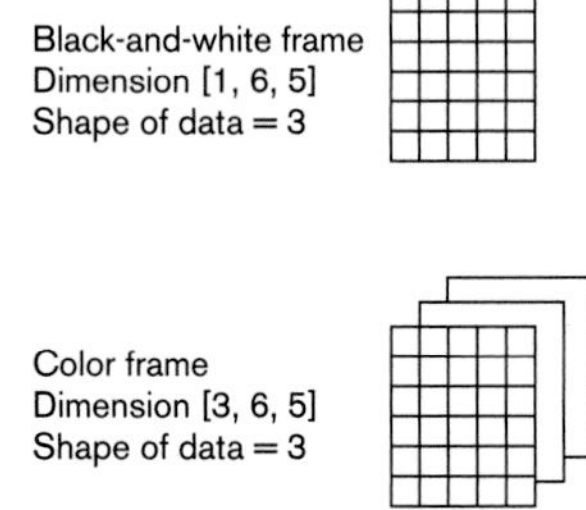

Figure 2.12 Above: Format of a frame and its channels. The top portion of the figure presents a black-and-white frame. The bottom portion presents a color frame that is represented by a 3D matrix containing red, green, and blue channels.

Figure 2.13 Below: Format of a shot. The top portion of the figure presents a shot consisting of black-and-white frames. The bottom portion of the figure presents a shot consisting of color frames, each represented by a 3D matrix containing red, green, and blue channels.

An alternative approach to unit duration is *center-unity duration*, which centers the origin (zero) of an interval at the temporal center of the interval, and defines the domain of the interval to continuously range from −1.0 to +1.0, for a total length of 2.0 (see Figure 2.14). In a center-unitized duration, the middle point of the interval is 0.0, the beginning is −1.0, and the end is +1.0 A value of −0.5 represents a time that is one quarter of the total interval time. This system is referred to as *center-unity time.*

Both normalized time and center-unity time are based on continuous time; hence the unit duration or center-unity duration can be "mapped" into any duration of time expressed in real-world units, for example, thirty seconds, one minute, five and a half years. Normalized time is widely used in *easing*, discussed in Chapter 10, because it enables the animator to approach a shot in terms of when things happen in a relative fashion. Because the shot is normalized, it can then be scaled to the actual length. Center-unity time is a more subtle concept, but is useful when there is a central event—for example, a countdown for a rocket launch, which counts down and then counts up.

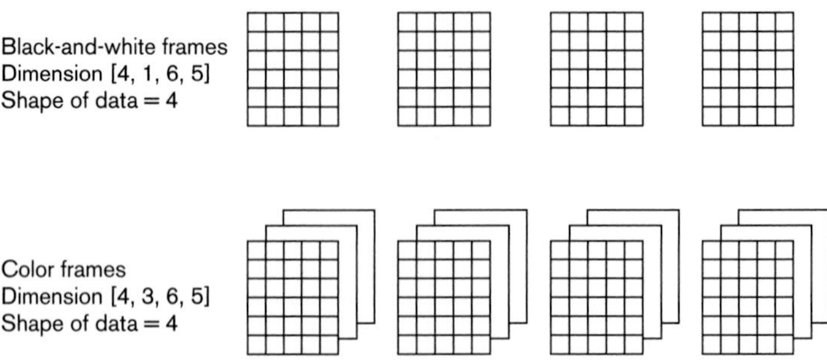

Absolute and Relative Time

Two other essential temporal concepts are ***absolute time*** and ***relative time***. Absolute time is a specific numeric time value, usually expressed in instants, for example, 3.21 seconds, but which can also be expressed in terms of a frame, for example, frame 301. In normalized and center-unity time, absolute time has a domain of 0.0 to 1.0 and −1.0 to 1.0, respectively. Relative time is a time expressed as a ratio of a time interval. For example, "Begin swinging the bat when the ball is halfway (50%) between the pitcher and the catcher." Relative temporal events have no implicit absolute time; they are relative to and subservient to an interval—if the interval becomes longer or shorter, the relative duration is made longer or shorter proportionally. For example, 30% of a shot 4.2 minutes long is 1.26 minutes, but 30% of a shot 4.3 minutes long is 1.29 minutes.

In motion pictures, there is an affinity between relative time and normalized intervals because the combination allows one to think in terms of overall rhythm and timing instead of in frames. It is best to design shots in terms of seconds and not in terms of the frame numbers of some particular recording media. (Remember, film and television have different frame rates.) This way, the shots can be easily transferred to the temporal resolution of another medium. Hence shots—especially in computer animation—can be conceived with some elasticity, or temporal stretch, to them, so that the events within the interval change proportionally as the shot is scaled longer or shorter. Only when shots need to be digitized and recorded need one resolve them into absolute time (see Figure 2.15).

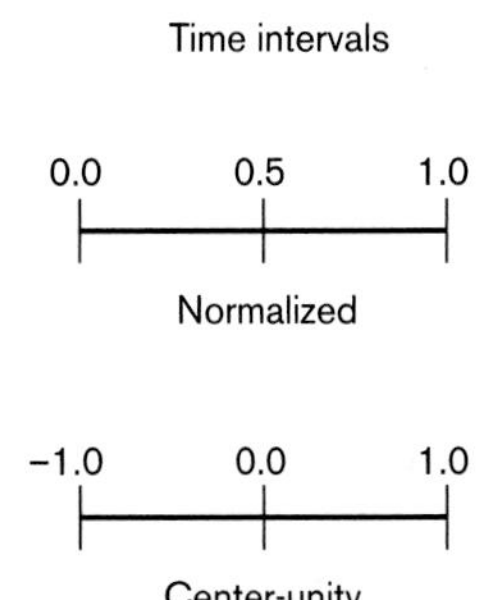

Figure 2.14 Above: Normalized time and center-unity time.

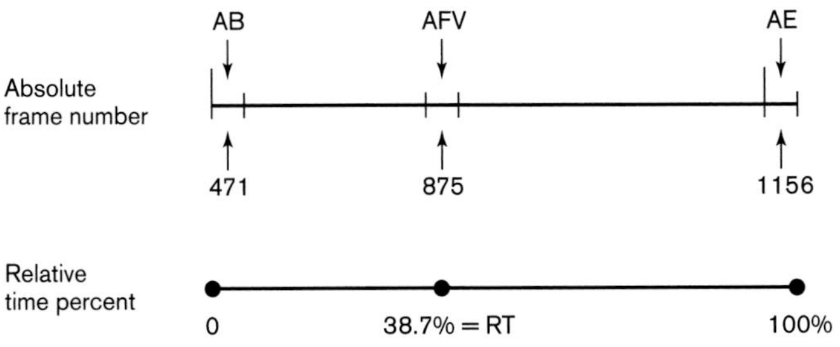

Figure 2.15 Below: Absolute and relative time, and a procedure for translating relative time to absolute time. The procedure requires as input the Absolute Beginning (AB) frame, Absolute End (AE) frame, and the Relative Time (RT), that is, the point in time for which an absolute frame number or value is being computed; the procedure determines the Absolute Frame Value (AFV). The algorithm calculates the absolute interval duration, scales it by the relative time, and adds it to the Absolute Beginning frame, AB. The final step of the algorithm is to add 0.5 to the previous result and then take the absolute value of the resultant sum; this final step correctly rounds off the result to an integer.

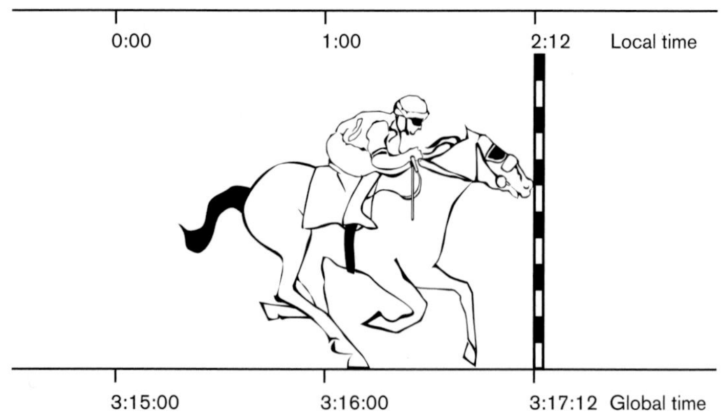

Figure 2.16 The horse race lasts 2 minutes, 12 seconds, its duration in local time. The race begins at 3:15:00 in the afternoon global time, and 0:00 local time. Thus 3:15 is the instant in global time that corresponds to the origin of local time. The race ends at 3:17:12 global time or 3:15:00 + 2:12.

Nested, Local, and Global Time

The concept of absolute and relative time leads quite naturally to the concepts of nested time intervals and local and global time. *Nested time intervals* are time intervals that can be contained wholly within other time intervals, that is, they begin after and end before the longer interval (again see Figure 2.11). If the nested intervals are relative, they can scale with their encompassing intervals. *Local time* is a duration with a local origin—for example, the duration of a horse race. The temporal event is expressed relative to its origin: the length of the race is 2:12 minutes. *Global time* is a larger frame of reference into which local time fits. For example, the time of day that the horse race starts is global time: 3:15 PM. Local time is converted into global time by adding the local time to the instance in global time at which local time began being measured (see Figure 2.16).

In practice, the concept of nested time intervals can become quite complex. For example, in motion picture practice, it is often useful to think of an independent shot as having its own local origin and length, and as consisting of several interval actions, each of which have their own local origins and lengths. Direction such as "fly the camera around the object, pause on it, then push it in closer" can create a shot such that each of the actions has its own local time, during which events are relative to its beginning and end: "lengthen the pause by a quarter second" or "make the pause 30% longer" or "add six frames to the pause." The time frame of the shot is global to the time frame of each action. Conversely, the time frame of the shot is local relative to the longer time frame of the program as a whole. For each shot, there is a correspondence between the shot's own

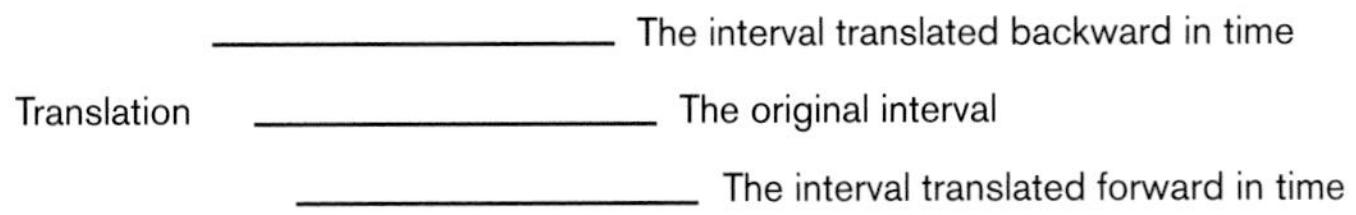

Figure 2.17 Left: Translating time. Translation advances an interval backward or forward in time.

Figure 2.18 Below: Scaling time. Scaling of continuous time is straightforward: simple multiplication by decimal numbers produces the new values. Numbers between 0 and 1 make events shorter, numbers larger than 1 make events longer, and negative numbers inverse the time flow and make events go backward. Hence, many computer animators feel it is easiest to work in a continuous time domain whenever possible, and convert to discrete time only at display time.

local origin and the program's global time. A temporal nesting scheme can involve many levels, and it applies to times both in the real world and within media.

Fundamental Temporal Operations

Equivalents of the fundamental geometric transformations, such as translation, scaling, and rotation, are also viable concepts in the temporal domain. All three of these transformations can be performed in either a continuous or discrete time domain.

Translation

Translation of instants, frames, and intervals is a process that moves events backward or forward in time; it makes events occur sooner or later (see Figure 2.17). With respect to moving pictures, translation involves moving events or shots forward or backward a fixed number of frames and is straightforward, provided one is sure that durations are correctly defined. Most of what an editor does involves the translation of frames relative to local and global time bases. Frames are moved backward toward the *head*, or beginning, and forward toward the *tail*, or end. Translation is trivial for continuous or discrete numbers and is performed by addition and subtraction; it is akin to moving objects in space.

Scaling

Scaling of time occurs during recording or replay when the duration of events are made to last longer or shorter (see Figure 2.18). In other words, action is sped up or slowed down relative to the viewer. Again, the process is akin to scaling graphics, where objects are

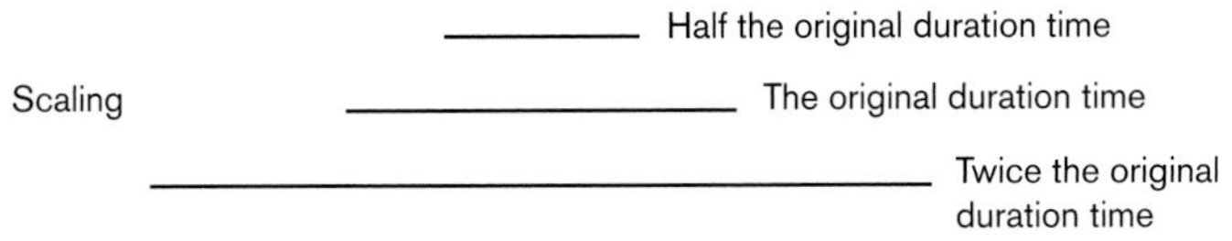

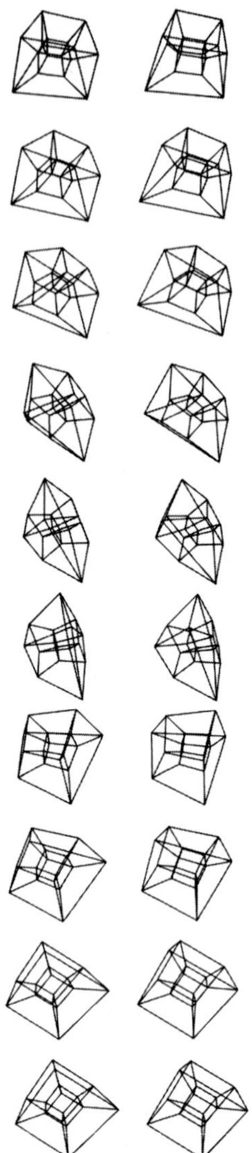

Figure 2.19 Four-dimensional rotation stereo pairs. Michael Noll's 1967 film *Hypercubes* presents a 3D projection of a 4D hypercube rotating in hyperspace. The movie is meant to be viewed by holding a sheet of paper between the left and right eye stereo pairs, with the viewer's head positioned in such a way that the two pictures merge into one image, which should appear as 3D.

made bigger or smaller. ***Reverse action***, that is, going backward in time, can be achieved by scaling an event by a negative quantity and is a unique creation of media that does not exist in the real world.

One way to scale time is to change the recording speed during the recording process and then play back the result at normal speed. For example, if a camera is run at a higher than normal speed—a process called *overcranking*—then when the frames are replayed at normal speed, the action appears to be in *slow motion*. *Undercranking* the camera produces ***fast motion***, faster than real-life action. When the time between frames becomes longer than a second or two—for example, when a growing flower is photographed once a day—the process is called *time-lapse photography*. In addition to letting the viewer see actions that are too fast or too slow for the eye to perceive in a normal way, temporal scaling can also be used in situations where it may be important to experience time at different rates.

There are instances in a discrete time domain where scaling time can also be straightforward. For example, frames, being indivisible and discrete, are relatively easy to scale in even-integer multiples and fractions. To make a shot twice as long, each frame is copied twice, a process called *double framing*. Conversely, to make a shot run twice as fast, one can *skipframe*, or omit every other frame when making a copy of the medium. Unfortunately, scaling shots by non-integer factors can get complicated and typically requires repeating frames in some sort of pattern. For example, a scaling factor of 0.666 is achieved by printing two frames, then skipping one—eliminating every third frame. Double framing every other frame scales time 150%. These approaches are surprisingly workable and have been used for years in optical printing. Note that the results produced are approximations and not completely accurate. The operational envelope is limited, and under many situations the methods produce unwanted side effects and cause an image to chatter. In addition, in order to scale a shot by an irregular quantity—for example, 46.21%—it is necessary to work out a more complicated pattern, such as skipframing plus skipping one extra frame every 25 frames.

Another technique for scaling time mimics an approach used when scaling pixels. This technique produces a frame that is a weighted mixture of two or more input frames—each of the input frames contributes its own percent of time to the result. For example, to make a shot run twice as fast, one might create a double exposed resultant frame, with half of the exposure coming from each of the two original frames that define it. This technique is particularly useful when converting between media, such as film and video, that have slightly different frame rates.

Rotation

Temporal scaling and translation are relatively easy to understand because they are axes-independent operations. Temporal ***rotation***, on the other hand, is not at all intuitive. As with temporal scaling and translation, time can be rotated in a manner that is analogous to spatial rotation. In 3D graphics, rotations hold one axis constant and vary the values along the other two axes. Rotation in space-time, that is, the fourth dimension, is more complicated than in 3D space.

Since the mathematics of temporal rotation is well understood, a computer can be programmed to perform 4D rotations (see Figure 2.19) by extending the idea of homogeneous coordinates and transformation matrices (see Figure 2.20).

$$\begin{bmatrix} 3 & 4 & 5 & 8 & 1 \\ 2 & 8 & 7 & 9 & 1 \end{bmatrix} \times \begin{bmatrix} 1 & 0 & 0 & 0 & 0 \\ 0 & 1 & 0 & 0 & 0 \\ 0 & 0 & 1 & 0 & 0 \\ 0 & 0 & 0 & 2 & 0 \\ 0 & 0 & 0 & 0 & 1 \end{bmatrix} \times \begin{bmatrix} 1 & 0 & 0 & 0 & 0 \\ 0 & 1 & 0 & 0 & 0 \\ 0 & 0 & 1 & 0 & 0 \\ 0 & 0 & 0 & 1 & 0 \\ 0 & 0 & 0 & 5 & 1 \end{bmatrix} \times \begin{bmatrix} .8 & 0 & 0 & .6 & 0 \\ 0 & 1 & 0 & 0 & 0 \\ 0 & 0 & 1 & 0 & 0 \\ -.6 & 0 & 0 & .8 & 0 \\ 0 & 0 & 0 & 0 & 1 \end{bmatrix}$$

Figure 2.20 Matrix mathematics may be used to transform time mathematically. These 5 x 5 matrices scale, translate, and then rotate the two-row, five-column temporal interval at the left. The result is an interval that is twice as long, five units advanced in time, and rotated around the *xt* axis. In 3D graphics, there are three possible rotations, each altering two axes at a time (*yz* rotated around *x*, *xz* rotated around *y*, *xy* rotated around *z*). But in space-time, there are six rotations, each altering two axes at a time (*yz*, *yt*, *zt* rotated around *x*; *xz*, *xt*, *zt* rotated around *y*; *xy*, *xt*, *yt* rotated around *z*; *xy*, *xz*, *yz*, rotated around *t*). Because spatial rotation about any axis affects two dimensions, any rotation about the time axis also affects either the *x*, *y*, or *z* axis. This approach provides some very novel ways to think about space-time. Research on how to visualize four dimensions is one of those topics that is perhaps only approachable with computer animation.

3 The Science of Moving Pictures

This chapter introduces the fundamental concepts of moving pictures, beginning with an introduction to media and corresponding technologies, then proceeding to a discussion of still-lensed imaging, with a detailed explanation of the imaging process and how it relates to light, the camera obscura, lenses, the shutter, and the still projector. Also discussed are recording and playback, continuous and discrete representation, persistence of vision, stroboscopic principles, and aliasing and anti-aliasing. This low-level world is very subtle, and the mechanics of lenses, shutters, and projectors imbue "signatures" into what is recorded and played back. Media technologies often blend continuous and discrete representation that produce aliasing in the recordings, and even well-formed recording can fool the eye.

The Search for Terminology

Moving pictures is a term used to describe a general system for the recording and playback of pictures that change over time, irrespective of the recording medium. Moving picture media include film, television, and, since the introduction of computer animation, digital media. The increased variety of media helps to focus our quest for general principles.

Early pioneers, such as Thomas Edison, developed terminology for very specific moving picture technologies. Many of these terms, such as kinetoscope, kinetograph, and kinematograph, incorporate the Greek word *kinēma*, meaning "motion" (see Figure 3.1), and were

Above: The Fort at Mashantucket: from a 3D interactive tour of the 17th century Pequot village and fort created for the Mashantucket Pequot Museum and Research Center.

kin-e-mat-ics (kin emat iks), *n. pl.* used as sing. [<Gk. *kinema,* motion], Phys., the science that treats the motion of bodies and systems without regard to the forces producing it: a branch of mathematics, but often included in treatises on dynamics. —*adj.* **kinematic; kinematical.**

kin-e-mat-o-graph (kin e-mat o-graf), *n.* **[cinematograph], 1,** lantern for projecting motion pictures upon a screen, as in a theater; **2,** a camera for making such pictures.

kin-e-scope (kin e-skop), *n.* [<Gk. *kinein* to move + *skopein,* to look], **1,** instrument for drawing a curve representing the resultant of several circular motions: also called *kinetoscope;* **2,** a motion picture made by photographing the image on the face of the CRT; **3,** the equipment (an interface device) used to make this transfer. —*vt.* **scoped; scoping:** to make a kinescope of.

Figure 3.1 Above: *Kinema* is a Greek root word meaning "motion"; its use as a moving picture term began about 100 years ago, and today we still talk about the art of the cinema.

used to describe cameras, projectors, and the process at large. While kinēma reflects the importance of the motion inherent in moving pictures, it does not acknowledge the importance of pictures, or graphics—derived from the Greek *graphein* meaning "to write" or "to draw" (see Figure 3.2). Combining the two produces the word *cinematography*, which has remained part of our vocabulary.

The word *video* came into being after the word *television*. The root word lies in the Latin *vidēre*, "to see," and video emerged as a visual correspondence to the word *audio*, the technology of sound transmission (see Figure 3.3). Video, like audio, implies an electronic as well as a temporal aspect; these two technologies, plus the technology of transmission, comprise television.

Although the words *cinematography* and *video* deserve consideration as general terms to embrace all forms of moving picture media, including film, video, and time-sequenced digital imaging, their history strongly connects them to specific technologies. Hence, this book will use the term *moving pictures*, which implies a 2D graphic that is changing over time and that is independent of any particular carrier or medium.

Media

Recording is the process of reorganizing matter or energy in a semi-permanent way so as to contain information. The information is expressed as a structure or pattern that has meaning for those using the recording to communicate. Recordings may be perceived—in the graphic sense, viewed—at different points in space-time and thus permit communication from the past into the future, possibly across thousands of years and billions of miles. Not only does recording allow communication between different individuals but also between different species and from an individual to the same individual at a different point in space-time.

A recording has two major components: the *medium* and the *message* (see Figure 3.4). The message, or information imprinted into a medium, is independent from the material of which the medium is built. The medium is the mass or energy used to transport the message through space-time. Recordings such as drawing, printing, and photography employ a physical carrier to support the image. The medium usually accounts for most of the mass or energy of the recording. The medium may support textual alphanumeric messages, sound, pictures, and holograms, as well as other information. Samples of common media include clay bricks, granite, paper, cellulose acetate, Mylar tape, vinyl, plastic, and constant radio frequencies such as those encountered in radio and television broadcasts. Classical media, such as vinyl for phonographs or wire for telephones, offer substantial physical support. During the last 5000 years, media have become increasingly compact and fragile, and we speak today of carrier waves, magnetic alignments, and short-lived phosphor decay. Increasingly, media requires sophisticated hardware to record and play back an image.

There are many variables that affect the viewing of an image. These variables often have psychological and sociological bases, and include screen size, viewing angle, total number of screens, amount of ambient light needed for viewing, number of viewers per screen, and total number of viewers. Thus, the psychological and sociological impact of a movie projected on a large screen in a dark room with many viewers is different from that of a small television in a well-lit room with two viewers.

Visual media fall into three broad categories: reflective, transmissive, and radiant (see Figure 3.5). With *reflective media*, light hits the media, bounces off, and travels to the viewer's eye. An example is a simple photograph. *Transmissive media*, on the other hand, let some, but not all, light pass through. If the medium is wave-length-specific, such as stained glass or a color slide transparency, then the image appears to contain colors. Transmissive media are widely used for projections, be they slides or motion picture film. *Radiant media* emit light and are energized internally. Common examples include the television, an oscilloscope, or a glowing 2D flat-panel display.

Due to the differences in the physical properties of these media, the creation of color is not the same in each of them. In reflective media, the creation of secondary and tertiary colors depends on subtractive primary colors (see Figure 3.6). Transmissive and radiant media depend on additive primaries (see Figure 3.7).

There are three predominant models for recording media: *roll, cylinder,* and *disk* (see Figure 3.8)—which can be either concentric or helical. For practical reasons, the disk is often favored because it is

graph (graf), *n.* [<Gk. *graphein,* to draw], **1,** diagram or curve representing successive values of a changing variable quantity; as, a *graph* showing the temperature each day at a certain locality; *Math.,* a diagram expressing a mathematical relationship between two or more variables of an equation; **2,** a suffix used to imply the making of a record thereof, as a monograph, photograph, phonograph, videographic. —*v.* **to graph, -ed, -ing,** to represent using a graph, or to plot data upon.

graph-ic (graf ik), *adj.* **1,** pertaining to the art of writing, making marks and drawings; **2,** illustrating by diagrams or charts; **3,** explicit representations of life-like behavior; graphic arts, arts that deal with working on the plane and represent objects or the real world on a flat surface; **graphics,** *n. pl.* used as *sing.* the art or science of making marks, paintings and drawings, and including mechanical drawing, creating and calculating from graphs, flowcharting, and mapping. —*adj.* **graph-**

Figure 3.2 *Graph* is a word meaning "to write" or "to draw," and its applications include words about symbolic writing systems as well as systems that operate on the plane. Note the general absence of the third dimension.

vid-eo (vid e o), *n.* [<Lat. *videre,* to see + *O* (as in audio)], **1,** broadly, a moving picture signal or media; **2,** the transmission, reception, recording, or reproduction of moving pictures; **3,** the picture-single channel of a television system (exclusive of audio).

vid-e-ol-gy (vid e-ol o gy), *n.* [<Lat. *videre,* to see + *ology*, the study of], term proposed by video artist Nam June Paik to encompass the study of video.

vid-e-o-phi-le (vid e-o-fiel), *n.* person who consumes, collects, and researches video communications, including both mass communications as well as private ones.

vid-eo-phone (vid e-o-fon), *n.* [video + phone], instrument to communicate visual pictures (along with audio) via a telephone exchange in a point-to-point mode so that users can see and hear each other in real time.

vid-e-o ta-pe (vid e-o tap), *n.* [video + tape], recording medium used to record video signals on a roll of magnetic tape; **video tape player,** a machine on which to record and play video tape.

Figure 3.3 *Video* is a newer word implying a real-time moving picture channel. Initially the word had an electronic connotation, but increasingly its connotation may include digital, film, or other media.

more compact and has a higher resistance to breakage. The surface of each of these models can be used to record information in several ways, through physical, magnetic, or optical alterations. When the recording process involves physically altering a surface, such as wax, a pressure, for example air pressure, causes a needle to wiggle so that an imprint is made. The surface is physically modified to represent the information. *Electromagnetic* media usually consist of a thin coating of metal oxide, which can be magnetized and demagnetized on a plastic surface. In electromagnetic recording, an electronic signal is fed into the head of an electromagnet, causing its magnetic field to modulate. When a surface or substance is passed across this modulation gap, the temporal sequence of the electromagnetic field is imprinted serially into the passing substance's magnetic charge (see Figure 3.9). Finally, *analog optical* recording places information onto a light-sensitive medium, such as film.

Each of the above possibilities can be used for recording sound, picture, data, and processes such as computer programs. In fact, several approaches can be combined into one product. For example, optical image recording and magnetic sound recording allow sound and pictures to merge onto a single carrier. Note that the film medium serves both continuous and discrete needs. Also note that in cylinder and disk media, the information can be recorded concentrically or helically. Recording technologies are evolving from serial to random-access technologies, and increasingly, roll, cylinder, and disk media are being replaced by chips.

Fundamentals of Lensed Imaging

In a technical sense, *lensed images*—images made with light and a lens, usually in real time (see Figures 3.10 and 3.11)—involve the recording and playback of light data. Light plays a critical role because it is the mediator that connects objects in the real world to the mediated image, and then in turn connects this image to our eye. The viewing and perception of the moving picture image is mediated by light, and light is employed on both sides of a recording medium to connect viewing to a sampling of space-time. It is worth noting that animation can short-circuit the use of a lens during the creation process by generating a recording without a lens—for example, by drawing directly onto film (see Figure 3.12).

Light

The presence of light is required in order for humans to see. Chapter 1 discusses how light interacts with surfaces in the rendering process. Here, the formal properties of light are explored. Light is a form of energy that travels in a straight line. A quantum unit of light is called a *photon*—a discrete, finite parcel of energy. Light can also be perceived as an analog wave form. A *ray* of light is a simple line of light coming from a luminous point. A *beam* is a collection of parallel rays; rays emitting from a point in different directions are called *diverging rays*, and the light is called *omnidirectional.*

Light travels very fast, and for distances in the thousands of miles it appears almost instantaneous. At 186,000 miles per second, light takes approximately two and a half seconds to travel to the moon and back again; it travels about one foot in a nanosecond. Light can communicate the position of an object. The distance of the object from the viewer can be calculated by the time it takes light to travel from the object to the viewer's eye. Light will go through a vacuum and is emitted and absorbed by matter in a multitude of ways. When light interacts with matter, it is slowed down, and it may be refracted, reflected, absorbed, or transmitted unencumbered. Light passes through transparent matter easily and is absorbed or reflected by opaque matter.

Light comes from many sources. Most natural light results from boiling nuclear reactions suspended in space, as with the sun. It can also be made artificially by molecular heating, as with a lightbulb, or fluorescence, as in a cathode-ray tube (CRT). Lights may be omnidirectional, floodlights, or spotlights (see Figure 3.13), and may be hard, creating sharp shadows, or diffuse, creating soft shadows.

Light can be described in terms of several parameters. A light wave has a *frequency*, or *wavelength*, which determines its color. It also has an *amplitude*, or *brightness intensity*, often measured relative to the brightness of candles, or *candle power.* The measurement

Figure 3.4 Above: A recording consists of two components, a medium and a message. The medium is the carrier, or supportive material; the message information is often layered on the surface of the carrier, and may subtly alter the carrier in some way.

Figure 3.5 Left: Reflective, transmissive, and radiant are three categories of media.

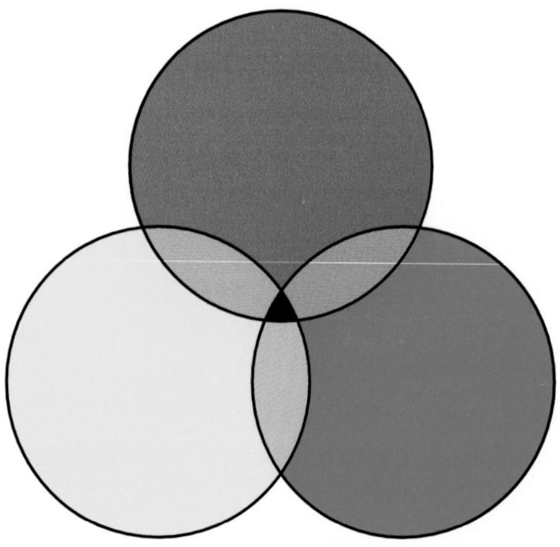

Figure 3.6 Above: Subtractive color/reflective artwork. The subtractive color gamut can be visualized as three circles of colored pigment that overlap in pairs to produce three areas of secondary colors; the three secondary colors overlap in the center to produce black. White is the absence of any pigment whatsoever.

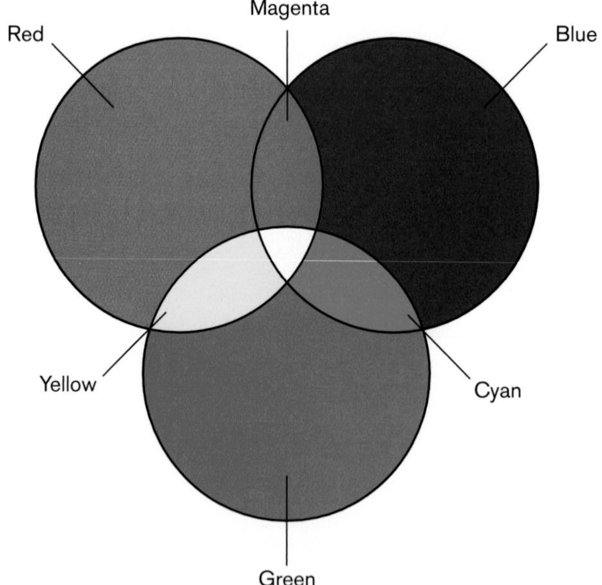

Figure 3.7 Below: Additive color/transmissive artwork. The RGB color gamut can be visualized as three circles of colored light that overlap in pairs to produce three areas of secondary colors; the three secondary colors overlap in the center to produce white. Black is the absence of any light whatsoever.

of intensity relative to surface area is the *lumen*, also known as a *foot candle*, which is equal to the amount of illumination falling on a surface one foot away from one candle (see Figure 3.14). The lumens per square foot is equal to the total intensity in candle power divided by the distance away in feet squared; this is the *inverse square law of light* (see Figure 3.15). The amount of light falling on a subject can be measured with a *light meter*, or *photometer*, and the science of measuring light is called *photometry.*

In the real world, there are two primary approaches to measuring light. *Incident light* is measured by going to the place where the light is falling and pointing a meter at the light source; it will measure the light falling on the scene and gives the overall illumination of the scene. *Reflected light* is measured by pointing a light meter at the subject from the point of view of the camera (see Figure 3.16). This will measure the light coming from the scene toward the camera and produce an average reading. A special kind of reflective meter, called a *spot meter*, has a narrow angle of view and is used to measure small areas in a scene, such as a face. The amount of incident light is greater than the amount of reflected light. A common light meter can be used to measure both incident and reflected light; a piece of translucent plastic placed over a reflective light meter will make its reading consistent with the incident light. The recording of light onto media typically requires that the ratio between bright to dark illumination, the *contrast ratio*, be constrained, because the contrast ratio of the recording medium itself is less than in nature. Beyond its quantitative, formalistic aspects, light is often used to convey mood

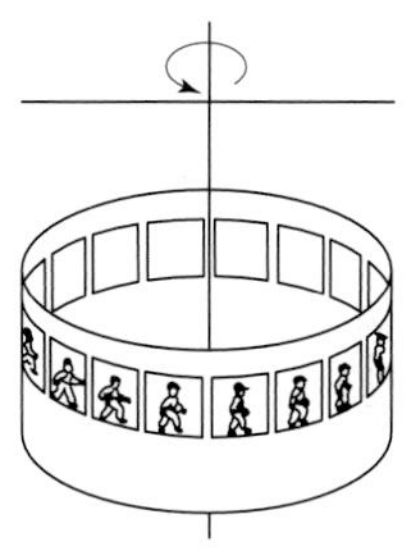

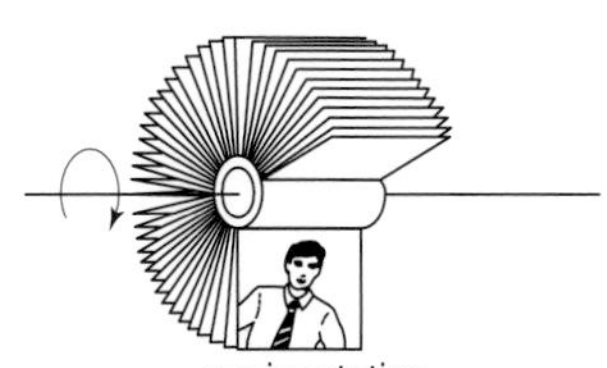

Figure 3.8 Above: Disks, cylinders, and paddles are physical structures for storing media; in the discrete cases shown here, the individual pictures are placed with a translation followed by a rotation about a major 3D axis (*x, y, z*). Disks and cylinders may also be used to record continuous, analog media, such as the phonograph record, which spirals from outside to inside, or cylinder, which helixes from one edge to the other. One profound difference between these viewing instruments and the modern moving picture viewer is that the pictures here are never held still.

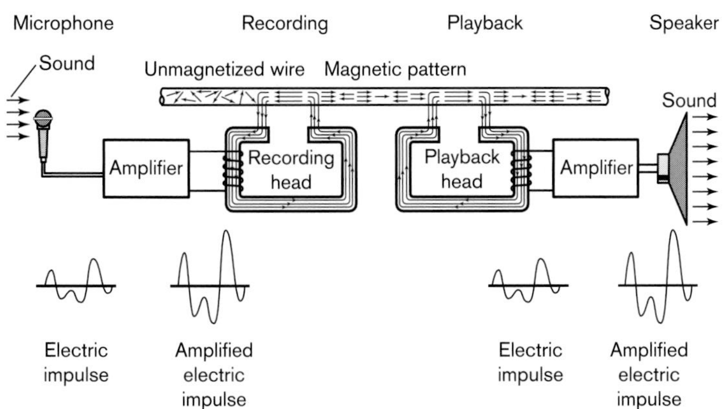

Figure 3.9 Left: Electromagnetic recording/magneto electronic playback.

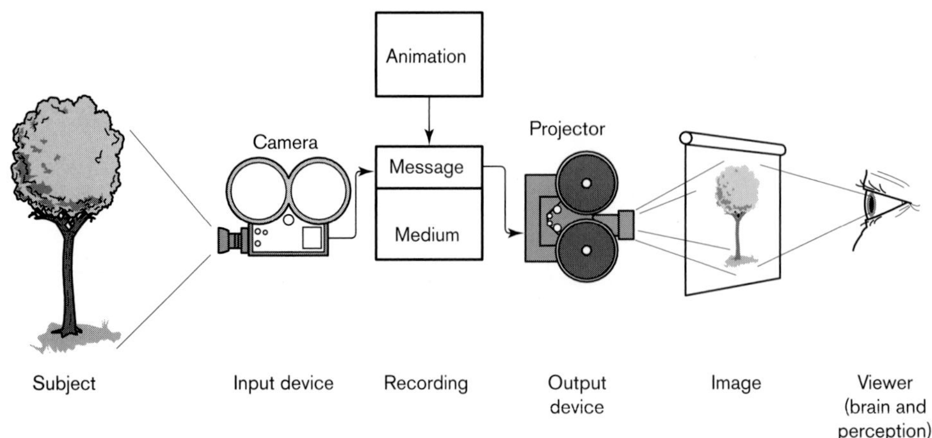

Figure 3.10 Input/medium/output block diagram of a temporal imaging system. The medium may be transmissive, moving the images in serial at up to light speed, or it may record the images for future playback. Animation can be made directly without the necessity of the input device by synthesizing a sequence of images by hand or by computer.

and set a psychological tone—consider daylight, twilight, overcast sunlight, starlight, moonlight, candlelight, gaslight, and so on.

The Camera Obscura and Aperture

The complement of light is *shadow*, that is, a space from which light is excluded, typically because it is being blocked by an opaque object. Shadow is the latent vehicle of a device called the ***camera obscura***—a device used to create images using light and shadows. Discovered during Aristotle's time or earlier, the camera obscura has no moving parts and no glass lens. Its mechanics are those of light itself. On a large scale, a camera obscura consists of a closed, darkened room with a very small hole (hence, the term ***pinhole camera***) in one wall to be used as an ***aperture***, and a white viewing screen on the opposite wall, with all the other walls painted black (see Figure 3.17).

The small hole of the camera obscura constrains the light coming into the room to a very small selection of rays. Unlike a window, where there is a substantial amount of incoming light spilling into much of the space, the pinhole limits the light so that for any occurrence of light in the outside environment only a small cone of it passes through the hole to collide with the viewing screen, where it is viewed. The ideal camera obscura hole is so small that only one ray of light, traveling in a straight line from its source, passes through it. At the center of the pinhole, the ray of light crosses through other similar rays from many points in the outside environment, and travels away from the pinhole until it strikes the viewing screen. The result is an image projected onto the viewing screen, upside down

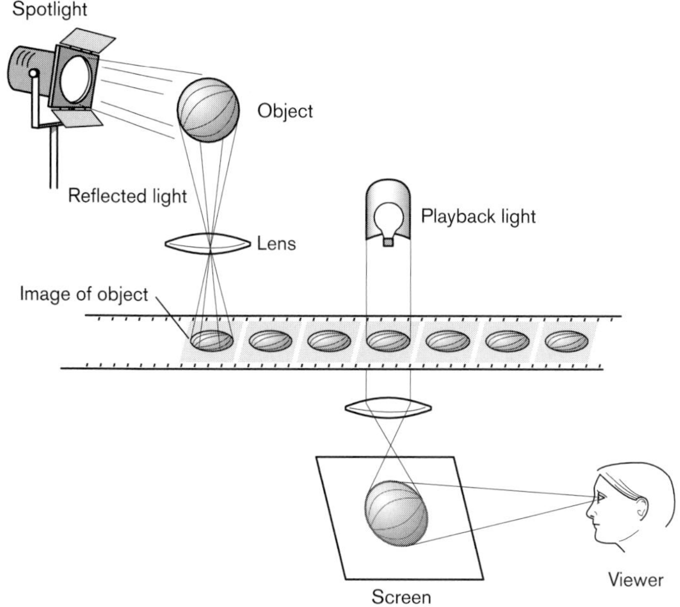

Figure 3.11 Left: Light plays a role on both sides of the recording medium. It is a mediator when moving picture systems are used to record the movements of objects in the real world; light transmits the information between the object in space and the recording medium. On the viewing side, light illuminates and transmits the image from the display screen (paper, glass, or whatever) to the eye.

(a)

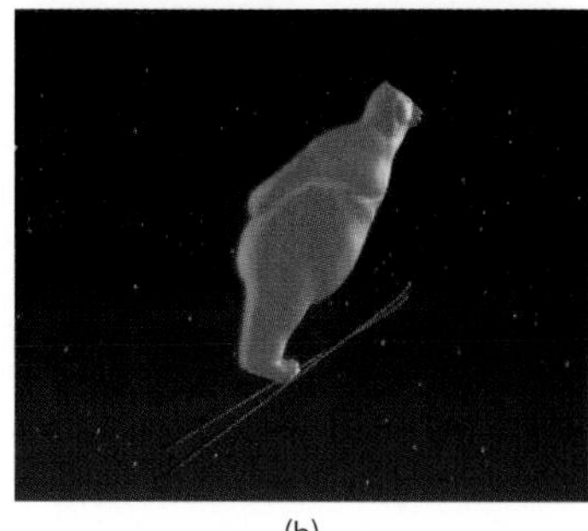

(b)

Figure 3.12 Above: Lensed imagery versus animated imagery. Animation can be made without a moving picture input device (a camera) by drawing directly on paper or celluloid. The image in (a) of the woman and the number 6 is *lensed*, that is, recorded with the use of a lens. The image in (b) is computer-generated.

and backward, of the outside environment. The resulting image is called a *real image*, because it exists in the real world.

Algorithms used to simulate the pinhole effect can be applied to both continuous and discrete data. Basically there are four variables, which are the same variables as the "simple lens" equation, described in the caption for Figure 3.18. First, there is the real world, often called the ***subject***, or ***object***—for example, a sunset or flower. Second, there is the ***subject distance***, the distance from the object to the aperture. Third, there is the image, formed by light hitting the viewing screen. And finally there is the ***focal length***, the distance from the aperture to the image (see Figure 3.18).

The focal length, the size of the subject, and the distance from the subject to the aperture determine the size of the image. The size of the image compared to the size of the subject is proportional to the distance from the aperture to the viewing screen compared to the distance from the aperture to the subject. The longer the focal length, the larger the size of the image. When the distance from the subject to the aperture and from the image to the aperture is equal, the image is 100% actual size. When the focal length is greater than the subject distance, enlargement occurs. When the subject distance is greater than the focal length, reduction occurs (see Figure

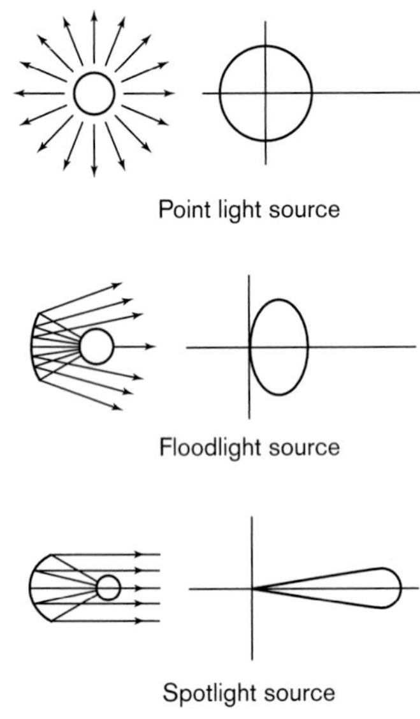

Figure 3.13 Above: Point, flood, and spotlights. Optical arrangements of three kinds of lights and corresponding polar graphs show equal luminance contours of each as a function of viewing angle.

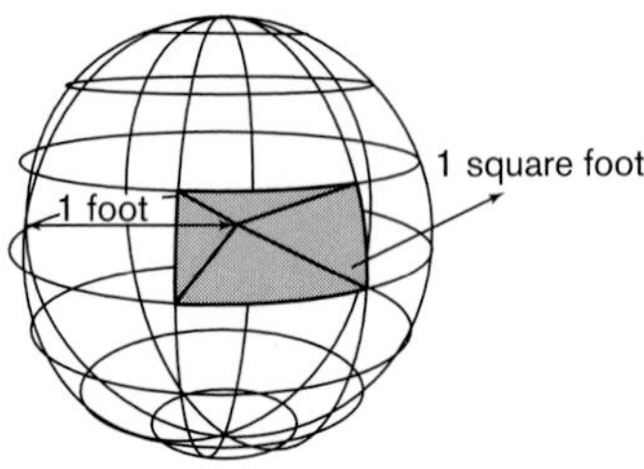

Figure 3.14 Above: Lumen defined. A 1-candle power light source at the center of a 1 foot radius sphere. The area of the sphere is 12.57 square feet. By definition, the total light emitted is thus 12.57 lumens, and the illumination on each square foot is one lumen.

Figure 3.15 Right: The inverse square law of light states that the illumination of a body is inversely proportional to the square of its distance from the light source. Doubling the distance away from a light source quarters the amount of light on each area.

3.19). A normal camera lens usually has a focal length slightly longer than the length of diagonal length of the image; thus a normal 35mm still-camera frame has an image diagonal length of about 44mm, and a focal length of 50mm.

The aperture area is calibrated as *f-stops* (see Figure 3.20). The f-stop is the value of the focal length divided by the diameter of the aperture. If the focal length is 50mm and the aperture diameter is 25mm, then the f-stop is 2. The f-stop number is inversely proportional to the square of the amount of light admitted. Smaller diameter f-stops are represented with larger numbers, let less light through, and provide greater depth of field. Larger diameter f-stops are represented with smaller numbers, let more light pass through, but narrow the depth of field. In photographic practice, variations in f-stops may be compensated for by changing the shutter speed, using a recording medium which is more or less sensitive to light, or by adding neutral density filters—colorless light-absorbing filters—in the optical path.

The *depth of field* of a lens is the interval of distance that appears in sharp focus and extends from a point in front of the subject to a point behind the subject. Depth of field depends upon the f-stop, the focal length of the lens, and the subject distance. The smaller the f-stop, the greater the depth of field. The farther away the subject, the greater the depth of field. Conversely, the larger the f-stop, the smaller the depth of field. The closer the subject, the smaller the depth of field.

The image formed using a pinhole camera has much less luminance than the subject in the real world because the image is composed of single rays of light only. If need be, the image can be made brighter by making the aperture bigger in diameter. In fact, doubling the area of the pinhole doubles the brightness of the image, but there are limits and liabilities in doing this. A bigger aper-

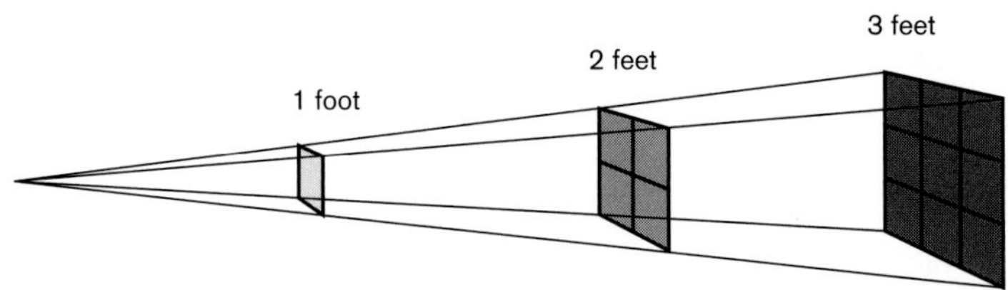

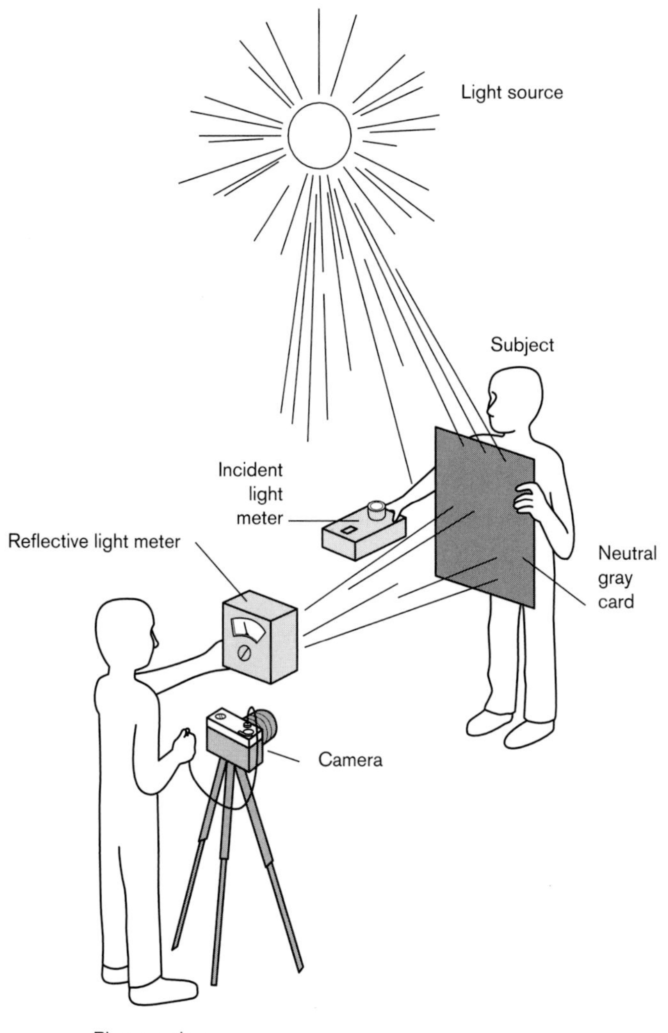

Figure 3.16 Left: Incident light is a measurement of light falling on a subject; reflected light is the light bouncing back off it.

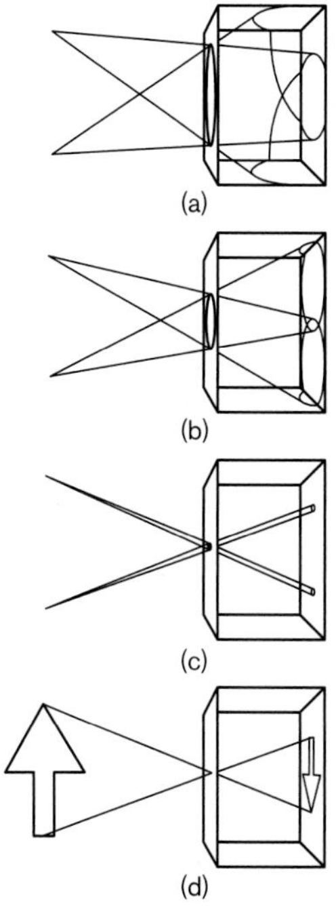

Figure 3.17 Above: A camera obscura forms a real 2D image of the real 3D world. In (a) two point sources of light pass through a large aperture and the rays fan out to flood the back wall, or screen, with light. Closing the aperture (b) creates shadows—places where there is no light. Points of light in the environment create large circles. Narrowing the aperture still further (c) makes the circles smaller still. While constraining the aperture to a pinhole (d), only single rays pass through. Shadows fall on almost all of the room and back wall except for where the light rays actually hit the wall or screen. The result is a real image that is proportional to the location of the light in the real-world environment. The pinhole camera is simulated using the lens equation.

ture diameter integrates a wider cone of light rays for each pixel of the screen, making the image less sharp and reducing the depth of field. Conversely, halving the area of the pinhole dims the image, but makes it sharper and increases the depth of field.

Rarely is a pinhole aperture larger than f/4 because the image information would be lost. At the other extreme, an infinitely small pinhole will have a depth of field from the pinhole to infinity. In other words, all subjects will be in focus no matter what the focal length of the lens. While infinitely small pinholes are possible in computer simulations, a real-world pinhole cannot be infinitely small and must be

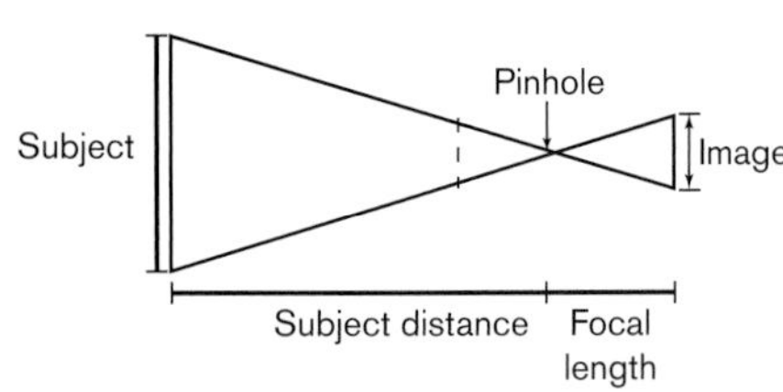

Figure 3.18 Above: The simple lens equation models the pinhole camera. Focal length is the distance from the pinhole to the real image and relates object size to the image size. The formula is

$$\frac{\text{subject}}{\text{image}} = \frac{\text{subject distance}}{\text{focal length}}$$

where subject distance is the distance of the subject from the aperture and focal length is the distance of the screen from the aperture.

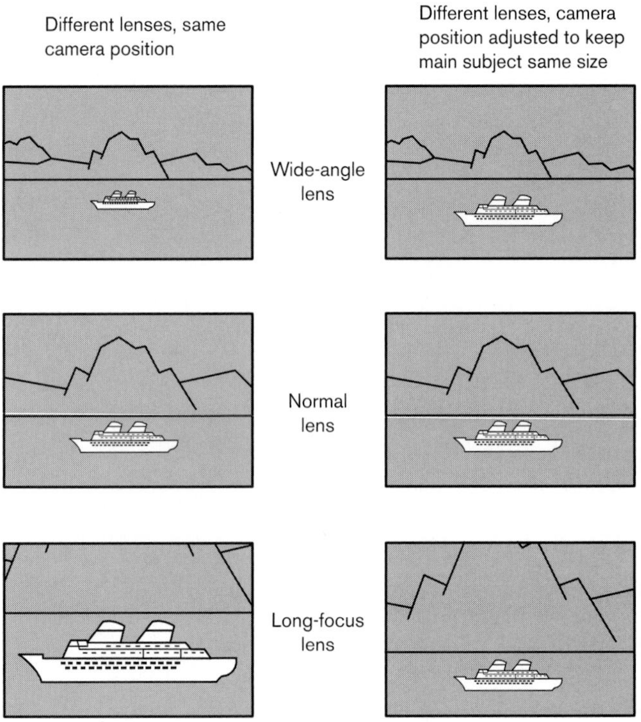

Figure 3.19 Right: Composition is altered by changing the focal length of a lens or changing the camera position. Keeping the subject the same size while using different focal lengths and object distances produces different compositions.

big enough to let visible light waves pass through. The practical limit on the smallest pinhole aperture is related to the wavelength of light:

SQRT(2 × WAVELENGTH × FOCAL LENGTH)

where WAVELENGTH is the wavelength of light and is dependent upon the color of the light, and FOCAL LENGTH is the focal length of the lens. In practical terms, for visible light and a 50mm focal length lens, the smallest f-stop is about f-225. Computer graphic software may allow f-stop manipulation in addition to changing focal length. This is important because controlling the depth of field is a classic creative aspect of cinematography.

The Simple Lens

Lenses are used in both the recording and viewing of moving pictures. At their simplest, they function like a pinhole, but in a more advanced system, a lens is a transparent substance used to form images of objects in space. In the real world, a lens is a piece of glass or other transparent substance with one or two curved surfaces.

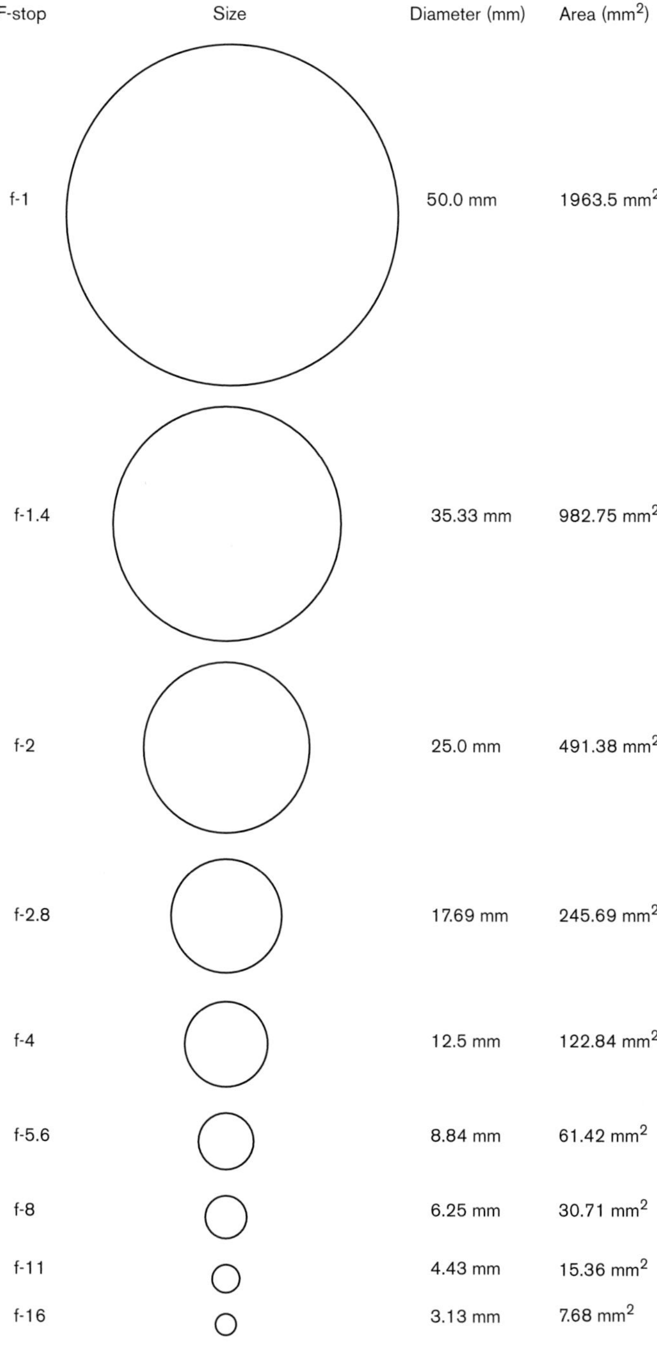

F-stop	Size	Diameter (mm)	Area (mm^2)
f-1		50.0 mm	1963.5 mm^2
f-1.4		35.33 mm	982.75 mm^2
f-2		25.0 mm	491.38 mm^2
f-2.8		17.69 mm	245.69 mm^2
f-4		12.5 mm	122.84 mm^2
f-5.6		8.84 mm	61.42 mm^2
f-8		6.25 mm	30.71 mm^2
f-11		4.43 mm	15.36 mm^2
f-16		3.13 mm	7.68 mm^2

Figure 3.20 The aperture, or iris, is a hole through which light can pass, usually circular in shape and usually of adjustable diameter. The drawing compares f-stop numbers, sizes, diameters, and actual f-stop areas. The table is based on a lens with a focal length of 50mm.

$$\text{F-stop} = \frac{\text{focal length}}{\text{diameter of the aperture}}$$

$$\text{area} = \pi \times (\text{the diameter}/2)^2$$

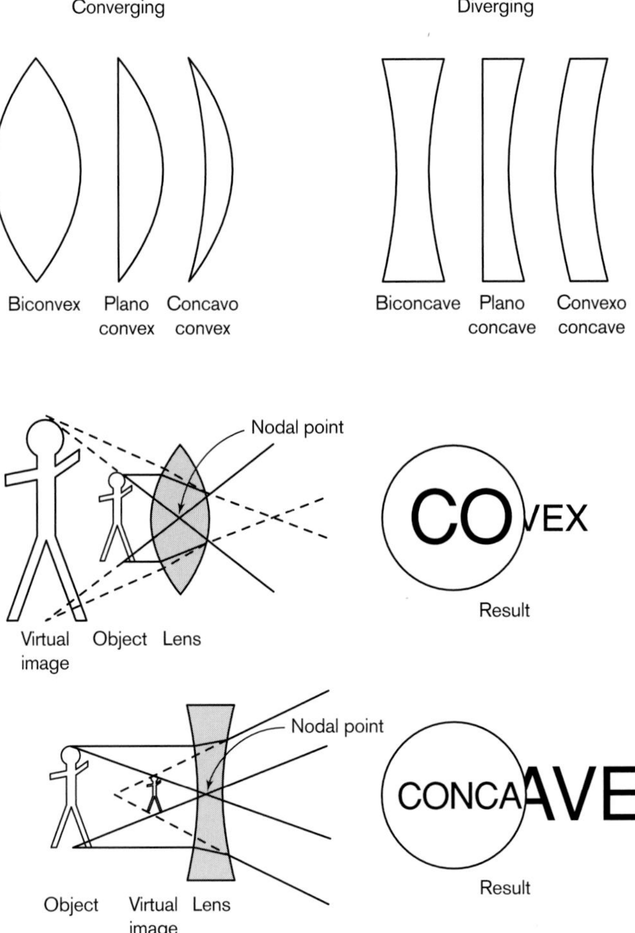

Figure 3.21 Six kinds of simple lenses: Biconvex, plano convex, concavo convex (convex meniscus), biconcave, plano concave, and convexo concave (concave meniscus). The concave lenses reduce; the convex (or positive) lenses enlarge. The cross-section views of a convex and concave lens show how the virtual image is created in each case. Refraction occurs twice—once when the light enters and once when it leaves. The nodal point is the geometric center of the lens.

Surfaces that curve outward are *convex*; those that curve inward are called *concave*. Lens surfaces that have no curvature are *plano*. An *identity lens*—that is, one that does not alter light whatsoever—is created using what is called a *plano-plano lens*. It has plano front and plano back surfaces, in other words, no curve. Altogether, there are six types of simple lenses (see Figure 3.21). The *nodal point* is the exact center of a lens.

A real-world lens is essentially an analog optical computer that algorithmically bends light rays according to its material and the curvature of the surfaces. A lens works by *refraction*, that is, a bending of light rays that occurs when light passes into a new medium. In a lens this occurs twice, once when the light enters the lens and once when it leaves.

The image that a viewer sees when gazing through a lens is called a *virtual image* because it is not physical, unlike a real image as found in a camera obscura.

Lenses are important because they can project the (3D) geometry of the real world into the (2D) plane, a technique called *perspective*, detailed in Chapter 6. But they also have tremendous value in manipulating images. A lens can be used to magnify or reduce the view of an image without any modification to the scale of the real-world object. Images can be viewed through a lens and thus reduced and enlarged, during both duplication and projection.

The Shutter

Understanding the basics of the still-camera shutter are a prerequisite for understanding the basics of the moving picture shutter. The *shutter* is a device in a camera for opening and closing the optical path through the lens and aperture for a defined length of time, for example, 1/1000th of a second. In doing so, the shutter allows the medium, such as photoreactive chemicals, access to light. In the trivial case, when all pixels have simultaneous access to light, the *exposure time* is how long the shutter is open and the recording medium is exposed to light. The *shutter release* is a control that initiates the shutter action. Over the years, different kinds of shutters have evolved, often enabling different visual recordings.

The *leaf shutter* opens rapidly from a center iris and remains open for as long as necessary before snapping closed (see Figure 3.22). Because of this design, it tends to give all pixels a simultaneous recording time. In a physical camera, the leaf shutter may be located just behind the lens and aperture, in front of the lens, or even between individual lenses, in a compound lens system.

Focal Plane Shutter

A *focal plane shutter* is located directly in front of the medium, or focal plane. It works by sliding a diagonal slit across the plane. As a result, pixels in the image are recorded sequentially (see Figure 3.23). Focal plane shutters are used in most single-lens reflex cameras because they facilitate interchangeable lenses. Like the leaf shutter, a focal plane shutter is activated by a shutter release and has an exposure time. But unlike the leaf shutter, not all areas of the

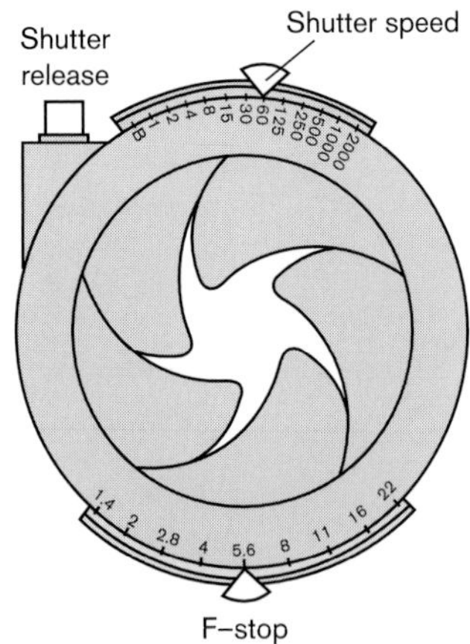

Figure 3.22 Above: Leaf shutter in the midst of opening and closing. The controls include two sliders—one for shutter speed, one for the f-stop. The shutter-release button is to the top left.

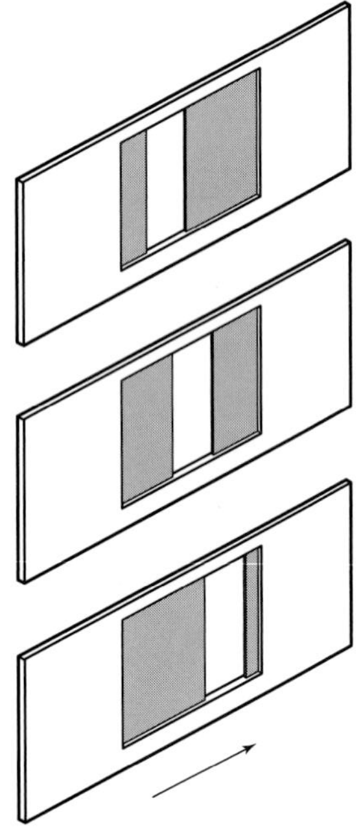

Figure 3.23 Above: The focal plane shutter translates across the images.

image are recorded during the same interval of real time. Because the slit is moving across the image horizontally, the parts of the image that are exposed at the beginning of its travel record events that occur before events that are exposed at the end of its travel. A side effect of this process is that an object's vertical motion will get warped in the direction of the shutter direction of travel, and an object's horizontal motion stretched or compressed, depending upon the direction that the shutter is traveling.

Rotary Shutter

A *rotary shutter* enables an exposure by rotating an angular opening, which typically rotates a full 360 degrees for each exposure (see Figure 3.24). The rotary shutter is found in the moving picture camera because the continuous motion of the shutter is necessary for motion picture recording. The rotary shutter has some of the characteristics of the focal plane shutter; oftentimes, it is near the focal plane, and both involve passing the shutter across the image (see Figure 3.25).

More advanced rotary shutters allow the angle (and the shutter speed) to be adjusted. This permits images of shorter exposure time and greater aliasing.

Nipkow Disk

Shutters can also take on unexpected forms. In television, for example, the scanning electron beam functions as a shutter. This principle is even more clearly illustrated with the *Nipkow disk*, a spinning disk with a series of holes or slits arranged in a spiral, scanning a shallow line below the line scanned by the previous hole so that as the disk turns one revolution, each hole successively passes across the focal plane (see Figure 3.26). As with the focal plane shutter, note that the time base of the resultant image varies across the image itself. In fact, the image is temporally scanned as the successive holes sweep arcs across the picture.

Note that one of the advantages of scanning—be it a mechanical or an electronic method—is that the resultant image is naturally represented as a serial linear stream of information, and thus can be readily transmitted over a linear transmission media such as a telephone wire or radio.

Shutters are an integral part of moving picture projectors and other forms of electronic displays. Because shutters function as an intermediary device between the continuous nature of the real world and the intermittent nature of media, they are prone to introduce aliasing artifacts into the recording, as discussed later in this chapter.

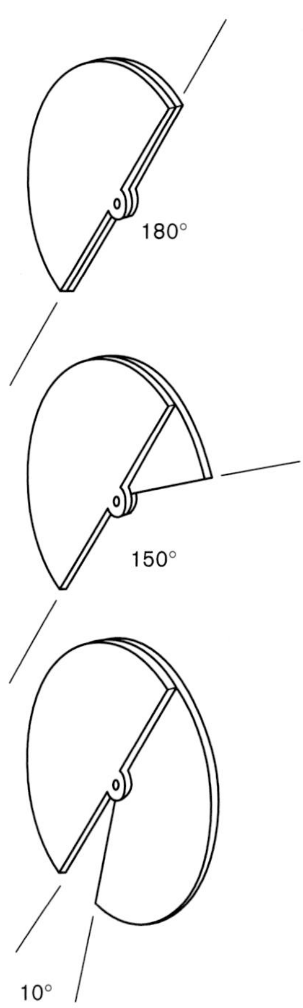

Figure 3.24 Above: In a film-based system, the shutter is often a rotary disk with an adjustable opening. Half open (180 degrees) is often the maximum exposure time, because the camera takes the remainder of that (blanking) time to advance the film. The shutter angle is related to the exposure time in seconds by the rule: Exposure time = (shutter angle in degrees / 360) × (1/ number of frames / second).

The Still Image Projector

Probably the first device for image projection was the magic lantern. Optically, a magic lantern forces light through an image, projecting it outward onto a 2D viewing screen. The resulting projected image appears upside down. Modern *image projectors* are similar to the magic lantern, but electric light and carbon arcs have replaced candle power, and the optical pathway is more complex (see Figure 3.27).

From the time of the magic lantern, one of the fundamental components of a projector has been the *feed mechanism* for loading the recorded medium (see Figure 3.28). There are three fundamental designs. As seen in the figure, the magic lantern uses a *horizontal feed* (a). Modern filmstrip projectors incorporate a similar design, but it is *vertical* (b). Modern slide projectors incorporate a *shuttle mechanism* that slides back and forth between a storage rack and the optical pathway. In a Kodak carousel projector, for example, the images are stored paddle-wheel fashion, the *y*-axis is rotated, and

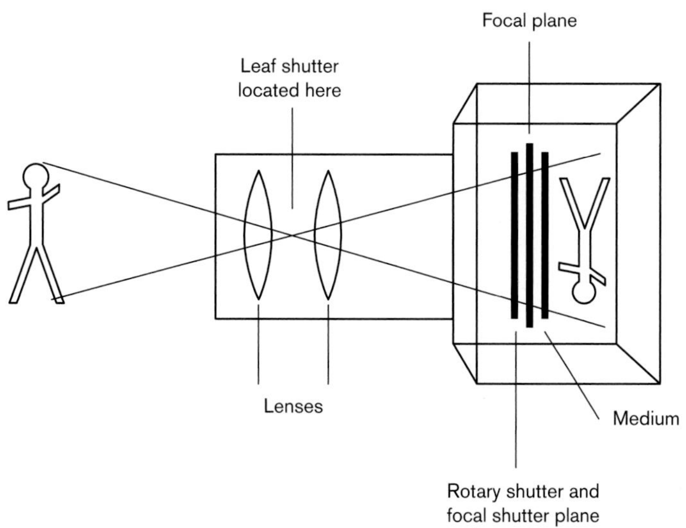

Figure 3.25 Left: A comparison of the different shutters.

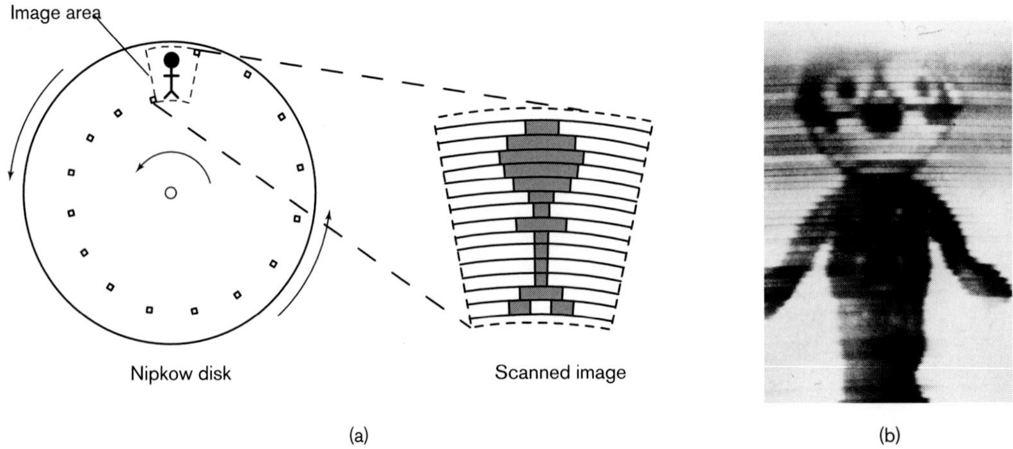

Figure 3.26 The Nipkow disk (a) is a scanning shutter with a spiral of rectangular holes. The shutter rotates once per frame and can be built with or without blanking. In one revolution of the disk, the 16 holes will zip across the image area, crossing it right to left, one row after another. Light, passing through the moving aperture, falls on film or a photocell behind the disk that in turn produces a varying voltage; the brighter the light at the moment, the higher the voltage. Thus the picture may be translated into a serial analog signal. The primary characteristic of the shutter is that only a small moving region is exposed at one time; the effect of this is that the effective shutter speed at any one part of the image is extremely fast. The disk can be built with many lines or only a few—as illustrated in the photograph of the image of Felix the Cat (b), which can be distinguished as gentle arcs.

the images are translated down and up (c). Another rotary feed mechanism is the ***Schott feed***, found in View-Masters, which use a rotary picture disk (d).

Before concluding this section, a brief comparison of the camera obscura to an image projector is appropriate. In particular, it is worth emphasizing that the image projector is not an exact complement of the camera obscura. The camera obscura creates a 2D image from 3D information. An image projector cannot do the opposite and recreate the 3D information; it can only project 2D images. In addition, while the image projector requires a recorded image in order for a projection to occur, the camera obscura does not create recorded images.

Recording and Playback

The process of recording and playing back moving pictures involves physics, mechanics, technology, media, and information. It is basically a computational process, and in a practical sense it reflects advances in industry, chemistry, and electronics. A general case model of this process involves collecting light and forming it into images, recording and/or transmitting these images, then displaying these recordings so that the images are visible to our eyes. The components of this process include a subject, a recording device, the medium itself, a display screen, and an observer.

The recording device, display, and medium must be able to handle moving pictures, as opposed to still pictures, and they are thus

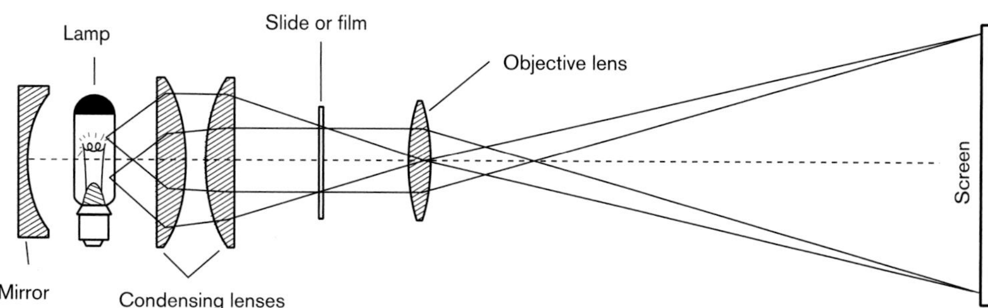

Figure 3.27 A cross-section view of the optical pathway of a modern image projector includes a light source, a parabolic mirror, two plano convex lenses, a convex lens, and a transparency.

more complicated than their static graphic counterparts by the factor of time. In many moving picture technologies, the imaged light is usually represented and recorded as a temporal series of discrete, two-dimensional images, or frames. These individual frames, recorded at successive intervals in time and played back at a consistent rate of speed, are fused in the viewer's mind, and hence appear continuous.

The input component of a temporal imaging system consists of a moving picture recording device, such as a film camera, video camera with a recording deck, or just a recording deck. These devices may operate mechanically, electronically, or digitally. All of the devices incorporate a mechanism that advances the recording medium, either intermittently as with a film shuttle, or continuously as with videotape or computer disk, and allows a sequence of individual images to be recorded onto a physical medium.

The output component of a temporal imaging system consists of either a viewer or projector, the former for looking directly at an emitted light image; the latter for looking at a projected, reflected light image. In both cases, light is used to present the image to the viewer's eye. In film, the light source is placed behind a transparent medium, and the light is forced through the medium and a projection lens. In electronic systems, the light source is either an electroilluminescent screen, as is found in the average television, or a solid-state flat-panel display. In these systems, the image is formed by varying the location and intensity of a moving light beam, or the brightness of a grid of very small solid-state, light-emitting pixels.

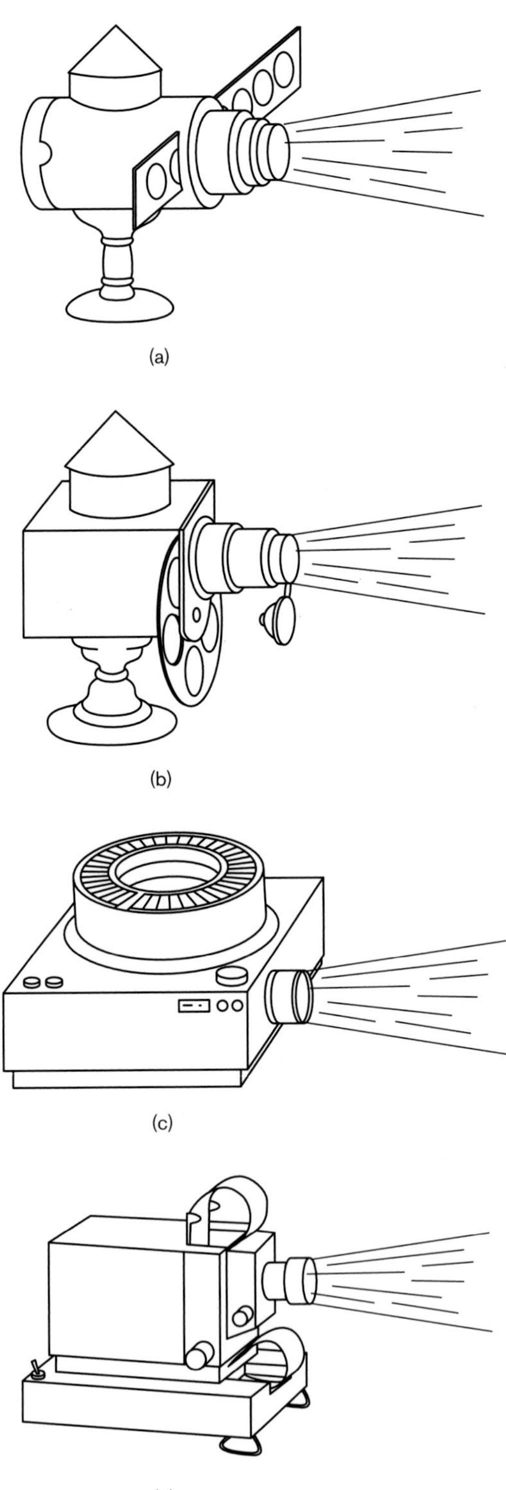

Figure 3.28 Slide projector feed mechanisms include horizontal (a) , vertical (b), and rotary feeds (c and d). Contemporary slide projectors usually also incorporate a shuttle mechanism to move the image in and out of the light pathway.

Continuous and Discrete Representation

A recording process that captures a sequence of discrete frames records a *discrete simultaneous representation* of continuous action. The frames are discrete representations because each frame records a brief finite amount of time and because there usually also exists intervals of time between the frames that are not recorded at all. In short, a series of photographs taken in rapid succession of continuous, real-world action is hardly a continuous representation of this action. In fact, a *continuous representation* of continuous action cannot be achieved using such a recording process. Discrete representation is not without value, but it is not without problems either, as will be presented in detail shortly in the discussion of *aliasing*.

Continuous simultaneous representation of continuous action is possible, but it is a technology that has not been explored since the early days of television. The continuous approach does not incorporate the concept of frames or finite temporal divisions. One method involves quantizing the image plane into a matrix of pixels whereby there is a photodetector for each pixel. The luminance and/or color of each and every pixel is output continuously and analogically, and all pixels are output—transmitted, recorded, and displayed—simultaneously and in parallel, each as a separate wire. The problem with this approach is that in order to represent even the simplest picture of modest resolution, the system needs tens or even hundreds of thousands of parallel wires.

Between these two extremes lie a myriad of other techniques. For example, *discretely scanned representations* read individual scan lines of an image or individual pixels in rapid succession, sequentially. Depending upon the system, the pixel may represent a discrete moment or interval of time, but no individual pixel represents time continuously. But unlike discrete simultaneous representations, each subsequent pixel is temporally offset from the previous pixel so that a frame consists of pixels that represent different moments in time. Again, these different methods have subtle effects when it comes to aliasing, as well as to perception.

Figure 3.29 The Faraday disk is a flat circle with a wedge cut out. If it is spun quickly on its center, scenes viewed through it appear whole, but with less exposure.

Persistence of Vision

Of primary importance to the perception of moving pictures is *persistence of vision*—a visual phenomenon in which the human eye and brain continue to perceive a visual stimulus for a short time after the stimulus disappears. The persistence of vision phenomenon was first observed by Ptolemy in Egypt, in 130 AD, when he observed that a bucket of fire swung in a circle appears to form a circle of flame. The phenomenon was experimentally explored in the early decades of the 1800s, with a simple apparatus called a *Faraday disk*, which is essentially a cardboard disk with a cutout wedge (see Figure 3.29). When the disk is spun around its center, a viewer can look at the disk and see the entire environment behind the disk. Persistence of vision is believed to occur because of *retinal lag*, a biological process that occurs in the eye when neurons keep firing for a brief period of time after a light source disappears. In 1824, Peter Mark Roget quantified the phenomenon and identified the rates at which individual, discrete images must be presented to the eye in order for the physiology/psychology of the eye/brain to perceive continuity of action. Roget established the concept of *critical fusion (flicker) frequency*, that is, a minimum speed of presentation of stimulus required to produce persistence of vision. At stimulus rates above the critical fusion frequency, the viewer perceives the moving image as continuous. Below the frequency, the flashing discrete images appear to be just that—individual image.

For humans, the critical fusion frequency is between 30 to 50 stimuli per second, with the range being a function of brightness. Brighter flashes must be presented at higher rates of speed to appear continuous. Weaker flashes fuse at slower rates because the lower-light-level rods in the eye take longer to discharge. With respect to moving pictures, it is therefore necessary for images to be presented somewhere between 30 to 50 frames/second. Thus, as a result of persistence of vision, a continuous process represented discretely may be perceived by the brain as a continuous process.

Roget next designed a second stimulus machine to explore issues concerning motion continuity (see Figure 3.30). At about the critical fusion frequency, Roget observed that the discrete spokes of a spinning wheel appear to fuse into one blurred spinning spoke,

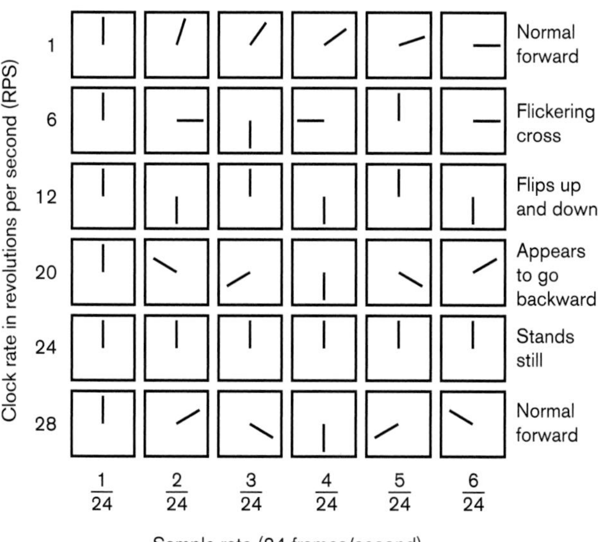

Figure 3.30 Temporal aliasing is an artifact of the movement of an object and the opening and closing of the shutter. The drawing depicts a spinning spoke in a wheel rotating at different speeds, varying from 1 to 28 revolutions/second. The sample rate is a constant 24 samples (frames)/second, and the samples are made with a short exposure time, so motion blur is not evident. When the spoke is rotating slowly, the motion in the recording appears normal. When the spoke rate is half the frame rate, the spoke appears to flicker up and down. As the spoke rate increases further, the spoke in the recording appears to go backward, then slows to a stop when the spoke rate and the frame rate are equal. This effect was first thoroughly understood by Roget, who constructed an experimental apparatus for his persistence-of-vision studies, which consisted of a spinning wheel and a spinning slot.

and apparent movement occurs. ***Apparent movement*** requires persistence of vision but also requires a second psychological factor, the ***phi phenomenon***, the distance displacement of an object from one frame to another. Roget observed that, depending upon the rate of speed of the wheel relative to the position of the spokes, situations occurred when the spokes appeared to reverse direction and rotate backward, even though they were rotating forward. This effect is called *temporal aliasing* and is discussed later in this chapter. Note that Roget also discovered that the sequence of images must be in registration—that is, perfectly aligned.

In subsequent years, the phi phenomenon has been quantified when it was discovered to be related to motion detectors in the eye that are triggered by adjacent objects in motion. Also be aware that the eye is capable of detecting and recognizing events that occur much faster than 1/50th of a second—for example, a person can identify photographs of people in less than 1/1000th of a second.

Stroboscope Principles

A ***stroboscope*** is a device that defines durations of light in terms of frequency, that is, number of flashes/second, as well as ***duration***, that is, how long the light flashes (see Figure 3.31). A stroboscope can produce a strobe effect one of two ways: through the use of intermittent vision, that is flashing an image using a shutter; or intermittent light, that is, flashing a light at a constant but adjustable frequency and with a constant but adjustable pulse duration.

In practice, we live much of our life bathed in strobe light. Almost all artificial illumination, incandescent lamps as well as fluorescent lights, blinks at us constantly. But at 60 times a second, the flashing occurs above the critical fusion frequency, and hence it is not perceived. The strobe effects resulting from fluorescent lights are easier to see than those produced by incandescent light because in an incandescent light, the metal filament that is heated to iridescence cools slower than fluorescent gas. Strobe effects can be illustrated in a variety of ways, including a simple waving of a pencil in front of your eyes. If waved in sunlight, the pencil will create a blurred image; if waved in front of a television monitor, the pencil movement will appear discrete.

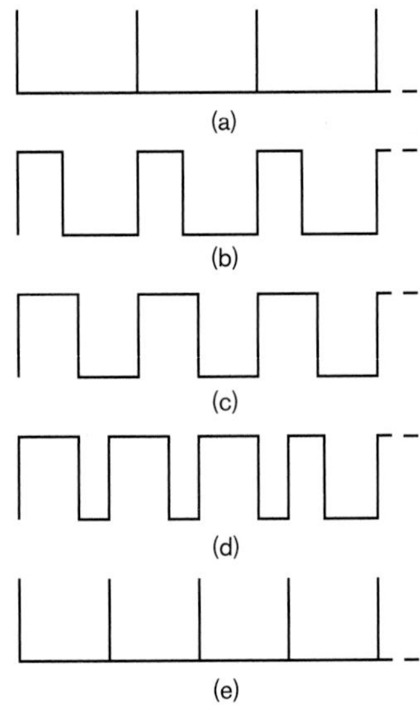

Figure 3.31 A stroboscope has at least two variables—pulse frequency and pulse duration—which are analogous to shuttle rate and exposure time. In (a), the duration of the pulse is very short. In (a), (b), and (c), the frequency of the pulse is the same, but in (a) the duration of the pulse is very short and in (b) and (c) it is longer. In (c) and (d), the duration of the pulse is identical, but in (d) the frequency of the pulses is faster. In (d) and (e), the frequency of the pulses is again identical. If the duration of the pulse equals the frequency of the pulse, the illumination is on all the time and there is no stroboscopic effect.

Aliasing and Anti-Aliasing

Aliasing is phenomenon that occurs when continuous data, for example a 2D image or continuous motion, is represented as discrete data. In 2D images, ***spatial aliasing*** results when a continuous still image is sampled as many discrete areas (pixels). The sampling process produces artifacts such as jagged edges along a line or moiré patterns. For example, sampling a black line on a white field will produce a digital image in which the line appears to have a jagged edge. Moirés result when patterns such as herringbone or plaid are coarsely sampled, so that new patterns are formed in the digital file. *Temporal aliasing* occurs when continuous motion is sampled discretely, as with individual frames, creating artifacts that provide false clues and interfere with a convincing portrayal of motion. It is manifest in objects that have temporal frequency, such as the revolving light on a police car, but it is also often a function of the movement of an object in motion, such as a spinning wheel, which appears to revolve backward or to stand still.

Spatial Aliasing and the Nyquist Limit

Because aliasing has been such a common problem in video, film, computer graphics, and computer animation, many techniques have

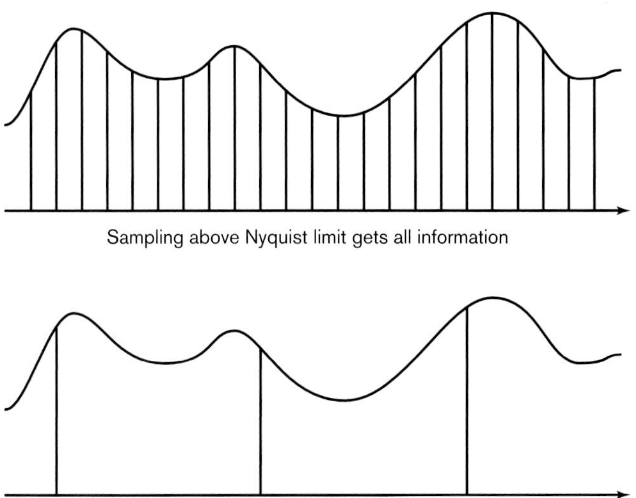

Sampling above Nyquist limit gets all information
Sampling below Nyquist limit misses information

Figure 3.32 Sampling and the Nyquist limit. Sampling above the Nyquist limit produces a digital signal that may be converted back to a similar analog waveform (a). Sampling below the Nyquist limit (b) misses things. All sorts of wiggles and waves, ups and downs, hills and valleys remain invisible to the frequency of the sample pulse; the sampling interval is too far apart, and critical events occur between samples.

evolved to minimize or eliminate it. All relate to the ***Nyquist limit***, which states that aliasing may be avoided if the number of samples is equal to at least two times the fastest frequency (the bandwidth) in the analog signal waveform. This theorem states that sampling at this rate will enable enough data to be collected so that the original analog frequencies can be reconstructed. In practice, it is common to sample at even higher rates. Based on sampling theory, when sampling occurs at the Nyquist limit or above, aliasing is null, or zero. Hence, aliasing occurs when sampling below the Nyquist limit, and in this regard, it is simply an artifact of sampling. More precisely, it results from insufficient sampling. If the sample rate is not at least twice the highest frequency in the corresponding signal, significant information can be missed during the sampling process (see Figure 3.32).

But just what is the highest frequency of a picture? A picture has two frequencies, one in the *x* direction and one in the *y* direction, and the highest frequency is considered to be the finest detail in the picture. This gets tricky: consider, for example, the lettering on a wine bottle held in someone's hand in a group shot. Essentially, the horizontal or vertical frequency is the number of different detectable horizontal or vertical elements. When dealing with multimedia, the frequency is determinable: in film it is the number of lines of resolution, in video it is akin to the channel bandwidth, and digitally it is the number of x or y pixels (see Figure 3.33). But in the real world, objects such as the line that forms the edge of the letter A or the arc that forms the letter O are in fact continuous, and do not have finite resolution. So, in these cases, going from the continuous to the discrete, aliasing will always be an issue.

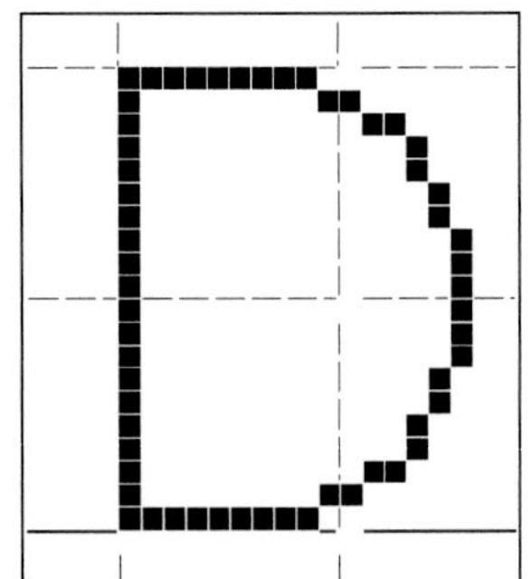

Figure 3.33 Above: The letter "D" is drawn with 20 pixels along the vertical axis and 16 pixels along the horizontal axis.

Anti-Aliasing

Anti-aliasing is the term given to a collection of techniques that can be used to minimize aliasing artifacts. Anti-aliasing techniques can reduce these appearances during the sampling process or afterward. For example, in the case of a diagonal line, an anti-aliasing technique would be to calculate new gray-scale values for the pixels adjacent to both sides of the line. The pixels' new luminance value would be relative to the distance from the center of the pixel to the line; pixels closer to the line would be a darker gray, and pixels farther from the line would be a lighter gray. The resulting image will appear smoother than the original aliased jagged line (see Figure 3.34).

At least two factors affect anti-aliasing; one is the resolution of the sampling frequency (in x and y, in luminance, in time) and its relationship to real-world frequencies. The other is the area or duration of the sample itself (see Figure 3.35). For example, in sampling an image, each pixel can be the intensity value of a point within the area of the pixel (e.g., the center point), or it can be a sample that integrates all the illumination within the square area. Obviously, the latter case incorporates more information about the analog source; hence the sample will be a closer representation of the source. The anti-aliased information is still incomplete, but it incorporates more knowledge about the original data and is perceived to be smoother. In fact, it is even possible to integrate some information from the surrounding pixels into the sample.

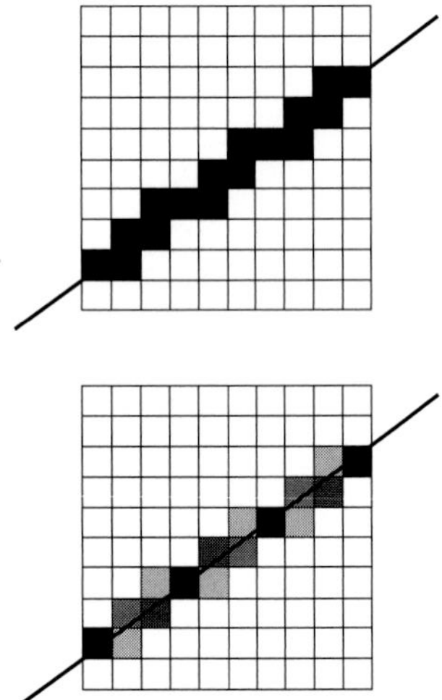

Figure 3.34 Above: A common technique for improving the definition of a line uses gray levels in proportion to the area of the grid occupied by the sampled line.

Temporal Aliasing and Anti-Aliasing

Aliasing works in a similar manner in the temporal domain. One easy way to think about the problem is to compare frames, which are discrete samples in time, to pixels, which are discrete samples on the plane. The careful reader is admonished that this analogy only works when a frame is simultaneously exposed and that scanning systems, especially video, provide some wrinkles to the discussion.

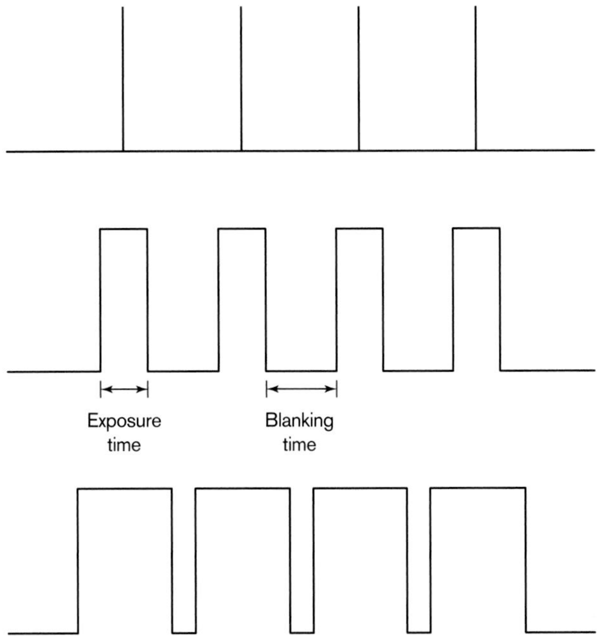

Figure 3.35 Frequency and duration of a sample are two major factors that concern us in anti-aliasing. The drawing illustrates successive point samples in time, where the exposure time is infinitely short, as well as samples of increasing length. In the bottom figure, sample time is longer than the sample frequency, an unusual but not impossible occurrence.

As with spatial sampling, sampling at frequencies above the Nyquist limit is necessary to avoid temporal aliasing. Temporal moirés will result when action such as a strobe flashing at 75 flashes/second is recorded by a movie camera running at 24 frames/second. The result appears to be a flashing light with different rhythms, a temporal analog to digitizing a picture of a pinstripe pattern at low spatial resolution. Objects in the real world also often exhibit continuous motion, and when they are recorded onto film (for example), as a series of discrete samples (frames), temporal aliasing also occurs. Here, too, the notion of frequency applies, especially when the motion involves things such as wagon-wheel spokes that, like the strobe light above, produce aliasing that grossly misrepresents the action—for example, the wheel appearing to come to a stop or to go backward.

Temporal aliasing manifestations include small details popping on and off the screen during action, chattering and strobing, juddering caused by change in frame rates, and forward action appearing to go backward. Aliasing is a problem in live action as well as in animation (see Figure 3.36), but strobing artifacts are particularly problematic in animation because frames are often point samples—that is, they represent an instant in time.

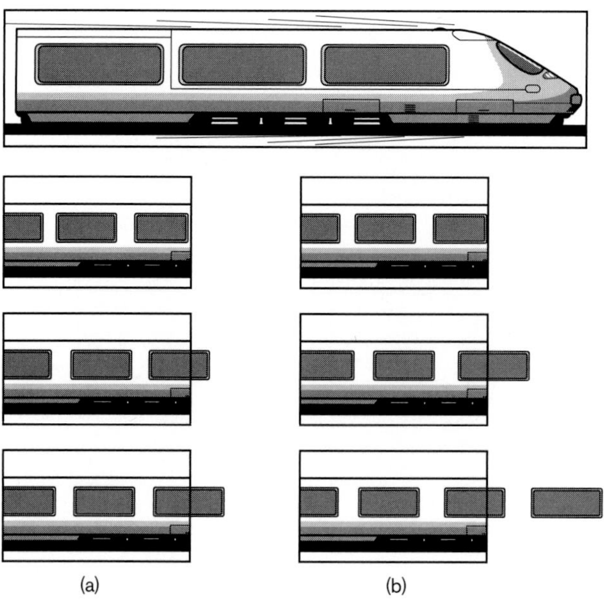

Figure 3.36 A three-frame sequence recording of a train moving slowly forward will appear to, in fact, move forward (a). But the same train may appear to move backward when moving at greater speeds (b).

Juddering Temporal aliasing is always a problem when media that have different frame rates are being duplicated or when a frame rate is unstable. These problems, called a *judder,* may be a side effect of the recording device—for example, when the recording device is unstable and instead of recording 24 frames/second it floats between 23.5 and 24.5 frames/second; yet the result is played back on a stable 24 frames/second device. Juddering is also manifested when media of different frame rates is interconverted, such as film to tape, or tape to film.

Chattering Temporal aliasing is also related to two human factors: the critical fusion frequency and the phi phenomenon. First, one must sample faster than the critical fusion frequency in order for persistence of vision to occur. But with regard to apparent movement, there are limits as to how far an object can move in the field of view and be perceived as moving. If the object moves too far, then no visual continuity of movement will occur or the object will be perceived to be in several places at once, or to *chatter* abruptly from one frame to the next rather than move smoothly and continuously. This chattering is easiest to see in rapid horizontal action. Only if an object moves within a reasonable range will the motion detectors of the human vision system be triggered by the adjacent positions and perceive movement.

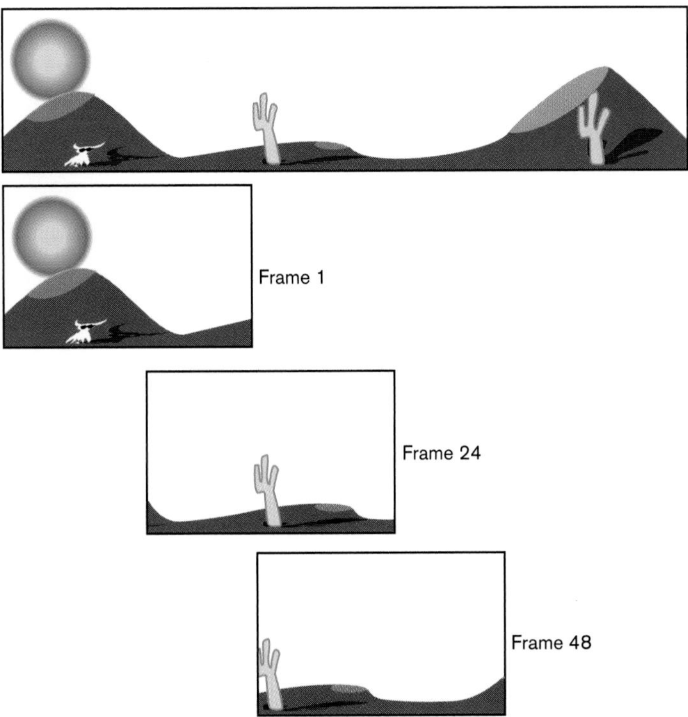

Figure 3.37 Panning at certain speeds will exceed the phi phenomenon. A test can be made to determine when the speed is too high—simply determine the difference between the initial and terminal position of a point in the scene and divide by the number of frames. When the distance traveled per frame exceeds 0.5% to 1% of the width of the field, then the possibility for chatter increases. It is also worth noting that the content of the frame significantly affects the manifestation of artifacts. Obviously, it does not matter how fast you pan across a perfectly white scene. Scenes of greater complexity require more diligence on the part of the cinematographer.

In moving picture media, the rule of thumb is that an object must move across the width of a field in more than seven seconds; conversely, panning speeds in excess of seven seconds across a field will create alias artifacts and should be avoided (see Figure 3.37). The total frames used, sometimes called the ***chatter factor***, may vary somewhat depending upon the size of the object and the sample rate. Translated into bandwidth terms, this means that the temporal bandwidth is more correctly thought of as movement bandwidth, and that the movement resolution is similar to the chatter factor, or on the order of 0.01 to 0.005 of the field width. Zooming action is more forgiving, but undersampled rotary action can produce particularly unusual artifacts (see Figure 3.38). Obviously, in all moving picture systems it is critical that the image be stable and not subject to motion jitter.

Blurring As with spatial anti-aliasing, temporal anti-aliasing involves the length of the sample (exposure) time. In the time domain, exposure times that are equal to the frame duration time have maximum anti-aliasing; conversely, very fast shutter speeds resemble point sample times and have no anti-aliasing. Longer exposure times produce

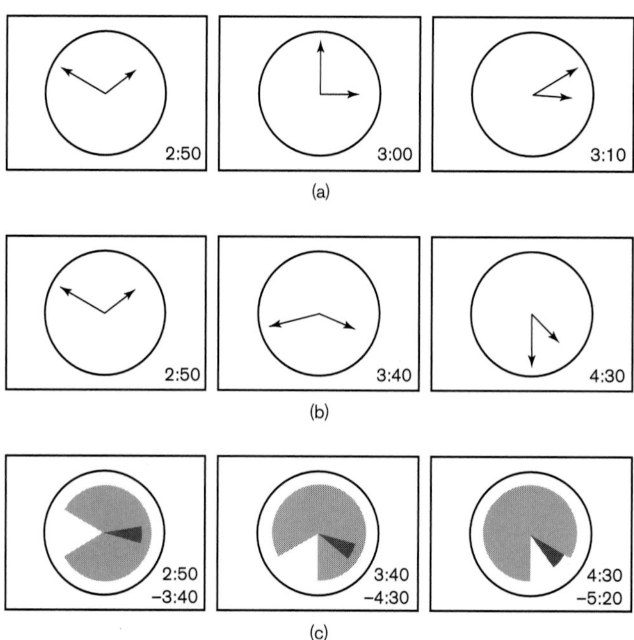

Figure 3.38 Right: The temporal frequency domain is presented here: a real-world clock consisting of hour and minute hands. The smallest unit of temporal space is the half-hour. Samples longer than this may produce aliasing—for example, the hour hand going forward and the minute hand going backward. In (a), observe that the sample grid is three times the bandwidth, one sample every 10 minutes, and this produces convincing motion. Once we begin to sample below the Nyquist limit, though, aliasing occurs, as in (b), where a sample is made every 50 minutes, creating the effect of the minute hand going backward while the hour hand goes forward. Again, the appearance of aliasing can be reduced by integrating the total luminance across time (c).

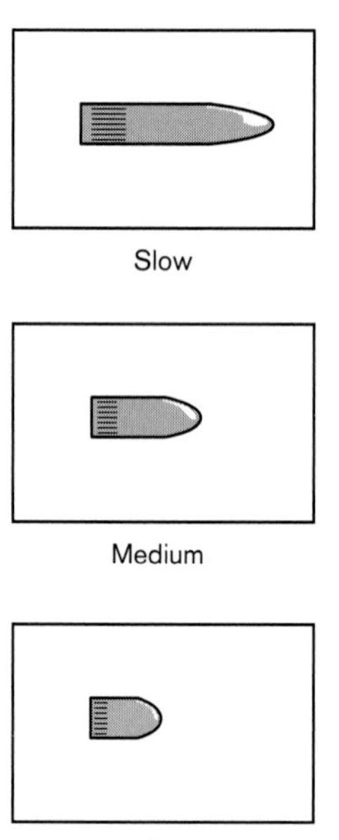

Figure 3.39 Above: The effects of shutter speed. Slower shutter speed increases the motion blur of a bullet traveling left to right.

motion blur—objects in the image that are in motion are recorded with smearing (see Figure 3.39). If an object moves during the exposure, its focused image moves across many pixels, forming a partially transparent image of the object smeared in the direction of motion. The recorded frame contains more information about what happened during that frame cycle than a frame that was recorded with an extremely fast exposure followed by a long blanking. The temporally anti-aliased, motion-blurred picture appears to the eye as having more continuous movement, perhaps because the motion blur provides a secondary clue to the velocity of the object, absent from a recording that shows only position. The faster an object moves within the frame, the more blurred it will appear to be along the direction of motion. Shorter exposure times produce less and less blur because the objects move a shorter distance while the shutter is open, but the individual frames are sharper.

Shutter Effects upon Aliasing

Practically speaking, anti-aliasing and the structure of motion blur is also a function of the type of shutter involved. Recall that a shutter is that part of the camera that determines the duration of time that media gets exposed to light. Furthermore, the shutter may determine

an order to the exposure time of pixels. A leaf shutter, which resembles an iris and is located near the aperture, theoretically exposes all pixels in parallel. The time spent opening and closing the shutter is small compared to the actual exposure time. The rotary shutter and the focal plane shutter are shutters located just in front of the light-sensitive recording medium, as in many 35mm still cameras. These shutters do not record all of the pixels in parallel. The exposure time for all pixels may be equal, but the durations the samples represent are sequential in time. This also produces aliasing artifacts (see Figure 3.40). Scanning shutters such as the Nyquest disk or those used in video scanning also produce temporal artifacts.

Figure 3.40 Distortion that is a result of the direction of the moving shutter and the direction of the moving object. A compressed image can result when the shutter and the object move in opposite directions (middle). An elongated image can result when the shutter and the object move in the same direction (right).

4 The Mechanics of Film

This is the first of three chapters devoted to the media and the recording and playback processes of moving pictures. This chapter explores photographic film pictures and its attendant camera and projector. Because film is a relatively old medium, many technologies that originated with it have migrated to subsequent technologies, such as video and digital imaging. But the motion picture film camera and the movie theater are steeped in a deep romance. Orson Wells, riding a boom of a jib arm, is like a cowboy atop a motion mechanism. Even though these machines and photochemical processes may be nearing the end of their life cycle, their impact will remain.

A photographic image is made by exposing film to light. Following a subsequent development process, the film is printed and then it can be projected. The invention of motion pictures did not come easily. The development of a camera able to record movement and the perfection of a device able to project it demanded the fusion of several technologies, particularly mechanics and chemistry.

This chapter covers the properties of film and photographic media in general, and includes a discussion of cyclic media and how roll media, such as film and tape, replaced cyclic media. It then examines the evolution of the moving picture viewer to the motion picture projector. There is a detailed look at the mechanics of the motion picture shuttle itself, the part of the machinery that is the discrete frame advance in a camera and a projector as well as a look at camera tripods and dollies and the fundamental ways to move them. Finally, the issue of film resolution is addressed.

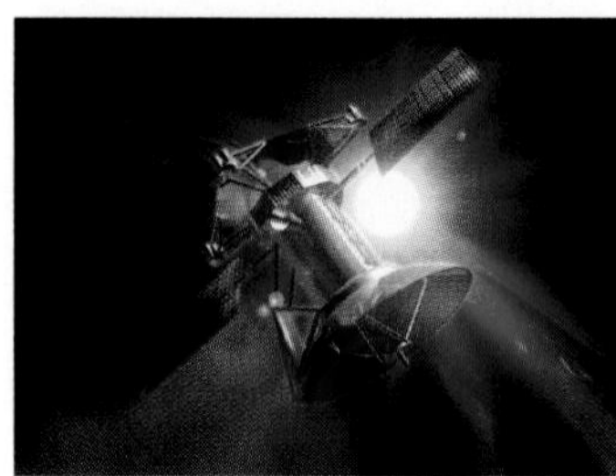

Above: Image courtesy of Mechanism Digital Inc.

Figure 4.1 Below: The photographic camera includes the black box, aperture, lens, and shutter, and a photosensitive film or CCD chip. The major controls are the film speed, the exposure time, the f-stop, the focal length, the subject distance, and the shutter release, to actually take the picture.

The Photographic Camera

While the camera obscura is an interesting imaging phenomenon, it lacks the components necessary to record the real image. The invention of the ***photographic camera*** allows an image to be permanently recorded. The photographic camera augments the camera obscura with two additional components: a recording medium, such as photographic film, which reacts to the real image over time, and thus provides a materialistic memory, and a shutter, which controls the temporal duration that the recording medium is exposed to light. This basic design remains the blueprint of the view camera, the Brownie, the Instamatic, and single-lens reflex cameras (see Figure 4.1). Photography has thus become the process by which a real image is recorded onto film or into a digital file.

The process of photography involves recording an image made of light onto a photosensitive material. Film itself comes in different ***gauges***, as well as different ***speeds***, that is sensitivities to light. Film speed is typically expressed as an ASA (American Standards Association), DIN (Deutsche Industrie Norm), or ISO (International Standards Organization) number; usually slower films (films with a smaller ASA number and less responsive to light) have a higher grain or spatial resolution. The ***exposure time*** is the length of time that a shutter is open. A full camera model thus includes the recording medium, a shutter that controls the exposure time, and an aperture, usually located inside a lens, which controls the quantity of light that reaches the film. The diameter of the aperture is expressed in f-stops. A modern viewfinder displays much of this information around the viewing frame (see Figure 4.2).

For a lens that can be focused, the diameter of the aperture controls the depth of field, that is, the distance in front and behind the

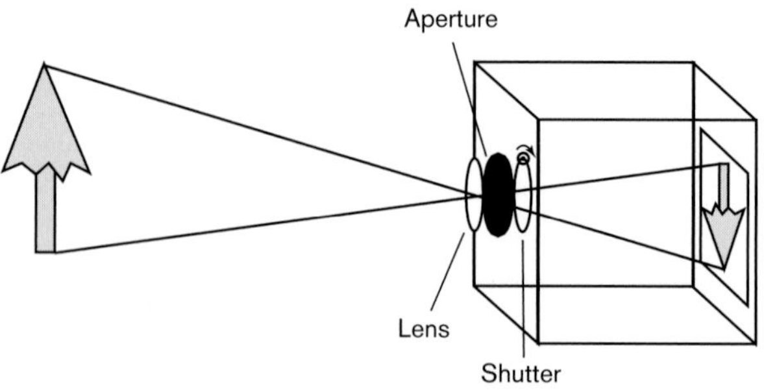

focal point, which is also in focus. Small f-stops have smaller diameter holes and produce a greater depth of field. Four variables do affect what the images look like: the amount of illumination on the scene, shutter speed, f-stop, and film speed. All must be in balance to make a correct exposure, but different combinations produce different results because exposure time relates to motion blur and an f-stop relates to depth of field.

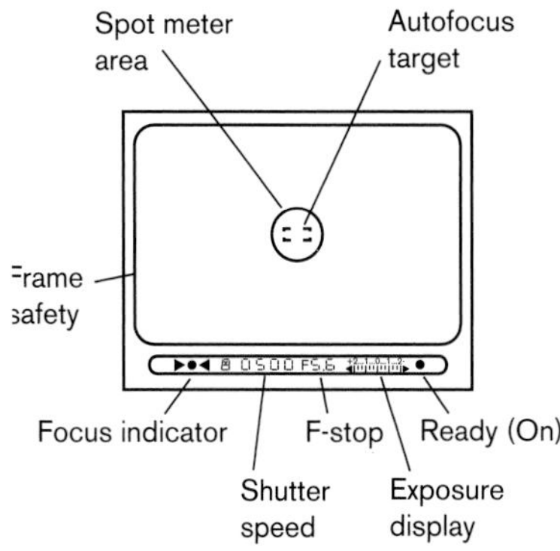

Figure 4.2 Above: A viewfinder display shows not only the picture, but also important related information about recording the picture. The auto-focus target is the object in the real world that the camera is focused on. The spot meter area is the center part of the image that may be incorporated into a light reading. At the bottom, the indicators include range indicators for focus and exposure, plus a readout of the shutter speed and f-stop.

Photographic (Film) Media

Photographic media consists of a thin *emulsion* of photosensitive material coated onto one side of a thicker, supportive material, usually called a ***carrier, base***, or ***substrate*** (see Figure 4.3). Carriers include paper, glass, and cellulose acetate (a clear flexible organic compound made from wood and acetic acid), as well as cloth, metal, and indeed any substance an emulsion can bond to. Carriers can be individual plates, discs, rolls of media, or even curved shapes.

In a typical photographic reaction, light is allowed to hit the surface of the emulsion. As the light hits, the photosensitive material is energized; the more the light energy hits the material, the more an electrochemical reaction is stimulated. The emulsion is a *transducer*, that is, it is a substance that converts one form of energy into another. In film, a developing process accelerates this reaction and the *exposed* portion of the material is made blacker. The reaction is then made lightfast, or *fixed*, by washing the unexposed emulsion away, leaving only the darker areas where light hit the emulsion. This remaining emulsion sits on the carrier and is dried. Thus an original *negative image* is formed.

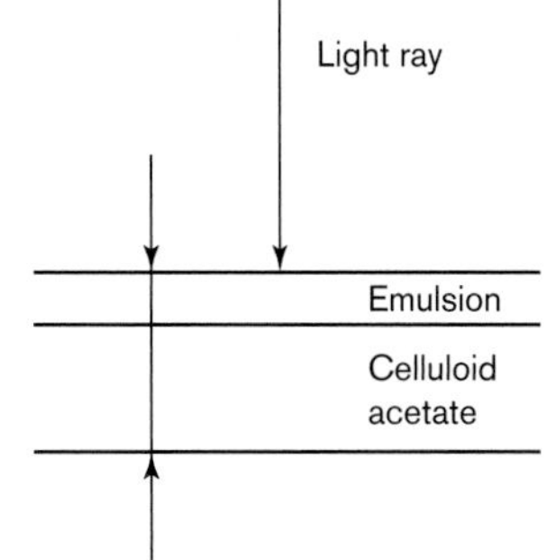

Figure 4.3 Above: A photographic recording consists of a carrier and emulsion. This is a probable cross-section.

A *positive* of the negative image can be made in several ways. Needless to say. during the process, the image can be cropped, enlarged, or reduced, and its exposure can be adjusted. It may be *contact printed* by placing the negative in contact with another carrier, such as glass, film, or paper, and then flashing light through the negative. The result is a ***positive image print*** made up of black and white (or black and clear if the positive is made on film instead of paper). The result is of opposite luminance to the negative and has gray values similar to the original photographed subject. An example of a positive image print is a common photographic paper print or, if

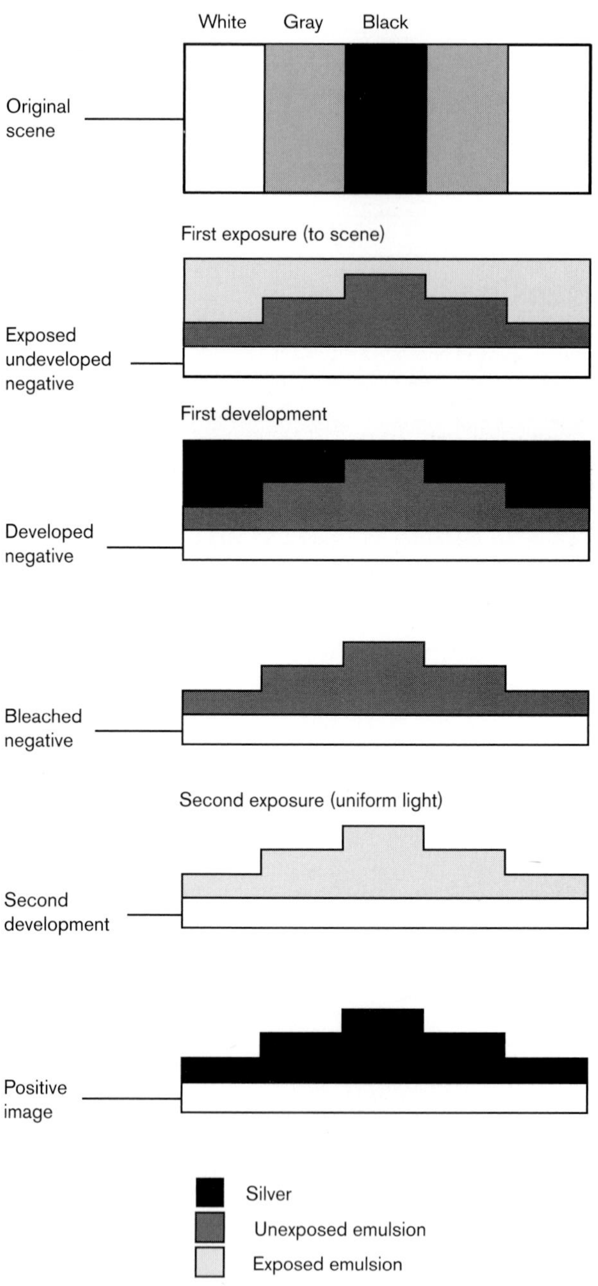

Figure 4.4 Reverse black and white uses a single carrier and single emulsion. After development, instead of fixing the image, the exposed silver is bleached away, and the remaining emulsion is flashed to light and developed. Then any surplus is fixed. The result is a positive image in one carrier generation.

the carrier is acetate, a black-and-white positive transparency, as used for projection in the movies. Another way to make a positive image is *projection printing*, in which the negative is projected, magic lantern style, onto film or paper, using an enlarger or *optical printer* (a camera that photographs film). Both of these are simply glorified magic lanterns.

The *reversal process* is also a way to create a positive transparency or print in one generation without separate negative-positive carriers. After the initial development, but before fixing, the processed emulsion is bleached away, and the complimentary, remaining emulsion is re-exposed to light, then the new positive image is developed and fixed (see Figure 4.4). The result is a positive image in which whites are white and blacks are black. Reversal processes are also used in video, where voltages representing color and intensity are duplicated.

Color pictures can be made in a variety of ways. The Technicolor process splits the light inside a camera into three beams and then filters the beams separately with red, green, and blue filters. The resulting red, green, and blue light is recorded on three *panchromatic separation negatives. Panchromatic* means "many colors," and *separation* means that the color information is separated into three luminance channels, each of which can be represented as a black-and-white image. Pan seps, as they are called for short, may be created as serial images—for example, when making animation, the red, green, and blue exposures can be shot one after another for each frame, and often on the same roll. But with live action, a *beam splitter* must separate the three beams of colored light, and the three separations must be recorded simultaneously and in parallel on three strands of film. Pan separations are also prepared optically to archive color material—it is assumed that black and white has a longer life.

Where subtractive primary color is found (in printing and reflective imagery), we encounter *subtractive color separations*, three in-register black-and-white negatives shot through cyan, magenta, and yellow filters. Prints can be made using pigments or transmissive emulsions that contain cyan, yellow, and magenta dyes. The pigments absorb, or subtract, light from all colors except their own, which they reflect.

Figure 4.5 Single carrier reversal color. Three layers of light-sensitive emulsions are coated on a film of cellulose acetate. The top emulsion is sensitive to blue, the next one to green, and the bottom one to red. The three negative images are reversed during development to form a positive image to which cyan, yellow, and magenta color dyes are coupled.

Color reversal stocks can also be used to record color images. With color reversal stocks, colors are recorded onto the medium as they exist in the real world. The medium records the true color image within one frame, as in slide film. In practice, the stocks form a three-layer color negative, and during development these layers are contact printed onto another triple layer of dyes on the same carrier, making the positive image (see Figure 4.5).

Although pan separations are still used in contemporary processes, such as blue screen compositing, pan separation recording, per se, has been replaced by the use of single-strand *color negatives* and complimentary color print stocks. Color negative film combines three filters and three color emulsions onto a single carrier; color print film—either paper or film—also contains three color layers and is contact or optically printed. Today, color negatives are employed almost exclusively for movie photography and outsell reversal stocks in the stills market.

It is worth noting that the negative-positive photographic process relates closely to the use of molds and castings and allows for mass production—many prints can be made from one negative. As a system of molds and castings, film, especially color film, provides a filmmaker with a network of pathways to go from an original negative to an end product, or print. One advantage of digital representation of imagery, as will be discussed in Chapter 6, is that it avoids a negative/positive mold strategy for the duplication of an image. With digital representation, there is only a positive image, and this positive image is used to make one or more positive images, each in just one step.

Cyclic Motion Picture Recording and Projection

One way to record moving pictures is to use *multiple cameras* to record sequential images (see Figure 4.6), a technique pioneered by Eadweard Muybridge. The advantage of this technique is that the recording instrument is simple; the disadvantage is that the recording must incorporate multiple viewpoints and becomes impractical for long scenes.

The viewing of short cyclic sequences of moving images was perfected during the 1800s. Almost all of these early *cyclic media*

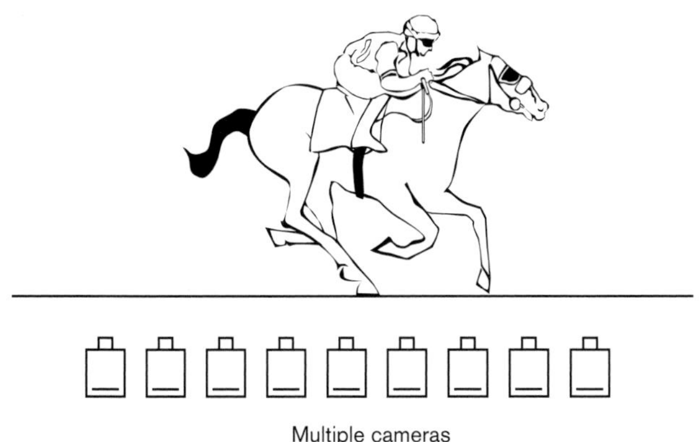

Figure 4.6 Multiple cameras fuse photography with motion pictures. The cameras are "tripped" as the moving object passes by, triggering the shutter release and recording the image.

image viewers were based on a cycle of discrete images arranged in a circular medium. There are three primary structures for image display, one corresponding to each axis of rotation: the disk, cylinder or drum, and paddles (again see Figure 3.8). *Disk viewers*, such as the phenakistoscope, display a series of discrete images radially. In *cylinder viewers*, such as the zoetrope, a paper band of images is mounted on the inside of a drum and viewed through slots in the circumference of the drum. The *paddle wheel viewer*, such as the Mutoscope, is similar to a flip book and depicts an individual piece of artwork on each page.

In the disk and cylinder viewers, the rotating image is viewed through a *rotating slit shutter* that sweeps in front of each picture. The slit shutters are often embedded in the same carrier as the pictures, usually between them. In the paddle wheel viewer, the pictures are in perfect registration, with each picture falling on top of the previous picture in rapid succession; in a sense each image shutters the previous image. Neither the zoetrope, phenakistoscope, or Mutoscope employs a lens, internal light source, or projection, although each of these technologies can be adapted to projection.

Disk and cylinder viewers animate *cycles*—the repetition of media viewed rapidly and in endless succession so as to create the illusion of movement (see Figure 4.7). Cycles are played over and over again, the end linking up with the beginning. Paddle-wheel viewers permit longer action times than disk or cylinder viewers, but even this technology does not lend itself to temporal domains longer than a minute or two.

Another early attempt to perfect animation was through the use of *dissolving views*, in which a transition between two related

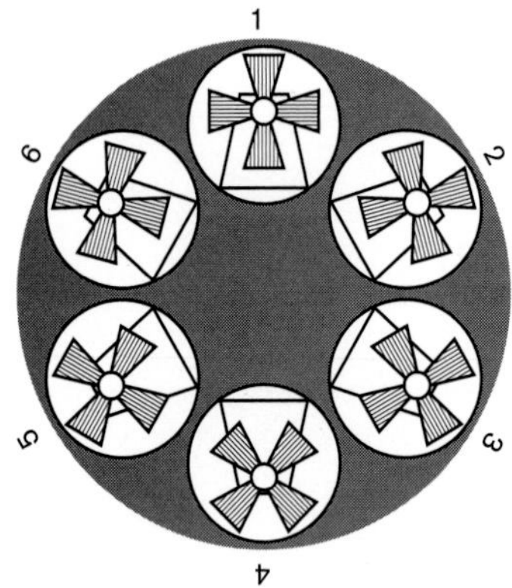

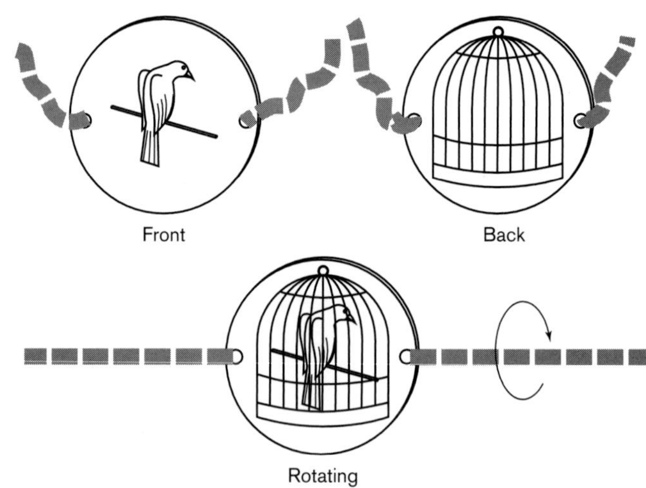

Figure 4.7 Above: Cycles occupy much of early animation—the medium and the action go round and round, repeating seamlessly. Here the windmills are drawn as they would appear on a six-picture disk.

Figure 4.8 Above, right: A thaumatrope disk is bistate, consisting of two images, one on each side. When the disk is rapidly turned over and over, the two images fuse together into one.

images is accompanied by ***cross-fading***. This technique remains popular in slide shows and has become part of the vocabulary of film. ***Stagger devices***, such as the thaumatrope, create animated effects by using a two-sided disk with different pictures on the front and back, for example a bird and a cage (see Figure 4.8). Two holes at the sides are threaded with string, which is wound up and pulled to spin the disk. When the disk is spinning, the eye sees the images from both sides of the disk and perceives them as one image. The thaumatrope is simulated in film or video by alternating every other frame, and is often used as a rhythmic device, sort of a visual drum-roll or trill, as well as a device to indicate mental disorientation.

Roll Media Recording and Projection

The primary limitation of cyclic motion picture media is the duration of the cycle; large disks were used to extend durations to hundreds of frames, and paddle-wheel viewers into the thousands, but eventually, a simpler way emerged to dramatically extend recording and viewing time. ***Roll media*** are essentially long strips of a medium such as film wound onto a core or spool, and used by winding them past the recording or viewing mechanism onto a second take-up reel. Because roll media can essentially be of arbitrary length, they are not constrained to repetitive cycles (see Figure 4.9). The size of a roll is specified in terms of ***gauge***, that is, its physical width, and length.

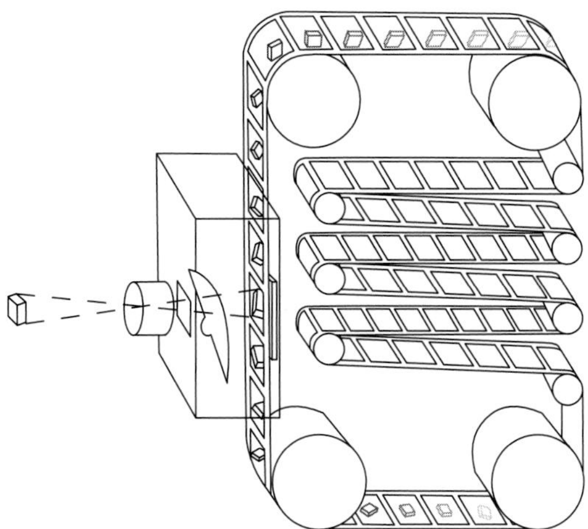

Figure 4.9 Roll media can be of arbitrary length.

Standard gauges of film include 35mm; 16mm, which was developed to be an industrial standard; 8mm, which was introduced as a hobby medium; and the grandiose 70mm (see Figure 4.10). A system of perforation holes, at one or both edges, ensures that individual frames are all registered.

Motion picture roll media have now been used in excess of 100 years. Perforated 35mm film has become an international standard, available in lengths ranging from 3-foot prepackaged canisters to fit into still cameras, to rolls thousands of feet long for use in motion picture cameras, laboratories, and theaters.

The Shuttle and Intermittent Movement of Media

A series of individual discrete images can be recorded onto continuously moving analog roll media because of a *shuttle*, which allows for intermittent movement of the roll inside the recording device. In order for the images to be evenly spaced and evenly exposed, the shuttle is synchronized to the shutter release. Mechanical power is provided by a continuously rotating shaft that is translated into a cyclic lateral mechanical action.

In motion picture recording, the shuttle is the part of the apparatus that physically positions the medium and holds the image area steady while the recording and exposure are made. Because the shuttle has a very low-level function, it is easy to forget about it. However, due to its precise, intermittent, automated movement, it is one of the few functionalities that differentiates moving picture from

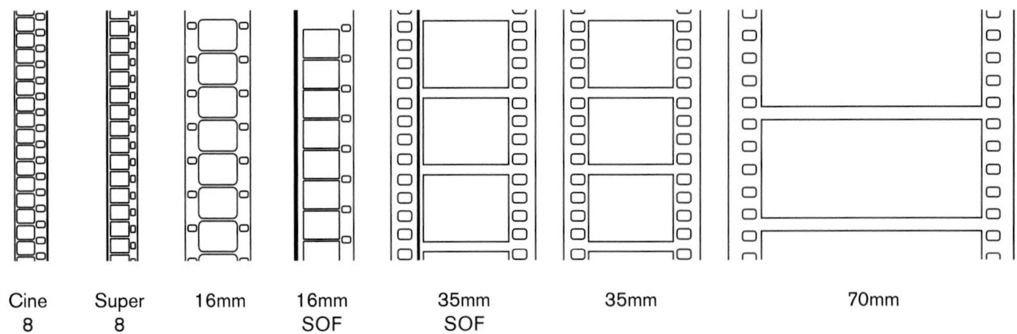

Figure 4.10 Film gauges. There may be several different locations of sound track and apertures for each gauge.

static picture recording. Shuttles are found in both motion picture cameras and projectors.

In order to photograph discrete images on roll media, the following steps must be taken: First, the shutter must be opened while the recording medium is held still and the recording is made. Next, the shutter must be closed and the recording medium must be moved so that the next frame of film is advanced into position and held still. Then, the steps are repeated over and over again. Note that during the time when the shuttle moves the film, the shutter is closed and no image is recorded (or projected), for the camera (or the projector). This part of the cycle is referred to as ***blanking***, because the image is blanked from view. The blanking time is equal to the duration of time that the shutter is closed. Due to persistence of vision, blanking is not perceived during playback.

Despite this start-and-stop strategy needed for image recording, one does not want to move the roll of film (or other medium) in discrete advances. Rather, it is preferred to rotate the medium's source and take-up reels continuously. This continuous approach is particularly necessary when sound is present. Sound is recorded continuously, with an analog method, and analogically, and must pass the recording and playback head at a constant rate of speed. In other words, in a film camera (see Figure 4.11) and a projector [see Figure 4.12(a)], roll media must move both continuously and discretely. This is accomplished by forming a loop of film on each side of the shuttle. Inside the loop, the shuttle advances film discretely using an intermittent movement device such as the Geneva mechanism or a claw, which provides a jerk-free intermittent motion. Before and after the loop (before and after the shuttle), sprocket drive rollers turn the medium forward continuously. A projector has a similar arrangement,

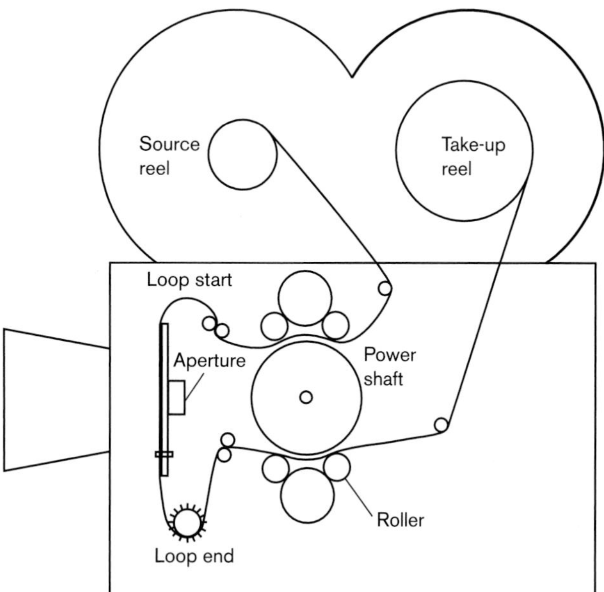

Figure 4.11 Left: The film camera. Sound and pictures are synchronized onto a common carrier that serves both analog and discrete needs, respectively. Because of the intermittent (or in video, the spinning head), sound is usually recorded physically ahead of the pictures.

except that it also has a sound playback head, physically located outside and after the loop. The sound is thus located physically ahead of the picture but plays synchronously [see Figure 4.12 (b)].

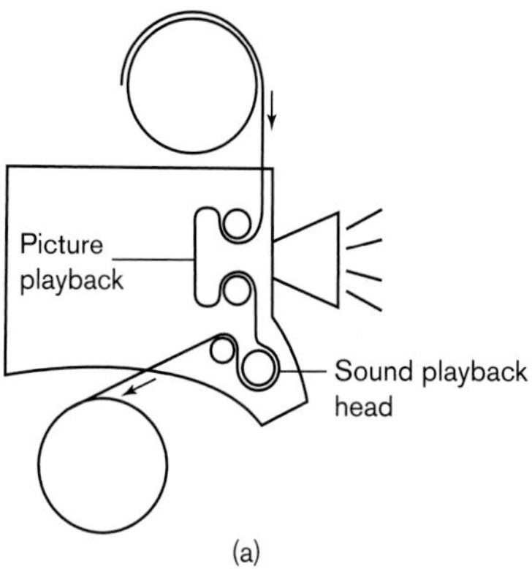

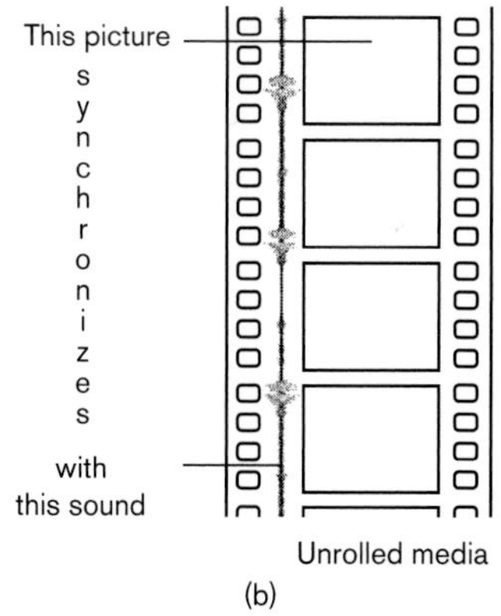

Figure 4.12 Above: The film projector (a). As shown in (b), the image appears on the film after the sound, and thus the sound-playback heads are placed before the picture playback area. The distance is actually made up of more frames than shown here (b).

Camera Movement

A camera may be mounted on several kinds of supports. The simplest is a *tripod*, a collapsible support with three legs (see Figure 4.13). The legs may be stuck in the ground, placed into a triangular frame called a *spider* so that they do not slide around, or rested on a dolly. A *dolly* is a support platform with wheels, often with a central pedestal to support the camera, and is typically used to move a motion picture camera. A *crab dolly* has wheels that can be set so that two of them are used to steer and two are locked, or so that all four can be locked or all four used for steering, and the dolly can thus be "crabbed" in any direction (see Figure 4.14).

A *jib arm*, also known as a boom, is a rotating arm attached to a dolly or fixed base that can be raised and lowered in a manner such that a camera, attached to one end, stays parallel to the ground as the arm is raised and lowered (see Figure 4.15). Longer arms permit greater vertical motion. The vertical motion of the camera does transverse a slight arc, but nonetheless, the camera always remains parallel to the ground; this is accomplished by a

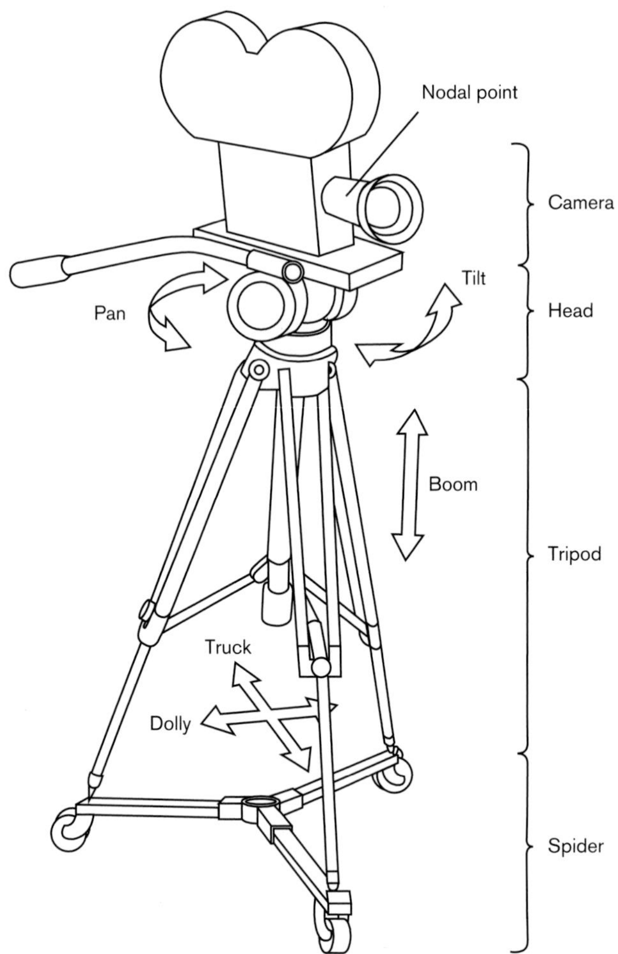

Figure 4.13 Right: The tripod head provides the ability to tilt the camera at an angle up and down, to pan the camera around an angle to the left and right, to lift, or boom, it straight up and down, and to move, or truck, it. The tripod is mounted on a dolly to allow for trucking.

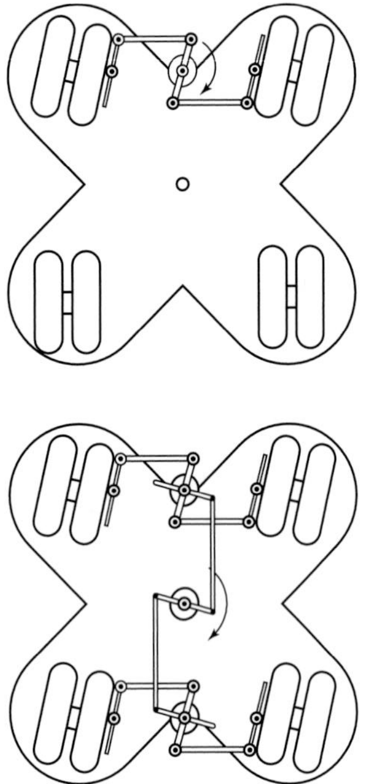

Figure 4.14 Above: The underside of a crab dolly. The design of the wheel mechanism allows the dolly to move in any direction.

four-bar linkage in the shape of a parallelogram. Although the primary purpose of the boom is to raise and lower the camera, it can also be used to sweep the camera through an arc motion, raising or lowering the camera in the process.

Often the camera operator (and an assistant) sit on the arm. Their weight, along with the weight of the camera and boom, are counterbalanced at the opposite end with a counterweight. A third assistant located near the counterweight raises and lowers the boom. A fourth assistant pushes and steers the dolly. The entire assembly of the dolly and jib is often called a *crane*; this term is also used to refer to many different articulated linkages capable of extended motion.

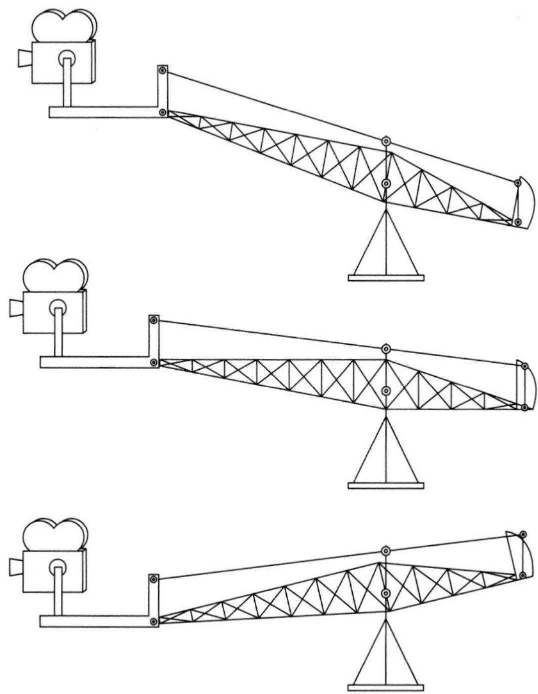

Figure 4.15 A jib arm raises the camera up and down while keeping it parallel to the ground.

The motion picture camera has 6 degrees of freedom, 3 of which involve rotations: pan, tilt, and roll (see Figures 4.16 and 4.17). A *pan* [Figure 4.17 (b)] is a rotary pivoting movement of the camera, from left to right or vice versa. In a 3D coordinate system where *y* is the vertical axis, a pan is a rotation of the camera around the *y*-axis. In pragmatic terms, a pan means rotating the camera so as to pass across a horizontal vista. A companion to the pan is the *tilt* [Figure 4.17 (c)] , which is an up or down movement of the camera, more specifically, a rotation of the camera around the *x*-axis. Finally, a *roll* [Figure 4.17 (d)] is a rotation of the camera around the *z*-axis, that is, the axis that goes through the center point of the lens. These terms are analogous to the aeronautical terms yaw, pitch, and roll, which are also occasionally used in 3D computer graphics software: *yaw* is synonymous with pan, *pitch* is synonymous with tilt, and *roll* has the same meaning in both nomenclatures (see Figure 4.18). Yaw, pitch, and roll are often used to describe the rotation of a free-flying object—such as a camera in flight—whereas pan, tilt, and roll imply that the camera is grounded.

The three degrees of freedom relate to moving the camera in space. A *dolly* (or the verb *to dolly*) refers to a translation of the

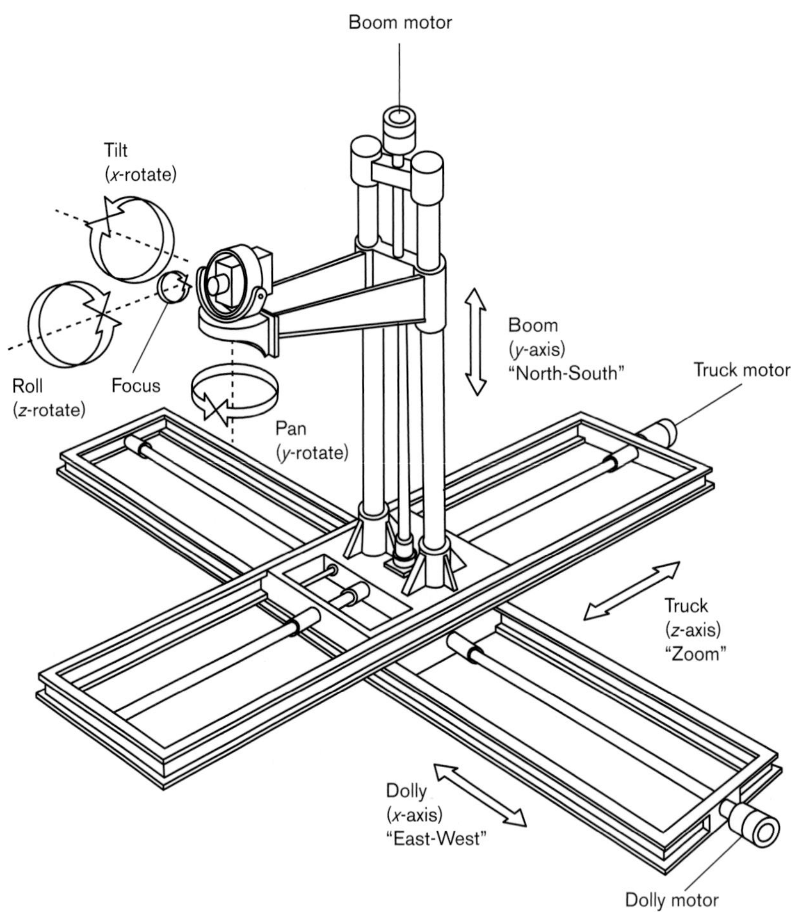

Figure 4.16 The six degree of freedom of a motion picture camera.

camera on the dolly into or away from the scene, that is, in or away from the direction of the lens. The movement is usually stated as "dolly in" or "dolly out". A *truck* is the movement of the camera from side to side. A *boom* is a vertical movement of the camera, named after its physical configuration. Note that in practice, the terms *dolly* and *truck* are often used interchangeably. Obviously, in computer animation, all six degrees of freedom are accomplished without the physical apparatus, although they may be accomplished by simulating a real-world apparatus. In live-action-simulation lockups—that is, when two scenes are required to be in perfect registration—this is necessary. But it may also be desired where a cinematographer wants to get the feel of classic camera movements.

Strictly speaking, a *zoom* is not a degree of freedom of the camera, although it is related. A zoom is a change in the focal length of the lens while the camera is running. A zoom requires a zoom lens,

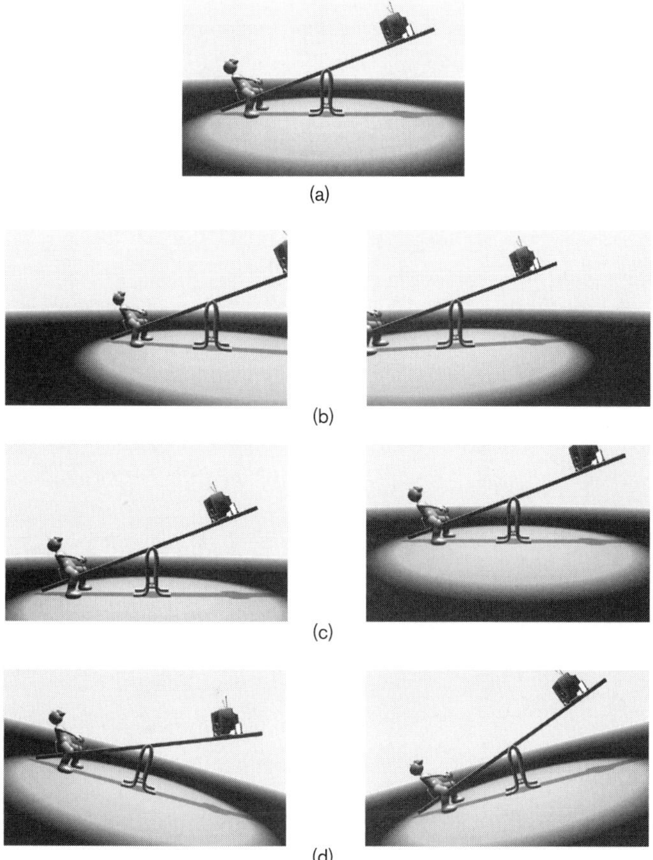

Figure 4.17 Original image (a). Pan (b)—the camera can pivot left and right, that is, rotate around the *y*-axis. Tilt (c)—the camera can pivot up and down, that is, rotate around the *x*-axis. Roll (d)—the camera can pivot around the center of the lens, that is, rotate around the *z*-axis.

that is, a lens capable of changing focal lengths. The effect of a zoom is to make objects in the field of view bigger when zooming into the scene, smaller when zooming out of the scene. It is worth noting that the images created during a zoom are not the same as the images created during a dolly. In a dolly, the camera moves closer, yet the focal length is constant; in a zoom, the actual focal length is changing, while the camera remains stationary. The difference is visceral: in a zoom, the resulting perspective of the images changes; in a dolly, the camera actually gets closer. Because the zoom requires less equipment and hence is cheaper to achieve than the dolly, many filmmakers use zooms instead of dollies.

An exception to this definition of zoom is the definition associated with a classic animation camera, where the camera sits above a platen and shoots down at it. When the classic animation camera dollies into the artwork, it is referred to as a zoom, even though there is no change to the focal length of the lens.

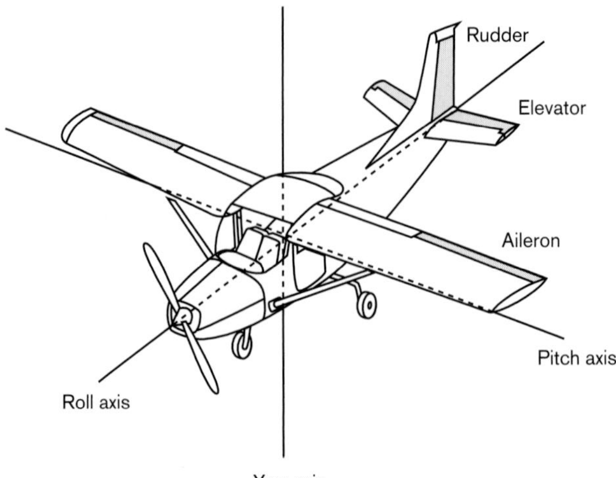

Figure 4.18 Yaw, pitch, and roll.

In practice, camera movements are often used in combination. For example, the camera might pan during a zoom. The many combinations can be used to enhance the emotional impact of the resulting shot.

As we have discussed, the *nodal point* is the exact center of a lens (see Figure 4.19). This physicality has ramifications to the digital cinematographer. Consider this example: when panning a camera with a standard tripod, the *pivot point* of the pan is typically located at the pivot point of the tripod, not at the nodal point of the lens. In normal practice, the camera is mounted on a *head*, which is a metal plate surmounting the legs of a tripod. When panning, the camera pivots around the center of the head, and the nodal point swings in an arc around it because the camera is centered on its own body, not on the center of the lens. The displacement between the nodal point and the pan axis is called the *nodal point offset*. In situations where a virtual camera must simulate the use of a real tripod, it is imperative to correctly implement the nodal point offset if the simulation is to be accurate. For a typical head, the simulation involves concatenating a translation before and after the pan rotations; the translation is equal to the nodal point offset. Note that tilt and roll (if it exists) may also have nodal point offsets. In the real world, on occasions when it is necessary to pan around the nodal point, a *nodal tripod* can be used. These special tripods mount around the camera to allow for the nodal point to lie on the axis of the pan, tilt, and/or roll.

Another kind of camera mount is a *gimbal mount*, which has three types of rotation—yaw, pitch, and roll—controlled by mechanical

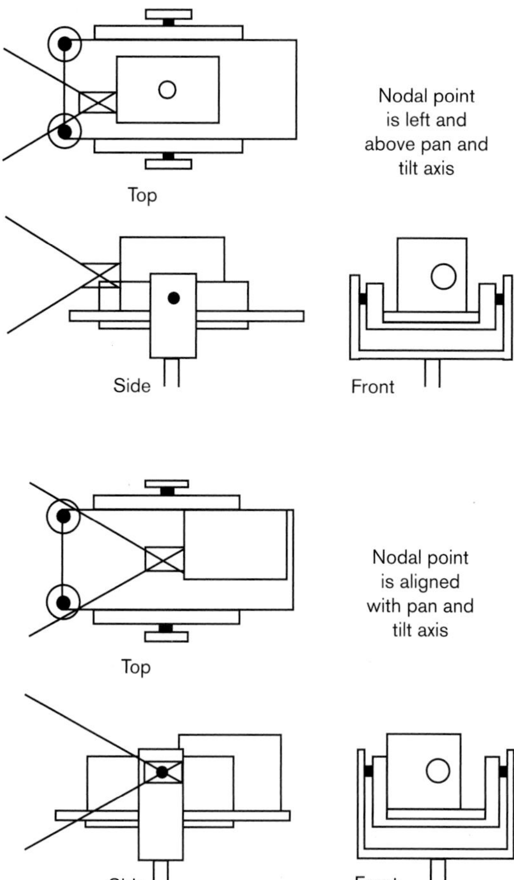

Figure 4.19 Nodal point offset. At the top, the nodal point is left and above the pan and tilt axis. At the bottom, the nodal point is aligned to the center of the lens.

parts (see Figure 4.20). These rotations can be described mathematically and therefore can also be used for virtual cameras.

The Moving Picture Projector

The *motion picture projector* is the machine needed for projecting film images. An intermittent shuttle inside the projector enables light to be projected through individual frames. With this method, the perception of moving pictures is dependent upon persistence of vision. That is, continuous motion is perceived because the discrete image frames are kept in precise and momentary registration while the remainder of the medium moves continuously. The eye and mind perceive the image for a fraction of a second, until the next frame is projected. Remember that flicker fusion occurs at about 30 frames/second, so an ingenious strategy is employed whereby the

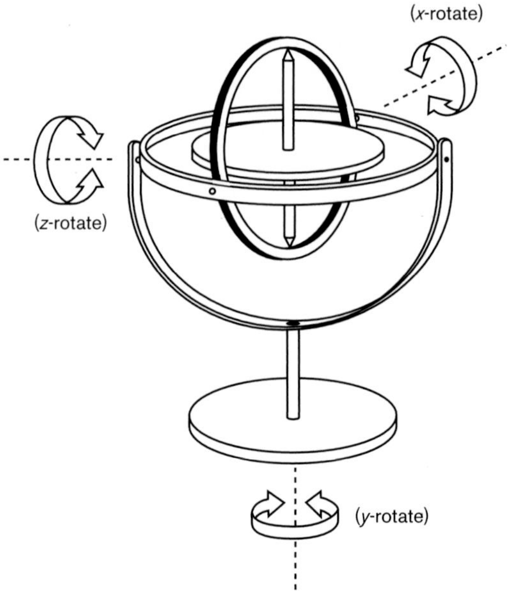

Figure 4.20 A gimbal mount.

film is shot at speeds from 18 to 24 frames/second, and then projected at the same speed, but each image is strobed two or three times while it is held in the gate, raising the number of exposures past the critical flicker-fusion frequency.

The coupling of a projection device with roll media made the first *movie theater* possible. The roll media projector created a new viewing environment and experience. The more simple one-person viewers only allowed the image to be viewed by an audience of one. The projector, on the other hand, permits many people to simultaneously view an image, creating an ***audience***. The additional factor is not only one of size, but also of audience response and behavior.

System Resolution

Many variables which determine the visual quality of a recorded image. First, there is the nature of the scene, especially how it is illuminated and how much smoke, haze, and dust particles are in the environment. Next, there is the quality of the lens. Several variables relate directly to the recording medium itself. These include, in the case of film, the amount of area available for recording the image, the fineness of the grain of the film in resolving detail (resolution is usually measured in the number of lines/millimeter), and the dynamic range of the medium in terms of light to dark. Obviously, the spatial resolution of the image as a whole is the product of the lines/millimeter times the width and height; the dynamic resolution is akin to the number of bits per pixel. While the details of the actual metrics may be debated, it is safe to say that spatial resolutions in the range of 100 lines/millimeter are practical; thus a 24.892mm full academy film frame has somewhere around 2500 pixels of horizontal resolution. Film has a dynamic resolution of 1000:1, or about 12 bits per pixel per primary color (red, green, and blue).

Because film is a temporal medium consisting of a series of many frames, the precise registration of the frames during recording and playback is also a significant factor in overall perceived resolution. There is also evidence to suggest that a motion sequence of frames has more resolution than any individual frame because the grain averages out and augments the information.

It is important to note that if the film is projected in a theater, additional factors also come into play in determining the perceived resolution of the film as it appears on the movie screen. These include, in addition to those described above, the loss of resolution (spatial as well as brightness) caused by duplication from negative to print (and any intermediate materials), registration wiggle during duplication and projection, unevenness of the light source during projection, artifacts created by the projector lens, smoke and dust in the theater, loss of contrast created by the presence of ambient light in the theater, and imperfections in the screen itself as a perfect reflector. Note that the ambient light in the theater not only includes actual lights such as exit lights, but also ambient light that is reflecting from the screen itself, bouncing around the room and back onto the screen. (The latter is a major problem in Omnimax, where the surface that is being projected on is the inside of a dome.)

Thus the resolution of film is very different depending upon whether one takes the perspective of an individual frame or the perspective of the entire system, from the movie set to the screen. Obviously the cumulative effects combine to lower resolution, an argument that has been advanced by proponents of ***high-definition television*** (HDTV) systems. With digital HDTV, neither the spatial nor the dynamic range of an individual frame equals that of film, but there are no sprocket holes, and no intermediate materials or projector to lower resolution, and no analog duplication, so from a system perspective, the "resolutions" are more equal.

The Electronics of Video 5

This chapter focuses on the key principles of electronic imaging, in particular video and television. An important characteristic of electronic imaging is that moving pictures are represented as electrical or electronic signals, often in analog form. The chapter addresses input and output devices, television standards, issues of raster images, video recording and editing, color, HDTV, video formats, and recording technologies. Special attention is paid to scanning techniques and the graphic and temporal structure of the video frame, because they are not obvious and because a thorough understanding is vital to the animator, whose job it is to render frames.

As a technology, video enormously expands our ability to record the world around us and to structure images and ideas. But video is not without baggage. As will be discussed, its limited color space, the artifacts of composite video, and the specifics of scanning and interlace present a demanding arena for those who deal with frames. However, the older technologies are not going to go away quickly, and the new ones are not without their own artifacts. The evolution of video into a digital system is also explored here, and although distinctions are developed between digitized video and other kinds of digital systems, a fuller exposition of this topic is reserved for the next chapter.

The Principles of Raster Scanning

Electronic images, such as video images, are images that are represented as analog data and involve the transmission and storage of

Above: From *Babe.* (© 1999, Universal Pictures. Image courtesy of Rhythm and Hues Studios.)

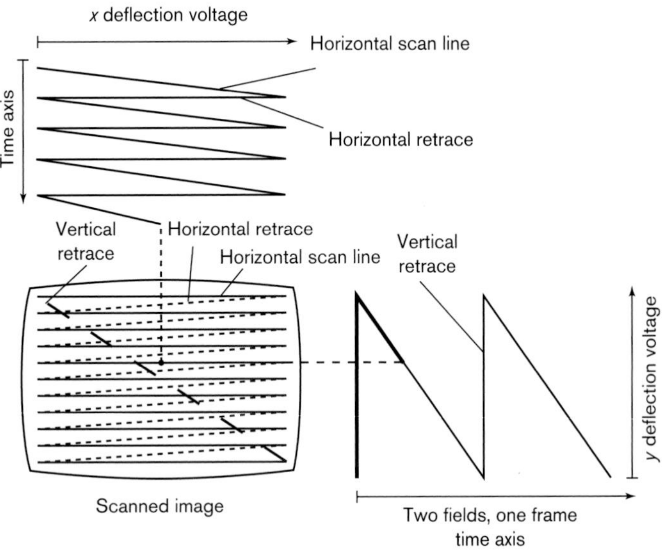

Figure 5.1 Right: Electronic scanning, be it used for a CRT or pickup tube, involves deflecting the beam with separate *x* and *y* voltage patterns. The scanning circuits only position the beam, they do not determine brightness.

varying electronic ***signals***. Two fundamental concepts of electronic imaging are the frame and the raster, and with them the concepts of phasing and sync. A ***frame*** is a representation of a 2D area, and a ***raster*** is the representation of a frame made by scanning successive rows of scan lines (see Figure 5.1). More precisely, a raster is the representation of a picture as a series of closely spaced parallel, usually horizontal, scan lines, where each line has varying intensity (brightness). A raster has a predefined number of scan lines, each scan line has height, and adjacent scan lines are in fact touching. Timing plays a critical role: each scan line lasts a fixed predefined temporal interval, and the luminance of the line corresponds to the temporal sequence of a continuously varying voltage. Finally, each line has a time that is unique to it, as lines are transmitted sequentially.

In order to accomplish a successful transmission of a raster image (such as a television image), the two machines—sending and receiving—must be *in phase* and *in sync*. In other words, input and output devices must be reading and writing at the same graphic location at the same time. To be in phase means that the two machines start together at the same place; to be in sync means that they must run at the same speed (see Figure 5.2). If their graph-time is not equal, is not in phase and in sync, the resulting picture gets at best skewed, and at worst, scrambled. Phasing is achieved when the transmitting machinery sends a special phasing pulse

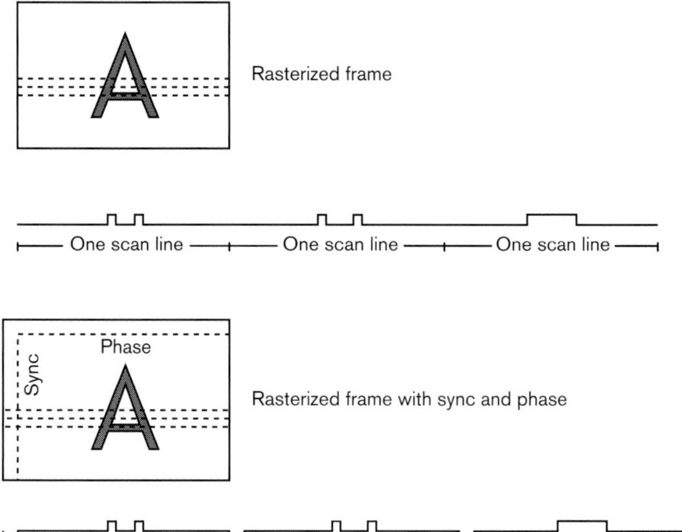

Figure 5.2 Left: Phasing and sync in a raster graphic are akin to frames and scan lines. Phasing aligns the playback unit and the recorder both at the beginning (such as the top left) of a picture; sync ensures that the transmitting and receiving units operate at equal speeds. The upper system is devoid of phase and sync. The lower system contains both. Note that the three scan lines each contain extra width, which is a negative signal; this is the horizontal sync pulse. Extra lines at the top of the picture contain a continuous negative pulse; this is the vertical sync, or phase pulse.

prior to sending the actual picture. Synchronization occurs between each line and requires that the input and output devices be running at the same speed.

A frame in an electronic image system therefore needs to be thought of in two ways: (1) as a static 2D graphic image, and (2) as a phasing and duration of time during which symbols or signals represent the image. It is common to merge the phase and sync information into the signal temporally. A small interval of time, called the *horizontal blanking interval*, and a *horizontal sync pulse* may occur between successive lines. A longer period of time, called the *vertical blanking interval*, and a *vertical sync pulse*, or phasing, may exist between frames—for example, the time needed to change paper on the receiver of a fax machine.

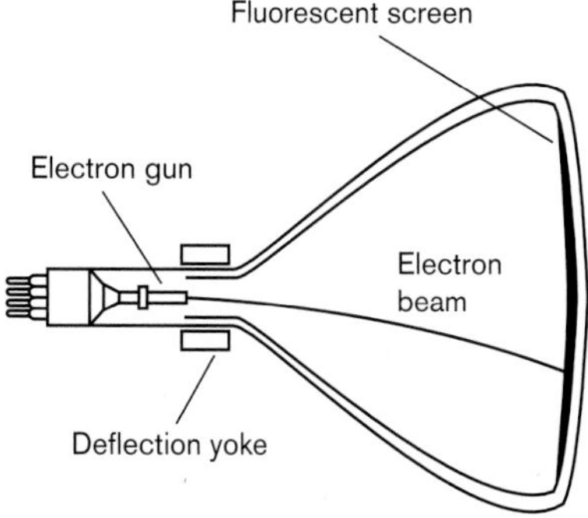

Figure 5.3 Above: A CRT.

Electronic Output Displays

Raster images are often displayed on a cathode ray tube (CRT), which is a vacuated glass tube, flattened at the back and covered with phosphors inside at the front (see Figure 5.3). The back end of the tube contains three electron guns, which release an invisible beam of cathode rays that flow from negative to positive inside the tube. The cathode rays are negatively charged subatomic particles of matter called electrons. When the electrons strike the phosphors, they cause a fluorescent glow.

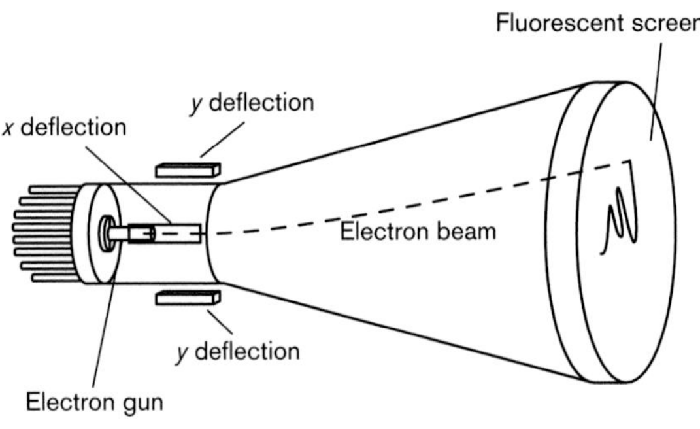

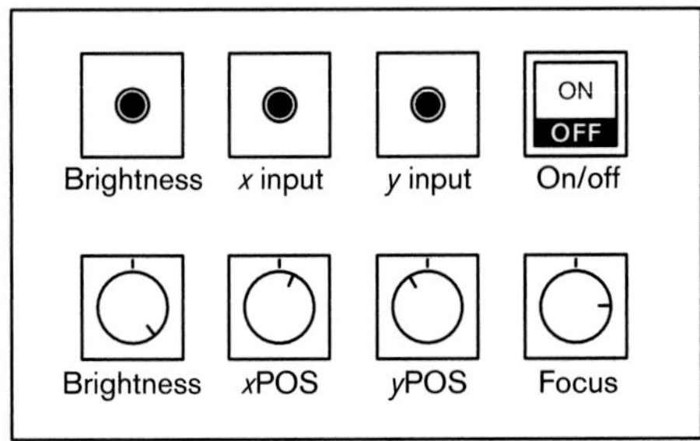

Figure 5.4 The oscilloscope is a general-purpose CRT that can visually display voltages or the waveform of any electronic circuit. This oscilloscope has three degrees of freedom. Input jacks (at the top left) receive the incoming signals: brightness (the intensity of the beam), and *x* and *y* axes deflections. The controls also include scalar knobs to adjust the overall brightness, and the horizontal and vertical centering of the beam (XPOS, YPOS), adjust focus, and power the unit on and off.

Raster images can also be displayed on ***flat-panel displays***, which utilize one of several solid-state technologies and have the advantage of being very thin. As with a CRT, images on a flat panel are produced by scanning. One difference between the CRT and the flat panel is that because the beam inside the CRT can be electromagnetically deflected, the beam can be positioned anywhere on the screen, and thus be used to trace graphic curves, as in an oscilloscope (see Figure 5.4), and draw graphic vectors, as with a vector graphics display.

In a raster graphics system, the beam is rapidly written as a series of parallel scan lines while the intensity (or brightness) of the beam is varied. Because the phosphors take a moment to fade, and because of persistence of vision, humans perceive the rapidly scanning electron beam as a color image. Because the beam is scanning rapidly, any changes in the scene are immediately incorporated in the changes in intensity of the beam, so humans perceive movement.

Electronic Image Input Devices

Electronic image input devices convert optical images into signals; if operated at high speeds, they are capable of capturing real images

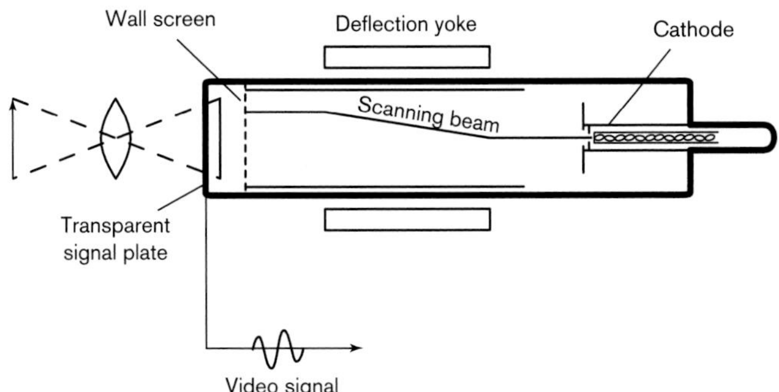

Figure 5.5 An orthicon and vidicon scan from behind the image and are more sensitive to light than the iconscope. The electron beam is also slowed down before encountering the stored charge on the tube face. A vidicon uses a slightly different photoconductivity principle with electronic scanning.

and motion. Examples of such devices include the ***orthicon*** and the ***vidicon***, which are vacuum-tube capture devices used in many high-end video cameras (see Figure 5.5). Like the CRT, the orthicon and vidicon employ a scanning raster beam of electrons to convert the brightness values in the image into electrical voltages. Unlike a CRT, the scanning surfaces of the orthicon and the vidicon are not coated with phosphor (which emits light when struck by electrons) but is with a photosensitive surface that accumulates charge when hit by incoming light rays. The accumulation of charge is stored locally (and microscopically) on the photosensitive "emulsion" of the surface; this accumulation matches the distribution of light in the image. As the electron beam scans over the surface, the accumulated charge is discharged and flows out of the tube as a signal—the brighter the image, the greater the amplitude of the signal (see Figure 5.6). One may think of the photosensitive surface as a matrix of microscopic capacitors, all gathering charge as they continue to be exposed to light. Brighter areas of the surface gather more charge, and charge at one location continues to be gathered while the beam scans the rest of the surface. As the scanning beam passes over a particular part of the surface, the stored charge flows out and into the output signal; the discharged surface then begins to accumulate charge again.

An alternative to vacuum-tube devices is the ***charged coupled device*** (CCD), a solid-state transistor device with a matrix of light-sensitive pixels. In a video system, the CCD is designed so that it is discharged in the raster scanning pattern of video. Some CCD chips combine red, green, and blue sensors; others are monochromatic so that the camera employs a beam splitter and three chips.

Note that the photosensitive surfaces of the CCD and the vidicon have exposure speed—just like the photosensitive surface in film

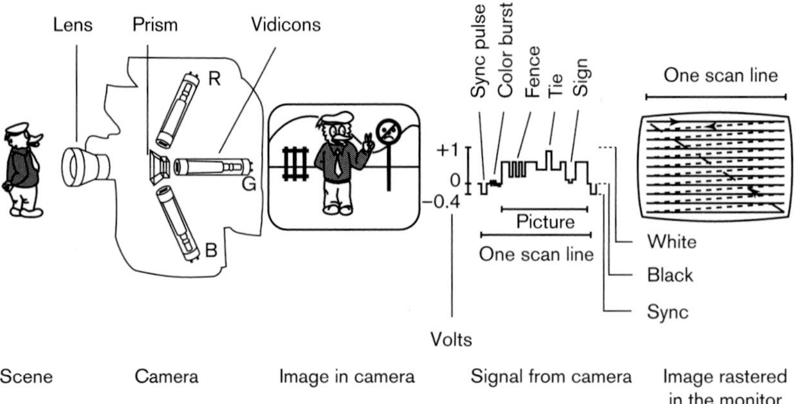

Figure 5.6 The full electronic television model. Incoming light from the real world passes into a camera through a lens and a prism, where it is split into primary colors. Three vidicons capture synchronous video signals, which are encoded in the camera and output as a composite signal that includes sync. The waveform to the right of the picture is of a single scan line. The signal is then transmitted to a display that uses the incoming picture and sync to scan out the raster. The principles are the same if the transducers are digital.

does. Exposure times, shutter speeds, f-stops, focus, and depth of field remain pertinent issues. Exposure times may be determined by the speed of the scanning process as well as by mechanical shutters placed in the optical path before the light hits the sensor. (Those scanning devices have some roles in scanning film and in media conversions, and are discussed again in Chapter 6.)

Electronic Television Standards

Television is a process of capturing, transmitting, recording, and displaying moving pictures in real time. It requires a transducer for converting light into electricity, a scanning methodology, a phasing and synchronization method, and a way to convert electricity back into light on a display screen. Television can employ discrete or continuous luminance signals, but electronic analog television uses continuous voltage.

Television was perfected during the late 1800s and became ubiquitous after 1941 when the American *National Television System Committee* (NTSC) standard was adopted by the Federal Communications Commission (FCC) for broadcasting. This standard, since extended for color and digital representations, resulted from a careful study of the spatial acuity of the eye, bandwidth, the vacuum tube, and spatial and temporal resolutions. The resulting system uses 525 lines per picture, 30 pictures per second, and a 2:1 interlacing and requires a bandwidth of 6MHz, the equivalent of 300 FM radio stations. It represented a dramatic jump in resolution, up from the 120-line system of the 1930s, and has remained surprisingly durable after 50 years of use.

Parameters	NTSC	PAL
Aspect ratio	1.33	1.33
Scan lines	525	625
Vertical resolution	483	575
Horizontal resolution	720	720
Frame rate	29.97	25
Interlace	2:1	2:1
MPixels/second	10.42	10.35
Color	Composite	Composite
Horizontal scan line (including sync)	63.5 μsec	64.0 μsec
Vertical scan line (including sync)	16.5 msec	20.0 msec
Number of lines/second	15,734.25	15,625.00

Figure 5.7 Television standards.

The NTSC standard defined all of the specifics for the transmission of a television image, including the aspect ratio, the number of scan lines, resolutions, frame rates, and scanning rate and frequency (see Figure 5.7). The ***aspect ratio*** is the ratio of the image width divided by its height. The ***scan line value*** is the total number of scan lines from the top of an image to the bottom, including the time for the raster to return to the top. The ***vertical resolution*** is the number of scan lines devoted to the picture. Determining the ***horizontal resolution*** of a television image is not straightforward. Since the horizontal lines are drawn in a continuous fashion, they do not have an inherent discrete number of samples along each line. Hence, to determine the horizontal resolution, the horizontal line must first be sampled. The resulting number of samples is limited to double the frequency (as per the Nyquest sampling theorem), which works out to be about 720 samples per scan line. What should be obvious is that the horizontal axis can be digitized at a wide variety of resolutions. NTSC is often digitized at 640 to make a 480-by-640 matrix of square pixels.

The ***frame rate*** is the number of frames/second. According to the NTSC standard, this rate for television is, strictly speaking, 29.97 frames/second, although we will use the number 30 here for convenience. The scanning rate is the time (in seconds) or frequency (in hertz) it takes the beam to scan side to side, or up and down. The ***horizontal scanning rate*** is equal to the number of scan lines times the number of frames/second divided by 60. The ***vertical scanning frequency*** is the reciprocal of the number of frames/second. The number of lines per second is the number of scan lines times the number of frames/second.

While the NTSC standard has been adopted by many countries to be used as a broadcast standard, it is not the only television standard.

Phase Alternation by Line (PAL), a European standard, uses 625 lines per picture, 25 pictures per second, and also a bandwidth of 6 MHz. It is often said that the PAL system is superior to NTSC because it has a higher resolution. In fact, there are more scan lines per frame and thus more spatial resolution. But conversely, there are fewer numbers of frames/second and thus less temporal resolution. If you multiply the total number of lines transmitted per frame times the number of frames/second, to derive the total number of lines transmitted per second, you will discover that the two standards contain approximately the same number of scan lines and are thus approximately equal in space-time resolution and bandwidth.

In more recent years, ***high-definition television*** (HDTV) systems have been developed with vertical resolutions upward of 1000 lines, wide screen aspect ratios, and progressive scanning. One characteristic of these emerging standards is greater variation in resolutions and scanning methods. Unlike NTSC or PAL, signals are captured, internally represented, and transmitted digitally. As the CRT fades out of use, and as flat-panel displays predominate, the system is likely to become entirely digital. (More information on HDTV is presented later in this chapter.)

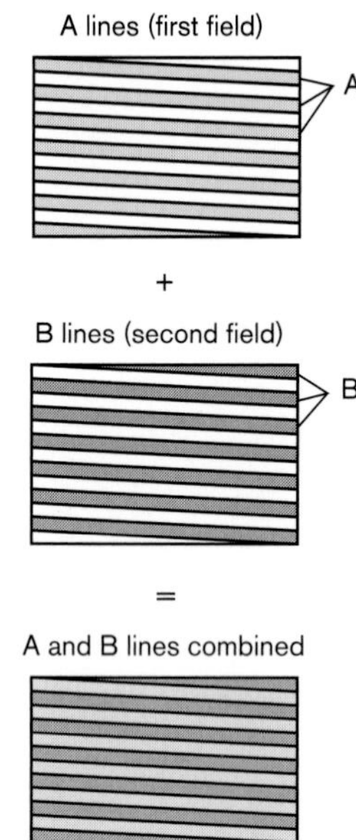

Figure 5.8 2:1 interlaced raster. Two fields compose each frame; the fields contain alternate scan lines. The raster pattern is formed by two scanning deflection circuits. The horizontal deflection waveform moves for 262.5 lines for each vertical deflection. There are two vertical deflections per frame, one for each field. The illustration is made with fewer scan lines for simplicity.

Raster Images, Fields, Interlacing, and the Video Shutter

Raster images present many subtle issues. For example, in a television, the electron beam is constantly being deflected from top to bottom as well as from side to side. Hence, although the individual scan lines are still parallel, the raster lines are actually at a slant. In raster systems, temporal consistency may be improved by transmitting two partial frames. The two partial frames, called ***fields***, are formed by ***interlaced rasters***, a scanning procedure whereby alternate scan lines are read and written (see Figure 5.8). This also increases the flicker-fusion frequency.

During recording, fields are created in the camera. That is, the camera outputs an image by first scanning the even lines of the picture, creating the first field. Then the camera outputs a second time, but this time only the odd lines, creating a second field. Because there are 2 fields/frame, there are 60 fields/second in NTSC and 50 fields/second in PAL. Fields, in themselves, are not complete spatially; in NTSC or PAL, each contains only half of the spatial information of the video frame.

Fields are somewhat akin to flashing each frame twice in a projector, but the analogy is not exact. Understanding the difference gives one insight into the nature of a ***video camera shutter*** and how it differs from a shutter in a motion picture film camera. Although the latter actually moves across the frame as it opens and closes, for all practical purposes one can think of the surface of a single frame as being exposed continuously and in parallel to the same light. Hence, in film, the time base of the entire image surface is identical because the entire surface is recorded simultaneously. During projection, the frame is flashed twice and the time base of the projection is the same for both durations of flash even though the flashes are sequential—in other words, an event recorded at time *t* is flashed at time *t* and again a fraction of a second later. In video, however, the situation is different. Fields increase the temporal sampling from 30 to 60 samples/second. The two video fields really do have different time bases—each is 1/60th of a second behind the previous one. Furthermore, the pixels within the individual fields are not recorded simultaneously: the exposure time of each pixel on the television pickup tube lasts from when the pixel is sampled (e.g., discharged by the electron beam) until it is sampled (discharged) once again 1/30th of a second later. The photoconductive materials of the camera's sensor (whether tube or CCD) are allowed to bask in the image light and to absorb and store up exposure (to charge). The subsequent discharge (for example, by an electron beam) marks the end of the exposure time and the beginning of a new exposure. Thus each pixel has an exposure time of 1/30th of a second, but each pixel is temporally displaced from its neighbor by approximately 100 nanoseconds (see Figure 5.9).

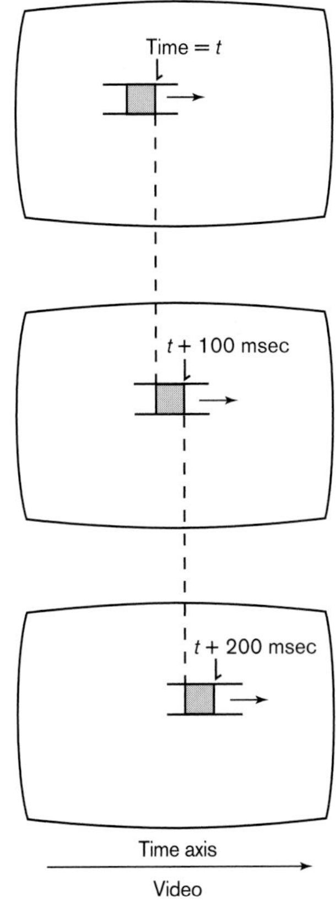

Figure 5.9 The shutter on a video camera is a shifting time window. The two interlaced fields are temporally displaced by a 1/60th of a second, and lines within a field advance downward in time.

If a camera is ***photoconductive***, it means that its electrical properties vary with the amount of illumination to which it is subjected. A ***photoelectric cell***, or ***photocell***, is an example of something that is photoconductive; its absorption of photons effects how much electricity it conducts. This is output as a varying analog waveform.

Fields, interlacing, and the nature of the video shutter significantly affect how we manipulate and simulate single frames of video. This particularly concerns the animator. One solution is to calculate a single frame and record it as two sequential fields. A better way is to calculate and record individual video fields, a technique called *field sequential recording*, which calculates 60 independent fields per second instead of whole frames. This makes a difference because a moving object is in different positions in field 1 and field 2 of a single video frame. In fact, moving objects are not in the same position at the top and bottom of the same field because the pixels at the bottom are later in time than those at the top; this lesser problem is usually ignored. Thus field sequential representation is inaccurate in that all the pixels have the same time base, but it is more accurate than calculating one image for both fields. One disadvantage of field sequential recording is that all geometry and lighting calculations are doubled, although the rendering resolution is identical to the frame resolution.

Note that in raster images, the beginning location of the scanning process can be any corner of the image; in television, it happens to be at the upper left. The scanning beam can be at any angle. In television, it happens to be slanted slightly downward, to the right. The raster lines can be drawn in different directions. They can be drawn right to left, or back and forth. In television they are drawn left to right, left to right, left to right. Also, the number of fields does not necessarily have to be equal to two. For example, *progressive scanning* is a raster technique in which each line is drawn sequentially and there is one field per frame without interlacing, as is the case in most computer monitors. Progressive scanning is also an option for HDTV systems. Progressive scanning produces a more stable image with less flicker, but also one that is less suited to showing high-velocity action, such as sports.

Video Waveform Structure

The *video shuttle* is a mechanical spinning-head assembly; the mechanism involves rotation and translation. As we pointed out, unlike frames in film, the flow of information in a video signal is constant, and there is no mechanical intermittent.

The *sync generator* is an oscillator designed to generate clock pulses in a temporally stable and predictable fashion. The sync generator fabricates a step-march of rigorously formed and predefined

Figure 5.10 Sync pulse and waveform as seen on a video waveform monitor, a specialized CRT tuned to video's horizontal and vertical frequencies. Video levels, phasing, and sync timings are observed against an overlay reticle.

pulses, essentially temporal structures of voltage variation, which time the entire video production (see Figure 5.10).

Inside the video camera and the monitor, sync pulses control the *x* and *y* deflection, so as to position the scanning beam and define the raster pattern. The *y*-axis deflection occurs continuously and slowly, from top to bottom once per field, and the *x*-axis deflection sweeps across the screen many times—282.5 times—during the journey from top to bottom. At the end of each scan line the beam snaps quickly back to the left side and commences to read or draw the next line. At the end of a field, the *y*-axis deflection returns the beam to the top left corner.

The sync signal can carry its housekeeping data quite independently of the picture, and can be routed and switched independently on a separate wire. During the 1930s, the sync and picture signals were designed so they could be merged together into a single ***composite video*** signal, which contained both the sync and picture intermixed. This is distinct from ***non-composite video***, which has its sync pulses removed or which never had sync pulses to begin with. *Composite* also refers to a color-coding-scheme (discussed shortly); like the merging of sync and picture into a single signal, composite color is a scheme for merging three colors into a single signal. The term is also used in the assembly of scenes, a technique explored in Chapter 13.

There are several different pulses produced by a sync generator, two of which are discussed here. A ***vertical sync pulse*** occurs at the beginning of each field; this phasing pulse occupies the duration of the last 40 scan lines of the picture. That is, the time needed for the beam to travel from the bottom right corner of the screen up to the top left corner of the screen is equal to the time needed to complete 40 scan lines. The result is a reduction of the vertical resolution from 525 lines to 486 lines. A ***horizontal sync pulse*** occurs at the beginning of each line. The time between two vertical sync pulses is the duration of one field, 1/60th of a second. The duration between two horizontal sync pulses is the duration of one scan line, about 63 milliseconds. Because the horizontal sync occurs before or in front of the scan line, it is theoretically visible on the left side of the picture. A typical television monitor is designed to place the pulses under the viewing frame of the monitor so they cannot be seen, but if the edge of the monitor is viewed at its brightest, the sync pulses can be clearly seen. The ***fly back*** of the vertical retrace—that is, the movement of the electron beam from the lower right corner of the screen back up to the upper left corner during the vertical sync pulse—may also be seen if the brightness of the monitor is turned up.

It is essential that the camera and monitor be driven in phase and in sync, that is, both pictures must start at the same time and each line must start at the same time. The process of phasing different video signals together is called ***genlocking***. In a video studio, it is common to either drive cameras and monitors with a single house sync, or if the equipment has its own internal sync generator, to genlock the internal sync generator to the incoming video signal. All the cameras, recorders, monitors, video output boards on computers, frame buffers, output from switchers, titlers, graphics devices, and paint boxes must be in phase and in sync if one is to cut between the image sources. Otherwise the edits will incorporate partial frames.

Finally, we want to relate the issue of blanking to video. As already discussed, blanking occurs in movie cameras while the shutter is closed and the film is being advanced. Typically, the minimum amount (180-degree shutter) of blanking is half the shuttle speed. Of course one can blank more; many events of life can occur during these times and never be seen by the camera. Like the movie camera, video uses blanking, but with video, there are two kinds: one at the end of each field and one distributed throughout the field and before each scan line. The ***horizontal blanking interval*** is a short period of time after each scan line to allow the horizontal timing circuit to return the beam to the left side of the raster. During this time, the beam is blanked—turned off. The ***vertical blanking interval*** is a longer period of time after each field to allow the vertical timing circuit to return the electron beam to the top of the screen; its duration coincides with scan lines 481 through 525, eliminating them. Of course, most of the time, a picture is being transmitted, but during these blanking intervals, no picture is transmitted.

Horizontal retrace—that is, the movement of the electron beam from the right side of the screen back up to the left side—is shorter than horizontal blanking, which is 10.5 microseconds, or about 16% of the total scan line length of 63.5 microseconds. Vertical blanking lasts 1333 microseconds, or 21 scan lines, about 4% of the total time. Other signals that are maintained during blanking include the color burst, vertical interval test and reference signals, vertical interval time code, closed captioning, and teletext (some as afterthoughts to the original design of the signal).

Video Time Code

Frame-accurate editing requires that individual frames be labeled in some way—for example, with time code. *SMPTE* (Society of Motion Picture and Television Engineers) ***time code***, also known simply as *SMPTE* (pronounced *simp*-tee), is a numbering system used to address the information on a videotape (Figure 5.11).

23:59:59:29

Figure 5.11 Time code. Each frame on a tape is assigned a consecutive number, where the counting starts at 00. The format of the time code is hours:minutes:seconds:frame number, where hours can range from 00 to 23, minutes can range from 00 to 59, seconds can range from 00 to 59, and frames can range from 00 to 29. Thus, examples of time code are 00:00:00:00, 23:59:59:29 and 23:20:20:00.

There are two modes of time code for NTSC video. ***Non-drop-frame time code*** counts 30 frames/second. Unfortunately, since color video actually runs at a rate of 29.97 frames/second, non-drop-frame time code is not perfectly accurate. ***Drop-frame time code*** corrects this problem by leaving out two frames per minute, except for every 10th minute.

Frame-accurate editing also requires that frames be tracked by an electronic editor, which performs the "cut" between the correct frame of the insert machine and the correct frame of the record machine. A computer is a superb controller for this task: it can monitor the time code in real time, direct the motors of the decks, and dispatch the edit. Furthermore, the computer can accept input such as edit types and edit times.

Color

There are three color strategies for television: RGB color, composite color, and component color. Understanding these strategies makes it much easier to produce graphics for television.

RGB Color

Color television involves three video signals, one for each primary color—red, green, and blue. As in film, the color frames can be recorded sequentially or in parallel. In the ***sequential color*** approach,

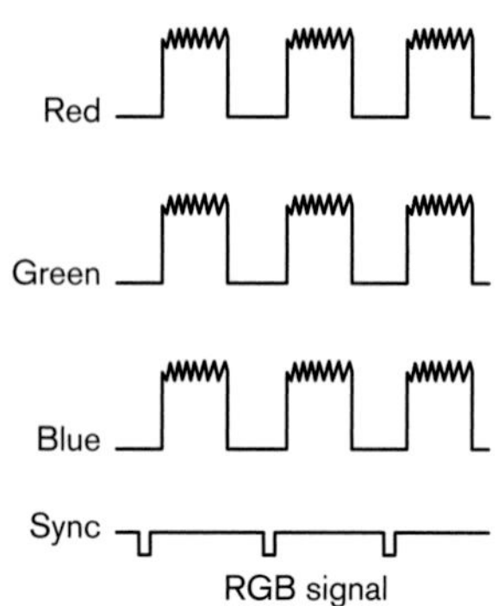

Figure 5.12 RGB color consists of three parallel signals. Often sync is carried as a fourth signal; sometimes it is composited with green. Each channel is independently modulated in luminance.

colors are transmitted in sequence, essentially as three fields. Because the three color fields are temporally displaced, color fringing occurs—that is, the three fields do not align, unless the image being recorded is static. This inadequacy is corrected using the ***parallel color*** approach, also known as ***RGB color***, which sends three color signals over three separate circuits. Unlike the sequential approach, the color-separated RGB parallel signals do not fringe, provided all the wires are the same length, so signals take the same length of time to travel through them. Unfortunately, the three parallel color channels require a threefold increase in bandwidth (see Figure 5.12).

Inside an RGB-color video camera, there are three pickups—imaging tubes or CCD chips—one for each primary color. A beamsplitter and colored filters placed in the optical pathway route light to the three pickups (see Figure 5.13). Systems also exist in which a single pickup is used, which, like color film, contains a laminate of internal filters and photoconductive substrates. But in either respect, three in-sync, simultaneous, and parallel RGB color channels emerge from the pickup(s). On the receiving end, the color monitor includes three electron guns, three electron beams, and three colors of phosphor—red, green, and blue. All of the beams are deflected together, in sync and in phase, but their brightness is modulated independently. Solid-state displays work in a similar fashion.

RGB color may be subject to a host of processing techniques. In the analog or digital domain, these techniques include color filtering, color correction, and conversion to ***Hue Saturation Luminance*** (HSL) space. One of the advantages of conversion to H-S-L space is that the L, or luminance, signal is essentially the same as a black-and-white signal. In other words, a black-and-white signal can be extracted from the color signal. In television, this luminance channel is called ***brightness*** and designated by the letter Y:

$$Y = (0.66 \times G) + (0.30 \times R) + (0.10 \times B)$$

After the brightness is determined, two additional color channels—collectively called ***chrominance***—are formed. The chrominance is equal to the red minus brightness (R – Y), and the blue minus brightness (B – Y), followed by a 33-degree rotation, making I and Q, so as to better align the color space to flesh tones. (I is the orange-blue axis; Q is the purple-green axis.) Visually, this can be best under-

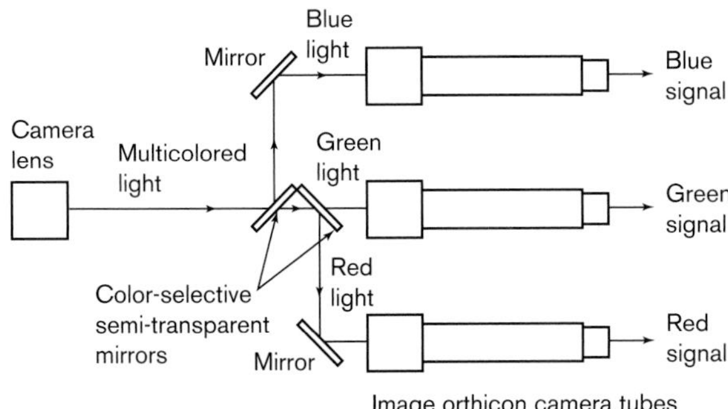

Figure 5.13 Detail of the three-tube camera, using prism and colored filters to split light.

stood by thinking in terms of a color wheel, or *vectorscope*, where the saturation of the color is depicted as a radius and the hue is depicted as the angle (see Figure 5.14).

Computer monitors are almost exclusively RGB color. Most are also progressively scanned and operate at rates above 60 frames/second.

Composite Color

In practice, video engineers can represent an RGB signal on one wire provided they are ready to make compromises. In 1953, the NTSC defined an electronic color signal standard that enabled color video to be represented on a single channel and also to be compatible with the 1941 black-and-white standard. This signal is commonly called *composite color.*

The composite color signal is essentially a compressed low-resolution color signal overlaid on the existing compatible black-and-white signal. If the signal being transmitted is black and white, then it plays on a color television as black and white. If the signal is in color, then it plays on a black-and-white television as black and white. Obviously, a black-and-white signal plays on a black-and-white set as black and white, and a color signal plays on a color set as color.

The RGB signal is converted to composite color by a process called *encoding.* During the encoding process, the chrominance channel is multiplexed, or added, to the luminance channel by modulating a sub-carrier (at 3.579545MHz) both in phase and amplitude, with the phase corresponding to the hue and the amplitude corresponding to the saturation. Upon reception, the signal is *decoded* and converted back into RGB (see Figure 5.15). Unquestionably, this process delivers less color information to the monitor than if RGB had been transmitted; the upside is that there is only one wire or transmitter involved.

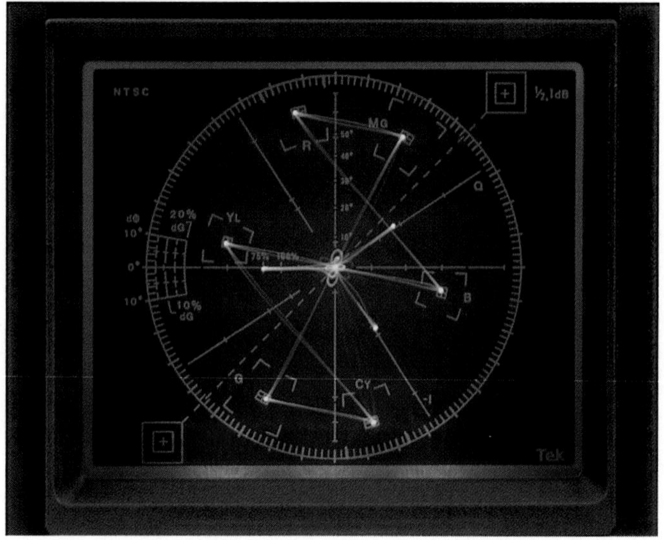

Figure 5.14 A vectorscope.

One of the rationalizations for composite color is that human perception of an object's color is influenced by the size of the object with respect to the size of the field in which it exists. Moreover, brightness (luminance) bandwidth is more important than chrominance (color) bandwidth and provides more information to the eye and brain than color. Therefore, bandwidth reduction can be achieved without a noticeable loss by lowering resolution of the hue and saturation, especially in smaller spatial details. Conventional NTSC composite-color television cuts hue and saturation bandwidths in half; together they equal the *luminance channel*.

In practice, the fundamental color waveform, including the vertical and horizontal sync pulses and the representation of luminance information across the scan line, remained unchanged from the original black-and-white signal. A receiver with a color detector recognizes an additional component in the video waveform called the *color burst*, a reference signal located between the horizontal sync pulse and the start of the scan line. The color burst is present whenever the multiplexed chrominance channel is present; otherwise it is absent.

Most television systems in the world today operate on either the NTSC standard or either of two incompatible European standards: the German-English PAL and the French *Système Electronique Couleur avec Mémoire* (SECAM). Both are 50Hz, 625-line systems.

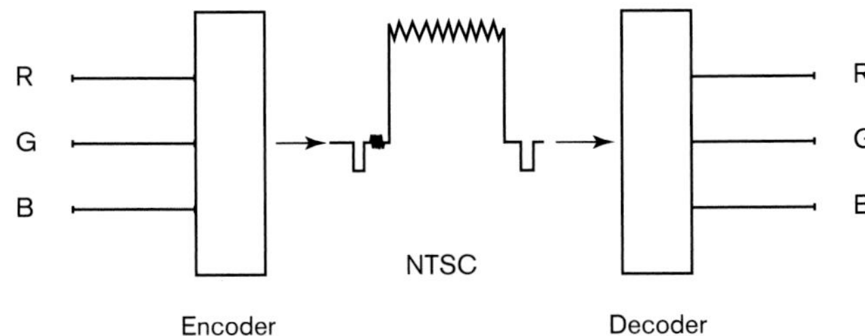

Figure 5.15 RGB/NTSC encoding and decoding block diagram, illustrating the color burst.

Obviously, composite television is not without problems. Beyond the lower color-resolution issue, other NTSC color problems result from the way in which the chrominance signal is multiplexed onto luminance: basically, they interfere with each other. Examples of interference are crosscolor and crosstalk. *Crosscolor* is the production of false colors in areas of high-frequency detail, for example pinstripes; white areas may also catch some of the color of adjacent objects. *Crosstalk*, interference between two different communication channels, occurs because the decoder is unable to determine if the signal is brightness or chrominance information. Another negative side effect is *chroma crawl*, which occurs at sharp changes of brightness. Chroma crawl appears as annoying wiggles crawling up the television screen. In less severe cases, the edge simply goes soft. Because of these and other problems, composite color is increasingly being shunned in production environments, and it is not used in computer displays. But it remains the technology for broadcast television, cable, and *video home system* (VHS) cassettes.

Component Color

Another approach to color implementation is referred to as *component color*. Unfortunately, there is no single standard definition of component color, but it almost always involves either two (brightness and chrominance) or three (Y, I, Q or Y, R − Y, B − Y) parallel signals. In the case of three separate signals, all forms of crosstalk are eliminated and the model is similar to RGB color. Also, production techniques such as *chroma keying*—the replacement of an entire image region by another image region—may be accomplished without impairments caused by the encoding process. And, since the color information for red, green, and blue is not composited, separate RGB information exists for display. Component color, even in full RGB channels, is facilitated by digital videotape recording technology, where the

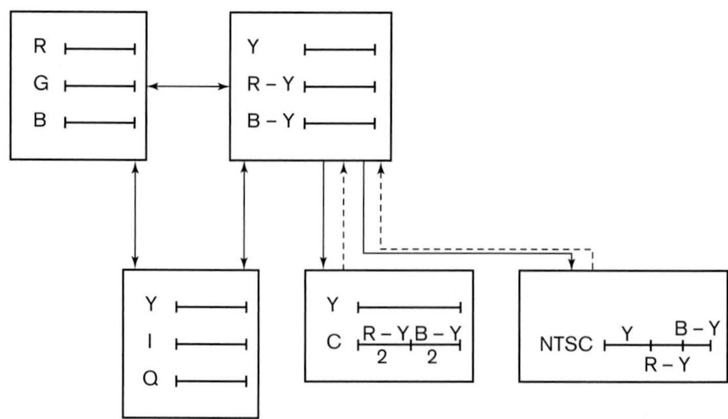

Figure 5.16 Component television conversions and data reductions. RGY, YIQ, and Y, R − Y, B − Y are transcodable with insignificant loss. When converting to composite, video loses half of R − Y (or I) and half of B − Y (or Q); inverting this function (the dashed line) requires stretching the two signals back out but they are still missing half of their data. Converting to composite video creates the most compact waveform, and coming back (the other dotted line), even less of the original data.

three color channels are represented by streams of binary numbers that may be intermixed—and extracted and reassembled later.

Converting back and forth between RGB, YIQ, and Y, R − Y, B − Y is possible and is called *transcoding*. In an analog setting, this process adds a trace of noise, but it does not impair the color as does NTSC composite coding/decoding.

When component color is recorded, the two color channels, I and Q, are often combined into a single chrominance channel that has half the resolution of I and half the resolution of Q. When this is the case, it is possible to run the video signal on two wires, and record chrominance 1:1 to luminance. Of course, when displaying the signal, the chrominance must be converted back to I and Q, and the I and Q must be stretched out temporally (Figure 5.16). With the advent of digital recording, one of the key variables is the relative resolution of the three color channels.

High-Definition Television

High-definition television (HDTV) is a term that refers to a new generation of television formats that, as a group, provide higher spatial resolution (more scan lines), better color, wider aspect ratios, and a digital representation (Figure 5.17). HDTV has also involved a bitter debate about progressive versus interlaced scanning, frame rates, square verses rectangular pixels, and compression.

In the United States, HDTV has been approved as a broadcast format in which the channel allocation and type of modulation is tightly defined, but where the broadcaster is given considerable freedom to

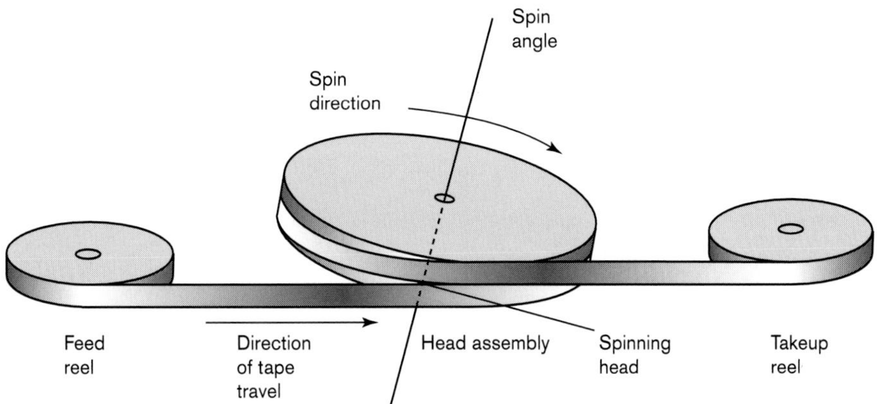

Figure 5.19 The spinning head. As the tape moves forward, the head also spins, writing or reading signals. The forward motion of the tape offsets the segment before it, as well as the one after. The head-to-tape speed is high; therefore the bandwidth is high.

of recording deals with the physical recording medium (e.g., tape width, recording head movement, etc.). But, as with film of different gauges, there do exist subtle relationships between the recording format and the image quality.

Unlike film, where all of the "pixels" are recorded simultaneously, in video, the "pixels" are recorded sequentially. Thus, a recording strategy may be employed that allows the medium to progress continuously without an intermittent motion. Of the many recording technologies explored, two have proven to be viable: magnetic tape and disks.

Transverse Versus Helical Scanning

The *videotape recorder* (VTR), or *videocassette recorder* (VCR), is the instrument used to electronically record and play back a television signal onto magnetic tape. In order to record the very high bandwidth video signals onto magnetic tape, it is necessary to raise the head-to-tape speed of 7 1/2 inches/second for voice up to about 500 inches per second for pictures. The trick in doing this is not to move the tape at a high rate of speed, but rather to move the tape at a modest speed (about 1 foot per second) and employ a rapidly spinning *recording head*, which is placed inside a drum at an oblique angle to the tape and moves quickly past the slowly moving tape (see Figure 5.19).

Two major spinning recording strategies exist: transverse scanning and helical scanning (see Figure 5.20). In *transverse scanning*, the heads are located at approximately 90 degrees to the moving tape, so that the combined motion produces slightly diagonal tracks,

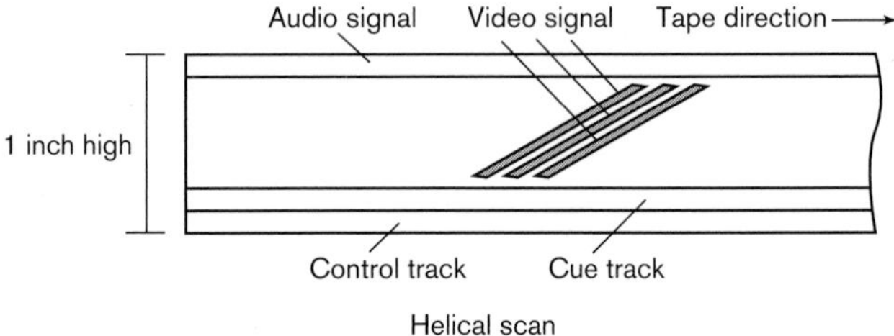

Figure 5.20 Transverse versus helical scan.

each of which records a segment of a video field. A major liability of this technique is that it is not possible to record an entire field in one pass, so fields must be reconstructed during playback.

Helical scan recording utilizes a spinning head positioned nearly horizontal to the tape, with the tape wrapping around in an almost 360 degree helix. This gives the spinning head a very shallow angle to the tape and permits an entire video field to be recorded in one long diagonal *nonsegmented scan*. Each passage of the head records a video field. Helical scan recording enables the ability to play back in slow or fast motion, view action either backward or forward, record single frames, and freeze a single video field, that is, hold the tape steady while spinning the head. In both methods, sound may be recorded continuously along the edge of the tape, as are control tracks.

Analog Videotape Formats

A variety of formats exist in which tape moves left to right as well as right to left, and in which heads spin at different angles to the tape. The first professional videotape format, called *2-inch quad* and introduced in 1956, recorded composite video using the transverse technique; it was called *quad* because the recorder had four heads.

Today, almost all videotape recorders use tape in cassettes and the helical scan technique.

Helical scan formats have been engineered in a wide variety of tape widths and electronics. One of the most significant formats is the industrial 3/4-inch helical non-segmented composite format called *U-matic* (introduced in 1971). The tape is contained in a self-threading cassette, hence the term videocassette. U-matic is a color format and, although not strictly a legal NTSC recording, it can be made into legal NTSC video by using a device called a *time-base corrector* (TBC), which in effect restores battered sync pulses and time-shifted scan lines and organizes them into an NTSC signal. As a format, U-matic revolutionized video production because it could be electronically edited using a command language and computer-controlled playback and recording decks. Although it was conceived as an industrial non-broadcast standard, the portability of the equipment encouraged its use in broadcast as well, particularly for news broadcasts.

All professional tape formats that have been introduced subsequently use the helical scan strategy. These include the 1-inch *C-format*, which records composite video and uses a reel-to-reel machine that records a non-segmented field and is able to play back and record single frames and fields, a necessity for recording many types of computer animation.

Miniaturization of the U-matic format to a 1/2-inch-wide tape cartridge resulted in *video home system* (VHS), the success of which has essentially brought a composite-video VCR into the home. Technologically, the VHS format is a scaled-down version of the 3/4-inch format. The major advantage is the extremely low media cost, under $3 an hour. Like U-matic, VHS can be time-base corrected into legal NTSC video. Enhancements to the VHS format include hi-fi sound, in which the audio is also recorded via the spinning head, and *super-VHS* (S-VHS) in which higher radio frequencies are used to increase the horizontal resolution from 240 to 400 pixels, and thus requires tape of greater density.

In the 1980s, helical scan formats were introduced that recorded component, as opposed to composite, color (see Figure 5.21). The most successful professional format was *Beta SP*, introduced by Sony, but consumer component formats, such as the *Hi8* camcorder, also emerged.

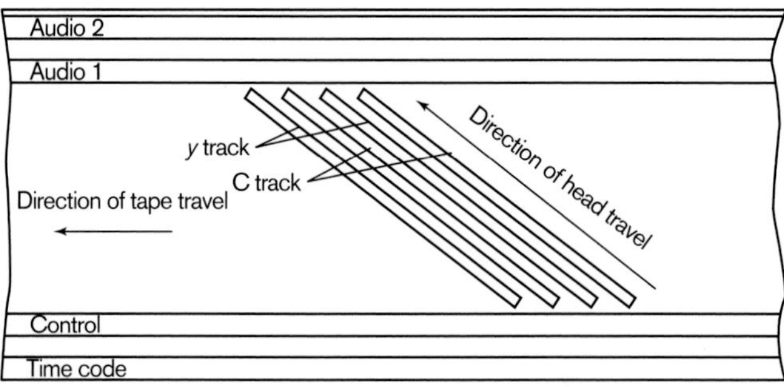

Figure 5.21 Component recording formats include Betacam and HDTV. Component machines may also be helical scanned, but are different from the classic composite helical scan recorders in that two scans are written for each field, one for the luminance information and one for the chrominance information. Remember that the chrominance channel contains half each of I and Q (or R − Y, B − Y) channels. There are a number of ways to do this, as suggested in the drawing.

Digital Videotape Formats

Digital video formats come in two varieties: ***Digitally sampled video*** involves digitizing the entire video waveform by sampling everything—the picture signal, sync pulse, color burst (when applicable)—and recording the stream of samples onto tape. ***Pure digital video*** involves treating each moving picture frame as a matrix of pixels. It is important to understand that digitally sampled video is nothing other than a digitized video signal—it can be converted to pixels but it is not natively pixels. Pure digital television represents the images as pixels, rather than scan line samples, and therefore does not include a sync pulse or samples made during horizontal and vertical blanking times. Unlike a sampled waveform, pure digital video is scalable and can range from streaming video on the Web to super-HDTV.

Examples of digitally sampled video include the ***D2 format***, which digitizes and records an NTSC composite signal on a helical scan cassette recorder. The sampling rate is at four times the frequency of the color subcarrier of 3.375MHz, or 13.5MHz. A companion format, ***D1***, records either digitized RGB color or component video, where the analog waveforms of the three color channels of video (red, green, blue, or luminance, and the two chrominance channels) are sampled and stored as digital waveforms. The digital transmission standard for D1 is called ***SMPTE 259M***; its data rate for 8-bit samples is 143 megabits/second for NTSC and 177 megabits/second for PAL. While D2 is used throughout the industry, the main use of D1 recorders is in postproduction.

Sampling, as you know, can be done at different sampling frequencies and different degrees of precision (number of bits per sample). The D1 format may use a sampling structure of 4:4:4, which means that the red, green, and blue channels are each sampled at four times the frequency of 3.375MHz, which is the frequency of the subcarrier of transmitted video. Alternatively, D1 and other formats may also use a 4:2:2 sampling, which means that the luminance signal Y is sampled at 13.5MHz, and that each of the two chrominance channels are sampled at half that rate, or 6.75MHz. The samples may have either 8 or 10 bits of precision. In practical terms, D1 produces 720 samples per scan line. Transmission of D1 is also governed by SMPTE 259M, which specifies a data rate of 270 megabits/second for 8-bit video and 360 megabits/second for 10-bit video.

In general, lowering the sampling frequency in the chrominance channels makes it possible to dramatically reduce the bandwidth of digital video formats. Two popular component formats, ***Digi Betacam*** and DV50, sample at 4:2:2 and use compression to reduce the bandwidth to 90 megabits/second. Taken a step further, a series of ***digital video*** (DV) formats sample at 4:1:1 and have bandwidth of only 30 megabits/second. These formats provide consumers with all of the capability of digital video.

Obviously, one advantage to all of these digital video formats is that they can be copied without generational loss. In addition, the D1 format eliminates some concerns about the different international color systems (NTSC and PAL), because the recorder can record either 525 or 625 scan-line pictures. They can also record both 4:3 and 16:9 aspect ratios. Many of the formats also involve compression, so unfortunately quality issues do emerge when different formats of different sampling rates and different compression ratios are intermixed. Another exasperating factor emerges from the fact that the 720 samples across a scan line create non-square pixels; since computers use square pixels, sampled images appear stretched on a computer monitor unless they are first resampled. Digitally sampled video has turned out not to be a panacea. Nonetheless, with the advent of digital video formats, the distinction between professional quality resolutions and consumer resolutions is becoming minimal and may very well vanish, just as it has done with 35mm color film. However, this full fusion still lies in the future.

Note, too, that because VCRs are usually designed to record composite or component video signals, for example, NTSC television, they are not able to record the signal that usually comes out of computers, which tends to have a different number of scan lines and frames/second. In order to record "video" from a computer, one must employ special videocards that output NTSC. Most recently, manufacturers have introduced consumer digital cameras that have CCD chips and record digital signals. The signals can be brought digitally into computers, edited, and returned to the digital videotape.

Video Disk Formats

While videotape is often used to record and store video, disks are also well suited for the job.

Magnetic Disk Technology NTSC video may also be recorded onto magnetic disks, both in analog form as well as digitally sampled video. Analog disk recording is no longer practical, but its introduction during the 1970s provided the first way to record individual fields and to provide "instant replay"—video recorded in real time and played back in real time, slow motion, or backward. Remember, one of the main benefits of disks over tape is that frames can be randomly accessed.

Sampling video and recording it onto magnetic disks is now a well-understood technology. The sampling, recording, and playback can all occur in real time. Obviously, it is necessary that the disks must have extremely high data transfer rates and storage capacity. The amount of video stored is dependent upon the quantity of disk space devoted to the task.

Laser Disk Technology Optical *laser disks* or *video disks* are a mass-replicated, read-only technology that stores a digitized analog NTSC (or PAL) signal including picture information, sync, color burst, and so on. As a spiral of information on the disk, the digital binary numbers are expressed as a series of pits or holes, either burned into the disk directly with a laser or produced via a mass-produced stamping process. The pits are embedded in a thick plastic substrate, or carrier, which is relatively impervious to surface handling—fingerprints, dust, scratches, and nicks. The disk is read by focusing a laser at the spiral of pits and catching the reflected light in a photocell. The input stream of zeros and ones, pulses and no pulses, are routed to a digital-to-analog converter and converted back into an NTSC (or PAL) composite waveform (see Figure 5.22). A laser disk can hold 30 minutes of information, at 30 frames/second, and may be frame-addressable.

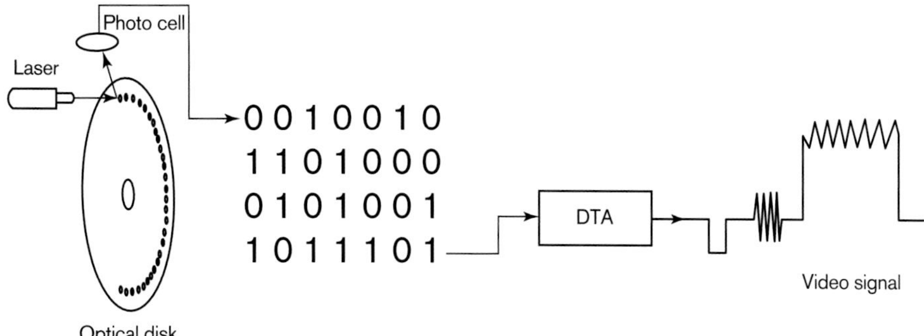

Figure 5.22 A digital optical disk records digitized NTSC in serial fashion, one sample following another. A DTA converter on output reconstructs the video. The digital optical disk is an extremely flexible device and can be used to record sound, still pictures, and computer data and programs as well as video. Some disks are erasable, some not.

The laser disk has superior horizontal resolution compared to U-matic and VHS formats. It is as simple to use as the videotape cassette, and relatively impermeable. Because the disk is spinning constantly, access time to any information on the disk is very quick, on the order of 1/100th of a second.

The laser disk is laid out as a series of concentric rings, or ***tracks***. Some disks play at a ***constant angular velocity*** (CAV), which means that the disk is always spinning at a constant speed. With this strategy, one frame or still picture is stored on each track of the disk. Along a radial edge of the disk, there is a sync pulse-like strip, which includes a start mark for each track. Constant angular velocity provides access on a frame-by-frame basis and allows the viewer to freeze frames and view still pictures.

Conversely, some disks play at ***constant linear velocity*** (CLV), which means that the disk is always spinning so that the linear velocity of the place where the laser is reading from is always the same. Remember that a disk has a bigger diameter at the outside than it does toward its center—thus, at a constant linear velocity, the disk runs at different speeds depending on where it is read; in essence, toward the center, it is spinning slower, and toward the outer edge, it is spinning faster. A side effect of this strategy is that more information can be stored on the disk. In particular, more than one frame can be stored on a track.

Because laser disks can be randomly accessed—something that is completely impossible to do with roll media such as tape—they provide a method to build applications that enable a user to interactively and randomly access still images and video scenes. In addition to storing video, the laser disk has a limited capability to store menus that can respond to a user's input; they can also be controlled by computers sending commands to the laser disk player. So, for example, the disk might store a menu that is displayed to the viewer; the viewer can respond to the menu by selecting an item, which triggers a command to the disk player to begin playing a particular video scene. These *interactive video applications* are characterized by a user determining the outcome of the experience. Examples include sales kiosks in department stores, interactive education systems that employ branching and interaction to help reinforce the learning process, museum kiosks, and games that involve non-linear navigation.

Digital Video Disk Technology There are several technologies that are called "DVD," but are different from one another; this section focuses on the DVD that is defined for video. The *digital video disk* (DVD) is one of a family of second-generation CD-ROM devices, in which the physical size of the disk is the same size as a CD-ROM but the recording capacity is increased to 4.7GB and beyond. The DVD is similar to disks that record music and to DVD-ROMS (discussed in the following chapter), but is tailored to the needs of video.

Video on a DVD is stored as an *MPEG-2* compressed digital video stream (derived from NTSC video). With respect to VHS videocassettes, this DVD has superior image quality (even with MPEG-2 compression), and therefore, it is targeted to be a replacement for the VHS cassette.

The DVD has lower manufacturing costs, is expected to be more reliable, and can be encrypted so that privacy and exporting are more easily controlled. The role of the rewritable DVD and the intricacies of MPEG-2 encoding and mastering for small-run distribution is not clear at present.

Digital Temporal Imaging

With classic media, information is closely coupled with its carrier, and film and video are no exceptions. During playback, the carrier itself is visible and/or audible. Digital media, on the other hand, provide us with a strategy to reproduce information without any taint of the carrier being mixed in—noise such as the crackle of phonograph plastic, dirt in the picture, or the hiss of magnetic tape are not present. This chapter examines the formal aspects of digital media images, including input and output devices, digital memory, the virtual camera, bandwidth, aspect ratio, compression, recording, and current media.

Digital Imaging

As previously stated, electronic images are images that are represented as analog data and involve the transmission and storage of varying electronic signals. ***Digital images***, on the other hand, are images that are represented as a collection of discrete numbers. Digital images can be represented as electrical images, which use the absence or presence of electricity to communicate or store an image—the electrical data is represented as On or Off signals, which can be interpreted as binary information or binary digits. But they can also be represented in other ways, for example, using bar code.

Digital Input and Output Devices

Digital input and output devices are a relatively recent technology and one of continuing research. The most significant digital input device is the ***charged coupled device*** (CCD), a solid-state transistor

Above: Image courtesy of Gennady Blanket, © 2000.

Figure 6.1 Below: A CCD is a light transducer. As a solid-state device, it has profound differences from a vacuum tube. No external scanning circuit deflects a beam—instead its photosensitive surface is itself physically pixelated; each pixel on the surface accumulates its own light independently of all others. Typically, an indexing process polls the CCD's pixels, perhaps marching them out in video sequence, where they are digitized and transmitted as serial strings.

that contains a grid of light-sensitive pixels (see Figure 6.1). A CCD is similar to a raster television tube except that it does not necessarily have to be operated raster style; it is different in that, in addition to being solid state (versus tube), it is truly discrete and digital—that is, each pixel is a separate physical entity (albeit very small).

A wide variety of CCD technologies exist for different kinds of imaging technologies. One distinction is between linear and areal CCDs. A *linear CCD* contains only one row of pixels and is used by either moving the CCD across the image plane, much like a focal plane shutter, or by moving the image past the CCD. Linear CCDs are widely used where an image is being copied—for example, in a modern fax machine or flatbed scanner—because the image that is being copied can move past the linear array, or the array can move past the image. A linear CCD has a single resolution—the number of pixels long. An *areal CCD* consists of a 2D matrix of pixels and captures all the light of an image simultaneously. Like linear CCDs, areal CCDs are made with different resolutions, only they have both an x and y resolution, typically a few hundred to a few thousand pixels along each axis.

Both linear and areal CCDs exist in monochromatic and color models. Color imaging systems choose between color single-chip designs and three-chip designs that employ a beam splitter, three filters, and three monochrome chips, sort of a digital version of the Technicolor process. Video cameras use specially designed areal CCDs that are designed with the exact spatial resolutions of the format and with the exact scanning requirements as well.

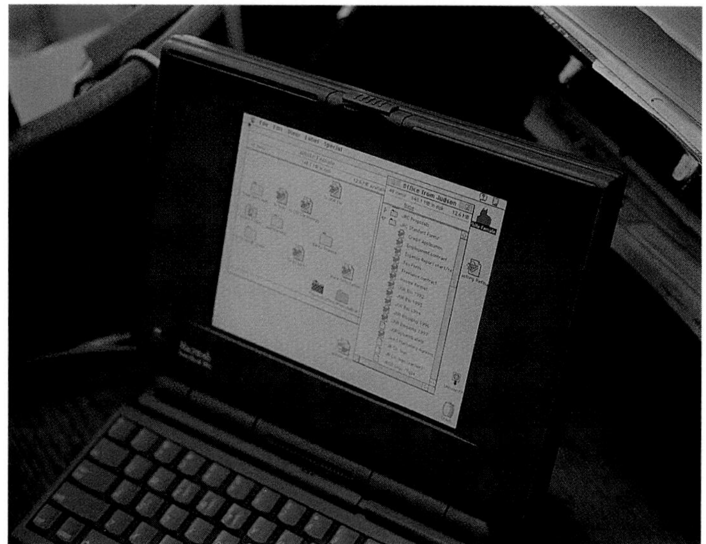

Figure 6.2 An LCD is characterized by a discrete matrix of light-emitting pixels.

CCDs have many advantages over tubes: they are smaller, weigh less, and require less power. They last a long time, and the registration of their images does not change over time. Other characteristics—such as contrast ratios, lag, capture times, burn-in, and electronic shutters—are competitive. Unlike tubes, their output is all digital. The adjustable electronic shutter in CCD cameras adds freedom to the recording process. The shutter makes depth of field compensation achievable without changing lighting. Faster shutter speeds can eliminate undesirable blurring that results from the longer exposure time. It is worth noting that the emulsion and carrier model of film also applies to the CCD chip—the carrier is the chip, and the emulsion is the part of the chip that is photoconductive. Like photographic film, a CCD has an exposure index.

Output devices that are complementary to the CCD flat panel are solid-state light-emitting devices, including ***light-emitting diodes*** (LEDs) and ***liquid crystal displays*** (LCDs) which are now integrated into televisions, games, and computer displays (see Figure 6.2). Solid-state displays can be monochromatic or in color and exist in a wide range of resolutions, sizes, and quality. Simple metrics include the number of pixels in the *x* and *y* dimensions, the contrast ratio of the displays, and (since this is a real-world device) the ***pitch***, or number of pixels per inch, often about 72 to 85. Solid-state screens are lighter and consume less power and rival the contrast and color separation of CRTs.

When using digital devices, there are many ways that an image can be scanned, because although pixels are usually transmitted and recorded in row and column formation, they do not necessarily need to be. In fact, many new ideas depart radically from the concept of sequenced raster televisions. The traditional approach is to march the pixels out of the CCD in sequence. However, with some CCDs, pixels may addressed in any order and read randomly. This process can be optimized by concentrating the sampling in areas of the image where the most change is occurring, much like the eye does.

The Frame Buffer and Color Lookup Table

The digits in digital images are numbers that represent the luminance of each pixel. The numbers are organized in a matrix format, where each position in the matrix corresponds to a location in the image. This matrix is typically stored in hardware called a *frame buffer*, sometimes also called *video memory* or *vram*, a random-access memory with two basic properties: (1) it is organized so that a computer can read or write to it as if it were a pixel array, and (2) this memory is continuously read from or written to and converted into a video signal (see Figure 6.3). Some frame buffers incorporate

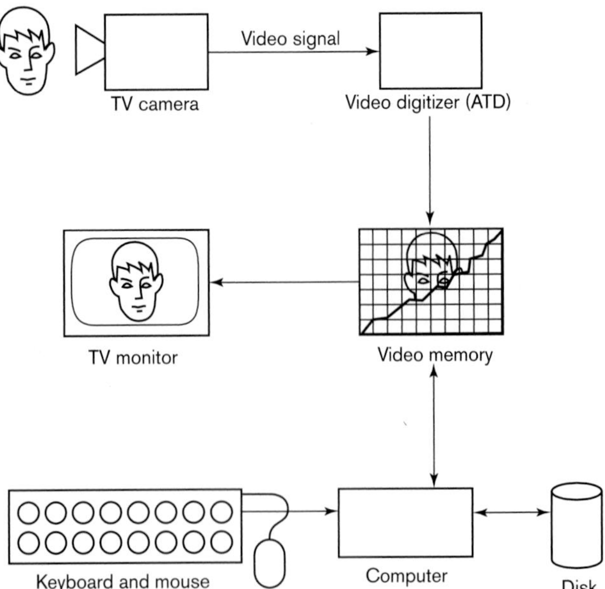

Figure 6.3 The recorded image is converted into digital data that represents the luminance of each pixel. The image is then stored in video memory as a matrix of pixels.

a *palette,* or *lookup table* (also known as a *color table* and *color look-up table*), used for indexing colors. Other synonyms for frame buffer include the terms *frame store, video still store*, and *graphics card.* A *virtual frame store* is one without any video output, essentially a software pixel matrix that cannot be viewed.

A frame buffer continuously coverts the contents of a fixed-size memory into a predefined raster image, such as a television or computer monitor. The frame buffer can be updated in batch or interactive modes; the changes a user or program makes to the frame buffer are immediately visible on the attached monitor. If the number of screen changes are modest, they may all be performed in real time, as with a desktop or paint system. For American broadcast television, if the changes require more than 33 milliseconds to compute, the output from the frame buffer must be single-frame recorded because the time is longer than the 1/30th of a second frame rate. An issue with many frame buffers is that the video signals they output are totally incompatible with the video signals used by broadcast television, since different monitors are used for computers and television.

In addition to representing an image as a pixel matrix, the image can also be encoded using a compression process.

The Virtual Camera

Of paramount importance to 3D computer imaging is the virtual camera. This section presents the related issues.

Lenses, Perspective, Windows, and Ports

When the source of digital imagery is 3D virtual worlds, then a method is required to convert the 3D data into a 2D world. This is accomplished using a virtual camera that records the 3D virtual world; the result is a 2D image. The virtual camera is (almost always) modeled after its physical counterpart and includes a simulation of the pinhole lens, depth of field (that is, the simulation of f-stop), and of the shutter and the attendant motion blur result. The virtual camera is used to record the images it sees in a virtual world. The images are recorded onto digital memory, which can be transferred to other media such as film, videotape, or CD-ROM. The virtual camera's lack of physical limitations enables new possibilities. For example, cameras in a scene can be invisible. The virtual movie camera includes all of the properties of the still camera, plus a virtual shuttle, often implemented as a frame advance command on a clock and having a frame rate expressed as frames/second or frequency of exposures.

Although most of these components have already been reviewed in previous chapters in the context of a film or video camera, their more abstract aspects are looked at here. The virtual camera is based upon the physics of the pinhole camera and simple lens, as described in Chapter 3. A lens in and of itself does not perform *perspective*, which is a formal process for representing 3D environments on 2D surfaces, such as the surface of a monitor or sheet of paper. Perspective requires a lens and a projection plane. Computer graphics can model many kinds of perspective, but this discussion will center on the single-vanishing-point perspective evolved during the Renaissance. When using a virtual camera in computer graphics, calculations for the creation of an image can assume the image is projected onto a screen behind or in front of the aperture (see Figure 6.4). The *point of view* (POV) is the position in space from which a 3D environment is viewed. It is defined by an *xyz* point analogous to the location of the center of the lens of a camera or an eye. The point of view is the location through which all perspective lines converge. Along with the point of view is the *aim point*, which is the point that the camera or eye is looking toward. Incidentally, the line from the point of view to the aim point may also be thought of as a *viewing normal.*

Many kinds of virtual lenses may be implemented, including all of the simple lenses described earlier, as well as compound and zoom lenses. *Anamorphic lenses*, such as those used in CinemaScope, compress the *x*-axis but not the *y*-axis, and are modeled by scaling the data in *x* after the perspective transformation. The many spherical-lens projections used in cartography can also be applied to cinematography—for example, a special projection used for screening onto the inside of an Omnimax theater.

Distortions that accompany increasingly wide-angle glass lenses, such as curved lines, and the fish-eye effect, do not always occur in computerized perspective, although these effects can be created. Many other kinds of perspective, including isometrics, the formal but

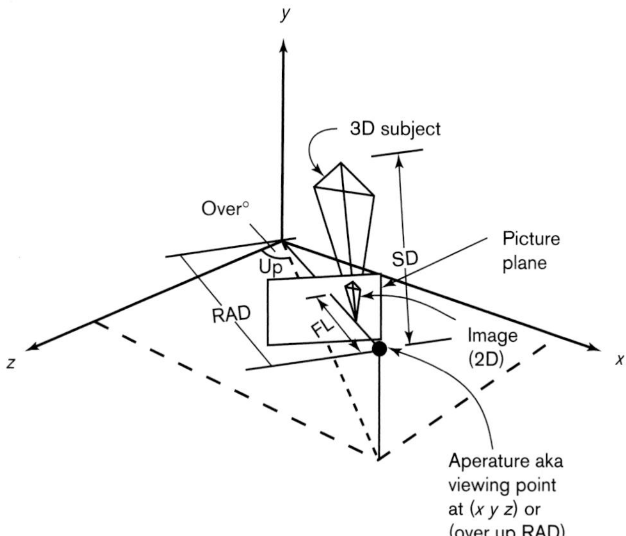

Figure 6.4 The typical computer camera simply projects the picture onto a plane in front of the aperture, which is now called a *viewpoint*; the image is formed where rays intersect the screen. The simple lens formula is unchanged.

pre-Renaissance perspective of Pompeii, and even the unreal imaginings of M. C. Escher, can be generated with computer graphics.

A *zoom* is a change in the focal length of the lens during a shot and is created by animating the position of either the window or the point of view while holding the other constant.

The aim point lies on the ***window***, a rectangular image plane perpendicular to the viewing normal and located within the viewing environment. The window is analogous to that part of the world that would be visible to film in a camera. The window, like the eye, may be moved; it may also be scaled bigger or smaller so that the imaginary computer camera can look at things on an atomic or interplanetary scale.

A window corresponds to what we see on a screen, but a window and a screen usually have different coordinate systems. The coordinate system of the window is related to the scale of the data; the coordinate system of a screen is dictated by the hardware. It is thus necessary to scale the image window into the address space of the device itself.

The point of view is connected to the four sides of the window to form a ***perspective pyramid***. All of the objects that are outside this pyramid are clipped and excluded from the final image. A perspective view is created by projecting each point of an object onto the window by drawing a ray between the point and the point of view,

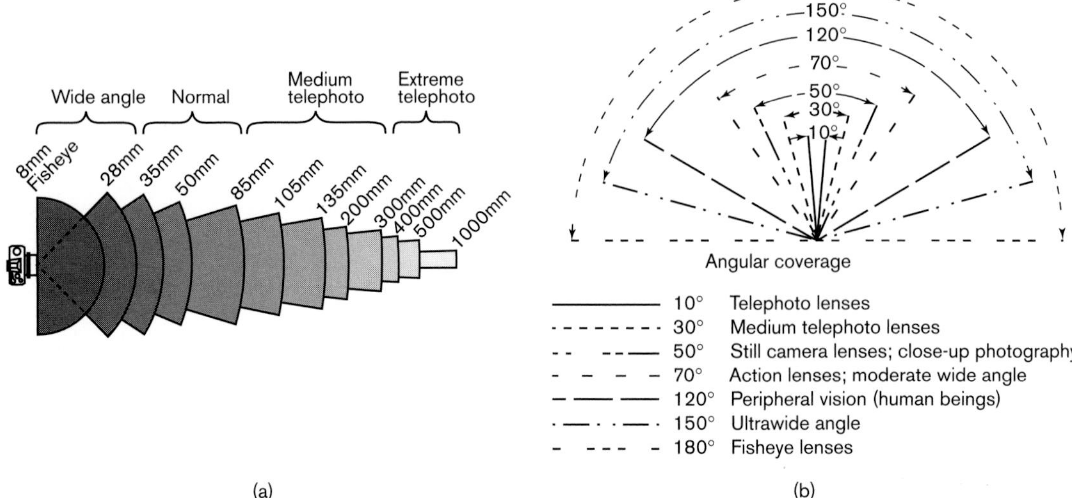

Figure 6.5 The viewing angle of a lens is the angle subtended by the horizontal width of the field (a). The longer the telephoto, the narrower the angle of view (b).

and determining where that ray intersects the window. Thus, points in the object coordinate system are transformed to the window coordinate system; the *z*-axis values are discarded.

The cinematographer can usually specify a lens in terms of focal length or viewing angle. The *viewing angle* is the angle between the viewing normal and the sides of the perspective pyramid and can be calculated for the lens parameters (see Figure 6.5) The focal length of the lens is (literally) the distance between the window and the point of view. For a "normal" focal length lens, the distance between the window and the point of view is equal to the diagonal of the window. A window that is close to the point of view functions like a wide-angle lens, and a window that is far away from the point of view functions like a telephoto lens. As the window pulls away from the point of view, the perspective gets flatter. When the window is at infinity, points orthogonally project, that is, the *xy* location of a point in the window is the same as the *xy* location in the environment.

A *port*, usually rectangular, is that part of the display screen where the window is presented. A port may be the full resolution of the display or may be smaller than the total area of the display. In a newspaper, for example, the full port is the total area of the newspaper with smaller ports used to display pictures; a traditional window-to-port conversion is done by cropping a photograph and scaling it. The activity is no different in computers—the crop is the window and the scaling is the ratio between the width of the window and the width of the port.

Remember that the computer is an elastic machine, and that a window and its port need not have the same aspect ratio, as, for example, in the anamorphic transformation used in wide-screen motion picture photography.

Shutters and the F-stop

Simulation of the f-stop and the shutter speed also affect how the calculated image appears. Digital shutters can be used to create images independent of any concern for a physical shuttle, which would be used to display them. In computational systems, the duration of time the shutter is open per frame may be completely independent from the frame rate. In the simplest computer simulations, it is typical to make the exposure time infinitesimally short—so short that it is only a point in time and all action is frozen. In the real world, this approach is impossible. When using a physical camera, increasing the shutter speed (shortening the duration of exposure time) requires that the aperture be made bigger, so that the same amount of light reaches the medium. If the shutter speed is cut in half, then the f-stop must be doubled; the disadvantage here is that the depth of field becomes narrower. Since a virtual camera is not constrained by physical limitations, shutter speeds and f-stops can be adjusted without concern for physics. A virtual camera can simulate all camera activity, including depth of field and motion blur (see Figure 6.6).

Virtual Camera Motion

It is helpful to begin this discussion of virtual camera motion by recalling the equipment used to move a real camera, including the tripod, dolly, and jib arms, as well as the movements of the real camera, including pan, tilt, roll truck, and dolly (all are described in Chapter 4). The virtual world contains virtual analogies of these; however, the virtual camera can also be moved in a more abstract, mathematical manner—for example, it can follow a spline pathway. An animator needs to remember that a moving camera is being used to record moving images and that the movement and timing associated with the camera is as much a part of the story as the movement of the objects it is recording. The animator needs to consider the motion pathway of the camera—that is, the path along which the camera moves—and the direction in which the lens points (see

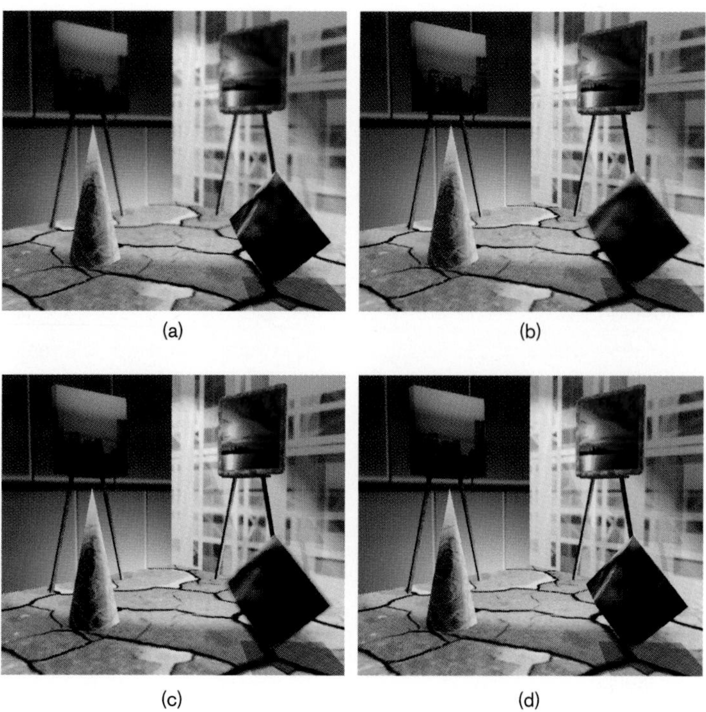

Figure 6.6 Examples of digital motion blur show its relation to simulated depth of field: no motion blur or depth of field (a), motion blur (b), depth of field (c), and motion blur and depth of field (d). More motion blur (slower shutter, smaller aperture), more depth of field; less motion blur (faster shutter, bigger aperture), less depth of field.

Figure 6.7). The direction of the lens can also be simple—for example, the lens might simply point in the direction of the camera's motion pathway. Unfortunately, most effective camera shots involve the camera looking in a direction other than the direction of the camera's motion. Even in a simple example such as a roller coaster ride, if the camera only looks in the direction of the motion, then most of the shots will consist of either the open sky or tracks. To achieve the effects of a dramatic ride, the camera movement will also need to incorporate changes in tilt along the ride. Hence, the camera motion can be described by an equation that describes the camera's motion pathway together with an equation that describes the tilting motion of the lens. In order to achieve the appropriate results, the two equations must be correlated. (Details regarding the specifics of the mathematics necessary to describe motion pathways are presented in Chapter 10.) The computer animator is also reminded that pans and tilts may often appear richer if they are made around nodal points instead of the center of the lens.

In computer animation systems, it is often useful to think about the camera's three axes of rotation as local to the camera and independent of the *xyz* coordinate system in which the camera is embedded. Like a real camera, the virtual camera may be moved in space and pointed in different directions and has six degrees of freedom (three position, three rotation) (see Figure 6.8). Yaw (*y*), pitch (*x*), and roll (*z*) rotations may be applied to real or virtual cameras, but in either case, the rotations are applied sequentially. In a real camera, this is defined by which gimbal pivots inside which gimbal; in the virtual camera, sequential rotations are defined by the order of rotation transformation matrices. Essentially, the transformation matrices simulate the construction of hardware. Changing the order of the transformations in software implies reconstructing the real-world gimbals.

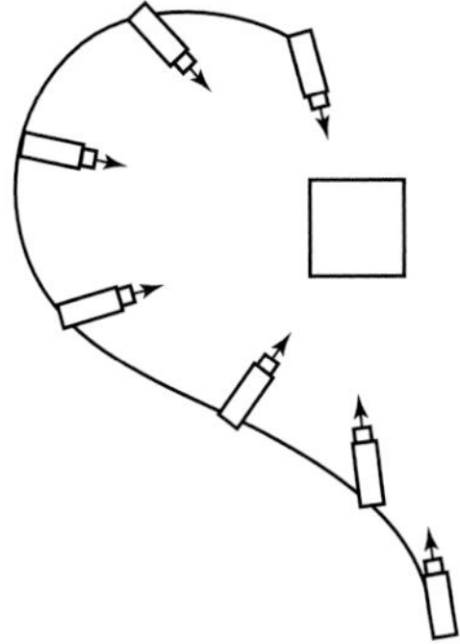

Figure 6.7 As the camera moves along the pathway, the direction in which the lens points changes constantly so that the aim point remains directed at the subject. Both of these movements can be expressed with mathematical curves and described with equations, such as this spline. Splines provide a way for the camera to move smoothly in a 3D space.

Bandwidth

With the advent of digital video and the limiting factors of CD-ROM, computer networks, and the Internet, the issue of ***bandwidth*** is becoming paramount in the computer industry. In the past, bandwidth was an issue only for radio and television engineers, but those who want to view moving images in real time now must understand this issue as well. The concept of bandwidth relates bits of information and time; specifically, it is the number of bits per second that can pass through a channel (see Figure 6.9). In a computer, a channel is a wire or group of wires between one location and another. An *Ethernet wire* and a *small computer system interface* (SCSI) bus are examples of channels, as are an ordinary telephone wire and the television cable that comes into a home. Channels can also be wireless: television and radio stations broadcast on a channel, and so do cellular phones. Each of these channels has a bandwidth, although the quantity of the bandwidth is different.

Bandwidth is measured in bits per second, or ***baud***; 1 baud is 1 bit/second. In other words, a 9600-baud channel can transmit 9600 bits/second. The relationship between the baud and the number of data bytes (characters) per second is that the number of bytes per second is typically 1/10th the baud rate. This is because there are 8 bits transmitted for each byte, plus a parity bit and a timing bit, for a total of 10 bits. In other words, a 1200-baud channel is able to transmit 120 bytes/second. Sometimes 7 bits are used for each character and the parity bit is bit 8, but the 1:10 ratio is a good rule of thumb.

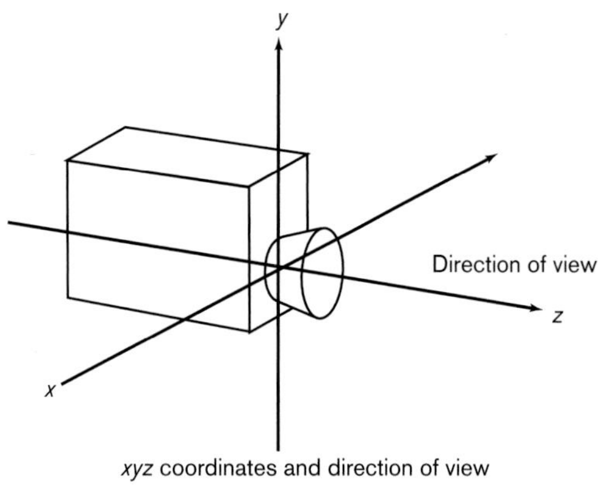

(a)

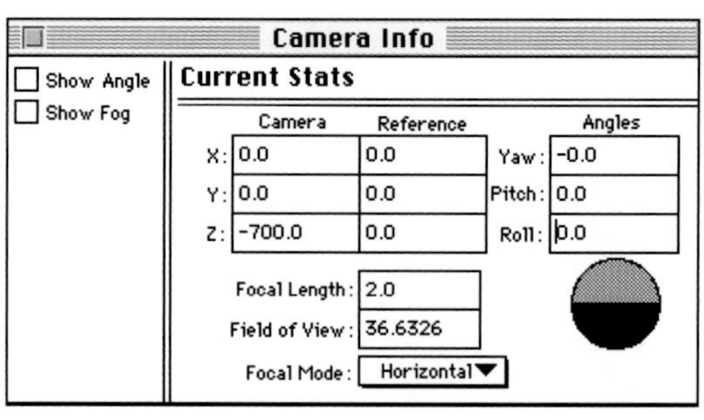

(b)

Figure 6.8 The virtual camera (a) has its own coordinate system, and it operates within the global coordinates of the environment. The Camera Info window (b) displays all relevant information.

The bottom line is that the speed of a network is critical, even when the task does not involve moving images (see Figure 6.10). Some of the networks currently available, such as the telephone network, have modest bandwidth but are global in scope. Local area networks, such as those installed within an office or building, can move digital data between computers at millions of bits per second. Bandwidth within a computer and along its busses can be even faster. A network able to move digital video must not only be fast, but it must also be able to have all (or a significant part) of its capacity devoted to the task, because any interruption would disturb the constant flow of images.

Be careful when discussing bandwidth so that you know if you are referring to bits per second or bytes per second, since both are abbreviated *bps* or *kbps*, but they are different by eightfold.

Formal Aspects of Digital Images

Fully digital moving pictures keep *x* and *y* discrete, as well as time, the lens, and often other things that exist in front of the lens, including objects, lights, and the camera itself. Hence, ***digital temporal imaging media*** are multidimensional information structures that define and/or record events over time, with all axes digital and discrete. Minimally, digital temporal imaging media must be capable of recording three dimensions—two spatial dimensions (the *xy* image plane) plus the sequence of images (or scanning pixels) in time. Color components expand the number of dimensions.

Typically, the pixel values stored for each image contain luminance information—the brightness of the picture at each pixel. The

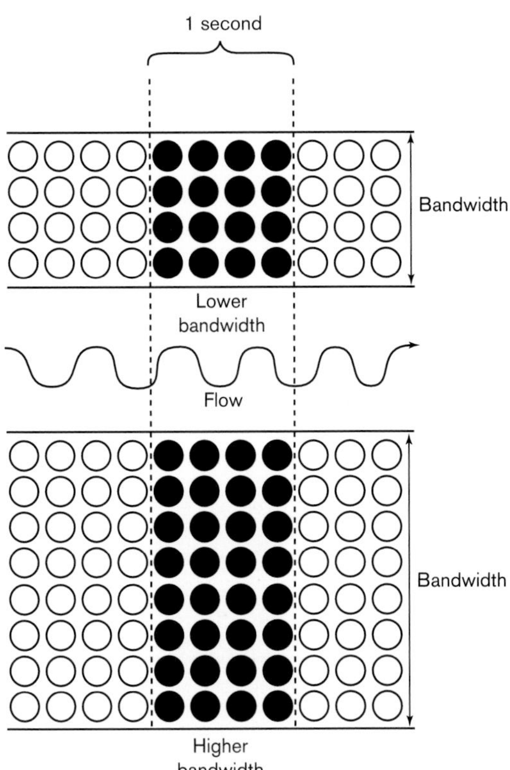

Figure 6.9 Bandwidth is the number of bits that can pass through a channel. In the top figure, 16 bits pass per second along the channel for a bandwidth of four. In the bottom figure, 32 bits pass per second along the channel for a bandwidth of eight.

numeric value stored at each pixel may be either an integer or a floating-point number, but in either case it has a domain, a minimum and maximum value, and, if floating point, an accuracy. Thus, like film or tape, the digital recording has a *dynamic range*, or *signal-to-noise ratio*, a lightness-to-darkness ratio. This is measured in *decibels* and is correlated to the number of bits, according to this formula:

$$\text{decibels} = 10 \log 2^{*} \text{ number of bits per pixel}$$

Eight bits, or 256 levels, is equivalent to 56 decibels. Note also that because each successively larger f-stop involves a doubling of light, the number of f-stops a medium will record is the same as the number of bits. In other words, eight bits, or 256 intensity levels, provides for eight f-stops of dynamic range.

The transmission rate of digital images is expressed in terms of baud rate, which is the number of bits transmitted per second. *Noise* is the term given to interference in the picture, which can be manifested as static, ghosts, dropout, and graininess, and it is found in both film and tape, as well as digital media.

Figure 6.10 Bandwidth table. (continued on opposite page)

Description	Megabits/second	Comments
Foot messenger	0.000,003	For 25-mile distance at 10 mph and 30,000-bit (~1000 words) message
Telegraph	0.000,030	70 wpm at 5 characters/word at 5 bits/character = 30 baud
Teletype	0.000,050	At 500 characters/minute at 6 bits/character = 50 baud
2400-baud modem	0.002,400	On ordinary (POTS) telephone line
Plain Old Telephone Service, (today)	0.064,000	Maximum capacity POTS 64kbps, voice, fax, modem, SSTV, ARPANET
DS-0 Data channel	0.064,000	Digital Signal Level Zero, this channels nets out 56kbps to the user
DSL	0.128,000	Conditioned leased telephone line for data transmission, scalable data rates to over 1 mbit/second
Basic ISDN	0.144,000	Integrated Services Digital Network, uses 2 DS-Os plus a 16kbps data channel
Switched 384	0.384,000	Also called Fractional T-1, this is used for videoconferencing
Audio CD disk, single speed CD-ROM	1.200,000	Two 20,000-hertz channels sampled 40,000 times/second at 16 bits
DS-1 (or T-1, Primary ISDN)	1.544,000	Equals 24 DS-Os, may connect to PBX; NSNET uses this
DS-2	6.312,000	98 DS-Os or 4 DS-1s
Xerox Ethernet	10.000,000	Local area network (LAN)
IBM Token Ring	16.000,000	Local area computer network
SCSI bus	20.000,000	Bus used for connecting peripherals on small computers
Compressed digital video	30.000,000	Bandwidth for various 4:1:1 MPEG compressed NTSC video signals
DS-3 (or T-3)	44.600,000	672 DS-Os, 28 D-1s or 7 DS-2s; used by the telephone company
Compressed digital video	50.000,000	Bandwidth for various 4:2:2 MPEG compressed NTSC video signals
OC1	51.840,000	Lowest SONET limit optical network

There are several advantages to storing an image in digital form. Because the image is ultimately stored as binary numbers, it is possible to employ error-detection and -correction methods that permit the data to be processed and reproduced without degradation. Noise, loss of contrast, and mechanical registration problems are not part of the digital reproduction process. Digital signals can be reproduced and copied exactly and endlessly. Digital images can also be easily digitally processed, that is, scaled, translated, or rotated about the *x*, *y*, or *z* axes. Digital images can be frozen, mirrored, flipped, replicated many times, or broken apart. Video in its native analog form, on the other hand, cannot be scaled, translated, or rotated. It also has no facility to employ optical operations during duplication. Also, while video typically stores images sequentially on tape, individual access to

Description	Megabits/second	Comments
FDDI LAN	100.000,000	Fiber Distributed Data Interface
Firewire	100.000,000	Computer bus, also used by 4:2:2 and 4:1:1 compressed digital video
D2 Videotape Recorder	114.000,000	Digital NTSC composite television
HDTV 1080i	120.000,000	HDTV 1080 lines interlaced
Broadband ISDN	135.000,000	Telephone company service
Asynchronous Transfer Mode (ATM)	154.000,000	Packetized switched mixed data wide area network, also faster models
OC3	155.520,000	Three OC1s
Ultra 160 bus	160.000,000	Fast version of the SCSI bus
D1 Videotape Recorder	214.000,000	Digital NTSC component television
Multi bus 2	256.000,000	For workstation computers
EISA Bus	264.000,000	Computer bus
Serial Digital Interface (SDI)	270.000,000	SMPTE 249M; serial routing of professional NTSC component 4:2:2 digital video signals
VME Bus	320.000,000	Computer bus
OC12	622.080,000	12 OC1s SONET protocol
HPPI channel	800.000,000	High performance parallel interface
Personal Computer Interface bus (PCI)	1,056.000,000	Internal computer bus in both 32- and 64-bit widths, with either 33 or 66 MHz speed. This is speed of 32 bit×33 MHz variety
HDTV Digital Recorder	1,180.000,000	Lossy SMPTE 240M HDTV, by Sony
Serial Digital High Definition (SDHDI)	1,485.000,000	Digital serial routing of professional HDTV component video signals
OC48	2,400.000,000	AT&T long lines fiber trunk capacity
Human eye-to-brain circuits	5,600.000,000	Estimate eye to brain data rate
OC 192	9.600.000,000	Currently the fastest bandwidth
Fiber Optic Capacity	64,000.000,000	Theoretical fiber capacity
Human eye-data reception	6,168,960.000,000	36,000×28,000 pixels×17 bits/pixel ×3 colors×2 eyes×60 frames/second (per Seth Shostack)

any given frame requires a sequential search of the tape. Digital media, on the other hand, can allow for random access so that individual frames can be stored and retrieved without a lengthy search.

Another digital advantage is that additional information associated with the image can be stored in a form similar to that of the image itself. This might include the date of creation, the camera operator, the camera, and a description of the scene. And finally, since the image is in a numeric form, it may be subject to analysis, which can apply to static images as well as moving ones. This analysis can be quite varied, ranging from counting the numbers of blood cells in an image to recognizing faces.

Unfortunately, digital signals are not perfect. When digital signals are mixed together, a little bit of precision is lost. So although they can be duplicated indefinitely, they cannot be composited (moved together) indefinitely.

Pixel Aspect Ratio

There is an issue that concerns the relationship of the aspect ratio of the screen to the aspect ratio of the individual pixels. ***Pixel aspect ratio*** is equal to the horizontal width of a pixel divided by the vertical height of a pixel (see Figure 6.11). If pixels are square, then the pixel aspect ratio is 1:1, and in this case, the aspect ratio of the screen may be defined as the number of horizontal pixels divided by the number of vertical pixels. But pixels need not be square; they can also be rectangular, and in these cases, the screen aspect ratio is not equal to the number of horizontal pixels divided by the number of vertical pixels. Sometimes pixels have the same aspect ratio as the overall image; thus the overall image has the same number of pixels in x and in y.

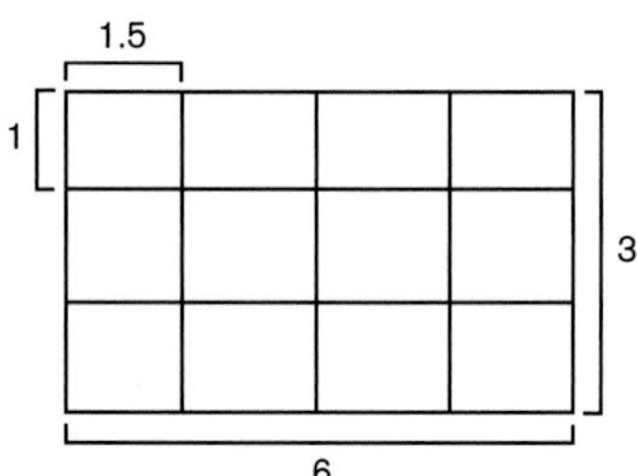

Figure 6.11 Rectangular pixels. Each pixel has an aspect ratio of 1.5:1, and the aspect ratio of the image is 2:1.

Square versus non-square pixels is a design issue that confronts standards committees. Computer professionals favor square pixels, because with square pixels, image processing operations, such as rotating an image 90 degrees, are trivial. If the pixels are not square, then the results must involve averaging pixels together to get the correct result. Television professionals tend to believe that resolution in x and y need not be equal and therefore see advantages in rectangular pixels. In the motion picture industry, digital imaging tends to be confined to computer animation and special effects work, which have both used square pixels. Prepress and the graphic arts also use square pixels.

In a truly general computer graphics system, software should be able to define an image in real coordinates (such as inches or millimeters) or virtual coordinates, or in square or non-square pixels, and then output an image on a device that has real coordinates (such as inches or millimeters) or square or non-square pixels.

Compression

The representation of digital temporal images can be based on the representation of all pixels for all frames, or the images can be represented in a way that is less memory intensive. *Compression* is a general term given to algorithms that reduce file size while maintaining some degree of data integrity (see Figure 6.12). Its primary purpose is to reduce file size, and thus storage space and transmission time. The opposite of compression is ***decompression***,

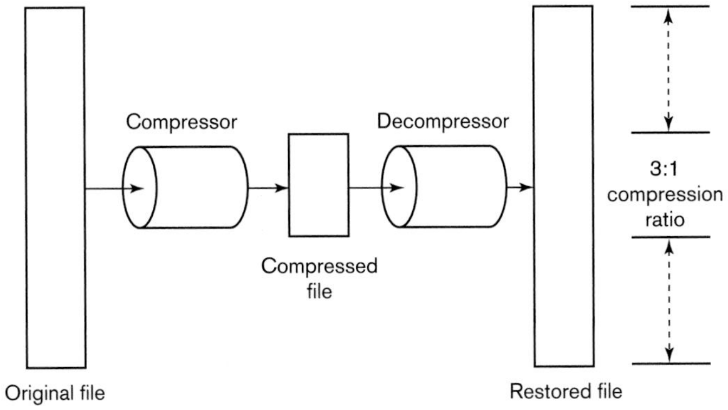

Figure 6.12 Compression is applied to a file to decrease its memory requirements. Compressed files can be decompressed, restoring the file to its original state while maintaining some degree of data integrity.

which takes a compressed file and restores it to its original form, typically for display. Thus a compression algorithm includes both a compressor and a decompressor; these two pieces of code (or hardware) are called a *CODEC* for short. Sometimes compression/decompression is done on the fly during transmission, and the compressed file is never stored.

There are two classes of compression, lossless and lossy. *Lossless compression* schemes compress and decompress the original data perfectly, without any loss of information; the decompressed result is identical to the original. *Run-length encoding* is an example of lossless compression. When using run-length encoding, not every pixel in the matrix is individually represented. Instead, sequences of pixels that have the same value are represented by the pixel value and a count of contiguous pixels that have that value. So, for example, if there is a sequence of 3 pixels of intensity 12 followed by 5 pixels of intensity 22, then the sequence is represented as 3 12 5 22 (as opposed to 12 12 12 22 22 22 22 22) (see Figure 6.13).

Another kind of lossless compression for graphics is *delta coding*, in which only the amounts of change in the intensity value from one pixel to the next are stored (or transmitted), rather than the full pixel value (see Figure 6.14). Because the changes in intensity values tend to be small, they can be represented in four bits, rather than a full eight-bit value.

Lossy compression schemes do not reconstruct the original data upon decompression, but seek to reconstruct the original appearance. In computer graphics, lossy compression involves understanding just what the eye actually perceives and, in theory, throws away what the viewer cannot see. For example, it is well known that the eye is more sensitive to luminance than to color, so color information is degraded before luminance information (see Figure 6.15). Both kinds of compression have their uses, and many systems support user-selectable compression schemes.

The *compression ratio* is the relationship between the size of the original, uncompressed file and the compressed file. A 100MB file that is compressed to 20MB has been compressed with a 5:1 compression ratio. Some data (such as a movie of a tree) may be almost identical on a frame-to-frame basis and be able to be compressed a great deal; other data may contain very little, or perhaps even no redundancy. With lossless compression, it is not always possible to determine a compression ratio in advance. With lossy compression, it is possible to scale the amount of compression one desires. Obviously, the more the data is compressed, the poorer the quality of the data after decompression, and there is a point, of course, beyond which it is not possible to recover a recognizable image. The trick with lossy compression is to find settings that maximize the compression ratio, yet that make the image look almost as good as the original when it is decompressed.

Another distinguishing factor of compression algorithms is intraframe versus interframe compression (see Figure 6.16). With *intraframe compression*, all the redundancies are removed within a single frame; this is an example of *spatial compression.* With *interframe compression*, redundancies and motion predictability between sequential frames is used to reduce the data; this is an example of *temporal compression.* It is believed that the human eye has different receptors to perceive static images or motion: for static images, the eye looks at details; for moving images, the eye perceives the structure of the motion.

Two compression standards important in multimedia are *Joint Photographic Experts Group* (JPEG) and *Moving Picture Expert Group* (MPEG). Both are lossy standards. JPEG is an intraframe still-image format. JPEG pictures suffer some quality loss—as seen in the JPEG compressed version compared with the original image—but in return they take up much less space. Despite the fact it is a still-picture format, JPEG is also utilized by some video systems; in these cases, each picture is individually compressed.

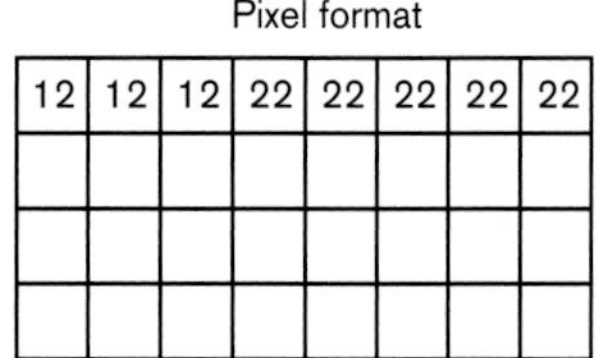

RLE format

3, 12, 5, 22, . . .

Figure 6.13 Above: Run-length encoding. Without run-length encoding, storing the image above would require that each pixel intensity be stored, for example, 12,12,12,22,22,22,22,22. With run-length encoding, runs of each color are stored, for example, 3,12,5,22.

Pixel format

112	112	112	122	122	122	122	122

Delta coding

112 0 0 0 10 0 0 0

Figure 6.14 Above: Delta coding. Without delta coding, storing the image above would require that each pixel intensity be stored. With delta coding, only the change in intensity is stored.

Like JPEG, MPEG is a lossy format, but it is an interframe technique, designed to compress video images. Video that is subject to MPEG compression suffers some quality loss but takes up a lot less space and has smaller bandwidth. MPEG is currently used in television distribution, and a variation, ***MPEG-2***, is used for DVD-ROMs. In general, MPEG compression is a non-real-time process, and MPEG decompression must utilize special hardware.

Figure 6.15 Above: The image on the left is the original image displayed at full size. The image in the center is an enlargement of the top right section of the original image. The image on the right is the same enlarged section after compression. The compressed image is blocky, the edges lose their clarity, and fine detail such as the branches of the tree lose resolution; these differences are referred to as artifacts.

Desktop and Streaming Video

During the 1990s, it became possible to display "video" on the desktop of a personal computer (see Figure 6.17). Faster CPUs, more bandwidth, bigger storage devices, digital sound, and compression techniques all contributed to the practice. We say "video" but the word itself takes on new nuances and meanings. Some of these conflict with ways we have defined the term and suggest new definitions. So for right now we will use the term ***desktop video***, and with this term connote a system technology that incorporates all of the facets of the following: an ability to input most forms of traditional video (NTSC, PAL, component, and various DV formats); an ability to save digital representations of this video, including the sound tracks and associated data streams, in memory and onto hard drives and CD-ROMs; an ability to display either the captured input stream or to play back its digital representation from memory, a hard drive, or CD-ROM. Finally, an idealized system also has an ability to edit the images using graphic user interfaces, and to convert the digitized files back into the traditional video medium.

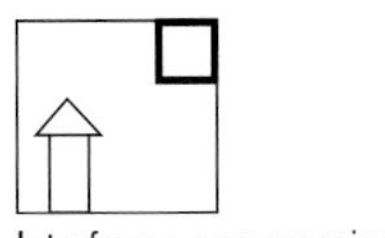

Intraframe compression

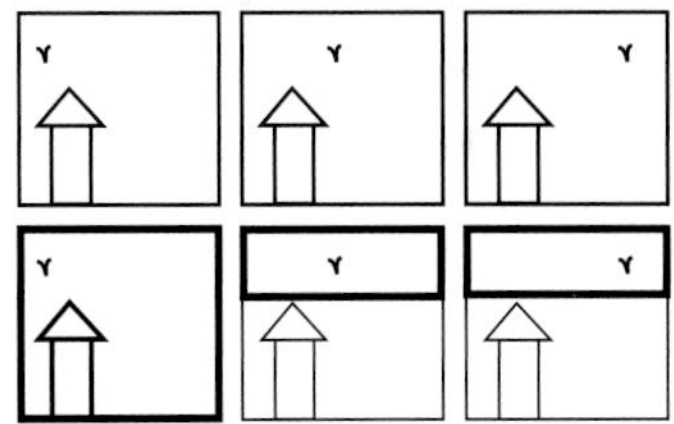

Interframe compression

Figure 6.16 Above: Intraframe versus interframe compression. Intraframe compression reduces rendering within an individual frame while interframe compression reduces rendering on a frame-to-frame basis by recording the changes from frame to frame.

This basic desktop video model implies circuits with video inputs and outputs, a screen, a storage unit (a place to store files), and a controller. The controller is a piece of software that displays on the

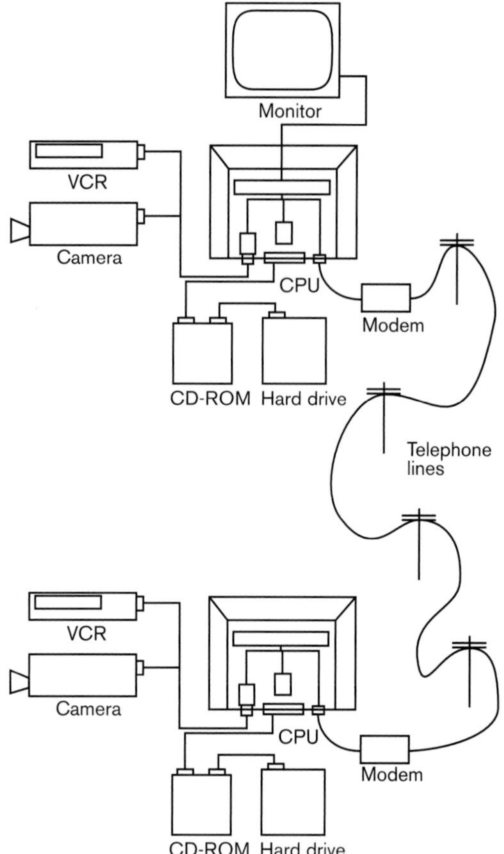

Figure 6.17 The figure shows both the physical configuration as well as the data flows of a two-person videophone system. The record/playback toggle determines source and directionality of the disk drive (to or from). The decompresser formats the data to the computer monitor. The controller software manages time.

screen and allows the user to select sources, view files, and to save and name files. Features of the desktop video system include an ability to compress and decompress the signal. Furthermore, the choice of compression/decompression may be set to any one of a number of standards. The system is resolution independent, meaning it can vary in size from postage stamps to full-screen, full-resolution video. It can vary temporally as well, and can run at frame rates from as fast as the monitor can go, to frames every few seconds. It can integrate sound, time code, and other narrow band data into the digital file.

Desktop video is important for a number of reasons. Because it is scalable, it can be deployed across a broad range of systems—from single-speed CD-ROM drives to the fastest hard drives available. Scaling is accomplished by adjusting spatial resolutions, frame rates, and compressions so the data rates fit into the available bandwidth. This idiom is a powerful alternative to the traditional carrier of video:

fixed-bandwidth analog channels. In a production sense, digital video makes non-linear editing possible.

Note that the desktop video system we have described thus far is just that—a desktop system that is local and confined to a single PC and its peripherals. But beyond the desktop, the addition of computer networks makes it possible to move "video" among computers. *Streaming video* is digital data that describes real-time moving pictures and that is transported from computer to computer via networks in real time. Real time is a key thought here, and it is the distinction between a digital stream and a digital file that distinguishes streaming video from desktop video. Now it is true that with desktop media, both in the case where the screen image is digitized on the fly and where it is played back from disk, that real time is a defining part of the system. The data processing for digitizing, playback, and display must all occur at the speed of the video medium. With streaming video, the source of the digital stream and its destination are separate computers connected via a network, and all must function together to ensure that the video is in real time.

Streaming is not the same as copying a file across a network. Copying a movie file across a network is no different than copying any file, and the time taken to transfer the file is not related to displaying the contents of the file at some rate. Once the file is on the other computer, it can be viewed with a desktop video system. This is the strategy in downloading movie files from the Internet, especially files in AVI (audio video interleaved), MPG (Moving Picture Experts Group), MOV (abbreviation for movie) and other desktop media formats. But streaming the file means processing and feeding it out onto the network at something approximating real-time rates. For example, consider a desktop video file of a movie that is 2GB large. In a desktop video scenario, in order to move the file over a network it is necessary to copy the 2GB across the network and only then can the recipient screen it. But if the file is streamed, then it is streamed from beginning to end, and the recipient can watch it as it evolves. The total bandwidth consumed is approximately the same in both cases—the difference is that in the streaming case, the recipient gets the file in real time, as it plays out.

Lets examine some of the implications here and some of the game plan. First, all of the ground rules about desktop video apply to streaming video. Both incorporate sound and ancillary data, both use compression, both are scalable in terms of special resolution, frames/second, available bandwidth, and compression of data rates. Both can digitize in real time, and thus afford a variety of sources, including live and VCR playback. Streaming video assumes that the NTSC-type video is digitized at its initial point of capture and is distributed throughout the system as a real-time, ongoing stream of digital information. This adds complexity and requires that the network part of the system deliver the data to the recipients in a clearly identifiable way and at a rate so that the recipient can display the "video" on the screen, also in real time.

Streaming video is employed in a number of applications. It is used in one-to-many broadcasts, where, for example, a traditional broadcast channel is digitized and distributed via a network such as the Internet. In a one-to-many situation, the source can be video or digital files, but the viewer has no freedom of choice to modify the stream other than to turn it off or switch to another channel.

A variation on this theme mandates that the data be prepped on random-access digital media and extends to the user the equivalent of a VCR controller, which permits fast-forwarding, rewinding, freezing, hunting and so on. Now the source is no longer outputting ("serving" in Web terms) the same data stream to everyone, but is outputting a unique stream to each user. This is a substantially more demanding CPU task. Other variations of streaming might include channels with multiple camera points of view, with the viewer having a selection control, and one-on-one (videophone) situations where two parties can see and talk to each other interactively, by running simultaneous input/output functionalities. With the data channels already on the streaming channels, these interactive participants can also control pan, tilt, and zoom of their complement's camera, adjust focus and zoom, and otherwise sense and alter each other's environment.

Desktop and streaming video differ from traditional video in several ways. The most obvious difference is that digital and streaming video do not require the production tools of traditional video, especially videotape editing. Imagery that is initially digitally synthesized (computer animation is a good example) never need be output to film or video if their destination is the desktop. While desktop and streaming video are extremely flexible technologies for delivering moving pictures, they are not without limitations; of particular concern is low-quality imagery caused by bandwidth limitations, including poor spatial and color resolution and jerky motion.

Once images are converted to digital video files, non-linear editors enable a user to cut, copy, paste, save, and load/replay sequences of images, recreating the traditional video editing on the desktop and enhancing it with the ability to instantly modify edit points, effects, and sound-track relationships and preview them in real time. Popular non-linear editors, including Avid and Premiere, and another class of products, such as After Effects, focus on transitions and special effects such as morphing, warping, color correction, pixelation, lens flare, posterization, and so on.

Because it is scalable, the desktop video model becomes the model for all video production, and the obvious model for HDTV and film postproduction, as well, although resolution and bandwidth have to struggle to catch up with the idea. Thus, the combination of desktop video and streaming video change not only the production landscape, but the distribution landscape as well. In a future that includes the Internet, we expect that a relatively common technology envelope will encompass applications as diverse as person-to-person interactive video, videoconferencing, broadcasting, and random access to movies.

Digital Media

The all-digital world of future media is arriving. Solid-state cameras, storage, transmission, and displays are being integrated into traditional film and video production, and a new genre that borrows features from both but is a generation beyond has moved from concept to mainstream. The new world is not without weak links—but resolutions will continue to increase and the development of CCD chips, solid-state displays, storage, and projectors will continue to be driven by purists in quest of images of clarity, dynamic range, and accuracy of color, and by an audience who is very attuned to presentation quality.

This section introduces digital media, including magnetic tape, magnetic disks, optical disks, and solid-state digital memories.

Factors in choosing digital media that concern the computer animator or digital artist obviously include storage capacity and cost, but also include the access time and sustained transfer rate. The *access time* is the latency time between the time that data is requested until the time that the drive returns the data. The *sustained transfer rate* is the bandwidth of the drive when it delivers data to the CPU over a prolonged period of time (minutes).

Magnetic Tape

Although we are prone to dismiss *magnetic tape* as antiquated—it was the first standard computer storage medium—it remains a viable part of the recording landscape. It is low in cost and reliable, and higher-density formats continue to be introduced, virtually all of them in a cartridge format so that loading and threading issues do not exist. Tape is, obviously, a sequential storage media and is therefore unsuited for random-access applications. But it remains viable for data backup and archiving; its serial nature also makes it very suitable for video recording, a topic discussed in the previous chapter.

Magnetic Digital Disks

Magnetic digital disks store information on circular platters divided into concentric tracks so that information can be recorded, erased, and recorded again in a random-access fashion. Traditionally the purview of text, sound, and pictures, they are now also viable for the storage of digital video in all of its forms and flavors. *Hard drives* are sealed drives that are connected to a bus—the wire system of a computer. *Mountable drives* employ mountable disks than can be put in and taken out of the drive; this drive is likewise connected to a bus. A hard drive has a fixed capacity; a mountable drive design separates the drive mechanism from the recording media and can mount any number of drives of a particular format. Mountable formats include the still-familiar 3.5-inch floppy, rigid media devices including products from Syquest and Iomega, and others. These have evolved in densities from a few hundred kilobytes to gigabytes. Mountable media is cheaper than hard drive media because it is only media, but the drive is more expensive because it has to incorporate the mounting mechanism. Disadvantages of mountable drives include slower speed and loss of reliability due to the fact that this kind of media is never sealed to the air (there has to be some way for the heads to get to it) and is always at risk of contamination, whereas hard drives are sealed environments.

For applications that require the recording or playback of digital or streaming video signals directly to a digital disk drive, the bandwidth of the drive is critical—the drive has to be fast enough to accommodate the stream of data. When the bandwidth requirement exceeds that of a single hard disk, one can turn to ***RAID drives***, short for ***redundant array of independent disks*** technology, to expand the data rate. A RAID system breaks up the digital bytes into pieces and records them simultaneously and in parallel on multiple hard drives (see Figure 6.18). Putting eight bits onto eight separate drives in parallel, instead of just one in serial, produces an eightfold increase in bandwidth. As disks of all formats shrink in size and cost, they increasingly displace serial tape media.

Optical Digital Disks

An alternative to the magnetic digital disk is the *optical disk*. The optical disk recorder writes information by using a laser to modify a substrate inside the disk, which is organized as a series of *lands* and

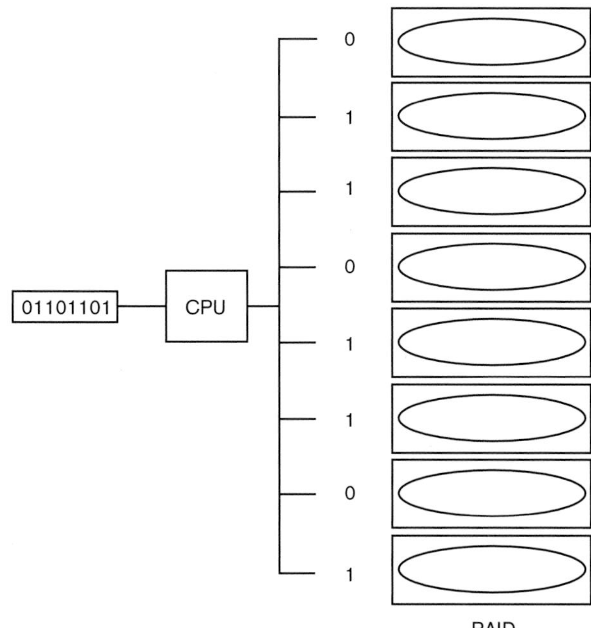

Figure 6.18 RAID technology. In this particular configuration, eight digital magnetic disks are used to record a single byte of video, one bit per platter. This is not a typical disk addressing scheme, and it requires special controllers and hardware.

pits, each of which represent a zero or one. Conversely, optical disk drives use the same laser to read the information. Optical disks come in three varieties: *Write-once, read-many time*, also known as *WORM* technologies, make a permanent, non-erasable recording that can be re-played many times. The CD version of this is called *CD-R*. *Write-many times, read-many times* are known as *WMRM* technologies or *rewritable disks*; the CD version is called *CD-RW*. And the third variant in digital optical disks are disks that are mass replicated, including the CD-ROM and the DVD. This third class of product allows disks to be replicated (stamped) at low cost, and mass distributed, whereas the WORM and WMRM disks must be written one at a time.

As with magnetic disks, storage capacity, access time, and transfer rates of optical disks vary. Storage capacity depends upon the wavelength of the laser and the number of layers on the disk. Data transfer speeds are determined by the linear data density and rotational speed of the drives. In general, optical disks are slower than magnetic disks and optical drives are more expensive than magnetic drives. The main benefit they provide is the low manufacturing cost of mass-produced disks. One variant of the optical disk—the video laser disk—was discussed in the last chapter; two others are discussed below.

A *CD-ROM* is an optical disk technology adopted from the music industry, mastered and manufactured on identical equipment, with a storage capacity of 650MB. The CD-ROM production cycle involves recording content—including text, pictures, sound, moving pictures, and programs—onto WORM masters, usually a CD-R or CD-RW. These are then duplicated onto mass-produced copies. Because the recordable CDs were originally gold-colored, they are often call *gold masters.*

CD-ROM drives come in several speeds. A 1X drive has a theoretical data rate of 150KB per second, and an actual data rate of 95KB in common practice. A 12X drive offers data rates of 1800KB per second, which allow movies to be played as big as 320 pixels at 15 frames/second (compressed). The CD-ROM is a mature technology and in recent years has been an integral part of every personal computer.

The next generation of CD-ROM is expected to be *DVD-ROM*, a sister technology to the DVD, discussed in the previous chapter. DVD-ROM has storage capabilities upward from 5.2GB. DVD-ROM drives play CD-ROMs and write once, and rewritable versions also exist. The DVD-ROM is used just like a CD-ROM—that is, something that can be used for multimedia and, because it has greater data capacity, can incorporate a full-screen, full-motion MPEG-2 compressed movie. The production pathway of the DVD is the same as the production pathway of the CD-ROM. A WORM drive can be used to build a master, which can be sent to a replication plant to manufacture distribution disks.

Solid-State Digital Memories

Beyond disk and tape, we expect that future storage technologies will evolve toward extremely high-density, non-volatile solid-state chip memories with no moving parts. These already play a role in digital still cameras, where their higher cost is outweighed by their fast access time, random access, and lack of moving parts. They contain no motors, no bearings, no capstans, and no servomechanisms to keep tape, heads, lasers, and the disks all moving at the right rates of speed. This enables a substantial reduction in power consumption as well as the size of the overall unit.

Solid-state densities have increased dramatically in the last decade or so, but if they are going to be used to store entire motion pictures, even at television resolutions, they will have to increase by orders of magnitude. Theorists and researchers are not without strategies, and it is not inconceivable that the moving picture recording medium of the future might well be a 1-inch solid plastic cube that might contain thousands of films or television programs.

7 Intermixing Media

Moving pictures can be created with film, with video, or in the digital domain. Which tools and media are most appropriate? Should the imagery be shot on film or tape? Which is easier to work with? What is the role of emerging high-definition video formats? There are many questions regarding media preference and no simple answers. And often the animator or technical director will not be presented with choices, but with problems where one media must be converted to another.

The variety of media and formats affect the production process as well as the perception of the final product. Motion picture products are increasingly hybrids of a multiplicity of source material, with digitized media becoming the preferred media of postproduction. Distribution choices continue to include film, video, digital video via DVD and the Internet, and HDTV (digital) projection. All of these options and choices bear subtle signatures—grain in film, the liveliness of the raster scan, the differences in gamma between film and CCD chips, to name a few—that connote subtle messages to audiences about quality, attitude, style, and even feelings about what they are seeing.

This chapter reviews issues of preference, including film versus video, and issues of conversion, including film to tape, tape to film, tape to tape, and tape and film to and from digital. An overview of the production process is also presented.

Issues of Preference—Film versus Video

There are many issues regarding the preference of film versus video: they range from the camera, to the medium, editing, and finally the message itself. Here is a review of some of those issues.

From *The Nutty Professor.* (Copyright 1999, Universal Pictures. Image courtesy of Rhythm and Hues Studios.)

Both film and video cameras can be self-contained, or they can be tripod or dolly mounted. Lenses for both are comparable. Both can be connected to the studio with electrical cables, picture signals, and control lines. Both cameras operate wireless, although the film camera must record locally, whereas the video camera is often recorded remotely. A film system is primarily a mechanical hardware technology, repairable with a lathe or milling machine and stock metal. Its electrical requirements include relatively unsophisticated motors and sync. Its electronic requirements do not exceed a simple audio amplifier, assuming that sound is employed. Conversely, video equipment involves precise synchronized motors, high-performance electronics, and, increasingly, microprocessors and digital chips, much of it fabricated at an inaccessible microscopic scale.

The nature of the film shutter and video (scanning) shutter provide subtle but profound differences in what the media can record. Classically, the film camera has had better control of shutter speed and motion blur (temporal anti-aliasing), which is much more complex in video and CCD systems. Newer video shutters address some of these problems, including a simulation of shutter speed. Interlace remains a confusing problem for classic NTSC and PAL video, as well as HDTV systems, where each half frame is temporarily advanced. Video, even progressive video, is still scanned, so the temporal structure of the image is quite different than that produced by the film shutter. Shutter speed implies that each pixel stores only a certain domain of time; this axis is independent as to whether or not the pixels have a uniform time base. In other words, a digital representation may include either a representation of a moment (in which all pixels represent the same moment in time) or of a scan (in which each successive pixel represents successive time). This is also true for completely synthetic images that need to be presented in either simultaneous time (as in a film flash in a projector) or serial time (as in a scanning display).

Both media can record images in low light. The film emulsions have higher spatial resolution and superior contrast (light-to-dark) ratios, in excess of seven stops in film compared to five for video. Color resolution of film is very good (at least 10 bits per pixel per primary color), whereas the color resolution of most video systems is very depressed (approximately 5 to 8 bits per pixel per primary color, with the best being RGB systems). Temporally, at 30 versus 24 frames/second, video has slightly higher temporal resolution than film, and its two fields double temporal resolution to 60 fields per second.

With respect to standards, film and video are rather different. Film is very standardized—one professional and one industrial gauge dominate the world. Tape standards also exist, but there are many formats and commensurate recording technologies. Almost all are incompatible. Furthermore, each format seems to have a rather finite lifetime. People and organizations have built up large bodies of work on media that have become obsolete, and playing them becomes increasingly difficult. More valuable properties are copied onto the newer formats, with corresponding generational loss, of course. As digital tape recording becomes more common, the duplication concern regarding video standards will be minimized, but the issue of evolving storage media is just as much at issue with digital storage devices.

One benefit of video, not available in film, is the short duration of time that exists between the capture and the viewing of the collected source material. Video has advantages of immediacy. What you see is what you get—now. There is no batch process involved, no laboratory, no print. Video records what the camera sees simultaneously with the viewer watching the monitor. Furthermore, a video recording can be played back immediately. Film, on the other hand, must be fully processed before the source images can be viewed. *Video assist* is a process whereby a live video feed is tapped out of a film camera; this allows film takes to be reviewed instantly.

There are also differences in the ease of handling the media. Video cassettes are easier to load and handle than roll film. Tape is not subject to damage from preexposure to light or X-rays, while film is very sensitive. Tape is magnetic and can be erased, accidentally or deliberately—a process that enables it to be used over and over again. Physical splicing of videotape is not practiced, and it is difficult to use a reel over if there is important material recorded in the middle of the tape. Film, on the other hand, may be separated and respliced to facilitate the management and storage of materials. Both media are susceptible to extremes of humidity and temperature, both can stretch and break, and both can be contaminated by physical dirt.

Costwise, tape stock, even top-of-the-line stock, is an order of magnitude cheaper than film on a per-minute basis. On a resolution basis (the number of bits captured), they are more equal. The producer must make decisions about the spatial and color resolutions. Consumer-grade video is very cost-efficient. VHS cassettes hold six hours of NTSC or PAL video. By contrast, an hour of 35mm film occupies six 10-inch-diameter reels. Video takes up less space but it also holds much less information.

There are also some things that can be done with film that cannot be done with video; these are due to the fact that film utilizes *accumulative chemical memory*, or, in digital terms, it sums successive exposures together. Like digital media, it can be overflowed, or rather, overexposed. For example, film can be double-exposed—something that cannot be done with video. Many special effects such as glows, streaks, and burn-ins involve a second exposure into the original image of selected regions. There are ways to approximate these film effects in video, but they cannot be applied directly to the tape—they must be "computed" and then recorded. It should be noted that there are also video effects that are a function of electronics and hence cannot be done in film.

With respect to editing, film editing is a physical practice. The film can be held and looked at directly, cut and spliced, and viewed on a Moviola or projected onto a screen. With film editing, it is easy to make scenes longer or shorter, to cut them out or insert them. With videotape, these tasks are not so easy, although it is relatively simple to erase a scene and then record it back onto the tape (an *insert edit*), provided the lengths of the old and new scenes are exactly the same. But with videotape editing, scenes cannot be made longer or shorter by extending or trimming them because there is no way to physically add or take away frames in the tape. To make a scene longer or shorter, the tape must be copied down a generation and edited. So the editing process, in this regard, is not as flexible with videotape as it is with film. Non-linear video editing overcomes many of these objections, but tape masters are not non-linear files. The primary advantage of editing on tape, and especially on a non-linear editor, is the ability to review the edits and effects immediately.

Film and video also have a different impact on the viewing audience. Film works well projected. It is ideal for a simultaneous presentation to a large number of viewers in a common audience, where the people are physically together and can interact as a unit.

Video projection, on the other hand, has very low contrast ratios and usually does not project as well as film (although a new generation of projectors, including HDTV projectors, is changing that). The television monitor is able to be viewed in medium-light environments, whereas motion picture projection must occur in the dark; video reduces the need for special screening rooms and screening situations, but it does require shade.

Above and beyond the purely technical aspects of film versus tape, there remain compositional and psychological factors that distinguish the two modes of presentation. Video typically employs a small, transmissive light screen, usually watched by one person to several people together in a lighted environment. Film employs a reflective light screen, usually watched by several people to a large audience in the dark. The difference in screen size is also a factor. Traditionally, composition in video tends to be more intimate. Small figures in big scenes get lost in the scan lines. Close-ups have a more visceral quality: they are not overwhelming, they are life-size. The small-box television is not a panorama of vast vistas. There is never a need for viewers to turn their necks to pivot from one side of the picture to the other, as they might when watching projected film on a large screen. In video, ideas need to be brought to the forefront and strongly displayed. The screen is so small that competitive foci are likely to get lost. Some of the psychological factors also occur in the nature of the medium—the scanning beam helps video be more "real" because it is always in the now, whereas with film, one views a succession of still frames. All of these factors—big size versus small, reflective versus transmissive, shutter/scanning technology—contribute to differences, and the result is that the semantics of communication are not the same. As new technologies evolve (e.g., HDTV), that which works best to communicate a message will evolve.

Conversions between Media

Before beginning a discussion of digital moving pictures, it is important to first understand issues related to the conversion of media, in particular conversions between film and tape. In practice, today's production environment often involves a mixture of media; there are at least six types of conversions that need to be understood (see

Figure 7.1). This section covers the general principles of film-to-video and video-to-film conversions.

Telecine—Film to Video

The *telecine* process—or film-to-video transfer process—is a common practice and has been around since the beginning of television. Film-to-video transfer provides a way to show movies on television and to fabricate material for television using film-recording equipment.

In scene-to-scene, color-corrected film-to-tape transfer, film can be transferred as positive or negative. The scene-to-scene color correction permits brightness and colors to be controlled within the context of a given scene and the hues of the various colors to be electronically manipulated. This eliminates the necessity of a color-corrected film print. Computers mediate the interface and the color-correction values, called ***timing lights*** or ***printing lights***, which may be saved in a computer file called a ***timing file***. Speed control (fast and slow motion), blowup and reduction, and repositionings may be made part of the timing file. All these effects are immediately visible on the video screen.

A telecine—the equipment used for the transfer—is composed of a projector, light source, shuttle, shutter, and photosensor. It syncs to the video signal, particularly the phase, or vertical interval (see Figure 7.2). Once a single frame is held stationary in the projection gate, several strategies are employed to scan the film image electronically. The ***flying spot scanner*** is an electronic device that uses a phototube as an input device, and a CRT with a bright white beam. The

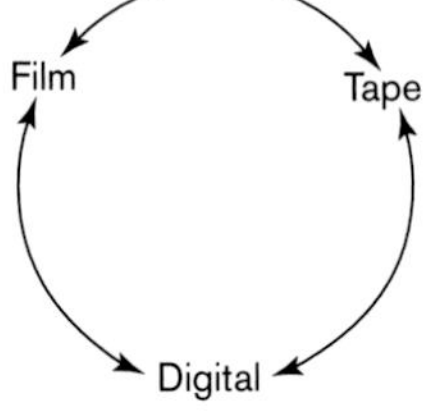

Figure 7.1 Above: There are six conversions illustrated here: telecine, also known as film to tape (FTT); kinescope, also known as tape to film (TTF); film to digital (FTD); digital to film (DTF); tape to digital, commonly called analog to digital (ATD); and digital to tape, commonly called digital to analog (DTA). More typically, the film and tape, to digital are grouped as analog to digital (ATD), while the conversions in the opposite direction are termed DTA.

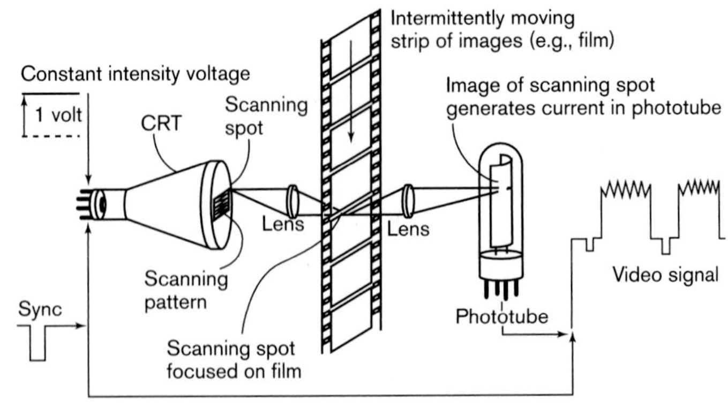

Figure 7.2 Right: Flying spot scanner telecine is one way to electronically capture a film image. The sync makes a scanning raster of constant (white) brightness. Density in the film (the darker areas) absorb some of the brightness, so less light reaches the phototube for that spot.

white beam, which is scanned onto the surface of the CRT, is simultaneously focused onto the film transparency, placed just outside the CRT surface. As the light passes through the transparency, it strikes a phototube, placed behind the transparency. The phototube measures the varying amount of light emerging from the point on the transparency illuminated by the "scanning spot". The output from the phototube becomes the video signal. When scanning color, the process must be repeated three times, using filters. Video output can be RGB, component, or composite. An alternate technology to the flying spot scanner is to use CCD pickups or normal television camera tubes.

Unfortunately, the film-to-video transfer process has its share of problems. In particular, a temporal aliasing problem sometimes called *judder* occurs as a result of the different frame rates of each format; film has a frame rate of 24 frames/second, whereas video has 30 frames/second, so the 24 frames/second must be transferred to an equivalent 30 frames/second. The solution to the problem, sometimes called a *louping intermittent*, involves a procedure that blends one frame of film into several video frames. There are a variety of ways to do this, and some produce better results than others. One of the most common ways is the so-called *three-two pulldown*, where each successive frame of film is alternatively transferred to two or three video fields. For example, film frame 1 is transferred to video fields 1 and 2; film frame 2 is transferred to video fields 3, 4, and 5; film frame 3 is transferred to video fields 6, and 7; film frame 4 to 8, 9, and 10, and so on (see Figure 7.3). Once again, a temporal aliasing artifact is introduced by this procedure in that it misplaces temporal events in the resultant transfer. Hence, an even better way may be to integrate the adjacent film frames temporarily, but this will require a frame store.

Film that is expressively made for television may also be shot at 30 frames/second, and then transferred one frame for one frame, eliminating all judder problems. In Europe, where TV runs at a rate of 25 frames/second, the 24 frames/second film may also be transferred at one-to-one. And conversely, certain new HDTV formats support 24 frames/second non-interlaced recording, so the film can be transferred; viewer perception does not seem to be significantly affected.

Do remember that all of these strategies differ from native video. This is especially true for NTSC and PAL, where in native video the two

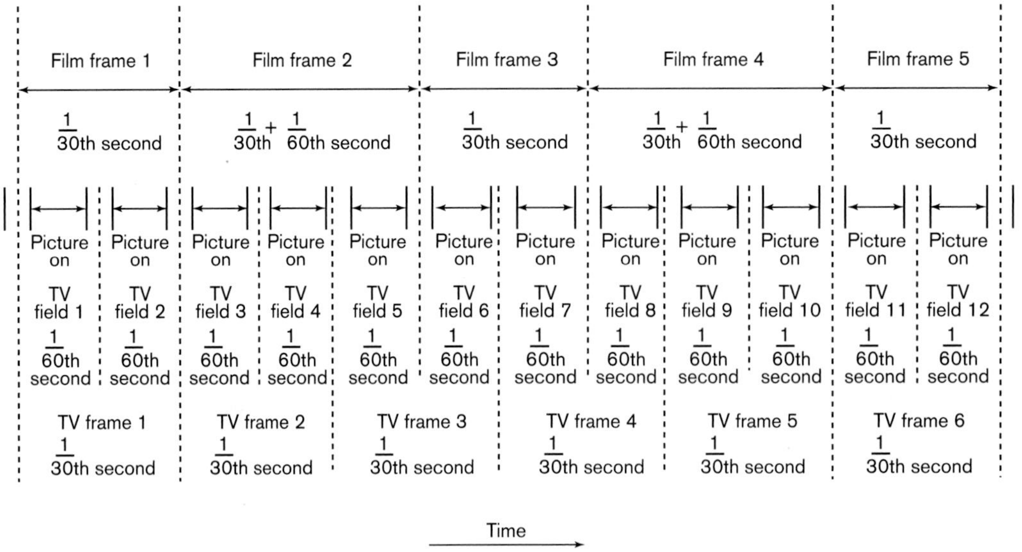

Film frame 1 | Film frame 2 | Film frame 3 | Film frame 4 | Film frame 5

$\frac{1}{30\text{th}}$ second | $\frac{1}{30\text{th}} + \frac{1}{60\text{th}}$ second | $\frac{1}{30\text{th}}$ second | $\frac{1}{30\text{th}} + \frac{1}{60\text{th}}$ second | $\frac{1}{30\text{th}}$ second

Picture on TV field 1, $\frac{1}{60\text{th}}$ second | Picture on TV field 2, $\frac{1}{60\text{th}}$ second | Picture on TV field 3, $\frac{1}{60\text{th}}$ second | Picture on TV field 4, $\frac{1}{60\text{th}}$ second | Picture on TV field 5, $\frac{1}{60\text{th}}$ second | Picture on TV field 6, $\frac{1}{60\text{th}}$ second | Picture on TV field 7, $\frac{1}{60\text{th}}$ second | Picture on TV field 8, $\frac{1}{60\text{th}}$ second | Picture on TV field 9, $\frac{1}{60\text{th}}$ second | Picture on TV field 10, $\frac{1}{60\text{th}}$ second | Picture on TV field 11, $\frac{1}{60\text{th}}$ second | Picture on TV field 12, $\frac{1}{60\text{th}}$ second

TV frame 1 $\frac{1}{30\text{th}}$ second | TV frame 2 $\frac{1}{30\text{th}}$ second | TV frame 3 $\frac{1}{30\text{th}}$ second | TV frame 4 $\frac{1}{30\text{th}}$ second | TV frame 5 $\frac{1}{30\text{th}}$ second | TV frame 6 $\frac{1}{30\text{th}}$ second

Time

Figure 7.3 Telecine timing: note 3:2 pulldown.

fields have different time bases; the telecine approach on the other hand creates fields that are temporally identical. Many people feel that this factor contributes to the "aliveness" of native video; in any respect, it is a subtle yet perceptible difference between native video and film-to-tape—even if the frame rates are identical. Intent plays a role here—if the intent, for example, is to transfer the 24-frames/second film to 24-frames/second video in order to edit and post it, and then transfer it back to film, the time-base differences are moot.

Be aware that real-time telecine transfer has loose registration; if compositing is involved, then the composited images will weave, or float against each other. This is especially noticeable when titles are being composited. The way to ensure a tight frame registration is to do a telecine transfer using a non-real-time Bell & Howell perf pin–registered shuttle. This process requires the addition of a frame store and single-frame video recording capability, but the resulting frames are steady and can be used for successful compositing. Remember that poor registration is one of the major factors in motion fusion, and that poor frame-to-frame registration dramatically decreases spatial resolution.

Kinescope—Video to Film

Television, ironically, was invented before there was a way to record it; there was no indigenous electronic media able to record the 6MHz bandwidth of television—no videotape. So in the early days of televi-

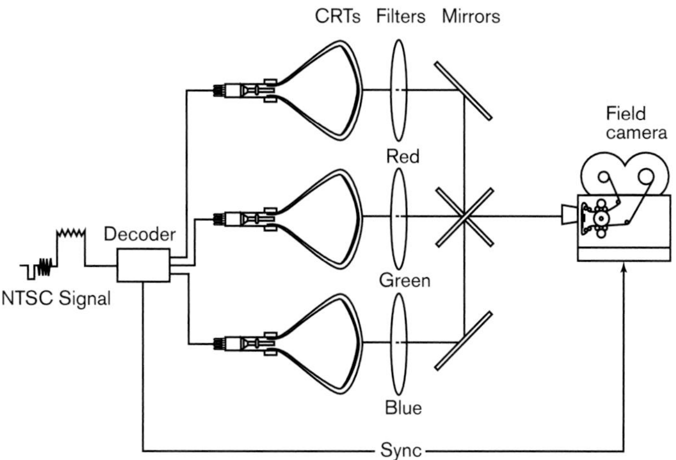

Figure 7.4 Color kinescope block diagram. The NTSC signal is decoded into red, green, and blue components and displayed on three monochromatic monitors. The monitor images are viewed through color filters and combined onto a single strip of film. An alternative design, not shown here, is to employ a single monitor, a spinning filter, and no mirrors. This simplifies the design and reduces the cost, but it also can only go a third as fast as this parallel arrangement (but may be fast enough for some applications).

sion, video images were recorded onto film. The machine that carried out this process came to be called a *kinescope*, and the films that were and are made on it are *kines* or kinescopes. The kinescope essentially utilizes a film camera to record a video monitor.

A kinescope machine includes a film camera and a monitor, which are synchronized (see Figure 7.4). Usually the video is electronically enhanced and displayed on a flat-faced monitor to improve the final film image. Aperture correction provides more apparent sharpness in the final film image by sharpening the monitor being photographed. Gamma correction modifies the gray scale of the video to enhance tonal reproduction onto film. The quality of the resulting kines is that of "The Honeymooners," "Milton Berle," or "Ernie Kovacs."

As a result of the difference in frame rates, a juddering temporal aliasing also occurs during the kinescope process. Typically, the video is photographed in half fields to allow for camera blanking. Using this method, every other film frame combines a bottom half field with the successive top half field (see Figure 7.5). The camera shutter may be mechanical or electronic, in which case the picture on the kinescope is turned on and off (blanked) electronically. Again, the change in frame rates places spatial events at the wrong time and creates motion discontinuities. Obviously, there exist more sophisticated ways to resolve the frame-rate differences, but the channel capacity and audience needs may not demand it. Europe, going from 25 to 24 frames / second, shoots one-to-one, and the different speed typically goes unnoticed.

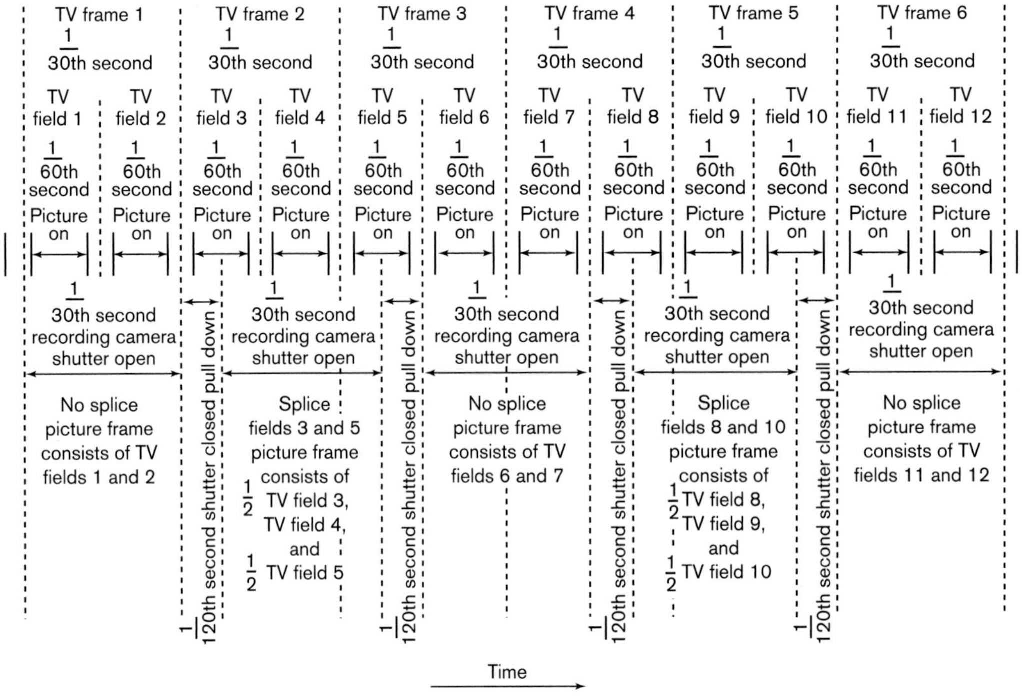

Figure 7.5 Kinescope timing.

In the more modern world, video-to-film transfers, including the multitude of HDTV formats, tend to be transferred by first digitizing the video, then transferring the digital video to film. These techniques are described generically in the film-to-digital conversion section below, although special algorithms are often employed to assist in frame-rate conversions, gamma adjustments, and other reconciliations between media. Clearly the strategy of using a digital intermediary will be the basis of all media conversions.

Conversions between Video Standards

Conversion problems also exist between different kinds of video. NTSC, PAL/SECAM, and HDTV all have different numbers of scan lines and frame rates and are functionally incompatible with each other. Conversions between these different types of media are possible, and all involve compromises of resolution and frame rates. Unfortunately, this is the realm of integer arithmetic, where scan-line resolutions and frames/second resolutions are not easy multiples of one another. Conversions between different frame rates and spatial resolutions may be accomplished by rescanning the image (the worst approach) or using digital algorithms to partially integrate frames (a better approach). In pragmatic terms, standards conversions between video systems leave a great deal to be desired, enough so that when doing film-to-tape conversions, it is advisable to do one film-to-tape transfer for each video standard. It is worth noting that one of the arguments in favor of HDTV is that it can be downward convertible into either NTSC or PAL/SECAM. And one advantage of digital video, discussed in a moment, is that video standards are best converted within the digital domain.

Video to Digital—ATD and DTA

One must be quite precise when talking about the conversion of video to a digital format. First, as you recall, video comes in a variety of flavors—component, composite, RGB, and others. And second, there is the issue of just what the digitized file represents. Chapter 5 reviewed a number of digital video formats in which the digital file is a digitized representation of the NTSC (or PAL) waveform. In this section, we assume that the file is a matrix of pixels that represents successive frames.

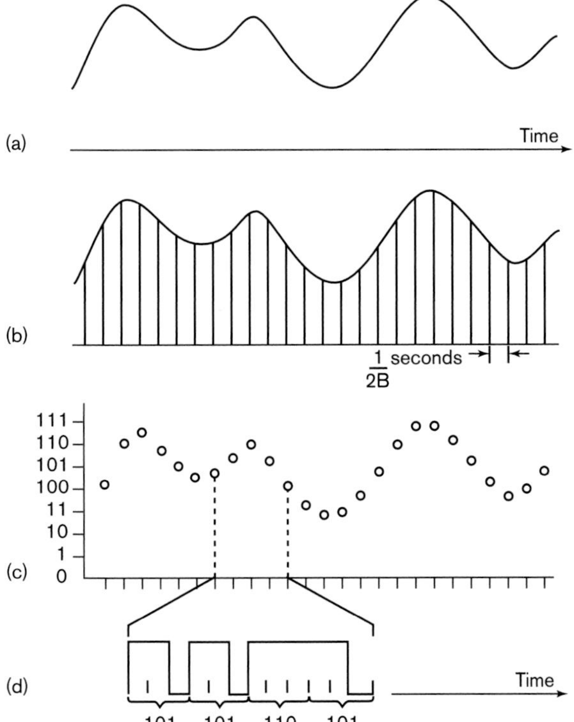

Figure 7.6 A sampling and quantization. An analog waveform (a) is sampled (b), quantized (c), and formed into a digital signal (d).

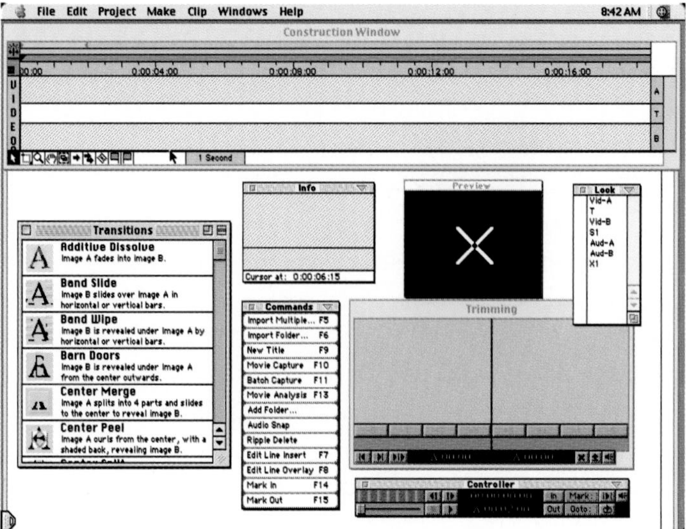

Figure 7.7 A Premiere video capture window along with time line, transitions selection, and controller.

A *video digitizer*, or *frame grabber*, is a system used to convert a video signal to a digital representation. It requires a video signal and, synced to it, an *analog-to-digital converter* (ATD), as well as a memory, or frame store. The source of the video signal may be a camera or other live device or it may be a recording. The ATD must be synced to the start of the video frame. The ATD samples the analog waveform periodically and quantizes those samples into numbers (see Figure 7.6). The numbers are deposited into the digital frame store, where they may be read by the computer. Conversely, converting the picture of digital numbers stored in the frame store back into a video signal is achieved by genlocking the video and the frame buffer, and clocking out the digital data through a *digital-to-analog converter* (DTA) at video rates, about 100 nanoseconds per pixel. The result is a video signal representation of the contents of the frame store.

A critical issue related to the conversion process is the time it takes to digitize one frame of video. Systems vary widely, ranging from the ability to digitize one frame in a minute or more, to video digitizers that grab sequences of images at video rates, that is, they can grab each successive frame in 1/30th of a second, as it goes by (see Figure 7.7). This kind of frame store is found in video equipment such as time-base correctors and ADOs (Ampex Digital Opticals). In all of these machines, one frame (two fields) gets digitized, buffered, and converted to analog. Because this process takes time, the output is delayed by 1/30th of a second—that is, it gets delayed by one frame.

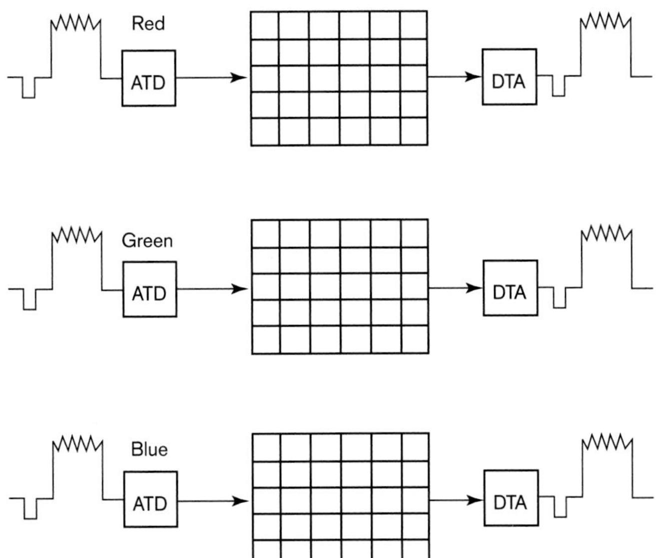

Figure 7.8 Digitized RGB is perhaps the most familiar video format to a computer animator. Essentially three parallel digital video signals, it is often held in a frame store or dimensioned memory.

Video digitizers require digital hardware for storing the frames. Practically speaking, in order to digitize action, a frame store must be complemented with a fast disk or a large block of fast RAM. Often the images are compressed after they are digitized and before they are stored, so that the bandwidth and data store requirements are reduced.

With respect to spatial resolution, most video digitizing assumes that the number of samples along the *y*-axis is the same as the number of scan lines in the image. But as previously stated, the resolution of the *x*-axis is not a predefined number. Sampling theory, in particular the Nyquist sampling theorem, states that a signal may be uniquely represented by samples no further apart than one half the fastest cycle. In other words, the number of samples / second = 2 × bandwidth in Hz (cycles/second). A 6 MHz video channel requires 12 million samples / second. At 30 samples / second, that is 400,000 samples per frame or about 833 per scan line. In practice, the CCIR (International Radio Consultative Committee) Video Standard 701 recommends 720 samples/second, whereas the slightly lower resolution of 640 pixels results in convenient square pixels.

Luminance resolution is almost always an integer power of two, and 2^8 provides 256 luminance values, although this is by no means representative of the limits of the dynamic ranges found in reality, or even of the eye.

Digitizing RGB Color Note that all of the discussion of video-to-digital conversion thus far has concerned black-and-white video. Color video is not so trivial, if only because RGB, component, and composite signals have very different representations. In RGB color, 8 bits (256 luminance levels) or 10 bits (1024 luminance levels) are typically used for each primary color. Three individual parallel sets of bit planes correspond to the three color channels (see Figure 7.8). Digital recorders used to record this kind of signal include tape drives and disks.

Digitizing Composite and Component Color Digitizing a composite-color video format such as NTSC or PAL involves a more complex process. Recall that the three parallel color signals R, G, and B are converted into a luminance channel and two lower-resolution chrominance channels that contains the hue and saturation. The chrominance signal is superimposed over the luminance signal to produce a single channel of composite video, which travels on one wire. This may then be digitized as a single waveform, such as the D2 format. Although it is true that in order to view the image, the composite signal must be decoded back to RGB to drive the monitor, it is also true that decomposition is not necessary if the digitized composite video is only to be converted back to video.

Component video is digitized by digitizing the luminance and two chrominance channels separately. Note that digital composite or component video cannot be stored in a frame buffer that stores RGB video—this is because the two chrominance channels, roughly speaking, only contain information for every other pixel, with fewer bits. That is because the information in hue and saturation is unequal to the information in luminance. Thus, many video frame buffers store a full matrix of luminance but only half a matrix for each of the two chrominance channels. In other words, the sampled composite video must be converted into an unequal spatial resolution. Digitized RGB can be converted to digitized component or composite color, but when digitized composite or component color is converted back into the RGB format, there is less information (resolution) than there was in the original RGB format. (Issues of compressing video are discussed in Chapter 6.)

A Caution About Recording Digital Video from Computers

While outputting video signals from computers is common practice, a word of caution is in order. Computer screens are often designed for detailed viewing of still pictures and have spatial and color resolution dramatically different from NTSC or PAL. Often the two forms are completely incompatible. CRT bandwidths may range from 20MHz to 100MHz (versus 4.7 MHz for NTSC), and color is often RGB with completely different numbers of lines, different scanning standards (interlace versus progressive), different timing, different voltages, different syncs, different blanking, and different color definitions. Do not assume that a computer's RGB output can be encoded into legal NTSC or PAL. Some computers do not even output video signals, and they use special signals to drive the monitor. In fact, output from computer screens, even color graphic cards, is often totally impossible to record as composite video.

Regrettably, much misleading representation is made in this area, but to be brief, in order for video to work on a VCR, television set, or transmitter, the video output waveform and sync must conform to Electronic Industries Alliance (EIA) Recommended Standard RS-170 and to paragraph 73.699 of the FCC rules. Any computer output signal that does not meet this standard is probably not usable for broadcast television and cannot be recorded with an ordinary VTR.

Film to Digital Conversion

Conversions between film and digital systems is an older topic than the fusion of digital and tape systems. Differences include the fact that film may be negative or positive, whereas video is only positive; that film represents intensities logarithmically and not in a linear fashion; and that film has richer spatial and luminance resolutions. Nor is film a scanning beam technology. Digitizing a 35mm motion picture frame implies a resolution upwards of 1600 × 2000 spatially and at least 3 × 8 bits per pixel for color. Digitizing at resolutions of 2000 × 3000 pixels and 12 bits per pixel per primary color are not uncommon. A 70mm frame requires at least 3000 × 4000 pixels per frame, or 36MB per frame, about 100 times a video image. The facts that the process is still not real time and that storage requirements are overwhelming discouraged its use until the mid-1990s. Still, once film has been converted into a digital form, there are major benefits

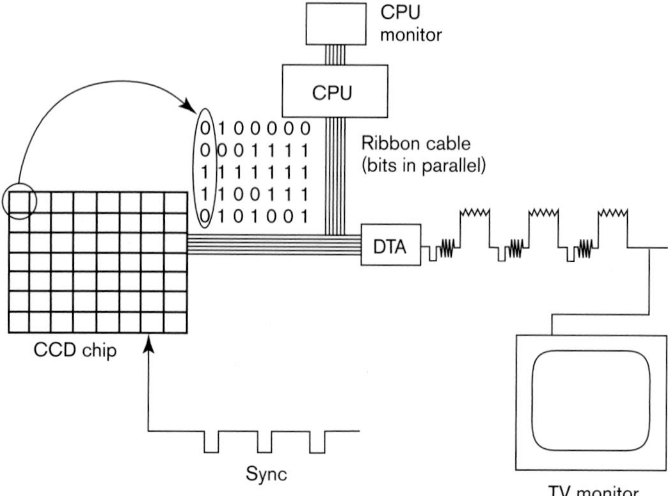

Figure 7.9 Film-to-digital conversion using a CCD.

in terms of compositing, matte work, and duplication that render it superior to analog postproduction techniques.

All film scanners and recorders require pin-registered shuttles and Bell & Howell perforations. The favorite shuttle designs are by Acme, Oxberry, or Mitchell. Cameras may be purchased new or used, and it is not unusual to find older precision cameras being mounted on brand-new displays. Registration and repeatability of the camera as well as the electronics and screen is of paramount importance, especially if the scenes produced are going to be composited. Software can assist in reducing noise and ensuring that the fields are uniform in brightness.

Scanning is often accomplished by focusing the image onto a CCD and making an exposure, then reading the pixels out (see Figure 7.9). There are two different strategies for the use of CCDs: the areal CCD and the linear CCD. As previously described, the CCD basically consists of a grid of pixels, and the grid is sampled with an ATD converter and presented to the CPU as binary numbers. High-resolution systems, such as a Kodak Cineon film-scanning system, uses a long linear CCD (with red, green, and blue built in). Film is moved past the CCD while it scans and then discharges. Note that there are two general scanning strategies: either the CCD is moved across the picture, or the picture is moved across the CCD. The movement may be continuous or may be made in a series of discrete steps. When scanning film, once the CCD is discharged, the film can be advanced and another frame captured.

As a side note, it is worth mentioning here that digitizing film does not really entail scanning it; although the equipment may be capturing the images in a scanning mode, the temporal base of the information being captured is not displaced. This is quite the opposite of what happens in a video camera: if the video camera CCD is run in real time, the CCD must be unloaded at a scanning rate. The CCD is actually scanning, because the CCD is being discharged serially at video time rates, and the result is not a simultaneous capture.

An alternate technology is the flying spot scanner, in which a scanning beam of light or laser light passes through the film and its exposure is measured. The flying spot scanner employs a CRT on one side of the film and a photocell on the other. The position of the "flying spot" is controlled by a computer program that positions the beam on the CRT and turns it on. The CPU simultaneously reads a digital value from the photocell behind the film and stores the value in memory. This value is the density of the film at the location of the flying spot. Once the value is saved, the computer advances the beam to the next sampled position and repeats the measurement. In recent years, three colored laser beams are used, one for each primary color.

The reverse process—digital to film—is relatively easily accomplished, typically using a very high-precision flat-face CRT, black-and-white style, with colored filters. Circuits in the film recorder convert digital addresses to *xy* deflection values, and digital luminance to CRT beam intensity. The source of the images can be digitized film, digitized video, or synthetic computer animation.

Another technique is to deflect a laser beam and scan onto the film directly. This eliminates the need to photograph the face of the CRT as part of the image and produces a more noise-free picture, since the glass surface and phosphor structure is eliminated.

This transformation from film and tape to digital moving picture media has positioned us at the beginning of a new age. Once digital, the same tools can manipulate images that differ in resolution, mix and match them, write them back to film or tape, or distribute them as purely digital formats. Digital recording is the first technology of this new age.

Production Flow

The relationships between and among individual media is constantly changing, and a bit of knowledge about film and tape production may help to provide an understanding of how media fit into the production environment. The decision of whether to choose film or tape is a difficult one because each has some clear advantages over the other. Which is better is often defined not by the characteristics of the medium per se, but by the characteristics of the situation in which the medium is employed. Often the subtleties of production, especially postproduction, influence the decision.

The choice of which medium to use may involve compromises and it may be a condition over which one has no control. Shots and segments may originate in different media; an animator may have to work with a variety of source material. In special-effects work, different elements of a single scene often come from different image sources, and from different media sources as well. Another common production strategy is to shoot on film, transfer to video using a telecine, and then edit onto tape. Another emerging pathway is to shoot on film or tape, digitize the image, and postproduce digitally. The output can then be recorded on film, video, or digital media. Blending media together is an art and a craft of the producer, director, editor, compositor, and animator.

Postproduction for Black-and-White Film

The mechanics of film have already been discussed; here we explore how the original film is transformed into a final product (see Figure 7.10). After photography, the original negative is processed and a *positive print,* or *dailies,* is struck. The dailies are screened by the editor, director, and others and scenes are selected. The editor assembles the individual selected scenes into a *workprint* (W/P). The initial complete W/P is called a *rough cut,* and the final W/P is called the *finished cut.* Optical effects, titles, and so on are physically marked onto the W/P with a grease pencil.

If there are no optical effects, a *printing negative* is prepared by splicing the original negative so as to match or conform to the W/P. If optical effects are indicated, a *fine-grain master print* of the scenes used in the effect is made from the original negative. This positive

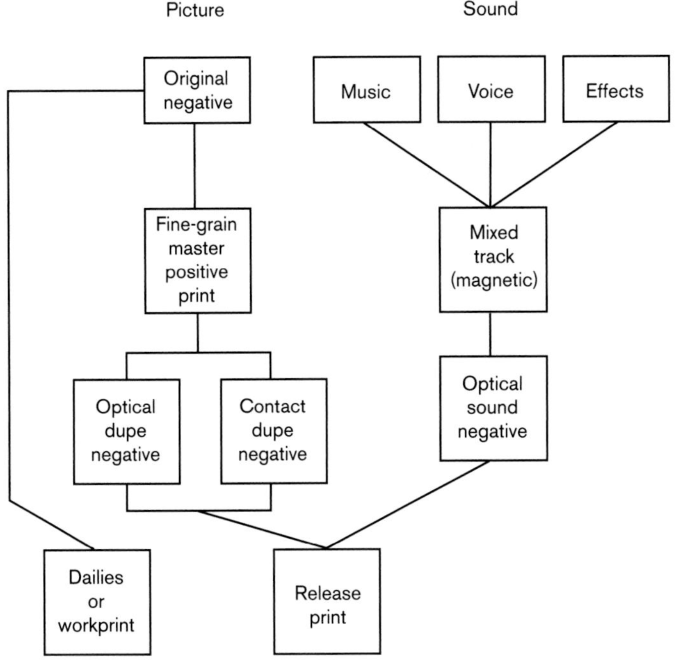

Figure 7.10 Black-and-white film production. The chart shows two major pathways. One has two steps or generations, the other has four steps. After photography and exposure of the raw stock, the original negative is developed. The simplest pathway to strike a print from the negative, usually called a daily (because it is ready within one day) or a workprint (because you use it to edit with). Many positive prints can be made from this negative, but if this negative needs to be protected, or if titles or effects need to be added, then it is necessary to strike a master positive print (also called a fine-grain master). From this a duplicate negative is made that also includes any effects, and then screening prints are struck from this duplicate picture printing negative. An answer print is a sample composite print made for client approval before many composite release prints are made.

print is then rephotographed by a special optical camera onto *optical dupe negative film*; fades and dissolves are added at this step.

To assemble a complete printing negative, the optical dupe negative is spliced or intercut with the original negative of the scenes without optical effects. Sometimes producers make optical dupe negatives of the entire show, whether the scenes are involved in optical effects or not. This is done to maintain consistent quality throughout the printing negative and to ensure that the master print does not need to be used during the duplication process—hence protecting the master.

A fine-grain or dupe negative may be either *contact duplicated* or *optically duplicated*. The former is made via the contact printing process and lacks tight registration; the latter is reproduced with tight registration, using a special optical camera and registration pins. Dupes must be in precise registration if images are to be composited accurately.

Finally, an optical negative of the finished sound track is synchronized to the printing negative of the picture, and an *answer print* (a test positive print) is made to check and approve what has been done. The answer print contains scene-to-scene brightness and color adjustments—the *timing lights*. Once the answer print is approved, many ***release prints*** are made for distribution using the same timing lights.

Color Film Postproduction

Color film postproduction, for example movie film postproduction, goes through steps similar to black-and-white postproduction. With color, however, there are additional choices of intermediate pathways, including negative/positive, reversal stocks, and pan separation masters (see Figure 7.11).

The color equivalent of a fine-grain black-and-white master is usually a single strand of color film recording referred to as the *intermediate positive* or (IP). The IP looks like a print except that it has lower contrast and the same orange tint seen in a negative. An alternative approach to the IP is to optically dupe three pan separation masters, called the *blue separation positive, green separation positive*, and *red separation positive*. The three pan separations make up the master. The dupe negative equivalent in color is referred to as an *internegative* (IN) and is made by duplicating the IP or photographing the pan masters through filters.

As with black-and-white film postproduction, to prepare a printing negative, the *original color negative* (OCN) and internegative are conformed to the W/P, and from this an answer print is struck, made

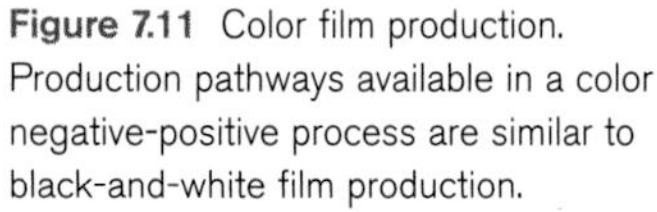
Figure 7.11 Color film production. Production pathways available in a color negative-positive process are similar to black-and-white film production.

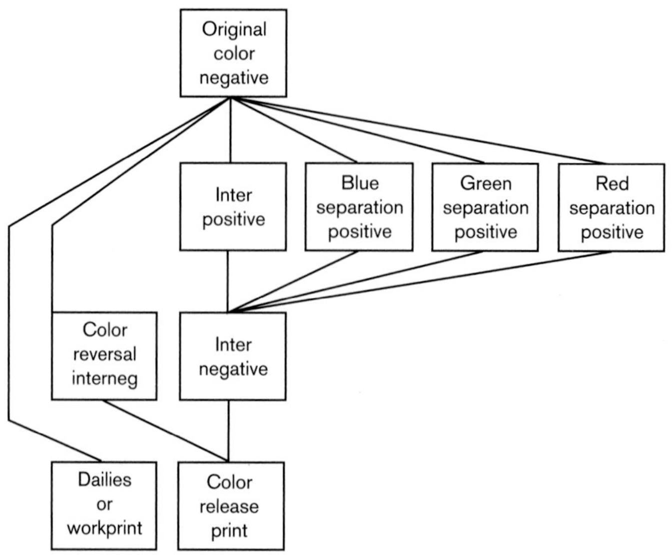

with scene-to-scene color correction and timing lights, which also includes an optical sound track similar to that which is used in black-and-white film postproduction.

Separation positives are rarely used in color film postproduction, but they provide the best possible color control with versatility in the use of opticals and titles; unfortunately, they take longer to do, cost more, pose more registration challenges, and use more physical medium. Because they contain no color dyes, it is believed that they have a longer life than color negatives, which fade with time. Therefore they are often used for archival protection.

When film-to-tape transfer is involved, it is usually preferred to transfer the OCN. If the OCN is not possible, then an IP or print from the OCN is the next preferred method. When an IP or print from the OCN is not possible, then an IN is used. Finally, the last method of choice is striking a print from an IN.

Video Editing and Postproduction

Video production, like film production, involves duplication of an original, only with video the duplication is an electronic process, not a physical one. The original is made using a high-quality format videotape. Often, screening copies of these original recordings are copied onto lower-cost media, for example ¾-inch videotape. There are now a number of pathways available to achieve the finished product.

Editing is the process of arranging the various shots into a certain order. In motion pictures, a continuous sequence of frames that describes or depicts an action is called a *take*; each take has a number, possibly a name, and a length expressed in frames. A ***head trim*** is the term used when a few frames are removed from the beginning, or head, of a shot. A head trim implies that the shot would slide forward, taking out the time in between. A ***tail trim*** is when a few frames are removed from the tail of a shot. A tail trim implies that the rest of the show behind the shot being trimmed is moved up. ***Extending the head*** means to add material in front of the head, pushing the show behind it backward. ***Extending the tail*** means to make the shot go longer and also to push the rest of the show backward.

A head trim can either trim and leave black in its place, or trim and tuck the show forward. Likewise, a tail trim can either trim and leave black, or trim and tuck the rest of the show forward. When extending the head, there are two possibilities: the tail of the previous scene can be written over, or the show behind the head can be pushed back. Likewise, when extending the tail, the head of the following shot can be written over, or the rest of the show can be pushed back. The implications of this play themselves out in how the editing is done.

The simplest way to edit video is an ***assembly edit***, in which the editor plays back a selected shot from the source tape on one video machine and copies it onto a destination, an edit tape being recorded on a second video machine. The process can continue for many source tapes, each being used to copy a shot to the edit tape. Eventually, the edit tape will contain a sequence of shots, edited back-to-back. To ensure that fields are recorded properly, the two machines must be genlocked.

One way that video editing is different than film editing is that because videotape cannot be physically cut, it is not possible to add or delete individual frames or scenes—that is, unless one is willing to duplicate the entire program up to the point of the change, make the changes, and then copy the balance of the show. This process produces excessive generational loss and degradation of quality, which has undesirable affects. Even the development of digital video machines in the 1980s did not completely fix the problem: They do provide a mechanism to copy endless generations of material, but it is still necessary to copy an entire show in order to add or delete a few frames—a very tedious process.

All of this radically changed with the introduction of the *non-linear editor* systems in the early 1990s. Non-linear editors utilize a computer, massive hard drives, and a video digitizer that enables the video to be captured and stored on the digital disk drive. As a result, shots are random-access material and may be assembled by a computer on the fly (see Figure 7.12) Trimming frames, adding frames, and moving scenes around are simple. No physical splicing (as with film) is necessary and no serial duplication (as with video) is required. Trimming and extending takes becomes a highly interactive process and is creatively enhanced.

Online editing refers to the use of (typically) three professional-quality video decks—two source decks and one destination deck—under the control of a computer, which manages them in a series of edits. The video may or may not be digital but it is stored

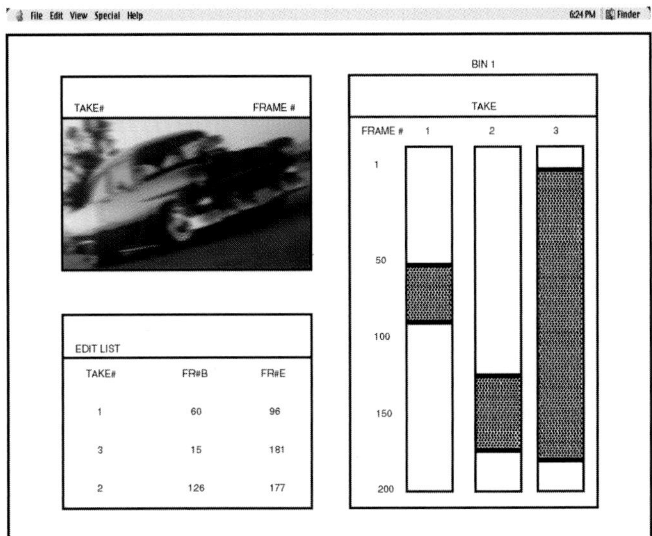

Figure 7.12 This virtual editing system shows the current frame plus the complete list of takes that make up a sequence in both graphic and alphanumeric form. The box at the right depicts three takes, each 200 frames long. In the lower left, an edit list specifies the order of the takes, and what frame numbers begin and end each take. The area at the top left allows the editor to preview the sequence of takes.

on tape. Some effects can only be done in online suites. With the advent of 3⁄4-inch tape (as far back as the 1970s), the concept of the *offline edit* suite emerged. In the offline scenario, the videotape is (initially) edited using 3⁄4-inch decks or some other inexpensive, low-quality technology; then, either the 3⁄4-inch product itself is used (especially common for creating newscasts), or an *edit list* was prepared (by the offline edit suite) that contains a description of the time codes for each of the scenes in the show—where they begin and end, and where they go onto the destination tape. The edit list can then be transferred to the computer that controls the online decks; the online decks automatically follow the edit list so as to conform the high quality of the tapes of the show automatically. Because some offline studios can only make cuts, or limited effects, the integration of titles, wipes, and effects such as repositioning are reserved for the online suite. Non-linear editors also play into this online/offline scenario. Some allow video to be digitized at full resolution and are able to integrate a very rich tableau of effects into the work. With these machines, the computer's output is simply directed back to videotape or to broadcast. Alternatively, if the video is low resolution, then an edit list is prepared and the high-resolution video is conformed in an online suite. The adept reader will observe that the offline non-linear editor may also be coupled with online HDTV tape decks, or it may be used to edit low-resolution digitized film, where the edit list that is produced is a guide for a person who actually cuts the original film negative. Most likely both the non-linear direct strategy and the non-linear offline/online conforming strategy will be around for quite sometime.

The final *edit master* containing all of the effects and titles is then used to strike third-generation copies, often in many formats (e.g., VHS), which are equivalent to release prints. In video, sound is usually adjacent to picture and copied with it, but it can be mixed separately.

Other Production Concerns

Hybrid productions—that is, those productions that involve film as well as tape—can work many ways. In a typical example, the original film negative is shot, processed, and transferred to video, where it is offline edited into a W/P. Upon approval, an edit list is prepared and the original film negative is conformed and release prints made. In another situation, original film negative may be shot, processed, and printed and a W/P assembled. Upon W/P approval, the OCN is transferred to tape, and an edited tape master is conformed to the W/P. The easiest way to do this is to transfer the W/P to tape also, which is used as the edit master, and record the good transfer on top of it.

HDTV television and digital scanning have sparked new thinking that goes beyond the typical shooting of a color negative at 30 frames/second and then transferring to create a one-to-one video hybrid. One strategy involves shooting in film, transferring to HDTV or digital files, editing and compositing the film electronically or in a computer, and then transferring the video or digital files back to film. Doing this with conventional NTSC produces a decidedly inferior quality of picture. But doing this with HDTV or digital imagery retains picture quality and provides a viable alternative to intermediate film formats such as IP/IN. The benefits of this approach include an ability to preview and see compositing effects in real time, simplifying the creation process.

The quality of third- or more generation release duplicates—film or tape—is a primary concern of production. Duplication, especially of analog media such as film or tape, where the signal is recopied, is problematic because aspects of the carrier are often replicated as information. Often it is more the quality of copies rather than the quality of the originals that differentiates an amateur medium from a professional medium. In the digital age, where duplicates are perfect copies of the originals, this distinction may become a forgotten problem.

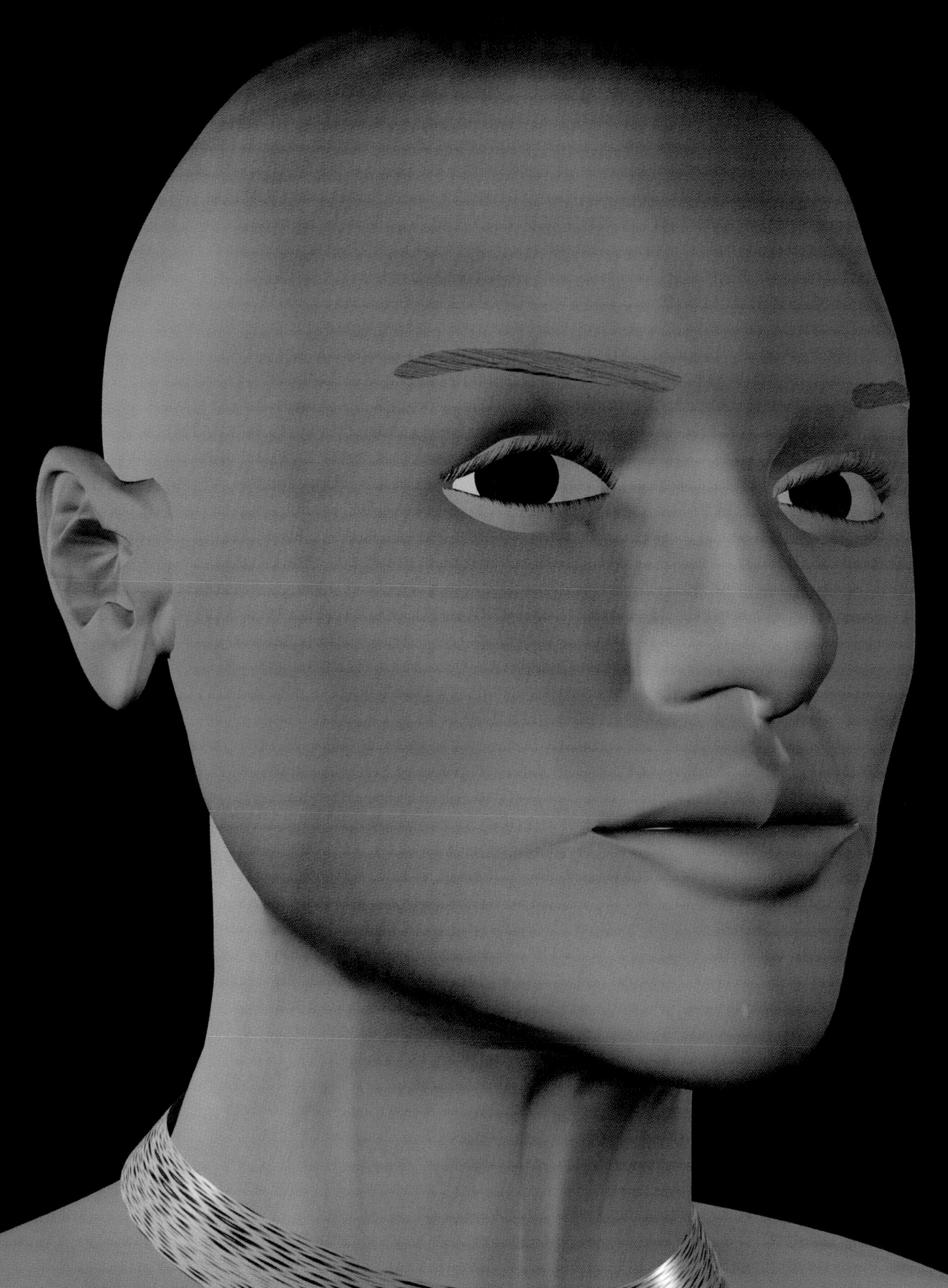

Animation Methods and Tools

It is important for animators to know the basic methods and tools of animation. A general knowledge will enable them to expand their skills and, therefore, expand the types of animation they can make. It will also enable them to interface more effectively with people who work in other parts of the animation process—for even today, many people are still using paper, pencil, and peg bar.

This chapter focuses on general animation methods and tools, such as fields and field guides, safeties, registration systems, and the animation stand. It also deals with a few issues of primitive action, including animating on twos, pan and scan, scaling, staggers, scratchons, and color table animation. These methods and tools apply to physical and virtual media. Many of them are dimensionally independent—that is, they can be applied to either 2D or 3D animation. This chapter also contains a section on 3D methods—some from the era of solid puppets, but most of them computational techniques. Before proceeding, it is worth noting that the in-depth discussion of *how* things move is left until Chapters 10, 11, and 12, which will present the fundamentals of easing, parametric motion, kinematics, and dynamics.

Fields and Field Guides

To direct animation, a system of ***fields*** is often employed. The animator's stage is the field—the 2D, usually rectangular, area where the image appears (see Figure 8.1). A field defines the boundary or perimeter of a frame and conforms to the aspect ratio of the medium

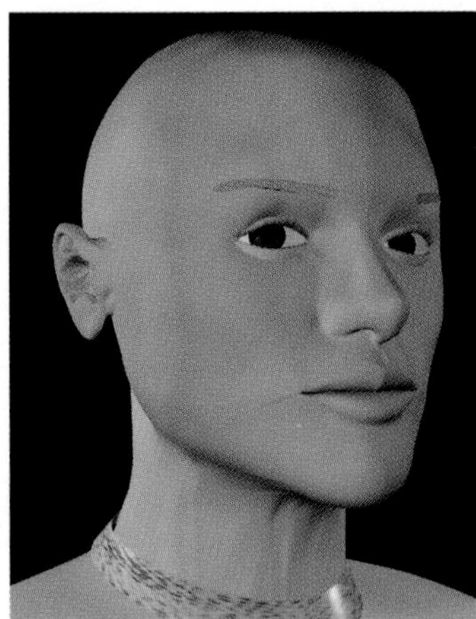

Above: Image courtesy of Gennady Blanket, copyright 2001.

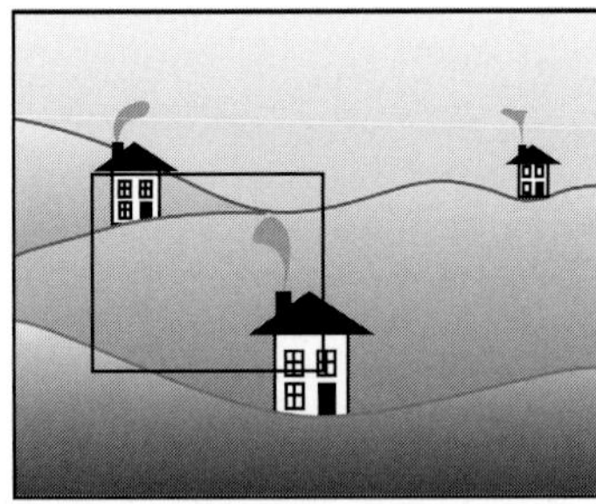

Figure 8.1 Above: A field defines the boundary of the frame.

being employed. It is the field of view, and it indicates what will be visible within the field of the recorded image and what will be outside of it. Essentially, the field defines the perimeter of the frame.

A *field guide,* also known as *panning guide,* is a reticle used to direct the position of artwork in the field of view. A field guide consists of a reticle grid, which may be toggled on or off over the top of the artwork or image (see Figure 8.2). In the real world, a field guide is referenced in terms of its actual size: a "12 field" is 12 inches left to right, a "10 field" is 10 inches, and so on; artwork is made a certain field size. In a mechanical environment, a field guide has punched holes similar to registration holes in artwork. These holes enable the guide to be registered on peg bars over the artwork, insuring that all material is aligned. Camera moves can then be empirically positioned, by using a field as a guide, and pan and zoom positions are noted. When the camera is in position, the field guide is removed and the shot is made.

Geometrically, the field guide's origin is at the center, and it is calibrated in decimal units, east-west and north-south. Field guides in the real world are transparent and calibrated in inches; in the computer, they may be calibrated in inches or pixels.

The area of the picture that is framed by the camera when a scene is shot is known as *field size* (see Figure 8.3). Field size is

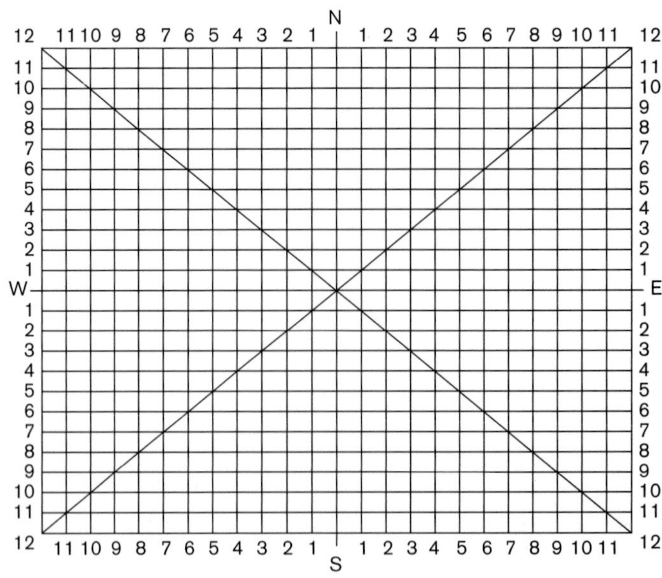

Figure 8.2 Right: Field guide. A 12 field is illustrated in the figure. In real-world practice, this field guide would be 12 inches. The field guide shown here is less than actual size, but all dimensions are in proportion to a film frame. Directionality is indicated as north (N), south (S), east (E), west (W).

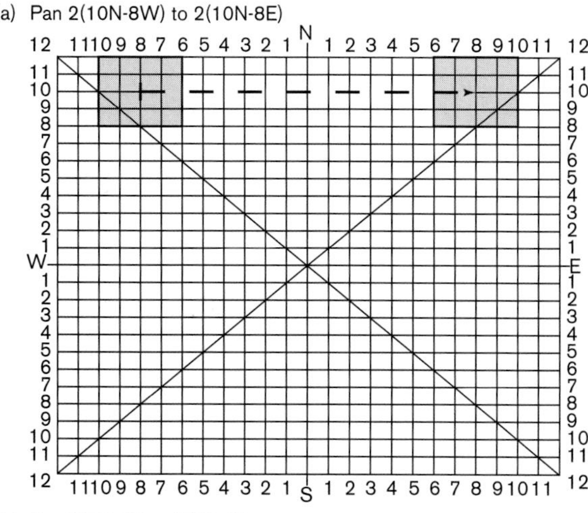

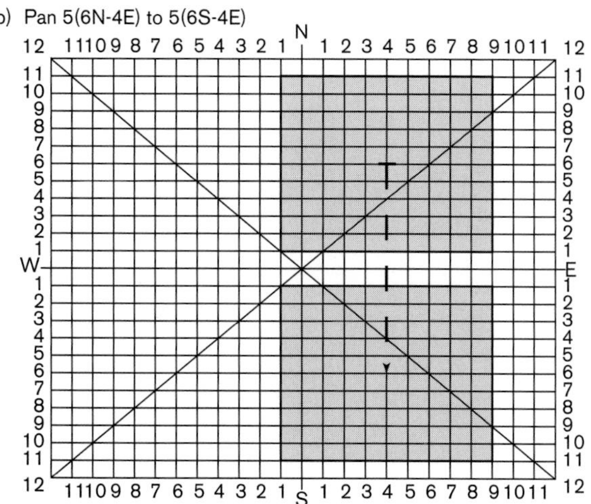

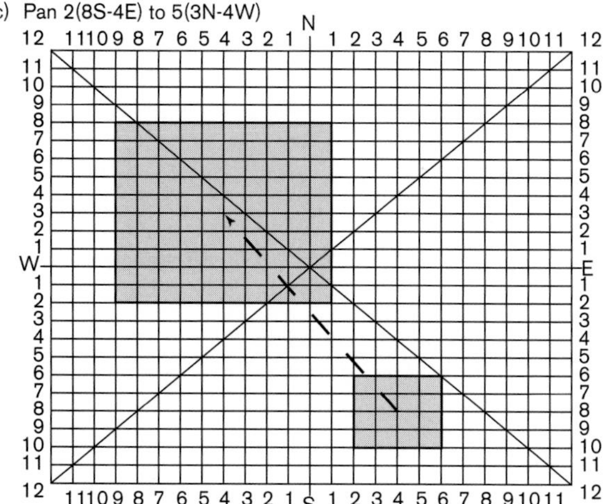

Figure 8.3 A field diagram showing a pan. In (a) the field size is 2 fields, which is what the camera is shooting. The initial position specification of 10N–8W indicates the location of the center of the field. The terminal field size is also 2, and the terminal position is 10N–8E. The syntax at the upper left indicates the full camera direction, but does not indicate duration. A vertical pan is depicted in (b); (c) depicts a shot that incorporates a pan in two axes, as well as a zoom-out.

indicated by a number that corresponds to the actual width of the field in inches. The field can be any size the animator chooses, but the standard sizes are 12 and 15 fields. A 12 field measures 12 inches from left to right, with a height approximately 8.75 inches from top to bottom. A 15 field measures 15 inches horizontally and is approximately 10.9 inches from top to bottom. A 4 field is 4 inches across and 3 inches high. Field sizes can, however, be as variable as the technical versatility of the camera being used. Some physical cameras can focus in as close as 2 inches wide and can pull back to more than 15 fields. Digitally, any field size can be used, even a 1 field, although it is common to employ a 10 field.

Since a field guide is a real physical guide, a 12 field is actually 12 inches wide. When photographing a 12 field onto a medium, such as 35mm film, it is still a 12 field, but it is no longer 12 inches wide; it is as wide as a piece of film. Similarly, if a 12 field is scanned into a computer, then it is still a 12 field, only it has dimensions in pixels. Therefore, when field guides are discussed with respect to image space, they are no longer referenced with respect to their real-world dimensions.

Fielding is a textual notation system for directing action on the 2D plane (see again Figure 8.3). Fielding instructions direct the animation in terms of platen *x* and *y* scroll and camera zoom positions. Since fields need not be centered at the origin of the artwork, fielding instructions tell the camera operator where to place the camera for each shot and where to move to. It is left to the camera operator (or a computer) to calculate the in-between shots.

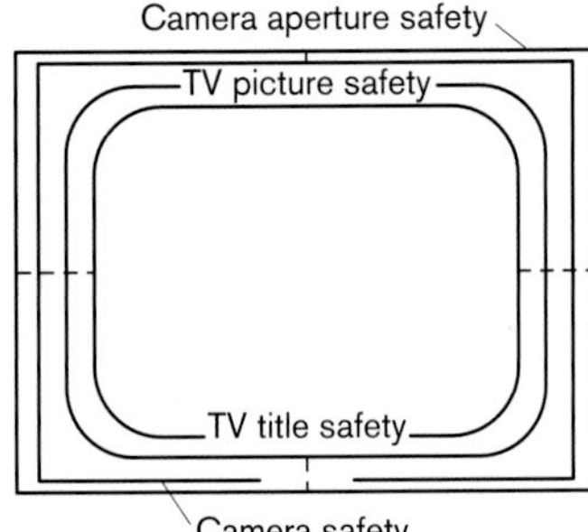

Figure 8.4 In film and video there are several safeties, each a different size, and sometimes with different aspect ratios. The outermost line (FULL) is the camera aperture safety. The next innermost line (CAMERA) is the camera safety. The third inner line is the projector safety. The innermost line is the TV title safety, a region that lies well inside the TV transmitted area to insure that even the most poorly aligned television will be able to display the image; it also accommodates for the rounded box that houses the television tube and obscures edges and corners. In film, the first three safeties are defined as part of the SMPTE standard. TV title safety is typically 70% to 80% of the camera aperture safety.

Safeties

Safeties are areas within the field of view that designate areas that are "safe" with respect to certain target media (see Figure 8.4). By safe it is meant that there is a chance that the target media may crop off part of the field and, should this happen, the material within the safety region will probably still be visible when displayed. For example, even if a television is poorly aligned, the text and action being displayed within the TV title safety area will be visible, whereas content outside this special region may not be. Hence, when designing titles and credits for television, designers need to know the boundaries of the TV title safety.

Essentially, the purpose of a safety is to acknowledge that the tolerances of equipment may not be exact and to allow for error. Not all safeties are equal, and some are more critical than others.

Registration Systems

Frame-to-frame registration is of paramount importance in animation and is achieved by registering everything—the drawings, the camera, the film, the projector, and any intermediate media in the process (IP, IN, ATD, DTA, as described in Chapter 7). ***Registration***—that is, the *x-y* alignment of one frame to another—may be accomplished mechanically, electronically, and optically.

Mechanical Registration

Mechanical registration systems typically use punched holes. For example, registration in traditional animation is achieved when the artwork is punched along the edges, with either ***Oxberry holes*** (East Coast) or ***Acme holes*** (West Coast), and mounted, or ***pegged***, onto registration peg bars (see Figure 8.5). ***Registration peg bars,*** or simply ***peg bars,*** are used to mount (and thus position) all materials in registration with each other and with the camera. Unfortunately, holes punched in paper wear out after several uses and tend to lose alignment with repeated repegging or movement. Registration with respect to the recording medium—for example, 35mm film—is more difficult, primarily due to the fact that the area of a frame of film is about 70 times smaller than the area of typical artwork, and it is at varying times both in motion and intermittently paused. The solution to medium registration requires standardization with strict tolerances so that the ***registration holes***, also known as ***perforation holes*** or ***perf holes***, in the film match exactly to mechanical ***registration pins*** in the camera shuttle (see Figure 8.6). This makes the photographed image steady, eliminates weave, and paves the way for more sophisticated special effects involving multiple exposures, since repeated exposures of one piece of film or composite exposures from many pieces of film can all be aligned.

In film, there are actually two kinds of perf holes: ***camera perfs***, also called ***Bell & Howell perfs,*** and ***projection perfs***, also called ***Kodak perfs.*** Intermediary equipment, such as optical printers, use

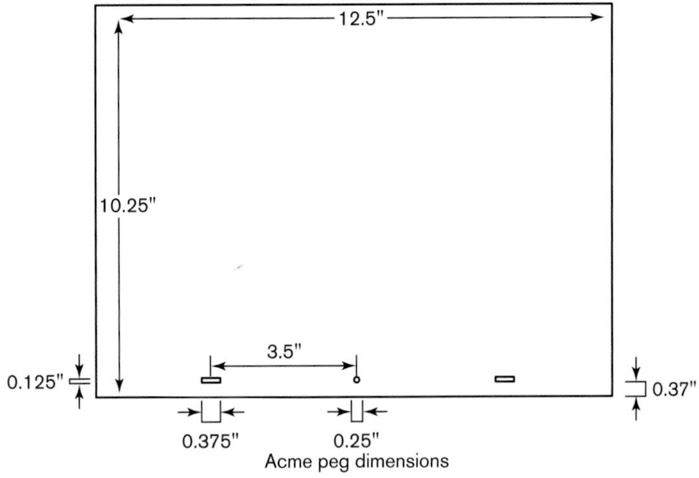

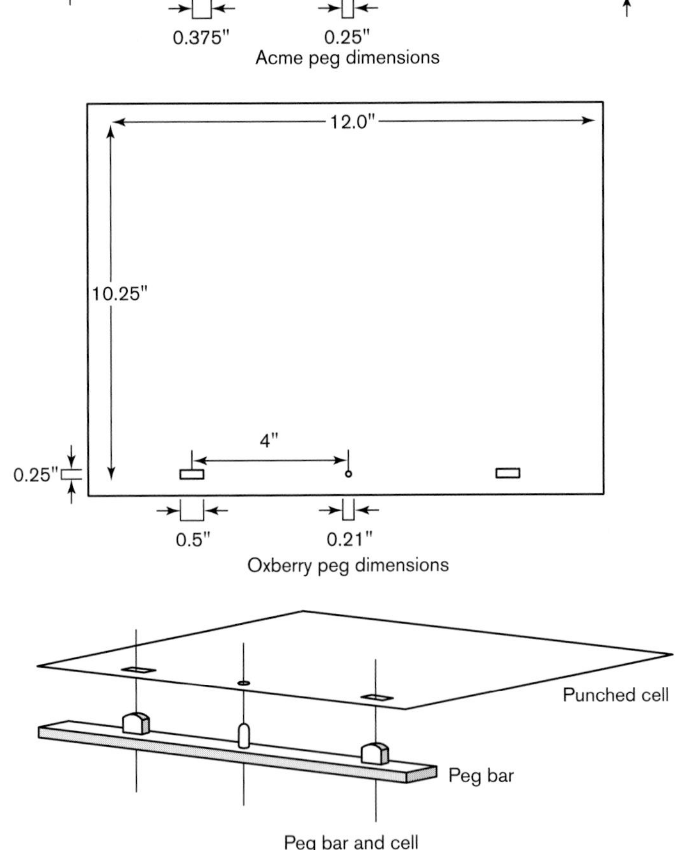

Figure 8.5 Peg bar and punch holes. Two different systems are illustrated: Oxberry and Acme. Note that the paper and peg dimensions are slightly different; the hole is narrower (to give the paper a good grip) and slightly wider (to let air pass during pegging). In practice the pegs also have curved tops, as you can see in the schematic at the bottom. Additional pegs and holes can be added for wide artwork.

the Bell & Howell perfs. The difference is that the Bell & Howell perf is an exact-fitting perf, tailored toward registration and slower-moving film. The Kodak perf has lower tolerances and is able to run in claw-type projectors. It may also be a little more reliable.

It is important to observe that the registration of a moving picture system is really no better than the registration of the system as a whole. Registration must travel from the camera, to film, to the optical printer, to the internegative, to the projection print, to the projector, and to the screen. Although each frame remains sharp, together these systems accumulatively degrade registration quality and allow individual images to drift left-right-up-down so that by the time they get to the screen, they are minutely off-center from each other. Since resolution involves flicker fusion, the fidelity declines. An argument presented by the HDTV community is that film as a system really only has a perceived resolution of 1000 or 2000 scan lines, due to the degradation that occurs as a result of cumulative small errors of registration culminating with the wiggle in the projector. Simply put, the perceived resolution as a whole is the product of the resolution of the weakest parts of the process.

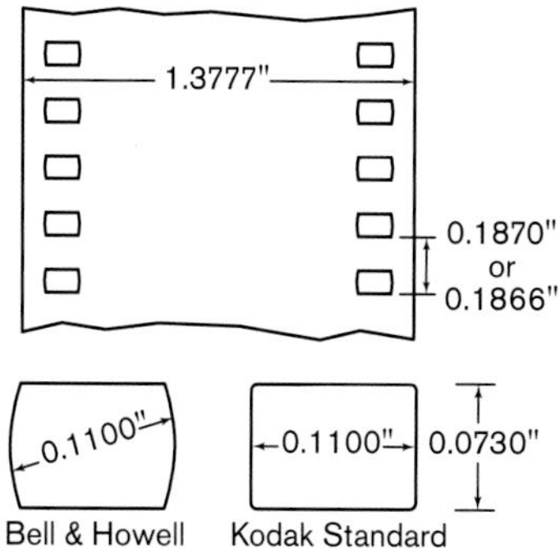

Figure 8.6 Dimensions of 35mm film and two kinds of perforation holes. Perf holes are found in many kinds of roll media, including paper tape and movie film. In 35mm film there are two major types: the Bell & Howell perf used in negative and intermediate stocks, and the Kodak Standard perf used in prints that are projected. The difference is that the Bell & Howell perf is designed to hold registration, whereas the Kodak Standard perf is optimized for repeated projection at higher speed. Stock is also manufactured in two different pitches, that is the distance from one perf hole to the next. The shorter pitch (0.1866 inch) is found in negative stocks, the longer pitch is used for release prints and is an artifact of how printing machines are threaded. In 16mm film (not shown here), there is only one kind of perf hole.

Electronic Registration

Registration must also be designed into electronic systems such as video. Horizontal and vertical sync in faxes and video provide fundamental registration. Misregistration occurs as these frequencies drift. Video is sometimes erroneously edited on fields instead of frames. Loss of synchronization can produce roll bars, partial frames, small *x*-axis shifts, and changes in color.

Optical Registration

Optical registration usually employs visual registration markers, such as a bull's-eye or crosshair (see Figure 8.7). These markers ensure precise visual alignment and also provide evidence of any deformation of the medium—for example, shrinkage of film. In computer graphics, registration marks (as well as safeties) are often carried on a channel separate from the image and thus may be toggled on and off.

The Animation Stand

One of the primary ways of capturing a sequence of images is through the use of an ***animation stand*** (see Figure 8.8), a machine onto which the artwork is fastened, moved on calibrated scales, and photographed (recorded, digitized). The animation stand consists of

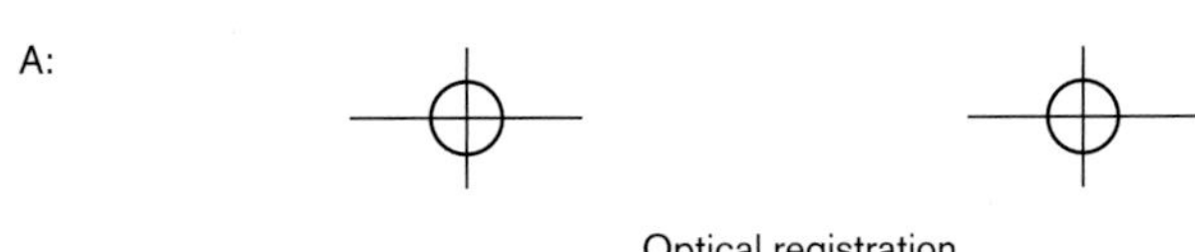

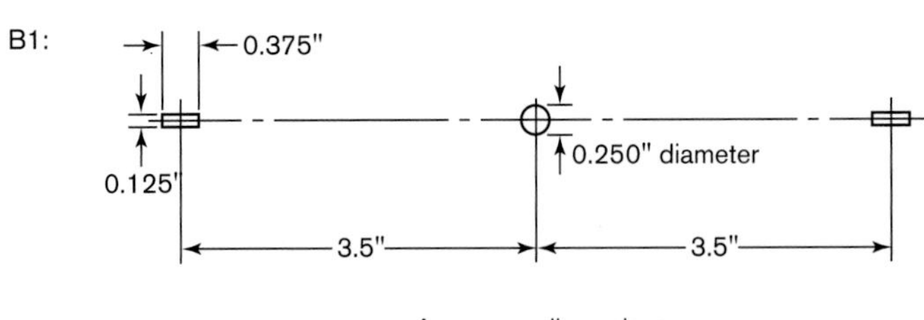

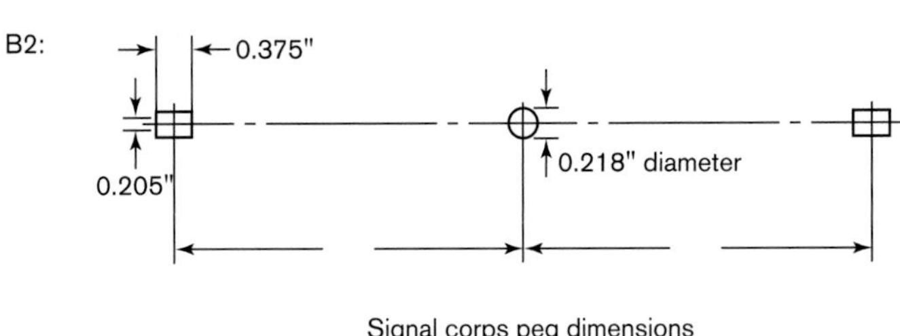

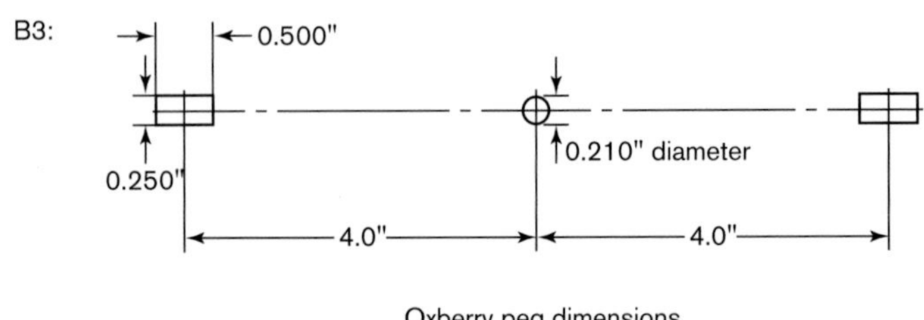

Figure 8.7 Bull's-eyes provide a method to visually align artwork. They need to be placed as far apart as possible—often in the four corners—to ensure optimal alignment.

several parts, including a camera mounted on a column and usually shooting downward, a compound table, and a platen. The resulting arrangement can be used to photograph 2D art or models, in a repeatable fashion.

The *compound table,* also referred to as simply the *table*, is a mechanical apparatus that lies below (or ahead of) the camera (see again Figure 8.8). The compound table usually consists of several parts, depending upon its level of sophistication. First, it can pan and tilt—that is, move in *x* and *y*. Next, a compound table might include

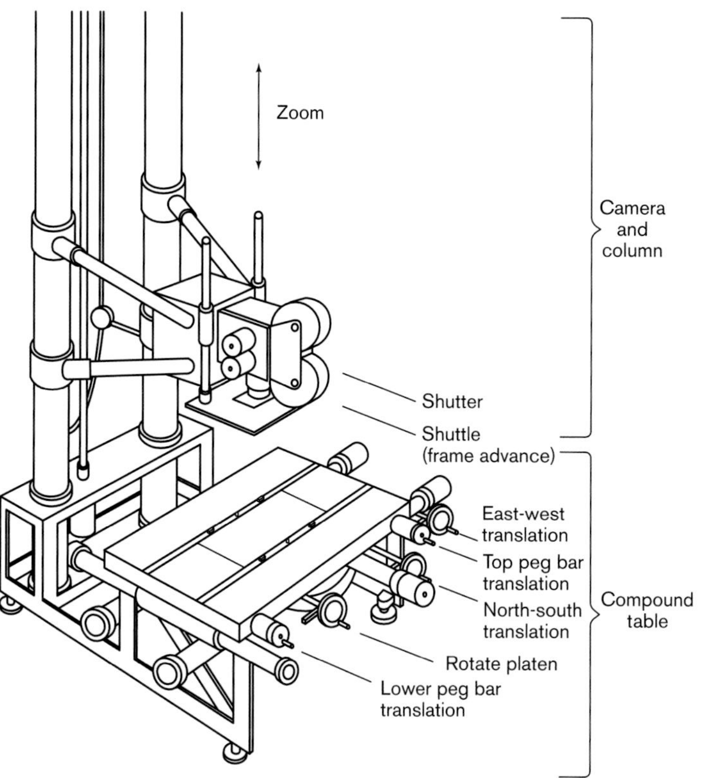

Figure 8.8 Animation stand. Five cranks along the front of the compound table allow five degrees of freedom independent of any movement by the camera on the up-down axis. The cranks on the front of the compound table allow it to be translated east-west (x), or north-south (y), and the table may rotate (z-axis); the two traveling peg bars mounted in the compound table translate east-west (x) relative to the table and are subservient to (nested inside and applied to the artwork data before) any global transformations of the table itself. One control on the column raises and lowers the camera. The camera contains a shuttle (which can advance frames forward or backward), a variable shutter (which allows one to make dissolves), an aperture (to control f-stop), and focus.

two registration peg bars—one above the shooting area and one below the shooting area—that can move relative to the table. This positioning, which insures that all visual material is aligned within the film frame, is extremely important if the resulting animation is to portray convincing motion.

The compound table just described has four degrees of freedom—the table may move right, left, up, and down (east-west, north-south); the top peg bar may move east or west; the bottom peg bar may move east or west. Therefore, the degrees of freedom are x translation on the table, y translation on the table, x translation on the top peg bar, x translation on the bottom peg bar. Some tables can also rotate, adding a fifth degree of freedom. Usually, the table does not move in the direction away from the camera, although some tables are equipped to do so. In most cases, however, the camera may move away from the table, adding another degree of freedom, called *zoom* (not to be confused with a zoom lens, where the focal length is changed). Certain animation stands also have an

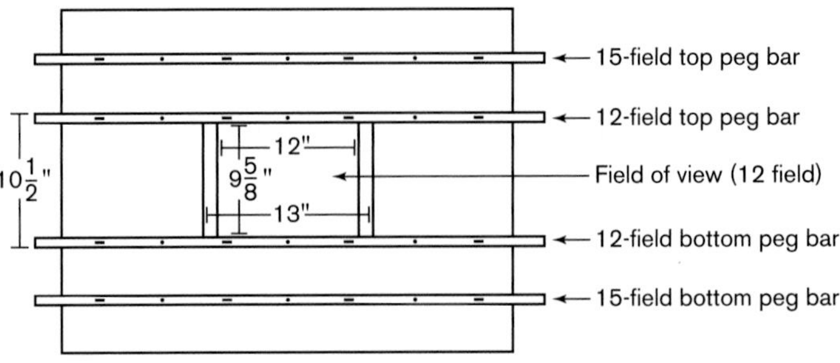

Figure 8.9 A platen viewed from above. A table light is located in the center; it is slightly wider than a 12 field; the top of the light table is flush with the table top and it is slightly wider than the field of view. Two pairs of traveling peg bars fit into the platen and allow the background and different cel layers to be moved independently. One pair is positioned to hold artwork that is drawn on a 12 field, and a second pair, farther from the center, can position artwork on a 15 field. Missing from the drawing is a glass plate, which may be used to cover and press down on the artwork so as to keep it flat and minimize flares.

ability to do gimbal or flip moves, that is, the ability to rotate the compound table and any flat art or model in yaw, pitch, and roll. (Gimbals, as well as more complex camera rigs, are discussed in Chapter 4.)

The *platen* is the part of the compound table upon which artwork is fastened. The platen usually consists of a flat plate and a sheet of glass with a handle, and is usually parallel to the ground (see Figure 8.9). The handle is used to raise the glass so that the artwork can be placed underneath the glass and pressed flat. Some platens have vacuum backs to help keep work flat. The platen can also exist in other forms; however it is constructed, it is thought to be the part of the table that holds the artwork. To insure consistent lighting, the animation stand is usually equipped with two side lamps to light from above, as well as a back lamp, which allows light to come from below.

The platen is generally set up with 12-field peg bars; the pegs are in a fixed position in relation to the center of the table. When the table is in its home position, that is, its zero position, the center of the table and the center of the camera are aligned. The 12 field is the largest field able to be photographed in this position; any larger will cause the peg bars to be visible in the field being photographed. In the platen depicted in the figure, the 12-field peg bars can be removed and replaced with 15-field peg bars in order to record larger artwork.

Manual animation stand practice dictates that the camera operator crank the stand to each extreme position, log the positions, calculate eases (as discussed in Chapter 10), and then use this produced table of positions to shoot each frame. A *computer-controlled animation stand* is an animation stand fitted with motors that are computer controlled (see Figure 8.10). The computerization of the stand brings all of its degrees of freedom under formal command-control. These include x and y translation, rotation, zoom, frame advance/reverse, and shutter angle. Readouts on the stand, whether

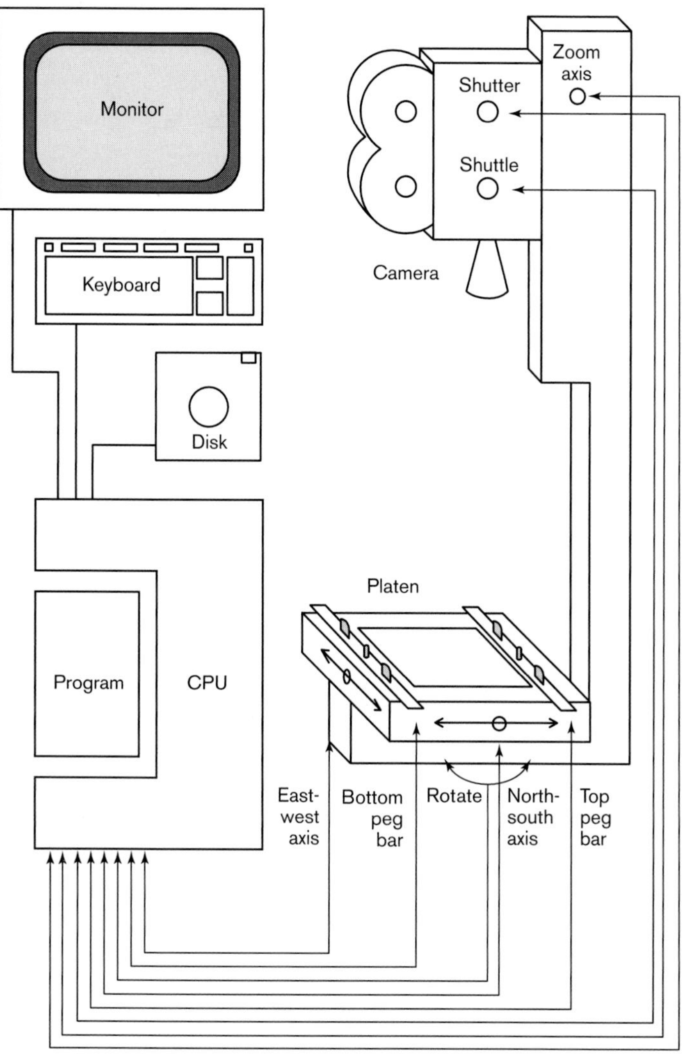

Figure 8.10 A computerized animation stand. In a minimal system, a computer-controlled animation stand consists of a computer attached to an animation stand consisting of a platen and a column. Most systems are equipped with a digital output device such as a disk drive.

they are physical scales or electronic number displays, correspond to the coordinate system of the commands entered by the operator.

On computer-controlled animation stands, the fielding positions are entered numerically or determined empirically by placing the platen, and the in-between positions are calculated by the computer. It is significant to note that the empirical positions can be edited, that new positions can be merged in and existing positions removed; timings may also be edited.

To photograph a sequence, the operator composes a series of commands, possibly incorporating some saved data positions; the computer interprets the commands and outputs a sequence of increments, which are sent to an input/output (I/O) port where they are translated into electrical signals that rotate motors. If need be, the commands and their corresponding actions may be previewed before actually shooting film.

The stand can be calibrated in either real or virtual inches, and the accuracy of a typical stand is about 0.001 inch. The shutter can be numerically calibrated to facilitate in-camera dissolves and fades. The accuracy needed to do repeatable work is significantly increased with a computer-controlled animation stand.

The computerization of simple animation equipment expands the productivity of the camera operator. Although human error is still a factor, once the cause of an error is discovered, it can be repaired without another error slipping in somewhere else during a reshoot. Also, one can shoot tests easily, encouraging more previewing and fine-tuning.

Computerized animation equipment can also be used to perform calculations, particularly fades, dissolves, and eases. Motions can be defined by their extreme positions, and the computer can calculate the intermediate positions for pans, tilts, rotations, zooms, and traveling peg bars and position the mechanics accordingly. Skip framing, double frames, holds, and fades of any length become trivial because of precise shutter control. The filming of cyclic action is also simplified. This approach dramatically reduces handling and extends the life of the artwork.

Analytical checks may be performed to determine where there may be problems—for example, to see if movement rates will produce strobe effects; if so, the computer can send back a suggestion to change the speed. Boundary conditions may also be verified, and actions, such as trying to move the camera through the floor, are restrained. The software can also alert the camera operator when the production rig is being mistakenly included in the photograph. The polite system also warns the camera operator if the shutter is closed or if the camera is set to shoot backward.

Cutouts and the Slash System

One advantage of using registration during the animation process is that individual drawings can be decomposed into static and moving parts, which can be handled independently. A simple example of this approach employs the use of ***cutouts,*** paper drawings laid overtop a background and incrementally moved and photographed (see Figure 8.11). This system is efficient because the entire image is not redrawn for each frame; in addition, the image is steady. In computer practice, the "cutout" is simply an object with an *x y* location in front of a 2D background. (This approach is discussed in greater detail in the next chapter under cel systems.)

Another example of the benefits of registration can be seen in the ***slash system,*** an animation strategy in which scenes are printed en masse on translucent paper (see Figure 8.12). The part of the field that contains changing action is "slashed out" with a razor blade and the paper laid overtop a clean sheet, onto which the changing action is drawn. The pair of drawings is then shot together. The cutout and the slash system reduce work because the entire scene is not redrawn every frame; furthermore, the line quality is stable, since the unchanging lines are the same on each printed sheet.

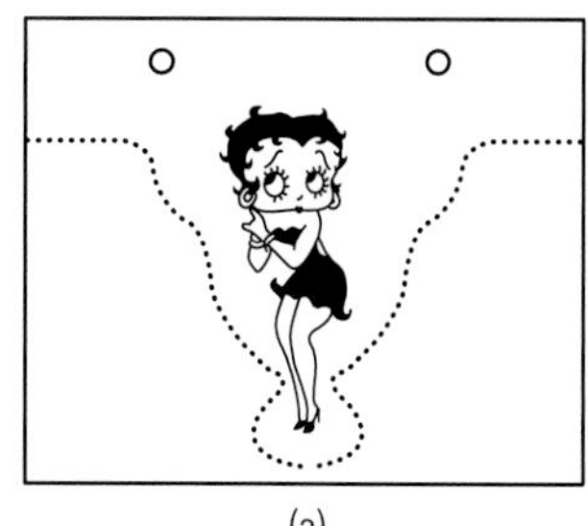

(a)

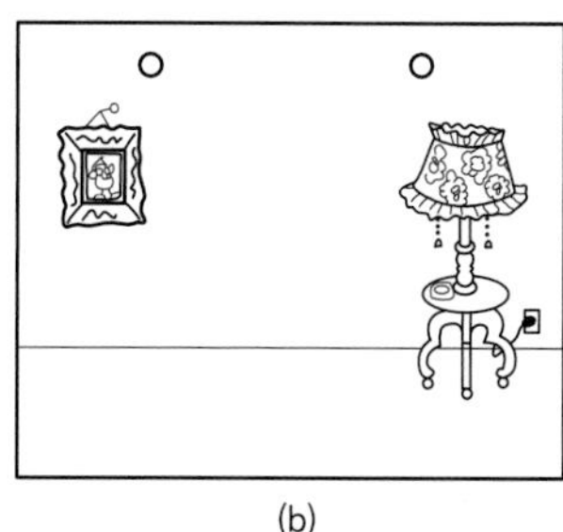

(b)

(c)

Figure 8.11 Cutouts, also known as the *decoupage system.* The moving part of the image (a) is cut out of the whole sheet along the dotted line and laid overtop a static background (b) and photographed (c). Nature performs hidden surface removal. Only that part of the image that moves is redrawn and cut out for each frame. Cutouts are not necessarily attached to a peg bar, but if they are free-floating, they do need some kind of movement guide. Some historians also call what is shown in this drawing the slash system—its only difference is that here the moving action is physically in front of the static. The reader is cautioned that the selection of Betty Boop to illustrate this technology may be placing her into a technology that is before her time.

Pan and Scan: Zooms, Pans, Spins

Basic camera movements can also be used as basic animation methods. The zoom is used to establish a shot, to serve as a transition between a long shot and a relatively closer shot, and to bring the viewer to a close look at the subject at hand. Zooms that end with a very close-up shot increase the dramatic impact of ordinary scenes, hence, they are often used when promoting a product. Regardless of why a zoom is used, the precise movement must be determined and calibrated before the shot is recorded.

Pan and scan animation, also known as ***photo montage,*** uses north-south, east-west motions, often coupled with zooms, when shooting flat stationary artwork (see Figure 8.13). It imparts a sense of movement to photographs and paintings and directs the eye of the viewer. This method employs the compound table, which has the ability to perform various incremental moves in relation to the camera. Start and end positions of the move are indicated, using fielding notation, along with the path of action, if it is not linear. The total timing of the move, expressed in seconds or frames, with notations of eases and holds, is marked. When very complicated paths of action

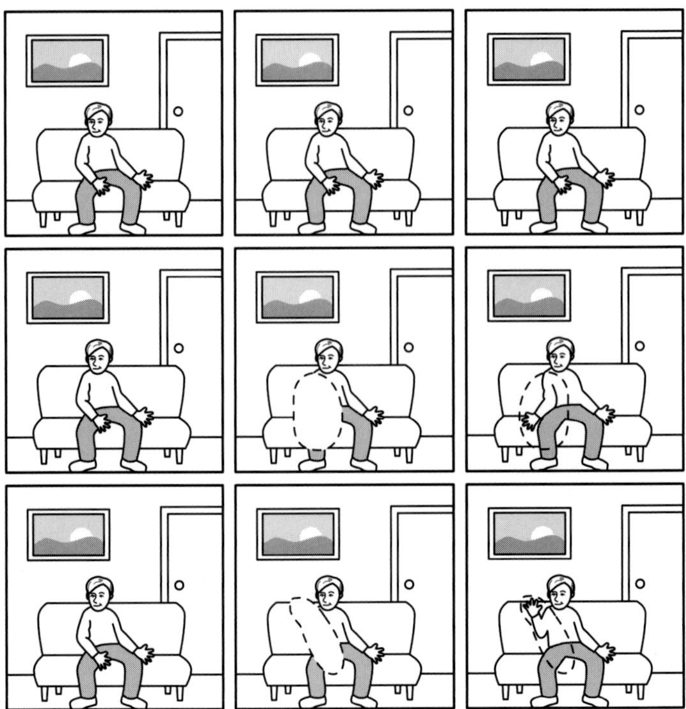

Figure 8.12 The slash system (also known as the *slash and tear system*) begins with identical drawings that have been printed onto paper and pegged. The figure shows three successive frames. Whenever action occurs, the drawing is torn away (leaving a hole in the paper) and laid over top a clean sheet of paper, and the area inside the hole is drawn in. This approach is the opposite of the cutout because the static action is laid on top of the changing element, rather than laying the changing element on top of the background. This setup is useful when the changing element wants to go behind things.

are required, with specific timings at key points, a drawing—with incremental markings—is made of each path.

The production of pan and scan animation depends on accurate control of the movement of the camera and the artwork. Which movements should be assigned to the camera and which should be assigned to the artwork? When moving a physical camera, minor alignment errors are greatly magnified when viewed. Therefore, high-quality equipment usually confines camera movement to vertical movement and relegates all horizontal movement to the compound table. This strategy provides great latitude in mechanical design and creates three axes of camera direction. Digital systems, of course, have different types of problems than mechanical systems, a main one being the pixel resolution of the artwork and how big it can become. But the animator must still decide which movements should be assigned to the camera and which should be assigned to the artwork.

Pan and scan animation allows for very controlled, smooth movement of artwork. Unfortunately, because each frame being photographed is of equally crisp focus, fast moves are subject to unwanted strobing and chattering. This side effect is most prevalent

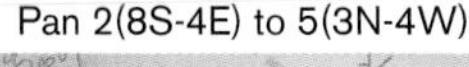

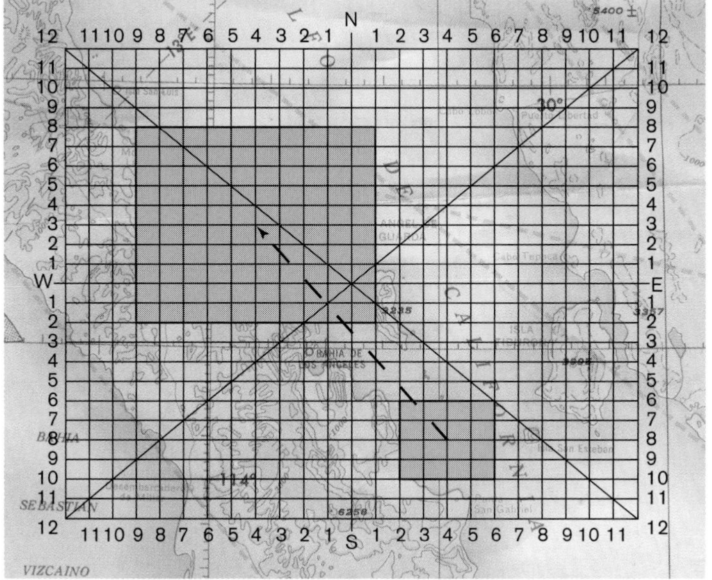

Figure 8.13 Left: Pan and scan animation. Panning the compound table while zooming is a common technique to breath life into static art—be it a push-in to one person in a group photo, or a pullback and horizontal movement on a map to imply travel. Compare to Figure 8.3(c).

Figure 8.14 Above: Staggers. Two extreme positions of this character are animated back and forth on ones. The images fail to create flicker fusion, so the viewer tends to see the images as vibrating and in both places at once.

when the artwork is perpendicular to the direction of the move. To eliminate the effect, it is best to move no faster than six and one half seconds for one full field of action, in any direction. It is possible to modify the strobe by creating a blur—keeping the shutter open as the move is executed, thereby simulating the kind of result that occurs normally in live-action photography. When shooting pan and scan onto video, it is desirable to move the table and camera in real time.

Scaling

Depending on the animation being made, artwork often needs to be *scaled*—that is, made larger or smaller—to achieve the desired animated results. When the artwork is physical, the effect of scaling can be achieved by zooming into the artwork or by drawing the artwork at the desired scale. When the images exist in a digital form, the answer can be a bit more complicated.

There are several ways to scale a digital image. In a computer animation, where all the frames are first created in non–real time and then stored and recorded to a playback medium, scaling is achieved during the creation process through the appropriate use of software tools. Vector-based art can be scaled continuously, but pixel-based art has limits—if it is scaled too big, the pixels become visible. In a situation such as a computer game, however, the images are determined and presented in real time, and hence can not necessarily be created in non–real time. Consider a computer game that might take place in an outdoor scene: as clouds move toward the player, the clouds get bigger, that is, they get scaled larger.

Scaling larger in real-time animation is a problem because the larger version of an image has more picture information than a smaller version, but where does the additional information come from when the image is scaled? One solution is to create all necessary animation frames at the time the animation is being created; all of the frames can be stored digitally. While this is a valid approach, it does, however, consume a lot of memory. A second possibility is to store only the largest frame for each scaled picture; when the smaller versions of the frames are needed for display, they can be calculated by sampling down the largest frame, that is, creating a new frame from the large frame by removing pixels. While this approach is also valid, it is time-consuming and therefore not appropriate for every real-time situation. A third possibility is to use custom-designed procedures for designing and displaying objects, at the right scale, on the fly. As CPUs get faster, this is more often the solution.

Animating on Twos

In the early days of animation, each frame was completely redrawn, even if several frames shared common imagery. Today, with some animation, especially computer animation, this approach is still in use. Because this approach is extremely time-consuming, however, techniques have been developed to reduce the required time both in manual and computerized systems.

One way to economize is to record each frame twice, thus recording half as many frames. In fact, animation can be made on ones, twos, threes, or whatever. When an animation is made *on ones,* the animation contains a different drawing on each frame. When an animation is made *on twos,* each frame is repeated twice—frame 1 and frame 2 each have the first drawing of the animation; frame 3 and frame 4 each have the next drawing of the animation, and so on. When shooting twos in film, the film runs at 24 frames/second and there are 12 unique frames. In NTSC video, these numbers are 30 and 15. Similarly, when an animation is made *on threes,* frame one, two, and three each have the first drawing of the animation. In many situations, the illusion of motion is almost the same whether an animation is made on ones or twos, and since animating on twos requires half the number of drawings, much animation is made on twos. There are situations, however, where animating on threes is possible, and situations where animating on ones is preferred, if not more correct.

The basis behind this discussion is largely the speed at which objects move in the field of view. The greater the distance traveled (rotated, scaled), the greater the need to animate each frame individually. Persistence of vision plays a role here also, and the eye readily accepts actions on twos as continuous, whereas action on threes may appear jumpy. Remember also that persistence of vision is affected by the number of times a frame is flashed on the screen, the brightness of light, steady registration, and other factors.

Staggers

What makes animation great is often the attention paid to details. A *stagger* is a two- (or three-) frame cycle that runs on ones and that looks to the eye like it is vibrating back and forth. For example, when one character hits another character in the nose, the appeal of the action is a result of what happens to the character once he is hit. Staggers are a way to exaggerate the action; the object of the action vibrates in response to the action (see Figure 8.14). Thus, in the figure, the use of a stagger would mean that the character's head would vibrate back and forth in response to the hit. In some regard, it is a completely a trick of the medium—staggers do not occur in real life.

Color Table Animation

Color table animation, also called *palette animation,* one of the simplest 2D computer animation techniques, creates the illusion of motion by changing the colors in an image in a regular fashion. It is a very low-tech approach to computer animation, yet it is often completely satisfactory for certain applications, such as news graphics, video games, and the Internet. Color table animation creates action by sequentially illuminating spaces that are positionally predefined, just as a theater marquee creates the illusion of motion by turning light bulbs on and off in a sequential order.

When using color table animation, the actual objects in the scene do not move. Rather, the area intended for animation is colored in such a way that when the colors are automatically changed by the animation software, the results appear to be moving or sparkling. For example, on a local news weather map, there may be an animated sequence to indicate the path of a weather system (see Figure 8.15). At close inspection, the weather path can be seen as a strip made of stripes of similar hue, possibly with darker hues at the head of the path and lighter hues at the tail. Starting at the head of the path, color table animation software will systematically change, or flip, the color of each stripe so that it becomes the color of the stripe just behind it. The software will repeat this process until directed to stop. Often the color of the animated area is arranged so that the sequence of colors is relatively short and repeated many times, for example, very dark blue, followed by blue, followed by light blue, followed by very light blue, followed by very dark blue, followed by blue, followed by light blue, followed by very light blue, and so on. This sequence is repeated throughout the strip, from head to tail. When the colors are flipped, the result is the illusion of a continuously moving blue strip.

Color table animation is related to the idea of painting-by-number. An object in the scene to be animated is assigned a color number, which corresponds to a color in a color table. The different positions of the object (for successive frames) are assigned successive color numbers; each number corresponds to a different color in the color table. The illusion of motion is achieved by modifying the contents of the color table, that is, by changing the color associated with each color number. Since the color table is used by the computer to determine which colors to display on the screen, modification of the color table modifies the colors on the screen. Practically speaking, the color table can be modified very quickly, and therefore color table animation can be used to create animation in real time.

While color table animation is rather limited, it can be used to animate simple changes to an object or scene, such as different times of day, different seasons, and different weather. When the scene is a sunny afternoon scene, the table is loaded with colors that reflect the desired results. When the weather is stormy, a stormy palette is loaded into the color table. When the desired effect is to show a sunny day turning stormy, the sunny palette is loaded first, then the

	R	G	B
0	150	150	255
1	0	0	255
2	50	50	255
3	100	100	255
4	150	150	255
5	0	0	255
6	50	50	255

	R	G	B
0	0	0	255
1	50	50	255
2	100	100	255
3	150	150	255
4	0	0	255
5	50	50	255
6	100	100	255

	R	G	B
0	50	50	255
1	100	100	255
2	150	150	255
3	0	0	255
4	50	50	255
5	100	100	255
6	150	150	255

Figure 8.15 Color table animation. A colored line marks the edge of a moving high-pressure system on this weather map. Screen action (left) and a seven-row color look-up table (right) depict three successive animation frames. Between each frame, each row in the look-up table is translated one row up, in a loop. The design and format of the objects, and in particular their color-by-number assignments, set up the animation. Because the computation only involves the table and not the objects, it can be completed quickly. The effect on the screen is the ribbon flowing upward.

palette is gradually changed, one color at a time, until the stormy palette is completely loaded. Since computers represent colors as numbers, the transition from sunny to stormy can be easily calculated with a simple program.

Scratchon

A *scratchon* is a type of animation created with a method that goes back to the early days of classic animation. When using the original

Figure 8.16 Right: Scratchon. Single-frame photography of a progressive blackboard scratchon drawing was used to make J. Stuart Blackton's *Humorous Phases of Funny Face* in 1907.

Figure 8.17 Opposite: Scratchon. The scene depicts a furnace tumbling into place while the lines are drawn on. To improve visibility, glowing dots are added to the head of the line currently being drawn. Once the wire frame is established, a second effect transits the wire frame to a solid view. Computer scratchons presume the preexistence of an image database and a procedure that can draw successively greater percentages of the database, in successive frames.

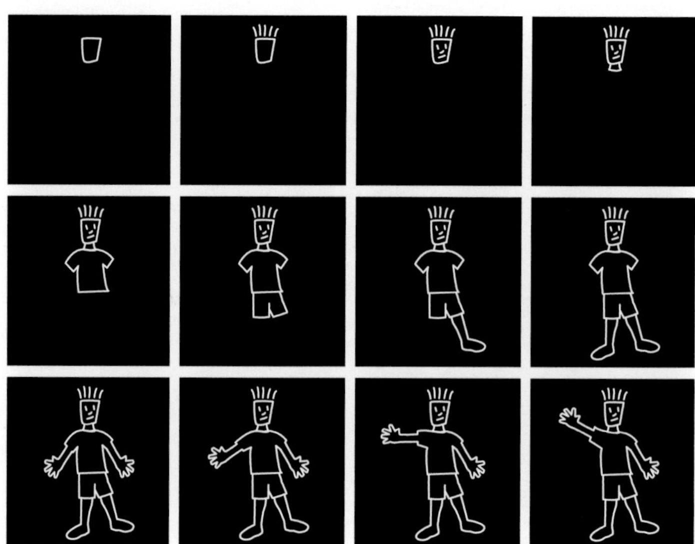

method, the animator draws the animation, often using chalk, on a blackboard. As each new part of the drawing is created, the entire drawing is recorded onto a frame of film (see Figure 8.16). Once the drawing is complete, it is then modified, and re-recorded after each new modification. For example, the artwork might consist of a background and character. As the background is drawn, it is recorded. Then the character is added, and recorded. When the basic artwork is done, the character's legs might be modified and recorded, creating the illusion of the character walking. The resulting effect connotes the process of something coming into being.

The inverse approach of this process can be applied to flat art: the final drawing can be covered with black tape and the tape removed, one piece at a time, as the frames are shot in reverse order. This creates an action that reveals, or establishes, the object.

While animators are no longer using chalk and blackboards, the visual language of a scratchon is still in use today, especially in 3D computer-animated commercials. Figure 8.17 shows a scratchon used to advertise a furnace. The scratchon can involve a linear drawing or a solid shape. Here, a wire-frame furnace is drawn onto the screen to simulate the effect of being drawn by a computer. To make this type of scratchon possible, a computer program breaks the lines or shape into small fragments; each fragment is drawn to the screen according to a predefined algorithm. The results can appear either random or choreographed in some way.

Shape Deformation

Shape deformation is a technique for changing the shape of objects; it is a primitive operation in which the individual points of one object interpolate to individual points of a second object. Examples include deforming a keyhole into a circle (see Figure 8.18) and deforming a soda bottle into a runner. As defined here, shape deformation is a deformation between outlines—either 2D or 3D.

If the geometry of the two objects is the same or similar and points on the two objects are correlated, then an interpolation process is performed for each points-pair that defines the two objects and the result is a sequence of frames that depicts a smooth change from shape 1 to shape 2.

In more complicated scenarios—for example, a keyhole to a circle—the points do not match well, so one must resort to *fragmentation*, the breaking of an object into lines or pieces. If the outline of a keyhole is to deform into a circle, then the straight lines of the keyhole must be broken up into many short fragments so that the number of points on the keyhole matches the number of points on the circle and the distribution of points is similar. There are many solutions on how to fragment the two outlines so as to interpolate them, and there are many ways to match them to their correspondents.

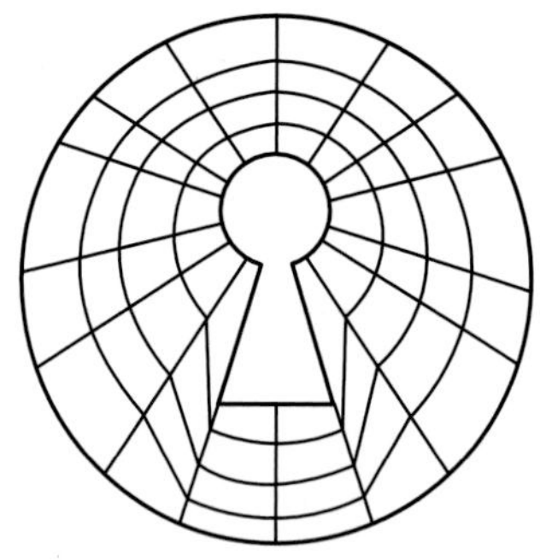

Figure 8.18 Above: Deforming a keyhole into a circle. If the number of control points in each shape is equal, then the deformation is straightforward. If not, then one of the shapes (in this case, the keyhole) needs to be fragmented to increase the number of control points to achieve a match.

Squash and stretch is an animation technique that uses shape deformation to convey information about motion and to help inject life into animation (see Figure 8.19). *Squashing* is the flattening of an object that occurs as it reaches a moment of zero velocity and maximum acceleration—the moment a ball hits a wall, for example. *Stretching* is the elongation of objects in the direction of rapid movement. In a technical sense, stretching is a drawing in of motion blur and shows the object as it is distorted by time. And in a comic sense, it is used to exaggerate the action.

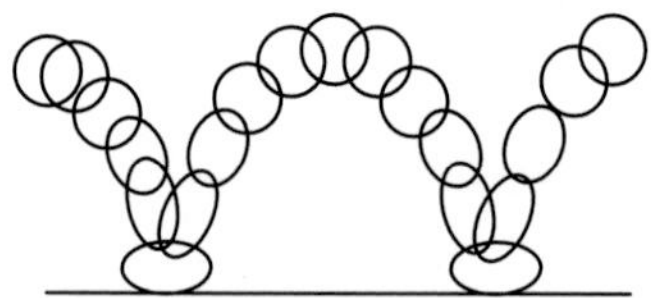

Figure 8.19 Above: Squash and stretch. Squash is the tendency of objects—especially non-rigid objects—to compress when they come to an abrupt standstill. Stretch is the tendency of objects to get longer in their direction of rapid motion.

Morphing

A *morph* is an approach to producing action and is a type of image-processing effect that produces a resultant image from two input images with similar features, where features on one image appear to transition into the features of the other. A morph may be done with polygon outlines and 3D volumetric objects, but it is most commonly thought of as operating on pixel data. In a morph, key points on two images are correlated, and composite images are computed and interpolated using the key points from the two images. During the morph, pixels migrate along different planar paths while a dissolve occurs. For example, one of the images might be a small boat and the other might be a large boat, and the resulting morph is the transition from the small boat to the large boat. The morph is an important part of cinema vocabulary because the geometry of the outgoing image is actually modified, creating a transition effect that is more dramatic than other types of transitions.

In digital morphing, the animator defines *control points*—special points in key locations of the image that play key roles in controlling the morph. For example, in a face these points would be the eyes, the tip of the nose, and points along the edges of the lips and ears. Control points may be digitized interactively by hand or they may be algorithmically determined using image-processing and artificial intelligence tools such as edge detection, region determination, and a knowledge base. The control points are then interpolated, and all the remaining pixels or points are moved to follow. The algorithm is a two-step process: First, the control points are interpolated between their initial and terminal positions. Then the remaining points or pixels are repositioned (and in the case of pixels, blended). The process can also work three dimensionally by locating control points on 3D models, interpolating the control points in 3D space, and allowing the geometry to follow.

Figure 8.20 Onionskin. Like physical onionskin, virtual onionskin allows an animator to see a virtual image of artwork on a previous frame or frames.

Onionskinning

There are some 2D animation tools that are commonly used in classic 2D animation but not always available in 2D animation programs. One such tool is often called *onionskinning;* it provides the ability to lay one cel over another in a semitransparent mode (see Figure 8.20). Tissue paper allows the animator to work on one drawing while viewing the previous drawings, which are under the drawing being worked on. This enables the animator to draw the images in an aligned position.

3D Animation Methods

Three-dimensional animation must not only be designed as a series of flat images, but must also be conceptualized in the context of a 3D environment. Objects are often designed with detailed blueprints, and instead of a 2D background, the environment is designed as a set, with lights, cameras, and objects (see Figure 8.21). The lights, cameras, and objects are initially set up. A recording is then made, and the lights, cameras, and/or objects are moved; the process of recording and moving is repeated over and over to create the illusion of animation. 3D animation can be created in the real world or in the virtual world of the computer.

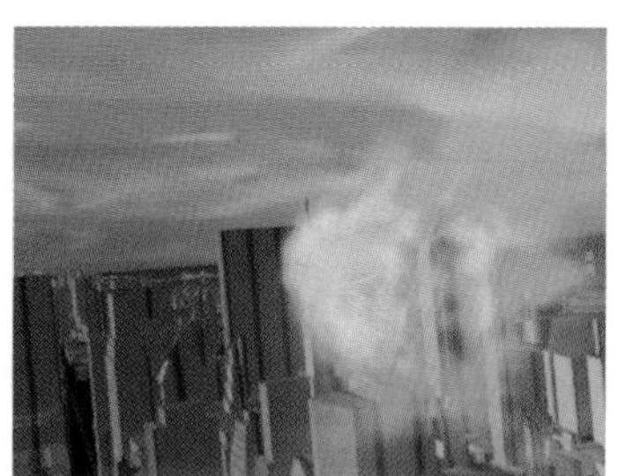

Figure 8.21 Three-dimensional computer animation.

Lights have several properties, including *xyz* position, directionality or omnidirectionality, color, scrims or cookies to modify the quality of the light, falloff, and inverse square properties. Lights themselves can be animated. Since lights are just another object in the 3D world, they can have many of the qualities of other objects—not only position, but also momentum, velocities, and trajectories.

In order to view the scene, a camera needs to be set up. The camera has an *xyz* position and directionality. Because the camera is just another object in the 3D world, it, too, has many of the qualities of regular objects. Only the objects within the camera's field of view are included in an animation.

In a practical sense, the foundation of 3D computer animation is the simulation of the camera and lens. Lens simulation allows one to describe an object with three spatial coordinates and to calculate its projection on an imaging plane. Like a real camera or eye, the synthetic or virtual camera may be moved in space and pointed in different directions. The virtual camera has six degrees of freedom—three position, three orientation. In addition to the lens, the virtual camera may also have a shutter and aperture.

In 3D computer animation, the virtual camera is modeled after its physical counterpart. However, due to the fact that it is not limited by physical forces or constraints, artifacts of traditional motion pictures are not always part of 3D computer animation. For example, in 3D computer animation, the result of a boom does not necessarily reflect an arc movement, whereas for a physical camera, it would.

In addition, there is an enormous amount of flexibility in terms of the ways in which a virtual camera can move. Because the laws that affect a physical camera are not present in the virtual world, almost anything is possible. For example, cameras can accelerate at unrealistic rates; they can pass through walls and other seemingly solid objects; they can move as if they are not tethered to cables and tripods.

Some computer animation systems provide a facility whereby it is possible to script more than one camera in an environment. One advantage of this approach is that it is possible to watch how the principal camera moves as well as to watch what is visible through its lens. It is also true that cameras placed in a shot can be invisible to other cameras.

The concepts presented here relate to both physical and virtual 3D animation. While the range of techniques are listed separately below for simplicity, in practice, they are often combined to create an animation.

Rigid Object Animation

The simplest type of 3D animation is *rigid object animation,* that is, animation that is conveyed through the frame-by-frame movement of objects that are rigid and unchangeable, except with respect to their position and orientation. While the animation of rigid objects is inappropriate for most convincing lifelike animation, it does have uses, especially for architecture and objects such as household products, appliances, and automobiles.

Flexible Object Animation

Flexible object animation is the animation of material things or computer models with well-defined shapes or geometry. While the objects are well defined, their shapes can be easily altered to convey action. Characters and props used in animation are often flexible objects. Animated objects made from jointed wood, rubber-coated wire, or hierarchies of computer primitives can be considered flexible objects. And, of course, the position and orientation of these flexible objects can be animated as well.

In the real world, *puppetry* is the use of articulated physical puppets, designed to be moved incrementally and photographed on a frame-by-frame basis in miniature 3D sets. Thus, puppetry is a way to build physical models and produce action. Puppets are usually built with an internal armature, or skeletal structure. The armature typically has articulated joints that can be moved into various positions.

Malleable Object Animation

Malleable object animation is the animation of material things or computer models that can be moved or have parts that can be moved, but that have shapes that are not well defined and not easily described by geometry. Animated objects made from real clay or virtual clay can be considered malleable objects.

Figure 8.22 Claymation.

Claymation, a method similar to puppetry, employs the use of clay to make animated characters and objects (see Figure 8.22). Characters and objects are first sculpted into shape, and then animated. Since they are made out of clay, they can be moved incrementally and photographed on a frame-by-frame basis in miniature 3D sets. In addition, since clay is extremely malleable, characters and objects can be made to move and change in all sorts of unnatural ways.

Virtual claymation can be created with metaballs—bloblike objects that are defined by density and blending ability. Like real clay, since metaballs are extremely malleable, characters and objects can be made to move and change in all sorts of unnatural ways.

Switchable Body Parts

Switchable body parts are those parts—especially heads and hands (see Figure 8.23)—that are created separately from the body and are used to provide variation in animation. Thus, a puppet often consists of a basic form, or body, plus a collection of switchable parts. Likewise, flexible *facial masks* can be used to provide a range of facial expressions. Figure movement can be accomplished by moving the joints of the armature or repeatedly interchanging body parts.

It is worth noting that the 3D computer animation process can sometimes be made more efficient with the use of switchable body parts. Multiple head and hand models, for example, can be built and attached to a model body. Transitions between body parts can be within one frame, or they can be made gradually as in the case of a morph.

The concept of switchable parts is quite powerful and can be applied to objects as well as to characters. For example, a sparkling 3D animated star can be created from two or three star-shaped objects that are repeatedly interchanged. As they are interchanged, they create a sparkling effect. When using switchable parts, the

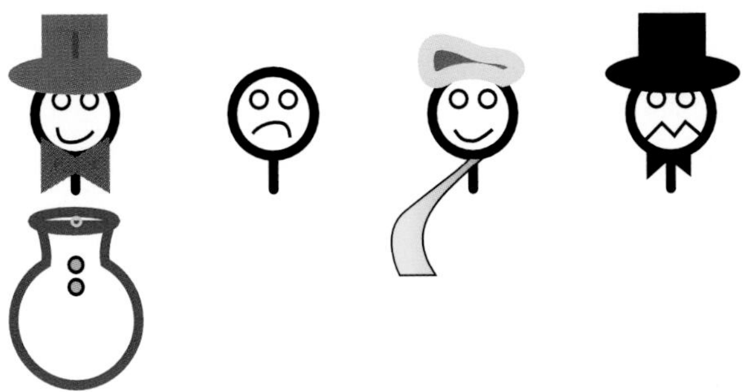

Figure 8.23 Switchable body parts.

scene and the characters must first be functionally decomposed into objects that have multiple swappable parts.

Special Considerations for Virtual Animation

Virtual objects can be animated in many ways. For example, the mathematics used to build computer models can also be applied to models to create action. Thus, a model can be rotated, scaled, and translated. It can move ad hoc or according to the path of a sine wave. Armatures can be moved kinematically, with velocity and acceleration, or dynamically, according to the laws of nature. (These approaches to action are presented in the chapters on easing, kinematics, and dynamics.)

The Integration of Two and Three Dimensions in Computer Animation

Most 3D computer animation utilizes 2D imaging programs. In the simplest of cases, 2D integration occurs when frames from a 3D animation are brought into a 2D imaging program so that the frames can be perfected in some way (see Figure 8.24). For example, the 3D animation program may have produced some unwanted artifacts that are visible in several frames. Those frames can be brought into a 2D imaging program, and the artifacts removed. Sometimes 2D animation is applied to frames produced three-dimensionally, such as blinking lights, animated signs, and so on.

Two-dimensional integration can also occur when 2D imagery is brought into the virtual 3D world (see Figure 8.25). Sometimes imagery is used in a rather static way, while at other times it is actually animated. For example, if an animation is to include a bee that is to fly throughout a scene, and if the bee is to appear striped, then the

Figure 8.24 Right: Two- and three-dimensional integration can take many forms—for example, a scene generated in a 3D program may be further modified in a 2D imaging program. In this example, the purpose is to enhance the readability of the label. The top section contains glare, which has been cleaned up in the bottom section.

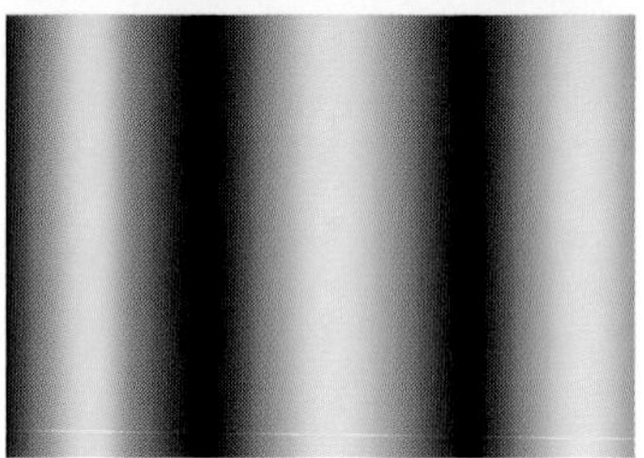

Figure 8.25 Above: Another way to integrate two and three dimensions is to map 2D images onto 3D objects, such as the markings of this bumblebee.

striped pattern can be achieved through the use of a 2D image of yellow and black stripes that is mapped onto a model of the bee's body. This is an example of using a 2D image in a 3D animation. Note that even though the texture will go with the bee as it flies around, the texture itself is rather static; it is the bee that is animated, not the stripes.

Another example of the use of 2D imagery in 3D animation is the following: Suppose that in an animation there is a scene of rippling water (see Figure 8.26). While there are many ways to animate water, one way might be to take 2D images of moving water and map them frame-by-frame onto an animated rippling surface. Hence, the 2D images provide the action. While both examples illustrate the use of the integration of 2D imagery in 3D animation, this second example illustrates how 2D imagery can also be used to create animation.

Figure 8.26 Many mapping scenarios are possible. In this example, a sequence of 2D frames of water is mapped into a 3D scene to create the illusion of water moving in 3D space.

Global and Local Actions

Animated objects—be they 2D or 3D, virtual or real-world—can be created as one single object or as a collection or group of objects. When animating objects, action can be applied to a single object or to a group of objects.

A *global action* is an action that is applied to an entire object or group of objects (see Figure 8.27). For example, if a computer model consists of a sphere, two long cylinders, two short cylinders, and one short fat cylinder—which together represent a robot—an action, such as translate, can be applied to the group of models so that all of the parts of the robot move together.

A *local action,* on the other hand, is an action that is applied only to a single object (see again Figure 8.27). For example, a rotation can be applied to the propeller on the robot's head. The propeller can then move independently of all the other parts.

Both local and global actions can occur simultaneously; thus, in the figure, the propeller spins around as the robot moves forward.

Procedural Animation

There are many objects that are difficult to create using standard tools, and hence are also difficult to animate using standard anima-

Figure 8.27 Right: Global versus local animation. A global action is applied to an entire object; a local action, on the other hand, is applied only to a single object. In the figure, the entire robot is translated to the left (a global action) and the propeller rotates independently of the rest of the robot (a local action.)

Figure 8.28 Above: This image of steam from a procedural animation was procedurally volume modeled and rendered.

tion methods. An example would be mist or steam rising from a cup of coffee (see Figure 8.28). Similar to procedural modeling, ***procedural animation*** uses programs to procedurally generate the visual information of an animation—either 2D or 3D. The difference is that procedural animation techniques will generate all of the frames in an animated sequence, not just one still image. These techniques can be used to create 2D as well as 3D animation.

Figure 8.29 Above: A particle system.

Particle systems, a procedural animation technique, can be used to model certain irregular animated objects, such as fireworks, explosions, fire, and fluid flows (see Figure 8.29). Particles are often volumeless pointlike objects that can be individually manipulated and animated. Not only does the point have an *xyz* coordinate and color, it also has a velocity. Thousands of points are needed to represent anything meaningful, but when a collection of particles is set into motion, they can be used to represent large objects, often with a convincing degree of realism. Other procedural actions include deformations, explosions, and melting.

While procedural animation can be used to simulate everyday events, it can also be used to create completely random animation. Because computers can easily generate random numbers, it is simple for procedural animation programs to create animation that is seemingly random.

9 The Cel System

Cel animation is a second-generation animation technique. It breaks the image into layers, minimally two layers, which must be held in registration and which can move (but need not) relative to each other. For example, a cel drawing can be moved over a background drawing. The basics of cel animation are reviewed in this chapter, including physical as well as virtual implementations. Methods on how to decompose graphic art objects into a series of graphic layers, and methods to introduce movement into these components, comprise much of the body of this chapter.

It is the cel system that propelled the Hollywood cartoons past cutouts and the slash system. Much as we would like to explore the direction of cartoon personalities and Technicolor animated features such as *Fantasia,* our message here is focused on technique. Although physical acetate cels may become a thing of the past and it is tempting to dismiss cel animation as obsolete, possibly worth simulating but nothing more, the techniques of the cel system are indeed applicable to all computer animation. For example, in 3D computer graphics, one might also layer 3D action in front of 2D backgrounds, or one might build 3D models and render them into 2D cels. It is especially useful in interactive formats, including CD-ROMs and the Web, where its economical approach to artwork (and thus bandwidth) make it a very pragmatic solution.

Cel Animation

Cel animation is an art-production method that enables a producer and director to construct action shots using cycles of drawings

Single-frame photography of successive paper drawings breaks away from cyclic phase drawing and is a pathway to the cel system. In Windsor McCay's *Gertie the Trained Dinosaur*, the entire drawing is recreated for each frame.

arranged as layers of artwork in which the drawings are layered front to back (in a z-buffer fashion). Each layer is referred to as a *cel* (from *celluloid*), which (in the physical domain) is a piece of transparent acetate, perhaps containing an opaque cartoon character inked on it (see Figure 9.1). The action of each animated character can be rendered on separate cels.

In computer terms, cels are often called ***sprites***. Like cels, the area around sprites is represented with a numeric value to indicate transparent, or clear, and like cels, which are registered on peg bar, they are registered graphically at a measurement or pixel address.

The concept of ***layers*** suggests that cels can be stacked one on top of another and composited into a single image (see again Figure 9.1). The concept of layers implies an ordering, and for this reason, layers are also called ***levels,*** or (as in virtual levels) ***channels.*** An image may be thought of as the combination of layers. The layers are used priority-style, so in a formal sense, cel animation is an *x-y* continuous, *z* orthogonal, and discrete graphics system; informally, it is a 2.5D representational system.

The cel process separates artwork into background (which gets drawn once) and foreground (which gets drawn for every frame), and allows the foreground cels to be translated relative to the background. In a cel system, the layer farthest away is called the ***background.*** Action is created by placing one or more cels over the background, recording the result onto film or tape, then changing and/or moving the cel artwork. A sequence of frames recorded in this fashion make up a cel animation shot.

In order to create a sense of fluid motion, the cels are kept aligned by the use of registration marks or pegs on an animation stand (or numbers in a computer). The imagery is rendered on separate cels, then combined by overlaying registered cels against a background drawing. Animation can be created in two ways: by changing the shape of the imagery across sequential cels, or by changing the position of a cel with respect to its background. The first strategy is much more expensive than the second.

Beyond a background and one level, the cel paradigm becomes very complex. Because the physical acetate absorbs light, classic animators are limited to less than seven layers, and in practice two or three. Dust, flicker, and wear and tear become exacerbated as the

Figure 9.1 The cel system. The background is drawn onto paper or artboard and painted. The foreground is drawn onto paper, then trace-inked onto one or more flexible transparent cels. The backside of the cels is painted with opaque colors, then laid face up over the background and photographed. Action that is static is drawn onto cels or backgrounds that are used for many frames; only the moving parts that are different for each frame are transferred to cels. In the figure, two cel layers are pegged over a background; both cels are pegged on the top pegs so they can move together yet independently of the background, which is pegged at the bottom. A typical scene might involve a changing, talking head cel and a single held cel for the body and arms.

levels increase; the absorption of light by successive levels requires that animators ***gray out*** the paint of colors of the topmost levels to match the colors closer to the bottom. Therefore, in classic cel animation, the number of cel levels used throughout the scene must be consistent. Otherwise, the change in cel density will cause a color change or visible flicker in the resulting animation at the point where the change occurs. The computer, on the other hand, allows for perfect transparency, and allows, in theory, the creation of many, many levels.

Three levels increase flexibility (over two levels) because three levels permit an object in a cel drawing with both a stationary and a moving component to move as a unit against a background, perhaps itself panning. The physical implementation is accomplished with the background and the cels connected to different sets of pegs—that is, they can be moved independently of each other. The action might involve a body and a head. The head could talk while the body stands still. Or the body could walk while the head remains silent. Or the character could talk and walk at the same time. The computer implementation works the same way.

Three or more cel levels increase flexibility but often become harder to handle than lower cel levels. Decisions as to what goes on which cel level involves artistic considerations, such as how to keep the colors true; production considerations, such as wanting to change certain cels more frequently than others; and the functional decomposition of a scene. Even with the computer and multiple channels, it is necessary to plan how animation is to be manifested and, especially, what is in front of what.

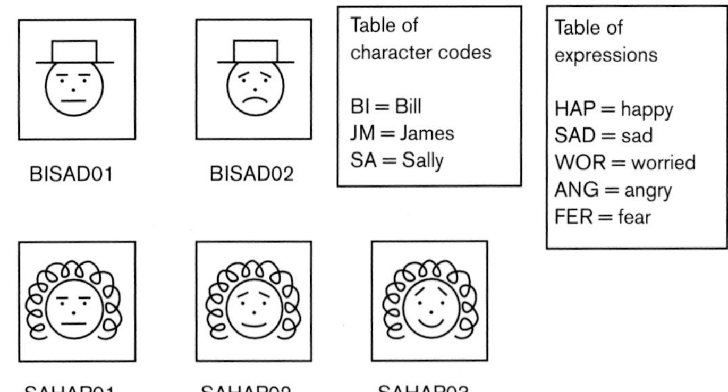

Figure 9.2 Naming systems. This naming chart for a character or object uses a two-letter code to indicate the character's or object's name, a three-letter code to indicate the expression, and a two-letter code to indicate the cel number. An ampersand at the end of the name indicates that this is the last cel in the sequence.

A naming system is usually devised in order to manage the drawings in an animation; the number, or name, often reflects its shot or scene or character. In computer systems, names and numbers may also indicate if the cel is at the end of a sequence, or if the sequence loops (see Figure 9.2). Names can also incorporate information about the cel level. Again, planning is paramount.

Doping of cel animation is done using a traditional *dope sheet* or the horizontal chart format. Doping involves placing cels at the intersection of a frame and channel; note that a dope sheet is a discrete environment. (The dope sheet is discussed in detail in Chapter 14.)

Action Technologies

Cel animation enables a few kinds of action. Here is an inventory.

Hold Cel

A *hold cel* is the term given to a cel that is repeated over several frames. Hold cels are used in situations where very little action is occurring—for example, where a character is standing still and speaking. In this case, the animator only need create the animation of the head, saving the time that would have been required to redraw all of the other objects.

Sliding Cel

A *sliding cel,* also known as a *traveling cel* or *panning cel,* is a cel that slides over the background, creating the appearance of motion (see Figure 9.3). Sliding cels are registered, the background is held stationary, and the cel is translated over the background. Action in x and y is possible, although most animation stands will slide only in x.

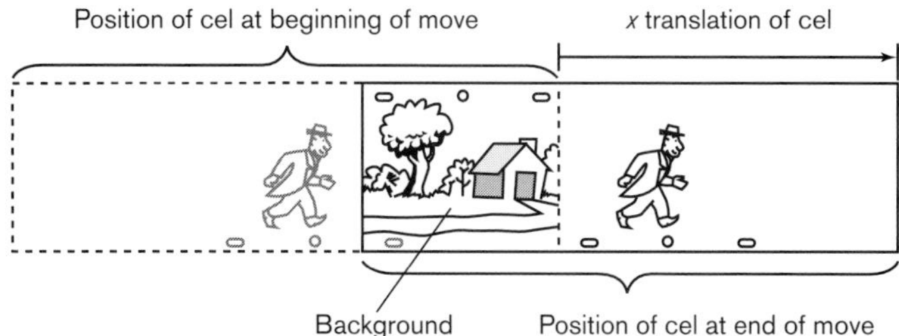

Figure 9.3 Left: A static background and sliding cels create the illusion of the subject moving through the scene. The background is fastened to the upper peg bar and held static, and the successive cells (perhaps from a walk cycle) are pegged at the bottom. For each frame, the bottom peg bar moves incrementally to the right and the next cel of the walk cycle replaces the last cel on the pegs. Note that the cel or the image database must be extrawide.

Figure 9.4 Below: A traveling background and a stationary walk cycle create the illusion that the subject is moving through the scene and that the camera is panning or dollying with the subject. Of course, the camera is not panning at all; the background is simply traveling in the opposite direction incrementally on a frame-by-frame basis. Note that here the background (or its database) must be extrawide.

Backgrounds and Background Animation

In cel animation, the background is at the bottom-most level; it establishes the place of action. In animated commercials, backgrounds must support the product being sold. They can be static or have lateral motion. ***Static backgrounds*** are backgrounds that remain still throughout the animation. ***Traveling backgrounds,*** also known as ***panning backgrounds,*** are backgrounds that translate during the recording process (see Figure 9.4), creating the illusion of movement.

Background animation in a real-time digital system sometimes incorporates the use of custom graphics display chips that enable the computer to move large areas of a picture without having to move large blocks of memory. Rather than moving the data, the hardware is designed so that the computer can scroll the image by looking into different parts of memory. The background is stored as one large image, and the screen becomes a movable window onto that memory (see Figure 9.5). This type of scrolling, ***hardware scrolling,*** enables a picture to be panned north-south and east-west. Hardware zooms enable the picture to be enlarged; rotations are also permitted. These operations are accomplished pixelwise in bitmap devices, and pointwise on display list devices. All traditional

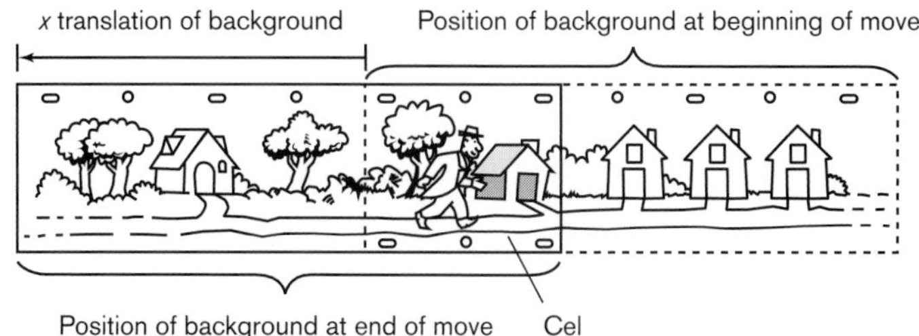

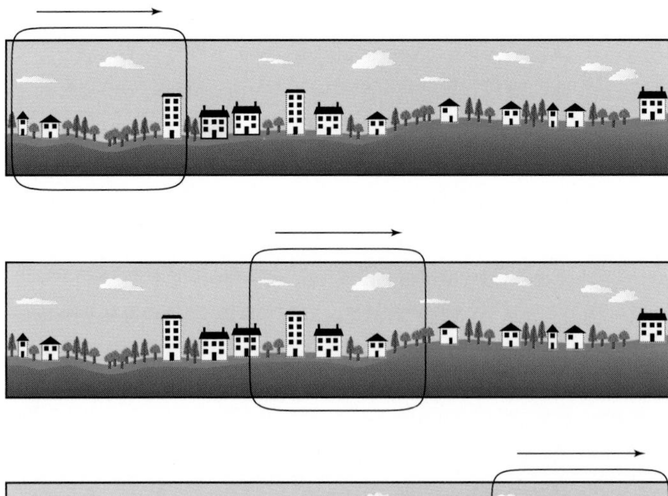

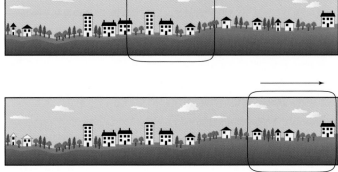

Figure 9.5 Hardware scrolling. An over-wide pixel image travels past the viewing window. This technique is widely used in some videogames, such as Nintendo's Game Boy. The images are called *side-scrollers.*

stand processes—zooms, pans, tilts, and rotation—are easily emulated and bring action to otherwise static artwork by moving the art through the field of view. Traveling backgrounds can also be created in 3D computer animation systems by moving the background past the camera.

Multiplane Animation

A *multiplane animation stand* gives the illusion of depth to 2D art by physically separating the layers by several inches (see Figure 9.6). In a typical situation, the animation foreground is a cutout and is mounted on the topmost level; a character (possibly two or more cel layers) is on the middle level; and the background is on the bottommost level. The distance between the levels can be varied; since the maximum illusion of 3D space is achieved when there is a discernible difference in focus between levels, it is best to set the lens at its minimum depth of field. When the foreground imagery pans or the camera moves, either away or toward the art, or as the focus changes, the maximum multiplane effect is achieved. Multiplane animation appears to have a realistic sense of depth, because the artwork at each depth level moves at a different rate of speed. In order to simulate multiplane animation with digital artwork, it is nec-

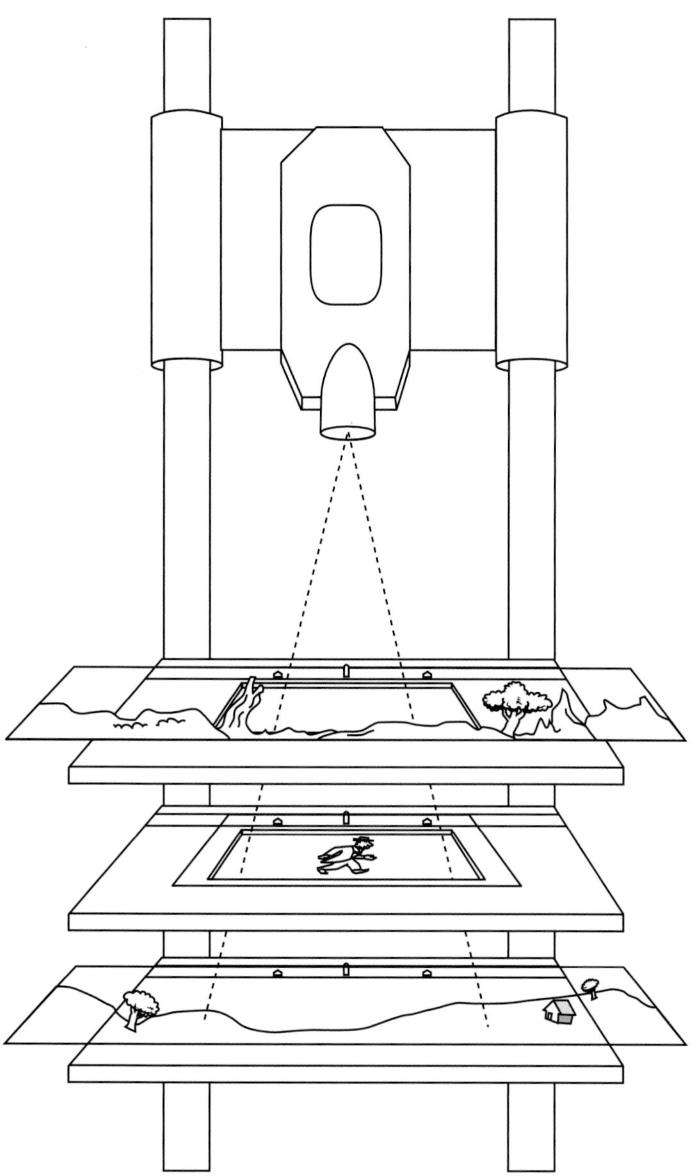

Figure 9.6 Multiplane camera, front view. In this three-plane example, the closest plane contains foreground elements, the second plane is where the major action is played, and the third plane is the background. Note that the field of view gets bigger on levels farther away. In a four-plane camera, an additional plane could be added above (in front of) these three planes, where it would be out of focus and could create mood, such as rain or fog. Note that depth of field plays a critical role.

essary to mimic the geometry of the platen and soften the focus of the foreground plane.

Movement Cycles

A *motion cycle* is a sequence of images depicting an action, where the first frame may be hooked up to the last frame, allowing the sequence to be repeated in a cyclic fashion (see Figure 9.7). The term

Figure 9.7 Motion cycle with hookup.

hookup is used to indicate that the first and last frames of the sequence are the same; it is worth noting that this identical first and last frame is not displayed at both the beginning and the end of the cycle; it is only displayed once. Otherwise, the frame would be displayed twice, and hence the cycle would appear to jerk on that image during display. This is a common mistake made by computer animators.

By repeating the sequence of drawings, the time of the sequence can be extended without the need for additional drawings. The animator need only create one sequence of drawings. Cycles can run on ones, twos, or whatever is appropriate. Motion cycles can be applied to many types of repeated motion, including a waving flag, the rotational movement of the hands of a clock, and the flapping of a bird's wings. Motion cycles are often coupled with other techniques—for example, the motion cycle might take place over an animated background.

Computer-Mediated Cel Animation

When the computer was discovered by animators, one of the first things that they envisioned was simulating the animation process. Animation seemed like an ideal use for the computer; it is repetitive, numeric in nature, precise, and it involves calculations. Toward this end, one of the first steps was to computerize the animation stand. The next obvious steps were to represent cels in a digital format inside the computer (either as vector representations or as bitmaps), to do the positioning of the imagery computationally, and to composite cels computationally. In other words, these pioneers computerized the cel animation process.

Currently, 2D animation systems range from implementations that computerize virtually all facets to hybrid approaches that combine traditional processes with computerization of certain stages.

From a production point of view, the cel process includes scripting, storyboarding, drawing cels and backgrounds, inking and painting the cels and backgrounds, doping, compositing the artwork, and recording. Cel overlays and backgrounds are either hand drawn and scanned into the system, or made using a digital-paint or polygon-based system. Text is keyed in via a word processor. Illustrations and text are merged to form electronic storyboards. Animated sequences are created. Finally, compositing or layout commands are added to specify which cels and backgrounds are to be combined and in what order. The results are output to film, video, or other medium, possibly purely digital and interactive.

A full-blown, computerized cel animation production system consists of many computers networked together that share and exchange files pertaining to different facets of the process. Many animation systems are interactive and screen-oriented, controlled with menus and mouse clicks; text input is also possible, especially since many of the processes are batch-oriented. Flexible systems can create, edit, and replay action sequences in real time, often with color, sound, and several cels moving over a background.

General Properties of Digital Cels

In general, digital cels can be made to act just like traditional cels: they can be held still or they can slide over backgrounds; they can contain images that look 2D or 3D; and they can be made to cycle and create animated sequences such as a waving flag, flapping butterfly wings, or blinking eye. In addition, digital cels can be embedded into interactive computer graphics and function as virtual buttons; they can have an up and down state and possibly one middle state.

Sprites and Polygon-Based Cels

Digitally, a cel may be simulated using pixels or polygons. In general, the movement of cels can be easily and automatically calculated by computers; all of the mathematics associated with kinematics and dynamics can be incorporated into a 2D computer animation system and applied to sprites and cels. Mathematics can also be applied to the shapes of the sprites and cels, deforming the shapes in infinite ways, as well as to their positions.

Polygon-Based Cels When polygons are used to simulate cels, the shape is represented by its point and vector perimeter form, as well as by any interior lines or divisions (see Figure 9.8). The color of

Figure 9.8 Above: Polygon-based cels have an outline, an outline color, an outline width, and a fill color. They can be created with vector-based illustration systems.

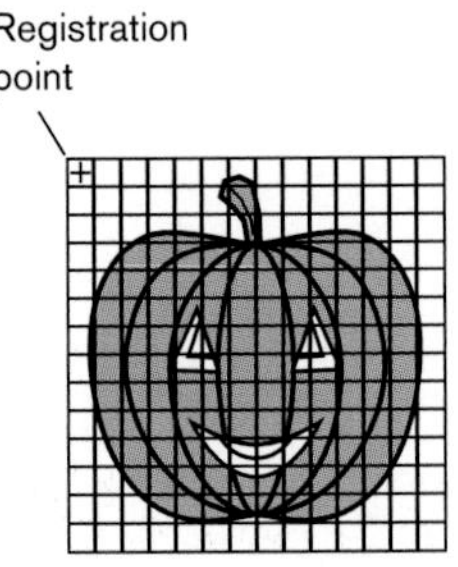

Figure 9.9 Above: Sprites have registration points and a grid of pixels.

each object is stored with its geometry, as may other properties, including transparency, outline color, and outline width. Polygon-based cels often exist in floating-point, continuous space and do not get quantized until display time. Because polygon-based cels are not stored as a matrix of pixels, they do not have a fixed resolution and are very zoomable. They can always be simulated in a 3D system by making all the polygons share a common normal, and simply using *z* positions to simulate levels or channels. One can shoot with orthogonal projections or with perspective, and one can alter the *z* distances to create multiplane effects. Polygon cels have no concept of clear regions around them—there is nothing around—but they can have regions within them that are clear holes.

Sprites—Pixel-Based Cels A cel represented by a matrix of pixels is also called a ***sprite*** (see Figure 9.9). The colors of the pixels in the sprite define the image, and the sprite has a fixed resolution. Sprites are pixel arrays that are smaller than the total area of the image and function as submodules. These small pixel arrays vary in size from a few pixels wide and one bit deep, to full-color areas hundreds of pixels square. Sprites exist in integer space, with all the attendant benefits and liabilities. They can pan fairly easily. Strictly speaking, a sprite looks best when its edges are anti-aliased into the background (but this takes extra CPU cycles). Unfortunately, the ability to zoom is rather limited, and extended zooming eventually results in a pixelized image.

Sprites usually incorporate the concept of transparency, in which one color value is reserved to indicate that the pixel is transparent, or clear. This is important because sprites in a computer are usually rectangular arrays, and it is often necessary to matte out the region surrounding the drawing in the sprite, creating a non-rectangular image. This also allows holes in the sprite artwork. Transparency is often indicated by assigning the value zero to a pixel. When the sprite is positioned over another image, the zero-valued pixels are assumed to have no color, and hence do not mask out the colors of the pixels in the image underneath. Hence, the resulting animated object does not have to appear rectangular (see Figure 9.10). Artists should take note, however, that this means that white (or black, depending on the system) is not represented by zero, but the value

Figure 9.10 Transparent pixels. Pixel-based cel animation software usually reserves one color, which the program recognizes as transparent. Unfortunately, 2D imaging software does not always recognize transparency. Thus, creating transparent pixels and maintaining them requires diligence on the part of the animator.

one, and that there is no such thing as a full eight-bit gray scale—there can be 255 intensity (or lookup) table values but not 256, since one value represents clear.

Sprites are easily animated and are a useful technique for creating limited real-time computer animation. First, a cycle of action is created and defined in terms of sprites. Sprites usually have a registration point, that is, an *xy* coordinate to be used for the registration of movement. Sprites are positioned and sized using parameters that specify the *xy* location on the screen and the size. Next, the sprites are sequenced to reflect the order of the action. Finally, they are displayed rapidly in sequence, either by the use of interactive commands or a scripting system, which specifies the sequence of sprites, their position, and the timing. Although today sprites often reside in software, it is also possible to design special hardware to manage them. In fact, the term *sprite* was originally associated with a sprite register in the computer, and operations such as put_sprite or draw_sprite.

Sprites Versus Polygon-Based Cels The choice of whether to work in a vector or bitmap format is often one of personal preference, but each approach does offer some advantages and disadvantages. Vectors, for example, exist in a continuous domain and hence are infinitely zoomable, and therefore, unlike sprites, offer great flexibility in terms of enlarging and reducing cels. Furthermore, polygons can be changed programmatically—for example, linear interpolation can be used to turn a circle into a keyhole. The disadvantage of polygon-based cels is that a real-time polygon system must maintain a display list, that is, a list of the geometry representing the image, and this requires fast hardware. For both formats, there are many good tools on the market—Illustrator and Freehand for vector images and Photoshop for bitmap images—hence the decision is usually not linked to the availability of tools. Often, it makes sense to work in the target format. For example, if the animation is to be embedded in an interactive bitmap-format product, then the process would be simpler if development were done using a bitmap format.

Digital Cels in Interactive Graphics

Cel/sprite animation is important not only to create animation as an end art form, but also as an element of interactive graphics and games. A very special case of this is *buttons*, which animate between up and down states when clicked, and possibly also include a rollover sprite. Remember that any animation in interactive graphics must take place in real time, and that it is not possible to create all possible animations in real time. The creator must engage in a cagey decomposition of artwork, separating moving elements from static elements, draw upon basic positions, and design cycles. Remember, too, that sprites can be produced by 3D programs and displayed as 2D cycles. This adds a look of three-dimensionality to the graphics.

Objects

Finally, it is worth noting that in addition to simulating the traditional cel process, both in data as well as in doping/direction, the computerized sprite may also contain "intelligence." That is to say, the sprite contains instructions, so that in addition to having properties such as its location, color, and transparency, it may also contain a process. For example, it might cycle on its own, changing speed depending upon external factors. It might be able to detect other objects in the scene and avoid or be attracted to them. A character might know how to move its lips based on the spoken dialogue.

Benefits and Practical Considerations

Once in a digital form, the cel and the process may be manipulated as a uniform digital file. Artwork can be created that is infinitely reusable. A traditional animation cel is prone to damage due to physical handling, and therefore has a very limited life, but a digital cel lasts forever (theoretically). We have explained how the layering of physical cels is not a perfect process; if the cel is not absolutely flat, it bubbles and will cause flares and flashes, whereas digital cels have no physical flaws. The transparent part of digital cels do not absorb light, since they have no physical component; they also do not get dirty. Also, the essence of the physical material associated with the image, such as brush strokes, is visible during tight zoom shots. Another benefit is achieved when the process involves moving cel layers in the real world; abrasion can occur between levels, causing mechanical problems. Moreover, the computation associated with motion of any kind, including pans, zooms, cyclic motion of animated objects, in-betweens, and movement of the cels, can be easily done with the computer. Therefore, in general, taking the animation process into the digital domain eliminates many of the physical problems involved in the animation process and eliminates many of the tedious jobs as well.

Cel Production

While many computerized processes have been widely adopted, many traditional methods remain popular. Hence, it is not surprising that much animation now incorporates tools and processes from both approaches. The union of the two schools has led to many new production pathways (see Figure 9.11).

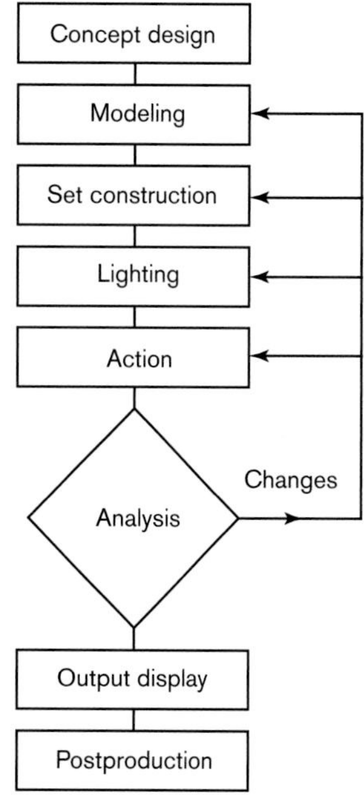

Figure 9.11 Production pathways.

Because drawing with pencil on paper is so popular, animation often begins with physical drawings of the characters. One of the reasons for this is that animators often find it natural to draw with physical tools; they respond to physical forces—the harder one presses, the darker the mark—while digital tools are less varied. The drawings are made on punched paper, in registration. When the drawings are complete, they are retouched to make the linework stronger, crisper, and cleaner. As black-and-white drawings, they may be scanned into the computer, where the linework will be solidified

Figure 9.12 Digital pen and ink. The software can automatically color all shapes in all frames as long as the shapes were present in the first frame. The process, therefore, begins with the animator coloring the first frame, then the computer colors the rest of the frames. Obviously, the software cannot handle new shapes or objects introduced to the scene. In practice, however, the software can color about 95% of the frames and will prompt the user for assistance with regions that it is unequipped to handle. It is worth noting that the colorization of old movies works in a similar way: regions in the first frame are colored in, then the program colors the rest of the frames accordingly.

and they will be colorized or painted. This is called a *digital ink and paint* process and can be done either with (1) a vector-based program that recognizes the line, converts it to polygons, and fills in the regions between the lines with uniform or gradient color, or (2) a bitmap-based program that can apply anti-aliasing techniques to the line and fill in with continuous or gradient color. Ink and paint software usually has the ability to recognize similarities between successive frames and can apply information from one frame to consistently color those that follow (see Figure 9.12). Once the cels are fully colored, they can be recorded.

While some production pathways may be more common than others, almost any pathway is viable, and many pathways have been explored. For example, one might start with 3D animation software to create the objects and calculate the animation. The 3D results can then be plotted onto paper, inked onto cels, hand painted, and shot with a camera. If need be, hidden lines can be removed during the inking-to-cel process; any unwanted lines can simply not be inked. This process can be modified in many ways—for example, by placing cels in the plotter, so that the result of the plotter is the inked cel, which then gets hand painted. Or the images can be plotted onto paper; the paper can be hand painted and photographed. And, for more experimental animators, the plotter pen can be replaced with a light-emitting diode, and the plotter can be replaced with a classic animation stand, and colored gels can be used instead of paper. The computer can drive the diode over the gel, creating a vector drawing on an original camera negative. We offer these older, approaches to make you aware that animators use varied tools and that the tools can produce varied visuals.

10 Motion Pathways, Key Frame Animation, and Easing

The focus of this chapter is on key frame animation, motion pathways, and easing. Motion pathways exist in the geometric domain; easing exists in the temporal domain. It begins with a rather formal review of action and associated concepts such as speed, velocity, and acceleration, which form the physical basis for traditional eases. The discussion continues with a presentation of motion pathways and an examination of several ways that they may be created. Next, key frame techniques are explored in detail, both in a classic "cartoon" sense, as well as a computerized implementation in which key frames are defined with parameters.

The chapter concludes with an inventory of easing techniques, which, although not necessarily always natural, are extremely useful. It is possible to design eases that have a variety of changes. For example, it is possible to speed up and slow down or to construct an ease that accelerates for a while, maintains a constant velocity, accelerates again quickly, breaks quickly, slows down, darts forward—in general, to produce a tremendous amount of liveliness of movement, and yet be very smooth. This kind of creative movement, coupled with engaging spline pathways, can produce action that is very dramatic.

Keep in mind that animation is an art form of movement, and movement is a key element in character. The manner in which a camera moves compels viewers to respond—it brings them into or out of spaces quickly, it provides them with exhilaration when moving throughout small spaces quickly, or it instills them with a sense of peace. The manner in which the camera moves is how the

Above: *The Smell of Horror*, by Mitch Butler.

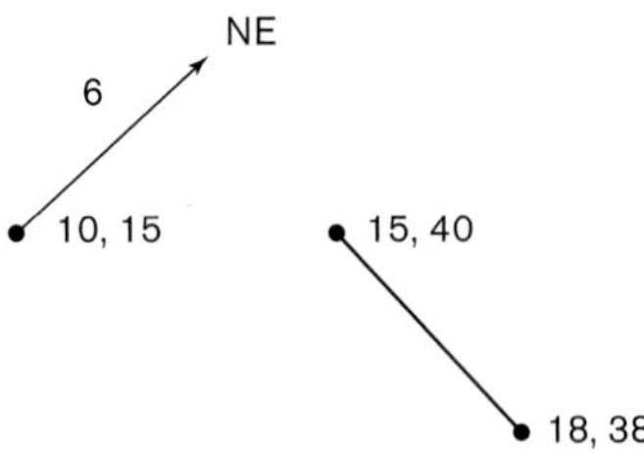

Figure 10.1 Above: Vectors. The left vector is six units, northeast.

audience members themselves move, since the camera is their eye into the animated world.

Some Basic Definitions

Before beginning the discussion of key frame animation and easing, let us first define a few concepts that present a basic foundation for how objects move.

Action

Action refers to any and all kinds of change that occurs over time, including the change of position of objects, changes in an object's shape, changes in the position of the camera, and changes in the position of lights. Action is also created by changes in an object's geometry, by the brightness of lights, by rotation of objects and cameras, by surface patterns that are changing, by changes in the focus and focal length of the lens, and by special effects such as fades and wipes. Action must always occur at certain rates if they are to appear natural.

The rotation of a cube about its local *y* axis is an example of an action. The action can be separated into an ***action type,*** for example, the local *y* rotation, and an ***action parameter,*** in this example, an angular value. The most basic of action types are scaling, translation, and rotation. Action parameters depend upon the action type—for example, for rotation, the parameter may be an angle specified in degrees, while for translation, the parameters might be *x*, *y*, and *z* distances. Producing a sequence of animated images requires computing values for each action parameter for each frame and displaying the resulting images. Computers facilitate the computation of the action parameter values.

Vectors

A ***vector*** is a quantity specified by a size (or magnitude) and a direction (see Figure 10.1). There are certain things that can only be fully represented with the use of a vector, for example, a force. When a force is exerted, it is exerted in a particular direction and with a particular magnitude. Often, vectors are expressed or represented with the use of an arrow.

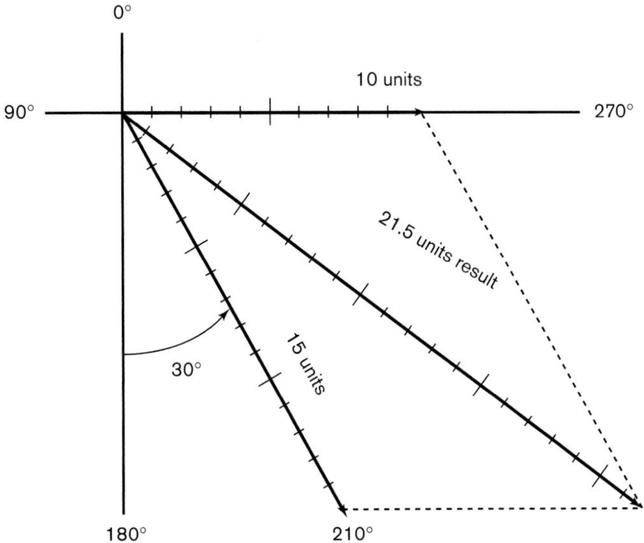

Figure 10.2 Left: A resultant vector. The resultant vector created from the 10-unit vector at 270 degrees and the 15-unit vector at 210 degrees is a 21.5-unit vector at 240 degrees.

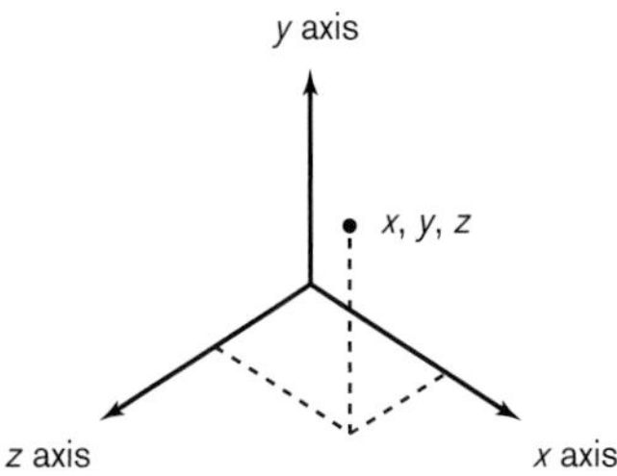

Figure 10.3 Above: A position is a 2D or 3D location in space, indicated in the figure by a point.

Any vector representation can be combined, or composited, with another vector. For example, a vector that represents force A can be combined with a vector that represents force B to created one *resultant vector* (see Figure 10.2). In the case of a resultant force, the result is a single force that is the equivalent of the force that would be produced if the original two forces were applied. Forces can augment each other, as well as cancel each other out. Mathematically, resultant vectors are simple to calculate.

Vector is a term that is often used to refer to lines, and *vector graphics* has come to mean line drawings. Strictly speaking, each line is an instance of a vector because it can be represented with an initial position and a bearing (or directionality) and a magnitude that represents the same information as would two endpoints. We say this only to address any confusion the reader might have about our definition of the term here, which is slightly different than the line vector definition; it is also a definition that we intend to apply to a different purpose—in particular, the definitions of velocity and forces.

Position, Motion, Speed, Velocity, and Acceleration

Position, Motion, and Speed A position is a 2D or 3D location in space, expressed as *xy* or *xyz*, respectively (see Figure 10.3). A *displacement* is a series of positions; it is not a single static, instantaneous position, but a set of positions that an object may take

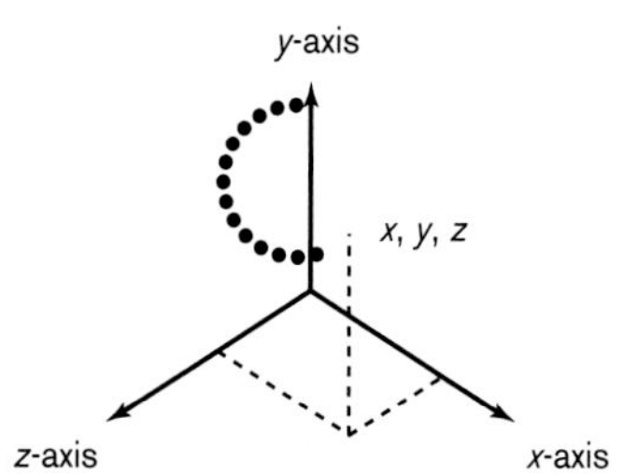

Figure 10.4 Above: A displacement is a series of positions. The positions may be on a straight line or a curve. The displacement illustrated here exists in the curve of a circle and goes around the y-axis.

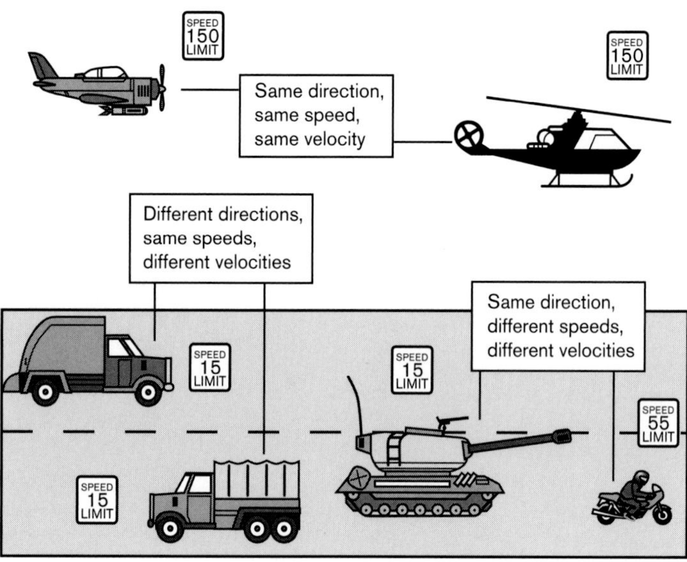

Figure 10.5 Right: Speed is the rate at which an object changes position—for example, a truck might travel 15 miles/hour. Velocity is the rate of motion in a particular direction; it is a vector quantity and involves speed and direction.

(see Figure 10.4). Motion is a continuous change of position (although in the digital domain, it is usually approximated discretely). When in motion, an object changes its position at a particular rate, referred to as speed (see Figure 10.5). Therefore, speed indicates how fast an object is moving. Speed is the rate of motion, a measure of distance across time, and is expressed in units such as miles/hour, feet/second, knots (nautical miles/hour), or mach (speed relative to the speed of sound). In more general terms, speed indicates how fast an action is occurring—for example, how fast lights are dimming.

Velocity *Velocity* is the rate of motion in a particular direction (see again Figure 10.5). That is, velocity is defined as the speed at which an object moves, together with the direction in which it is moving. Therefore, velocity is a vector quantity; it has a magnitude and a direction. Because velocity is speed *and* direction, it is therefore expressed in 2D terms such as "60 miles/hour northwest"—a two-element vector of speed and compass heading (e.g., 60 miles/hour, 330 degrees). In 3D terms, velocity may be expressed as a four-element vector of speed and a direction normal. *Uniform velocity* occurs when velocity is constant; that is, when an object moves the same distance in the same direction at the same rate (see Figure 10.6). A graph of uniform velocity distance versus time produces a straight line.

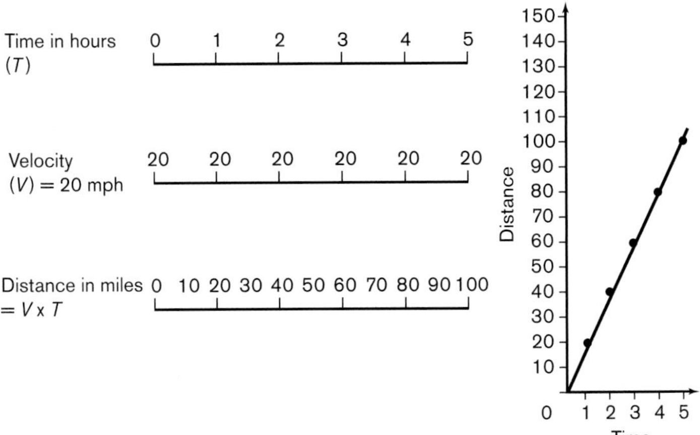

Figure 10.6 A vehicle traveling at a constant 20 miles/hour for each of the five hours travels at a uniform velocity.

Acceleration In life, an object such as an automobile at rest begins to move slowly and gains speed, or accelerates, before reaching a constant, uniform speed. The physical explanation is that it is necessary to overcome the inertia of the resting object. Conversely, objects decelerate and slow to a stop. *Acceleration* is the rate of change of velocity over time (see Figure 10.7). A drag racer accelerates quickly; a blimp accelerates slowly. The Roadrunner operated with exaggerated parameters—he accelerates very fast! These differences in acceleration reveal differences in the object's character—differences that are crucial to animation. Objects in nature often begin to move in small increments that become larger until the object approaches a constant velocity; the increments might become smaller as the object decelerates to a stop.

Because acceleration is the rate of change of *velocity* per time, time enters the equation twice and it is therefore expressed in units such as miles/hour/hour. It may also be expressed in forms such as miles/hour/second, feet/second/second, feet/second^2, or mile × hours^{-2}. Animated objects that move in equal distances from the start to the finish of a motion do not accelerate and appear to start and stop with an unsightly jerk. Simply put, it is necessary to accelerate the object in order for it to appear real. Furthermore, because velocity is a measure of both speed and direction, any time there is a change in direction, even though the speed is constant, there must also be an acceleration. It is important to note that acceleration also pertains to actions that do not involve a change in position—for example, when lights are faded down, the decrease in brightness must accelerate.

Figure 10.7 Right: A blimp changes velocity slowly; a dragster changes velocity quickly. Acceleration occurs whenever an object speeds up or begins moving in a new direction.

Figure 10.8 Below: Linear acceleration. A vehicle beginning its travel at 0 miles/hour, and then uniformly accelerating 10 miles/hour for each of 5 hours, will eventually be traveling at 50 miles/hour.

Acceleration may be uniform or variable. *Uniform acceleration* is motion in which an object is accelerated at a constant rate; it is sometimes also called *linear acceleration* (see Figure 10.8). Uniform acceleration simulates the manner in which many objects in the real world gain speed. An object that moves 2 feet in the first second, 4 feet in the second second, and 6 feet in the third second is an example of uniform acceleration: it is gaining velocity, but the rate of acceleration is constant at 2 feet/second/second. It has been experimentally determined that the distance traveled during an inter-

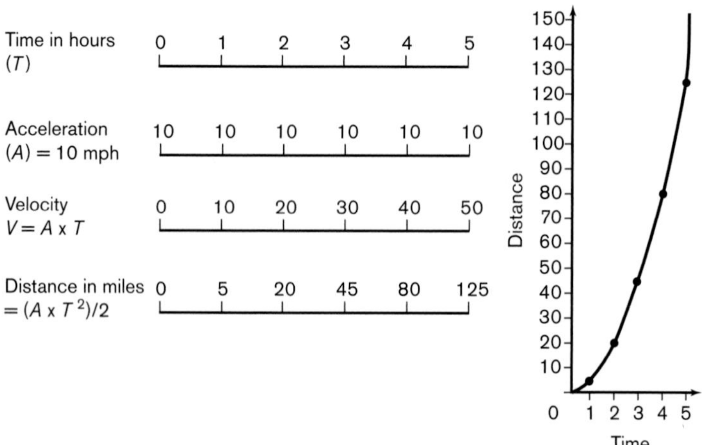

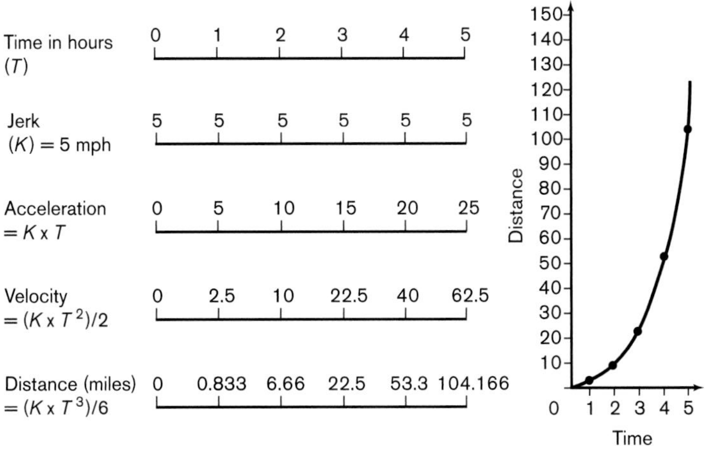

Figure 10.9 Variable acceleration. A vehicle beginning its travel at 0 miles/hour, and then accelerating to 5 miles/hour at the end of the first hour, and then accelerating to 10 miles/hour at the end of the second hour, and then 15 miles/hour at the end of the third hour, is accelerating at a variable rate.

val of time is equal to one-half the acceleration times the duration of time squared, or in classic notation:

$$s = \tfrac{1}{2}\, at^2$$

Acceleration produces a parabolic curve when distance is plotted against time. Note that although the rate of speed for linear acceleration is constantly increasing, the rate of acceleration is constant.

It is also possible for an object to accelerate so that the rate of acceleration is increasing. This is called *variable acceleration.* One case of variable acceleration is ***exponential acceleration,*** when acceleration is increasing at an exponential rate (see Figure 10.9). One example of where this occurs in the real world is with a rocket: the rocket weight primarily consists of its own fuel, so as it burns the fuel, the rocket engine has less mass to push and is therefore able to propel faster.

Several pertinent equations involving velocity and acceleration are as follows. The average velocity equation is only for the case where velocity is increasing at a steady rate. The last equation implies uniform acceleration.

$$\text{velocity} = \text{acceleration} \times \text{time}$$
$$\text{distance traversed} = \text{average velocity} \times \text{time}$$
$$\text{average velocity} = (\text{initial velocity} + \text{final velocity})/2$$
$$\text{position at time } t = \tfrac{1}{2}\, at^2$$

Derivatives

Closely allied to acceleration is the concept of a derivative, especially with regard to changes in the rate of motion. In this context, a

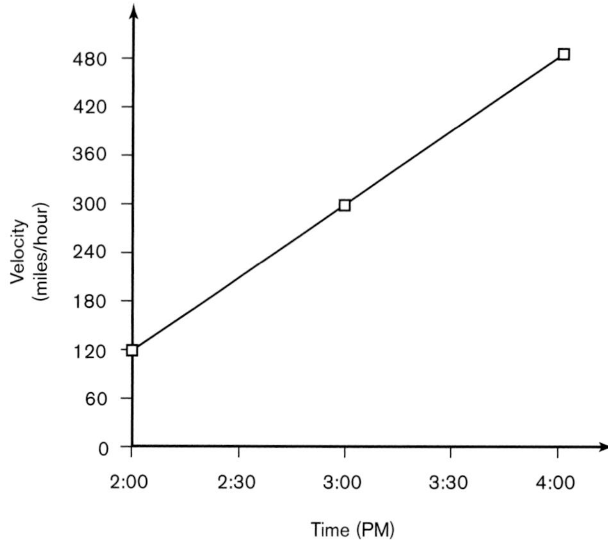

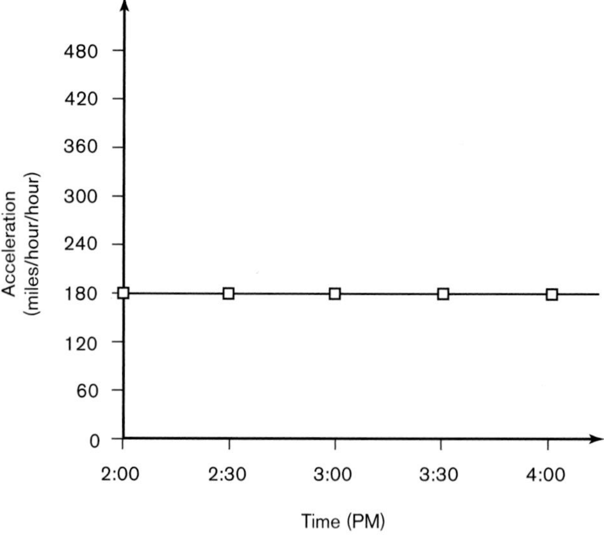

Figure 10.10 The first derivative of velocity is acceleration. The lower graph shows an object accelerating at a constant rate of 180 miles/hour for a duration of 2 hours. The top graph shows the same object with an initial airspeed of 120 miles/hour. Assuming the acceleration rate shown in the lower graph, the object in the upper graph will have an airspeed of 300 miles/hour at the end of the first hour and one of 480 miles/hour at the end of two hours.

derivative is a rate of change (see Figure 10.10). Thus, the first derivative of motion is the rate of change of the velocity, in other words, the acceleration. A constant-velocity motion is devoid of acceleration; it has no change in velocity and therefore its derivative is zero. The second derivative of velocity is the rate of change of the rate of change, or, in motion terms, any change in the rate of acceleration. When the value is non-zero, the result is called *jerk;* other synonyms might include *lurch* and other words to suggest an abrupt change in speed, direction, or rate of curvature. Obviously, in a formal sense, the jerk may be zero, as is the second derivative of a constant-velocity motion. Note that the first derivative of velocity (acceleration) contains time twice, and that the second derivative of velocity (jerk) contains time three times, for example, miles/hour/hour/hour.

In the example of uniform linear acceleration (again see Figure 10.8), the change in velocity is 10 miles/hour/hour; thus, the first derivative is 10 miles/hour/hour and the second derivative, the change in acceleration, is zero. In the example of exponential acceleration (again see Figure 10.9), the velocity has both a first and a second derivative, because not only is the vehicle accelerating (changing velocity), but also the rate of acceleration is increasing. Here the first derivative of velocity is 5-10-15-20-25 miles/hour/hour and the jerk (the second derivative of velocity, or first derivative of acceleration) is a constant 5 miles/hour/hour/hour.

This process of rates of change of rates of change can continue indefinitely, and yes, there are third derivatives, and fourth derivatives, and so on. The reason that this matters is because humans can perceive change, and can perceive the rate of change. Hence, something that is changing will not appear smooth if the rate of change is not continuous; that is, the action will appear jerky if the rate of change varies. Examples of jerk and jerk-free action can be perceived while driving on clover-leaf exit ramps on roadways. On a well-designed ramp, the driver can turn the steering wheel into the turn and can increase the turn of the wheel at a continuous rate. On a poorly designed ramp, the driver must rotate the position of the steering wheel at various rates in order to move in the direction of the curve. Although both ramps curve (have change in direction), the well-designed ramp has a uniform rate of curvature, while the poorly designed ramp does not. Moreover, when the end of the ramp reconnects to a straight roadway, well-designed ramps connect in a continuous fashion.

Understanding derivatives is essential for creating smooth action, and in general, action must contain a first-derivative continuity in the temporal domain and a second-derivative continuity in the spatial domain in order to appear smooth. It is sometimes necessary to determine the derivatives of a sequence of values, and this is done by subtracting adjacent values (see Figure 10.11).

```
REPEAT WITH I=1 TO (N-1)
    RESULT [I]=(P[I+1]-P[I])
END REPEAT
```

Figure 10.11 To determine the derivatives of a sequence of values, subtract adjacent values.

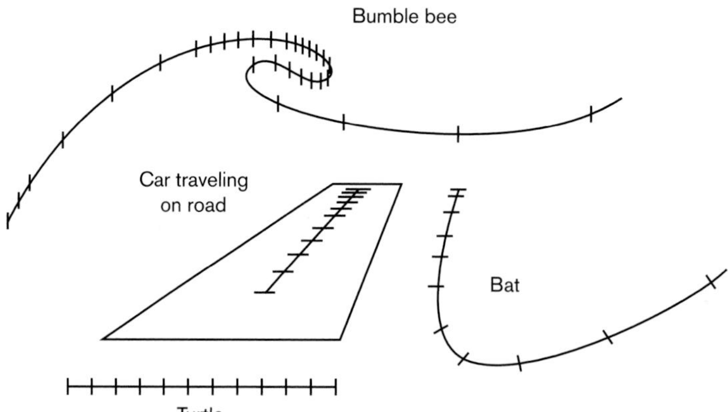

Figure 10.12 Motion pathways. Motion pathways can be straight or curved, simple or complex, 2D or 3D.

Motion Pathways

A ***motion pathway*** or ***motion curve*** is the route along which an object moves (see Figure 10.12). More specifically, it is a line or a curve along which an object moves through a sequence of frames. In mathematics, the term ***trajectory*** is used to mean the same thing, but the meaning is independent of media.

A motion pathway can be extremely simple, or it can be complex, such as a fractal pathway. Motion pathways can exist in 2D or 3D space. They are usually independent of whatever data describes the traveling object, and they are designed as an entity in their own right, independent of objects. Thus, many different objects can travel along the same motion pathway. This separation of motion from object is a feature of most computer animation systems. Finally, motion pathways can be used for the path of any object, including a camera or lights.

Motion Pathways in Practice

The simplest motion pathway is a straight line or a simple curve that describes a sequence of positions in space (see Figure 10.13). In Figure 10.13(a), the object moves along the path without any change to the object itself. Notice that the orientation of the object remains the same as the object traverses the entire motion pathway. A slightly more complex situation is presented in Figure 10.13(b), where the same object travels along the same pathway, but where the object rotates as it travels so that the object remains tangent to the curve at all times. In Figure 10.13(c), again the same pathway is used, but this time the object rotates as it travels, so that the object remains oriented on an external object. The approaches presented in Figures 10.13(b) and 10.13(c) are extremely useful when the object moving along the path is a camera. In Figure 10.13(b), the camera interest remains fixed on the pathway. In Figure 10.13(c), the camera interest remains fixed on an object.

A slightly less typical approach uses the same pathway from the previous example, but involves the object being scaled as it moves along the path (see Figure 10.13(d)).

In Figure 10.13(e), the same pathway is used again, but this time not only is it used to position the object, it is also used to deform the object as the object travels; this approach is called *path deformation,* also known as *spline deformation* and *curve deformation.* The curvature of the pathway itself is used to deform the shape of the object, at every corresponding position along the curve.

Finally, the pathway itself (whether simple or complex) can be extruded into a surface, such that the surface becomes a pathway see Figures 10.13(f) and 10.13(g). In the figures, the pathway has a ribbonlike quality and twists and turns through 3D space; in mathematical terms, the surface normals along the path change orientation in *xyz.* Thus, the twists and turns of the pathway can be used to twist and turn the object as it moves along, as shown in the figure. In Figure 10.13(f), the object moves along the pathway, remaining tangent to it, but not deforming. In Figure 10.13(g), the object moves along the pathway and is deformed accordingly as it goes.

Any combination of the approaches listed above (translation, scale, rotation, and deformation) can be applied to any object as it moves along a pathway.

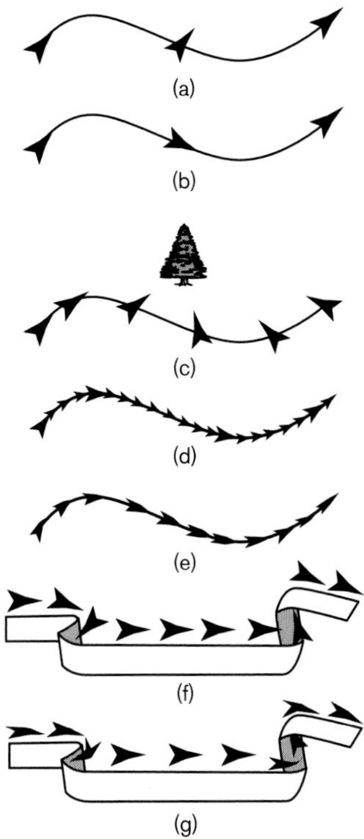

Figure 10.13 Motion pathways. In (a) the triangle does not rotate as it traverses the pathway. In (b) the triangle rotates to remain tangent to path. In (c) the triangle rotates to remain fixed on an external object. In (d) the triangle scales up and down as it moves along the path. In (e) the triangle deforms as it moves along the path. In (f) it rotates as it moves, but does not deform. In (g) it deforms as it moves along the path. Note that in (f) and (g), the path rotates in three dimensions (*xyz*), and thus the triangle rotates in *xyz.*

Motion Pathway Vocabulary

Some motion pathways are so common that they are given names. The idea of a vocabulary of motion pathways is hardly unique to computer animation. In many specialized fields—skiing, aviation, dance—compound motion pathways are important enough to be given names. For example, in aviation, which consists of free-form navigation of a 3D object in a 3D space, there are numerous standard motion pathways, which almost always involve translations (because the plane is flying) and rotations. Examples include a *loop* (a translation incorporating a 360-degree rotation about the *y*-axis), a *roll* (a

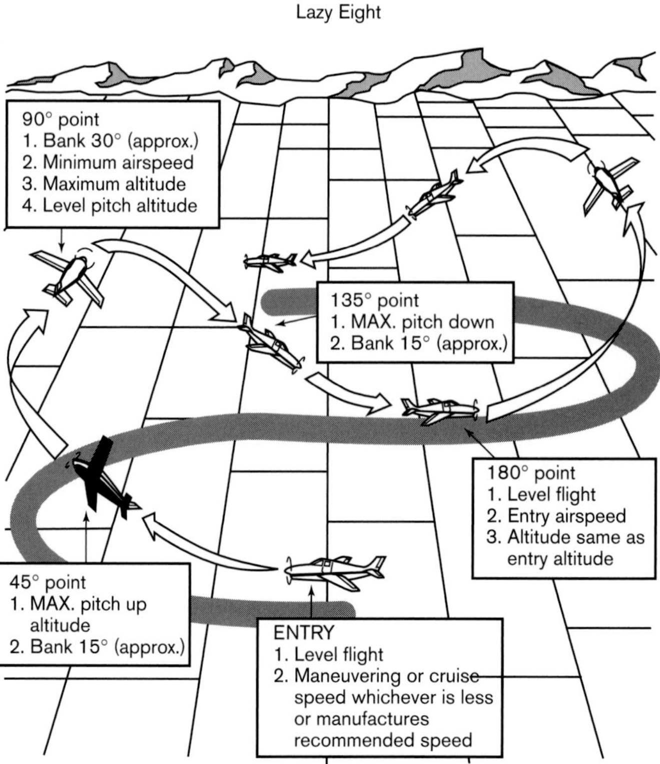

Figure 10.14 Right: Lazy eight. This maneuver derives its name from the manner in which the airplane is made to trace the figure of an eight lying on its side. A lazy eight consists of two 180-degree turns, in opposite directions, while making a climb and a descent in a symmetrical pattern during each of the turns.

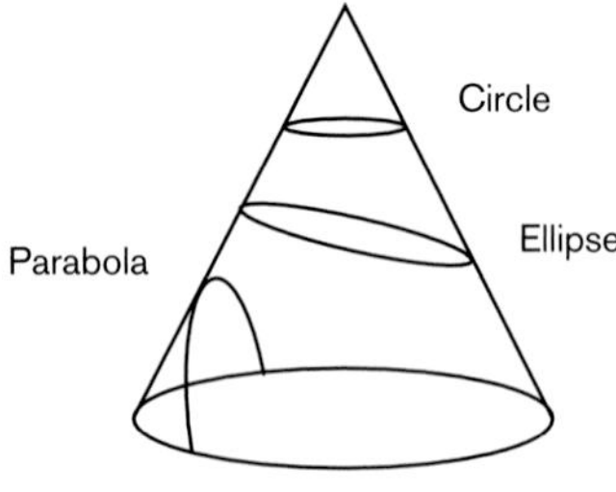

Figure 10.15 Above: Motion pathways based on a circle: circle, arc, ellipse, and parabola.

translation incorporating a 360-degree rotation about the *x*-axis), a spin (a translation incorporating a 360-rotation about the *z*-axis), a two-turn spin, a stall, and a lazy eight (see Figure 10.14).

The idea here is that motion pathways may often be thought of as entities with names, and directed accordingly. With respect to directing computer animation, one goal is to employ a high-level language and have the programs break down the action.

Motion Pathway Primitives and Functions

There are an infinite number of motion pathways, the most common of which are based on a circle (see Figure 10.15), including a circle itself, an arc (part of a circle), sine wave, ellipse, parabola, and hyperbola. Some of these are available as primitive curves in computer animation programs.

Beyond the circular functions, a rich collection of mathematical functions can be used to create pathways as well (see Figure 10.16). One of the reasons that functions are so useful to the animator is

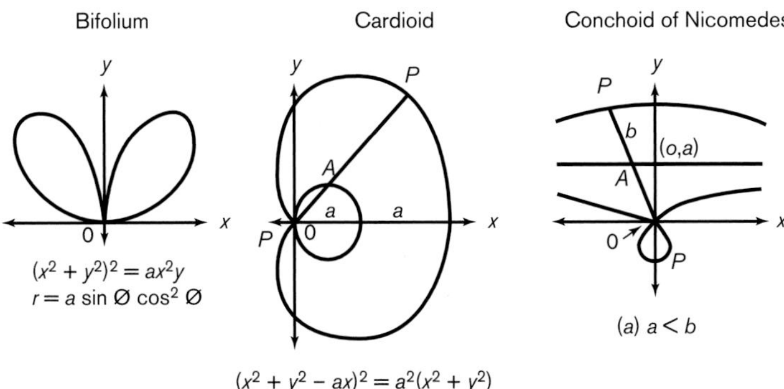

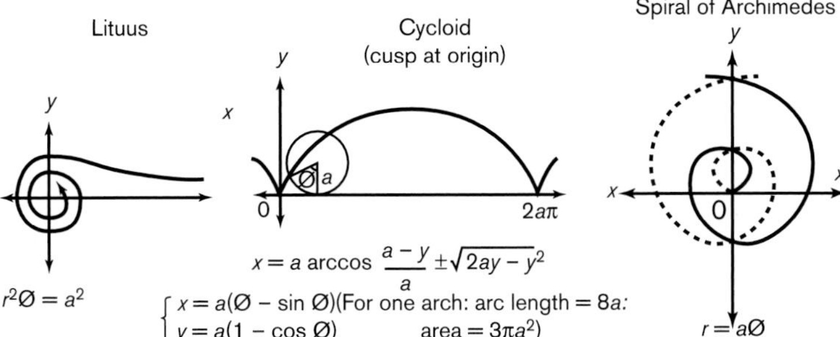

Figure 10.16 Mathematical functions used to create pathways. The corresponding functions are presented with each curve.

that they are parameterized so that the incrementation of one or more input parameters produces a new position on the curve. A word of caution, however, is in order: equal increments of an input parameter to a function do not necessarily produce equally incremented points on the corresponding curve. Thus, to produce curves using functions, it is useful to know about the relationship between input parameters and the resulting curve.

Motion Pathways and Splines

Possibly the most versatile motion pathways are those created with splines. When using splines, just a few control points can be used to create and edit a complex curve. In addition, and possibly most importantly, splines can be used to create smooth, jerk-free motion pathways. Any of the standard splines can be used to create motion pathways. Acceleration and speed can be maintained as an object travels down the spline, as when a car drives over a road. An object can also be rotated so that it always stays normal to the pathway.

Straight-Ahead Animation

Straight-ahead animation is animation that is created by drawing the beginning frame of the animation, then the next frame, and animating continuously through until the end. The action has a beginning frame, but it is not bounded by an end frame, as is key frame animation. There is no predetermined destination; there is simply a flow of action. The first frame is drawn, then the second, then the third, and the action evolves, unfolding itself, as the frames progress.

In computer terms, straight-ahead animation may be produced kinematically, procedurally, dynamically, or behaviorialistically. It may certainly involve acceleration mechanisms as long as they are not predeterminant. It may involve a motion pathway and a destination, but it does not involve a definition of a destination time, for if it did, it would be a key frame approach, not a straight-ahead approach.

Key Frame Animation

The term *key frame animation* originated in the days of manual animation and defined a production process whereby the principal animator broke down all action into a series of key actions. In the traditional cel studio, the key action frames were drawn by the senior animator, whereas the in-between frames were drawn by an assistant. This specialization of labor is typical of industrial processes.

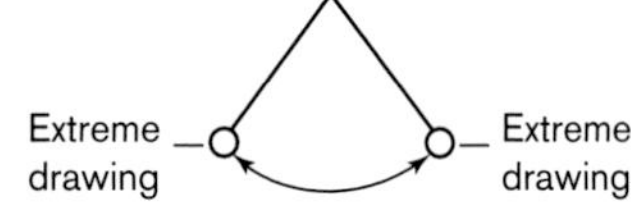

Figure 10.17 The key frames of a swinging pendulum.

Key frame animation is an animation method where the action is bounded by a pair of *key positions*—also known as *key frames, keys,* and *extremes*—that represent the extent of action with a duration of time (see Figure 10.17). For example, the key positions of a clock pendulum would be the leftmost and rightmost positions of its swing. A more complicated example might be the key positions of a football player throwing a football: two key positions might be the player's hand positioned behind the player's head, holding the ball, and the player's hand positioned in front of the player, at the moment of releasing the ball. A key is often typified by (1) a moment of rest and no acceleration, or (2) a moment of maximum position, zero velocity, and maximum acceleration.

Typically, the keys are created by the master animator. The frames between the keys are called *in-betweens,* and their images are formed by a breakdown of the information contained in the keys, plus additional information about the nature of the object in motion. Appropriately, the process of making the in-betweens is called *in-betweening* or *tweening.* The *in-betweener* is a person (or computer program) who creates all the in-between drawings.

In computer animation, key frame animation can be created in both 2D and 3D systems. The 2D approach is often a direct simulation of the cel process whereby an animator draws the extremes and a computer calculates the intermediate shapes and positions; the goal here, to eliminate the human in-betweener, has proven more difficult than anticipated because often the in-between drawings are not simply a blend of the two extreme positions. When applied to 3D graphics, the key frame concept involves parameterizing the world, setting (either explicitly or interactively) the parameters of the extremes, letting the computer calculate the in-between parameters, and using these parameters to move (or deform) the object.

It is worth emphasizing that in key frame animation, the information for the start frame and the end frame is predeterminant. The in-betweens can be calculated at any interval and in any order; there is no dynamic relationship between them; the present is not dependent upon the past. Thus, the conceptual difference between straight-ahead animation and key frame animation is that in key frame animation, the action is bounded by the extremes, and straight-ahead animation is not. The key frame animator animates from these extremes and sees the world as a sequence of gestures and movements that have beginnings and ends. The key frame animator knows that as they draw the 2nd drawing of a series, the 15th drawing of that series is already predetermined. The straight-ahead animator simply lets the action manifest itself, without a predetermined destination. Both techniques are useful approximations of the real world.

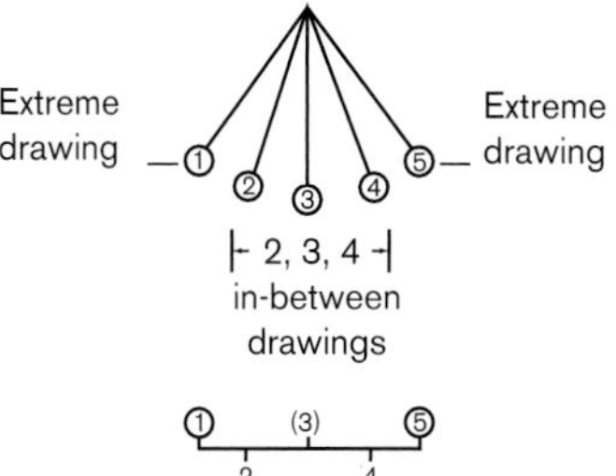

Figure 10.18 Key chart. The key chart specifies where the key frames will fit into the sequence of an animation, and the length of the sequence in frames. There are five frames in this sequence.

Key Charts and Breakdown Drawings

To assist in the in-between process, the animator often designs a *key chart,* which accompanies the first key frame (see Figure 10.18). The chart specifies where the key frames will fit into the sequence of an animation, and the length of the sequence in frames. In this example, there are five frames in the sequence; the odd number assures that there will be a middle frame. The chart also specifies which in-between frame is to be drawn first; this frame is called the *breakdown drawing*

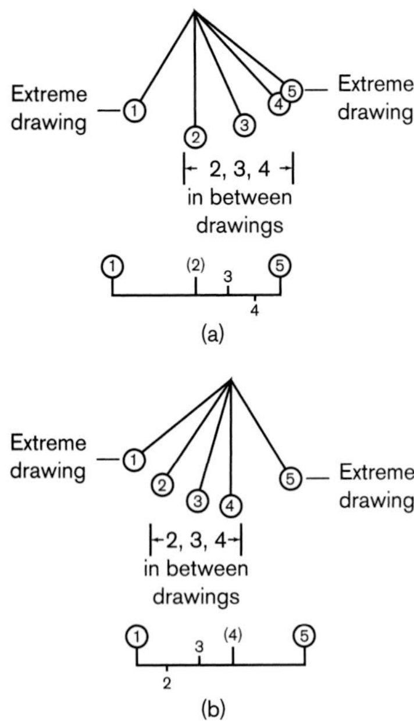

Figure 10.19 Above: The key chart indicates changes in speed—for example, the top chart (a) indicates that most of the in-betweens are used to represent the right part of the swing, creating a quick start and a slow stop. The bottom chart (b) indicates that most of the in-betweens are used to represent the left part of the swing, creating a slow start and a quick stop.

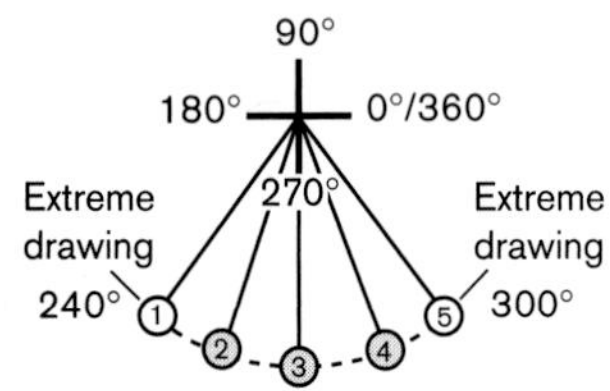


```
ANGLE = 240 DEGREES
REPEAT
    DRAW PENDULUM
    ADD 15 DEGREES TO ANGLE
END REPEAT
```

Figure 10.20 Above: Parametric key frame animation. The animated pendulum is created through the manipulation of the angle parameter, which begins at 240 degrees, ends at 300 degrees, and is incremented 15 degrees for each frame.

and is sometimes the frame exactly in the middle of two given key frames; in this example, the breakdown drawing is frame 3. The more in-betweens, the more frames it takes to present an action, hence, the slower the action. The key chart may also be used to designate changes in speed—for example, the chart can specify where (when) the in-betweens lie in the animation (see Figure 10.19). Remember, animation is not always a science, and like other art forms, can exaggerate, distort, and warp not only geometry, but also timing.

Drawing Representation: Discrete Cels Versus Action Parameters

Key frames can be 2D, 3D, pixel- or voxel-based, or polygon-based. A key frame drawing may be a 2D outline drawing, be it a pencil line drawn by hand or a digital 2D polygon outline. It may be a sprite, that is, a pixel grid able to be moved over a background. It may also be a 3D vector object or voxel object. How the object is represented affects the key frame process.

An alternate approach is to not define the keys and in-betweens in terms of drawings, but rather in terms of parameters that define the shape and position of the object. In this approach, in-betweening involves the interpolation of the parameters from initial to terminal values. These parameters, or ***action parameters,*** are any parameters that define the object, including those that specify position, scale, rotation, and so on.

Parametric Key Framing of Action Parameters

Parametric key frame animation is animation that is represented by and created through the manipulation of action parameters, which change over time and which are defined by start and end values and a rate of change (see Figure 10.20). In the parametric key frame approach, the parameters are modified and the drawing is calculated; the start and end values are analogous to the start and end drawings.

Three-dimensional computer animation that is accomplished using parametric key frame animation involves the following steps: First, the key objects are created and positioned. Then, the in-between values of the action parameters are automatically calculated by the animation software and applied to the object, creating the in-between drawings.

In 3D computer animation, everything in an animation set is parameterized—for example, the position of objects, lights, and camera; the color of lights and objects; textures and reflections; degrees of transparency; density of atmospheric haze; and so on. The computer animator's art lies in the manipulation of these parameters on a frame-to-frame basis. Just as objects and lighting require design, so, too, must action be sculpted in space.

Keep in mind that although each controllable degree of freedom in a model or animation can be assigned a parameter, there are many ways to define key values. Obviously, they can be defined interactively, by creating an object and then positioning it. But they can also be defined explicitly, by typing in values at the keyboard. And an object's shape and position can be derived from the real world, using rotoscopy or even sophisticated 3D motion tracking.

The parametric approach to key frame animation allows at least two ways of achieving action: (1) by parameterizing the object and interpolating from an initial object to a terminal object, changing its geometry (see Figure 10.21), and (2) by parameterizing an action transformation, which gets applied to the object; the parameters being interpolated are usually those of the three axes transformations—translation, rotation, and scale. The translation transformation moves objects left, right, up, down, in, or out (see Figure 10.22). The scale transformation makes the object bigger or smaller (see Figure 10.23). And three-rotation transformation pivots an object around one of three axes (see Figure 10.24). Transformations can be combined, or concatenated, creating one transformation that combines the successive order of two or more primitive transformations. For example, there may be one transformation that can perform a rotation followed by a scale.

Do note that parametric methods in general are widely used in computer animation, and that many parametric methods (inverse kinematics, dynamics, procedural) do not require key framing. In the key frame system, although the model may be fully parameterized, it is always constrained by the extremes.

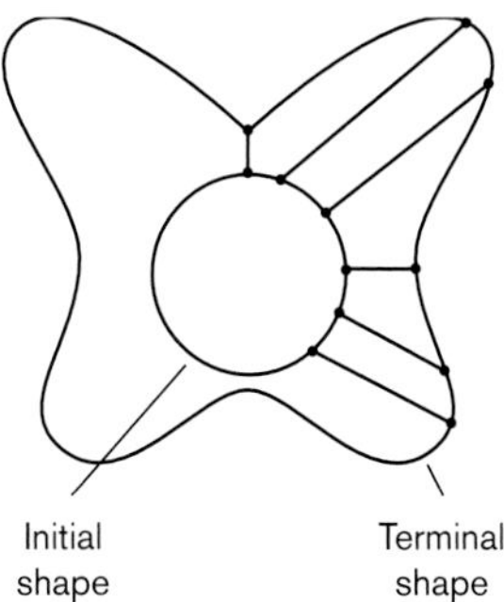

Figure 10.21 Above: The object's shape is parameterized, then interpolated from an initial shape to a terminal shape.

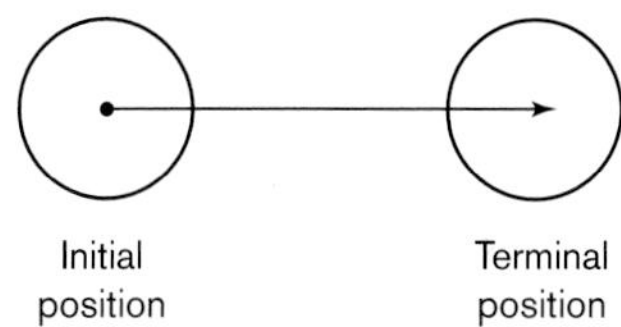

Figure 10.22 Above: Translation transformation.

Figure 10.23 Above: Scale transformation.

Easing

It is important to understand that the quest for reality is only partly in how objects look; reality must also involve believable action. Animators

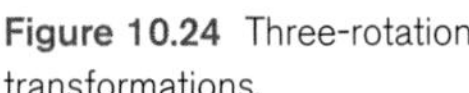

Figure 10.24 Three-rotation transformations.

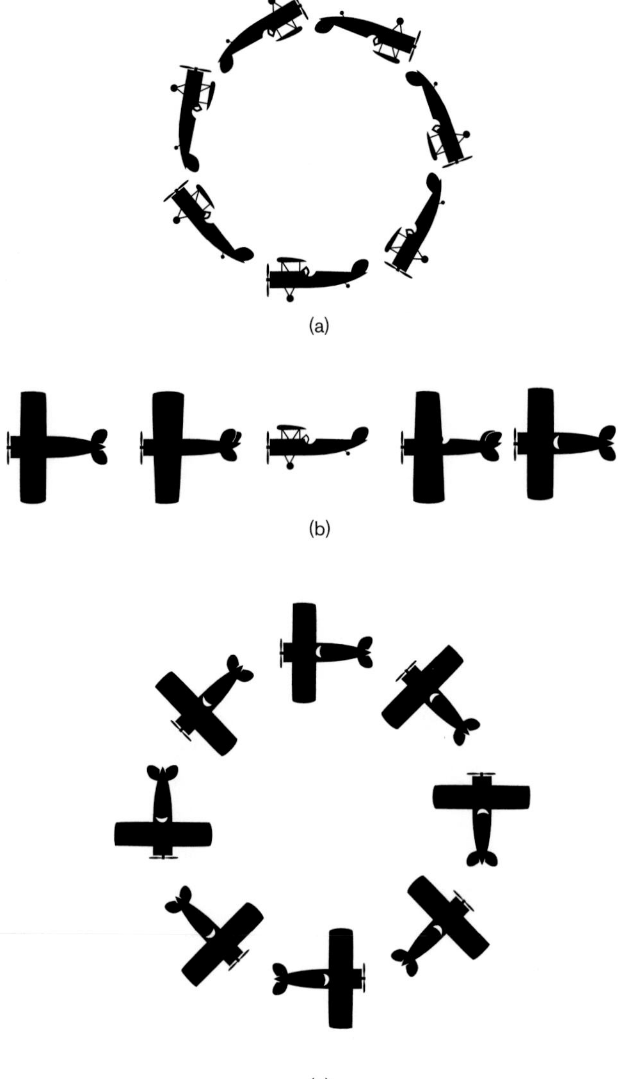

need to understand how action really occurs and how to approximate it. The focus of this section is on easing methods that achieve believable action, albeit not necessarily natural action. This section examines both ad hoc methods as well as eases that mimic nature.

Easing and key framing are both about action and, hence, easily bound together, but are definitely not the same thing. Key frame animation requires a start state of the action, an end state of the action, a start time, an end time, and a rule, called an *ease,* or *faring,* which specifies how the in-betweens are calculated. For example, an ease would determine whether an action will begin slowly and end quickly, or begin quickly and end slowly. Eases also provide a way to depict acceleration and deceleration. In other words, eases are functions that calculate rates of change.

If, for example, the key frames define a start position and an end position of an object, and if there is a defined motion pathway, then an ease will dictate the individual positions of the object for each frame as it moves along the pathway. Most natural action starts gradually, and then increases speed. When an ease starts off slowly, it is said to *ease in.* Conversely, when an ease ends slowly, it is said to *ease out.*

In formal terms, easing is a 1D time-to-curve mapping; it maps a point in time to a point on a curve. There are two ways to define an ease: (1) it can be defined so that it returns a set of solutions for a given number of frames (times), or (2) it can be defined to return a solution for a given percentage value, where the percentage value represents a percent of the time along the action. In both cases, the function takes even divisions of time and returns uneven divisions of action.

Eases are used in all approaches to animation, whether hand drawn, motion graphics, or computer-generated. Eases are used to control the movements of objects, cameras, zooms, focus, color and lighting changes, and special effects such as fades, dissolves, and glows (see Figure 10.25). Practically speaking, everything that changes, eases. A camera that is meant to move, eases; the camera must be pushed, and it has to gain momentum and speed. Similarly

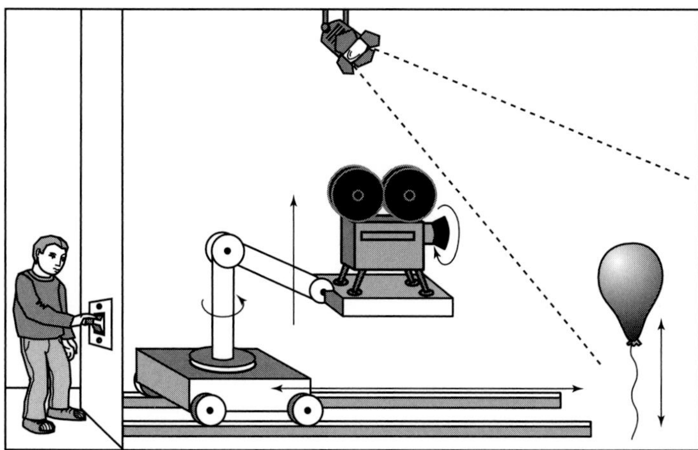

Figure 10.25 An easing world. The dimmer switch at the left can be eased up and down; thus, the spotlight at the top can be eased on and off. In the middle of the scene is a camera on a dolly, which can be eased up and down, and in and out; its rotation can also be eased. At the right is a balloon, which can be eased up and down.

for zooms, the zoom ring has to be turned and eased. Lights fading in or out, or changing color—all have to be eased. Morphing—changing from one image to another—requires easing in and easing out on the control points. Any transition effect must be eased.

In a practical sense, the only time one does not need to ease in or ease out is when an object—a moving car, a meteor—enters into the frame already at full velocity; the object is moving at a constant velocity because it must have already reached constant velocity before it entered the frame. Hence, not everything moving in the field of view is in a moment of easing in or out. A camera panning a scene may already be at rotational velocity before there is a cut to the scene. But if a cut to the scene is made before the camera starts moving, it must ease-in when it first starts to move. It is important to note that a scene starting with the camera at rest followed by an ease-in has a different feeling than a scene in which the camera is already in motion.

It is important to emphasize that when the ease being performed is with respect to a change in position, the ease assumes that the pathway along which the object is moving is already defined.

The creation of eases is quite open-ended; some produce better results than others.

Percentage of parameter being eased
100
90
80
70
60
50
40
30
20
10
0
1 2 3 4 5 6 7 8 9 10 11 12
Time in frames
Ease in 20%
Coast 60%
Ease out 20%

Figure 10.26 Above: An ease diagram is a curve that indicates the rate of change of an action. The curve begins with a gradual incline, which indicates a slow ease-in. A steady speed is indicated by the straighter, middle part of the curve. And finally, deceleration to a stop is indicated by the right part of the diagram. The more vertical the curve, the faster the corresponding action; the flatter the curve, the slower the corresponding action.

Figure 10.27 Below: The car accelerates, coasts, then decelerates to a stop, according to the ease diagram in Figure 10.26.

Ease Diagrams

An *ease diagram,* also known as a *timing curve* or *function curve,* is a plotted curve with time along the *x*-axis and the parameter being eased along the *y*-axis (see Figure 10.26). In Figure 10.27, the car accelerates slowly (eases in), as shown in the left part of the ease diagram. The car then moves at a steady speed, as indicated by the straight, middle part of the curve. And finally, the car decelerates to a stop (eases out) as indicated by the right part of the diagram. In computer animation, the ease diagram might be automatically created when an action is created, or it can be drawn by hand. Every action has a corresponding ease, and every ease has a unique ease diagram.

It is important to note that timing curves are entities in themselves and exist independently of an action. They can be saved, retrieved, translated, scaled, reversed, cut, copied, and pasted (see Figure 10.28). Points can be added to or deleted from the curve, and points on the curve can be edited as well. Each change applied to the curve alters the action that might be associated with the ease. Finally, an ease diagram can be applied to any number of different actions.

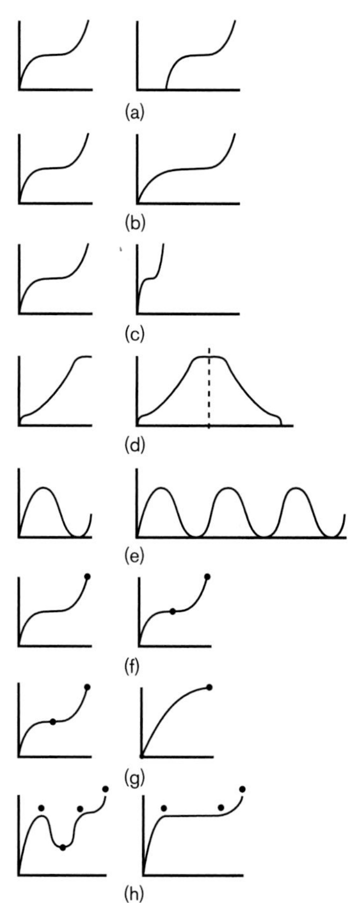

Figure 10.28 Editing timing curves. In (a) the curve is translated; translating the ease curve is the same as translating the action in time—a curve that is translated to the right causes the action to happen later. In (b) the curve is scaled larger in *x*. In (c) the curve is scaled smaller in *x*. Scaling an ease curve is the same as making an animation longer or shorter—when a curve is scaled smaller, the animation is made shorter; when a curve is scaled larger, the animation is made longer. In (d) the curve is copied and reversed. In (e) it is copied and repeated. In (f) a point is added to the curve. In (g), by moving the new point, the curve is modified. In (h), given a curve with several points, one point is deleted.

Issues of Continuity

Easing is a rate-of-change problem. If an object is motionless, for example, and then is suddenly in motion, the rate of change has been discontinuous, so the action will jerk. If an object is traveling at a constant 60 miles/hour one moment and the next moment is traveling at a constant 70 miles/hour, even though both speeds may have been constant, the rate of change of speed is discontinuous, and thus the motion will jerk. In order for the action to appear natural and continuous, the rate of change of action must be constant. Actions can change speeds, but they must change speeds at a constant rate of change to appear natural. In cases where the acceleration is not consistent, then the rate of change of the acceleration must be consistent.

Types of Eases

An action can ease in an infinite number of ways. It can begin quickly or slowly, or it can proceed at a constant rate, or it can happen at a random rate. This section presents types of commonly used eases. The reader is cautioned that not all of these eases are designed to produce a smooth continuity of action, and that our definition of ease is that it is a rule to define a continuity of action, and that a rule to mimic smooth action is but one case.

Linear Interpolation Ease *Interpolation* is a method used to calculate intermediate values that are between two existing values, where the quantity of in-between values is specified, and where the values can represent anything from position to shape, time, or behavior. Interpolation is a technique widely employed in computer graphics for a variety of purposes, including animation.

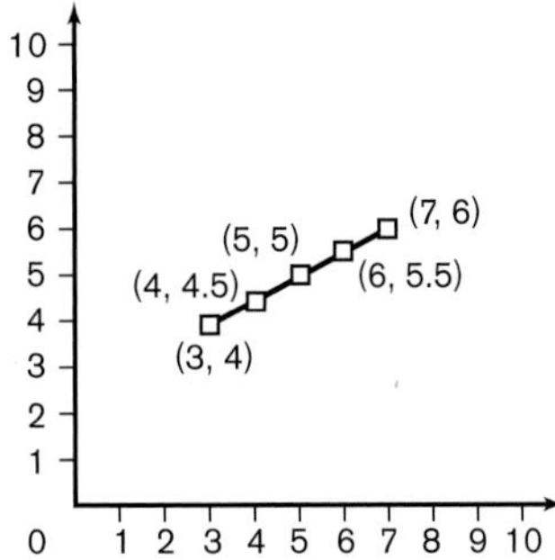

Figure 10.29 Above: Linear interpolation.

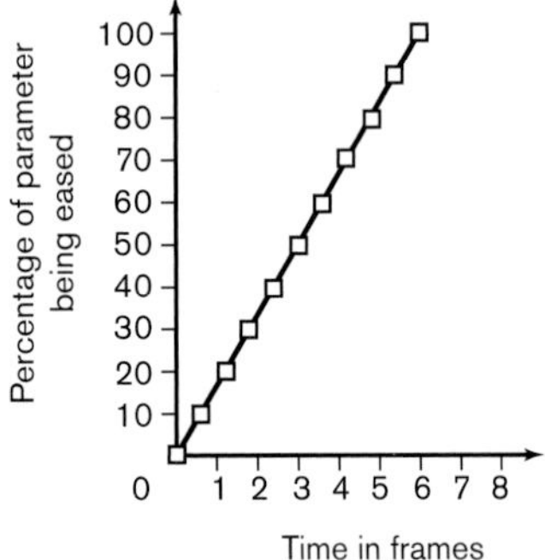

Figure 10.30 Above: A linear ease.

Linear interpolation is an interpolation in which the calculated values are equally spaced between the two existing values (see Figure 10.29). Linear interpolation is perhaps the simplest way of getting from one state to another in a designated amount of steps, and hence is used to create eases, in particular, *linear interpolation eases,* or *linear eases* (see Figure 10.30). The parameter being eased can represent anything that can be parameterized—for example, a distance along a curve or an angle around an arc. In a linear ease of distance along a curve, an object would increase its distance toward the end position in equal increments for each key frame. In a linear ease of an angle around an arc, an object would increase its angle toward the end angle in equal increments for each key frame.

While this solution is valid, it does not produce natural-looking results because it does not simulate acceleration or deceleration as manifested in nature. That is, most objects in the real world do not move in a linear fashion—for example, they decelerate to a stop. A linear ease produces a jerk in the action (a second derivative discontinuity) at the start and end of the shot and are not acceptable for most cases. This does not mean that it is without uses. It is fine for handling action that is passing through the screen, assuming that one is viewing an object already in motion. It is often used by scientific visualizers for whom even steps are often more important than those that mimic Newtonian physics (involving acceleration and mass).

Anything that can be represented numerically—position, scale, angle of rotation, color, and surface normals—can be interpolated. All that is needed is the initial value, the terminal value, and the number of in-between values that are to be calculated. Figure 10.29 presents a simple example of linear interpolation, suppose that there are two points on a plane, the initial point (3, 4) and the terminal point (7, 6). And suppose that three in-between points are needed, totaling five points. A linear interpolation is calculated by subtracting the initial point values from the terminal point values, creating a total x displacement value and a total y displacement value, in this case 4 and 2. Each in-between x and y displacement value is equal to the total displacement value divided by the total number of interpolation points minus 1 (in this case 5 – 1, or 4). Thus, the x displacement value for each in-between is $^4/_4$ or 1, and the y displacement value for each in between is $^2/_4$ or 0.5. These displacement values are then successively added to the original point values, to create a sequence of linear interpolated positions:

3, 4 initial point; 4, 4.5; 5, 5; 6, 5.5; 7, 6 terminal point.

Linear interpolation can be described in more formal terms as such. Given two points, P_1 and P_2, and t, where t is time relative to the two points and $0 \leq t \leq 1$, any in-between point can be calculated according to the following formula:

$$P(t) = (1 - t)P_1 + tP_2$$

The equation $P(t) = (1 - t)P_1 + tP_2$ is the parametric definition of a line, used to calculate the in-between values for linear interpolation. Therefore, in the previous example, the midpoint—$t = 1/2$—could be calculated as:

$$P(1/2) = (1 - 1/2)P_1 + (1/2)P_2$$

For x: $P(1/2) = (1 - 1/2)3 + (1/2)7 = (1/2)3 + 7 = 5$

For y: $P(1/2) = (1 - 1/2)4 + (1/2)6 = (1/2)4 + 6 = 5$.

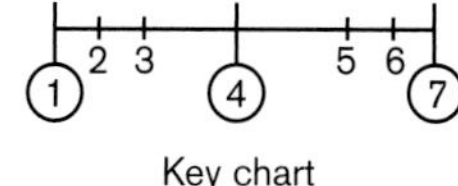

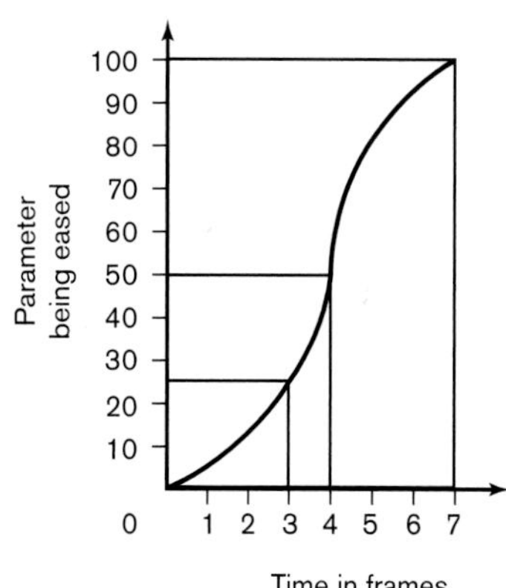

Figure 10.31 The classic breakdown ease. The percentage of the parameter being eased is first divided into half, then the outer halves are divided in half, then the outermost quarters are divided in half, and so on. The results resemble natural acceleration and deceleration.

Other kinds of eases can be more complex, such as eases that change according to sine waves or logarithmic progressions, or those that are calculated using the mathematical formula for acceleration, so that actions occur in a natural way.

Classic Breakdown Ease The *classic breakdown ease* is an ease that is created by recursively subdividing from the center of the action outward toward the two extremes. That is, the percentage of the parameter being eased is first divided into half, and then the outer halves are divided into halves, and then the outermost quarters are divided into half, and so on (see Figure 10.31). Action is often drawn on an odd number of cels so that there shall be a middle frame. This subdivision process produces a multiframe sequence with a slow ease-in, rapid velocity in the middle of the action, and a slow ease-out. Classic breakdown eases are simple to create and the results resemble natural acceleration and deceleration, but they are not mathematically accurate. Applied recursively, subdivision is a basis of thousands of computer algorithms, including rendering, compression, hidden surface removal, and anti-aliasing.

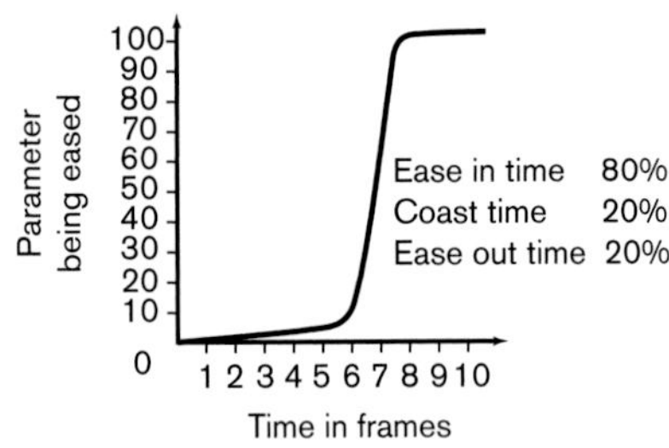

Figure 10.32 Linear acceleration ease.

Linear Acceleration Ease A commonly used ease, certainly whenever a computer is being used to calculate it accurately, is the *linear acceleration ease* (see Figure 10.32), which uses the formulas of velocity, acceleration, and deceleration (presented earlier in this chapter) to ease parameters. That is, these formulas are applied to a parameter, such as an angle, and the parameter is eased accordingly. The parameter can be eased either indefinitely, or until a desired velocity is reached (when accelerating), or until the action achieves a state of rest (when decelerating). The linear acceleration ease diagram illustrates a smooth transition from zero velocity, and hence is useful for animating an action that starts at a rest state. It can also be reversed to animate an action coming to a stop.

Linear acceleration simulates the way action behaves in the real world. When an action begins, it usually begins in small increments, which become increasingly larger as the action approaches a constant speed. For example, when a camera starts to dolly, it begins to dolly slowly, until it achieves the desired speed. When an action ends, it becomes progressively slower as the action slows to a stop—as an ordinary automobile might gradually slow down, eventually braking to a stop.

Remember that when in-betweening, the origin and destination are known; therefore an ease must calculate the acceleration based on the change incurred during the ease-in. The deceleration is based on the change incurred during the ease-out. And the *coast*, or constant velocity portion of the ease, is based on dividing the remaining change in action into equal increments. We must solve for the velocity and acceleration parameters so that the acceleration, coast, and deceleration all work together such that the in-between values lie between the two extremes.

Sine Wave Ease Sine waves provide a convenient way to create action, especially action that is oscillating (see Figure 10.33). A *sine wave ease* is an ease derived from a circle and can be used to approximate many biological and natural manifestations, especially for objects in a steady state of motion—a dog's tail wagging, a person breathing, ocean waves, swaying trees, a walking person, a cork bobbing on water, and certain types of machinery such as pistons connected to rotating shafts.

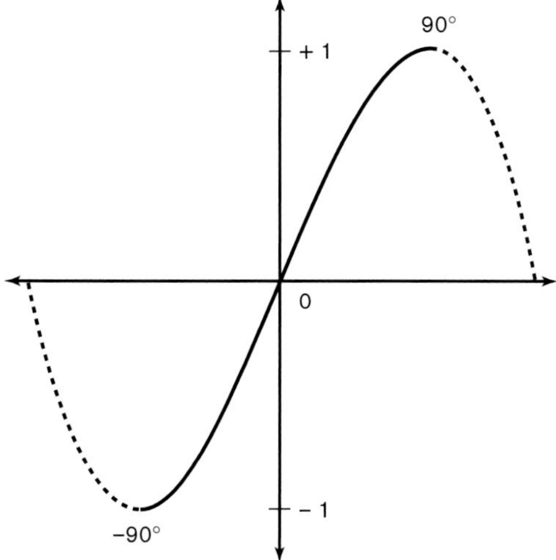

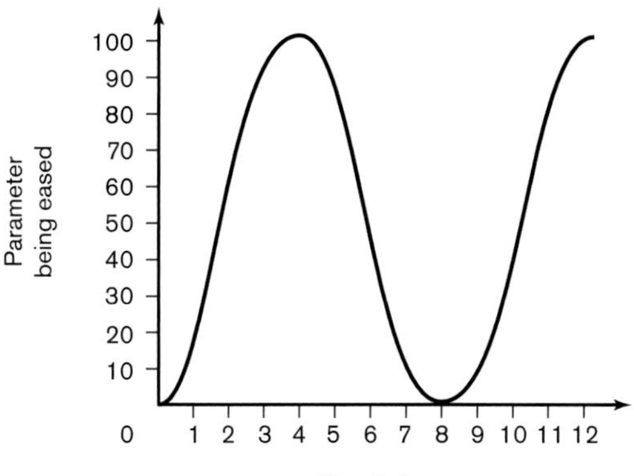

Figure 10.33 Left: Sine wave ease. The sine wave is created from a function that uses an angle as a parameter; the angle has a range of –90 to +90 degrees, domain of the sine is $-1 \leq \text{sine} \leq 1$.

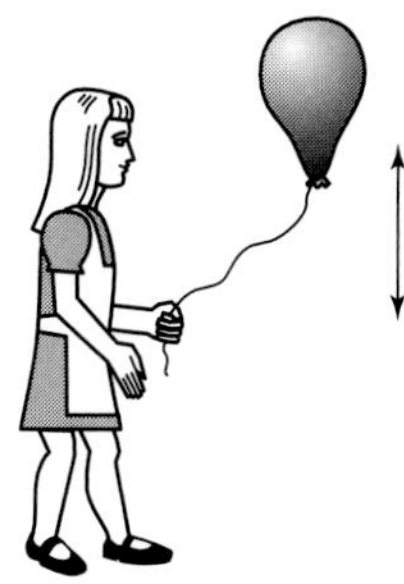

Figure 10.34 Above: A balloon bobbing up and down on a straight line according to a sine ease. The action produced by a sine wave ease begins slowly, achieves a fairly constant velocity, slows to a stop, then reverses direction.

A sine wave ease is most applicable for action that oscillates between two extreme positions. The action produced by a sine wave ease begins slowly, achieves a fairly constant velocity, and then slows to a stop. For example, a little girl might be holding a balloon that is bobbing up and down in a smooth fashion. The balloon moves along a straight line (the assumed pathway) between a lower point and a maximum height (see Figure 10.34).

The action based on a sine wave ease is markedly similar to the action based on a linear acceleration or deceleration ease, but it is not the same. The sine wave motion starts to slow a little sooner, and it has a more rounded toe and shoulder that creates a more organic feel to the motion.

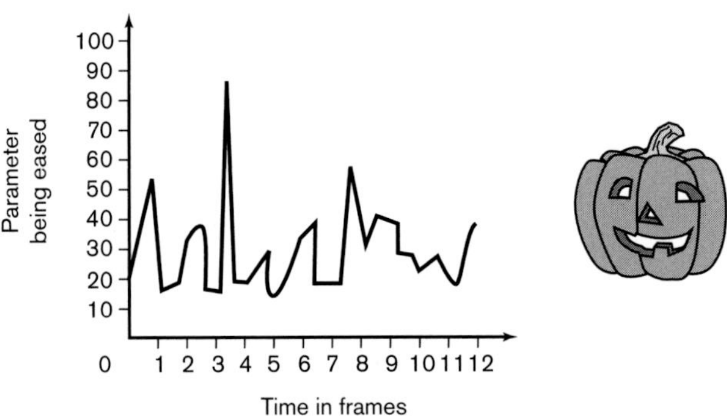

Figure 10.35 Right: Random ease. The glow of the lantern fills the room with randomly flickering light.

Figure 10.36 Below: Empirical ease. The timing of the ball may be analyzed to create an ease for an animated ball. The action has a slow start; then it accelerates quickly, stops at the maximum height, and accelerates back to the ground.

The sine function is attractive because it is centered at zero, and it has a domain of –1 to +1. Hence, it is ideal for doing oscillatory motion around a center (although this can be normalized to a 0 to 1 domain). But because it has an initial and terminal speed of zero, it can also be used to ease between two extremes.

Random Ease While it is often the case that eases impose some logical, orderly progression on an action, this does not necessarily have to be the case. An ease can be completely random—that is, a *random ease* (see Figure 10.35). For example, suppose that the scene is a room that includes a jack-o'-lantern; the glow of the lantern fills the room with randomly flickering light. To animate the light as seen inside the room, the change in the lighting might be extremely fast at first, followed by very slow, followed by another fast change, and then an even faster change. This sort of random ease might be necessary in order to achieve a particular emotional impact. Because computers are very good at computing random numbers, computers are also good at creating random eases, and any action parameter being eased can be eased randomly.

Empirical Ease Eases can also be designed empirically. An *empirical ease* can be designed by observing natural action (see Figure 10.36). For example, if the action in a scene is to simulate the throwing of a ball, then an actual pitch can be photographed and then

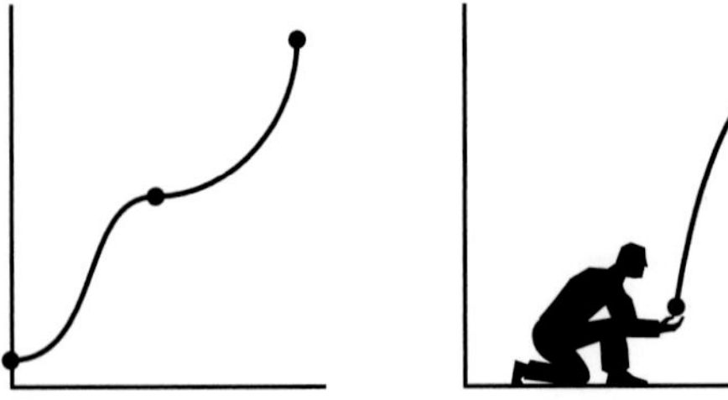

rotoscoped to determine the position of the ball in each frame. The rotoscoped positions of the ball may then be digitized and analyzed to create an ease for an animated ball; they can also be used to create a motion pathway of a real ball.

Spline Ease Eases can also be created by hand: the animator draws the ease diagram or the points that compose it. In today's world, it is more efficient to draw only a few points and employ the computer to construct a spline—the spline may or may not pass through the points, depending upon the type of spline used.

The beauty of this method is that a spline allows for the ease to progress smoothly. This is because the spline not only curves smoothly, allowing for continuous acceleration and deceleration, but it also progresses smoothly between different rates of acceleration and deceleration. This means that action easing on a spline will not jerk, which is often a critical requirement. Any of the various spline forms, such as Bezier splines or B-splines, can be used. This method allows one to create action that might move and rest—consider the flight of a hummingbird, for example.

Figure 10.37 Above: Anticipation. Before moving forward, a train first goes back a short distance, then proceeds to go forward.

Subtleties in Easing—Anticipation and Overshoot

Anticipation is when a large action is preceded by a smaller action, in the opposite direction, that sets up, or anticipates, the larger action (see Figure 10.37). For example, before moving forward, the motion first goes back a short distance and then proceeds. More precisely, when throwing a ball forward, a person pulls their body back first, and then moves forward. Conversely, *overshoot* is when a large action is followed by a smaller action in the reverse direction. For example, a forward motion comes to a rest by rocking a bit, as one might do on a train when it is coming to a halt (see Figure 10.38). Such subtleties can be built into eases (see Figure 10.39).

Figure 10.38 Above: Overshoot. A forward-moving train comes to a rest by first rocking forward a bit.

An Advantage of Easing

In an animation, some frames are more important than others—they represent a point in time that is critical to the action or story. Thus, sometimes, animators need to look at one frame in an animation before the entire animation is made. When easing during key framing, the in-between frames can be solved in any order. For example, easing

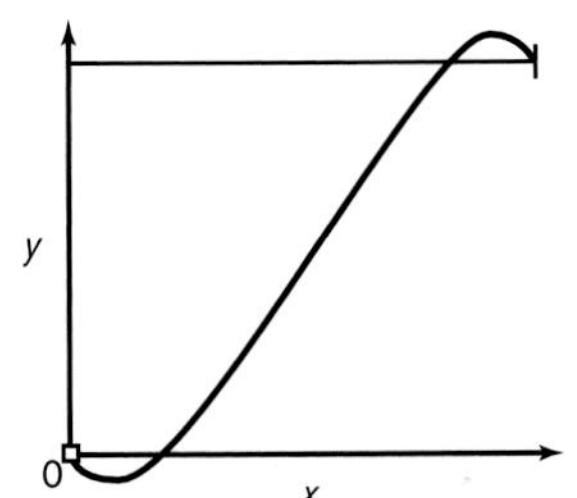

Figure 10.39 An ease that incorporates anticipation and overshoot. Notice that the start of the curve dips below the bottom horizontal line, and the end of the curve arches above the top horizontal line.

enables the animator to calculate the position of an object at a frame 60% into the ease, without creating all of the preceding frames first. It is also possible to calculate all of the positions for all of the objects in the frames before creating the frames, which is a common practice. Once all of the parameters are calculated, the parameters can be stored and used to create the frames; if any particular frame needs to be re-rendered, the data for that frame will be available.

A Final Word on Easing and Key Frame Animation

It is important to note that easing techniques need not necessarily be bound to key framing. For example, an object can be made to accelerate without any predefined terminal position. Also, in-betweening is not the only way to do realistic motion with 3D parametric objects. For example, motion can be calculated dynamically—a rocket ship could be launched into space, where the rocket has a simulated rocket motor and a steering mechanism and the Earth has simulated gravity that is exerted on the mass of the rocket. As the rocket is launched into the dynamically modeled atmosphere, the animation that is created is a result of the forces of the environment. These dynamic approaches are discussed in greater detail in Chapter 12.

11

Kinematic Motion and Mechanisms

This chapter presents a brief, formal review of kinematics, the study of motion in terms of position, velocity, and acceleration, without regard to actual masses or forces. Kinematics focuses on the mechanism, and the transference and transformation of motion. In 3D computer animation, much of what gets moved are kinematic mechanisms. The approach taken here is to introduce the computer animator to the concepts of physical mechanisms that move or permit movement—a cuckoo clock and a marionette are both kinematic structures. Toward these needs, this chapter defines kinematics as a study of the movement of rigid objects. It also inventories elementary kinematic mechanisms such as levers and gears and shows how to construct them using a computer. Presented are ways to create mechanisms that will produce a specific movement, as well as ways to analyze movements to understand what mechanisms might create them.

This chapter is closely tied to Chapter 10, which presents the concepts of speed, velocity, and acceleration. All mechanisms involve speed, velocity, and acceleration, and sections here show how actions can be designed to achieve particular velocities and accelerations, and how velocity and acceleration are analyzed. Also covered are the concepts of degrees of freedom and constraints, and how they can be used to modify action. The chapter concludes with a discussion of inverse kinematics, where goals are used to evaluate how an action occurs, rather than to specify it a priori.

At first glance, kinematics may seem like arcane 19th-century science, but in fact it is the formal basis of almost all

Above: From *Bunny*, a short animated film by Chris Wedge.

Figure 11.1 Above: A link.

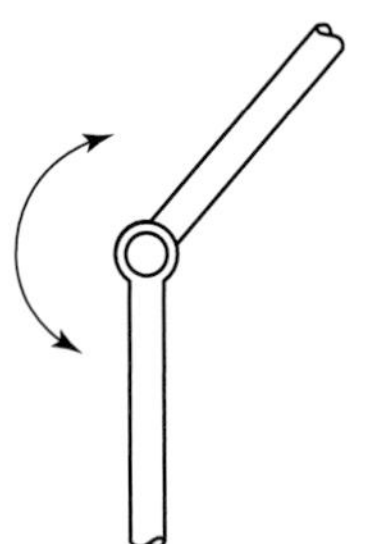

Figure 11.2 Above: Kinematic pair. The two links are connected with a joint that permits planar rotation.

translation/scaling/rotating motion. Kinematics provides a model of the human skeleton as well as of a steam engine. A keen awareness of its concepts and terms should provide the computer animator with insights into directing action, as well as understanding what one sees on the screen. Kinematics is a fundamental science for the computer animator because it studies and catalogs knowledge about motion—the continuous change of place or position. It is upon a kinematic foundation that almost all sophisticated action is built. The techniques presented in this chapter are general and may be applied to any animation, including that of a complicated robot (as seen in a Lucas film), which involves lots of linkages. The techniques here are, by and large, indifferent to whether the model is real or virtual—the rules are well understood and similar.

Links, Joints, and Chains

The most basic kinematic element is the *link*. A link is a rigid moving part (see Figure 11.1). Links are joined together into *linkages* (see Figure 11.2) by the use of joints. There are two basic types of *joints*—those that slide (translate) and those that pivot (rotate) (see Figure 11.3). Pivoting joints can be either 2D or 3D: 2D pivoting joints have a

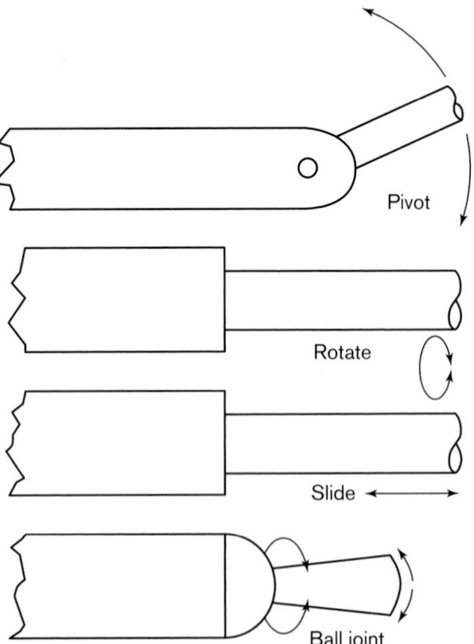

Figure 11.3 Right: The basic types of joints—those that slide (translate) and those that pivot (rotate). Note that in the ball joint, the casing that holds the ball limits the angle of rotation.

single degree of freedom and act like a hinge; 3D pivoting joints can rotate freely and are called *ball joints*. Note that while these terms are taken from the general field of kinematics and also relate to the everyday use of the terms, they may be defined differently in some computer animation programs—for example, the term *joint* might be used to refer to what we called a *link*. Thus, caution should be taken when using these terms.

The simplest kind of linkage is the ***kinematic pair***, which consists of two links organized so that one is constrained to rotate about a pivoting joint (see again Figure 11.2), or to move back and forth inside a slide. The kinematic pair is the nucleus of kinematics.

Connecting kinematic pairs with joints (see Figure 11.4) produces a ***kinematic chain***, also called ***articulated chain*** or simply ***chain.*** Many computer animation programs incorporate the use of these fully jointed kinematic chains—moving one link will result in the flexible movement of all attached links (see Figure 11.5).

It is worth noting that while a simple hierarchical model is not necessarily a kinematic chain, it can be defined and arranged to be a chain; the definition of the hierarchy can be such that the hierarchical connections (combined with the use of strategically placed objects' centers of rotation) behave similarly to joints, and the models in the hierarchy behave similarly to links (see Figure 11.6). Unfortunately, the movement of the links will not result in flexible movement of all attached links as in the case of the fully articulated chain described above; the attached links have to be individually placed (see Figure 11.7). Thus, because animating hierarchical chains

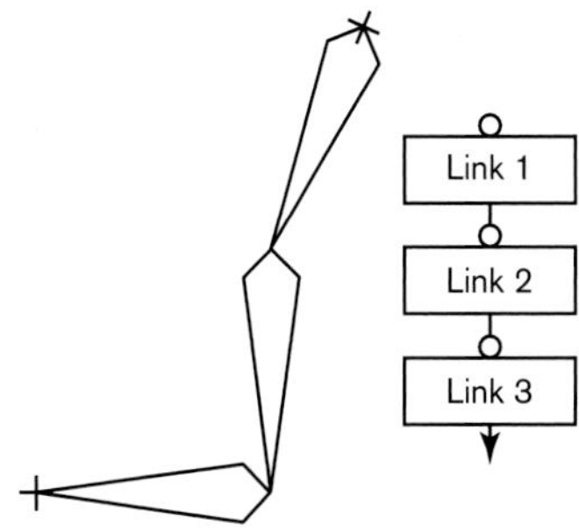

Figure 11.4 Above: The kinematic chain. The left side of the figure presents a jointed chain; the right side presents the corresponding schematic representation.

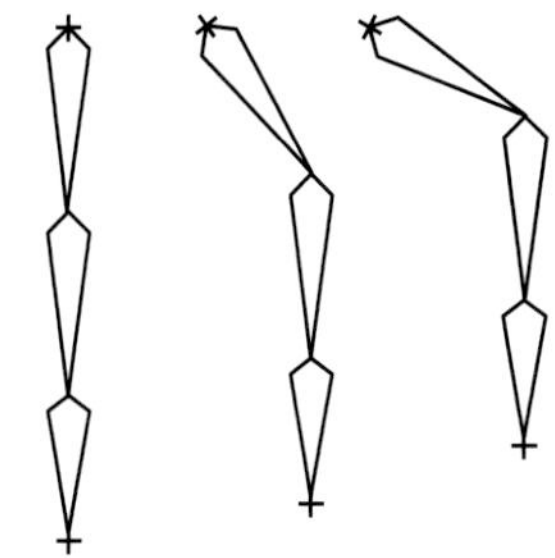

Figure 11.5 Above: Fully jointed kinematic chains.

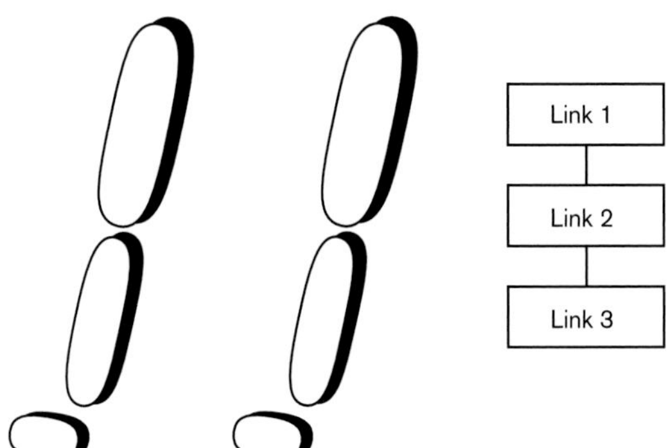

Figure 11.6 Left: A simple hierarchical model is not necessarily a kinematic chain. The figure on the left is a collection of individual models, arranged to look like a chain. However, due to the fact that there is no virtual connection between the parts, the collection of models is just that—a collection, not a kinematic chain. The figure on the right looks exactly the same. However, the models are defined as part of a hierarchical model, and therefore can be defined to behave like a chain.

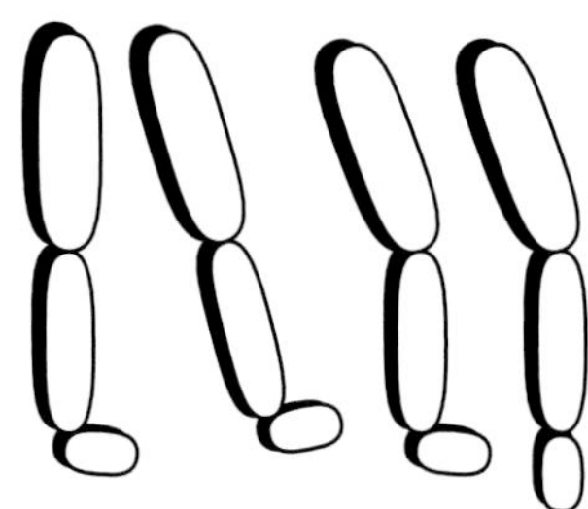

Figure 11.7 Above: Although the figure on the right in Figure 11.6 was defined to behave like a chain, the movement of the links will not result in flexible movement of all attached links as in the case of the fully articulated chain.

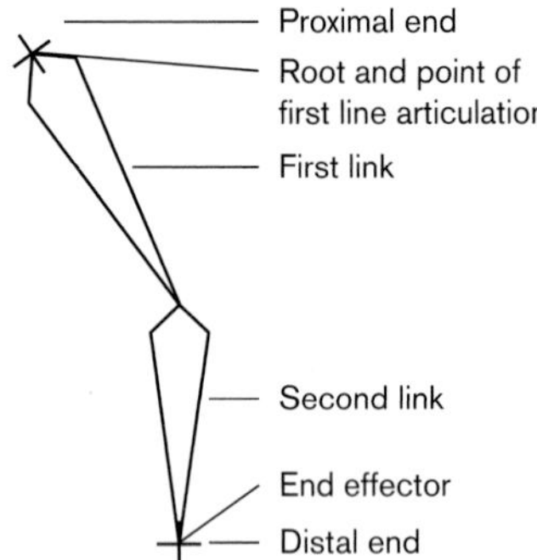

Figure 11.8 Above: The parts of a kinematic chain.

Figure 11.9 Right: Two schematic diagrams illustrating different meanings of the term *root.* The left side of the figure illustrates the schematic diagram for a skeleton; the root is represented by a nodule at the top of the topmost node. The right side of the figure illustrates the schematic diagram for a regular hierarchical model, the root being the topmost node in the hierarchy.

can be difficult, and because many computer animation programs include fully jointed kinematic chains, the discussion that follows will assume that kinematic chains are not just simple hierarchical models.

The endpoints of the different links in the kinematic chain have special names (see Figure 11.8). The *proximal end* is the fixed end of the first link in the chain. The *root* is a point at the proximal end that is the point of articulation of the link; thus, the root is a joint. The *distal end* is the end of the final link in the chain. The *end effector,* or just *effector,* is the point at the distal end that can be used to move the link and chain.

It is worth noting that the term *root,* as defined here, is different than it was defined in Chapter 1 in the discussion of hierarchical models. Recall that in a hierarchical model, the root is a model, and thus possibly a link. With respect to a kinematic chain, as defined here, a root is a joint in the chain. The difference is noticeable in their diagrammatic representations (see Figure 11.9).

From the concept of kinematic chain grows the concept of the *closed kinematic chain,* which is a closed mechanical connection of kinematic pairs (see Figure 11.10). A closed kinematic chain consists of a set of links, connected together by joints, so that the proximal end connects to the distal end; note that this connection in essence eliminates the presence of a distal end and proximal end. In a closed kinematic chain, at least one of the links is immobile, but the remaining links are able to transmit motion throughout the mechanism. The simplest closed kinematic chain is the *four-bar linkage,* which consists of four links and four pivot joints (see again Figure 11.10). One link is held in a fixed position, and the remaining three links are able to swing freely. The link that is immobile is referred to as the *fixed link* (1), the *driver link* is the link that drives the motion (2), the

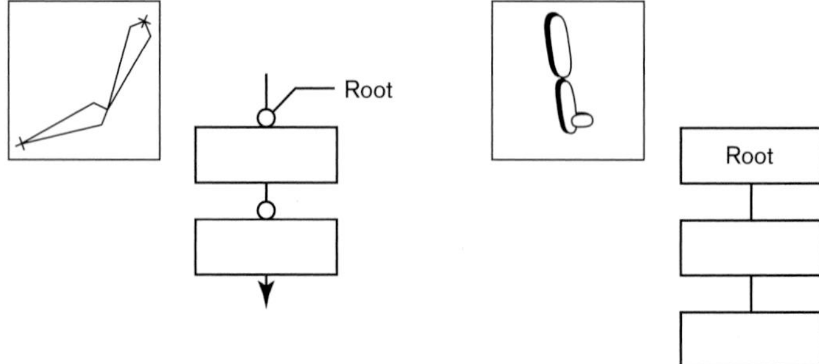

follower link (4) is the link that moves as a result of the driver link, and the *coupler link* (3) is the link that connects the driver link and the follower link. Depending upon the various lengths of the links, the movement of the driver link produces a predictable movement in the coupler and follower link.

As a side note, *sliders* also have equivalent four-bar linkages. A slider may be thought of as a special case of a four-bar linkage in which one pivot point is replaced with the slider.

A *skeleton,* also known as an *armature,* is a hierarchy of articulated chains (see Figure 11.11). A link in the hierarchy is said to be a *parent* link if there is a link or structure of links below it in the hierarchy—it is said to be the parent of the link or link structure. Similarly, a link is said to be the *child* of the link just above itself in the hierarchy. Each child can be transformed independently of other nodes in the hierarchy. Transformations applied to a parent propagate down to all of its children. Each level of the hierarchy has its own coordinate system and its own local origin. Objects rotate around their own center. A branch rotates around its parent's center. In mathematical

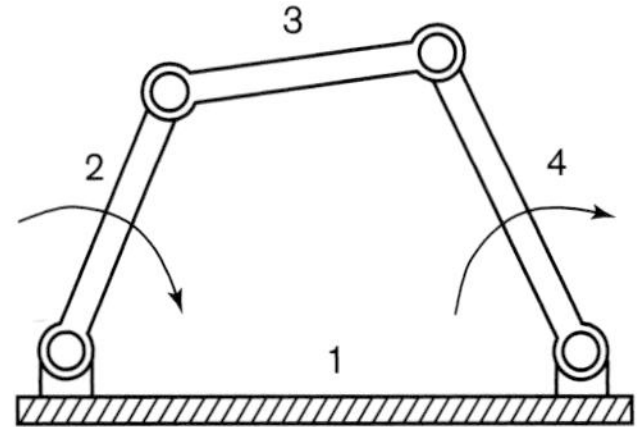

Figure 11.10 Above: The closed kinematic chain. The simplest closed kinematic chain is the four-bar linkage, which consists of four links and four pivot joints. One link is held in a fixed position, and the remaining three links are able to swing freely. Incidentally, any closed four-bar linkage can be uniquely described by only knowing the angle between any two links; the positions of all the other parts can be determined simply by knowing the position of any one part. A four-bar linkage has fully constrained motion, and once any one link is positioned all points on all the links can be determined.

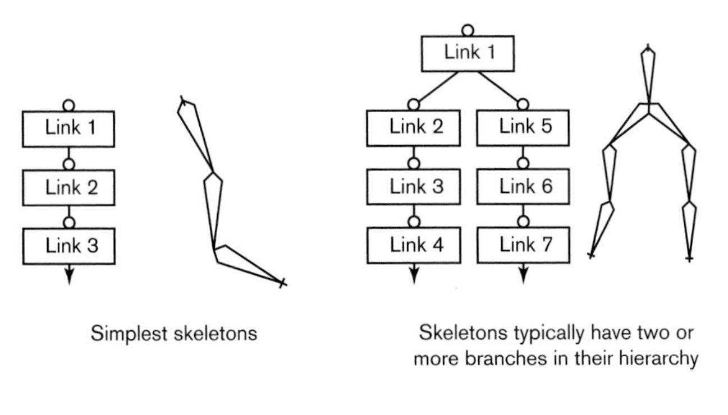

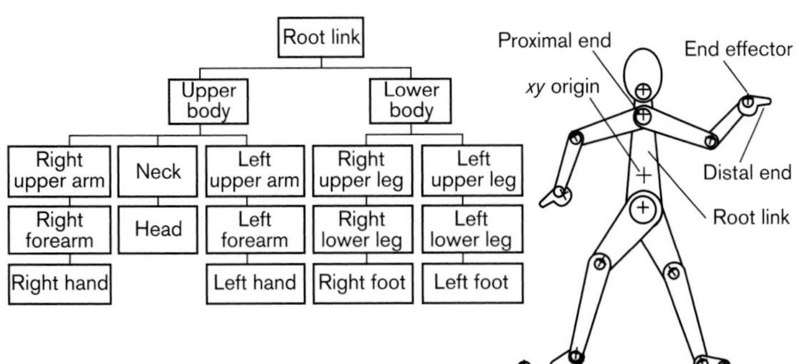

Figure 11.11 Left: A skeleton is a hierarchy of articulated chains. Skeletons can have one, two, or more branches. The 2D human skeleton has several branches, and 15 angles define the joints in the chain (left and right wrists, elbows, shoulders, hips, knees, ankles, and toes, which rotate against the floor, plus the neck). The data structure for this skeleton could also include the lengths of each link, should you want to tailor the armature to a particular person or body type.

terms, the kinematic chain is represented as a concatenated sequence of translation, scale, and rotation, most typically calculated using matrix algebra.

Note that the human armature in the figure is 2D and is composed of 16 joints, each with a single degree of freedom. The armature can be mathematically modeled by the concatenation of transformations, where each successive rotation describes a pivot and each successive translation describes the length of a link. While the armature resembles the mechanics of a real person, much greater subtlety is needed in order to really model a human. And while skeletons occasionally resemble the human form, it is not a requirement.

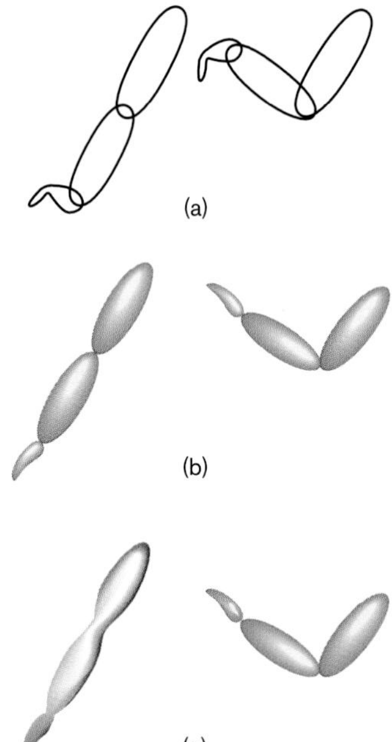

Figure 11.12 Three types of arms, each in an open position and a closed position. The arm presented in (a) has a rigid geometry that does not change when the arm bends. The arm presented in (b) has a more natural-looking geometry that also does not change when the arm bends. The arm presented in (c) has a natural-looking geometry that does change when the arm bends.

Kinematics deal with the geometric positioning of these kinds of articulated chains. They may deal with how to position the various links, or with analyzing the positions of the links. For example, kinematics address how to swing at a golf ball as well as how to examine a swing at the ball. It is important to note that there are many ways to swing a club. One may swing only the shoulders, with the elbows and wrists rigid. Or one may bend the elbows and wrists, and rotate them as the shoulders pivot around. One may start rotating the elbows and wrists at different moments in time, and one may change the rates of rotation for all three joints independently of each other. Therefore, for the animator, there are a variety of ways to animate kinematic chains.

The Kinematic Model

A *kinematic model* is a kinematic chain together with the geometry that surrounds the chain; the chain defines the relationship between the parts. There are two basic types of kinematic models: those that incorporate a rigid geometry and those that incorporate a flexible geometry (see Figure 11.12). This flexible geometry, sometimes referred to as a *skin* or *envelope,* moves and deforms as the underlying chain moves.

Different Types of Mechanisms for Different Types of Motion

Closely related to the concept of kinematic chains is the concept of machines and mechanisms. A *simple machine* is a simple device

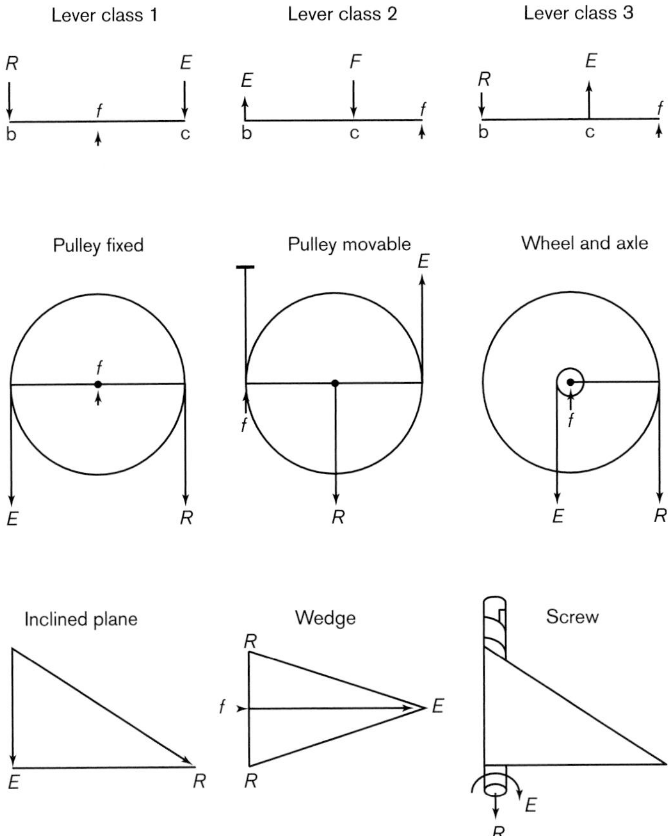

Figure 11.13 Left: Simple machines and how they work. The lever has three forms, all of which obtain balance depending upon the relationship between the distance from the fulcrum (f) of a resistance (R) and a force (E), and the relation of the strength of the resistance and force. In the diagram $Rb/Ec = bf/cf$, Hero's Rule. The three classes of lever distinguish different arrangements of force and resistance and fulcrum; a scale is an example of class 1, a wheelbarrow is an example of class 2, and a treadle is an example of class 3. The pulley and the wheel and axle have many manifestations, including the windlass, the block and tackle, and the crank, but they too may be organized in terms of the same three variables. The inclined plane is a slanted surface. A wedge is really a double inclined plane. A screw is an inclined plane wound on an axis.

	Translatory	Rotary
Continuous		
Reciprocal		

Figure 11.14 Above: Positional aspects of motion. Positional analysis may classify motion into a cross reference table. Motion may be either translatory or rotary, and it may be either continuous or reciprocal.

such as a lever, pulley, or inclined plane that alters the magnitude or direction of an applied force (see Figure 11.13). A *machine,* or *mechanism,* is a system of connected (usually) rigid bodies that alter, transmit, and direct force in a predetermined manner; it is an aggregate of simple machines. In a formal sense, a mechanism can also be a closed kinematic chain that describes an envelope of motion.

Motion can be produced by a variety of mechanisms and it comes in a variety of forms (see Figure 11.14). *Translatory motion* occurs along a straight line. *Rotary motion*—for example, motion generated by windmills, treadmills, or waterwheels—occurs along a circular or curved path. For translatory or rotary motion, the motion is either *continuous* and omnidirectional, or it is *reciprocal* and oscillates in a back-and-forth manner—for example, the up-and-down or back-and-forth motion generated by early steam engines. A survey of mechanisms is presented below.

Figure 11.15 Right: A rocker arm is a reciprocal motion mechanism that switches the direction of force with a lever that pivots near its center. In the first steam engines one end of the rocker was connected to the piston and the other to a pump.

Figure 11.16 Above: A bell crank is a rocker arm bent at the pivot point so as to amplify the distance of motion.

Figure 11.17 Above: A crank may be thought of as an axle with two right-hand bends; in simple machine terms, it is a wheel and axle.

Motion can be reversed with a *rocker arm,* a lever mechanism that pivots near the center of the motion mechanisms and transmits motion in the opposite direction (see Figure 11.15). A *bell crank* is a lever that can be used to amplify motion (see Figure 11.16).

A *crank* is an axle connected to an offset shaft; it can be thought of as an axle with two right-hand bends (see Figure 11.17), and is used to transmit rotary motion. In terms of a four-bar linkage, a crank is defined as a link that can make a complete 360-degree revolution about a fixed pivot. Figures 11.18, 11.19, and 11.20 contain single cranks. There are eight basic configurations of the four-bar linkage (see Figure 11.21). In broad terms, they can be classified as to whether they contain zero, one, or two cranks; how they convert directionality of motion; and velocity ratios. Important four-bar linkages include the *double-lever,* which converts oscillating arc motion to oscillating arc motion, as in Figure 11.21(a); the *crank-lever,* which converts continuous rotary motion to reciprocal oscillating rotary (arc) motion, as in Figure 11.21(b); and the *double-crank,* which can convert continuous rotary motion to continuous rotary motion, as in Figure 11.21(c), either in a forward or reverse manner. Figure 11.22 shows the names of these eight configurations along with the number of cranks that are able to make a full 360-degree revolution (0, 1, or 2), the nature of the motion conversion, and whether their velocity ratios change.

A *connecting rod* is a mechanism used in conjunction with a crank to convert reciprocal, up-and-down, motion into rotary motion or vice versa (see again Figure 11.18). A variation of the connecting rod is the *slider-crank*—a mechanism used to convert reciprocal motion to rotary motion, and vice versa (see again Figure 11.20). The

Figure 11.18 Left: The connecting rod links a reciprocal motion to a crank. The mechanism is bidirectional and can either convert reciprocal motion to rotary motion, or rotary motion to reciprocal motion. One of the first uses of the connecting rod may have been foot treadle-powered machinery, also known as a treadmill, a mechanism constructed in the form of a lever class 3. The figure presents a treadle sewing machine. Granny places her foot on the peddle and pumps it up and down, which drives the shaft and eventually drives the needle up and down.

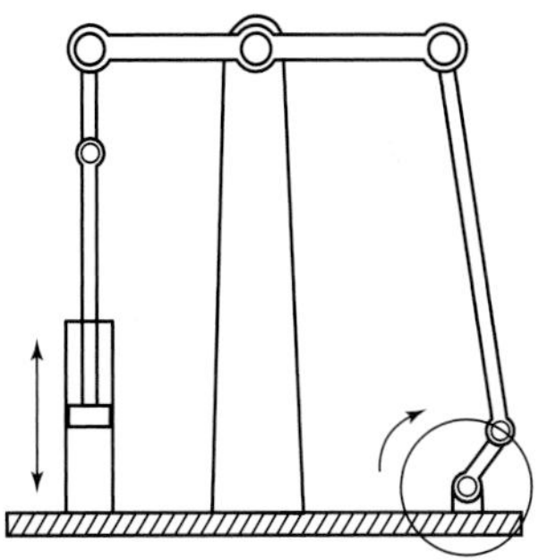

Figure 11.19 Above: Watt's steam engine combines a slider, a connecting rod, a rocker arm, another connecting rod, and a crank.

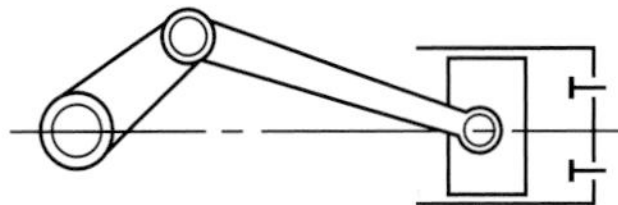

Figure 11.20 Above: The slider-crank also incorporates a connecting rod and can convert reciprocal to rotary motion, or rotary to reciprocal motion. The ratio of the depth of the stroke to the radius of the crank determines if the crank revolves fully or simply reciprocates. The illustration shows only one of several variations.

ability to convert rotary motion into reciprocal motion may also be accomplished with the use of a *cam* (see Figure 11.23), which is a mechanism used to lift a link up and down. A cam is a circular object with a shaft that can be rotated in a circular direction.

Note that there are two types of cams: those that produce continuous motion and those that produce continuous acceleration. In addition, cams can be designed with both features. A continuous-motion cam has the problem of discontinuity of motion at two extremes: it rotates upward, moving continuously, but when it reaches the end of its pathway, it stops abruptly and then starts descending. This design causes the cam to change direction instantaneously. The alternative is an equal-acceleration cam, which accelerates at an even rate; it does not move equal distances in equal amounts of time, but its rate of change is constant.

The various mechanisms may be placed into the 2 × 2 cross-reference table of positional aspects (see Figure 11.24). They can be combined together in an infinite number of ways to build more complex machines. One particularly interesting mechanism is one that enables its end effector to move freely within a 3D space. Slides and pivot joints can be combined to create such a mechanism, and the

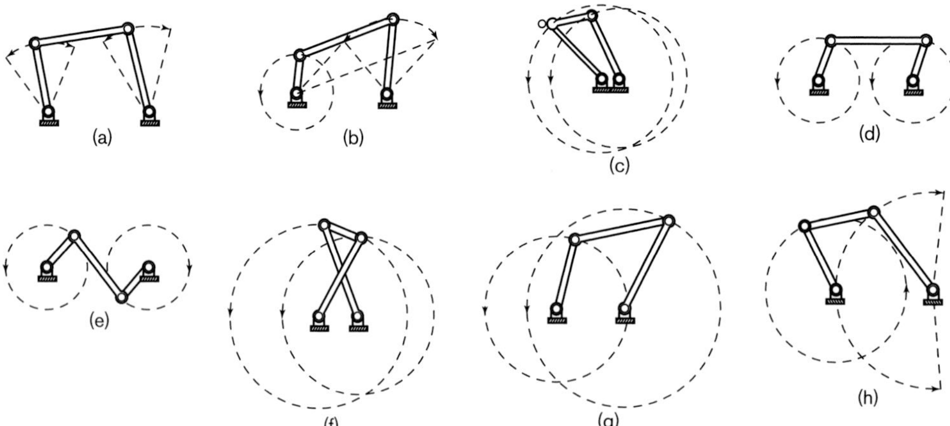

Figure 11.21 Above: Eight four-bar linkages. Three basic templates: double-lever (a), crank-lever (b), and double-crank (c) plus five special cases: parallel double-cranks (d), reverse antiparallel cranks (e), converse antiparallel cranks (f), isosceles double-crank (g), and isosceles crank-lever (h).

Figure 11.22 Right: Four-bar linkages as illustrated in Figure 11.21. A crank implies full 360-degree rotation. A lever implies constrained angular motion. The parallel cranks are like the sidebars of a steam locomotive and work in unison. The reverse antiparallel cranks reverse direction. The converse antiparallel and isosceles double-crank are also special cases of double cranks and function like gears down and up. The isosceles crank-lever rotates the follower up and down from the axis of the fixed link, which is why it is sometimes called a double leveler. The isosceles cranks derive their name from the fact that the length of the fixed link equals the length of the driver, and the length of the coupler link equals the length of the follower. In all the drawings, the cross-hatching under the pivots define the pivot as fixed and immobile.

results include the Cartesian robot arm (see Figure 11.25), the cylindrical robot arm (see Figure 11.26), the spherical robot arm (see Figure 11.27), the Selective Compliance Assembly Robot Arm (SCARA) (see Figure 11.28), and the revolute robot arm (see Figure 11.29). In the special effects business, often one of these assemblies is used to hold and move cameras as well as props.

Kinematic Synthesis and Analysis

Kinematic synthesis is the conversion of a motion idea into a geometric model or mechanical assembly that can carry out the motion. Kinematic synthesis employs methodologies to design models and assemblies that can perform certain motions; it involves linkages to

Four-bar linkages	Number of 360° cranks	Motion converted	Velocity ratio
Double-lever (a)	0	Reciprocating arc motion to reciprocating arc motion	Not constant ratio
Crank-lever or crank-rocker (b)	1	Continuous circular to reciprocating circular (arc) motion	Not constant ratio
Double-crank or drag-link (c)	2	Continuous circular to continuous circular motion	Not constant ratio
Parallel double-cranks (d)	2	Continuous circular to continuous circular motion	Constant ratio, equal velocity
Reverse antiparallel links (e)	2	Continuous circular to continuous circular but in opposite direction	Constant ratio, opposite velocity
Converse antiparallel cranks (f)	2	Continuous circular to continuous circular motion	Constant ratio, equal velocity
Isosceles double-crank (g)	2	Continuous circular to continuous circular motion	Constant ratio, unequal velocity
Isosceles crank-lever (h)	1	Continuous circular to reciprocating circular (arc) motion	Not constant ratio

produce a mechanism that engages in a certain motion with certain velocities. In matrix algebra terms, this involves concatenating a series of translation, scaling, and rotation operators; the key idea is that kinematic synthesis provides tools to design motions both in terms of their pathways and their velocities.

The conversion of a motion idea into an assembly that can carry out the motion has resulted in the creation of many drawing tools. Some simple examples include the ***compass*** for drawing circles, the ***elliptical trammel,*** the ***pantograph*** to draw parallel curves and to enlarge or reduce drawings, the ***ellipsograph*** for drawing ellipses, the ***volute compass*** used to draw spirals, the ***straight-line linkage,*** which draws a true straight line during its cycle (see Figure 11.30), and the ***harmonic synthesizer,*** which uses cranked eccentrics and reconfigurable links to move a drawing pen (see Figure 11.31). All of these can be simulated with computer drawing programs.

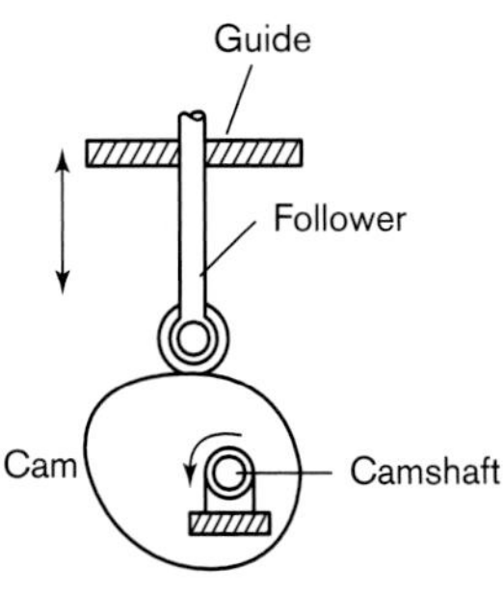

Figure 11.23 Above: Rotary to reciprocal motion is accomplished by mechanisms like the cam that lift a follower up and down. The profile of the cam is not centered, and as it rotates, it lifts the follower up and down.

Figure 11.24 Below: The positional analysis cross-reference table is expanded here with mechanisms used to convert between input motions (as rows) and output motions (as columns). Mechanisms to convert the input motion to the output motion are shown in the intersection box.

Kinematic Analysis

Kinematic analysis is the examination of motion pathways to determine the mechanisms that produce the curve in the first place. Some of these mechanical devices physically trace curves to analyze them for sinusoidal harmonies; other mechanisms determine the area bounded by the curve and display numeric readouts. Mechanisms and the motions they produce may be classified into three primary categories based on position, contact, and velocity. Hence, mechanisms and their corresponding motions are each associated with a particular type of analysis: positional analysis, contact analysis, and velocity analysis.

Positional Analysis A *positional analysis* of motion classifies mechanisms in terms of how they move, with the classifications

Motion Types and Conversion Mechanisms

		To			
		Continuous		Reciprocating	
From		Translatory	Rotary	Translatory	Rotary arc
Continuous	Translatory				
	Rotary		Double-crank, parallel cranks	Cam, crank-slider	Crank-lever
Reciprocating	Translatory		Slider-crank	Rocker arm	Slider-lever (toggle)
	Rotary arc		Lever-crank	Lever-slider	Double-lever

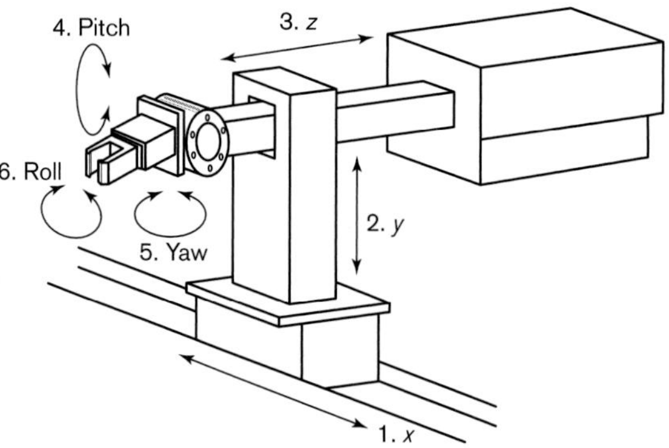

Figure 11.25 Right: Cartesian robot arm and robot hand. The numbers indicate the sequence of joints. The work envelope is a rectangular region, and the position of the wrist is represented by an *x, y, z* translation coordinate.

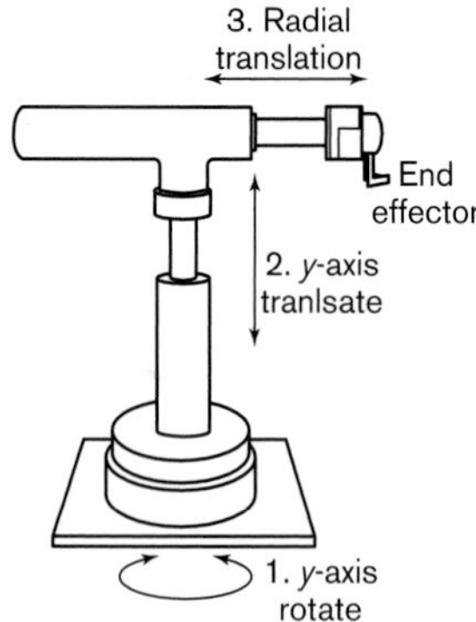

Figure 11.26 Above: Cylindrical robot arm and robot hand. The work envelope of the arm is a hollow cylinder, and the position of the wrist is represented by a rotation, translation, and radius.

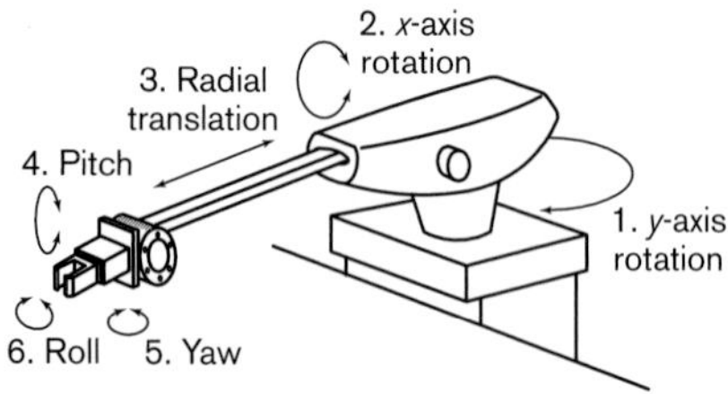

Figure 11.27 Above: Spherical robot arm and robot hand. The hand contains three degrees of freedom: yaw, pitch, and roll. The work envelope of the arm is a hollow sphere, and the position of the wrist is represented by two rotations and a radius.

Figure 11.28 Right: SCARA. The work envelope of the robot arm is a hollow cylinder, and the position of the wrist is represented by a rotation, an offset to a second rotation, and a translation at right angles.

being translatory, rotary, continuous, and reciprocal. This type of analysis is the most familiar to the animator.

Contact Analysis *Contact analysis* classifies mechanisms by the type of contact that exists between the driver link and the follower link. This schema produces three classes of contact: flexible ***wrapping contact,*** as found in a belt, rope, cable, or chain; ***direct contact,*** sometimes called ***rolling contact,*** as found in rollers, cams, gears, and friction wheels; and ***rigid contact,*** as found in the turning pair of the four-bar linkage or the sliding pair of the crank-slider (see Figure 11.32). In all of these cases, there is a fixed link (link 1), a driver and follower link (links 2 and 4), and a connector link (link 3), and in all cases, both the driver and follower links are rotating or reciprocating.

Velocity Analysis *Velocity analysis* classifies motion in terms of velocity—in terms of speeds of rotation between the driver and the follower, and in the ratios of the two speeds (see Figure 11.33). In the case of a wrapping contact mechanism, the driver and follower links are not necessarily rotating at the same speed, but the ratio of their speeds is constant. In the cases of the direct contact and linkage

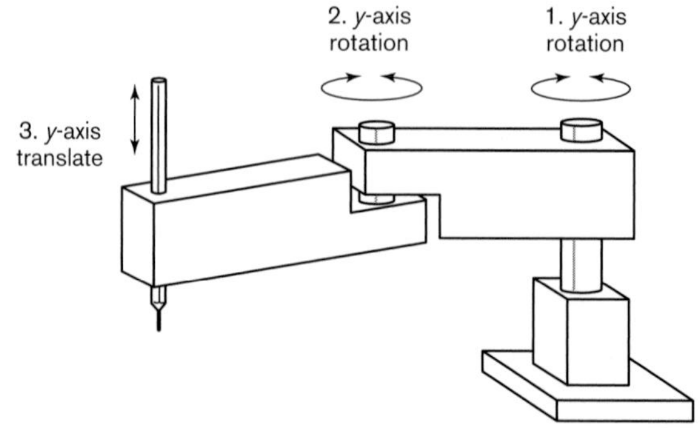

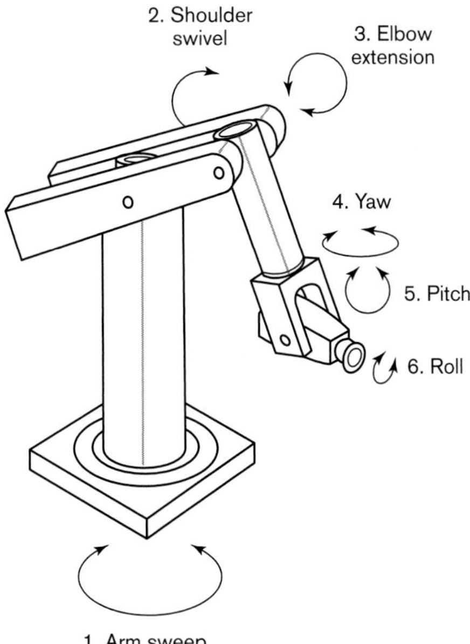

Figure 11.29 Left: Revolute robot arm. A yaw-pitch-roll hand is attached to the arm at the wrist, and the numbers show the sequence of rotations. The work envelope of the arm is a hollow sphere, and the position of the wrist is represented by a rotation, a fixed distance to a second rotation, and a fixed distance to a third rotation.

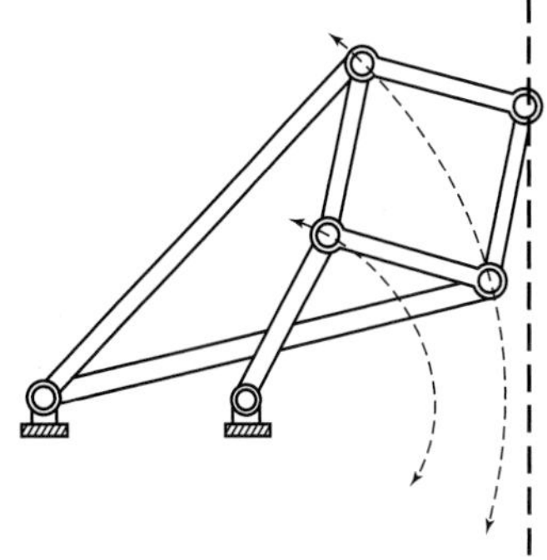

Figure 11.30 Above: James Watt invented a four-bar straight-line motion to drive the indicator of a pressure gauge in his steam engine, but only part of its cycle approximates a straight line. Peaucellier's mechanism to convert a rotary motion into a straight line is a six-link mechanism that uses a parallelogram. It has one degree of freedom.

mechanisms, not only do the driver and follower rotate at different speeds, but the rate of rotation of the follower to the driver is not constant; the follower is gaining and losing rotational speed as it pivots around its fixed pivot. Because the driver's velocity is constant and the follower's velocity is not, the ratio of the two speeds is not constant. Velocity analysis is of interest to animators because it provides a method of creating cyclic, repetitive actions that move at varying speeds.

The velocity of linkages can behave in unusual ways. For example, if a linkage is modeled after a crank-lever mechanism, the angular velocity of the driver will be constant, but the velocity of the

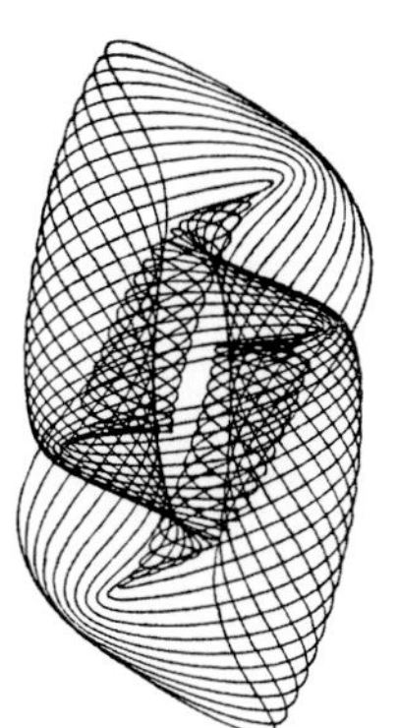

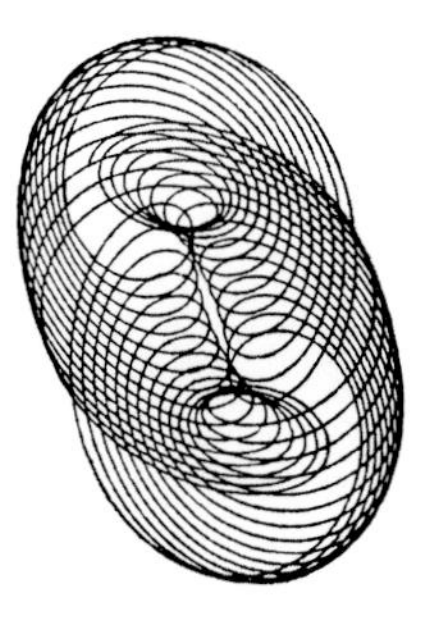

Figure 11.31 Left: Harmonigraph patterns. If the frequency ratio of the horizontal and vertical frequencies is an integer multiple, then simple patterns result. This is the same as computing sin(x) and sin(y) in a do-loop, where the domain of y is $0 \leq y \leq 360^\circ$, and where $x = y$, $x = 2y$, $x = 3y$, $x = 3y/2$, and $x = 4y/3$ (left to right).

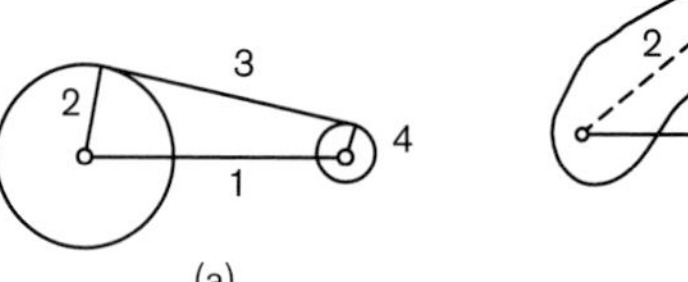

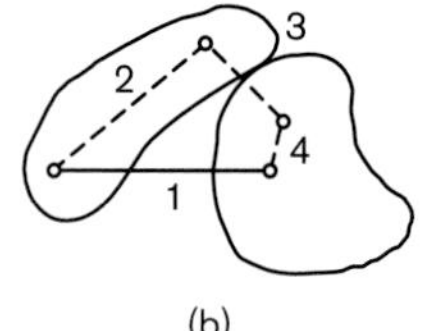

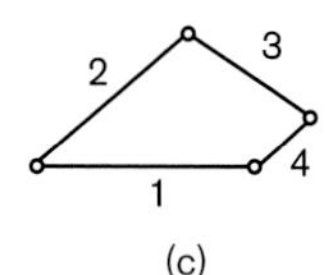

Figure 11.32 Right: Three types of connections (wrapping, direct, and rigid) between driver and follower: wrapping contact, direct contact, or rigid contact. In (a) the driver and follower are rotating at different speeds and the ratio of speeds is constant. In (b) and (c) the driver and follower are rotating at different speeds and the ratio of speeds is varying. This is because the follower is speeding up and slowing down as it rotates.

Velocity Analysis

Class	Directional relation	Velocity ratio
A	Constant	Constant
B	Constant	Varying
C	Periodic	Constant
D	Periodic	Varying

Figure 11.33 Above: Mechanisms for transmitting motion may have variation in velocity as well as direction. The directional relationship between the driver and the follower can be constant and in the same direction, or be periodic and oscillatory. The ratio of the two velocities may be constant or varying.

oscillating follower will be changing; in fact, the follower will slow to a stop before it reverses direction. When a follower is in its extreme positions, and momentarily motionless, it is said to be in *toggle position.* The crank-lever can also be engineered so that the time it takes the follower to travel in one direction is different than the time it takes to travel in the opposite direction. A linkage with a slow velocity in one direction and a fast velocity in the opposite is called a *quick return mechanism.* Velocity ratios can also change in linkages that do not oscillate—for example, in a double crank in which both the driver and follower make the same number of revolutions in the same time, but the rotational velocity of the driver is constant while the rotational velocity of the follower is not. In fact, the rate of rotation of the follower slows down during part of the cycle and then rushes ahead faster later on to catch up. Hence, these mechanisms are sometimes called *drag-link mechanisms.*

Kinematic Diagrams and Coupler Curves

Kinematic diagrams are a way to visualize the entire sequence of positions of a mechanism, the complete cycle, as a continuous curve on a graph (see Figure 11.34). Kinematic diagrams may be made to show several different relationships, in particular not only the relationship between displacement (position) and time, but also that between velocity and time, acceleration and time, velocity and displacement, and acceleration and displacement (see Figure 11.35).

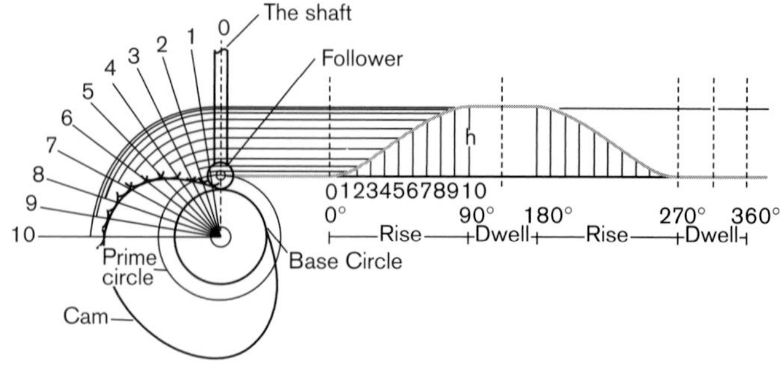

Figure 11.34 Right: The construction of a displacement diagram of a cam follower shows the radius at various angles plotted as a function of angle. Note that the scale is broken during the two dwells. In this curve, a continuous rotary motion of the cam is converted into an up-and-down motion of the follower. The cam is carefully designed with a changing radius so that during part of its cycle, it drives the follower up and down; and with a constant radius so that during part of its cycle, the displacement of the follower is constant. The resulting motion is not unlike that produced by the timing curve; the drawing suggests that the timing curve may have a mechanical basis, and it suggests that the timing curve can be synchronized to a 360-degree cycle and animated with an angular input.

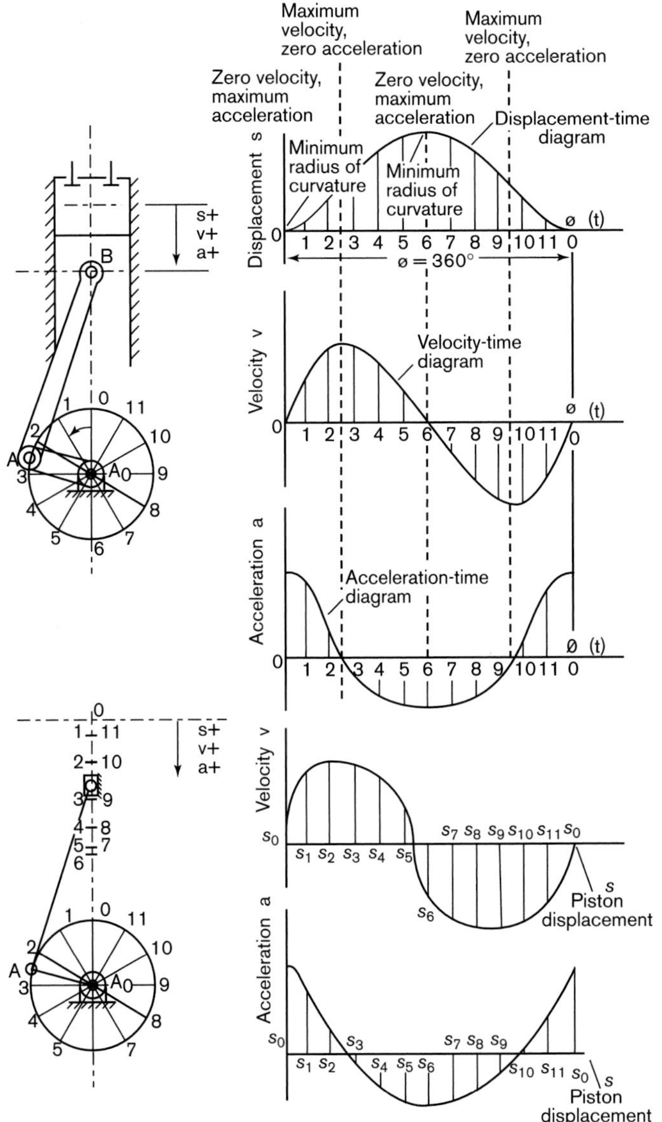

Figure 11.35 Five velocity diagrams of a crank-slider mechanism. All the diagrams illustrate a full 360-degree counterclockwise rotation of the crank and the action of the slider follower oscillating down and up between two extreme, dead-center positions. The first diagram plots displacement-time (note that as the slider descends, the displacement is plotted as increasing). The second and third diagrams plot velocity-time and acceleration-time, and the fourth and fifth diagrams plot velocity-displacement and acceleration-displacement. Some of the most interesting coincidences are noted at the top of figure: velocity is zero when displacement is maximum or minimum; acceleration is zero when velocity is maximum or minimum! Velocity is proportional to the slope of the displacement-time curve. Acceleration is proportional to the slope of the velocity-time curve, or inversely proportional to the radius of curvature of the displacement-time curve. A six-station Geneva movement is shown at the bottom of the figure.

These curves provide essential information to analyze or to design mechanisms. They show the maximums of displacement, velocity, and acceleration, as well as provide a continuous picture of just how displacement, velocity, and acceleration are indeed changing.

Note that the curves in Figures 11.34 and 11.35 are akin to timing curves, described in Chapter 10, and can be used to design a cycle of motion. These diagrams require strong understanding but contain insight about the essence of motion, especially in key positions where

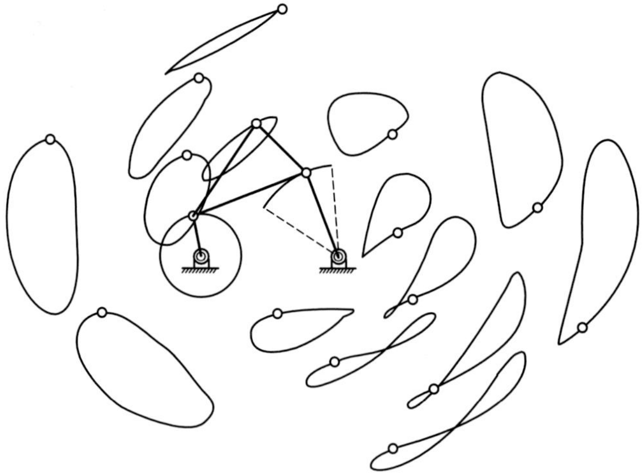

Figure 11.36 Right: Coupler curves can be designed to contain arcs or straight lines, or pass through a series of points.

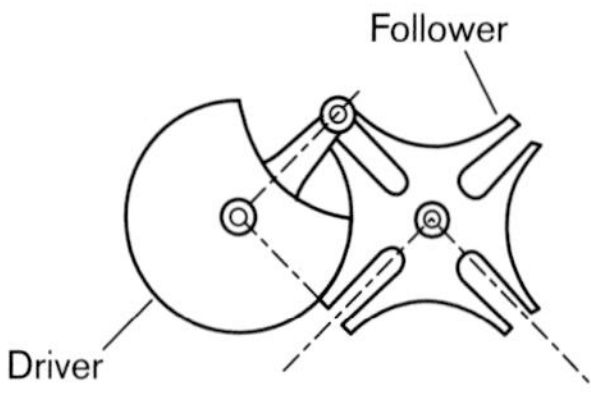

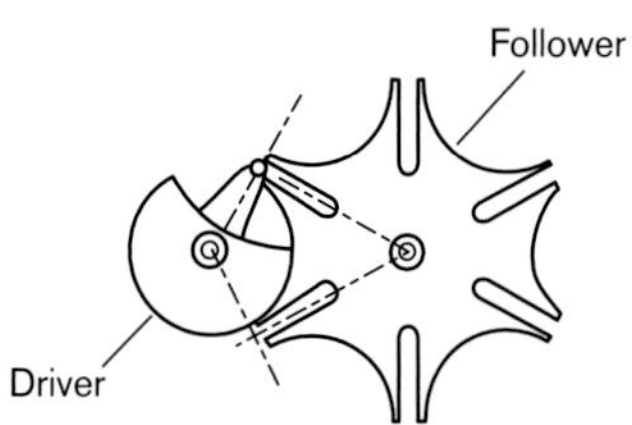

Figure 11.37 Above: A four-station, jerk-free Geneva movement converts rotary motion to intermittent rotary motion with no reversal of direction. The crank at the left rotates continuously. A pin on the end of the slide enters the slot of the follower and rotates it 90 degrees before disengaging. The follower then dwells, that is, stands still, while the driver rotates the remaining 270 degrees. The mechanism is sometimes used in motion picture shuttles to advance the film while the shutter is closed. A six-station Geneva movement is shown at the bottom of the figure.

action is reversing. Because action is not just about position, the fact that acceleration is at a maximum as an object comes to rest is responsible for much of the feeling of a situation, such as the moment an amusement ride comes to rest before hurling its riders in a new direction. The ride—itself a kinematic assembly—obviously incorporates position as part of its appeal, but the thrill is in the acceleration!

A *coupler curve* is a type of kinematic diagram; it is the motion described by a point on, or rigidly attached to, the coupler link as it moves through a cycle of action. Coupler curves are created by constraining the fixed link, moving the assembly, and tracing out the path of the point. Coupler curves may be designed to contain arcs or straight lines, or to pass through a series of points. Any point on the coupler, or rigidly attached to the coupler, may be plotted during the entire cycle of the driver; every four-bar linkage can produce an infinite number of coupler curves (see Figure 11.36).

A *double point* is defined as a point on a coupler curve where the curve passes over itself. A *cusp* is a point on a coupler curve where the velocity of the coupler point is zero and the mechanism is momentarily at rest before changing direction. Cusps are formed at the toggle positions of a mechanism. A *dwell* occurs when the follower stays motionless while the driver part of the mechanism continues to rotate. There is a dwell in the coupler curve of Figure 11.34, as well as in the follower in the mechanism in Figure 11.37.

Incidentally, there are always three different planar four-bar linkages capable of drawing identical coupler curves, and those curves are algebraic curves of the sixth order. Plus, it has been shown—

by the *equivalency proof*—that any algebraic relationship may be described by a linkage. Practically speaking, this means that a linkage can function like a computer, and that equations have a geometric, physical basis, as well as an algebraic one. Thus the computer animator confronted with a task of building an action may think about the solution either from the standpoint of manipulating algebraic equations built out of symbols, or manipulating physical linkages.

For the computer animator, linkages provide a way to generate motion pathways, which are a type of kinematic diagram. In addition, some computer animation programs allow the animator to design a curve that can then be associated with a chain, such that the distal end of the chain follows the path of the curve (see Figure 11.38).

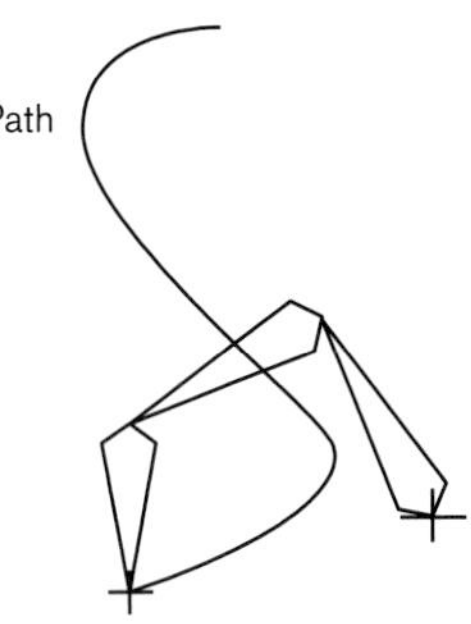

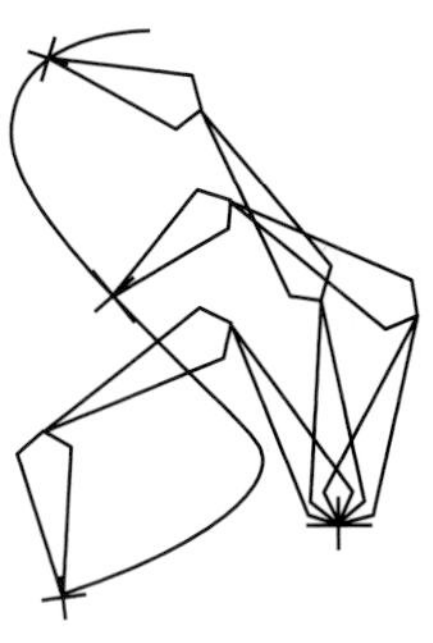

Figure 11.38 Above: The distal end of the chain follows the path of the curve created by the animator.

Figure 11.39 Below: Grubler's equation. The number of links, NLINKS, is equal to the number of "links" with two pivots plus the number of "links" with three pivots, and so on. Irregularly shaped links or links arranged in triangles are really only single links, because they are a rigid structure. The analysis is entirely dependent upon the number of joints attached to each rigid link. A three-bar linkage has three links with two joints each; NLINKS = 3, JOINTS = 3, DOF = 0. A four-bar linkage has four links with two joints each; NLINKS = 4, JOINTS = 4, DOF = 1. The five-bar linkage has five links with two joints each; NLINKS = 5, JOINTS = 5, DOF = 2. The six-bar linkage has six links, four of which have two joints and two of which have three joints; NLINKS = 6, JOINTS = 7, DOF = 1.

Degrees of Freedom

In an intuitive sense, the number of *degrees of freedom* is akin to how many different ways a linkage can move independently. Joints such as a 2D pivot or a slider connecting rigid links have one degree of freedom. A 3D pivot joint or ball joint, as is found in a joystick, may have three degrees of freedom, two directional and one rotational (twist of the handle). A rigid object in 3D space, for example an airplane, has six degrees of freedom: three specify position (*x*, *y*, *z*) and three specify rotation (yaw, pitch, roll).

In closed chains, the number of degrees of freedom can be calculated using a mathematical equation called *Grubler's equation,* a function based on the number of links in the chain and the number of pivot joints (see Figure 11.39). A closed three-bar linkage is immobile and unable to transmit motion; thus it has no degrees of freedom (hence may be thought of as a *structure*). In order to move, a closed mechanism must consist of at least four links; a four-bar linkage has only one degree of freedom.

```
NLINKS = N2 + N3 + ... + Nj
JOINTS = (2 * N2 + 3 * N3 + ...j * Nj)/2
DOF = 3 * (NLINKS - 1) - 2 * JOINTS

where

N2, N3,...,Nj is the number of links with j joints
NLINKS is the number of total links
JOINTS is the number of total joints
DOF is the number of degrees of freedom of the linkage
```

Parameter table

Shoulder angle	0		45		90		90		0
Elbow angle	0		40		0		30		0
Wrist angle	0		0		0		10		0
Frame	1		48		72		100		120

Figure 11.40 Right: A parameter table is a matrix that contains one column for each joint angle parameter in the body and one row for each joint, such as shoulder, elbow, and wrist.

Figure 11.41 Below: Forward kinematics. The animator specifies each joint angle for each pivot in an articulated chain or hierarchy, starting from the root of the chain and working downward. This virtual arm can move its shoulder, elbow, and wrist. This approach implies that the elbow, and all the other joints that are rotating, have an initial bend angle in the first frame and a terminal bend angle in the last frame; each action has its own parameters. The computer calculates the rotations of the joints for the intermediate frames and draws the arm as it is seen by the virtual camera. It is worth noting that it is not the *xyz* values of the objects that are being in-betweened; rather, it is the angles of rotation that are being in-betweened, and it is the angles that are used to determine the amount of rotation, and hence the position of the object.

Parameter Tables

A chain may be animated with the use of a ***parameter table,*** a matrix that contains one column for each joint angle parameter in the body and one row for each joint (see Figure 11.40). A computer program can evaluate the table, construct the appropriate transformations, and calculate intermediate frames; the parameter values for in-between frames are determined by easing each parameter individually. A parameter table is not unlike a dope sheet used in traditional animation, except that it is transposed and contains parameters, not cels. It should be obvious to the computer graphics veteran that one method of implementing kinematic systems is a system of transformation matrices.

Forward Kinematics

One of the most elementary ways to animate chains is to use *forward kinematics*, a technique whereby the animator specifies each joint angle for each pivot in an articulated chain or hierarchy, starting from the root of the chain and working downward (see Figure 11.41). That is, the transformations being applied to the chain are applied to the root first and then work their way down to the distal end. Complex chains—for example, a robot character—can be hierarchically organized so that action transformations propagate from the trunk of the body out through the limbs. The animator or computer animation program needs to determine all of the angles and posi-

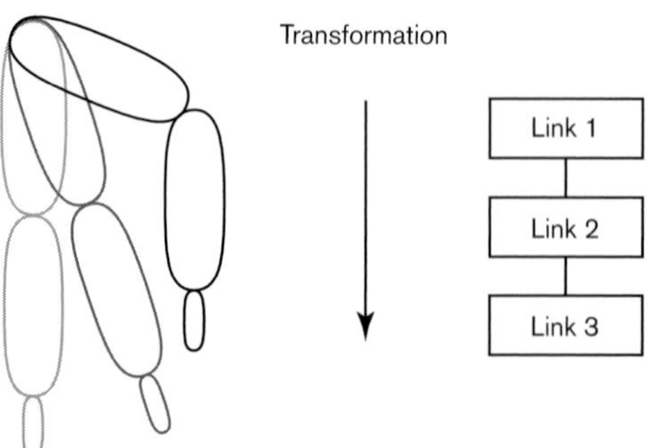

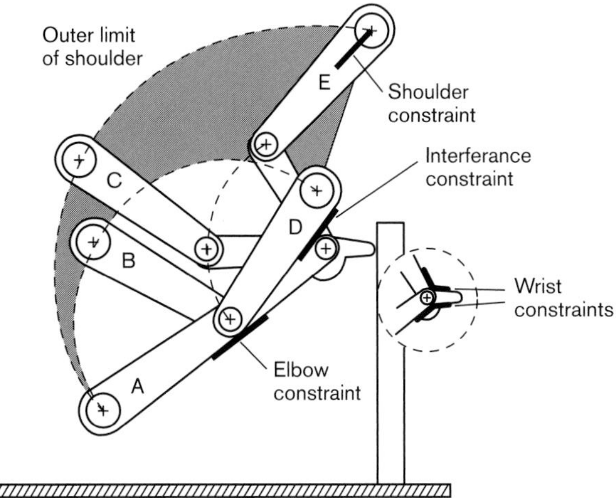

Figure 11.44 Left: The envelope of permissible solutions. Given that the position of the wrist joint is constrained, it is possible to examine the domain of possible positions for the elbow and shoulder. Given the conditions of the wrist, observe that the domain of the elbow is limited to an arc. Given also the constraints of the elbow and shoulder, and the constraint between the shoulder and hand, it is possible to define an envelope of all possible shoulder positions (shaded area). This area is bounded by an arc, the "outer limit of the shoulder" which is actually a compound curve, and a straight line. The extremes of this area are seen in positions A, D, and E; positions B and C are in-between positions that lie on the edge of the envelope. There are an infinite number of algorithms that can determine an infinite number of different positions as to where to place the shoulder inside the envelope. A careful reader is correct in observing that the body of the person must be floating in space in order to get into positions like E, and that if the person is constrained to the floor, the envelope of shoulder positions is a smaller area.

tered. Thus, constraints can be defined with an activation time and a duration time or deactivation time.

A constraint may be used to express a physical situation. For example, consider a spring attached to a door. The force of the spring physically constrains the door to keep it closed, but the force can be overcome in order to open the door. In mathematical terms, a constraint may be specified with a vector, which would include the geometry associated with the constraint. Following is an inventory of several common types of constraints available in computer animation programs.

Position Constraints

A *position constraint,* sometimes called a *boundary constraint,* dictates the position of objects. The constraint is assigned to a given object, and its effects are applied to the position of other objects. For example, a position constraint may be assigned to a mother duck, and its effects are applied to a group of baby ducks. As the mother duck swims away, the position of the baby ducks changes to follow the mother duck (see Figure 11.45). A position constraint might also be defined so that when the mother duck swims back, the baby ducks stop, wait for the mother duck to pass though, and then begin to follow her again. That is, the babies will only follow the mother if she is

Figure 11.45 Below: A position constraint is a constraint that dictates the position of objects. In the figure, a position constraint is assigned to a mother duck, and its effects are applied to the baby ducks. As the mother duck swims away, the baby ducks follow the mother duck. The constraint is also defined so that when the mother duck swims back, the baby ducks stop, wait for the mother duck to pass though, and then begin to follow her again.

getting farther away and is beyond a given distance. Or the constraint might be defined so that the baby ducks are always swimming away from their mother. A position constraint is any constraint that dictates the positioning of objects relative to one another. An example of a position constraint that is more kinematic in nature might include a slider that is constrained so it can only move back and forth in the slide. In a mathematical sense, a position constraint is a condition imposed on a parameter that limits its domain of variance.

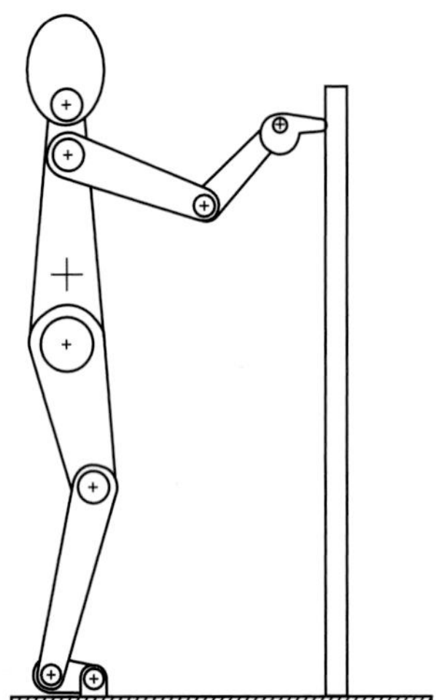

Figure 11.46 Above: Interpenetration constraints prohibit collisions between objects.

Related to the concept of position constraint is *interpenetration constraint,* which is a condition that determines if more than one object can be in the same place at the same time (see Figure 11.46). For example, a model of a human can either have its left hand or its right hand placed at a position three inches in front of its nose, but it cannot have both of them there at the same time. Interpenetration constraints will limit the mechanism from having its right hand move into this position. The constraining factor is one of interaction; interpenetration constraints are enforced by knowing where the rest of the model is and testing to make sure collisions are avoided, a process related to collision detection and contact analysis.

Scaling Constraints

A *scaling constraint* dictates the scale of objects. The constraint is assigned to a given object, and its effects are applied to the scale of other objects. For example, a scaling constraint may be assigned to a character in the scene and its effects applied to a second character (see Figure 11.47). As the first character increases in size (along a particular axis) to express an emotion, the second character increases in size as well (possibly along the same axis). A scaling constraint can also be used to limit the scale of an object. For example, the maximum or minimum size that a given object can get can be constrained by the size of another object.

Figure 11.47 Below: A scaling constraint dictates the scale of objects. The constraint is assigned to a given object, and its effects are applied to the scale of other objects. In the figure, as the leftmost character gets larger, so does the rightmost character.

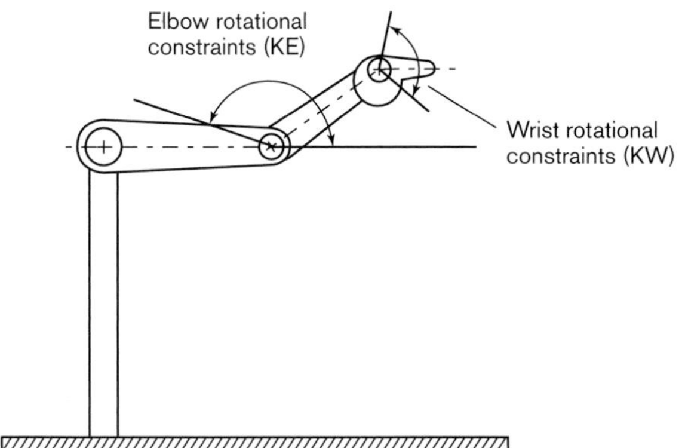

Figure 11.48 Left: A rotation constraint dictates the rotation of objects. The constraint is assigned to a given object, and its effects are applied to the rotation of other objects. In the figure, the elbow cannot bend beyond a certain angle. When we parameterize the rotations of the joints of the human body, we may constrain them to a certain domain of angular rotation. In the human body, the axes of rotation of the elbow joint is constrained so it can only pivot not quite 180 degrees and is unable to bend backward. In other words, the domain of the elbow constraint, KE, is such that $0° \leq KE \leq 160°$. The domain of the wrist constraint, KW, is $-30° \leq KW \leq 75°$.

Rotation Constraints

A *rotation constraint* dictates the rotation of objects. The constraint is assigned to a given object, and its effects are applied to the rotation of other objects. The simplest example of a rotation constraint is constraint on an elbow joint—the elbow cannot bend (or rotate) beyond a certain angle (see Figure 11.48). A slightly more complex example would be the case of a car driving along a flat winding road (see Figure 11.49). A rotation constraint could dictate that the car remain tangent to the direction of road at each point along the way. In this case, the shape of the road dictates the rotation of the car.

Related to rotation constraint is the concept of *orientation constraint*, which dictates the orientation of objects in *xyz* space. The constraint is assigned to a given object, and its effects are applied to the orientation of other objects. In the previous example, the winding road might also be hilly, so the orientation constraint might dictate that the car remain normal to the surface of the hilly road as it drives along (see Figure 11.50). In this case, the orientation of the car in *xyz* space is affected.

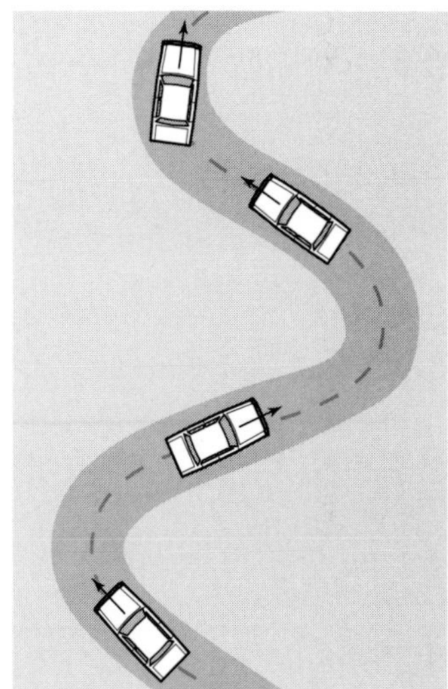

Figure 11.49 Above: A complex rotation constraint would be the case of a car driving down a flat winding road. A rotation constraint dictates that the car remain tangent to the direction of road at each point along the way. In this case, the shape of the road dictates the rotation of the car.

Figure 11.50 Left: An orientation constraint dictates the orientation of objects in *xyz* space. A winding road might also be hilly and the orientation constraint might dictate that the car remain normal to the surface of the hilly road as it drives along.

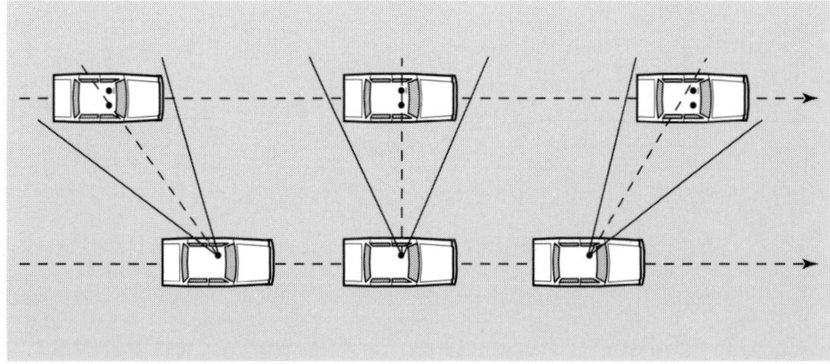

Figure 11.51 Right: Combining constraints. A constraint may be assigned to a car moving along a hilly, winding road, and its effects can be applied to the orientation of the heads of characters sitting in a second moving car. As the first car passes the second car, the orientation of the heads change to remain fixed on the first car as it passes. Both position and orientation constraints are applied to achieve the desired effect.

Combining Constraints

Constraints can be combined in any number of ways in order to satisfy the needs of a given situation. Going back to the previous example, a constraint may be assigned to a car moving along a hilly, winding road, and its effects can be applied to the orientation of the heads of characters sitting in a second moving car. As the first car passes the second car, the orientation of the heads change to remain fixed on the first car as it passes (see Figure 11.51). In this example, both position and orientation constraints can be applied to achieve the desired effect.

Priority of Constraints

A given constraint may be specified in terms of its importance relative to other constraints; the ***constraint strength*** is the measure of the relative importance of a constraint. A constraint strength may be expressed in a real-world quantity such as pounds, or in neutral, normalized terms, such as a 0-to-1 scale. A 3D animation constraint may be specified using a vector: K[StartTime, EndTime, *x*, *y*, *z*, Strength]. For a constraint that is always true, the start time would specify the beginning of the animation sequence, and the end time would specify its end.

A system with an equal number of degrees of freedom and constraints is said to be ***fully constrained;*** this is necessary for a mechanism to transmit predictable motion. If a system has fewer degrees of freedom than it has constraints, it is considered ***overconstrained,*** such as the six-bar linkage in Figure 11.52. If a system has more degrees of freedom than it has constraints, it is considered ***underconstrained,*** or redundant; the difference between the degrees of freedom and the number of constraints is considered to be the ***degree of redundancy.*** An underconstrained system, such as

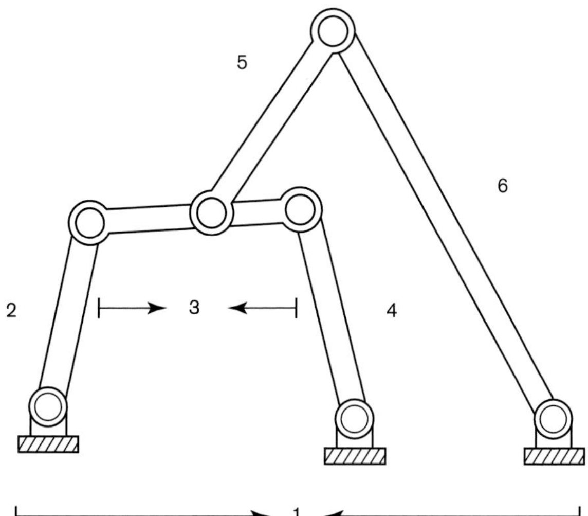

Figure 11.52 A six-bar connected chain, partly constrained.

the five-bar linkage in Figure 11.53, has no definite pattern of motion. Underconstrained systems are of special interest to the animator because interesting linkages, such as the human armature, are often underconstrained.

Constraints that are isolated or narrowly focused in scope, for example, position constraints, can be easy to maintain. However, working with multiple interacting constraints is more difficult and sometimes impossible. This is the case because a solution that satisfies one constraint may violate another. Hence, in order to solve the problem with multiple interacting constraints and/or goals, it is often necessary to implement a *functional control system* to evaluate the strengths of each constraint and determine the best solution. This requires not only establishing the relative strength to each constraint in the system, but also defining an evaluator that makes choices. This is a serious strategy for animating an underconstrained chain with many degrees of freedom, such as a human armature. In order to solve these more complicated problems, it is necessary for animation software to have a control system that examines larger issues, such as balance and quest for stability, or energy efficiency.

A Constrained Hierarchical Skeleton

Constraints can be applied to hierarchies to create many types of models with sophisticated motion. There are an infinite number of ways to combine constraints and hierarchies, and there are

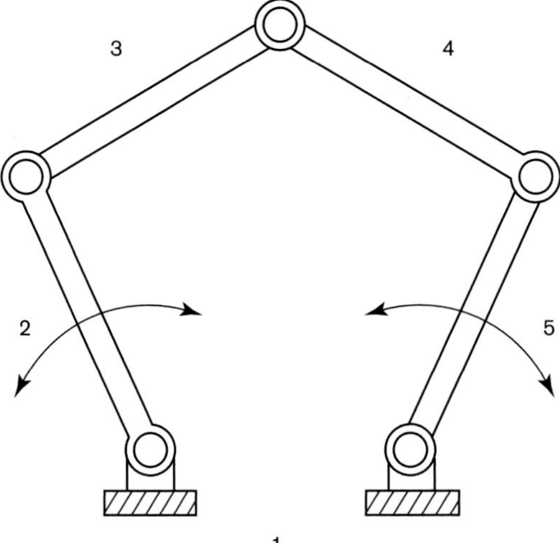

Figure 11.53 A five-bar linkage in which the links form a serial connected chain.

many good ways to achieve the same results. One of the most frequently animated models is that of a human character, with elbows, knees, and other jointed parts. It is important that the model be created appropriately so that the character can walk and bend correctly (see Figure 11.54).

There are many good ways to create such a model; the figure presents one such way. Here, the model is simplified in order to show the underlying structure. The character has a head, torso, hips, hands, and shoes, each of which are represented as a simple model. In addition, the character also contains four skeletons, two of which control the arms and two of which control the legs. The position of each skeleton is constrained to a model: the tops of the leg skeletons are constrained to the hip model, and the tops of the arm skeletons are constrained to the top of torso model. The trick to making the skeleton behave correctly is to construct the ends of each limb—the hands and feet—in such a way that the animator does not have to move the end effector when defining the key frames. Thus, the hands and feet are positioned at the end effectors and then constrained to the position of the end effectors. To include the hands and feet in the hierarchy, they can be parented to the torso and hips, respectively. This way, the character's limbs can be animated by key framing the hand and feet models. If, instead, the end effectors had been used to define the key frames (instead of the

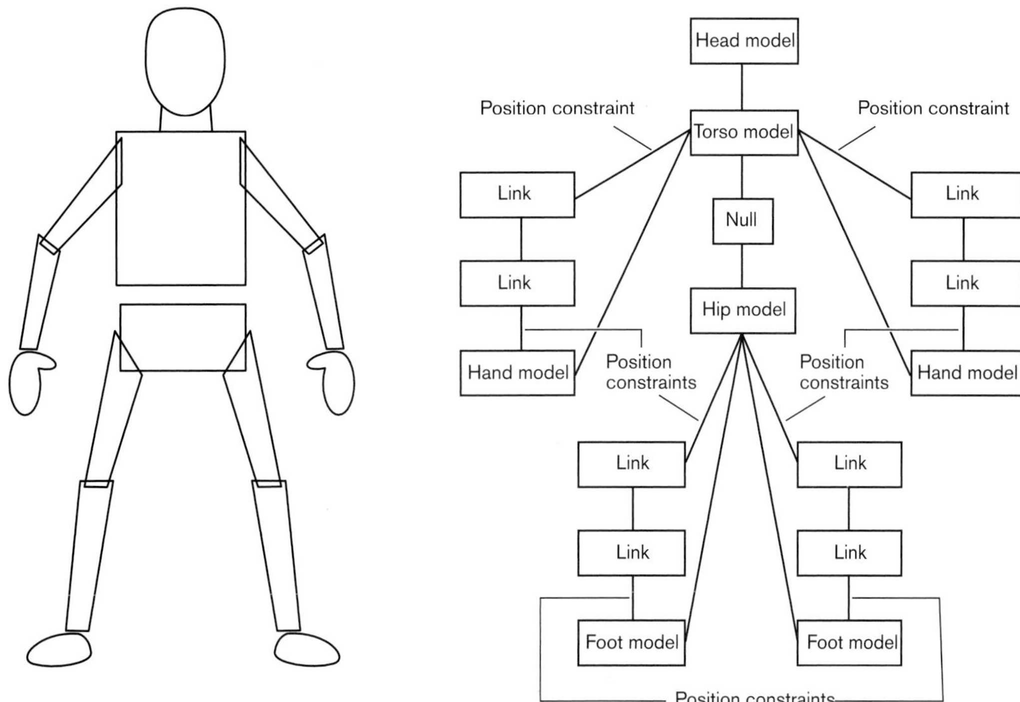

hand and feet models), then, if the entire character was translated, the limbs would act as if they were still positioned at the key frame locations and would not translate freely with the character. The addition of the hands and feet at the end effectors eliminates this problem. Since they are parented to a node higher in the hierarchy, a translation applied to the parent is also applied to hands and feet so they can translate freely with the parent. Understanding how the skeleton of a body works and what sort of limitations it has is a good first step toward rigging muscle, skinning, and weighting it.

Figure 11.54 A constrained hierarchical skeleton. In the figure, the simplified human character (left) and its schematic diagram (right) resemble a human. To allow for greater control of the upper and lower halves of the character, a null is inserted into the hierarchy. A null is the equivalent of a model that has no geometry, and is available in modeling software. Although the null is positioned between the upper and lower halves of the character (to maintain the resemblance to a human), it is actually the parent of both halves; each half is a branch in the hierarchical tree. This way, each half can be selected independently of the other, giving the animator greater control over the movement of the character.

12 Dynamic and Behavioral Modeling

This chapter reviews the essentials of dynamic approaches to animation, which are characterized by the modeling of forces. The review of basic forces presents relevant terminology, and discusses types of forces and how they interact in life and in animation. Dynamic methods are critical if a complex animation is to behave in a believable way. They enable the computer to take on much of the tedious work involved in animation, but more importantly, they provide a powerful tool set to go beyond classic methods.

While the methods presented thus far are well suited for many types of animation, they are not suitable for all. For example, animating a chair falling down a flight of stairs using kinematic methods is almost impossible. Certainly an animator, using a succession of in-betweens, can animate a chair tumbling down, hitting a stair, bouncing off in a new direction with a new spin, falling and hitting another stair, and so on until it finally bounces to rest at the bottom. But it is unlikely the result will be visually satisfactory, let alone realistic. Other situations where kinematic approaches to motion fall short include the modeling of physical phenomena, such as the blowing of leaves in the wind; cloud animation; and the locomotion of animal figures, including human figures. Although in each of these cases, it is theoretically possible to individually animate thousands of translations and rotations, it is not practically possible to specify meaningful parameters.

Luckily there is a superior way to animate complex environments: instead of animating objects directly, the animator instead creates a

Above: *Greek Gods*, by Gavin Miller and Ned Greene. Cyberware-scanned heads of Gavin Miller and Ned Greene spout particle-based water into a height-field-based fluid simulation. Rays from the light source are used to create caustics in the bottom of the pool.

Figure 12.1 Above: A dynamic animation of a chair falling down stairs. A force is applied to the chair so that the chair falls off the top of the stairs, and gravity pulls the chair downward. The calculation for this action includes factors such as the distribution of mass in the chair, the speed and direction of travel when the chair hits, and the angle of the stair, and it may include factors such as how much of the energy gets absorbed when the contact is made.

more sophisticated environment and then lets this environment calculate the action (see Figure 12.1). This new environment augments the world of geometry and surface properties with a world of forces—in particular, gravity, momentum, and mass—and it employs dynamic techniques, rather than kinematic techniques, to achieve action (see Figure 12.2). For example, in the case of the falling chair, the environment might be augmented with mass, gravity, and momentum. The chair is launched into motion by applying a sideways force so that the chair falls off the top of the stairs. Gravity pulls the chair downward, and at each frame-time interval, a collision detector determines if any part of the chair has contacted any part of the stairs. When a contact is detected, the current trajectory of the chair is terminated, and a new direction of motion, spin, and rate of speed is determined. The calculation for this action includes factors such as the distribution of mass in the chair, the speed and direction of travel when the chair hits, the angle of the stair, and perhaps how much of the energy gets absorbed when the contact is made. The same chair behaves differently when falling down stairs covered with carpet than it does when falling down stairs that are made of wood or concrete.

This chapter defines dynamics and begins with a review of the physics of force and the definition of variables the computer animator may be called upon to manipulate or implement in this new world. It includes an explanation of how forces are represented and how they can be combined. The chapter surveys different types of dynamic animation and expands the concept of dynamics to incorporate behavioral forces. These tend to be less grounded in classic physics and involve parameterizing social and psychological variables such as intelligence, dexterity, learning ability, population densities, spheres of influence, money, and so forth.

Force and Dynamics

A *force* is something that acts on an object (or a joint) and either causes it to move or prevents its movement. Forces in the real world include gravity, mass, friction, momentum, and inertia. *Dynamics* is the study of forces and the rules that describe their relationships.

In a computer, forces such as gravity, mass, and friction are modeled by assigning them numeric parameters. This process is not

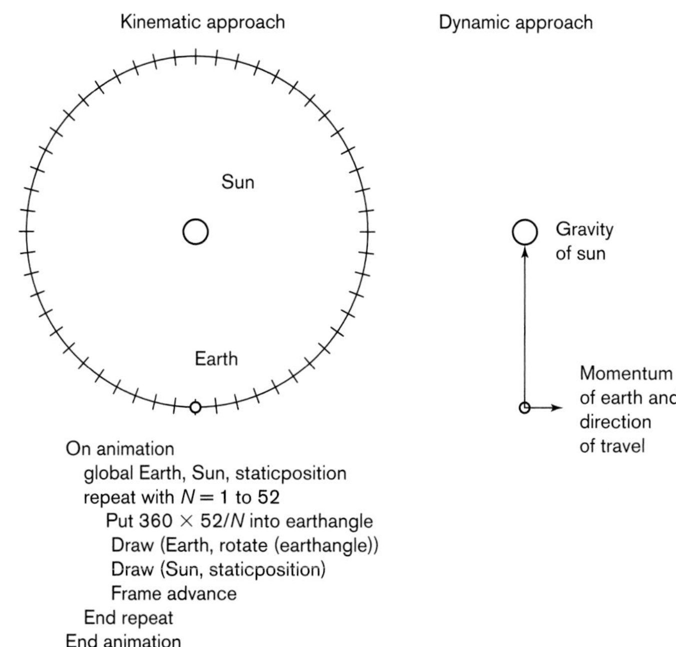
Kinematic approach
Dynamic approach
Sun
Earth
Gravity of sun
Momentum of earth and direction of travel
On animation
global Earth, Sun, staticposition
repeat with N = 1 to 52
Put 360 × 52/N into earthangle
Draw (Earth, rotate (earthangle))
Draw (Sun, staticposition)
Frame advance
End repeat
End animation

Figure 12.2 Kinematics versus dynamics. Animating the Earth traveling around the sun by incrementing the Earth's position by $^{360}/_{52}$ degrees per week is a kinematic approach: it may approximate what occurs in nature, but it by no means describes what actually happens, such as the interaction between the sun's gravity and the gravity, momentum, and direction of travel of the Earth.

unlike building models of objects in the computer, except that objects are modeled in units such as centimeters or inches, whereas forces are modeled in units such as kilograms or pounds. So in this regard, forces are simply additional parameters attached to an object; an object has geometric properties such as length, width, and height; surface properties such as color, transparency, and texture; and dynamic properties such as weight, density, and slipperiness.

The approach of creating computer animation by modeling how forces act on objects is called *dynamic animation* and is also known as *physical modeling* or *simulation.* Dynamic approaches actually model how masses and physical forces interact to produce movement—for example, how gravity affects planets and determines their positions. Dynamic action is produced by forces acting on objects. This approach is a completely different strategy from a kinematic approach, in which objects are simply positioned where they are supposed to be. And unlike key framing, the object is not being moved between two positions: the force is simply applied to the object, and the object responds until another force is applied. For example, the animation of an automobile engine would consider the physics of engine operation; it would calculate the rate of exploding gas and the resistance of the piston and connecting rod, and determine how far the piston gets pushed. The position of the parts are calculated for each successive discrete frame in time, creating animation.

In a dynamic computer animation model, the animation of a space shuttle returning to Earth is no longer simply an animation that involves simple translation, rotation, and easing of color change. In a dynamic model, the animation involves complex calculations of trajectories, velocities, time interval changes, positions, speed, direction, friction, and heat and its effect on color change of the model.

Dynamic models are a very reliable way to model and animate natural events, such as fog or billowing smoke (see Figure 12.3). Dynamic computer animation is also useful for animating the human figure, which can be built with a kinematic armature that is bound by the same kinds of forces that bind humans. For example, the armature is subject to the force of gravity but strives to stay upright even when moving over different terrain, and therefore, calculations must be made continuously to keep it upright. Dynamic computer animation is useful for animating most organic actions, such as flowing fluid and waving flags.

Another pertinent example of dynamic animation might be that of a closed room filled with gas molecules (see Figure 12.4). At the start of the simulation, each molecule has a location, a direction in which it is moving, and a speed. For each frame of the simulation, the computer advances the molecule the distance in space along the direction of its motion. The computer then tests to see if (1) any molecule has collided with any other molecule, or (2) any molecule has collided with the exterior of the room. When two molecules collide, they ricochet away from each other, and the simulation program calculates the new direction vector and speed for each molecule. Should a molecule hit a wall, it will bounce off the wall and travel in

Figure 12.3 Dynamically animated smoke by Nick Foster and Dimitris Metaxas, from research originally published in the SIGGRAPH 97 Conference Proceedings.

a new direction. Using this model, various aspects of the nature of molecules can be simulated, including what happens to molecules when heated and cooled. Basing motion on accurate physical models produces realistic action, much different than action that is determined by hand.

The advantage of dynamic animation is that by incorporating factors such as balance, support, and center of gravity, the motion can be made physically more accurate. The disadvantage is that a dynamic world requires a richer parameter definition, and although it can confer naturalistic behaviors to objects, its lack of predetermination can produce animation that is not predictable and fails to satisfy cinematic considerations. For this reason, dynamic approaches often employ forward and inverse kinematics, as well as constraints.

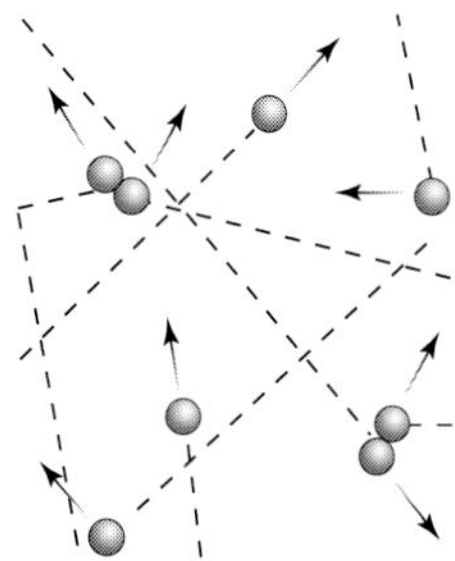

Figure 12.4 Dynamically animated gas molecules. Each molecule has a location, a direction in which it is moving, and a speed. The dynamic animation system advances the molecule and tests to see if any molecule has collided with any other molecule or the exterior of the room. Upon collision, the program calculates the new direction and speed. There is no prior determination as to where things end up.

Dynamic tactics may draw from formulas that describe a wide range of physical phenomena. These may involve relative solid objects, such as the orbits of planets or the drop of a pin, or more fluid substances, such as a waterfall, an explosion of a smoke bomb, or the formation of a cloud. Dynamics enables a computer animator to tackle a vast range of tasks that kinematic approaches simply cannot address.

Thus, for the computer animator, dynamic modeling is a powerful tool because the animator need not manually craft action but instead can program the physical attributes of the world (in factors such as mass, center of gravity, stiffness) and then let the computer carry out reality. This method for generating motion is therefore analogous to how motion is generated in the real world; the motion of objects is simulated by the physical dynamics of reality. As animation seeks to replicate phenomena that are visually or temporally too complex to be adequately reproduced by the animator's skills alone, dynamic models become a way to achieve a higher degree of naturalism.

The Basics of Force

As previously defined, a force is something that acts on an object and causes it to move, or that prevents movement. Common forces in the real world include gravity, mass, friction, momentum, and inertia. We have defined dynamics as the study of forces and suggested that dynamic animation may be produced by implementing forces and the laws governing how they act on objects. The visual result, like life, is the solution produced by the forces acting on the objects according to the rules.

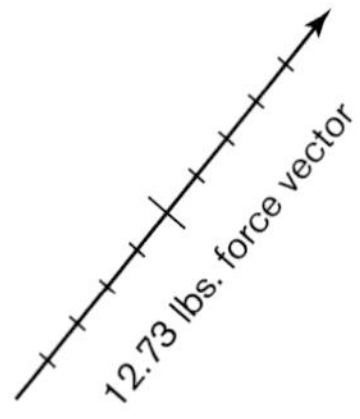

A force is usually exerted on an object via contact with another object, but there are forces, like gravity and magnetism, that may act on an object with no actual physical contact. A force may act alone on an object, or several (or many) forces may act in combination; certain combinations of forces may balance each other and cause an object to remain stationary. Other combinations of forces may move an object at a constant speed, or increase or decrease a rate of speed.

Force is a vector quality, meaning it has two components, a magnitude (or quantity) of force, and a direction in which the force acts. In this regard, force is similar to velocity, which also has magnitude and direction. A force may be represented graphically with a *force vector,* a line with a convenient scale and an arrowhead pointing in a certain direction (see Figure 12.5).

A *composition of forces* occurs when two or more forces act on the same point (see Figures 12.6, 12.7, and 12.8). In practice, the two or more forces augment or subtract from each other and act to produce a single *resultant force.*

An *equilibrant force* is a force of exactly the same magnitude but opposite direction as the initial force (see Figure 12.9). The effect of an equilibrant force is to completely counteract the effects of the force and ensure that the point upon which the forces are acting is in *equilibrium,* that is, immobile because the opposing forces are balanced. Equilibrium is the condition of a body when no unbalanced forces act upon it. This is the state achieved in an arm-wrestling contest when neither party is able to force the other party over, or in a rope-pulling contest when neither side is able to pull the other side over the line.

Parallel forces are two or more forces with the same or opposite direction applied to a common point (again see Figure 12.6). In the case of parallel forces, the resultant force is the sum of the two forces in the common direction. If two forces are applied to the same point from opposite directions, the resultant force is the difference of the two forces, in the direction of the larger magnitude (again see Figure 12.6).

Indeed, two or more forces acting on a common point can be pointing in any direction. The result of two forces acting at right

12.73 lbs. force vector

Figure 12.5 Above: A force, represented graphically with a vector, of 12.73 pounds acting northeastward.

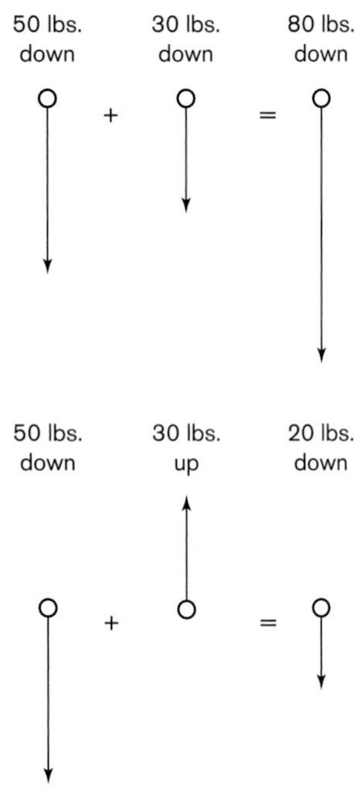

Figure 12.6 Above: Parallel forces add and subtract from each other. A hanging 50-pound weight plus a hanging 30-pound weight add up to a hanging weight of 80 pounds. A 50-pound hanging weight plus a 30-pound lift adds up to a 20-pound downward force.

angles is a force with a magnitude equal to the square root of the sum of the squares of the two forces, with a direction equal to the diagonal of the square formed by the two force vectors (again see Figure 12.7). In the general case, the result of two forces of arbitrary magnitude and direction is the diagonal of a parallelogram formed by the two forces (see again Figure 12.8). If there are three or more forces acting on a point, then the problem is solved by successively solving pairs of forces.

Whereas the composition of forces deals with cumulative effects of individual forces into an aggregate force, the ***resolution of forces*** is the decomposition of a single force into two or more forces; it is the inverse problem. Any force may be separated into two forces that act in definite directions and magnitudes upon the same point; these forces may be parallel, at right angles, or at arbitrary angles, such as the rafters of a house resolving the downward force of gravity (see Figure 12.10).

Relevant Terms

In Chapter 10, motion was defined as a continuous change in place or position. In a dynamic model, ***motion*** is the result of forces acting on masses. In a gravitational field, the mass of an object is the same as its weight, but in outer space this definition is insufficient; hence

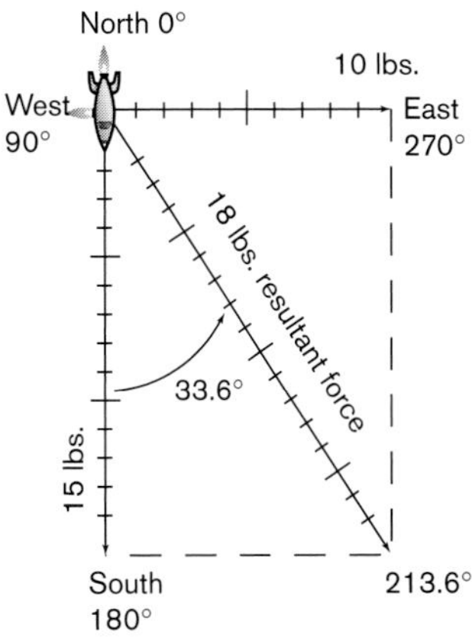

Figure 12.7 Above: In this example, two forces are simultaneously applied to point P. If you wish, you may think of P as the center of a space shuttle in stationary orbit, looking at it from above. The shuttle is pointing south. The force is applied by firing thruster rockets from the aft and the starboard side. Ten pounds of thrust from the starboard rocket push the shuttle to the east, and 15 pounds of thrust from the aft engine push the shuttle south. The magnitude of the resultant force is 18.03 pounds, and equal to $((10^2) + (15^2))^{**}0.5$. The direction of the resultant is equal to the arctangent of the two forces and is rotated 33.6 degrees east of south, which is arctan ($^{10}/_{15}$). The craft now has a heading of 213.6 degrees, assuming north is 0 degrees.

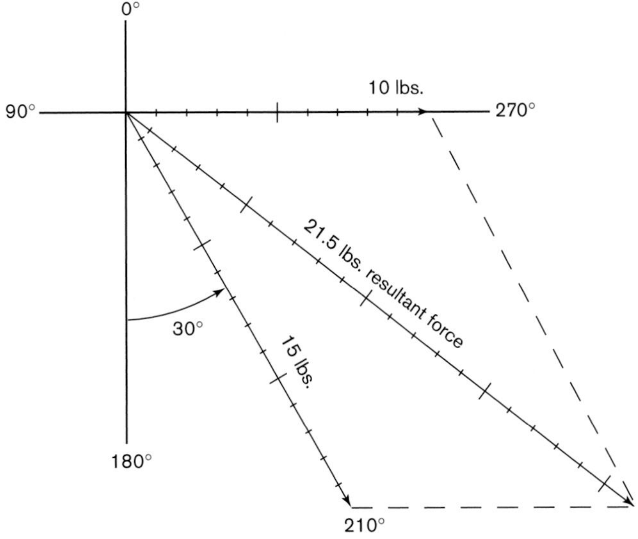

Figure 12.8 Left: The general case for the solution of two forces. Given two forces, one applied with a force of 10 pounds due east (a heading of 270 degrees), and one applied with a force of 15 pounds in a heading of 210 degrees, the solution is a force of 21.5 pounds.

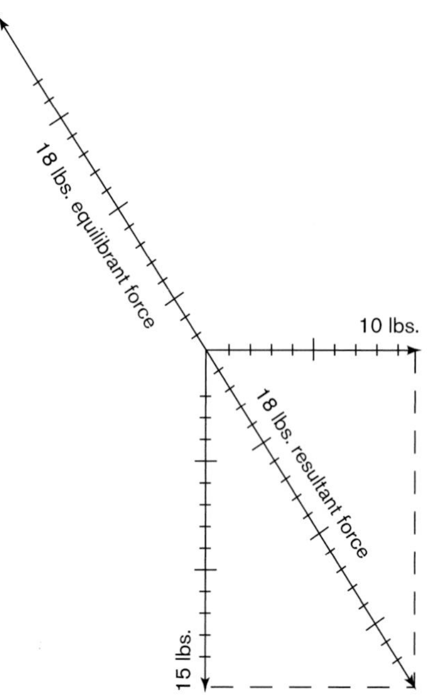

Figure 12.9 Right: Resultant and equilibrant forces balance each other out. They have equal magnitude and opposite direction.

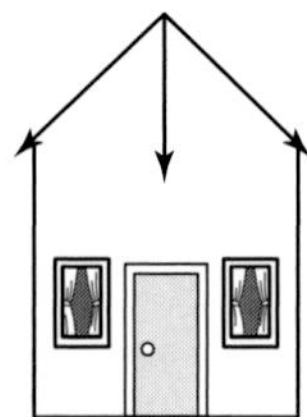

Figure 12.10 Above: The resolution of forces is the decomposition of a single force into two or more forces. Here, the downward force on the roof is resolved into two forces—each represented by a rafter.

Figure 12.11 Above: Inertia is the amount of force necessary to move an object. In the figure, the character applies much force as he attempts to move a large box.

mass is more correctly defined as the amount of inertia possessed by a body, where *inertia* is defined as the amount of force necessary to accelerate (move) an object (see Figure 12.11). Inertia is the tendency of objects that are at rest to continue to stay at rest, or for objects in motion to continue moving in the same direction at the same rate of speed. For example, a space shuttle in orbit has no weight but it does have mass, and in order for the shuttle to move in any direction, it is necessary to apply force to it, usually via a rocket motor (see Figure 12.12). The consolidation of this understanding was first advanced by Isaac Newton's three laws of motion (see Figure 12.13).

Thus there is a relationship between mass, force, and acceleration. In fact, the acceleration of an object is directly proportional to the force exerted on the object, inversely proportional to the mass of the object, and is in the same direction as the force:

$$\text{force} = \text{mass} \times \text{acceleration}$$

In the metric system, mass is measured in kilograms, acceleration is measured in meters/second/second, and force is measured in Newtons, measured in kilograms-meters/second/second. One Newton equals the weight of approximately 0.1 kilogram at sea level on Earth. Another metric system measurement of force is called the dyne; one Newton equals 105 dynes. In the English system, force is measured in pounds, which is inconsistent with the common view that pounds measure the mass of an object, which they do not; mass is measured in units called slugs. In a dynamic model, kilograms cannot be converted to pounds because they are not equivalent units of measurement. In a gravitational field, a balance is an instrument that may be used to measure the magnitude of force.

If the formula for acceleration,

$$a = v/t$$

is substituted into the formula for force,

$$F = m \times a$$

the result is

$$F = m \times v/t$$

and transposing produces

$$F \times t = m \times v$$

This product of force times the length of time it acts is called *impulse,* and the product of the mass times its velocity is called *momentum.* Impulse and momentum are equal. Mass is a scalar quantity, but velocity is a vector quantity, so consequently the product, momentum, is also a vector quantity, with both magnitude and direction. Thus a ferryboat has a lot of mass and moves very slowly, but it has a lot of momentum. A rifle bullet is very light but it moves very quickly, and it too has a lot of momentum.

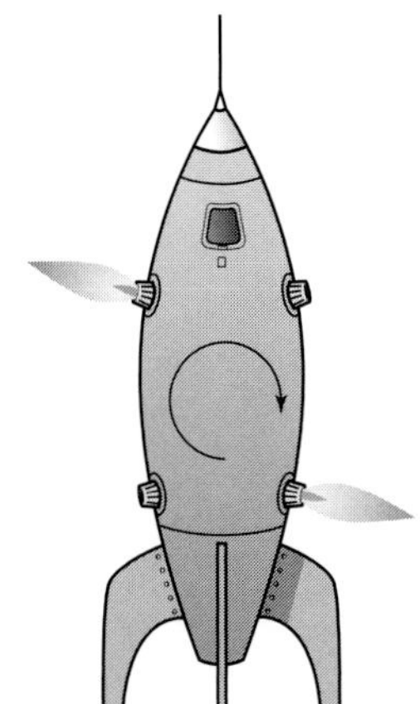

Figure 12.12 Above: A rocket motor is required to move the space shuttle—which has no weight but it does have mass. Firing the two motors will cause the rocket to pivot clockwise.

Figure 12.13 Below: Isaac Newton's three laws of motion.

Newton's Three Laws of Motion

1. An object at rest or in uniform motion stays at rest or continues to move in a straight line unless acted upon by a force.

2. Force = mass × acceleration (F = MA).

3. For every force exerted on an object, there is an equal force exerted in the opposite direction.

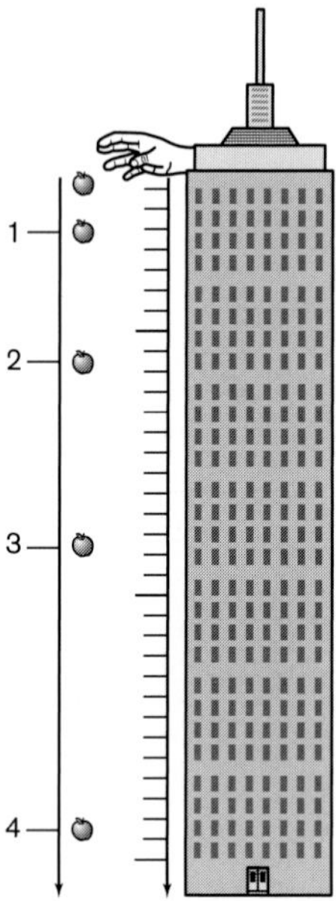

Seconds Feet

Law of universal gravitation

$F + G \times M1 \times M2/R \times R$

G = Gravitational constant
M1 = The mass of one body
M2 = The mass of the second body
R = Distance between the centers of M1 and M2
F = The attractive force

Figure 12.14 Above: Gravity. As the apple drops out of the window, gravity pulls it to the ground.

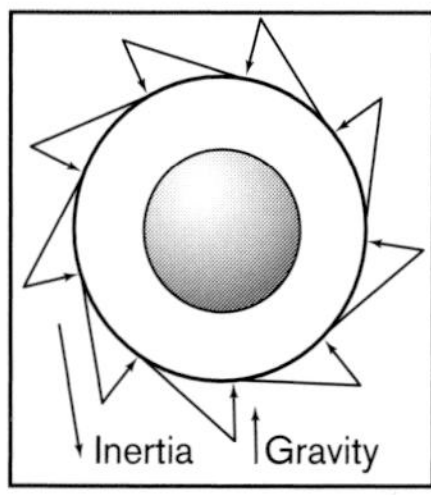

Figure 12.15 Above: The figure illustrates the effects of gravitational force combined with inertia. As the object falls straight away from the planet via inertia, gravity pulls it back in toward the planet; together they create an orbit.

Types of Force

There are various types of force in the universe; physics identifies several, including gravitational force, centrifugal force, centripetal force, friction, wind, and spring force. These forces affect the way that an object can move, and hence are the building blocks of dynamic models.

Gravitational Force

Gravitational force, or *gravity,* causes bodies to fall toward the Earth (see Figure 12.14). It is a natural phenomenon of mutual attraction between massive bodies. Gravity is the force that is measured when the weight of an object is being determined. The *center of gravity* is that point in or near an object at which all the weight of that object appears to be concentrated. Because gravity is such a critical force, there are many numbers, equations, and laws associated with it that can be used to predict motion. In addition, because it is so critical, it is available in some computer animation programs; gravity is applied to the environment and affects everything, including human characters.

Gravitational forces (and inertia) are clearly illustrated by the concept of an *orbit*, an elliptical path traveled by one object around another, for example, a satellite around a planet. In a dynamic sense, an orbit is the balance between an object's inertia, for example, the tendency for a satellite to fly straight off into space, and the gravitational attraction of a central object, for example, the tendency for a satellite to be pulled directly toward a planet. The balance keeps the satellite moving around the planet (see Figure 12.15).

Centrifugal Force

There are also forces associated with circular movement; these are less common in contemporary animation programs. *Centrifugal force* is a force acting away from a center, or the force on a body that is in curvilinear motion, where the force is directed outward from the center of the movement. Centrifugal force occurs in many everyday situations, such as the force one feels when a car turns quickly around a tight turn, or during an amusement park ride designed around circular motion (see Figure 12.16).

Figure 12.16 Left: Centrifugal force occurs in an amusement park ride designed around circular motion. Here, the person riding in the teacup is pushed against the back of the teacup as the ride goes around in circle.

Centripetal Force

Centripetal force, on the other hand, is a force acting toward a center, or the force on a body that is in curvilinear motion, where the force is directed inward toward the center of the movement. Centripetal force is less common in everyday situations, but does occur in the flow of vortexes such as tornadoes and whirlpools (see Figure 12.17). Along a similar line, ***torque*** is a turning or twisting force that is defined as the product of a force times the length of the arm on which it acts.

Figure 12.17 Above: The centripetal force of a tornado is directed inward toward the center of the movement.

Friction

Like gravity, ***friction*** is commonly found in computer animation programs. Also called ***roughness,*** it is the force that opposes motion (see Figure 12.18). Friction results from two bodies in contact, either completely separate objects or two links connected at a joint. It is specifically a result of the surface qualities of the two bodies: the smoother the surfaces, the less friction and the less opposing force; the rougher the surfaces, the greater the friction and the greater the opposing force. The ***coefficient of friction*** is the ratio of the force of friction to the normal force pressing the surfaces together. Sometimes friction is broken down into different types: ***static friction*** is the friction that determines how one objects slides on the surface of another; ***kinetic friction*** is the energy that is lost by an object as it slides on the surface of another. All of these forces are measured in Newtons or pounds, depending upon whether you are using metric or English measures.

Figure 12.18 Above: Friction. The right skater is on a pond moving swiftly; there is little friction between the ice and the blades of the skates. The left skater is moving slowly on a path; there is much friction between the surface of the path and the blades of the skates.

Wind Force

Another type of force becoming more available to computer animators is the force of the wind (see Figure 12.19). ***Wind force*** is the natural movement of the air; it has a magnitude and a direction.

Similarly, *fan force* is the local movement of the air, created by something other than nature, for example, a fan. When wind force is suitably high, it can affect the other objects in the scene.

Figure 12.19 Wind force and fan force. Wind is the natural movement of the air and has the ability to alter the scene—for example, by blowing leaves in a tree. Fan force is human-made, local movement of the air, as illustrated by a circular fan.

Spring Force

Finally, the last type of force presented here is *spring force*, the force stored by a compressed or overextended spring. When a spring is relaxed, there is no spring force (see Figure 12.20). Along a similar line is the concept of elasticity. *Elasticity* is the amount of energy lost from one object when it collides with another object. In the case of the falling chair, which is not very elastic, its elasticity factor is vastly different from the elasticity of a rubber ball.

Behavioral Systems

Behavioral animation extends the concept of dynamic modeling to the modeling of behavior. A *behavioral system* is a program that enables behavioral modeling. *Behavioral modeling* is when aspects of behavior are modeled: personality, physical factors, social behaviors, and environmental factors.

Personality variables can include static variables, such as gender and birth signs, as well as qualities that change over time, such as age, weight, and eyesight. Personality variables can be psychological, such as shyness, assertiveness, fear, happiness, or stress. Creatures can also be described in terms of *physical variables,* such as hungry or tired, where such things affect behavior. In addition, certain behaviors might relate to parameters—for example, qualities that relate to one's age, such as innocence and playfulness.

Social variables represent another kind of behavioral quality and can describe a creature's social behavior. For example, some creatures have a tendency to stay within a group (for protection, perhaps), while others tend to stay by themselves (predators, perhaps).

Environmental variables represent aspects of the scene, and include temperature, air or water pressure, the amount of fuel or energy available, and radiation levels. Environmental variables can directly and indirectly affect the objects in the scene.

Obviously, all of these variables are represented digitally, either numerically on a scale, often normalized from 0.0 to 1.0, or as a finite

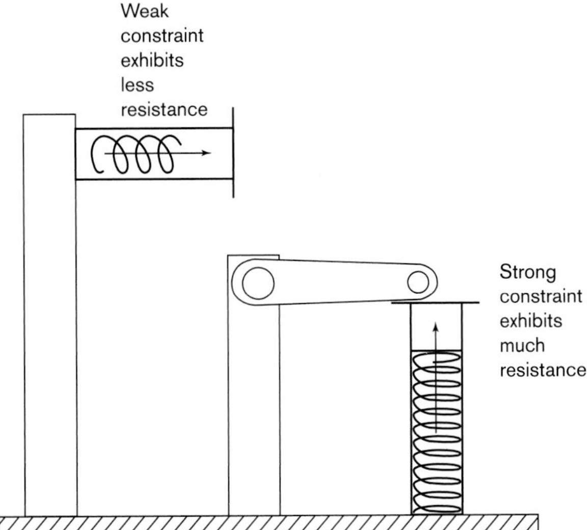

Figure 12.20 When a spring is compressed, it stores force, which can be used in many ways—for example, to move objects.

set of choices [plant, animal, bacteria, virus, and so forth]. For example, hunger might be represented as a value between 0.0 and 1.0. When a creature is created, it might be assigned a default value of 0.0 for hunger. After a designated interval of time, the value is automatically incremented by a small amount. When the value increases above a threshold, for example 0.6, then the creature begins to hunt for food, which is the second part of the behavioral dynamics concept: the modeling of goals and constraints.

In this context, ***goals*** are conditions that want to be met, and attendant behaviors and constraints are restrictions on when, where, or why a behavior can execute, for example, within a region of space. For another example, most creatures strive to avoid collision with other creatures or objects. Therefore, collision avoidance is a common behavioral goal that must be modeled in a behavioral system.

To continue the previous example, the creature possesses a variable (hunger), a condition (if hunger $\leq$ 0.6), a behavior (hunt for food), and a goal (not hungry). The behavior involves some kind of foraging activity. When food is found, the eating process can decrease the hunger variable. Once the goal is met and the creature is filled (hunger $\leq$ 0.4), it stops eating and foraging for food (see Figure 12.21).

As you can see, one of the key features for behavioral models is that the creatures instilled with the behavior can be completely autonomous. Properly equipped, they can move about their environment, maintain stability, avoid collisions, and function socially with other virtual creatures. This is true for any virtual creature, whether it

Figure 12.21 Goals. The goal is for the character to satisfy his hunger. In the first panel, the character is watching television at 4:00 PM, and his hunger level is below 0.4. In the second panel, the character realizes that he is hungry shortly after 4:00 PM, and his hunger level has risen to 0.6. In the third panel, the character is looking in the refrigerator at 4:05 PM, and his hunger level has risen even higher (0.8). In the fourth panel, the character is eating at 4:10 PM, and his hunger level has dropped to 0.5. In the fifth panel, the character is closing the refrigerator at 4:15 PM, and his hunger level remains the same. Finally, in the last panel, the character is watching television and his hunger level is again rising (0.6).

is based on a real-world creature or is completely imaginary. As with kinematic goals and constraints, behavioral goals and constraints may be interdependent, and they may be set up to have strength, so that goals may compete with each other. For example, defending hostile attacks may take precedence over feeding. Note that once interrupted, feeding might not continue; the creature might not be full, but until hunger rises above 0.6, foraging behavior will not begin again.

Note that according to the way we are describing them, behavioral models may have a rich or very little geometry. Much of the craft of behavior simulation comes from the game industry, where a creature may be no more than a variable name with a list of possessions. But remember that an animator who wishes to control part of a behavioralistic virtual world must direct the models behavioristically. Examples of such schema can be seen in the form of flocks of birds, schools of fish, and groups of humans.

It is possible to fuse dynamic and behavioral systems, which combine goal-directed behavioral models and dynamic motion control. Animators can direct in terms of higher-order parameterized commands, such as forage or feed, and the motion is calculated by the computer using dynamic models to control kinematic linkages at the lowest level.

While many of the behavioral concepts presented here are not commercially available, researchers are making great progress toward their implementation, and thus they may be available in the near future.

Behaviorally Modeled Characters

Behaviorally modeled characters, also known as *avatars* or *virtual actors,* are animated (often user-directed) characters that are defined in terms of personality and physical variables (see Figure 12.22). Once defined, these characters can be set free in an animated computer environment. Behaviorally modeled characters can each be defined in terms of a list of properties that describe personality traits such as temperament. Characters can modify their own traits, as well as the traits of their fellow characters.

Figure 12.22 Above: Behaviorally modeled characters. Animation systems may include an animation engine, to create physically convincing actions among actors, and a behavioral engine, which invokes rules that control the actors' behavior. The animation engine may respond to commands such as "walk" and "wave," while the behavioral engine may respond to higher-level commands such as "go to the store."

Keep in mind that behaviorally modeled characters can also be dynamically modeled. As such, the dynamic system operates the body of the actor, and the behavioral system operates the mind. The behavioral system impacts the animation system, which, in turn, can modify the geometry of the actor. The result is a system that can enable interesting behavior among characters and smooth, convincing action.

Behaviorally Modeled Groups

For creatures that have a tendency to exist in groups, the behavior of the group itself often needs to be animated and can be as interesting as the behavior of the individuals themselves. A *behaviorally modeled group* is a collection of creatures, such that the behavior of the collection is modeled in terms of social variables. These creatures can all be of the same type, or there can be a variety of types. Depending on the type of creature, the individuals react a particular way when placed in a group. Typically, each individual has its own personal behavior definition; in addition, it has a group behavior definition.

Figure 12.23 Above: Behaviorally modeled groups. In a flock of geese, the behavior of each individual bird affects the group. Here, each goose finds its position in the formation.

For example, consider a flock of birds (see Figure 12.23). The group behavior of each individual bird can be specified in terms of goal rules; imbedded in the rules is information about the birds' desire to stay within the flock, and at the same time, to avoid collision with other birds in the flock. Thus, collision avoidance, velocity matching, and flock centering are all stated in terms of rules. Creating many such birds results in a flock of birds, which, because of the behavior of each individual bird, behaves like a flock of birds in the real world.

A behaviorally modeled group can be implemented as an extension of particle systems—a group of small objects or particles, with each particle having its own behavior. They can get created, have a life, and die; they can have color, opacity, location, and velocity.

It is worth noting that the creatures being animated do not necessarily need to be physically accurate. In the case of the birds, each bird could be represented by a sphere; in this case, it is only the behavior of the birds that would be worth seeing in the resulting animation. However, to complete the realistic quality of the animation, the creatures could also be physically dynamically modeled—they could travel through their environment according to the laws of simulated physics or aerodynamic flight.

Behaviorally Modeled Ecosystems

A *behaviorally modeled ecosystem* is an ecological community together with its physical environment, which are behaviorally modeled in terms of environmental variables. Behaviorally animating an ecosystem means considering the ever-changing state caused by the interaction between the community and the environment.

Examples of ecosystems include a tropical rainforest, a pond, and a simple collection of plants interacting with their environment (see Figure 12.24). As in the real world, plants are affected by the global properties of the environment, including daylight, rain, and temperature, as well as local properties of the environment, such as obstacles affecting the growth of branches and roots, shadows, and water. Rules describe how the plant interacts with its environment—for example, if water is present, the plant's root absorbs the water and the plant grows; the water in the environment is depleted. This, in turn, affects the direction and growth of the roots in the next time interval of the simulation. Similarly, access to sunlight is affected by the season, time of day, and forest canopy. By simulating plants and the environment, the system enables the development of plants to be visualized. Too much or too little rain or sunlight stunts growth for normal plants, but may enable growth of plants adapted to extreme conditions. Note that the simulation is bidirectional: the plants and the soil interact with each other. (Although, at the other extreme, plants affect the sunlight insignificantly.) In the simulation, the plants and the environment can each be treated as separate processes (programs) that communicate with each other. The ecosystem produces plants that are physically responsive to their environments, and the effects can easily be seen in the resulting animated plants.

Figure 12.24 Above: A behaviorally modeled ecosystem.

Combining It All—Some Examples

Dynamic and behavioral modeling can get quite complicated, especially when dynamically modeled characters are behaviorally modeled and then placed into a group, which is then placed into a behaviorally modeled ecosystem. Once all of the variables are defined, a self-contained world can be created.

As an example, consider a school of fish that has been modeled in terms of appearance, movement, and behavior, and that is then placed into a dynamically modeled environment (see Figure 12.25). The individual fish can be realistically modeled, both in terms of their appearance and basic physics. They can swim realistically in dynamically modeled water, by contracting muscles (perhaps muscle springs). The movement of the fish reacts with the volume of water

Figure 12.25 Left: Behaviorally modeled fish. Dynamic and behavioral modeling can be combined to create dynamically modeled characters, which are also behaviorally modeled. They can be placed into a group, which is then placed into a behaviorally modeled ecosystem.

that surrounds them. The fish get propelled forward by a calculation that utilizes the inertia of the displaced water to produce a reaction force normal to each fish's body and proportional to the volume of water displaced per time unit.

Each fish in the school can also be behaviorally modeled—by providing it with properties that mimic cognition. Thus, their perception of their environment will determine their behavior. Each fish can have basic reflexive behaviors, such as collision avoidance, and motivational behaviors, such as fear, hunger, and libido. Their behavior can also be modified by their perception of their environment, and they can sense their local surroundings with their vision and temperature sensors.

In order to maintain the action of such fish, a control system would calculate the status of relevant variables at a series of periodic time steps. The control system could check for collisions; if no collisions, then it checks for predators; if the fear threshold is low, then hunger and libido states can be calculated. Finally, many such fish can be placed into a physically modeled marine environment.

The combination of dynamic and behavioral animation is also a valid strategy for solving problems such as animating a walking human figure. The human figure and other legged creatures are not only the most interesting things to animate, they are also among the most complex. Animating limbs in a convincing way, with all the degrees of freedom, presents the animator with many challenges, especially coordinating all the angles of even a simple kinematic armature. Consider a walk—hands swinging, hips, knees, and ankles bending—with some simple obstacles, ramps, inclines, potholes, uneven ground, and stairs. The challenge is enormous.

In this case—leaving aside the behavioral properties—the animated character wants to stay upright, move in a direction, and minimize the energy it uses to move. Here is a case where dynamics can solve the problem. Because we can imbue a kinematic armature with dynamic properties, for example mass and friction, a resolution of force will impact how the limbs and torso move. This produces action similar to real-world movement.

Dynamic behavioral models can assist with autonomous locomotion of real, as well as imaginary, creatures, and the same theory applies to a biped, a quadruped, and a six-legged insect. Personality, physical, and social variables can be defined for each creature. In addition, the character can be placed into an environment that is defined in terms of environmental variables. In all of these cases, a control system is necessary to coordinate a complex pattern of behavior and movement. This is achieved by evaluating goals and constraints, and evaluating force and resistance—this must be done for each frame of the simulation, if not more frequently.

Learning

As models become more complex, they get harder and harder to animate; even dynamic behavioral models require careful construction. Animation would be much simpler if the model could learn to animate itself. ***Intelligent models*** are models that are capable of learning from their own action.

For example, highly flexible models with many degrees of freedom, such as snakes, fish, and sea mammals, can learn to move (see Figure 12.26). Locomotion can be learned through action and perception, and much repeated trial and error on the part of the animated model. After many attempts, the model can learn to move effectively, and essentially learn to control its own body and learn higher-level motion.

Animated models can also evolve and adapt to their environment. They can be equipped with a virtual brain, which, depending upon what it senses, determines the model's behavior. Dynamic simulation can be used to control the creature's movement. Such a model could be responsible for the automatic generation of new models, with survival of the fittest being a driving force. Creature evolution could be driven by specific goals, for example, jumping—survival of the fittest would mean that the better jumper would stand a greater chance of evolving. Creatures could reproduce, and depending upon the specific goal, the offspring would either survive or not survive.

Dynamics and Computer Animation Programs

A dynamic computer animation program enables the modeling of forces and is the most appropriate approach to non-deterministic (but repeatable) animation. Virtual forces are implemented as part of the animation system and are automatically applied to virtual objects that are placed into the virtual environment. Minimally, forces that are

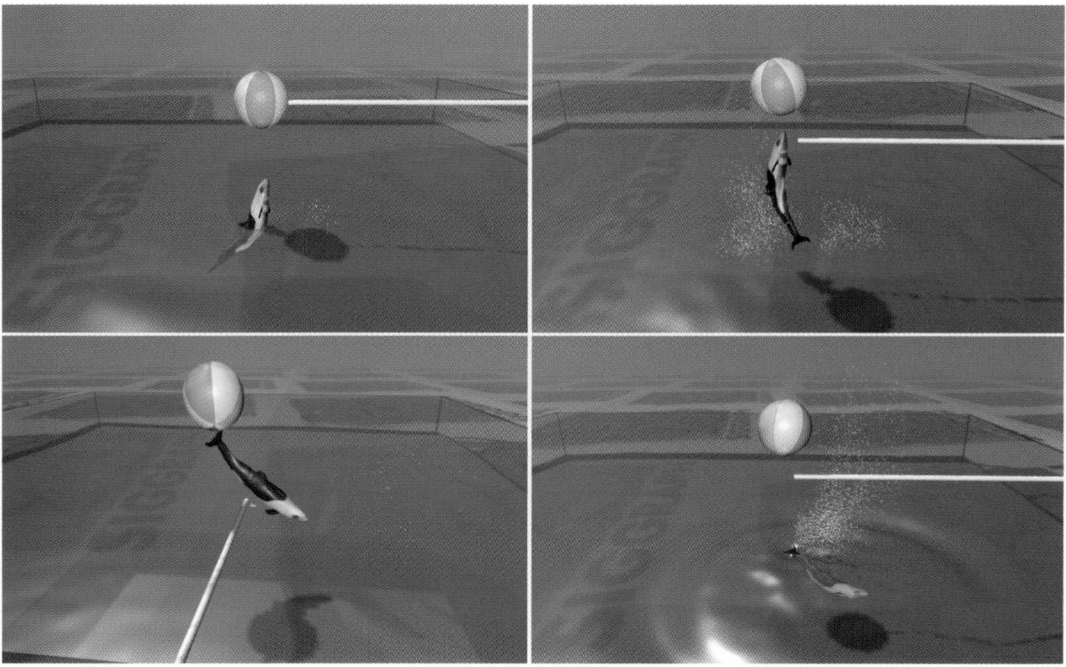

Figure 12.26 Intelligent models are capable of learning from their own action.

pertinent to the situation are implemented; these forces might include gravity, momentum, mass, energy, friction, and pressure. Objects are defined with mass, solidness, velocity, and other relevant qualities. A computer animation program that supports dynamics must support commands that enable an animator to place forces into a scene, attach forces to objects, and calculate the results.

A dynamic animation system knows about all of the models in the virtual world—it knows all the forces and properties of all the models, where they are, and where and how they are moving. Hence, when an additional animated model is introduced to the virtual world, the dynamic system automatically handles the qualities of the movement—Will objects collide? Is the new object affected by gravity? Does it pass through other objects?

Dynamic approaches have both advantages and disadvantages for the animator. One of the advantages of a dynamic model is that it can be explored experimentally. For example, a dynamic model of a car engine can help determine if the car will run faster if more gas is put into the cylinders, if the engine will flood, if the engine will stall, and so on. The results should be similar to those obtained if a real engine were used in the experiment. The crux of the dynamic approach is that the animation is controlled by manipulating its dynamic, not kinematic, parameters. If the engine wants to spin faster, it must be given more gas; it is not controlled by specifying a crankshaft angle.

In a dynamic system, the number of frames needed to animate a particular action is determined by the dynamic model. It is gravity that determines how long it takes a ball to fall to the ground. This is a very different approach than a kinematic approach, in which the number of frames is specified in advance. In animation, unlike the real world, it is often time that is constrained and predetermined, locked in dialogue, sound effects, adjacent shots, and visual rhythms. Dynamics can easily get in the way.

Dynamic solutions require precision in their setup and execution. Animators working in a kinematic domain have the liberty to cheat a lot—for example, an object that is too big can be moved farther away to make it look smaller (instead of sizing it smaller), or perhaps a slight twiddle on a motion pathway improves the composition at a special moment during a scene. But in a world that simulates the physics of reality, virtual nature has little tolerance for such adjustments. Units of measurement must be accurate and internally consistent. This can create real problems for animators who like to build in center-unity (–1.0 to 1.0), normalized (0.0 to 1.0), or convert coordinates to integers (e.g., 0 to 1023) coordinates.

Many other issues must be considered when working with a dynamic system. For example, in the real world, time is continuous, but in computer simulations, time is ultimately represented as a series of discrete frames. In kinematic animation, one can solve the frames in any order, but in dynamic simulations, one cannot—the future depends upon the past. Furthermore, dynamic calculations made with different time intervals produce different results, so the process of calculating motion tests on twos or sixes produces different results from an animation calculated on ones, or for that matter an animation where the time steps are more frequent than the frame rate. If the time steps are too coarse, events can happen between the time steps that would otherwise be critical—for example, two balls on a collision course could pass by each other if the time interval were not sufficiently short to detect them colliding.

The most effective computer animation programs incorporate both kinematic and dynamic features. In an integrated system, kinematic structures such as a human armature can be created, but they can be controlled by dynamic forces, as opposed to kinematic methods. In other words, the figure would have a "muscle" capacity (force) that would enable it to lift (or not be able to lift) an object with a certain mass. This combined approach gives control to the animator and may enable convincing results, but remember that the problem of animating how a flag blows in the wind is not necessarily the same as making sure a logo on the flag is readable.

In summary, the topics presented in this chapter may be applied to many animation production strategies. Which methodology to deploy depends upon the effect one wants to achieve. There are many instances when kinematics provide full control for a desired effect. However, when naturalistic simulation is required, the dynamic approach, perhaps coupled with behavioral simulation, may be preferred. Dynamics can be difficult to direct. Furthermore, the physically correct results it produces may well be antithetical to the results one seeks, especially when caricature of motion is often the quest of the animator. Because animation is an art as well as a science, there is no single solution to an animation problem.

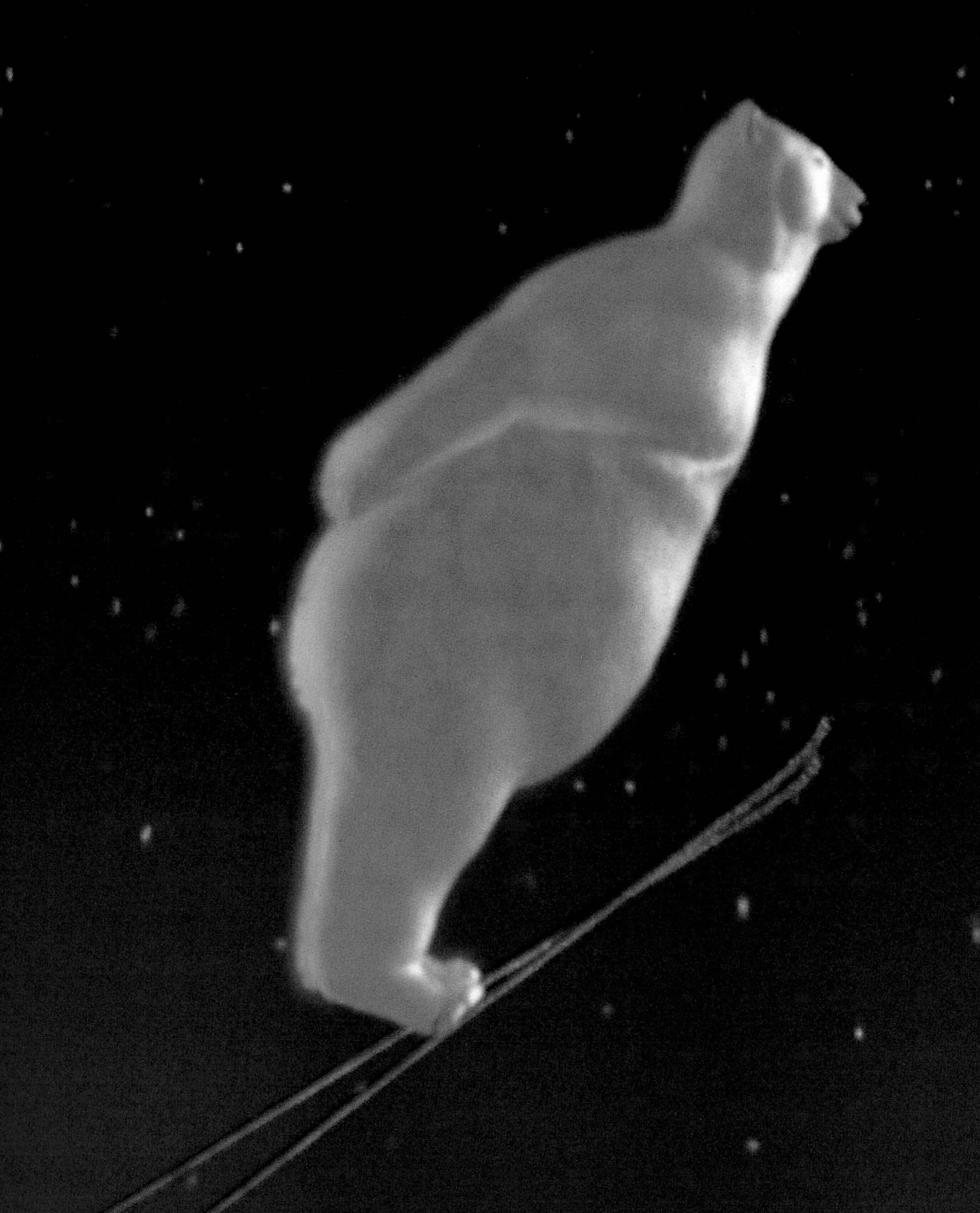

13 Digital Special Effects

Special effects are visuals that are difficult or impossible to achieve with standard imaging techniques. They can be created with standard equipment or highly specialized equipment, including computers. The topic of special effects is broad, ranging from optical effects to pyrotechnics. In order to narrow the focus, this chapter does not cover effects that occur entirely in the real world, such as stunts, makeup, or pyrotechnics. While these topics do affect the computer animator, they usually do so in terms of compositing and hence will not be discussed. The use of computer-controlled models called *animatronics* is also not covered here. In addition, since this book does not address modeling techniques, this chapter does not include algorithmic special effects techniques, such as those used to model fireworks, water, and other non-rigid geometries.

What this chapter does focus on are optical effects and those special effects that involve image processing. With few exceptions, the vocabulary here is borrowed from the film tradition and an era where effects were crafted by sculpting light directly onto film. With a computer, of course, the mechanics of this process are greatly simplified, but the vocabulary—for example, the *slow dissolve* as an indication of the passage of time—remains. Today, the computer has made possible hundreds of distortions, squeezes, and repeats. But complicated effects work still relies on basics such as the rotoscope, multiple exposures, compositing, and mattes.

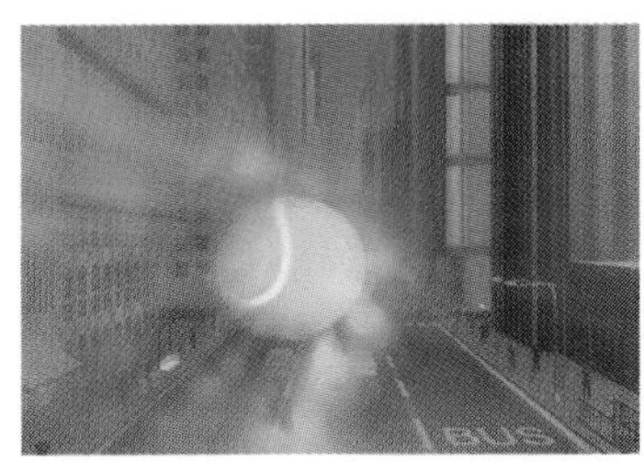

CBS 1998 U.S. Tennis Open. Image courtesy of Manhattan Transfer. Creative director: Micha Riss; 3D animation and compositing: Paul Lipsky; Software: Softimage 3D, Softimage particle, and Softimage eddie.

Non-Real-Time Live Action

We begin with a discussion of special effects that are created with a camera that is not recording in real time.

Time-Lapse and High-Speed Photography

Time-lapse photography, also known as *stop-motion photography,* is a special effects technique in which a sequence of recordings is made at infrequent intervals, and then played back at a standard frame rate, for example, 24 frames/second. The effect of time-lapse photography is that the resulting images appear to be happening at a speed faster than normal. If the object being photographed incurs small amounts of change over a long amount of time—for example, a blooming flower—then the resulting images enable the eye to see movements that it would not normally be able to (see Figure 13.1).

High-speed photography, on the other hand, is when a camera records at speeds much higher than normal and the resulting sequence of frames is played back at a standard rate. The effect of high-speed photography is that the resulting images appear to happen in slow motion. If the object being photographed incurs large amounts of change over a small amount of time—for example, an exploding bomb—then the results enable the eye to see things that would normally happen too fast to be perceived (see Figure 13.2).

Squeeze Action

Squeeze action is a special effects technique that uses sequentially shot still photographs to convey action, rather than using a subject that is moving in real time (see Figure 13.3). Obviously, the individual stills must have a sense of continuity, but their individual character makes the action jumpy. Typically, each still is repeated for two to five frames; different stills can be held for different durations to build rhythm. The resulting filmed action is unreal, usually staccato, even jerky, which is both the signature and the shortcoming of the technique. It is similar to time-lapse photography, but the time intervals are not equally spaced (even).

A variation of this technique employs making 8-by-10-inch or 11-by-14-inch photocopy blowups of 16mm or 35mm live action sequences or the use of individual digitized frames of film or video. The animator

Figure 13.1 Time-lapse photography. A bouquet of tulips was photographed every five minutes. When the sequence of photographs is played back at 24 frames/second, the tulips appear to be wilting at a speed faster than normal.

Figure 13.2 High-speed photography. When an explosion is recorded at speeds much higher than normal and then played back at a standard rate, the explosion appears to be happening in slow motion.

then "pegs the action" by either using the photocopied film sprocket holes or *witness points* in the background. Digitized images can be treated as photographic stills—color and additional graphics added. The animator can eliminate frames, cycle sequences, zoom or offset, and adjust the timing of the frames to fit the sound track.

The advantage of the squeeze action technique is its ability to make use of the traditional photographic image to produce animated results. The economic savings of using a still-photographed subject is often a factor in the choice of this technique, and the reuse of stock or previously used live action material, enhanced and rerecorded, is often a cost-saving factor as well. Unfortunately, the unreal, often erratic quality of the motion precludes the use of this technique for many projects. It is never advisable to employ this technique strictly as a low-cost substitute for live action photography. To make effective use of squeeze action, its shortcoming must be exploited.

Figure 13.3 Above: Squeeze action. Careful timing and composition can blend a sequence of related still pictures into a meaningful action.

Pixilation

Pixilation is the extension of animation techniques into live action photography; it is the manipulation of live action on a single-frame basis (see Figure 13.4). All of the animation is done with a live action, single-frame camera. Pixilation involves shooting actors or models as a series of individual frames, much as animation would be shot. The technique usually involves the creation of a 2D planning diagram such as is shown in Figure 13.4, which depicts the movement of the actor in the real-world set. This drawing is then overlaid on the camera view of the scene and the actor is positioned and shot in the indicated

Figure 13.4 Left: Pixilation. This technique involves the creation of a planning diagram as shown here, which depicts the movement of an action in a real-world scene. This drawing is then overlaid on the camera view of the scene, and the actors are shot on the positions indicated.

positions. The live characters are moved slightly from frame to frame, with the director using the prephotographed plan as a visual guide. This technique is also used with puppets and clay animation, substituting inanimate objects for people. Obviously, since pixilation is not photographed in real time, the sound track must be handled separately, as in any animation. As the result of this technique, action can be relatively smooth, yet patently unreal; it works best when it presents the visually impossible. Pixilation with human subjects works best in a completely controlled environment, which is both its strength and its weakness. Pixilation is sort of like inverse rotoscopy.

Rotoscopy

A *rotoscope* is a 2D tracing of a 2D or 3D image. After actors and 3D objects are recorded, a rotoscope is created by projecting individual frames, one at a time, and then tracing the images in the frame, either on paper or digitized into a computer. An animation stand can be used to project film images, or the images can be digitized and then traced. Tracing can be done by hand or with the assistance of edge-detection and spline-based illustration software. Exactly what gets traced depends upon the task at hand. For example, rotoscope drawings can be used to assist in the positioning of computer graphics objects that are to be composited with live action. Rotoscopy is often employed when animated characters need to interact realistically with live action, as in *Who Framed Roger Rabbit,* as well as when effects must be integrated, such as the light sabers in *Star Wars.* Rotoscopy is often used to create mattes that isolate one region of the screen, such as outlining a live action character so that an animated character can be made to pass behind. It is also used to gauge the positions of puppets during stop-motion photography such as pixilation. The rotoscoped drawings are not part of the final product; the original film images are composited with the computer graphics imagery. In order to achieve convincing results, rotoscopy requires time, skill, and precision.

Optical Effects

An *optical effect* is an effect created with an *optical printer, optical camera* (i.e., a camera that photographs film), or with a video switcher or computer that mimics this process. We endorse the term *optical* here because it implies a class of effects that can be accomplished with a lens, shutter, and shuttle. In general, optical effects imply an amalgamation of one or more scenes into a common resultant scene. In film, this is achieved by exposing the same length of film two or more times. In computer terms, a *double exposure* is performed numerically: for each pixel

$$\text{result} = \text{imageA} + \text{imageB}$$

If each image contributes to one-half the exposure, then for each pixel

$$\text{result} = (0.5 \times \text{imageA}) + (0.5 \times \text{imageB})$$

Optical effects techniques include fades, dissolves, wipes, and matte composition. These operations are all pixel-by-pixel operations and usually involve an incoming image and an outgoing image. They may also involve a transition device that marries the two input images into a single resultant image, as in a split screen or wipe. Special effects can be implemented optically in film, electronically in video, or algorithmically in the digital domain.

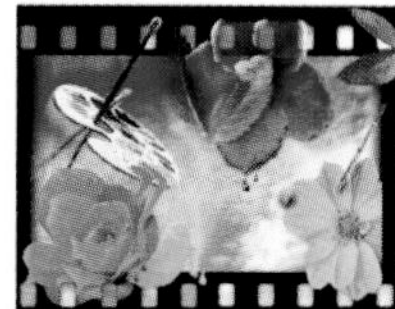

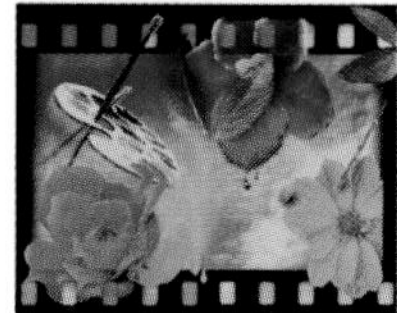

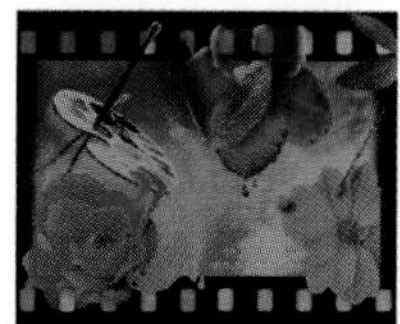

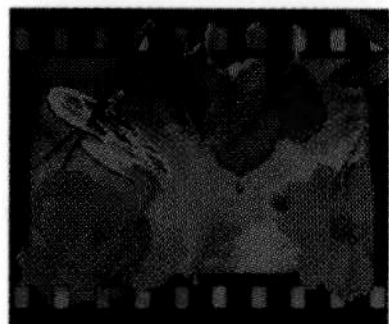

Figure 13.5 A fade is a multiframe transition, starting from an image and turning into black (fade-out) or starting from black and turning into an image (fade-in). Fades can be achieved optically, electronically, and digitally.

Fades, Dissolves, Wipes, and Double Exposures

Many special effects have been created to communicate the idea of a transition from one scene to another—for example, wipes, fades, dissolves, and double exposures, which are all operations that involve the use of two images. In the digital domain, these operations are accomplished by applying a mathematical operation to the sequence of frames.

Fades and Dissolves One of the simplest transition effects is the *fade,* that is, when the brightness of an image diminishes to zero, a black screen (see Figure 13.5). A fade is a multiframe transition, starting from an image and turning into black (fade-out) or starting from black and turning into an image (fade-in). For digital images, a fade is the result of multiplying each pixel in the image by a value between zero and one, resulting in an image of changing intensity. Built upon the fade is the *dissolve,* a transition produced when a scene fading out is simultaneously combined with a scene fading in, creating a dissolve transition between the images (see Figure 13.6).

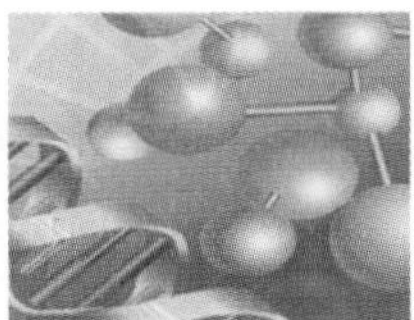
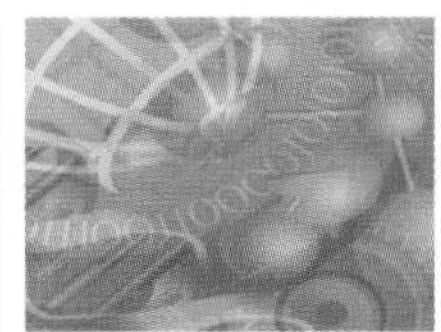

Figure 13.6 A dissolve is a transition produced when a scene fading out is simultaneously combined with a scene fading in.

Wipes A *wipe,* which is a similar effect to dissolves, is when the outgoing scene is replaced in the frame by the incoming scene (see Figure 13.7). The wipe itself has a geometric definition, defined by the way that the incoming image replaces the outgoing image—for example, by wiping along a straight line from top to bottom. A *push* involves both a wipe and an image transition (see Figure 13.8).

Double Exposures Another optical effect is the *double exposure,* which melds two images to create one resultant image, which contains all the imagery from both input images (see Figure 13.9). In film, a double exposure is created by exposing a piece of film twice—once while recording one input image, and once while recording a second image. In order not to overexpose the double exposure, each of the two recordings must be made at partial exposure. In the digital domain, double exposures are achieved by calculating pixel averages. For example, the pixels in the resultant image are determined by calculating the average color of the pixels in the two source images, that is, for each pixel add the numeric values of the two pixel colors, then divide by two.

It is a good practice to shoot or compute a test of different exposure possibilities since the best solution may not be

$$(0.5 \times \text{imageA}) + (0.5 \times \text{imageB})$$

A better equation might be

$$(0.6 \times \text{imageA}) + (0.6 \times \text{imageB})$$

This is because of the structure of the two images and where the brighter regions of the picture are located. Note that in this example, it is quite possible that some pixels (just like some part of the film) may overflow (become overexposed), because their values will be too large for bitmap storage. It is important to trap the overflow and cap them at the maximum brightness values, otherwise they may appear as ghosts.

This principle of overflow does have some utility, especially when placing type and logos over backgrounds. The type must be com-

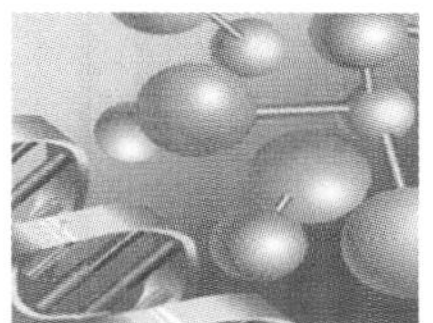
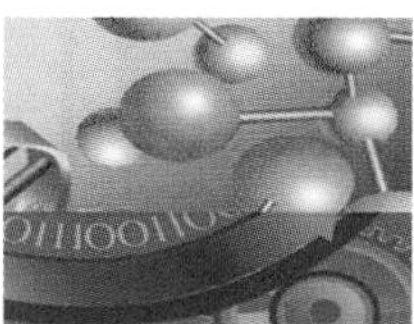

Figure 13.7 A wipe is when the outgoing scene is replaced in the frame by the incoming scene. The wipe itself has a geometric definition, defined by the way that the incoming image replaces the outgoing image—for example, by wiping along a straight line from bottom to top.

pletely white in order to overflow (burn out, double expose) any background image. Double exposures are used to create ***glows*** (a double exposure with a soft edge), ***streaks*** (movements that make a smear), and ***strobes*** (discrete streaks). Double exposures have become part of the vocabulary of moving pictures, often connoting dreams and memories. When designing the double exposure, the combined composition of each of the input images must be considered so that the resultant image is well composed. ***Multiple exposures*** are similar to double exposures, except that they involve three or more input images.

When preparing these kinds of effects, be encouraged to test systematically. Vary one thing at a time—brightness, color, and so on—and study the results. Often you can identify the desired combination as much by studying the adjacent frames as the target frames. These tests are variously called ***stepwedges*** and ***cinexes,*** short for *cinema exposure.* When in doubt, cinex it.

Mattes

There are also special effects that do not involve transitions, but that are integral within a scene. ***Matting*** is a process used to insert one image into another. In the television industry, mattes are called ***keys;*** in the print industry, they are called ***holdbacks*** and ***knockouts.*** The most common of these techniques is the ***matte composite,*** an optical effects technique in which two or more separate image streams are merged together into a single resultant image stream (see Figure 13.10). Compositing utilizes mattes, which are essentially operators that determine what content from which image stream is to be included in the resultant image stream.

Mattes can be either black-core or clear-core. A ***black-core matte*** is a matte in which the region defining the shape of interest is black and the remaining region is clear; the image is printed through the clear core, and the black region does not get exposed, as in Figure 13.10(a). In a ***clear-core matte***, the region defining the shape of interest is clear and the remaining region is black; as with the

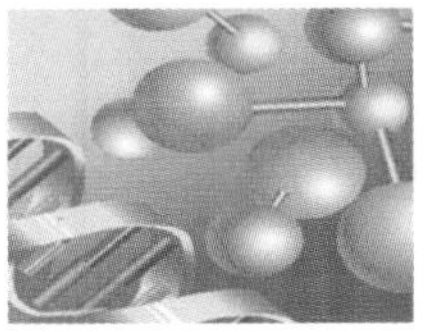

Figure 13.8 Above: A push is like a wipe, except the incoming image pushes its way in—for example, you can see the left side of the incoming image entering at the right-hand side; the image continues to push into view, pushing the original image out the left side of the viewing window.

Figure 13.9 Above: A double exposure melds two input images to create one resultant image, which contains all the imagery from both input images.

Figure 13.10 Below: A matte composite is when two or more separate image streams are merged together into a single resultant image stream. In (a) the black-core heart is composited with stripes to create one image of a striped heart, surrounded by clear. In (b) the clear-core heart is composited with stripes to create one image of stripes surrounding a clear-core heart. The end result is an image of a striped heart surrounded by a striped background.

black-core matte, the image is printed through the clear core and the black region does not get exposed, as in Figure 13.10(b). In a computer, black cores are represented as black and clear cores are represented either with white or a special value used to designate clear, or transparent.

Matting has become a common tool and can be used to create realistic images or images that are impossible in the real world. Matting can also be used to eliminate unwanted artifacts in an image—for example, the elimination of wires that were used to support an actor or prop during a shoot (although once the image is digitized, these are often simply painted out).

The simplest way of in-camera compositing is with the use of a single piece of film that is exposed several times. The resulting film combines all the imagery onto a single, original camera negative. In contrast, postproduction compositing relies on the use of pre-shot imagery—on film, video, or digital media. In film, composites are usually made with an optical printer; projectors are used to transfer images directly to a receiving camera. In video, composites are accomplished by mixing video signals. Only two signals can be mixed at one time.

In the digital domain, digital processors composite images by mathematically manipulating their numeric representations. Two input bitmaps contain the source images, and a bitplane contains the matte, which specifies which pixels from each image will be used to form the composited image. Matting and compositing processes that involve more than two input images are reduced to a sequence of

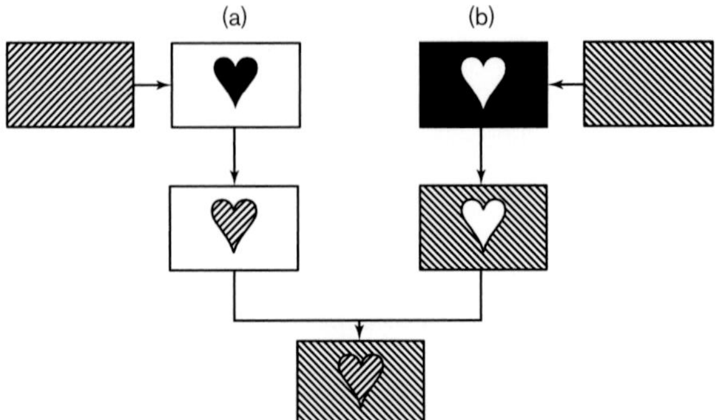

individual composites, each with two inputs, a matte, and one composited output sequence. One of the advantages of having the input images in digital form is that there is no generation loss or degradation through the succession of composites.

Matte Shapes

Mattes can be almost any shape. Some matte shapes are predefined, independent of the images being matted; some are dependent upon the content of the images involved in the matting process. Predefined matte shapes include rectangles, squares, triangles, binoculars, keyholes, and hearts (see Figure 13.11).

Mattes that are dependent upon the images being matted are called ***self-mattes*** or ***keys*** (see Figure 13.12). Self-mattes are shaped by the foreground object. The foreground components are photographed against a flat field of black or of a color, often a bright blue, white, or green, which is easily referenced by a computer. In postproduction, the computer detects these background pixels and replaces them with full black pixels. Next, all of the remaining pixels, depicting the objects in the foreground, are changed to white, producing a matte. The two images are then composited. Given two input (self-matte) images and a single matte, there are 12 possible ways that the images can be composited (see Figure 13.13).

High-Contrast and Variable-Contrast Mattes

The edges around mattes and the matte itself can be either high contrast or variable contrast. A ***high-contrast matte*** contains only zeros and ones (or black and clear); the composite is determined

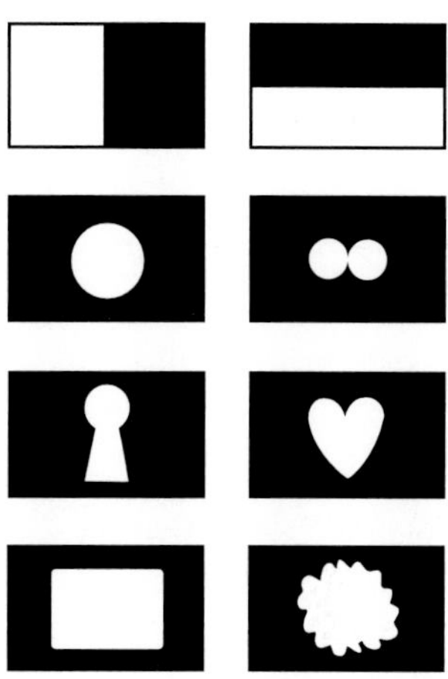

Figure 13.11 Above: Static mattes can be almost any shape.

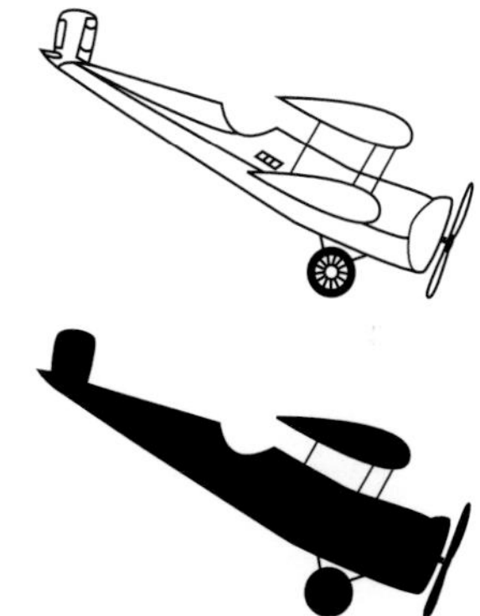

Figure 13.12 Above: Self-mattes, or keys, are defined according to the images in the scene. In the figure, the black-core self-matte is created by tracing the image of the airplane in the picture.

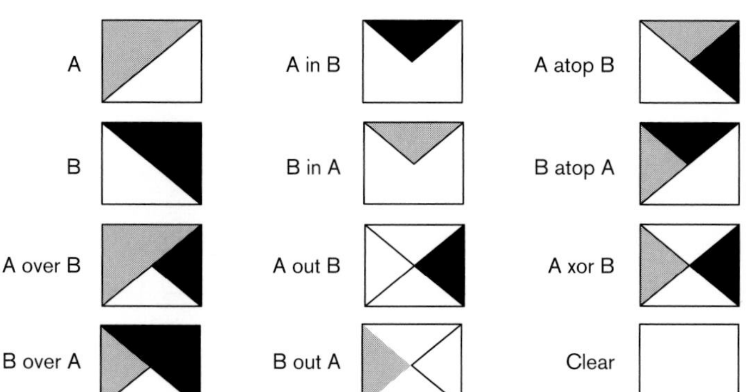

Figure 13.13 Left: Compositing operators illustrate all possible combinations of images.

Figure 13.14 A high-contrast matte. While these mattes are useful for many situations, they are not suitable for things that are not hard-edged, such as hair. Here a high-contrast matte was created from the original picture, then used to matte out the background. As you can see, a hard edge is created around the hair, creating a very unconvincing result.

on an either/or basis (see Figure 13.14). When a high-contrast matte is created from a continuous-tone image, the ***threshold*** is the intensity value that determines what turns to zero and what turns to one. It may be determined empirically or via some computational analysis of the image.

Variable-contrast mattes incorporate continuous gradations of gray from the clear regions of the matte to the black regions (see Figure 13.15) and permit two images to be blended; transparent objects, such as glass, can be matted over a background. In the digital domain, variable-contrast matting does not select a resultant pixel from one or the other of the source images; rather, the color of a resultant pixel is a blend of the two source pixels. Variable-contrast mattes allow objects with soft edges or objects in motion to be combined without hard matte lines dividing the foreground and background. Hair, for example, has a soft, fuzzy edge that is difficult to matte without some degree of quantization to determine what is and what is not part of the hair, but when the matte is partially transparent, the soft edges of the foreground hair blend into the background.

Variable-contrast mattes have become so essential to the special effects industry that hardware has been built specifically for that purpose. Ultimatte is a company that builds hardware to perform the function of variable-contrast mattes in video, as well as software to create the mattes on digital files.

Static and Traveling Mattes

Mattes can be either still or moving. ***Static mattes*** are mattes with no motion. For example, in the case of a split screen, the matte would specify that the left half of the picture is to come from one input image and the right half from another input image. Static mattes are also used to crop a picture—the part of the image that corresponds to the matte is not reproduced.

Figure 13.15 Left: A variable-contrast matte. These mattes are useful for things that have soft or blurry edges, such as hair. Here, a variable-contrast matte was created from the original picture, then used to matte out the background, creating a very convincing result.

There are several types of special-purpose static mattes. *Overlays* are a type of static matte used for field guides, safety grids, and registration (see Figure 13.16). A *garbage matte* is a static matte use to conceal unwanted portions of an image. For example, if, during a shoot, the camera rigging got in the way, a garbage matte would be constructed to conceal the rigging in the final image.

Traveling mattes are sequences of mattes applied to a series of frames and are used in motion pictures and television. A wipe is a traveling matte used to create a transition between two scenes (see Figure 13.17). A wipe is usually identified by a name or number, and its duration. In fact, any matte that contains motion is said to be traveling, including contrast mattes, self-mattes, and keys.

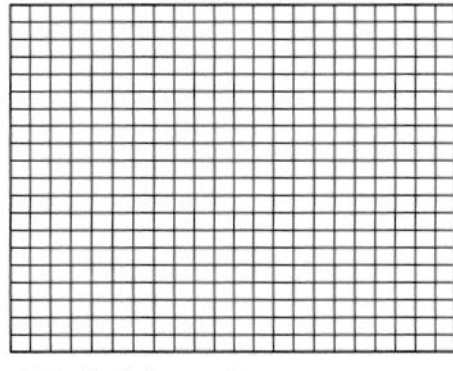

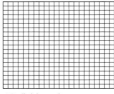

12–field overlay

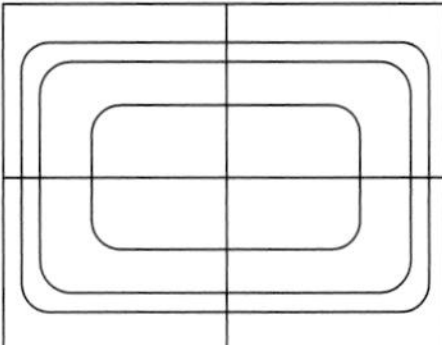

Safety grid

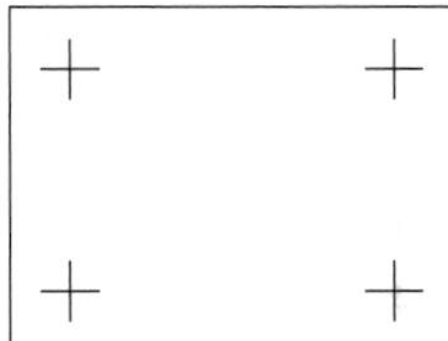

Registration marks

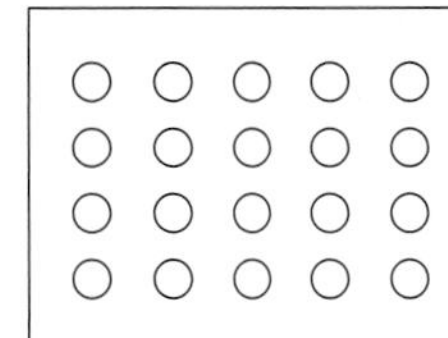

Counting reticule

Figure 13.16 Above: A 12-field overlay, a safety grid, registration marks, and a counting reticule.

Live Action Matchup Mattes

Live action matchups are composites that involve live action and computer animation in the same scene. In the simplest cases, the live action imagery and computer animation are separate—for example, the background is computer animation and the foreground is live action, or vice versa. In this case, one of the first steps in the production process it to blueprint the stage, the camera position, the lenses, and so on. The corresponding positions and data are entered into the computer, so that a virtual representation can be created. The physical stage and the virtual stage are used, in sync, to create the computer animation and live action source imagery, which is eventually composited.

The Optical Bench

An *optical bench* is much like an animation stand, except that it is used to photograph film instead of artwork (see Figure 13.18). Computer-controlled, motorized optical benches are frequently used to create special effects because they allow precision of matte work,

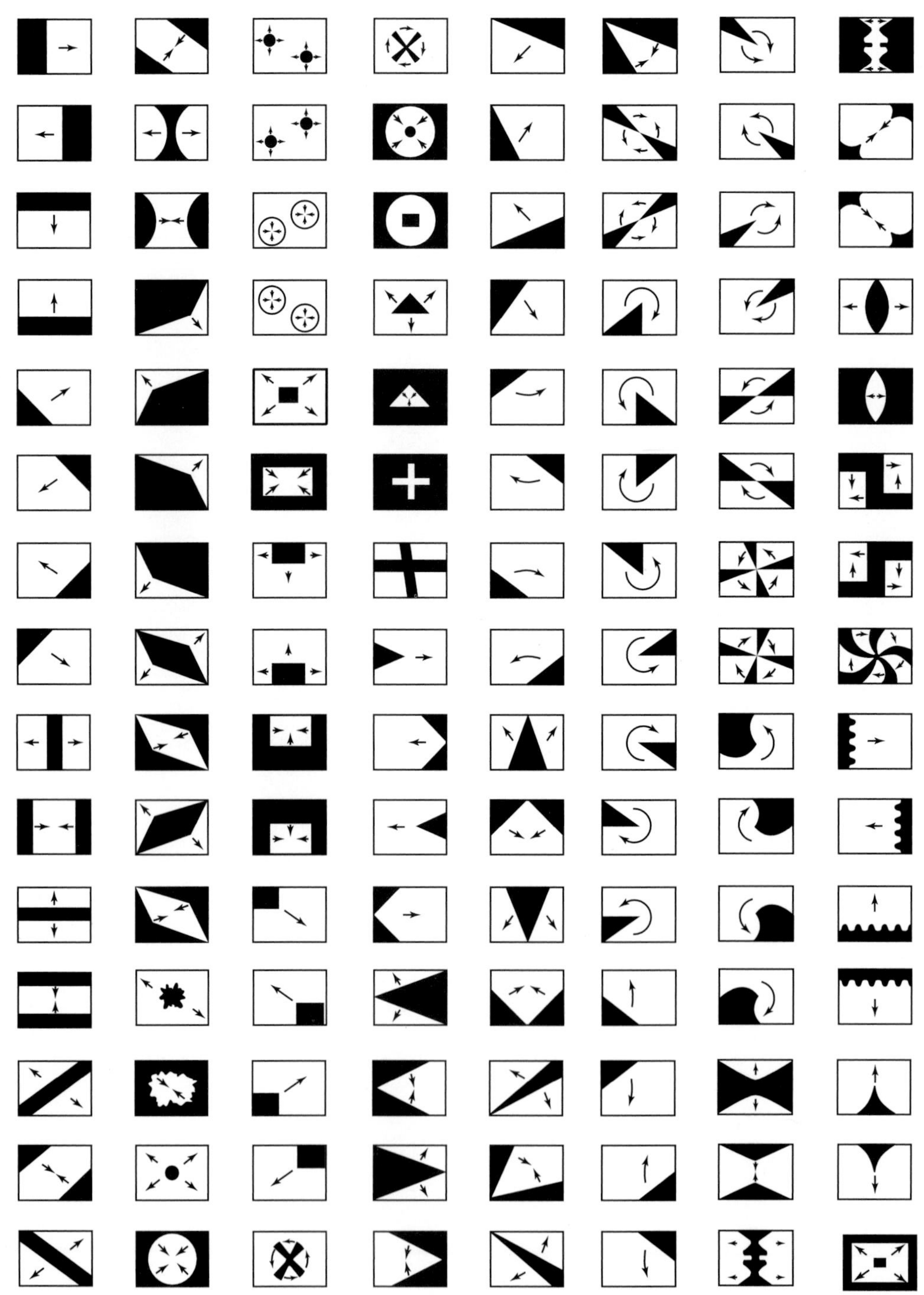

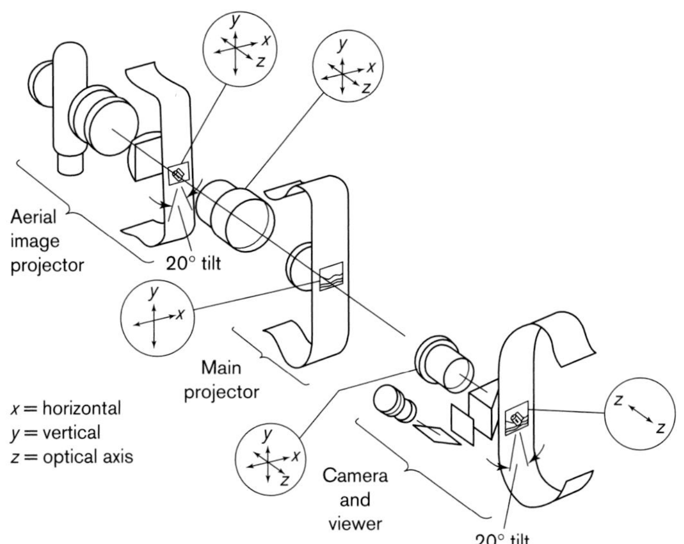

Figure 13.17 Opposite: Wipe effects are used in film, video, and computer graphics to create smooth transitions.

Figure 13.18 Left: Optical printer. The film image is projected by the main projector, then recorded onto another piece of film. The photographic axis is usually horizontal, and the field of view is a film frame. The camera, projector, and aerial heads can each translate in *xyz* and may rotate. The aerial image projector is optional and is used when necessary to carry a matte roll.

and a host of effects—including multiple exposures and superimpositions, reverse action, fades, dissolves, repositioning, enlarging or reduction, and freeze frames. Like the animation stand, the optical bench is motorized and hence can be automated. In recent years, as digitizing a sequence of film frames at film resolution has become possible, many of these optical bench effects are performed on bitmaps in the computer, and the physical bench is being phased out.

Motion Control

Motion control systems, or *rigs,* are a collection of techniques, software, and computer-controlled hardware, such as an animation stand or live action camera, that photograph real-world artwork and props and repeat their movements precisely. The rig usually exists within a large space. It contains a platen that can move models and other objects weighing hundreds of pounds throughout the space, as well as a camera that is also able to move anywhere inside the space. The result is an arrangement that can be used to photograph real objects in (almost any) motion, with almost any camera motion, in a repeatable fashion. A motion control system is very similar to an animation stand; the primary difference is that a motion control system has a full six degrees of freedom and thus is capable of full three-dimensionality.

Motion control involves recording camera positions and angles generated in the real world. During live action photography, motion control systems record all camera changes, such as pans, tilt, focus, shutter angle, dolly movement, or even the consecutive angles of a crane.

Similar to the animation stand, repeatability of a motion control rig is of paramount importance. For example, there may be a need to shoot a scene of a spaceship several different times—once to record the spaceship, once to record the lights on the spaceship, and once to record the background. In order to achieve the best possible results, each shot might need to be recorded at different exposures. Unless the process is repeatable, the power of a motion control rig is quite limited.

The fact that it is repeatable and is controlled by a computer enables a motion control rig to be correlated to a computer, where a camera and a model are represented virtually. Hence, motion can be planned and previewed in the virtual world, and the results can be used to move physical models in the real world. The elements of the computer environment can also be matted into the recording of the physical scene, or elements of the real environment can be matted into the recording of the virtual scene. Conversely, when a physical camera is moved throughout a real environment, that motion can be recorded and then used to drive the motion of the virtual camera in the virtual world.

It is worth noting that the geometry and the mechanical hardware to achieve six degrees of freedom are well understood. In the virtual world, the necessary mathematics involve simple matrix multiplication. In the physical world, the corresponding mechanical setups require six different rigs, one for each order of rotation.

The effect of motion control systems expands the visual vocabulary of model photography. Very small f-stops and long exposure times can deepen depth of field. Some motion control systems may permit exposures to be made while the camera and/or artwork is moving, so that motion blur may be introduced into shots. Some video animation stands are designed to move the camera and table in real time, creating natural motion blur. Some old-timers call the process *go motion* or *totalized animation.* Unfortunately, stop-motion footage with motion blur is particularly challenging to composite with other elements, and requires the use of a compositing system with continuous-contrast mattes.

The introduction of a computer into the motion control complex accomplishes the same benefits as computerizing the animation stand. Aside from the repeatability and automation factors, the user may now direct the camera in terms of a language that describes the camera in a real-world manner and with real-world terms. Another advantage is that actions of the system, captured by the input mechanism and recorded, may now not only be played back, they may also be edited. It is also possible to elude either the input or output side of the full-motion control model. For example, one might employ a virtual camera and props to plan moves, and then use the motion control system to execute those moves with a real camera and props. Conversely, one might capture the parameters of a real camera move, and then use those parameters to move a virtual camera in a totally virtual set. Hence, the motion control paradigm is a general-purpose design.

Figure 13.19 Above: Motion graphics.

STROBE EFFECT
STROBE EFFECT
STROBE EFFECT
STROBE EFFECT

Figure 13.20 Above: A strobe is a multiple exposure made by moving the camera or platen from position to position while the camera shutter is closed. The images are exposed multiple times on a single frame of film. The result appears to be that the object is in motion and has been illuminated by a strobe light multiple times on each frame.

Motion Graphics

Motion graphics are a genre or style of graphics that became popular during the 1960s and are characterized by a production methodology in which relatively few pieces of art are photographed multiple times to create geometric repetitions and patterns (see Figure 13.19). It involves a formal, algorithmic, repetitive process, either done by hand or by computer; it usually involves patterned repetitions, coupled with zooming or translation, and occasionally rotation. In general, the motion graphics genre is technology-bound, because it requires a platen device, a formal layout and planning notation, and pattern repetition, which is best served by technology. Examples of motion graphics include strobes, streaks, glows, and slit scans.

Strobes and Streaks

A *strobe* is an effect achieved when discrete images of a moving subject are exposed multiple times on a single frame (see Figure 13.20). The multiple exposure is made by first shooting the artwork, then moving the camera or platen to the next position, and then shooting the artwork again. The process is repeated until the desired

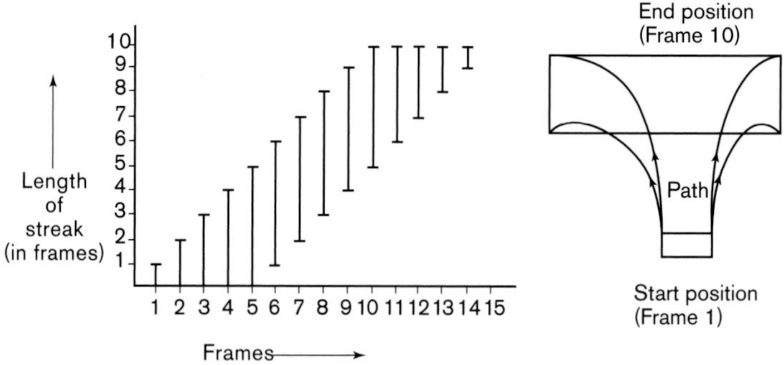

Figure 13.21 When making a streak, the shutter is opened, the camera or artwork is moved, and the shutter is closed. The result is a streak of image or light on the frame of film. In a streak, the sequence of frames usually involves at least one streak for each frame. If the streak is to appear to move at all—for example, to grow or recede—the composition of the streak on each successive frame must be different. The figure illustrates data for a 15-frame animation where the streak grows, travels a distance, then constricts. For this particular animation, the head—the leading edge of the streak—grows away from the tail—the part of the streak that is trailing behind—leaving the tail stationary. Then at frame 6, the head and tail both move forward together through frame 10, at which time the head stops, while the tail catches up to the head from frame 11 through frame 15. Time or frames are represented horizontally, and the length of the streak is represented on the vertical axis. Streaks work best with linear graphics, lit from below.

number of multiple exposures is achieved. Testing of value and color becomes a valuable and often necessary requirement in order to achieve a desired result.

Live action strobes are achieved by rephotographing the same sequence of action over itself, while changing the action. Depending on the speed of the original action, the strobe's effectiveness varies with the closeness of the increments chosen: the faster the action, the smaller the increments. Because the strobe employs multiple exposures, it is most effective if the subject is photographed against a black background, so that there is a minimum buildup of extraneous tones. In other words, the action plays in the dark and is illuminated by strobe light so that each frame contains multiple exposures.

Closely related to strobes are ***streaks,*** where the exposure is made while the camera or object is moving (see Figure 13.21). To create a streak, the shutter is opened, the camera or artwork is moved, and the shutter is closed. The result is a streak of image or light on the frame. Next, the frame is advanced, and the process is repeated, but with some variation—either the artwork is moved a little bit, or the starting and ending positions of the camera are different from those used to shoot the previous frame. The process is repeated for the required number of frames, and the resulting images appear as a continuous streak that smears and unsmears as it is played back. Note that if the camera is moved and then the shutter is opened and closed, the result is a strobe that appears as a sequence of discrete streaks.

Glows

Glows are soft-haloed emanations that can be achieved in a number of ways (see Figure 13.22). They simulate glowing light, street lamps in the fog, and so forth. One way to create them employs an optical printer, with a black core in front of an out-of-focus clear core. Combined with a color filter, this method produces a brilliant, narrow band with a medium outer bleed. On an animation or motion control stand, similar techniques can be applied. Clear-core art in front of an underlit setup (lighting is placed below the artwork), combined with various filters, provides numerous possibilities. Opal and frosted glass, placed directly on the art or positioned above it to increase the spread of the glow, can also be used. Digitally, glows can be simulated in a variety of ways, typically involving setting values for constant shading, diffuse color, and static blur.

No matter what the technique, testing is a necessity to determine both the intensity of the glow, which varies greatly depending on

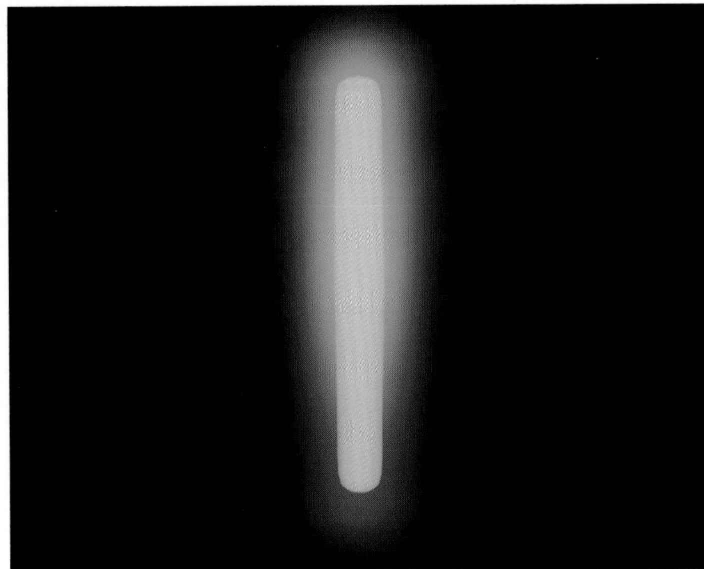

Figure 13.22 Glow. The glow in the figure is a 3D object created in Softimage. The result looks like neon.

color and background, and the spread, or diffusion. Sometimes it is desirable to have the subject remain crisp and intense, with a relatively weak halo. At other times, the subject may need to appear almost as one with the glow effect. To test for intensity, a cinex is used that varies the amount of the glow. The subject is first exposed or calculated without any glow using a range of exposures, from wide open to closed down, in half-stop increments, usually 20 to 30 frames. When this is completed, the subject is held for an additional amount equal to the number of frames needed to execute the cinex, at normal exposure. The film is run back in the camera to the start of the cinex, and the glow instruments added. Next, a double exposure of the run is shot, first at "normal," for the number of frames of the original cinex, and then at quarter-stop increments. The glow run is usually performed at a speed slower than that of the subject, usually at a half-second/frame, to increase the range of the intensity when color filters are used.

The opal- and frosted-glass techniques, as well as various-strength fog filters, can be tested using the method above. The clear-core art is placed on the table, with the opal glass on top. The opal glass itself has a softer side and a more diffused side, both of which should be tested. Where more spread is desired, a clear ⅛-inch or ¼-inch glass can be placed between the clear-core art and the opal glass. If an out-glow is the desired effect, then a black core of the subject can be positioned on top of the opal glass. Specially milled extralong pegs are required for this operation to insure registration, and it is also necessary to refocus the lens to account for the glass levels placed on the table surface. An in-glow is achieved by reversing the black and clear-core art.

Slit Scans

A *slit scan* effect is a contemporary variation of the original pinhole lensless camera; the slit scan technique makes use of a moving slit to expose the image (see Figure 13.23). The camera shutter is held fully open while the slit moves across the field. The shutter then closes while the film is advanced, only to be held open again to expose the next frame. (Note the similarity to the focal plane shutter.) The variety of effects possible with this technique have to do with the two basic movements involved in creating a single frame:

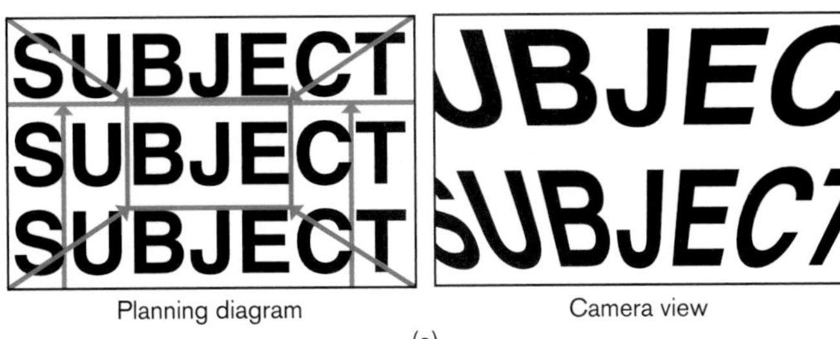

(a)

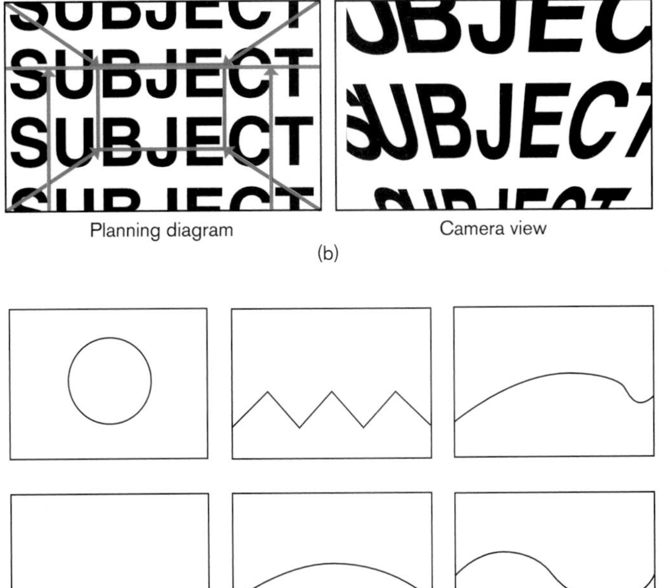

(b)

(c)

Figure 13.23 A slit scan. Slit scan technique makes use of a narrow line (the slit), which travels across the artwork or the recording medium (the scan) while the exposure is made. The slit is a narrow opening cut into a piece of very thin metal. The regular camera shutter remains open while the slit is in motion, although it is closed while the film is advanced.

The slit functions like a focal plane shutter. If the camera and artwork (or prop) are held steady during the exposure scan, then the newly recorded image looks normal and undistorted. But if the camera or artwork are moving during the scan, something magical occurs. For example, if the slit is a horizontal line progressing from the bottom of the scene to the top, indicated by the green lines shown in the left portions of both (a) and (b), and the camera moves closer to the image while this is happening, indicated by the red lines shown in the left portions of (a) and (b), then the resulting image appears in tilted perspective, closer to the viewer at the top of the screen shown in the right portions of both (a) and (b). Different effects can be achieved with different shaped slits (c).

the movement of the slit and the movement of the subject. For example, if the slit is a horizontal line that progresses from the bottom of the frame to the top as indicated in green, and the camera moves closer to the subject being photographed as it is photographed as indicated in red (the field gets smaller from the start through the end as in the left portion of Figure 13.23(a)), the resulting image appears in tilted perspective—closer to the viewer at the top of the resulting image, as in the right portion of Figure 13.23(a). If, as the frames are advanced and the slit movement repeated, the position of the subject is moved vertically, the resulting image will appear to progress along the plane of the tilted perspective, as in

Figure 13.23(b). Variations of this technique include variations in the thickness of the slit (a wider slit produces a softer, less focused image); in the shape of the slit—straight curve, sine curve, circular, sawtooth, free-form, and so on, as in Figure 13.23(c); in the movement of the slit—unidirectional, varying speeds, or free-form—all of which produce different effects. Similarly, the image or camera moves can vary within the normal vernacular of zooms, pans, rotations, and combination moves. Slit scan, as a film technique, tends to be expensive, due to the length of time required to photograph a frame (minutes as opposed to a fraction of a second). The other difficulty is that the slit must be perfect; any aberrations, even the most minute, result in a flawed and streaky picture.

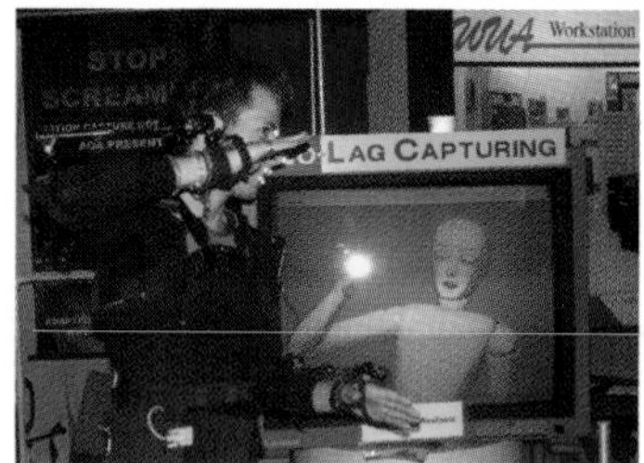

Figure 13.24 Above: Motion tracking system. The body is tracked optically with cameras or other optical devices and the positions or outlines of points, objects, or people are recorded and digitized.

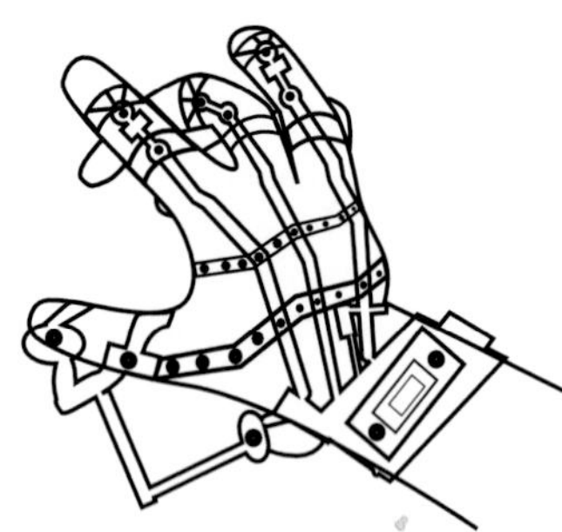

Figure 13.25 Above: Motion tracking system. Physical hardware moves with the object or actor. The position of the hardware is tracked, and digital data is streamed to a computer.

Tracking Systems

Tracking systems are the devices and methods used to track motion in the real world so that it may be converted into digital data and used to create animation, and to control physical machinery such as cameras. Tracking systems exist that can work in real time as well as non–real time.

There are at least two classes of motion tracking systems. The first class is where the body is tracked optically with cameras or other optical devices, and the positions or outlines of points, objects, or people are recorded and digitized (see Figure 13.24). When this involves people, the person being tracked wears special clothing—for example, a white bodysuit or body paint with markers used to mark the ***witness points*** on the body. In the simplest approach, the figure is recorded, and the frames are rotoscoped and then digitized. A more sophisticated approach employs a computer program that automatically recognizes where all of the witness points are on the frames and extracts the values—either of the witness points or of the outlines.

The second class of motion tracking system incorporates physical hardware that is able to move with the object being tracked and will provide streams of digital data to a computer (see Figure 13.25). For example, a person might wear an ***exoskeleton,*** a physical armature that fits on the body and contains sensors to track movement. Older devices, which look like braces, employ ***shaft encoders*** at the joints and measure the rotary angles of the exoskeleton. With the

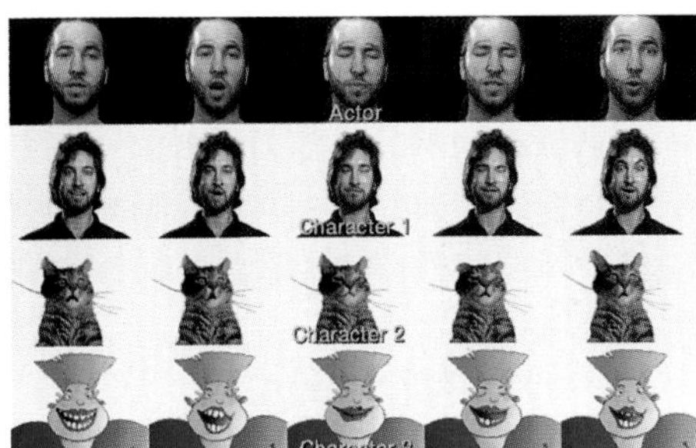

Figure 13.26 Automatic facial-expression mapping, as exemplified in the animated short *The Art of Talking Pictures,* by Peter Litwinowicz.

advent of the ***Polhemus***—a six-degree-of-freedom motion tracker—there is now a way to track points in space without wearing a mechanical armature. Polhemus tracking units are small wireless electronic units that may be placed on the parts of the body that need to be tracked. The units return a stream of data in real time consisting of 3D coordinates plus a three-element normal vector to indicate directionality (where it is pointing). By using a sufficient number of tracking units, say 20, one can capture data that can be used to produce accurate figure animation. Thus, the production method involves directing, say, an actor or dancer, accurately capturing the data of their movement, and then reconstructing their geometry with 3D animation software and rendering a virtual representation. This technique has also been used to animate facial movements such as lip movements (see Figure 13.26). Facial expressions are extremely difficult to animate but are of paramount importance to the telling of a story. Tracking techniques can assist with lip-syncing and facial expressions in general.

In these cases, the basic idea is to sample in real time and then use those samples to control virtual actions; a system can be configured to do this interactively and in real time, or the values may be saved, edited, smoothed, or otherwise worked before doping and computation of final output.

While tracking systems are extremely useful for capturing and reproducing natural motion in a quick and inexpensive way, in many situations, tracking systems are best used sparingly, especially in situations where the characters are interesting because they move in unnatural ways: they stretch, they wiggle, they have an unnaturally long or short gait, they accelerate and decelerate extremely fast.

Often these qualities are achieved via exaggeration and anticipation that transcends what a human actor is capable of. Many of the most beloved animated characters ever made—Bugs Bunny, Road Runner, Goofy, to name a few—acquire their charm from exaggerated gestures and nuances. Hence, tracking devices should not be used to remove creativity from the creative process!

Possibly one of the most creative uses of tracking systems is in driving the animation of inanimate objects. For example, in the creation of a television commercial, dancers were tracked and their motion used to drive the animation of gas pumps. The tracked points were mapped to points on the pumps, which were then set into a waltzing motion. The union of natural movement and inanimate objects makes this approach especially striking.

Digital Effects

Digital effects are effects produced by computer systems that involve special image manipulations. These include, for the purpose of this discussion, digital video effects that are available in switchers and can manipulate video images in real time, as well as a class of similar effects that can operate on HDTV or motion picture-resolution digital files in real or non-real time. The technology of these effects—in particular resolutions and real timeness—remains in a state of flux, but the ideas behind them transcend the medium.

Digital effects include the facility to size and reposition images, to freeze frames, and to leave trails. Some can be performed with film and video techniques, but when the image manipulation enters the third dimension, as with images tumbling in perspective, it is necessary to employ either custom hardware, such as the Ampex Digital Optics (ADO) system if the effect is to be done in real time at video resolutions, or a general-purpose computer system that can do the calculation at a wide variety of resolutions and aspect ratios. It is worth remembering that, prior to the invention of digital-image memories, there was no way in video to resize or reposition an image.

Besides the methods that manipulate images as ridged 2D objects, another class of digital effects involve *image warping.* In a more modern, computer graphics sense, we think of these as image-mapping techniques. The difference here is primarily one of intent:

the images are not patterns or textures on objects but manipulations of images in their own right. These include images that behave like venetian blinds, flow like water, or wave like a flag. Their artistic use varies from the purely baroque to effects with connoted disorientation (a wavy space), computer point of view (the image blocked into squares of color), animal or monster vision (strange mapping of colors), and so on.

This distinction extends to the design of the effect. Internally, an image is represented as a matrix of tiles that are programmable in a 3D space; the hardware or software maps the image onto the tiles. Each tile can be manipulated independently, and it may be connected to its adjacent tiles or separated from them. As the tiles of the mesh are stretched and rotated, the image that is mapped to them distorts accordingly.

This area of effects continues to add to the moving picture vocabulary as audiences are tantalized with effects such as morphs, which transmogrify one character into another, or distortions, which mimic the viewpoint of a fish (see Figure 13.27).

Finally, it would be incomplete not to inventory the 2D *paint box.* This interactive tool, initially the product of the interface between computers and video, allows digital images to be manipulated by a rich tableaux of classic painting techniques, including the ability to draw, mix colors, fill areas, and cut and paste. Today, a paint box, coupled with high-resolution digital film images, enables live action imagery to be retouched in the same way a photograph may be retouched, and then output back to film or any other moving picture medium.

Figure 13.27 Many 2D image effects can be applied to running action, even this fish-eye lens effect.

In summary, special effects have become an important part of cinema vocabulary. Their use helps enable the suspension of disbelief as our cinematic adventures explore the realm of both history and science fiction. Special effects techniques such as dissolves have also become a part of the vocabulary of moving pictures and stand on their own. With digitized cinema, it is possible to simulate all of the traditional optical effects and to deploy a host of new techniques as well. Digital special effects eliminate a raft of pragmatic problems that effect film and video technologies—generational loss, dirt, lens flair, and pinholes in mattes, to name a few—and facilitate faster testing and preview. This is especially true for a process such as matte compositing. Special effects can be startling in their own right, but more often their success lies in their invisibility.

14 Animation Languages

The scope of this chapter is the languages of animation. Language is manifested in many ways, from the tactical act of writing a subroutine to the more strategic mission of directing. The languages of animation involve, as a prerequisite, both the language of graphics and the language of space. However, animation languages are predominantly languages of action, to direct events over time. Thus, the focus of this chapter is on temporal controls unique to animation.

The chapter begins by establishing the fundamental language of cinema, from the play down to the frame. Classic approaches to animation languages are reviewed, including bar sheets and dope sheets. The chapter shows how tracks and actions are represented graphically on time lines and discusses classic scripting methods as well as virtual ones.

A taxonomy of computer animation languages is also presented. Computer animation languages have emerged for the creation, manipulation, and display of visual images; they are used to specify and control animation. Computer animators have a variety of languages to choose from, some based on classic approaches. Modern computer animation languages allow for an animation to be edited through the use of text editors or a graphic user interface (interactively moving a graphic element with the use of a mouse), and for the results to be presented on the monitor. The difference between textual animation strategies and interactive graphic approaches is also reviewed here.

Above: *Ocean Voyager*, a CD-ROM game. (Image courtesy of the Judson Rosebush Company.)

The Language of Moving Pictures

Much of the languages of computer animation stems from film and traditional animation. Hence, their languages must be reviewed before presenting the languages of computer animation. This section covers terminology related to the screenplay, as well as to the tools of animation.

Dramatic Temporal Subdivisions: Plays, Acts, and Scenes

The scripting of temporal events from small to large starts with the frame and ends with the scripting of long durations of time. The longest temporal interval, especially in classic dramatic media such as the stage, film, and television, is the ***play,*** a presentation designed to be consumed in one viewing, rarely longer than 150 minutes or shorter than 30 seconds (in the case of a television commercial). The play is a story told cinematically and incorporates temporal devices, including cuts that change the time or the point of view; close-ups, which take the viewer in for a detailed look; shots that reveal different players' perspectives; and crosscuts between parallel temporal actions.

The play is composed of ***acts,*** which are the major dramatic divisions and are usually delineated by a ***turning point,*** a dramatic event that closes out some options for the players and motivates the next act (see Figure 14.1). For example, in the movie *Star Wars,* the end of the first act occurs when Luke returns from his visit to Obe Wan Kenobe and discovers that his foster parents have been murdered. This event demands that Luke reconsider his option of staying on

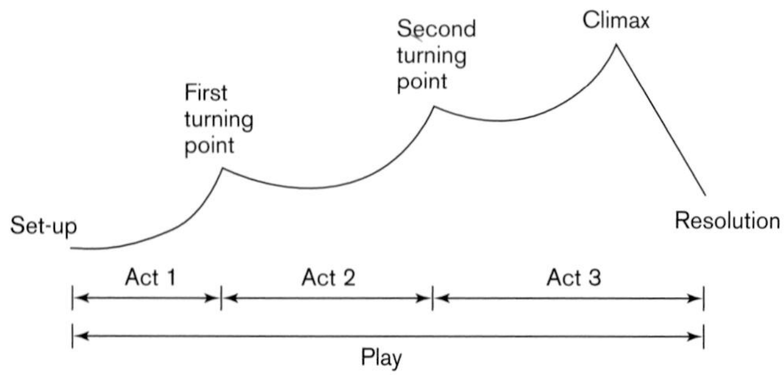

Figure 14.1 Below: The play.

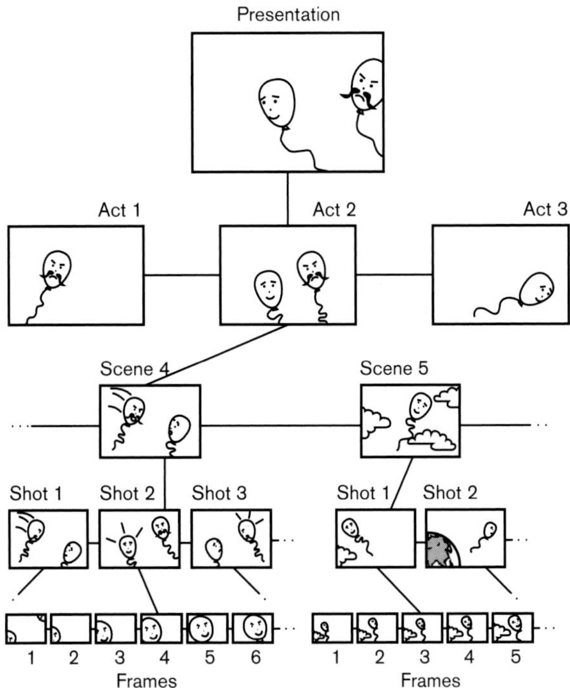

Figure 14.2 Temporal hierarchy of moving picture media. Frames make up shots, which make up scenes, which make acts, which make a play.

the farm, and the murder motivates him to behave in new ways. Most Hollywood movies and television shows consist of three acts.

Acts, in turn, are composed of ***scenes,*** which are equivalent to a paragraph in literature and which are characterized by one or more shots in a single location, about one topic. In theater, a scene is bounded by any addition or subtraction of a character on the stage (see Figure 14.2). As mentioned in Chapter 1, a ***shot*** is a continuous sequence of frames, made with the camera running without break in time or point of view. The shooting of a shot often begins with a ***slate,*** that is, a page containing notes on all relevant shot information, which is trimmed off in the final production. A ***frame*** is a discrete unit of a moving picture, and is essentially a still image, or, in the case of video, one raster.

Some classification schemes also include the term ***serial,*** a set of closely related plays, usually of similar length and with a similar set of characters and settings, and the ***sequence,*** a group of scenes composing a major expository unit that is subordinate to the act. At these levels of temporal magnitude, how durations are nested in a moving picture is primarily a function of storytelling, directing, and acting.

Actions

It is also convenient to define another kind of temporal interval, one that is subservient to the shot but longer than a frame. This is an *action*, which is a single parameterized change within a shot. For example, a shot in which a ball enters the screen from the left and travels to the center of the frames, stops, and then grows in size consists of two actions—the translation followed by the scaling. An action can also be an effect applied within a shot, such as a fade. Like a shot, an action is bounded by a ***start cue*** and an ***end cue*** and has a duration equal to the difference in time between those two cues (see Figure 14.3).

The most minimal shot consists of one action. But more typically, many actions occur during a shot: cameras move, lenses zoom, actors read lines, and props animate (see Figure 14.4). Note that actions can be contained inside of a shot and contained inside of other actions, and that the temporal control can be expressed absolutely or in relative terms. Also note that actions can overlap each other, and that an action can span across more than one shot, assuming the action is continuous and we cut between multiple cameras with different points of view. This relationship between shots and actions is built upon issues raised in Chapter 2 regarding global and local time, and relative and absolute time.

Normally, in a production, all the actions are scripted on a *time line,* a beginning-to-end representation of the show, often in floating-point space (see Figure 14.5).

Tracks

A fundamental concept in all temporal media is that of a *track*—an independent, 1D carrier of information along the time dimension. For example, a monaural audio tape has one sound track; tape with stereo sound has two tracks; and television or movies usually have

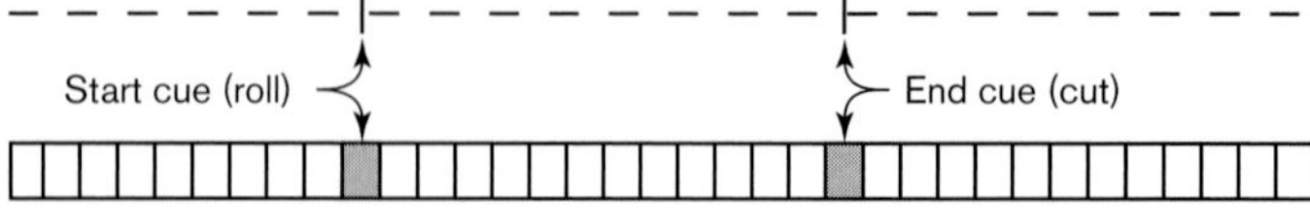

Action recordtype

Actionname	Startcuename	Endcuename	Processtoexecute	Activebit

Figure 14.3 An action. In the computer, an action recordtype contains two cues and also some process definition, and perhaps an active/off bit.

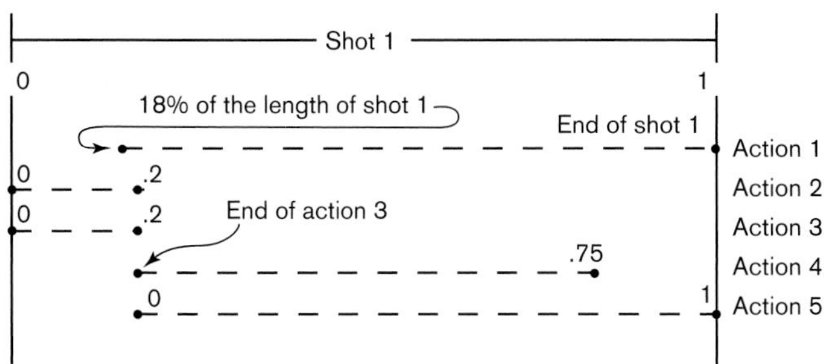

Figure 14.4 Left: A shot consisting of five actions. Shots are built out of actions. Actions may affect other actions and may themselves be affected by other actions. Single cues may trigger events or serve as sensors to other processes.

Figure 14.5 Below: Time line and actions. Consider an animated fan; the fan's blade rotation is represented by action 1, and the fan pivots back and forth, which is represented by action 2. The camera begins to zoom three seconds into the shot, which is represented by action 3; and the camera is simultaneously drifting to the left, which is represented by action 4. Finally, action 5 represents a fade. Each of the actions have start and end information, be they angles or positions.

at least one picture track and one sound track. In all of these examples, the tracks are synchronous and parallel.

In classic media, picture and sound tracks follow different production lines. And even when (in film) they are wedded back together on a common carrier, they remain separate—the pictures recorded discretely and the sound recorded analogically. During the editing process, picture and sound are stored on separate rolls, which are synchronized in parallel (see Figure 14.6). In digital media, picture and sound are both digitized and stored separately on a common carrier; the dramatically different bandwidths of picture and sound create files that have vastly different amounts of storage requirements for equal durations of time.

The concept of tracks applies especially well to animation. The most obvious example is classic cel animation, which involves a background that is overlaid by one or more cel layers. In this paradigm, the background constitutes a track, as does each cel layer. Another example of the use of tracks is in titles, which consist of text that is overlaid on top of moving pictures. The titles and the pictures each constitute a track. Pan separations also incorporate tracks: the red, green, and blue components may each be considered a track. Finally, tracks play a role in special effects, especially in the use of mattes.

Action		Values
1	Rotate	0 → 36,000
2	Pivot	45° → −45° → 45° → −45°
3	Zoom	25mm → 250mm
4	Dolly	0 → −20'
5	Fade	100% → 0%

Frames 0, 72, 120, 240, 360, 480, 600, 672, 720

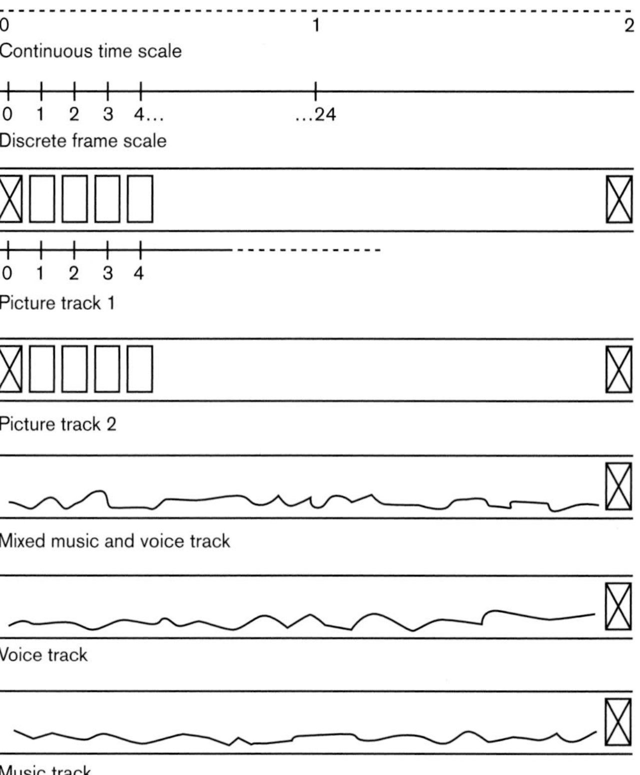

Figure 14.6 A track is an independent, 1D carrier of information along the time dimension. Picture and sound tracks may be recorded on a single carrier or on multiple carriers. Synchronization may be obtained mechanically or electronically.

The concept of tracks can also apply to actions, where each action is thought of as a track. Unlike the cel-level model, where the tracks denote a composition order, with actions the tracks denote degrees of freedom.

Cues

A *cue,* also called a *mark,* is an instant or frame at which a temporal event occurs. A cue may mark the beginning of an action, or it may schedule a future temporal event. For example, the villain enters a room, points a gun, and demands that everyone raise their hands in the air; the hero, in turn, pulls out his gun and shoots the villain's gun out of his hand. In this example, the raising of hands in the air might be the cue for the hero to draw his gun.

Tracks and cues can be easily implemented on a computer, and they are typically implemented within off-the-shelf software. For example, a track can be a named variable that contains a list of cues; a track is a vector of cue names (see Figure 14.7). An empty track is one that contains no cue names. A cue can be a named variable that contains time, the event, and a track list (for example, a list of cels that will be affected by a fade) (see Figure 14.8). A cue may initiate a new process or end an existing one. Two cues (a start and a cut) are required to define an interval or, in media vernacular, a shot. In practice it is best to refer to tracks and cues by names and not by numeric value; in most animation programs, cues are manipulated via graphic user interface (GUI) time lines.

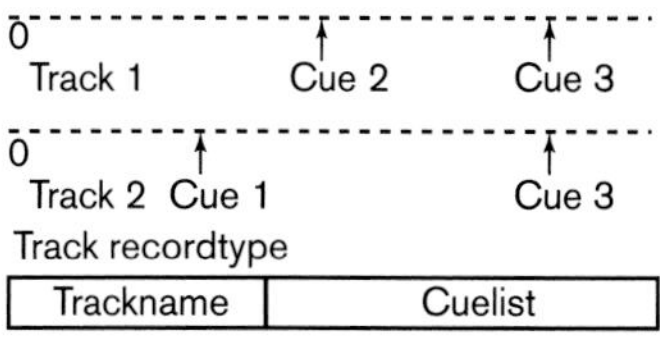

Figure 14.7 Above: A track recordtype. A track has a name and a list of cues.

Cue recordtype

Cuename	Time value	Action	Tracklist (cel levels)

Figure 14.8 Above: A cue recordtype includes a cue name and time. It may also contain a field indicating what track or tracks it refers to and a field indicating what action is to be activated at the cue.

Scripting Temporal Information

Frequently, graphs are used to assist in scripting temporal information. Time scripting predates computer animation, and it is important that the computer animator understand classic notation processes since they are still a major vehicle of communication inside most animation studios, as well as between animators and directors. There are three or four widely used notation methods that are similar but are used by different subgroups of the studio. Their similarities and differences illustrate some of the division of work and provide clues as to what is required in virtual systems.

Bar Sheet A *bar sheet,* also known as a *time sheet,* is a time line that presents dialogue and cues in a horizontal format. A typical bar sheet might be divided into horizontal thirds; a single sheet would represent 30 seconds of time, and it would consist of 10 seconds across the sheet three times, with the seconds divided into half- and quarter-seconds. The script would be written at the bottom, and the cuts would also be indicated.

Bar sheets might show a brief description of action and fades and dissolves, or might only show cuts. They are used to analyze and time a sound track and to show four things: time, sound track (including musical accents and the syllables of the voice track), the shots, and any camera and transition effects. The time is expressed both in seconds and frames. The voice track is written on a frame-accurate basis that shows the exact length of each syllable of each word. The beginnings and ends of shots are indicated, with the action described textually. Finally, camera moves, such as pans and tilts, and effects, such as fades and dissolves, are also indicated. Bar sheets are a primary tool of the animation director because they give

PROD. NO	CLIENT	PICTURE NAME	NO.	SCENE	FOOTAGE	SHEET NO.	NO. SHEETS

SYNOPSIS:

ANIMATOR:

ASSISTANT:

ANIMATION
STAND NO.
FILM

DIAL	TRACK	ACTION	DIAL	BKGD.	1	2	3	4	5	FLD	PAN				
1			1												
2			2												
3			3												
4			4												
5			5												
6			6												
7			7												
8			8												
9			9												
0			0												
1			1												
2			2												
3			3												
4			4												
5			5												
6			6												
7			1												
8			2												
9			3												
0			4												
1			5												
2			6												
3			7												
4			8												
5			9												
6			0												
7			1												
8			2												
9			3												
0			4												
1			5												
2			6												
3			1												
4			2												
5			3												
6			4												
7			5												
8			6												
9			7												
0			8												
1			9												
2			0												
3			1												
4			2												
5			3												
6			4												
7			5												
8			6												
9			1												
0			2												
1			3												
2			4												
3			5												
4			6												
5			7												
6			8												
7			9												
8			0												

a total view of the animation and serve as a guide for every phase of production. They can then be used by the animator during the production process to synchronize the animation to the sound; they are also used by the editor to sequence the shots. Bar sheets do not include a representation for cel levels.

Lead Sheet A *lead sheet* is similar to a bar sheet in that it too contains space for several tracks of information, including visual direction, dialogue, camera and effects, and musical score. The difference is that time on the lead sheet is expressed in terms of musical measures instead of seconds or frames. A *beat* defines the duration of a note and hence defines the tempo—the rate of speed at which a musical composition should be played—of the action. A beat may be referred to in terms of number of beats/minute, just like a metronome beat, or in terms of a number of frames per beat. For example, in film 30 beats/minute is the same as one beat every 48 frames. In both cases, there is one beat every two seconds.

Dope Sheet A *dope sheet,* also called an *exposure sheet, animation sheet,* or *score,* is a time line that represents frames and their corresponding cel levels (see Figure 14.9). In the classic animation studio, successive rows represent successive frames, and columns can represent cel levels or parameter settings on a frame-by-frame basis.

Doping, that is, the act of composing a dope sheet, applies certainly to compositing of cel animation and effects. In computer environments, the dope sheet is implemented virtually. Doping is almost always done with the sound track in mind, represented textually or, in a truly interactive system, textually, aurally, and in waveform.

Doping is always a frame-precise procedure and exists in integer space or rank order, as with the concept of cel levels. Frames can be numbered with time code (e.g., 16:54:02:26) or numbered absolutely (e.g., 5141). The doping of effects requires specifying the effect, its start point, and duration (or endpoint).

A dope sheet may also contain camera direction, which may indicate the pan and zoom positions of the compound table and camera. Thus, the dope sheet is also a procedure for the animation camera operator—it contains all of the information about what is to be shot and how it is to be shot. It may specify gels, lighting effects, spins, glows, or anything else that requires a parameter.

Figure 14.9 Opposite: A dope sheet represents frames and their corresponding cel levels. A dope sheet is the most common scripting tool used in the animation industry, especially for cel animation. A classic dope sheet contains one row for each frame and 10 or more columns, and is not unlike a computer spreadsheet. Each page of a dope sheet represents three seconds of running time, which is the same as 4.5 feet of 35mm film or 72 frames. On a dope sheet, time can flow down, as in the classic model, or it can flow to the right.

Let's look at how the dope sheet fits into production. Normally, information from a bar sheet is transferred to the dope sheet before the animator animates. The dope sheet is a more tactical device than the bar sheet. The bar sheet is used by the director, editor, and animator. The dope sheet includes the sound track, a description of the action, a table of all cels, background information, and camera position, and is used by the designer, animator, in-betweener, inker, colorer, checker, and camera operator. The dope sheet formalizes the relationship between animator and camera operator and centralizes production. Whereas bar sheets are part of the preproduction process, dope sheets are part of the production process and are created along with the animation itself. Bar sheets remain in the director's possession; dope sheets travel with the backgrounds and cels. Dope sheets are similar to bar sheets in format, except that they are frame and cel specific. Dope sheets indicate which cels are to be placed at what level for each frame. In a sense, cel animation really consists of two elements: the artwork (consisting of cels and backgrounds) and the rules (presented in the form of dope sheets, which state how the cels are to be organized and recorded).

Dope sheets tend to manifest in either of two different formats: time can flow down, as in the classic model, or flow to the right (see Figure 14.10). Many computer animation languages, such as Softimage, implement dope sheets so that the animator can graphically represent temporal commands, and organize and develop them independently of the order in which they might be executed.

Doping Parameters Of course, no animator wants to fill in values for each parameter for each frame. This is a job for the computer to do, but in order for it to be accomplished, we need a higher level of conceptualization. And this brings us back to the concept of an action, which is the value of a parameter across continuous time. An action has start and end values, a duration, and it may have rules (e.g., eases) that define how to determine the in-between values. In 3D computer animation, it is the in-between values that become the values in the dope sheet; in 2D computer animation, it is either the in-between values or bitmaps.

Effects and Layout Notation A *fade* is accomplished by a gradual opening or closing of the camera shutter. In a computer, a fade

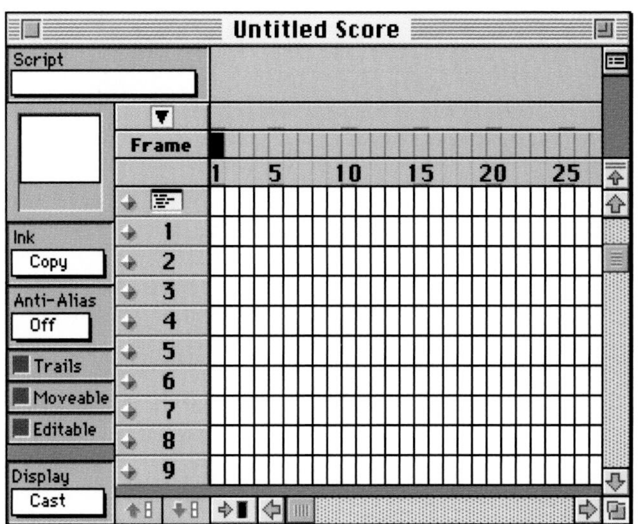

Figure 14.10 In some computer programs, the dope sheet (sometimes called a score) resembles a classic animation dope sheet, transposed about the top left corner, with each column representing a frame, each row representing a cel layer, and each intersection being a candidate location for a cel.

is generally calculated as a percentage of exposure. The dissolve involves a double exposure and is accomplished by fading out, rewinding the film, and fading in the new scene. In the language of cinema, a *fade-out* implies a bringing of a dramatic idea to rest, whereas a *dissolve* implies a gradual change of events.

Effects notation for fade-ins, fade-outs, dissolves, and double exposures in animation and editing is fairly standardized (see Figure 14.11) and usually appears on dope sheet, on any physical film workprint, and on notation for laying out effects for optical camera photography. *Layout notation* is a special scripting language used for optical photography, to describe the actions of an optical camera or its digital counterpart. It is prepared by a layout person upon inspection of the workprint and is executed by the optical or digital camera operator. Layout notation includes special symbols for fades, wipes, out-of-focus effects, zooms, pans, and shutter control. Similar notation is also used in video or digital postproduction to lay out complex multipass sequences. When computers are used to control optical processes, the graphic notation must be translated into a command language to run the machine. Note that layout notation is not standardized and varies from studio to studio.

The Languages of Computer Animation

With the advent of computers, many aspects of animation have been automated, and many others have been parameterized and

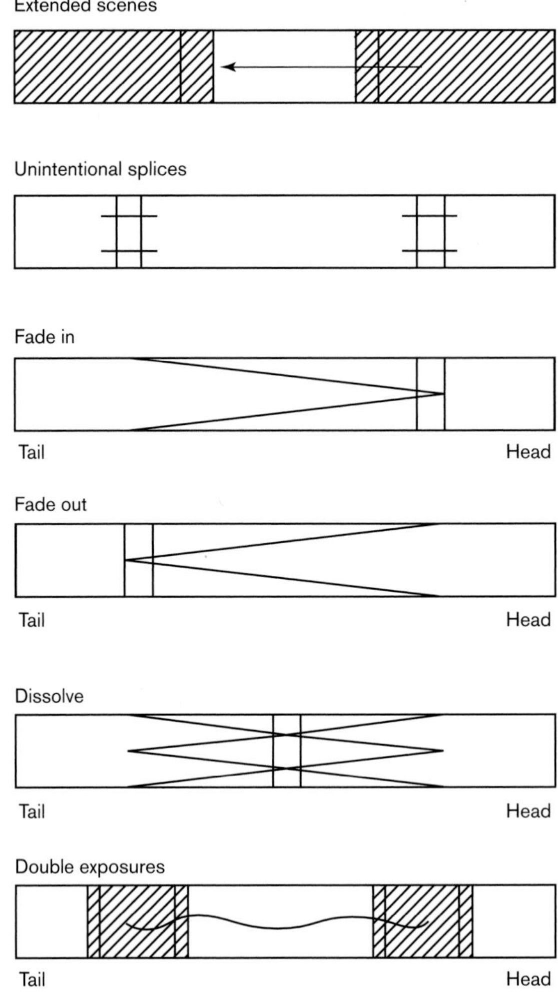

Figure 14.11 Fade-in, fade-out, dissolve, double exposure, extended scene, and unintentional scene markings are made directly on the workprint itself and are the exact physical length of the effect. Note that in the figure, time flows from right to left because this is the way the physical medium appears on the editing table.

enjoy interactive control. Our interaction with these controls—textually and graphically—impacts how we think about and direct animation, how we talk with an animator, and how an animator operates the system. Making animation is a procedural task that can be described with a series of steps. Animation involves manipulating both the data of the image, as well as temporal variables such as velocities and accelerations.

Computer animation languages are specialized languages with predefined functionality that are used to create computer animation. A computer animation language is an unambiguous vocabulary of interaction that is manipulated textually or graphically and that is ultimately expressed as a series of binary commands and arguments. A computer animation language, as distinguished from an ordinary language, is a language that includes a specialized set of commands that deal with issues pertaining to animation—that is, issues pertaining to time. Hence, all computer animation languages must include some sort of temporal controls or commands. An example would be a command that specifies an action type (e.g., translation, scale, or rotation), start and end values (e.g., beginning and end rotation values), an easing rule, and a duration (in seconds or frames). Computer animation languages may also include commands and controls that connect an object and an action to a set of frames, commands to specify image change, elementary arithmetical operations, iteration, and frame advance.

A computer animation language permits images and events to be specified temporally. Sophisticated languages organize actions in continuous time as opposed to discrete time, and incorporate concepts related to time—for example, instants, intervals, and actions—and nesting relationships, as described in Chapter 2. A computer animation language enables the animator to define the beginning and end of an interval, as well as what happens in between. Actions may be thought of as entities and may be scaled and translated. In a superior language, actions can cue other actions. Actions can usually be addressed via an assigned name, and movement is often accomplished by specifying initial and terminal conditions, and calculating interpolants for each new frame. Animation languages can be used as a tool for picture representation, enhancement, and analysis, or as a tool for moviemaking.

A typical computer programming language, such as Basic or C, does not include commands that address issues related to time. They simply execute instructions one after another, and the operations are largely numeric processes involving variables. Hence, although most typical programming languages can be used to make animation, they are not computer animation languages. Similarly, computer graphics languages include operations that have to do with graphic entities, but not time. Again, computer animation languages are distinguishable from graphic languages in that they include operations that have to do with temporal entities. A computer animation language may contain graphic capabilities (e.g., the ability to create graphic objects), and they need to contain general language basics (variable names, conditionals, assignments, iteration). But it is time-based tools that distinguish an animation language from a graphics language.

An example of a time-based tool is

```
in_between(x, y, x_prime, y_prime, number_of_frames)
```

The command may also include parameters for the amount of time to ease in and ease out and the type of ease. An animation language is designed in such a way that action is defined as an entity, and not as a graphics command inside a loop. An action, such as a movement or rotation, is treated as an entity that occurs over time. Therefore, a computer animation language is a time-based language where time is a parameter in an action command. Time is expressed as a variable in terms of cinematic time—for example, frames or seconds—and can reflect relative time, absolute time, start and end times, and time differentials such as acceleration, deceleration, and velocity. Animation languages provide controls and commands for actions, where the actions can be parameterized and one of the parameters represents time. Examples of animation language commands are

```
walk(character, point_A, point_B, number_of_frames)

rotate(object, start_angle, end_angle, number_of_frames)
```

One of the advantages of computer animation and computer-controlled animation over classic approaches to animation is the repeatability of the process. The direction of the animation exists as a formal description that can be carried out by the computer any number of times, exactly the same way each time.

Most computer animation languages incorporate some degree of kinematics and dynamics. In a kinematic model, computer animation is driven as if it is a giant gear train of events—everything proceeds with predictability and precision. In a dynamic model, the animation proceeds according to the forces of nature. The most effective approaches to animation incorporate both kinematic and dynamic approaches.

Attributes of a computer animation language that should be taken into consideration include the tools for image and model building, object hierarchies and grouping capabilities, adjustability of frame rate, a variety of action types, animated cameras and lights, feedback upon parameter input, parameter grouping, kinematic capability, dynamic capability, constraint capability, and the overall production environment—for example, pencil testing, scripting capability, and text- or menu-driven interface.

A Taxonomy of Language

Before turning to specific languages, here are three different ways by which computer languages may be organized: they can be (1) textual or graphic, (2) batch or interactive, and (3) compiled or interpreted.

```
Begin
  Fetch Fred
  Position Fred 0, 0, 0
  Walk Fred to 0, 50, 0 in 200 Frames
  Turn Fred YRO-90 in 50 Frames
  Wave Fred in 60 Frames
Cut
```

Figure 14.12 A textual computer animation programming language. Animations are created by typing a sequence of commands into the computer. In this example, the character Fred is first loaded up from memory, and then positioned in the virtual world. Next, Fred walks, turns, and waves.

Textual versus Graphic A *textual computer animation programming language* is used to communicate to a computer and enables direction through the use of predefined, textual commands, with a predefined syntax and a predefined functionality. Animations are created by typing a sequence of commands into the computer (see Figure 14.12); the sequence, also known as a *program,* might contain hundreds or thousands of commands. As the commands are executed, the resulting animation is created. A complete textual animation programming language requires syntax to express logic, store and manipulate variables, and create graphics.

Textual languages describe action with words and numbers and use predefined animation commands such as

in_between(x, y, x_prime, y_prime, number_of_frames)

which are typed into a computer and then executed.

The use of textual programming languages during the animation process has several advantages—for example, commands allow for the computer to calculate and use formulas and equations to determine temporal changes, such as change in position or change in shape. They also make repeatability easier—for example, a command can be written to make a door open; each time a new character enters the scene, the command to open the door can be executed.

Sophisticated textual programming languages are available that can manipulate complicated multiaxis cameras and multiaxis props, both virtually and in the real world, and perform previews and test shots. In these languages, the camera can move independently of the artwork or model. Terms used to identify motion may be drawn from the film industry (pan, dolly, zoom), or they may be computerese (translation, rotation, scale). Arguments are expressible in real-world or virtual-space coordinates.

The advantage of the programming approach to animation is that programming gives substantial power to animators—they can write their own programs to do whatever they want. The disadvantage is that for simple tasks—for example, drawing a line—it may be slower and less intuitive to create a program. To make the line, the animator must know the coordinate system of the animation system in which they are working, and the line must be drawn in terms of the coordinates using the appropriate syntax; the task would be simpler if done with a pen or mouse. Another problem can arise if the commands become very syntax-bound and expect data in specialized formats. Learning the protocols takes time.

Although many computer animation languages are currently implemented as interactive computer animation languages, the programming language approach remains a fundamental approach. In fact, it will probably always be a viable tool for certain members of a computer animation team, especially those who are developing new effects and methods.

Graphic computer animation languages are used to communicate to a computer where the primary mode of interaction is a *graphic user interface* (GUI), consisting of windows, pull-down menus, icons, and tool bars, and with drag-and-drop technology (see Figure 14.13). Communication is facilitated with the use of a pointing device, such as a mouse. The interface provides the user with virtual controls that can be used to build and direct animation in a virtual world. Often, temporal events are represented graphically using a dope sheet-like interface, which allows animators to place sprites or polygon-based cels at their appropriate frames. In a parameterized key frame model, actions can be dragged around on a virtual time line.

While the textual command approach and the graphic approach seem vastly different from one another, they are closely related on the inside, and many systems present both approaches to the animator; some do so in a unique way. The types of controls available in a graphic computer animation language often provide the same functionality as the commands available in a textual programming

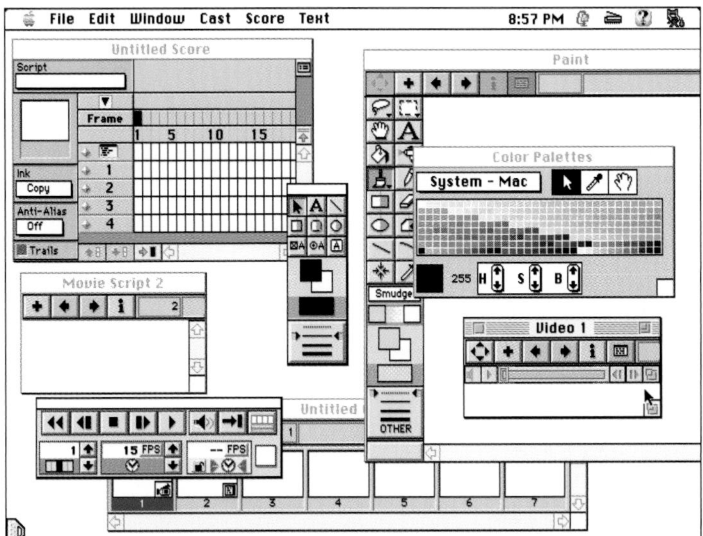

Figure 14.13 A graphic computer animation language. Animations are created by interacting with a graphic user interface.

language. The mode of communication—menus, windows, and icons versus text—is the primary distinguishing factor. In textual languages, commands are typed in with a keyboard; in graphic languages, commands act directly on the image or are selected via menus. In textual programming languages, parameters are typed in as part of the command; in graphic languages, parameters are manipulated by dragging objects or control points.

Although the textual programming language approach dominated commercial animation in the 1970s, graphic computer animation languages emerged all-powerful during the 1980s. The most significant factor contributing to this trend was the introduction of moderately priced, interactive display list workstations from Silicon Graphics that combined an off-the-shelf microprocessor running the Unix operating system, a raster frame buffer and CRT, special-purpose chips for display list processing, and an Ethernet port for communicating with the world. Its open architecture enabled a small cadre of third-party software products specializing in computer animation to evolve, including packages from WaveFront, Alias, Softimage, and others.

Softimage, for example, features extensive use of graphic windows and menus, with controls for object placement, lighting definition, and ease construction. A virtual dope sheet allows the animator to employ a spread sheet-style matrix to specify values for parameters, much the same way the classic animator uses a dope sheet to specify cel contents. Values for extreme positions may be entered, easing rules are defined, and the computer calculates the values for the individual frames and stores them in the dope sheet. One major advantage of the virtual dope sheet is that changes made to parameters—for example, the values of an ease—can propagate forward into the dope sheet immediately.

Batch versus Interactive The second of these distinctions between computer languages, interactive versus batch languages, describes whether the language is executed on the fly, as instructions are presented to the computer, or whether a sequence of many instructions may be executed without intervention. In *batch mode,* an entire set of commands is specified and stored in a digital file. When the set is complete, the file is executed—that is, all of the commands are run one after another, uninterrupted (see Figure 14.14). In *interactive mode,* commands are created and run one at a time—that is, before the second command gets created, the first command has already been executed (see Figure 14.15). Both approaches use controls, possibly the same controls, but the relationship between the time spent operating the controls and the visual depiction of the resultant action varies significantly. In addition, both approaches can be either graphic or textual.

An example of a language (albeit not an animation language) that has both interactive and batch capabilities is the command language for Unix. Unix instructions can be interactively typed into the computer one at a time; as each instruction is entered, it is executed. Unix instructions can also be entered in batch mode; that is, it is possible to construct a file of one or more instructions, using a word processor. As the instructions are typed in, they are not executed.

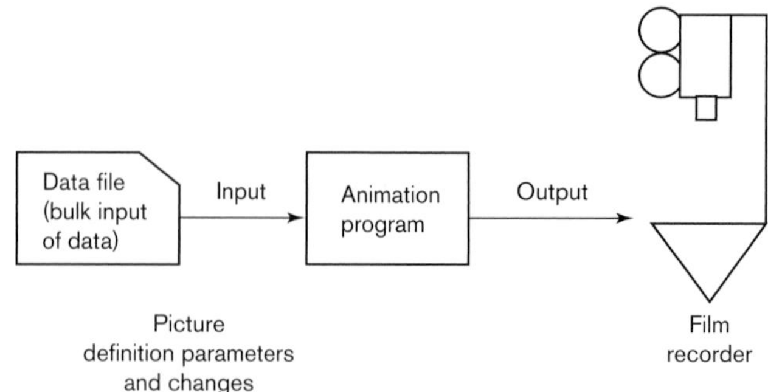

Figure 14.14 Batch mode. An entire set of commands is entered and stored in a digital file—for example, "create a cube," "create a sphere," and "create a cone." The file is then submitted as input to an animation program; all of the commands are then run one after another, uninterrupted.

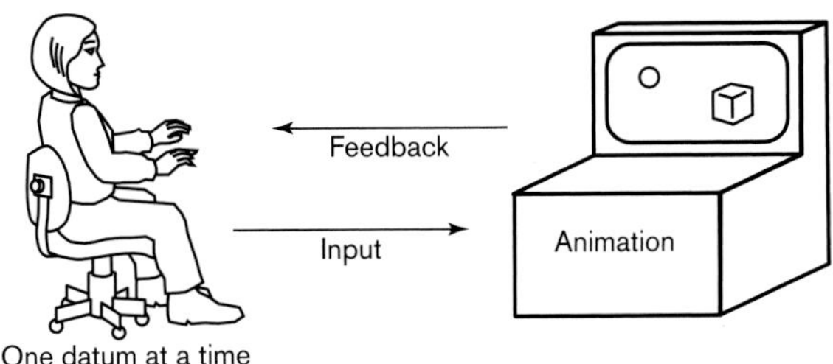

Figure 14.15 Left: Interactive mode. Commands are created and run one at a time. The animator enters a command; the result of the command—for example, the creation of a graphics primitive—is present to the animator as feedback; the animator then enters in another command.

Figure 14.16 Below: Interpreted and compiled languages. When using an interpreted language, a command is entered into the computer; the command is immediately translated into machine language, and then executed; the next command can then be entered. When using a compiled language, a series of commands is entered into the computer and stored in a file; the entire file undergoes a process called compilation, which checks for syntax errors; once the file is error-free, it is translated into machine language; once translated, the file is then linked to create an executable file.

Rather, once the file is completed, it can be presented to the computer, and the sequence of instructions is processed as a batch.

The advantage of an interactive approach is immediate feedback—for example, seeing the immediate changes when color-correcting an image or seeing an action that will become part of an animation. The advantages of a batch approach is the ability to apply a large or long process with little hands-on effort, such as color-correcting thousands of frames of an animation—the procedure is defined, the frames are designated, and the batch job is begun.

Interpreted versus Compiled Finally, computer animation programming languages may be either interpreted or compiled (see Figure 14.16). For *interpreted languages,* each command is executed as it is entered into the computer. For example, a command to move a sphere can be entered into the computer; once entered, the command is immediately translated into another language, a language equivalent to the original command yet closer in nature to the computer's machine language. The translated command is then immediately executed and the sphere is moved. Commands are invoked one after another, and the visual results will be displayed accordingly. The command can be textual or graphic.

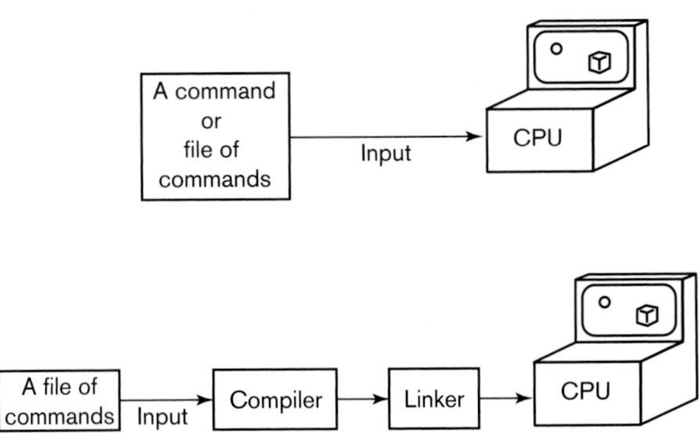

For *compiled languages,* each command is entered into the computer (textually or graphically) and saved as a file, creating a program. Once a program has been entered, the contents of the file must be compiled. During the compilation process, the contents of the file are analyzed to determine if any syntax errors exist. If there are errors, the compiler displays a notice of the error and will not proceed until all of the errors are corrected; once the errors are corrected, the file can be recompiled. Once the file is free of all errors, the compiler translates the program into its machine language equivalent. This translated program is usually stored in another file, which must then be linked—a process that creates the final executable program, which can be executed to create an animation.

From the user's point of view, the primary difference between these two approaches is in the development process. For interpreted languages, individual commands can be executed and the results viewed immediately. For compiled languages, a sequence of commands must be entered, compiled, and linked before results can be viewed. While compiled languages appear to be more cumbersome than interpreted languages, they usually make up for the inconvenience by being much faster. In practice, programs written in interpreted languages can also be compiled, which improves the speed of the program.

Animation Stand and Optical Bench Control Languages

A primitive example of textual language is language used to control animation stands and optical benches and optical printers. The syntax of these languages tends to be defined in terms of the machinery involved—for example, counters and fields—and not in terms of virtual images. After all, the artwork is in the real world, and the cameras are physical equipment. Typical commands include table pan and tilt, camera zoom, shutter, and frame advance or shuttle. Computation is employed to calculate eases, simplify skip and repeat framing, and alert the user to problems such as potential temporal aliasing or photographing the stand itself. The language can often be interactive or can run in batch mode.

Subroutine Libraries

Another approach to animation languages is to complement a language (be it an animation language or not) with a library of specialized animation functions. *Subroutine libraries* are a collection of small programs—functions—that can be used with and called by a preexisting high-level language, thereby retaining the full repertoire of the high-level language's capability, while providing additional functionality (see Figure 14.17). Subroutine libraries are available for textual as well as graphic programming languages, where they are often called *plug-ins.* Subroutine libraries usually have data structures supported by the host language—for example, dimensioned arrays in Fortran, structures in C, or records in HyperTalk. If the functionality of particular subroutines is highly demanded, it is not uncommon for the subroutines to be implemented as native commands in the next version of the animation language.

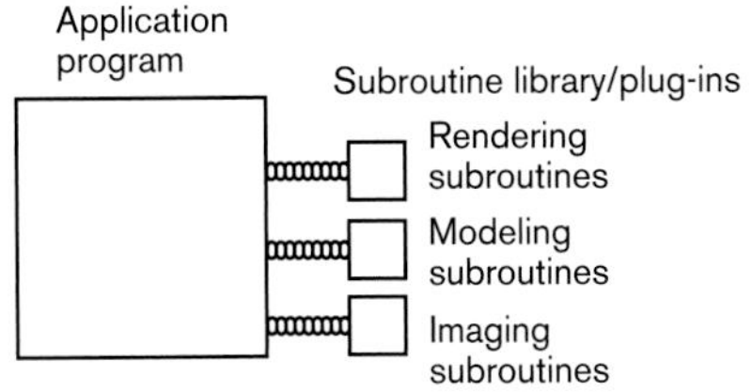

Figure 14.17 Subroutine libraries. A collection of small programs can be used with and called by a preexisting high-level language, providing additional functionality. In this example, rendering, modeling, and imaging subroutines are made available to the application program.

In animation domains where there are few well-developed products, as in the area of voxels, subroutine libraries are common. When new animation ideas are introduced, each new idea is implemented as a subroutine; the accumulation of subroutines creates the subroutine library. Over time, this migrates to a series of commands and gets surrounded by a graphic user interface.

Special Systems for Figurative Animation

The human figure is a very complex subject, and it is extremely important in animation for a number of reasons. First of all, it is important because we are people, and, as people, we are the number-one subject of all literature. Figures are sometimes represented as cartoon characters, they are occasionally represented by animals, and they are occasionally represented by abstract forms (see Figure 14.18). In any case, the figure is often represented by something that resembles a human form—with a head, arms, and legs—which can be presented elastically or with kinematic detail. Hence, it is not surprising that figures are treated as a special case, nor that special systems for figurative animation are still evolving (see Figure 14.19).

Figures are also special with respect to the models built to represent them. Natural figures are not built out of flat polygonal surfaces; they are not mechanical, they are not cast, but rather, they are grown. Their biology and physique are the antithesis of what computers are good at. Figures move in complex ways. They do not move along fixed paths, and character is often conveyed through the way a figure moves. A young man moves differently than a middle-aged man, a middle-aged man moves differently than a middle-aged woman, and a light man moves differently than a heavy man. Figures have a very wide range of movement: they can walk, run, crawl. They are usually clothed, and the sheet of clothes around a body creates another level of complexity.

Figure 14.18 Figures represented by abstract forms.

From all approaches, the figure is complex (see Figure 14.20). Starting with a simple kinematic armature, the figure has a body, head, upper arm, forearm, and so on. In reality, the human figure has 107 bones connected by joints. The rotation of the joints is rather complex. For example, when the arm rotates at the shoulder, the point around which the rotation occurs changes during the rotation. That is, not only is the arm rotating, it is rotating around a point that is itself traveling on a curve. Although we can approximate the body as a set of rigid links (limbs), in fact, it is elastic—the arm is actually longer when it is reaching than it is when brought back to the body, since the joints separate to accommodate the reach. Even the bone structures themselves are not rigid—the backbone compresses in order to absorb the impact of certain movements. In fact, the spine itself is an extremely complicated kinematic structure, consisting of vertebrae, which rotate in many different ways.

To make the situation more complex, the skeleton is surrounded by muscle, which moves as well (see Figure 14.21). Hence, when an arm is moved, the shape of the flesh changes. In fact, the entire shape of the body undergoes constant transformation—muscles flex, weight shifts, skin moves. If that is not enough, the body is constantly breathing: expanding when inhaling and contracting when exhaling. So the body is an organic shape that is in constant motion and constantly affected by outside influences such as gravity. Hence, it is an extremely complicated shape to create.

Today's figure animation systems take into consideration only some of these issues. Even with the simplest of inverse kinematic approaches, there are a tremendous number of ways that the human figure can achieve an end goal. Therefore, special handlers—which are high-level processors—are needed to enable figure motion direction, such as skip, jump, walk, fumble. With this strategy, a model can be built and then directed, much in the same way that a human actor can be directed. The virtual actors are not manipulated and directed at the joint level; they are directed using the higher-level handlers.

Figure 14.19 Left: Figurative animation systems are still evolving. The figure presents a still image from a virtual dance performance—*Hand-Drawn Spaces*—which uses an advanced figurative animation system.

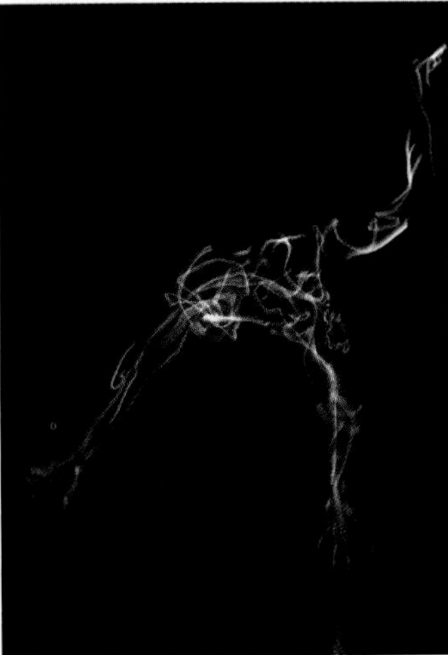

Figure 14.20 Above: The human body is composed of bone, muscles, and nerves. Here is a still image from a virtual dance performance, *Ghostcatching*.

When several handlers are operating simultaneously, their effects must be integrated in a natural manner.

This approach to a solution for figure animation requires a dynamic model that obeys certain constant principles, such as the figure's quests for balance. When building a body model, the model must dynamically attempt to stay erect. Hence, commands such as walk can be applied to the model, even when the action occurs over rough terrain. The quest for balance will keep the figure erect as it walks. With this approach, the model can navigate through the virtual environment, more or less on its own, just like an actor can navigate through the real world. A complete solution is achieved when the dynamic approach is coupled with some inverse kinematic approaches—for example, the virtual actor can be directed to achieve a goal such as reaching the bottle, and the figure can then rotate, translate, and reach the bottle in an integrated manner that satisfies all constraints. Because the figure is such an important and complex entity, it is worth building special tools to portray it in a convincing way.

Event-Driven Animation

Another tactic for scripting action is *event-driven animation,* in which actions are instigated as the result of certain conditions. The condition may be something that happens in the environment, it may be the result of the completion of another action (a door closes), or it may be the result of a user action (clicking something with the mouse). Event-driven animation, unlike key frame animation, is not determined a priori, and one of its prime uses is in computer games, where the action is a result of user input as well as the state of the world. Unlike dynamic animation, the conditions that instigate the actions do not necessarily relate to the physics of the real world. In event-driven animation, events get scheduled by people making appointments, by timetables for trains, and so on, and goals are met when we make purchases, catch trains, and so on. This section focuses on defining terms and explains how events are scheduled and get played.

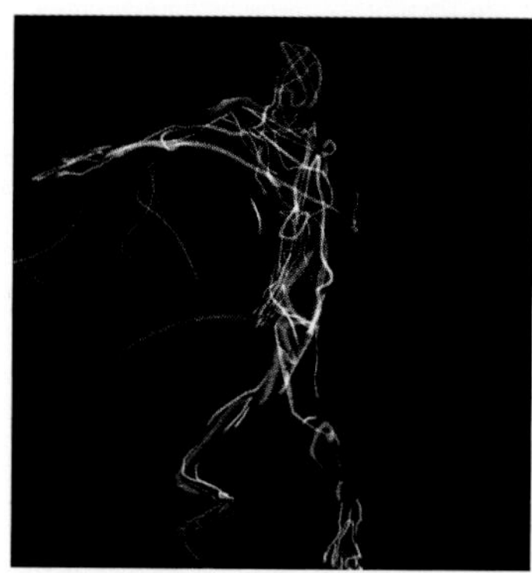

Figure 14.21 The skeleton is surrounded by muscles, which flex to move the skeleton.

Strategic Overview and Terms The strategy of event-driven animation is centered around scheduled events and goals. A *scheduled event* is an action that does not occur immediately but rather is scheduled and then executed at a later time (see Figure 14.22). The result of the execution may be an action that plays out on the screen, or something that is not visible, such as scheduling still another event or scheduling a goal. The scheduling of an event can occur as the result of a mouse click or as the result of a program calculation, but the action is scheduled and not played until it is evaluated and executed. The duration of time between scheduling an event and executing it may be less than a frame, or as long as minutes (or, for that matter, hours or days).

In data-processing terms, an event is an object with properties. A game may contain a database of many events, and at any time, the status of any one of them is one of three conditions: the event is currently scheduled, the event is available to be scheduled, or the event has been used up. An *event scheduler* is a piece of software that determines what events get scheduled when.

A *goal* is a condition not yet met but which may or may not be fulfilled by the player (see Figure 14.23). It is similar to an event, but it has two possible outcomes that depend upon a condition in the

Event table

Name	When	Where	If conditioned	Handler
London trip	Anytime	Not London	If ticket = true	Golondon
Call boss	9AM–5PM	Near phone	If late = true	Bossphone
Attend reception	7PM Oct. 21	Civic Center	If invitation = true	Reception

Figure 14.22 Left: Scheduled events. An event table contains information regarding when the event can happen, where it can happen, upon what condition it will happen, and the name of the program that will handle the event when it occurs.

Figure 14.23 Below: Goals. A goal table contains information regarding what the goal is, when the goal can be pursued, where it can be pursued, upon what condition it will be pursued, and the name of the program that will be called to finalize the goal.

future—it can be met or not met. Examples of goal conditions include behaviors to be realized, locations to be reached, puzzles to be solved, and so on. Goals may be scheduled just as events are scheduled. In data-processing terms, a goal is an object with properties. A game may contain a database of many goals, and at any time the status of any one of them is one of three conditions: the goal is currently scheduled, the goal is available to be scheduled, or the goal has been met and is no longer relevant. A ***goal scheduler*** is software that determines what goals get scheduled when.

Event-driven animation presupposes the existence of a ***main loop,*** a continuously running function that periodically evaluates any and all user input and that, in turn, manages the virtual world (see Figure 14.24). In pragmatic terms, the main loop executes once every frame. In event-driven animation, the main loop is coupled with the concept of scheduled events and goals, with the software that schedules events and goals, and with the procedures that test whether the goals have been met. The main loop determines if there are any goals that the player has achieved, any scheduled events that need to be executed, or any events that need to be scheduled. If it is appropriate, it updates the location of the player, tests for proximity to objects, and updates any dials, gauges, or views that appear onscreen.

Tacit in this discussion is the concept of a clock, counting in frames or fractions of a second, that provides a temporal time line to

Goal table

Goal name	Test	Handler	Retry time	Priority
Eat	If hunger < 0.5	Go eat	10 minutes	2
Sleep	If tired > 0.8	Do sleep	20 minutes	2
Don't crash	If Proximity < 0.6	Stop	$\frac{1}{20}$ second	1

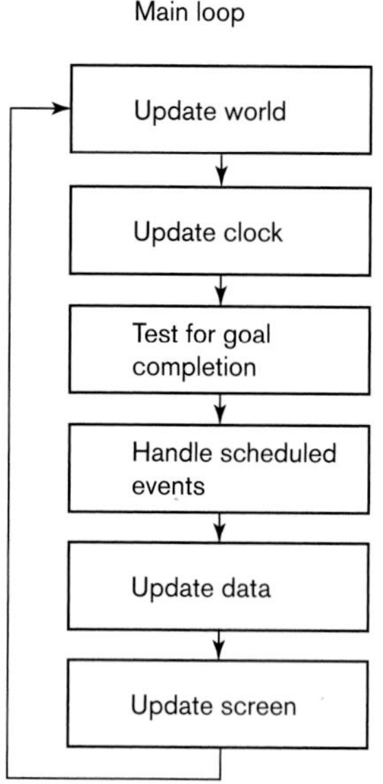

Figure 14.24 The main loop executes once every frame and updates the clock, tests for goal completion, determines if there are any scheduled events that need to be executed or any events that need to be scheduled. If it is appropriate, the main loop updates relevant data and the screen.

connect the present to the future and, if necessary, to the past. The whole concept of event-driven animation assumes the concept of time now and in the future, and assumes that time is quantifiable.

Event-driven animation works as follows: the main loop examines the status of all currently scheduled goals and tests to see whether each goal has been met or not (see Figure 14.25). If the goal has been achieved—perhaps the player has been filling a vehicle up with fuel—then the main loop clears the goal off the queue and out of the game, and it may schedule an event, such as playing an animation or sound file ("Okay, Captain, you gotter filled up, now let's get outta here!"). If the goal has not been met, the goal-failure function may do nothing, or it may schedule an event or a goal ("Hey, Captain, hurry up with that gas!").

In fact, a goal may be thought of as an if ***conditional***, which, when tested, is either true or false. It is important to note that the *if* conditional is not the direct result of a player action, but, in fact, is a test of a condition or state in the virtual world. The state of affairs tested by the *if* conditional may or may not be the result of a recent player action. Often it is the result of inaction: in the real world of driving an automobile, the engine "tests" to make sure there is gasoline in the tank and should this "goal" equal false, it stops running. The subtle point is that the game does not react to a player clicking a button; the game reacts to a goal test of whether a condition is met. The goal mechanism is a general-purpose mechanism that examines a property for a condition (e.g., "the highlight of button 36 is true"), and makes a true/false determination.

In event-driven animation, the flow of action is a sequence of goals and scheduled events that, depending upon their outcome, provides the player with a narrative flow that is not predictable. The overarching action begins with one or more goals and events being scheduled at the onset of the game, and the outcomes, in turn, schedule successive events and goals. Thus, there is more than one way to navigate from the beginning to the end of the game.

Scheduling Goals and Events Event-driven animation requires that we schedule the events and goals, and in order to do this, we need a special mechanism. The beauty of event-driven animation is that all the action in a game can be represented using a common

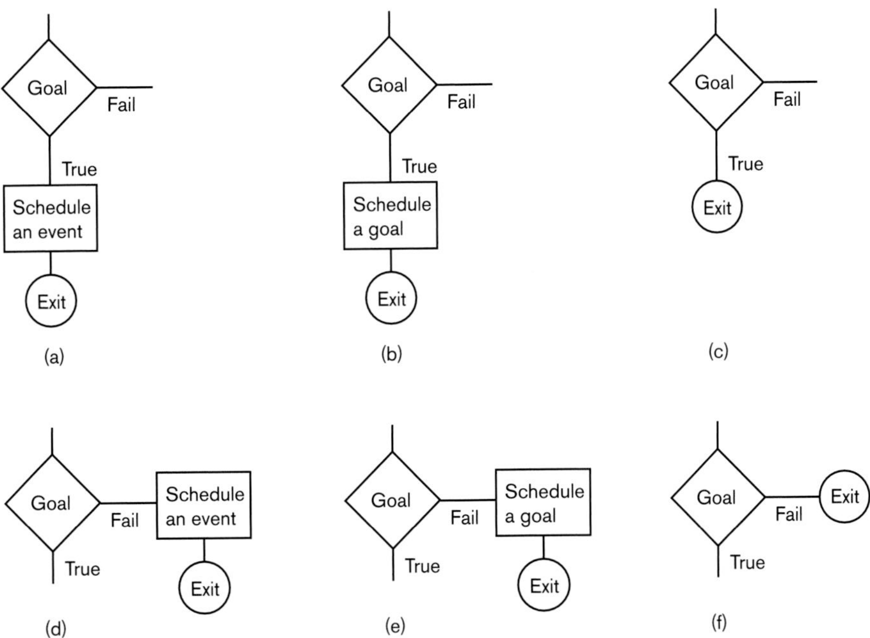

Figure 14.25 There are six possible outcomes of a goal. A goal gets evaluated by the main loop and either a fail or a true handler is executed. The true handler either schedules an event (a), a goal (b), or nothing (c). The failure handler either schedules an event (d), a goal (e), or nothing (f).

data structure handled in a common manner. A simple function can schedule or cancel an event or goal. In both cases, its primary function is to augment a goal or event variable with a time value. What is more critical is what causes an event or goal to be scheduled. Goals and events may be scheduled at the beginning of the game, at certain temporal points in the main plot, by changes in the time of day, by changes of locale, by the accumulation or loss of assets or environmental resources (fuel, air or water pressure, money, weather, etc.), by random factors (luck), as the result of events terminating, as the result of goals being met or not met, by characters and any artificial intelligence built into them, by player actions, and, in the event of multiplayer games, by the actions of other players. In all cases, the scheduling of a goal or event will involve a determination of what goal or event to schedule along with the time at which the goal or event becomes active—ranging from immediately to the distant future.

We assume, upon occasion, that more than one goal or event may get scheduled during a frame interval. Scheduling of goals and events may occur at any time, so the soonest the animator can assume a goal or event will be evaluated is the next frame (although it is possible to cycle through the main loop more than once per frame). Usually the main loop will have several goals and events that are actively scheduled, and it may have several that need evaluation. If this is the case, it may well process them by evaluating the most aged event first, or turn to the concept of priority and work the highest-priority events first. Realize that in a real-time system, it is quite possible to schedule more events than the computer can evaluate in real time. It is quite possible that a goal or event can become scheduled, and then canceled, before its time ever comes up. But the bulk of goals and events will be scheduled as the result of actions, including actions by the player and actions resulting from events that, in turn, schedule another event. Goals and events may also be scheduled as the result of goals being completed, and of goals not being met.

In summary, languages for computer animation are distinguished from graphic languages and general-purpose languages in that they contain built-in functionality to express the temporal dimension. The command may be a simple textual statement such as "Move the dot from A to B in 32 frames," or a sophisticated graphic implementation with motion diagrams for eases and a spread sheet-like database of parameters on a frame-by-frame basis. With an animation language, time is always part of the system. The decision regarding which particular language to use for a specific animation task is often based on the needs of the task and the functionality that a language has to offer—the more appropriate the language, the more likely it will be chosen for the job!

15 The Production Process

Production is the process of taking a concept and turning it into a final product. It begins with the preproduction phase, during which the concept is defined, then flushed out into words, developed visually, and planned financially, legally, and with respect to time. Following preproduction, the production phase itself involves the fabrication of sound and visuals according to the plans laid out during the preproduction process. Finally, during the postproduction phase, the parts created during the production process are assembled into a final product and prepared for distribution. This chapter presents an overview of these three phases of the production process.

Production involves four components: people, facilities, time, and money. The people are those that make the product. The facilities are the tools—cameras, computers, video decks—used to make it. Time is the non-reversible dimension that moves from the past into the present and then into the future. And money is the vehicle of control in the production process. In exchange for money, the client receives a few ounces or pounds of videotape or film containing the final product. One hundred dollars might buy a few ounces of videotape, and $20 million might buy 50 pounds of film. Hence, the final product—the tangible, material goods—is more valuable than most, if not all, precious metals. Commercial computer animators need to be familiar with the steps and have an understanding of how computer animation fits into the overall process.

Above: An opening scene from *Area 51*, a CD-ROM game. (Image courtesy of the Judson Rosebush Company.)

Figure 15.1 Opposite: This concept for a CD-ROM game, *Area 51*, briefly describes the plot, the locale, and the goal—that is, how the player wins the game.

Preproduction

Preproduction, the planning and designing phase of the overall production process, occurs before any of the product is fabricated. It includes creating the concept, writing a treatment document, developing characters, designing sets or scenes, creating the storyboard, writing the story and script, defining the budget, scheduling the job, and finalizing the contract. Only once the preproduction process is complete does the actual production begin.

Concept Development

In advertising terms, and sometimes in filmmaking terms, the idea behind a commercial or film is called a ***concept.*** A product, whether it is a 30-second commercial or a feature-length motion picture, usually has a concept, and typically this concept is describable in one sentence. Minimally, it can be described in five or six words, and at most it can be described in one paragraph (see Figure 15.1). For example, the concept of Alfred Hitchcock's *Psycho* can be described as a woman being stalked by a maniac and murdered in a shower, followed by the tracking down of the killer. Another example might be a television commercial, in which the concept is a mother feeding her baby a particular brand of baby food, and the baby growing up to be strong and healthy. Concepts also apply to still media—for example, the concept of a milk advertisement might be famous people wearing milk mustaches.

There is often a tendency to define the product concept according to the current visual technology. However, the concept is usually strongest when it is based on content, not tools. The technology may support the concept or become part of the concept, but it should not be the driving force. For example, in *Terminator 2*, the nature of the villain that can transmogrify its liquid character is supported by digital imaging technology, and not the opposite.

The Treatment Document

Once the concept is defined, it needs to be expanded into what is typically called the ***treatment document,*** or simply, the ***treatment.*** The treatment turns the concept into several pages of description (see Figure 15.2). If the product is an advertising campaign, the treatment might state how the campaign addresses issues such as

Project Concept

The *Area 51* CD-ROM is an interactive adventure game where the player becomes a journalist investigating top secret military and extraterrestrial activity. The game will demand that the player solve a series of interlocking puzzles in order to piece together the mystery surrounding *Area 51*, a top secret military installation in the southwestern desert of the United States.

Treatment

Area 51 casts the player as an investigative reporter on the trail of a secret government program. The game begins with an anonymous late-night phone call that points in the direction of Groom Lake, Dreamland, and *Area 51*, deep in the Nevada desert. The player is given a name or two, a phone number, a post office box key, and a ticket to Las Vegas.

The player is on her own and must follow leads, gain the confidence of those with information, avoid surveillance and death, sort out truth from misinformation, and break the story before a rival reporter does.

Along the way, the player encounters a bizarre collection of characters. The Leak is the mysterious voice on the phone who passionately wants the player to succeed but whose motives are unknown. Slippery Jim is the player's researcher and confidante. Ted Hunter is the rival reporter. Salt Flat Mo is the proprietor of the Salt Flat Cafe near *Area 51*. Sandra Pikesmith is the daughter of a local rancher who mysteriously died several years ago. Queequeg Zabblebrox is an outsider who wandered into town one day–his incoherent dialog hides deeper meaning. Jack Connors is the celebrated test pilot who is too scared to talk.

The look of the product is "render-realistic." The environment will have elements of realism but will also be obviously computer generated. Characters will be represented in a style somewhere between comic art and video capture.

The visual elements for *Area 51* straddle a strange dichotomy. *Area 51* is located in one of the bleakest and most unforgiving locations on earth, yet *Area 51* is also the site of some of the most technologically advanced projects in history. Physically the buildings and other evidence of *Area 51* will stand out in stark contrast to the weathered and dilapidated buildings and pitted roads of the surrounding regions. This place is powerful, organized, well kept, and well controlled.

The player's search for a story will take them from the corridors of the intelligence community in Washington D.C. to the barren Nevada desert. Clues abound in every location, but so do deception, misinformation, treachery, and even death. The consequences of failure range from humiliation and ruination of one's career to government sanctioned "removal."

people of different races, different genders, different ages. Some products are aimed for a broad range of appeal. Conversely, some products are aimed toward a narrowly focused market. Depending on the concept, the treatment indicates the specifics of the campaign—for example, the people in the advertisement are bodybuilders, or young women, or senior citizens. The treatment also specifies the character of the people: they may talk extremely fast to emphasize the fast delivery service being advertised.

Figure 15.2 Opposite: This treatment document for *Area 51* expands the plot, the locale, and the goal as they are defined in the concept statement.

The treatment can address the details of the characters, the plot, and the types of production technologies that might be involved. The treatment for a feature-length, computer-animated film must include the plot and characters, the tools needed to create the animation, the voices that are to be used in the film, and distribution strategies. The treatment for a television series might include the descriptions of the cast, some of whom are played by the same actor every episode, such as the hero, and some of whom are played by different characters each week, such as the villain who gets caught and sent to jail at the end of each episode.

It is often the case that the production company and the animators never see the treatment document, which typically resides inside an advertising agency or inside a studio or with the client. However, the production company is usually given more specific documents that are far more developed.

Production Design Issues: Character Development and Set Design

In order to proceed in the preproduction process, the characters and the world they inhabit must be designed. *Character development* is the process where the characters are designed, developed, and created. Typically, a document much like a biography is created that profiles each character to a certain degree of detail, which is dependent upon of the complexity of the project (see Figure 15.3). For example, in a modern soap opera, the character document would profile the character: where they were born, where they went to high school, and information about their family, their education, their love interests, their hobbies, and so on. While sometimes this information does not manifest itself in the final product, it is still a significant part of the preproduction process.

Character Document

Slippery Jim: A disbarred lawyer from "back east," Slippery Jim is the proprietor of the Hummingbird Motel, one of the few remaining inhabitable structures in Niles. Jim knows more than he lets on, and although he will purport to be the player's confidante, he is cunningly deceitful in advancing his own agenda.

Slippery Jim is knowledgeable of all things bureaucratic and all things legal; above all, he knows how to get information that people don't want him to have. Harvard educated, raised in Boston with a mellow Boston accent, Slippery Jim is 40 years old. His speech drips with cynicism and contempt for those he is tricking and combating. Slippery Jim never seems to sleep. When he is not working, he is drowning his frustrations at Mo's. He can help the player, but whose side is he really on?

Physical description: 5'10". Dark hair, pale skin. A sour and cynical look on his face at all times. Slippery Jim is fond of Hawaiian shirts and even flashier sport coats.

In conjunction with the textual description of the character, a visual description is also created (see Figure 15.4). In the case of animation, sketches are made of the characters—for example, what the character will look like, what the color scheme will be, and how textures might be used. In addition, motion sketches are made to present a description of how the character will move—for example, how the character will walk and talk. Production renderings of the visual treatment might also be created to give a sense of the finished quality (see Figure 15.5). In addition, actors are cast for the characters' voices. In the case of live action, actors are cast for specific characters.

The preproduction process also calls for ***set design,*** that is, the design of the locations or sets where the action will take place and the design of the objects in the sets, those that move and those that are static (see Figure 15.6). The design often begins with a text description and then proceeds to a visual design. Sketches are made of all locations, giving a sense of the specific look of each. General qualities such as atmosphere, coloring, and landscape, as well as details such as surface textures and patterns, are fully designed. In productions that emphasize objects, such as a television commercial for a product, designs are made of all relevant objects.

As with character designs, production renderings of the visual treatment might also be created to give a sense of the finished quality. Decisions are made to define the look and production

Figure 15.3 Opposite: This character document profiles Slippery Jim, presenting a brief history of the character, as well as his purpose within the game.

Figure 15.4 Above: Character sketch. This sketch shows what the character will look like, including the type of clothes he'll wear.

Figure 15.5 Left: Production renderings of the visual treatment give a sense of the finished quality. Here, the rendering includes two characters, an interior, and several props.

NILES LOCATION FIGURES

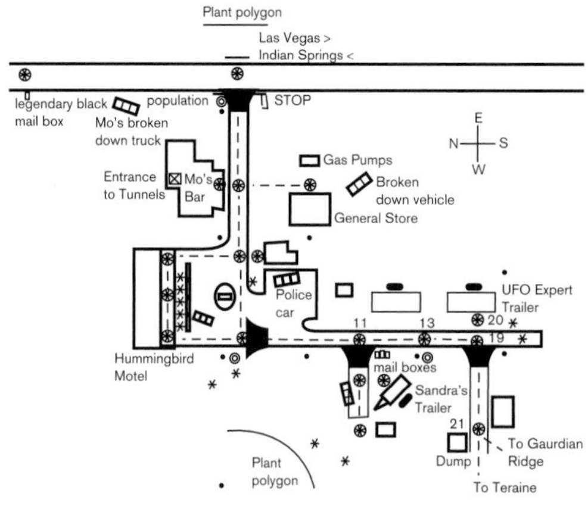

(Figure 18, Site Plan – Niles, Nevada)
Area 51 Functional Specification September 1, 1995

- ▬ = Propane tank
- • = Electrical post
- ◎ = Light post
- * = Plant (Joshua, Yucca, Cactus, Scrub)
- ⊛ = Location for 8 views
- – – = Navigatable movement

24

BAR EXTERIOR – NILES
CINDER BLOCK (ADOBE) WITH TILE FRONT.
SIDE BASEMENT DELIVERY ENTRANCE
FIGURE COULD HURRY/STUMBLE BACK IN
UPON OUR ARRIVAL OR SHADOW IN
WINDOW COULD DISAPPEAR

MOJAVE MO'S – REAR END OF BUILDING
POSSIBLE ADDITIONAL BACKGROUND LOCATION
BARBER... GIVES CLUES – SITS IN CHAIR
"BULLET" HOLES IN WALL
DUMPSTER FOR CLUES

27

BAR BACK ROOM
SAFE, DEFORMED SKULL
PERSONAL EFFECTS, ALCOHOL
TOOLS LOCKED BINS SCULPTURE
COBWEBS, GUNS GEIGER COUNTER

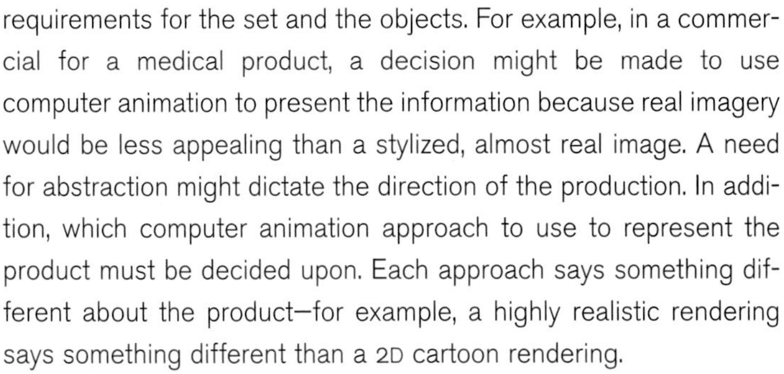

requirements for the set and the objects. For example, in a commercial for a medical product, a decision might be made to use computer animation to present the information because real imagery would be less appealing than a stylized, almost real image. A need for abstraction might dictate the direction of the production. In addition, which computer animation approach to use to represent the product must be decided upon. Each approach says something different about the product—for example, a highly realistic rendering says something different than a 2D cartoon rendering.

Figure 15.6 Opposite: Set designs. The set designs here include a floor plan and artwork for all the scenes in the story. Attention is paid to texture, lighting, and color.

Figure 15.7 Above: Costume design is the design of all garments worn by the characters in the production. Texture, pattern, and color are all part of costume design.

Closely related to set design and character design is ***costume design,*** that is, the design of all garments worn by the characters in the production (see Figure 15.7). The fabric pattern and flow are an intricate part of the design. In order to unify the final product, the costumes are often dictated by the quality of the characters and the overall look and feel of the sets. As with set design, costume design is a specialized guild craft, with a tradition of professionals and a large body of literature.

Finally, all visual treatments should consider the resolution of the target medium. For example, design decisions may vary depending on whether the product is made for television, CD-ROM, IMAX movies, or some other medium. Different degrees of detail may affect storage requirements as well as readability.

Storyboards and Scripts

Upon completion of the concept and the treatment, the next step usually involves the creation of a ***storyboard***, a document that describes the look and time progression of the final product and is

Stboard_03/01/01 Page 3

5	6	7

00:00:17:00 **00:00:20:00** The Chameleon looks down at the Robot from above in anticipation of the ensuing encounter of Robot and Doll. The camera drifts slowly forward.	**00:00:20:00** **00:00:27:00** Cut to an over-the-shoulder two shot as the Robot and Doll begin a flirtatious interaction. Camera drifts very slowly forward.	**00:00:27:00** **00:00:32:00** The Chameleon rotates, ending on an image of the Cyclist which the Robot and Doll have been watching.The Chameleon is illuminated from within, and a mysterious sound of music plays. The sound of pedalling fades in.

Figure 15.8 The storyboard describes the look and time-progression of the final product. The series of panels presents the story, a description of the audio, the timing of the story, camera instructions, and special effects.

presented as a collection of drawing panels and dialogue (see Figure 15.8). Depending on how elaborate the project is, the storyboard varies in length and complexity. Typically, it will have at least one drawing for each scene in the final product. A storyboard reads from left to right, top to bottom, with each page containing the same number of panels, which usually varies from one to six. A storyboard can be as short as three pages for a 15- to 30-second television commercial, or quite long, for example, 240 to 1000 panels (or more) for a feature-length film, assuming one to four panels per shot, and an average shot length of four to six seconds. Storyboards range from being thin and diagrammatic to dense and profusely illustrated. Prices of each storyboard panel can range from $30 to $1000. The price reflects the amount of treatment within the panel.

In general, storyboards must show several things: the content of the scene, that is, what the camera sees; the action, that is, how actors and things change relative to each other; what the frame is to look like in terms of rendering treatment; transitions; and how the camera moves. Since the movement of the camera directs the audience's attention to specific locations and actions in the scene, much of what is conveyed in motion pictures is conveyed through camera movement. Hence, camera movement is carefully annotated within the storyboard. Camera movement is occasionally indicated by drawing on top of the storyboard, possibly creating a panel within a panel. Sometimes it is indicated by a sequence of two or more panels, depicting the key frames and possibly some in-betweens.

Transitions between scenes, such as cuts, fades, dissolves, wipes, and morphs, are all indicated in the storyboard. These indications are used in postproduction, when the transitions are incorporated into the assembled final product. The type of transitions to be used is integral to the compositions of the scenes on both sides of the transitions; hence it is necessary for transition decisions to be made during preproduction.

It is often the case that storyboards do not show the rendering treatment; the storyboard is often accompanied by a treatment document that presents what finished frames are to look like. So, for example, if the scene is to be an on-site, live action shot of New York City, then the storyboard might be accompanied by photographs of locations in the city where the scenes are to be shot. If the scene is to be shot on a set, then paintings of the set might accompany the storyboard.

In most cases, it is best to describe the details of the storyboard in words rather than leave the explanation entirely to the panels. Hence, storyboards also include a textual portion, which includes dialogue, description of the music track, and an indication and list of sound effects and timing notes; it should include as well a redundant description of the camera action and transitions, and any necessary descriptions of the action, such as "the actor enters the scene, stops and turns, and then says his dialogue." A better storyboard will include the times of each panel. Timing notes, however, are not always included, and when they are, they are not directed at the level of a frame—a storyboard is not a dope sheet. Moreover, timing is often not completely finessed until postproduction.

The storyboard is the primary vehicle of communication between the writer, director, and producer. It is the vehicle of presentation to the client as well as the guide to production. Hence, the storyboard needs to be clear and well defined. Every aspect of it is subject to a *breakdown analysis*—that is, an analysis of all the imagery in each shot identifying backgrounds, objects, effects, logos, type, characters, transitions, and actions—in order to determine what has to be made in order to realize the shot. The breakdown also determines staffing and materials estimates, including labor, CPU, and camera time. Success at the breakdown phase is central to budgeting, scheduling, and integrating the final production.

Figure 15.9 Opposite: In the script, each character's lines are presented in the order that they will occur. Brief descriptions of actions may also be included.

Pragmatically speaking, the role of the storyboard is the same in computer animation as it is in traditional animation and live action—it shows the sequence of the final product. However, when designing 3D computer animation, the storyboard is often accompanied by a blueprint of the set, which includes the location and movement of the objects and camera. The blueprint clarifies sequences of action that may not be obvious from storyboard panels alone, assuring that the client, director, and animator all share a similar conception of the action.

Storyboarding programs can be used to simplify the storyboarding process, providing the tools and forms. Timing, effects, drawings, and other requirements can be specified and stored with these programs. The visual results can be played back and viewed as a sequence, or printed to paper.

As the storyboard is being developed, a *script* is also created. The script is the text that will be used by the performers to create the dialogue in the final product (see Figure 15.9). The script contains all the dialogue and screen direction of a moving picture product. It includes lines spoken by the characters, descriptions of the sets, and screen direction for characters and camera actions. Typically, the script is made available to everyone involved in the project.

Building the Parts and Planning for Action

When creating animation, one of the most important parts of the process is the planning and creation of the artwork and models. In particular, if a model is to animate, then it must be built to animate. If a model is to animate in a particular way, then it must be built so that it will be able to animate appropriately. Animators must plan ahead what objects are to move as a group and what objects are to

Script

SAMPAH
(suddenly realizing)
So where's Molly?

MCTAVISH AND XYFRIEND
That's what I'd like to know.

SAMPAH
That's weird...she was right–

Out the window (or via exterior camera seen on the monitor) another dolphin can be seen swimming towards us.

SAMPAH
There she is...with Flippy.

XYFRIEND
Flippy?

MCTAVISH
I take it that means we just met, Dee Dee.

SAMPAH
The one and only.

At the last second it veers, revealing a young women in Scuba gear swimming alongside it. She waves at us.

XYFRIEND
Oh my circuits, it is Molly!

MCTAVISH
Open the hatch, she's coming onboard.

Budget			
Production Company:	Pocock Productions		
Address:	123 Merry Lane New York, NY 10000		
Job Name:	Acme Hair Replacement for Men		
Job Number:	1400		
Date:	October 16, 1998		
Due Date:	November 25, 1998		
Producer:	Nancy Schneider		
Director:	J. Handler		
Quantity	**Description**	**Units**	**Amount**
6 weeks	Producer	$5000.00	$30,000.00
4 weeks	Director	$5000.00	$20,000.00
10 days	Art Director	$800.00	$ 8,000.00
10 days	Technical Director	$800.00	$ 8,000.00
1 flat rate	Story Board Artist	N/A	$ 2,000.00
1 flat rate	Writer	N/A	$ 2,000.00
Sub Total Above the Line:			$70,000.00
4 weeks	Computer Animator	$800.00	$3,200.00
4 weeks	Production Manager (1/2 time)	$350.00	$1,400.00
1 flat rate	Editor	N/A	$2,500.00
1 day	Narrator	$750.00	$ 750.00
1 flat rate	Music and Effects	N/A	$5,000.00
1 flat rate	Sound Mix	N/A	$2,000.00
1 flat rate	Stock and Media	N/A	$ 500.00
4 weeks	Overhead	$2000.00	$8,000.00
Sub Total Below the Line:			$23,350.00
Total Above and Below the Line:			$93,350.00
Mark up (25% of Total)			$23,337.50
Total Price:			$116,687.50

Figure 15.10 Example of a budget.

move independently. The types of animated action must be known in advance, and the models must be planned accordingly. Without sufficient planning, it is very likely that models will be constructed in such a way that they will not be usable during the animation process. In that case, new models would have to be built.

Another important consideration is whether to use 2D image maps or build 3D models. For example, if a particular action is to take place within a city, should a 2D image of a city be used as a backdrop or should the city be modeled three-dimensionally? Questions such as this often depend upon the nature of the shot—if there will be camera movement, if there will be close-up shots, and if convincing three-dimensionality is required, it might be best to model the buildings. However, if the city is seen in the distance, it might be sufficient to use the 2D images as texture maps on the buildings.

When 2D artwork is to be used to create animation, there are additional considerations. For example, when using a texture map to animate water, the primary consideration might be creating a map that can be used to create a cycle of motion, so that the motion cycles seamlessly. Unless the nature of the animation is taken into consideration before the artwork is created, the animation will be flawed.

Finally, it is important to remember that the purpose of the artwork and the model is to romance action. Therefore, it might be necessary to build subtleties into the model to enhance the motion or to enhance the object for those times when it is not in motion.

The Budget

Preproduction also involves budgeting. The ***budget*** is a document presenting a detailed list of costs associated with the production of the final product (see Figure 15.10). A fixed sum total of costs is derived and agreed upon by all parties before production begins.

For computer animation, the budget usually addresses the cost in terms of the time needed for modeling, animating, and rendering. Obviously, the running time of the final product is always a factor, but it is only one of many. For example, given a rendering technique and a polygon count, the budget might present an estimate of the modeling, rendering, and animation time required to create the final product. Or the budget can simply be presented as the number of hours of various staff members to create the product, coupled with a cost per hour. Both approaches take into consideration the time needed for modeling, animating, and rendering, as well as the running time of the final product, but they come to the final figures using different methods. Often a job is budgeted in several different ways; if the results are all similar, then the results are thought to be consistent, but if they are vastly different, then the budgets and budgeting methods must be reconsidered.

In terms of budgeting computer animation, the cost of rendering is the primary expense (not including salaries). Typically, the more sophisticated the rendering technique and the greater the range of techniques being used, the longer the rendering time. Techniques that take less time cost less, those that take longer cost more.

Budgeting can be based on simple calculations. For example, the number of polygons times the running time creates a reasonable result on which to base a budget—the greater the complexity of the objects, the greater the cost, and the longer the running time, the greater the cost.

One might argue that the majority of production demands occur during the modeling phase, and hence, the length of the animation should have limited affects on the budget—that is, creating an animation that runs twice as long should not double the price. For most real productions, however, animation segments are not repeated over and over; the additional length of the animation is required because additional unique animation in needed for some meaningful purpose. Therefore, the time to produce twice the animation is usually twice as long, and hence costs twice as much.

Also addressed in the budget are two kinds of costs: fixed costs and variable costs. ***Fixed costs*** are those costs associated with developing the project, which include the cost of the office and other overhead, writers, design production staff, and most of the things that go into the preproduction process. ***Variable costs*** are those costs associated with production and postproduction, including voice talent, sound recording, mixing, synchronization of sound and image, recording stock, editing, dubs, release prints, and some distribution expenses. For live action, the costs might also include camera rental, crew, cast, extras, and all other costs associated with shooting. For computer animation, the costs might include modelers, animators, equipment rental or the per diem expense of equipment, house staff, digital sound recording and editing, and all other costs associated with animation production.

In commercial production, there is a standard budget called the American Institute of Certified Planners (AICP) form, which is a multipage form used by all advertising agencies for bidding. This standardized production agreement defines budget lines and markup rules regarding the terms of profit taken by the production company. In the motion picture industry, there is a wider variety of standard budget forms, most between 12 and 15 pages long. It is not uncommon for a smaller computer animation company to run a budget one to two pages long, and a CD-ROM budget might run three pages. Because the computer animation business is so intertwined with other parts of the industry, it is important for computer animators to be familiar with all of the budgeting issues related to production.

The Schedule

The preproduction process also involves the development of a *schedule,* which is basically a time line with dates noting when jobs are to be completed and when deliveries are to be made (see Figure 15.11). For large projects, computerized scheduling software is often used to assist in the scheduling process. A primary concern during the scheduling process is determining whether conflicts occur within the schedule. For example, determining if job A is due before job B and if job B is due before job A; or determining if jobs A, B, and C are due all at once when it might be more efficient if the jobs were staggered. Certain jobs can run in parallel while others are dependent upon one another, hence these connections must be coordinated in the schedule. A good producer will understand the interdependencies and design the schedule accordingly.

The Contract

The preproduction process also includes the writing of a *contract,* which marks the final stage of preproduction and the beginning of production. The contract is a legal document that defines the terms of production of the product, and is a legal agreement between the party desiring the work and the party fabricating the work (see Figure 15.12). In it, the client specifies what they want to buy and the fabricator specifies what they are going to deliver. All of the materials generated during preproduction—the schedule, budget, and product description—are typically bound with the contract as attachments. When approved by both parties, the contract is signed and is legally binding.

Specifically, the contract includes a definition of the parties: who they are and what they are. It also includes a definition of the work, which is usually very detailed or references attachments, and includes as well the treatment, the techniques and tools used to create the product, and the number of seconds, minutes, or hours of product being purchased. The terms of the contract may address the production of a few dozen frames of film, or it may address the production of an entire feature-length film.

Time Life Books

Schedule

10/07	Finalize budget and procure client approval.
10/09	Contract with live-action and computer animation companies. Record scratch track.
10/12	Commence work on computer and 2D animation.
10/19	Preproduction meeting for live action.
10/21	Shoot live action.
10/22	Select takes.
10/23	Deliver all selected live-action takes to computer animation company.
10/26	Edit work print and rotoscope product shots.
10/28	Review pencil tests of computer animation shots.
11/02	Conclude man and book scene. Conclude all 2D and 3D animation scenes.
11/03	Commence pre-opticals of man and book, mummy and head, shoe, cockpit, and screen inserts.
11/06	Deliver remaining animation stand scenes and edit into work print.
11/11	Conclude pre-optical. Prepare final assembly.
11/19	Deliver final optical negative.
11/20	Prepare bar sheet of finished picture.
11/23	Record announcer voice over.
11/24	Record music.
11/25	Transfer to tape and mix music.
11/30	Ship to TV stations.

Time-Life Books
"Seeing the Unseen" 1:20

October/November

T.V. Production Schedule

Sunday	Monday	Tuesday	Wednesday	Thursday	Friday	Saturday
October	5	6	7 Finalize estimate	8 Estimate to T-L books for approval	9 –Award job –Record guide-track	10
11	12 Start computer graphics & editorial	13 Prep Virus, Shoe, Head Research 4D	14 Prep –Polaroids Set materials to NYC	15 Pre-production meeting with T-L Books	16 Prep	17
18 Fly to L.A.	19 Prep	20 Pre-pro at Coleman Group	21 Shoot (live-action)	22 Return to NYC	23 Prepare Rotomats –Start man/book scene	24
25	26 Start scene of head, shoes, monitor inserts cut w/p	27	28 Pencil test virus, shoe, head Review of 2-D animation: Tornado, book covers, cockpit, eyes lite up, man/book	29	30 Deliver additional optical scene events: Tornado, saturn, airplane, cockpit insert	31
1 November	2 –Conclude man/book scene cockpit, head, shoe, virus –Conclude 2-D & 3-D scenes eyes lite up, book cover	3 Pre-optical man/book/mummy/ head, shoe, cockpit screen insert	4	5	6 Deliver any remaining scenes: Tornado, book covers, partial head, saturn	7
8	9	10	11 Conclude preopticals, commence final optical	12	13	14

Time-Life Books
"Seeing the Unseen" 1:20

October/November

T.V. Production Schedule-Page 2

Sunday	Monday	Tuesday	Wednesday	Thursday	Friday	Saturday
15	16	17	18	19 Deliver optical negative	20 –Music counts	21
22	23 Record V.O.	24 Record music	25 Film-to-tape transfer –Add supers and phone numbers	26 THANKSGIVING	27 HOLIDAY	28
29	30 Deliver to stations P.M.	1 December				

Figure 15.11 Opposite and left: Examples of schedules. Every deadline should be accounted for.

Figure 15.12 Overleaf: Example of a contract. This contract for a television commercial describes the services and product being sold, the prices, and the delivery dates. The contract also addresses other legal issues, such as what happens to the artwork given to the animation company by the client.

The contract also includes the schedule of payment, which might be based on a regular calendar; for example, payment might be made on the first of each month, or it might be based on milestones, that, is special dates such as delivery dates. Whether the contract is based on a regular calendar or milestones, it specifies what is to be delivered and what the payment is for each delivery. Typically, delivery proceeds in phases; certain parts are due before others, hence, the contract specifies the details of all phases.

☐ Request for Quotation
☒ Production Contract
☐ Purchase Order

Date 6 February 2001 # 7757 Ref. # ______

For Cadbury's Dollops Ice Cream TV Spots (4 x 20 sec)

To: Name Jamshed K. Vakeel, Creative Director

Company Mudra Communications Pvt. Ltd.

Street Third Floor, Court House, Tilak Marg

City Dhobi Talao, Bombay State India Zip 400 002

Phone 255-877 Fax 022-290172

212-398-6600
ROSEBUSH VISIONS CORPORATION
25 W 45 STREET NEW YORK NY
10036-4902

Given: Your four storyboards.

Provide: Four finished :20 commercials made with standard animation, in color.
Price includes all animation, pencil test, ink and paint, and photography.

Item	Quantity	Description	Unit Price	Total Price
1)	-1-	Director (George Parker) for all four spots	$6,500.	$6,500.
2)	-1-	:20 animated spot #1 (Flying airplanes)	27,300.	27,300.
3)	-1-	:20 animated spot #2 (Truck and helicopter)	22,100.	22,100.
4)	-1-	:20 animated spot #3 (Submarine)	19,500.	19,500.
5)	-1-	:20 animated spot #4 (Wagon)	19,500.	19,500.
6)	-1-	Live action tag for use on all spots	5,400.	5,400.
7)	-1-	Editorial for all four spots	1,600.	1,600.
8)	-4-	OPTIONAL Film to tape transfer 1" plus 3/4" cassette	300.	1,200.

Terms	Delivery Date/FOB	Delivery Medium/Size	Rendering
Thirds (1/3 start, 1/3 pencils, 1/3 on delivery)	6–8 weeks	35mm negative and print if #8 then 1" tape and 3/4" cassette	Color cel animation With 3 or 4 levels. Front inked, back side painted.

Signature ______ Date ______ Signature ______ Date ______

Judson Rosebush
This quotation subject to terms and conditions described on the back.

TERMS AND CONDITIONS

1) Type of document: This is a request for quotation: a production/quotation, or a purchase order depending upon box checked.

2) Date: This is date of document creation.

3) Number: This is our unique number.

4) Reference Number: This is a backward pointer to your number, if any.

5) For: This project name.

6) To: This is your name, address, and phone number. If this is a RFQ or PO, you are the producer; if this is a PC, you are the buyer.

7) Given: This is a list of materials buyer will provide to the producer in order to more fully define the task, and otherwise contribute to production. These materials may include storyboards, blueprints, data, scripts, talent.

8) Provide: This is a list of materials the producer will provide to the buyer. This includes, for each item, a quantity, an item description, a price per item, and a total price. Prices do not include sales tax.

9) Terms: Those are the dates of payment. "Halves" are 1/2 upon commencement of job and 1/2 net 30 delivery. "Thirds" are 1/3 upon commencement, 1/3 after keys and motion test but before final computation, and 1/3 on delivery.

10) Delivery Date: This is planned date of delivery; no warranties are given or implied.

11) Rendering: This is a description of representation (e.g. wireframe, solid, hidden line). It may also include descriptions of the lighting model (polygon shaded, smooth shaded) as well as surface parameters (e.g. colored, transparent, texture, or image mapped).

12) Delivery Medium and Size: This is the material and format (e.g. 35mm slides, 35mm cine, 1 inch videotape). Delivery consists solely of the medium and images thereupon it and it does not include any intermediate images or elements, programs, manufacturing procedures, databases, or props. Designs may be reused at our discretion.

13) Signatures: Signing parties indicate acceptance to terms of document. Requests for quotations do not imply a purchase order. A production contract offer is valid for sixty days. A purchase order will be followed by payment upon receipt of goods and invoice subject to terms.

14) Production cancellation charges: If production is cancelled at the customer's request prior to scheduled dates the following proportion of the contract price shall be charged and due from the customer as a cancellation fee.

after recording	100%
after final computation	90%
after keys and motion test	60%
after database completion	30%

15) Error, Notice, and Suit: No production standard of aesthetics is defined. If any technical errors occur from Rosebush Visions Corp.'s failure to use due care or from malfunctions of machines of Rosebush Visions Corp. or subcontractors, customer shall notify Rosebush Visions Corp. in writing within 30 days after receipt of the completed work. After notification, Rosebush Visions Corp. shall correct such errors at its own expense. Such correction shall be the customer's sole and exclusive remedy. Such notification by customer shall be a condition precedent to any claim or the commencement of any legal proceeding against Rosebush Visions Corp. Customer shall not commence any legal proceeding of any kind against Rosebush Visions Corp. more than one year after accrual of such cause of action. If the customer is present during the production and accepts delivery of the completed product, the customer warrants to Rosebush Visions Corp. that the product meets all standards including but not limited to quality, format, accuracy, and aesthetic standards.

16) No Warranty: Rosebush Visions Corp. makes no warranties express or implied as to merchantability, fitness for a specified purpose, or any other matter. There are not warranties that extend beyond the fact hereof.

17) Right to dispose of or use artwork and materials: Unless otherwise notified prior to production date, Rosebush Visions Corp. may dispose of any artwork or other materials provided by the customer upon completion of the production. Rosebush Visions Corp. may use materials produced for delivery to client for demonstration, publicity, and educational purposes not connected with this project. The customer further agrees to hold harmless Rosebush Visions Corp. from any damage, loss of liability, including attorney's fees, resulting from unauthorized uses of music and/or artwork, film and videotape supplied by the customer. Subcontractors may employ work produced for product demonstrations provided credits for Rosebush Visions Corp. are displayed with any other credits.

18) Uncontrollable Events: Rosebush Visions Corp. shall have no liability to customer for any failure to perform its obligations hereunder if such failure is occasioned by fire, Civil disorder, war, strike, lock out, energy or materials shortage, equipment failures, governmental actions, inflation, or other events beyond reasonable control.

19) Total agreement: Customer acknowledges that he has read this agreement and does agree to be bound by its terms. This agreement is the exclusive statement of the agreement between the parties and supercedes all proposals, representations, and other communications (oral or written) relating to the subject of the agreement. This agreement may not be modified except by a writing signed by the duly authorized representatives of the parties. This agreement shall be governed by the laws of New York.

The contract also specifies ownership and rights. In particular, the contract specifies what the client is buying: they may buy the finished product, a license to use the finished product, any technology developed during the production of the product, trademarks, licenses, or characters. All of these issues are defined in the contract.

In almost all computer animation contracts, the client buys the final product. They often also buy all of the parts of the final product. For example, if the product is a composited scene of an animated character walking along a live action shot of a beach, then the client buys the product, plus the uncomposited live action footage, plus the walking character. The client almost never buys the technology that is used or developed during production of the product. Hence, ownership of source code and production methodologies usually remains with the production company. In fact, even if the contract defines that the ownership of technology is to be transferred to the client, in many cases, the production company does not have any right of transfer.

If the client brings their own characters to the product, they may wish to retain ownership of the characters. There are, however, some negotiable issues. For example, if the production company develops a special move or dance for the client's character, then the ownership of rights to that move must be addressed in the contract.

Production contracts usually have a *term,* which is the time period defined by beginning and end dates, where the beginning date is the day when the contract is signed and the end date is the delivery date. The terms of some contracts, however, go beyond the final delivery date. For example, a contract may include conditions for a sequel project or maintenance, and if so, the terms of the contract would address these issues.

The contract also includes a section referred to as *indemnification.* In this section, all parties make representations of themselves to each other. For example, all parties represent the terms of ownership for the things that they bring to the project. If the client brings a trademark to the production company and asks them to animate it, the client needs to represent legally that they own the rights to the trademark. Hence, the client indemnifies the production company: if the production company gets sued for engaging in a trademark violation, the client would have to take on the lawsuit and legally defend the production company. Conversely, if the production company violates laws (such as labor laws) during production, and this results in a lawsuit against the client, then the production company indemnifies the client and is obligated to legally defend the client. Occasionally, contracts flow indemnification entirely in one direction—either toward the client or the production company—depending on which party drew up the contract. In this situation, one party agrees to indemnify the other party for everything. Since there is rarely a situation where this sort of indemnification is reasonable, such contracts should be renegotiated.

Finally, one of the most important parts of the contract addresses *termination*—what the parties do if things go wrong or if one or both of the parties no longer wishes to go forward. Relevant issue are: what to do if the work produced by the production company is substandard or late; what to do if the client does not pay the production company on time or at all; what to do if one of the parties goes out of business; what to do if one or both of the parties wants to cease production. The contract can define the terms under which the contract can be terminated, such as failure to deliver and failure to pay. In these situations, the contract must state what to do upon termination. For example, does the client keep all materials delivered up until the point of termination? Must the company return all unfinished materials in their current state? How is final payment to be handled? Note that contracts sometimes include a clause stating that one of the parties can terminate without any reason at all. For example, the client might include a clause that states that they can choose to terminate at any time, without cause, and if so, the client might agree to generously compensate the production company for services rendered thus far and agree that ownership of the product remains with the production company. There may be a situation where the client and production company have a perfectly good working relationship, but outside factors might cause a termination; a well-defined contract will set out termination conditions that are mutually agreeable to both parties, so that their working relationship is not destroyed.

Production

The *production* phase of the overall production process is the time during which the actual parts of the final product are built. Typically, this phase is the most time-consuming part of the overall process. Production includes shooting scenes if the production contains live action shots, creating animation if the production contains computer or traditional animation, recording and mixing sound, and synchronizing the sound and the picture.

During production, all of the plans and designs agreed upon during preproduction are used to guide the film- or video-making process. Hence, the work done during preproduction is critical to the success of the final product. During production, changes made to the original plan often cost time and money, and can cause negative side effects. For example, suppose that during the preproduction process of a computer animation, an original scene is designed to include a static flag. The budget and schedule, therefore, reflect the type of tools and techniques needed to create the scene. Suppose that during production, it is decided that the flag will have to blow in the wind. This is a small but non-trivial request. Furthermore, the side effects of such a seemingly small change can be extensive—for example, other objects in the scene may need to blow in the wind as well. Thus, design changes during production can have very costly effects and should be avoided.

More and more, the production process involves both live action and computer animation. Therefore, it is important that the computer animator understand all aspects of the process. This section presents the overall production process, with an emphasis on computer animation.

Sound Tracks and Dope Sheets

The production process usually begins with the recording of a *sound track,* that is, the recorded sound to be used in the final product. It is common for an initial sound track to be rough, so it is called a *scratch track.* The scratch track is used as a guide, usually involves amateur voice artists and minimal use of musical instruments to create a rhythm and beat, and eventually gets replaced with a final recording. For the most part, sound production usually leads picture production, and the visuals are then synchronized to the music and dialogue. This is especially true in cases where animated characters speak; voices are recorded and analyzed before the characters are animated and synchronized to the voices. In situations where the sound track is recorded after the animation, the sound track is referred to as a *postsync track;* in this case, animators are provided with times to be used as a guide when animating.

The sound track is also read, that is, listened to on a frame-by-frame basis, and transcribed onto a dope sheet (see Figure 15.13). The transcription is presented in either a horizontal or vertical format, which maps individual words and syllables onto the time line. For example, every word of a 30-second television commercial, containing 720 film frames or 900 video frames, is mapped onto a chart, which has either 720 or 900 frames. The syllables of each word are mapped to their corresponding frame, so that the animator will know what mouth position to use.

Figure 15.13 Overleaf: The sound track is transcribed onto a bar sheet, which specifies exactly when each word of the script will be heard in the final production.

The initial dope sheet is then expanded, creating a slightly more detailed shot layout, which contains an indication of where and when the imagery occurs. In this action-planning phase, a diagram of the imagery is mapped onto the dope sheet, parallel to the sound. The doping shows all shots, all actions, all camera actions, and all camera transitions and where they begin and end on a frame-by-frame basis.

Animatics

The creation of an *animatic* is often the next step in the process. An animatic is a rough approximation of the final product, created by recording individual storyboard panels in synchronization with the sound track. An animatic provides an impression of the final show as it will exist in time and presents an opportunity to review pacing. Animatics are used in live action films as well as animation; in live action, as shots are produced, they are spliced into the animatic, effectively making an initial workprint of the production.

Artwork Creation and Model Construction

At this point in the process, the artwork is created. When a production involves cel animation, the animators draw the key frames. If the product includes 3D computer animation, models are constructed. This stage may also require that artwork be scanned into or printed from the computer. If type is required, then it is created; if live action shots are required, then props and sets are made; if effects are required, then they are generated.

In animation that involves hand drawings, the creation of artwork sometimes includes inking, that is, the process of applying ink

CLIENT SCIENTIFIC AMERICAN	DATED March 21, 2001	TV COPY
PRODUCT	STATION	
COMM'L NO. "CRICHTON"	LENGTH :30	MARSTELLER INC.

866 THIRD AVE. NEW YORK, N.Y. 10022

VIDEO — AUDIO

ANNOUNCER: 24 Michael Crichton makes the 47 future happen.

64 He's a Harvard Med School grad who operates on the imagination. 137

142 As an author and film maker. 174

192 Crichton's works include 216 The Andromeda Strain, Terminal Man, 258 The Great Train Robbery. 293

305 All became major motion pictures. 342

360 Crichton's fiction brings the future into focus. 420

430 And he reads 444 SCIENTIFIC AMERICAN. 470

480 As a working tool, for background, for pleasure. 540

551 To reach Crichton and two million other readers each month.. 625

SUPER: 643 SCIENTIFIC AMERICAN 665

676 We reach the people who make the future happen. 714

CW-Kevin O'Neill

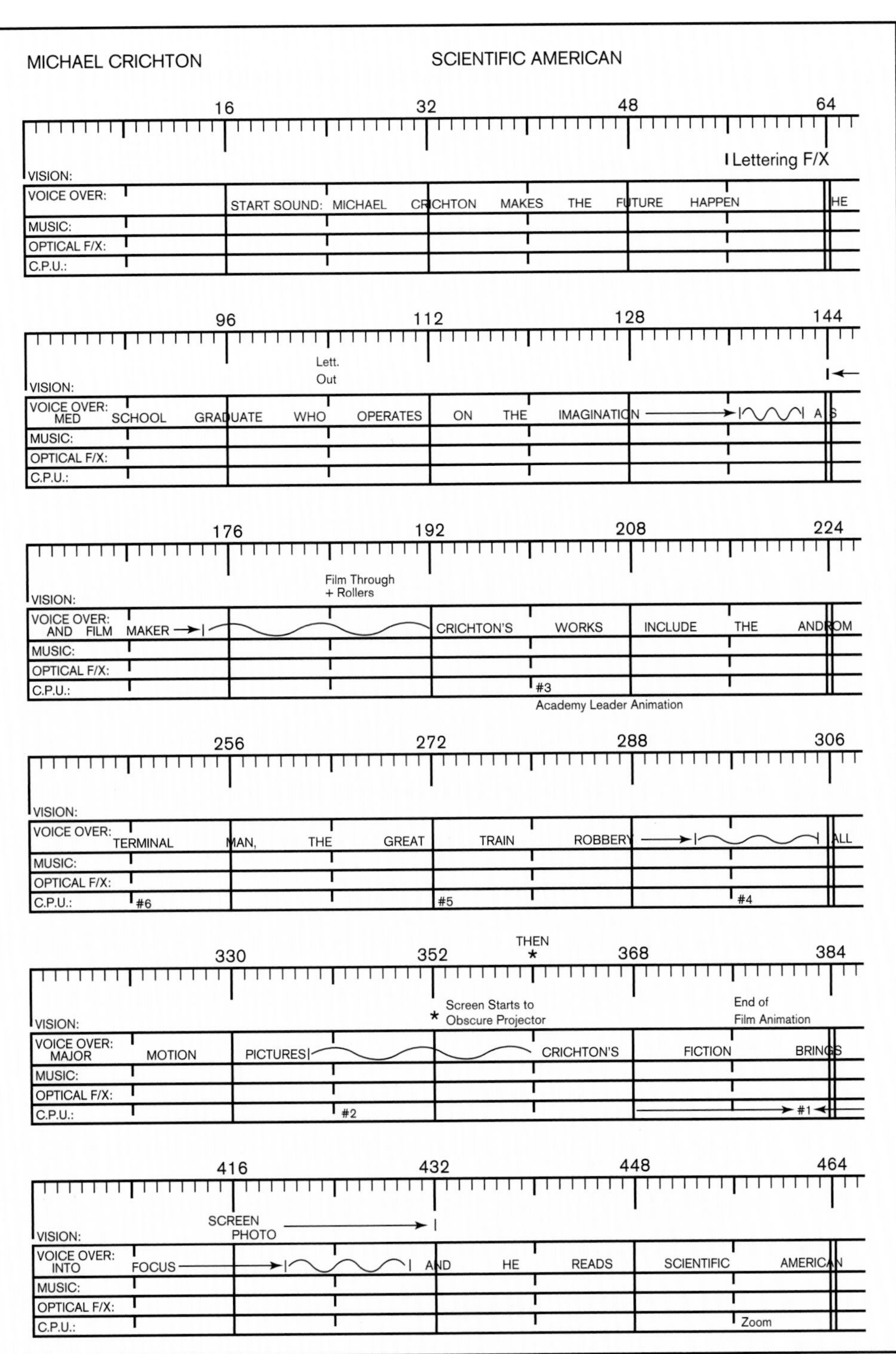
MICHAEL CRICHTON
SCIENTIFIC AMERICAN
16 32 48 64
Lettering F/X
VISION:
VOICE OVER: START SOUND: MICHAEL CRICHTON MAKES THE FUTURE HAPPEN HE
MUSIC:
OPTICAL F/X:
C.P.U.:
96 112 128 144
Lett. Out
VISION:
VOICE OVER: MED SCHOOL GRADUATE WHO OPERATES ON THE IMAGINATION AS
MUSIC:
OPTICAL F/X:
C.P.U.:
176 192 208 224
Film Through + Rollers
VISION:
VOICE OVER: AND FILM MAKER CRICHTON'S WORKS INCLUDE THE ANDROM
MUSIC:
OPTICAL F/X:
C.P.U.: #3
Academy Leader Animation
256 272 288 306
VISION:
VOICE OVER: TERMINAL MAN, THE GREAT TRAIN ROBBERY ALL
MUSIC:
OPTICAL F/X:
C.P.U.: #6 #5 #4
THEN
330 352 368 384
* Screen Starts to Obscure Projector
End of Film Animation
VISION:
VOICE OVER: MAJOR MOTION PICTURES CRICHTON'S FICTION BRINGS
MUSIC:
OPTICAL F/X:
C.P.U.: #2 #1
416 432 448 464
SCREEN PHOTO
VISION:
VOICE OVER: INTO FOCUS AND HE READS SCIENTIFIC AMERICAN
MUSIC:
OPTICAL F/X:
C.P.U.: Zoom

outlines (or their digital equivalent) onto cels. The ink can be applied to the cels by hand, by computer, by photocopy machine, or by some other manner. Inking is often followed by a step where the *opaquer* applies opaque watercolor paint onto the reverse side of each cell, usually in a color-by-number fashion. This can be done by hand or by computer.

Once the artwork is created, the next step involves setting the camera, artwork, and actors/characters into position. For the in-between process, this step involves initial and terminal positions within each shot. Any and all kinematics and dynamics must be defined, that is, how objects and cameras will move, including rates of change, acceleration, and deceleration.

Motion Studies, Pencil Tests, and Motion Previews

The next step of production is referred to by several names: *motion studies, pencil tests,* and *motion previews.* It is the part of the process when the motion is tested for accuracy. In 2D animation, the objects are set into motion and analyzed for corrections and improvements. In 3D computer animation, virtual models and the virtual camera are placed into the virtual world and set to move. As the models and camera move, the details of every movement is analyzed to determine correctness of motion. Depending on the available technology, previews of 3D computer animation can be done in real time using wire-frame models or low-resolution shaded models. For tests, the viewing window can be small or large. For higher-resolution cases, the preview needs to be built in non-real time before it can be previewed in real time.

For all forms of animation, once the motion study is perfected, it is spliced into the corresponding segment of the animatic. In a product with many scenes, the animatic will increasingly include more of the perfected motion studies, eventually creating the workprint.

Lighting

Lighting is another step in the process, involving the illumination of objects and the effect that illumination has on the look of the scene (see Figure 15.14). It involves colors, often of different intensities, from different locations, often with different degrees of focus. Not all production requires artificial lighting—for example, live action productions that involve natural lighting and wire-frame computer graphics animation, which is usually not lit.

Lights are positioned and oriented in particular directions. In computer animation, lighting is closely associated with surface properties such as color, reflection, luster, texture, and pattern. The characteristics of the lighting, such as position, can also be modified, creating animated lighting effects. Like set design, lighting is a rich craft, and it sets the mood of the piece.

Figure 15.14 Lighting is critical for most productions. It defines the overall quality of the scene and creates atmosphere. Here is a still image from Petrosain's *Rainforest* scene.

Rendering

Rendering is the process that gives representation to surface and light (see Figure 15.15). The rendering step often proceeds concurrently with the animation process. It is a batch process that involves the animator, the client, and the director. Because rendering is time-consuming, at first only key frames are rendered and presented to the animator, the client, and the director, who give feedback, fine tuning, or approval. With feedback taken into consideration, the process continues. The cycle continues until the rendering is complete.

Takes

Toward the final stages of production, ***takes*** are created. A take is a given version of a shot. In computer animation, in order to save time, takes are often rendered at resolutions lower than the intended resolution of the final product, especially if they are complicated. Low-resolution takes are brought to the client for approval before final-resolution takes are rendered. When the low-resolution takes are approved, then full-resolution final takes are made.

A common computer animation production problem is the creation of final takes too soon in the process. What is often needed are more rendering and more motion studies. Otherwise, an enormous amount of time can be wasted doing takes with resolutions that are way too high, way too soon. It is usually best to do small-scale tests, for example at 240 pixels wide, so that the rendering time is fast. Many types of errors and flaws can be detected at low resolutions. Plus, if a test can be rendered at a quarter of the final size, then it will take a quarter of the time to render, and hence four times as many tests can be done in the same amount of time. Once a low-resolution test is approved, the test can be rerendered at a higher or final resolution. It is important to remember that a 320-pixel-wide rendering takes one quarter of the time of a 640-pixel-wide rendering, which takes 16 times longer than the time needed to render a 160-pixel-wide test—the difference can mean a turnaround of the test three or four times in a business day compared to a turnaround once every two days, which is a very big difference.

Checking

Checking is a quality-control and correctness examination that occurs prior to postproduction. The checker inspects the parts created thus far to make sure that all frames are accounted for, all backgrounds are correct, all colors are consistent, and dopings sensible. The checker also insures that elements being composited fit together correctly. Failing to carefully inspect the work product and having defective work flow forward in production can be particularly costly.

Postproduction

Postproduction is the part of the overall production process when all of the parts made during production are assembled into a final product.

Editing

After final takes are created, they are viewed and analyzed very carefully. Once they are complete, they are shown to the client. If the work is part of a series of scenes, then the work is edited together and, if need be, composited. These processes are described in Chapter 7.

During postproduction, fades, dissolves, double exposures, wipes, and titles are constructed, all by combining existing material into a new-generation copy or dub, which includes all effects. For film, this used to be done with optical photography; now for both film and video, it is done by digitizing scenes and rerecording them. Often, this final generation is color-corrected to harmonize the scenes.

Sound tracks and voice dialogues are mixed together and then synchronized to the imagery; workprints are made, screened, examined, and fine-tuned; the final master is created; and copies of it are made and distributed.

Figure 15.15 Rendering gives representation to surface and light. The figure presents a still image from Petrosain's *Oil Rig* scene.

Paperwork and Cleanup

The final steps of the process can include billing, returning materials to the client, cleaning off disk drives, backing up and archiving the work, cleaning out file folders and storing any important papers, finalizing databases, analyzing finances, and possibly performing business analysis to determine whether the production was profitable. It is important to close the project in an orderly fashion so that the next project can begin effectively, and so that in the event that there is a sequel project or if the client wants something changed, the materials associated with the project can be easily retrieved.

Often associated with the paperwork is a list of credits naming everyone who worked on the project, and a press release announcing the product (see Figure 15.16). At the end of the process, it might also be necessary to mend some of the working relationships (see Figure 15.17). By its very nature, the structure of the production process can create adversarial relationships; the production company may want to produce as little as possible for as much money as possible, and the client may want to receive as much product as possible for as little money as possible. This structure can cause friction, and therefore the working relationship may need to be mended so that an ongoing relationship ensues.

A Word of Caution

During production, it is important to remember that it is possible to build professional-quality products that are not necessarily perfect. This does not mean that one should not quest for perfection. Rather, one should be humble about trying to achieve it. The reason for this is that as one gets closer and closer to achieving perfection,

Figure 15.16 Opposite: A press release announces the product, and often includes the names of significant people involved in the production. It never hurts to include too many names.

the cost of getting even closer to perfect skyrockets—it is the law of diminishing returns. In fact, the last 1% of the perfect product might cost as much as the first 99% of the job, which is probably not the best way to spend money, especially if the details of what is perceived as "perfection" are too small to be noticed. It is important to learn what level of quality is required of a particular medium and audience, and, from an artistic and business point of view, it is important to achieve this level of quality and not spend excessive time, effort, and money trying to achieve a quality that goes above and beyond professional excellence.

It is also important to remember that the production process is about building a product that is needed by the client. Production crews need to remember that the job is not to build what they, themselves, want, but to build according to the client's requests. This is especially true in advertising where the advertiser really does know their customers best.

Production Staffing Model

Production, to some extent, may be segregated into people who create content, and people who integrate content into a product. People who create content include writers, photographers, graphic designers, illustrators, animators, videographers, songwriters, and sound effects specialists. People who process this content into a product include editors, proofreaders, scanner and color-correction specialists, video digitizers, sound editors, and programmers. And who manages all of these people and processes? Typically, management is coordinated by a producer, who assembles and manages the finances of the project, and by a director, who manages the creative assembly.

There is no one staffing model that covers all computer animation studios. They vary from organizations employing hundreds of people to one-person studios. Hence, this section presents the discussion of staffing in terms of functionality rather than in terms of a typical company.

The Producer and Production Manager

Of paramount importance in the staffing model is the *producer,* the person who is responsible for the finances of a project. In a feature-film organization, the producer is the person who raises the money

Digital Effects Inc. 321 West 44th New York, N.Y. 10036 (212) 581-7760 March 1, 2001

PRESS RELEASE

DIGITAL EFFECTS GOES TO BRAZIL FOR FORD ESCORT SHOOT

NEW YORK: A unique sixty second spot has been completed by Digital Effects Inc. for Ford/Brazil through J. Walter Thompson which utilizes Digital Effects advanced image generating capabilities and live action photography.

Designer/Director, Jeffrey Kleiser, supervised the shoot in Sao Paulo which involved a specialized form of blue screen photography unique to this project. "The real challenge was lighting the car, an ESCORT, in such a way as to allow clean mattes to be derived from the negative while keeping the blue background from spilling onto the silver finish, which tended to be highly reflective," said Kleiser.

A futuristic computer generated city was created to insert behind the live action photography of the car. The idea is that upon entering a new Escort, one enters a "new dimension." Only through optical compositing of live and computer generated imagery could such an effect be realized.

Digital Effects Chief Animator, Don Leich, was responsible for building the sophisticated databases of the ultra-modern building in the cityscape and programming the animation.

The Brazilian studio work was produced by Espiral Cinema under the direction of George Jonas. The Director of Cinematography was Kimihiko Kato.

For J. Walter Thompson, Jose Caetano was Art Director; Raul Cruz, Copywriter; Claudio Correa, Creative Director; Nelson Salles and Maria Herminia Weinstock were Consultants for Radio/TV.

For Ford Brazil, Tom Drake was General Sales Manager, Tom Shanahan, Marketing Manager, and CR Mesanelli, Advertising Manager.

For further information please contact DIGITAL EFFECTS INC. at 321 West 44th Street, NY, NY 10036. (212) 581-7760.

###

WUNDERMAN
WORLDWIDE

Rosebush Vision Corp.
25 West 45th Street
New York, NY 10036

March 1, 2001

Dear Judson:

RE: "Seeing The Unseen" :120

Well, all the reviews are in now, so I thought you'd like to know how delighted everyone at Time-Life Books and Wunderman was with our computer spot.

I have to confess to you that at the outset of this project, I was more than a little dubious about our prospects, considering our limited budget and the time available. But thanks to you and your crew, the spot surpassed my wildest expectations.

I would like to take this opportunity to extend my personal thanks to the boys and girls in room 1203 – to Gail, Dave, Lester, and Michael for all the painstaking work that went into programming the spot. Also, to Dick Rauh for the wonderful 2-D animation and Dick Swanek for putting it all together. And of course, to Gwen who remained forever helpful and cheerful.

Finally, I would like to thank you, Judson – it was your true professionalism that held us all together when shoes didn't quite fit and mattes didn't quite match. But most of all, it was your vision and direction that made our commercial work so well.

Sincerely,

Stephen

Stephen Labovsky

cc Judy Keane
Fred Slobodin
Joan Barton

Wunderman/New York 575 Madison Avenue New York New York 10022 Telephone (212) 909-0100 and who supervises the hiring, and who is ultimately the boss. In a smaller production company, an advertising agency, or a video house that is doing computer animation, the producer might be called a *production manager* or *operations manager.* If the production staff is already part of the company's staff, then the producer's responsibilities focus less on raising money and more on administrating during production, budgeting for time and materials, and overseeing the project to monitor the progress in terms of time and money. Pragmatically speaking, as a person becomes less of a producer and more of a production manager, they become more concerned with tactical concerns, such as deciding how many candelabra must be used on the set, rather than strategic concerns, such as finding individuals to finance the project.

Figure 15.17 Opposite: Mending relationships. At the end of production, it is often necessary to mend working relationships; thank-you letters are often part of the process.

Upon the receipt of a script and storyboard, the production manager performs a *functional decomposition* of the project. That is, the production manager counts the number of shots, sets, setups (each set may be shot several ways—a setup is the set with a specific camera position and lighting), analyzes and possibly itemizes the components of a set, and enumerates the characters. The production manager will also create a list of tasks that need to be done, that is, break the project into craft-specific jobs. Tasks include modeling of objects, rendering, creating action, recording sound, and performing postproduction activities. In order to impose a structure, tasks can be organized in a variety of ways—for example, in terms of foreground and background object production, or in terms of sets and props production. This sort of structure is appropriate because, depending on how they are organized, objects have a different level of importance in the final project, so their treatment during production varies accordingly. For example, if a product being sold is the foreground object, then the background is simply a means to support that product. Other types of functional decomposition might include the identification of the texture map tasks, for example, the creation of 2D artwork that is to be mapped onto the model of the product, or the creation of 2D artwork that is to be mapped onto the set models.

The result of functional decomposition is a set of lists of tasks associated with everything that has to be made. The producer or production manager will keep track of the project from concept through completion, using the lists to monitor the process.

The Director

The *director* is the person who orchestrates the visual aspects of the project, works with and reports to the producer, and possibly assists with the functional decomposition. A director can be thought of in two different ways—one that originated during the early years of film and one that has come into being more recently. From the early definition, the director is the person who assembles the pieces of the project in a visually creative manner. First and foremost, the director is responsible for action. The director is also an artist and a craftsperson, and must be trained in the graphic arts, motion picture composition, sound, character design, timing, camera and character movement, action, and kinematics. While directors are responsible for assembling the parts, they are not responsible for the design or the visionary aspects of the parts. In this model, their role is to bring the script to life. The more recent definition of "director" incorporates the concept of visionary; hence a director today can also be responsible for the overall creative success of the project.

Normally, the creative production staff reports to the director, and the director reports to the producer. The creative production staff, including the camera operator, lighting person, modelers, and actors (real or synthetic), report to the director with creative issues. However, creative staff might report to the producer with administrative issues. The producer tends not to make creative decisions, such as those regarding modeling and lighting; this is the job of the director.

The Art Director

Assisting the director toward the goal of completing the task is, first and foremost, the *art director*. The art director is responsible for the look of the imagery that is produced, the composition of the shots, and the styling of the sets. Art directors are hired based on their ability to create a particular look, whether it be contemporary, gothic, or baroque; cheerful, haunting, or mysterious. The art director decides which visual elements are to be used in order to achieve the look, and so must understand all visual elements, including text, color, composition, costuming, and texture. When directing computer animation, the art director must also understand concepts related to computer imaging—for example, the different looks that can be achieved through the use of different modeling techniques. Decisions made by the art director are often written up into a set of guidelines, which are followed throughout production. In large studios, the art director defines the look and manages the creative production staff to create the corresponding imagery. In a smaller studio, the art director might actually be responsible for production.

The Production Staff

The ***production staff*** is the group of people who produce the final product. This staff can include blueprint artists, animators, and production assistants. All of these people work together under the direction of the art director and director to create the pieces needed in order to assemble the final product.

Proceeding in the order of the production process, the first person on staff is the ***blueprint artist***, who looks at the storyboard sketches and from them constructs blueprints of the actual objects and sets to be made. Sometimes, the blueprint artist can be eliminated, especially if the objects being constructed are computer models; it is felt that the ***modeler***—that is, the person doing the modeling—is sufficient, particularly if the software allows the creation of plans and elevations and has the capability to go back and forth between two and three dimensions. Once built, the 3D objects are handed off to a rendering operator, who is responsible for rendering, and setting the camera positions and lighting.

Concurrent with the job being done by the blueprint artist is a 2D image-assembly line, where ***2D artists*** fabricate and flow forward any 2D elements that are to be used in props or in the set. Such elements might include pictures on the wall, texture maps to be used in conjunction with 3D objects, and background paintings to be used instead of 3D sets.

Once the images and objects are constructed, the ***animator*** might be the next person involved in the process. This is the person responsible for creating the action and motion. For 2D images, it involves the creation of 2D cels that show a flow of action. For 3D models, it involves setting up the motion of the objects and the camera, and exercising the motion until it is right.

The division of labor is critical to the success of the production process. Because the labor is divided, the process can also be divided, so the process can be structured in such a way that certain tasks can be carried out in parallel. Moreover, *dummy art* is often used as place holders so that certain tasks, such as setting the lighting, can be carried out before the final artwork is ready. This structure is critical for an efficient use of time and therefore is financially prudent.

The Client, the Advertising Agency, and the Production Company

While there are many possible relationships between client, advertising agency, and production company, it is worth noting how these entities might interact. In situations where there is a client, it is the client who pays for the complete or partial product, and the others work for the client. In situations where an advertising agency is involved, it is usually the case that the client has hired the agency, and the agency is responsible for creating, designing, and writing the concept or commercial. It is the agency who has the day-to-day relationship with the client, understands their needs, and devises vehicles to fulfill those needs. Therefore the agency, which understands the entire picture, hires the production company, which, in turn, produces the product. While the production company may be especially creative, its job is often simply to carry out the creative ideas of a client or agency. Hence, in a situation where there is an agency, the producer of the project at large often resides with the agency. It is also possible that the director resides with the agency. However, for special projects—for example, a completely computer-generated commercial—the director may reside with the production company. In fact, sometimes computer animation production companies are hired simply because of an in-house director. In situations where the producer and director reside outside the production company, there are typically an in-house producer and director to manager the project from inside the production company.

Afterword

Time, one of the underlying themes of this book, has also exerted its effects upon us as writers, as we have sought to share our experiences and research on the topic of computer animation. Like many things in the world around us, the tools of this craft are ever-changing, and it has been a challenge to keep this book current, even in its prepublication stages.

Our goal has been to bring you a book that, amidst the turmoil of change, is one you will cherish as a classic in your collection. Now that it is finished, we finally understand it may be impossible to write a book on computer animation that is relevant beyond the day it is printed. Nonetheless, we have tried to cut to the essence of a multitude of techniques (many developed before the computer was perfected) and present an atlas of concepts, techniques, and thinking about the craft. Because we have the hindsight of traditional methods, we believe that our treatments of them may be the only chance to contextualize them in the digital world, where formal notation replaces the ad hoc. We have also tried to provide a way of thought for the professional as well as the novice, and to approach an art and craft that is one of the great achievements of the last half of the 20th century.

We sometimes forget that the magic wrought by animators is to create images out of nothingness. It is a task worthy of sorcerers, illusionists, and artists, especially when the images become realistic, 3D, and flowing in real time. When our interaction with them versus our interaction with the real world becomes blurred, then a certain line has been crossed. We are engaged in a pact to alter the fabric of society. Our contributions include the transference of consciousness—the "suspension of disbelief"—that has always been a part of cave art ritual, theater, movies, and television.

It has become clear that computer animation, as a craft unto itself, is a sort of way station to a future reality in which what was once considered science fiction is rapidly becoming social fact. As a

From *Bunny*, a short animated film by Chris Wedge.

tool, computer animation has become an integral part of a myriad of applications—from designing and building airplanes before they are physically realized, to resurrecting dinosaurs for the movies. Psychologically, some of the most potent possibilities lie in the fusion of computer animation with interactive techniques that propel users into a shared virtual reality that they can freely navigate.

The tactics of the new world order are filled with surprises. Who, a decade ago, would have predicted the explosion of the Web and its potential for interactive 3D graphics, in which people from all over the world participate in shared virtual experiences? Who would have predicted the radical changes in the Web business model, with its concepts of traffic management, click-through banners, and search engines?

The downside of this revolution is that we need to learn—constantly. As downsides go, things could be a lot worse. And as for the upside, just look ahead of you. Contemplate the possibilities. Get courage. Go for it.

Recommended Reading

Abramson, Albert. *The History of Television, 1880–1941,* McFarland, Jefferson, NC, 1987.

Adamson, Joe. *Tex Avery: King of Cartoons,* Da Capo Press, Cambridge, MA, 1985.

Alhazen (Ibn al Haitam). *Opticae,* Thesaurus Alhazeni Arabis, 1038; Basel, 1572.

Allen, F. A. "Maintaining Knowledge About Temporal Intervals," *Communications of the ACM* 26 (11), 1983, 832–843.

Barrier, Michael. *Hollywood Cartoons: American Animation in Its Golden Age,* Oxford University Press, 1999.

Battista della Porta, Giovanni. *Magia naturalis, sive de miraculis rerum naturalium,* Naples, 1558–1589.

Bendazzi, Giannalberto, and Anna Taraboletti-Segre (translator). *Cartoons: One Hundred Years of Cinema Animation,* Indiana University Press, 1996.

Billups, Scott. *Digital Moviemaking.* Michael Wiese Productions, CA, 2001.

Birn, Jeremy, and George Maestri (editor). *Digital Lighting & Rendering,* New Riders Publishing, Indianapolis, 2000.

Blinn, Jim. *Jim Blinn's Corner: Dirty Pixels,* Morgan Kaufmann Publishers, San Francisco, 1998.

Blinn, Jim. *Jim Blinn's Corner: A Trip Down the Graphics Pipeline,* Morgan Kaufmann Publishers, San Francisco, 1996.

Calder, Nigel. *Timescale: An Atlas of the Fourth Dimension,* Viking Press, New York, 1983.

Ceram, C. W. *Archeology of the Cinema,* Harcourt, Brace & World, New York, 1965.

Collier, Maxie D. *The IFILM Digital Video Filmmaker's Handbook 2001,* Lone Eagle Publishing Company, Los Angeles, 2001.

Computer Graphics Proceedings series, ACM SIGGRAPH, ACM Press, New York.

Crafton, Donald. *Before Mickey: The Animated Film 1898–1928,* University of Chicago Press, 1993.

Culhane, Shamus. *Talking Animals and Other People,* Da Capo Press, Cambridge, MA, 1998.

Culhane, Shamus. *Animation from Script to Screen,* St. Martin's Press, New York, 1990.

Cundy, H. Martyn, and A. P. Rollet. *Mathematical Models,* Oxford University Press, 1961.

Cunningham, Steve and Judson Rosebush. *Electronic Publishing for CD-ROM and Multimedia,* O'Reilly Publications, Sebastapol, CA, 1996.

Davidoff, Jules B. *Differences in Visual Perception,* Academic Press, New York, 1970.

DeFanti, Tom (editor). *Siggraph Video Review,* Association of Computing Machinery, New York, 1980 to present.

De Leeuw, Ben. *Digital Cinematography,* Morgan Kaufmann Publishers, San Francisco, 1997.

Del Tredici, Robert. *The History of Animated Film Resource Book,* Concordia University, Montreal, 1992.

Dull, Charles, H. Clark Metcalf, and William Brooks. *Modern Physics,* Holt, Reinhart and Winston, New York, 1955.

Dunn, Lynwood, and George E. Turner. *The ASC Treasury of Visual Effects,* The American Society of Cinematographers, Hollywood, 1983.

Durrett, John. *Color in the Computer,* Academic Press, Harcourt Brace Jovanovich, New York, 1987.

Eberly, David H. *3D Game Engine Design: A Practical Approach to Real-Time Computer Graphics,* Morgan Kaufmann Publishers, San Francisco, 2000.

Ebert, David S., F. Kenton Musgrave, Darwyn Peachey, Steven Worley, and Ken Perlin. *Texturing and Modeling,* Morgan Kaufmann Publishers, San Francisco, 1998.

Encyclopedia Britannica, Chicago, 1955. Articles on mathematical instruments, mathematical models, mathematical notations, matrices, mechanics, and general mathematics.

Encyclopedia Britannica, "Geometry, Analytic and Trigonometric," Chicago, 1979.

Encyclopedia Britannica, "Machines and Machine Components," Chicago, 1979.

Eves, Howard. "Curves and Surfaces," in *Standard Mathematical Tables,* Samuel Selby (editor), CRC Press, Cleveland, 1974.

Faigin, Gary. *The Artist's Complete Guide to Facial Expression,* Watson-Guptill Publications, Toronto, Canada, 1990.

Felding, Raymond. *The Technique of Special Effects Cinematography,* Hastings House, New York, 1965.

Fielding, Raymond (editor). *A Technological History of Motion Pictures and Television,* University of California Press, Berkeley, 1967.

Finch, Christopher. *The Art of Walt Disney,* Abrams, New York, 1973.

Fleming, Bill. *Advanced 3D Photorealism Techniques,* John Wiley & Sons, New York, 1999.

Fleming, Bill. *3D Modeling & Surfacing,* Morgan Kaufmann Publishers, San Francisco, 1999.

Fleming, Bill, and Darris Dobbs. *Animating Facial Features and Expressions,* Charles River Media, Hingham, MA, 1998.

The Focal Encyclopedia of Film and Television Techniques, Focal Press, London and New York, 1969.

Foley, James D., Andries van Dam, Steven K. Feiner, and John F. Hughes. *Computer Graphics: Principles and Practice,* second edition, Addison-Wesley Publishing Co., Reading, MA, 1992.

Fraioli, James. *Storyboarding 101: A Crash Course in Professional Storyboarding,* Michael Wiese Productions, CA, 2000.

Franke, Herbert. *Computer Graphics Computer Art,* second edition, Springer-Verlag, Berlin, 1985.

Furniss, Maureen. *Art in Motion: Animation Aesthetics,* John Libbey & Co Ltd., London, 1998.

Gallier, Jean H. *Curves and Surfaces in Geometric Design: Theory and Algorithms,* Morgan Kaufmann Publishers, San Francisco, 1999.

Gardner, Martin. *The Annotated Alice,* Bramhall House Books, Clarkson N. Potter, New York, 1960.

Gascoigne, Robert Mortimer. *A Chronology of the History of Science, 1450–1900,* Gerland Publishing, New York and London, 1987.

Gifford, Denis. *American Animated Films: The Silent Era, 1897–1929,* McFarland and Company, Jefferson, NC, 1990.

Gifford, Denis. *British Animated Films: 1895–1985,* McFarland and Company, Jefferson, NC, 1987.

Giloth, Copper and Lynn Pocock-Williams. "A Selected Chronology of Computer Art: Exhibitions, Publications, and Technology," *Art Journal,* Vol. 49, No. 3, pp. 283–297, College Arts Association, New York, 1990.

Glassner, Andrew S. *Andrew Glassner's Notebook: Recreational Computer Graphics,* Morgan Kaufmann Publishers, San Francisco, 1999.

Goodman, Cynthia. *Digital Visions, Computers and Art,* Abrams, New York, 1987.

Halas, John (editor). *Computer Animation,* Hastings House, New York, 1974.

Halas, John. *Graphics in Motion,* Van Nostrand Reinhold, New York, 1981.

Halas, John. *Masters of Animation,* Salem House, Topsfield, MA, 1987.

Halas, John, and Roger Manvell. *The Technique of Film Animation,* Hastings House, New York, 1968.

Hale, Judson (editor). *Old Farmer's Almanac,* Yankee Publishing, Dublin, NH, 1991.

Hambly, Maya. *Drawing Instruments,* Sotheby's Publications, Philip Wilson Publishers Ltd., London, 1988.

Hart, John. *The Art of the Storyboard: Storyboarding for Film, TV, and Animation,* Focal Press, Woburn, MA, 1999.

Haviland, Robert. *Build It Book of Digital Clocks,* Tab Books, PA, 1986.

Heiserman, David. *Experiments in Four Dimensions,* Tab Books, PA, 1983.

Herr , Laurin and Judson Rosebush. HDTV and the Quest for Virtual Reality, SIGGRAPH Video Review #45 (two one-hour programs), Association for Computing Machinery, New York, 1990.

Holman, Bruce. *Puppet Animation in the Cinema,* A. S. Barnes and Co., South Brunswick and New York, 1975.

Hooks, Ed. *Acting for Animators,* Heinemann Publishing, Westport, CT, 2001.

Hurtenberg, Richard S., and Jacques Denavit. *Kinematic Synthesis of Linkages,* McGraw-Hill, New York, 1964.

International Teleproduction Society, *Handbook of Recommended Standards and Practices,* New York.

Jasmin, Pierre. "Human Treatment of Temporal Information," in Rosebush, *Advanced Computer Animation,* SIGGRAPH, Association for Computing Machinery, New York, 1987.

Johnson, Dave. *How to Use Digital Video,* Sams Publishing, Indianapolis, 2000.

Kerlow, Isaac Victor. *The Art of 3-D: Computer Animation and Imaging,* second edition, John Wiley & Sons, New York, 2000.

Kerlow, Isaac Victor and Judson Rosebush. *Computer Graphics for Designer and Artists,* Van Nostrand Reinhold, New York, 1985, second edition 1994.

Kilmer, David (editor). *The Animated Film Collector's Guide: Worldwide Sources for Cartoons on Videotape and Laserdisc,* John Libbey & Co Ltd., London, 1997.

Kircher, Athanasius. *Ars Magna Lucis et Umbrae (The Great Art of Light and Shadow),* Rome, 1646, Amsterdam, 1671.

Knowlton, Kenneth. *A Computer Technique for the Production of Animated Movies,* Bell Telephone Labs, New Jersey, 1964.

Kramer, Edward. "Analog to Digital Conversion: A History of Video Animation," in *Computer Animation Using Video Techniques,* SIGGRAPH Course Notes #9, Anaheim, CA, 1987.

Lasseter, John. "Principles of Traditional Animation Applied to 3D Animation." *Computer Graphics,* Volume 21, Number 4, July 1987.

Lauzzana, R.G. and Lynn Pocock-Williams. "A Rule System for Analysis in the Visual Arts," *Leonardo,* Vol. 21, No. 4, pp. 445–452, Journal of the International Society for Arts, Sciences and Technology, Pergamon Press, Great Britain, 1988.

Laybourne, Kit. *The Animation Book,* Crown Books, New York, 1979.

Laybourne, Kit. *The Animation Book: A Complete Guide to Animated Filmmaking—From Flip-Books to Sound Cartoons to 3-D Animation,* Three Rivers Press, New York, 1998.

Leavitt, Ruth (editor). *Artist and Computer,* Harmony Books, New York, 1976.

Lee, Robert, and Robert Misiorowski. *Script Models,* Hastings House, New York, 1978.

Levitan, Eli L. *Handbook Animation Techniques,* Van Nostrand Reinhold, New York, 1979.

Lewis, William D., Henry S. Canby, and Thomas K. Brown. *The Winston Simplified Dictionary,* John C. Winston Company, Philadelphia, 1929.

Lindsay, Peter, and Donald A. Norman. *Human Information Processing,* Academic Press, New York, 1972.

Long, Ben, and Sonja Schenk. *The Digital Filmmaking Handbook* (with CD-ROM), Charles River Media, Hingham, MA, 2000.

Lord, Peter, and Brian Sibley. *Creating 3-D Animation: The Aardman Book of Filmmaking,* Harry Abrams, New York, 1998.

Lutz, Edwin George. *Animated Cartoons: How They Are Made, Their Origin and Development,* Applewood Books, Bedford, MA, 1998.

Madsen, Roy. *Animated Film,* Interland Press, New York, 1970.

Maestri, George. *Digital Character Animation 2: Essential Techniques,* New Riders Publishing, Indianapolis, 1999.

Malina, Frank J. (editor). *Kinetic Art Theory and Practice,* Dover Publications, New York, 1974.

Maltin, Leonard. *Of Mice and Magic: A History of American Animated Cartoons,* New American Library, New York, 1990.

Martin, Andre. "Origines et Age d'or du dessin Anime Americain 1906–1941," *Cinematheque Quebecoise,* Montreal, 1967.

Martin, Quigley, Jr. *Magic Shadows,* Harcourt, Brace & World, New York, 1965.

Menache, Alberto. *Understanding Motion Capture for Computer Animation and Video Games,* Morgan Kaufmann Publishers, San Francisco, 1999.

Menzel, Donald, and Jay Pasachoff. *A Field Guide to the Stars and Planets,* Houghton Mifflin Company, Boston, 1983.

Millerson, Gerald. *Video Production Handbook,* Focal Press, London, 1987.

Moller, Tomas, and Eric Haines, *Real-Time Rendering,* A. K. Peters Ltd., Natick, MA, 1999.

Muybridge, Eadweard. *Horses and Other Animals in Motion,* Dover Publications, Mineola, NY, 1985.

Muybridge, Eadweard. *The Male and Female Figure in Motion: 60 Classic Sequences,* Dover Publications, Mineola, NY, 1984.

Muybridge, Eadweard, and Anita V. Mozley (designer). *Muybridge's Complete Human and Animal Locomotion: All 781 Plates from the 1887 Animal Locomotion (volumes 1–4),* Dover Publications, Mineola, NY, 1979.

Muybridge, Eadweard, and Lewis S. Brown (editor). *Animals in Motion,* Dover Publications, Mineola, NY, 1957.

Muybridge, Eadweard, and R. Taft (designer). *The Human Figure in Motion,* Dover Publications, Mineola, NY, 1989.

Myers, Dale K. *Computer Animation,* Oak Cliff Press Inc., Milford, MI, 1999.

Newman, William M., and Robert F. Sproull. *Principles of Interactive Computer Graphics,* McGraw-Hill, New York, 1979.

O'Rourke, Michael. *Principles of 3D Computer Animation: Modeling, Rendering, and Animating with 3D Computer Graphics,* W.W. Norton & Company, New York, 1998.

Perrin, Porter G. *Writer's Guide and Index to English,* Scott Foresman, Chicago, 1950.

Pilling, Jayne. *A Reader in Animation Studies,* John Libbey & Co Ltd., London, 1999.

Pocock, Lynn. Visual Proceedings, "Ongoings: The Fine Arts Gallery," ACM SIGGRAPH, Association for Computing Machinery, New York, 1997.

Pocock, Lynn, Guest Editor. Ongoings: SIGGRAPH 97 The Fine Arts Gallery Slide Set, ACM SIGGRAPH, Association for Computing Machinery, New York, 1997.

Pocock, Lynn. "Touchware: The SIGGRAPH 98 Art Gallery," Computer Graphics, ACM SIGGRAPH, Association for Computing Machinery, New York, November 1998.

Pocock, Lynn. *Leonardo* (cover image), Vol. 34, No. 2, Journal of the International Society for Arts, Sciences and Technology, The MIT Press, Cambridge, MA, 2001.

Pocock, Lynn and I. Benado. "Computer Graphics in Context: One Student's Project," "An Interview with Ken Snelson," Computer Graphics, ACM SIGGRAPH, Vol. 29, No. 1, Association for Computing Machinery, New York, February, 1995.

Pocock-Williams, Lynn. *Computer Graphics* (cover image), ACM SIGGRAPH, Vol. 22, No. 2, Association for Computing Machinery, New York, April 1988.

Pocock-Williams, Lynn. "Towards the Automatic Generation of Visual Music," *Leonardo*, Vol. 25, No. 1, pp. 29–36, Journal of the International Society for Arts, Sciences and Technology, Pergamon Press, Great Britain, 1992.

Pocock-Williams, Lynn. "A Certain Uncertainty," *Leonardo*, Volume 26, No. 3, p. 58, Journal of the International Society for Arts, Sciences and Technology, Pergamon Press, Great Britain, 1993.

Pocock-Williams, Lynn. "SIGGRAPH 93 The Small Animation Theaters," *Pixel Vision*, No. 11, pp. 43–45, New York, 1994.

Ratner, Peter. *3-D Human Modeling and Animation,* John Wiley & Sons, New York, 1998.

Ray, Sidney. *The Lens and All Its Jobs,* Focal Press, Woburn, MA, 1977.

Rea, Peter. "The Perception and Presentation of Time by Analog and Digital Formats," in Peter Wildbur, *Information Graphics,* Van Nostrand Reinholt, New York, 1989.

Read, Oliver, and Walter L. Welch. *From Tin Foil to Stereo,* Howard W. Sams and Co., Indianapolis, 1976.

Reichardt, Jasia. *Cybernetic Serendipity,* Praeger, New York, 1968.

Reuleaux, Franz. *The Kinematics of Machinery,* originally published by Macmillan and Company, London, 1876; currently published by Dover Publications, Mineola, NY, 1963.

Reynolds, Craig. *Advanced Computer Animation,* SIGGRAPH Course Notes, SIGGRAPH, Association for Computing Machinery, New York, 1985.

Reynolds, Craig. "Computer Animation with Scripts and Actors," *Computer Graphics,* Volume 16, Number 3, July 1982.

Rosebush, Judson. "Computer Animation: An Historical Survey," *NCGA Proceedings,* NCGA, Baltimore, 1981.

Rosebush, Judson. "Pixel Handbooks #1 through #13," *Pixel Vision*, New York, 1989–94.

Rosebush, Judson. Chronology of Computer Graphics, Association for Computing Machinery, New York, 1992

Rosebush, Judson. Computer Animation: 1960–1980, ACM SIGGRAPH Video Review (Video collection plus Filmography and Chronology), Association for Computing Machinery, New York, 1992, 1997.

Rosebush, Judson. *The Story of Computer Graphics* (film), Association for Computing Machinery, New York, 1998.

Rosebush, Judson, and Isaac Victor Kerlow. *Computer Graphics for Designers and Artists,* Van Nostrand Reinhold, New York, 1994.

Rosebush, Judson and Gwen Sylvan. Filmography of Computer Generated Film: 1960–1980, ACM SIGGRAPH and the SIGGRAPH Video Review, Association for Computing Machinery, New York, 1992, 1997.

Rosebush, Judson, Mark Voelpel, Bill Kroyer, Craig Reynolds, Mark Vickers, and Philippe Bergeron. "Annotated Bibliography Computer Animation," Advanced Computer Animation Course Notes, SIGGRAPH 86; also SIGGRAPH 85, Association for Computing Machinery, New York, 1985.

Rubin, Michael. *Nonlinear–A Field Guide to Digital Video and Film Editing,* Triad Publishing Co., Winfield, IL, 2000.

Russett, Robert, and Cecile Starr (editor). *Experimental Animation: Origins of a New Art,* Da Capo Press, Cambridge, MA, 1988.

Schott, Gaspar. *Treatise on the Magic Lantern,* circa 1690.

Siden, F. W. *Force, Mass, and Motion,* Bell Telephone Labs, New Jersey, 1965.

Simon, Mark. *Storyboards: Motion in Art,* Focal Press, Woburn, MA, 2000.

Speer, Rick, Bill Kovacs, and Ruth Kovacs. *An International Guide to Computer Animated Films,* Reseda, CA, 1979.

Stanton, Julia, and Michael Stanton. "Bibliography: Video Production Techniques," *SMPTE Journal,* August 1987.

Sweeney, Daniel. "The Age of Mechanical Television," *Perfect Vision,* issue 3, Indian Summer, 1987.

Tao, D. C. *Applied Linkages Synthesis,* Addison-Wesley, Reading, MA, 1964.

Tao, D. C. *Fundamentals of Applied Kinematics,* Addison-Wesley, Reading, MA, 1967.

Thalmann, Nadia, and Daniel Thalmann. *Computer Animation Theory and Practice,* Springer-Verlag, Tokyo, New York, 1985.

Thomas, Frank, and Ollie Johnston (contributor). *The Illusion of Life: Disney Animation,* Hyperion, England, 1995.

Utz, Peter. *Video User's Handbook,* second edition, Prentice-Hall, New York, 1989.

van Musselonbroek, Pieter. *Physicae Experimentalis,* Leyden, 1729, and Venice, 1756.

Vineyard, Jeremy, and Jose Cruz (illustrator). *Setting Up Your Shots,* Michael Wiese Productions, CA, 2000.

Ward, Peter. *Picture Composition for Film and Television,* Focal Press, Woburn, MA, 1996.

Watkins, Adam. *3D Animation: From Models to Movies* (with CD-ROM), Charles River Media, Hingham, MA, 2000.

Watt, Alan H., and Allan Watt. *3D Computer Graphics,* third edition, Addison-Wesley, Reading, MA, 2000.

Watt, Alan H., and Mark Watt (contributor). *Advanced Animation and Rendering Techniques: Theory and Practice,* Addison-Wesley, Reading, MA, 1992.

Wein, Marcelli, and Nestor Burtnyk. "Computer Animation," *Encyclopedia of Computer Science and Technology,* Marcel Dekker, New York, 1976.

Wells, Paul. *Understanding Animation,* Routledge, New York, 1998.

White, Tony. *The Animator's Workbook,* Watson-Guptill Publishing, Toronto, Canada, 1988.

Youngblood, Gene. *Expanded Camera,* E.P. Dutton & Co., New York, 1970.

Zajac, Ed. *Simulation of a Two-Gyro Gravity Gradient Attitude Control System,* Bell Telephone Labs, New Jersey, 1963.

Index

E

T

W

X

Y

Z

Figure Credits

Introduction, Chapter 11, and Afterword opener details courtesy of Blue Sky Studios, Inc.

Chapter 1 opener courtesy of Lynn Pocock.

Chapter 2 opener detail by Thomas Banchoff, David Laidlaw, Fred Bisshipp, and David Margolis at Brown University.

Chapter 3 opener courtesy of Nicholson NY.

Chapter 4, 9, 12, 14, and 15 opener details courtesy of Rythm and Hues Studios.

Chapter 10 opener detail courtesy of Flimsy Entertainment, Inc., copyright 1998. *www.flimsy.com.*

Chapter 12 opener courtesy of Gavin Miller and Ned Greene. Copyright 1993, Apple Computer, Inc.

Figures I.1, 1.1, 1.5–1.7, 1.10, 1.21, 1.22, 1.29, 1.36, 1.41, 2.6, 2.16, 3.5–3.7, 3.25, 3.40, 4.6, 4.9, 4.11, 4.12, 4.20, 13.22, and 15.8 based on illustrations by Lina Yamaguchi.

Figure I.2 based on an illustration by David Anderson Deane in *A Time for Love*, a film by Carlos Saldanha, 1994.

Figures I.3, I.4, and 3.20 based on illustrations by Lina Yamaguchi and David Anderson Deane.

Figures 1.14, 1.52, and 15.13 courtesy of Digital Effects, Inc.

Figures 1.15, 1.27, 1.28, 1.53, 1.54, and 1.57 courtesy of Lina Yamaguchi.

Figures 1.19, 1.20, 3.36, 3.37, 6.6, 7.12, 8.16, 8.23–8.26, 8.27, 13.4, 13.6–13.9, 13.14, 13.15, 13.19, 13.25, and 13.27 based on illustrations by David Anderson Deane.

Figures 1.23 based on an illustration by Isaac V. Kerlow and Andrew Holdun.

Figure 1.24 courtesy of Immersion Corporation.

Figure 1.31 courtesy of Cyberware, Monterey, California.

Figure 1.33, *Carolina*, courtesy of F. Kenton Musgrave.

Figure 1.35 courtesy of Wei-Yi Lin.

Figure 1.50, *Last Call*, courtesy of Jaime Castaneda.

Figure 1.55 from Raydream software.

Figure 1.60 courtesy of Blue Skies Studios.

Figure 2.10 based on a drawing from Jasmine, 1987, expanding on Allen, 1983.

Figures 2.12, 2.13–2.15, 2.18, 11.30, 11.52, and 11.53 based on illustrations by Gwen Sylvan.

Figure 2.19 courtesy of Michael Noll from "Computer Generated Three-Dimensional Movies," *Computers and Automation*, November 1965.

Figure 3.8 based on an illustration by Felipe Morales, Suk-Il Hong, and Lina Yamaguchi.

Figures 3.9, 3.29, 3.32, 3.35, 3.39, 4.1, 4.2, 4.10, 4.15, 5.1, 5.2, 5.4–5.6, 5.8, 5.9, 5.12, 5.13, 5.15, 5.16, 5.21, 5.22, 7.1, 7.2, 7.4–7.6, 7.8, 11.31, 11.36, 14.3, 14.4, 14.6, 14.7, and 14.11 based on illustrations by Luis A. Camargo.

Figure 3.12(b) (and Chapter 13 opener detail), *Coca Cola Jump*, courtesy of Rhythm and Hues Studios.

Figure 3.13 based on an illustration by Raymond Stivala, Luis Camargo, and Lina Yamaguchi.

Figure 3.14 based on an illustration by Raymond Stivala and Lina Yamaguchi.

Figure 3.15 based on an illustration by Dick Rauh and Raymond Stivala.

Figures 3.21 and 4.14 based on illustrations by Luis A. Camargo and Lina Yamaguchi.

Figures 3.22–3.24 based on illustrations by Felipe Morales and Kathy Konkle.

Figure 3.30 based on an illustration by Luis A. Camargo after Isaac V. Kerlow and Judson Rosebush.

Figure 3.38 based on an illustration by Brenda Garcia and Lina Yamaguchi.

Figures 4.3, 4.4, 7.10, and 7.11 based on illustrations by Joanna Morrison.

Figure 4.8 based on an illustration by Felipe Morales and William Costello.

Figure 4.13 based on an illustration by Dick Rauh, Suk-Il Hong, and Lina Yamaguchi.

Figure 4.16 based on an illustration by Dick Rauh, and Suk-Il Hong.

Figure 4.17 based on an illustration by Lina Yamaguchi and Wei Yi Lin.

Figure 4.18 based on an illustration by Suk-Il Hong.

Figure 4.19 based on an illustration by Suk-Il Hong and Lina Yamaguchi.

Figures 5.10, 5.20, 6.3, 6.7, 6.8(a), 6.13, 6.14, 6.16–6.18, 7.9, 8.1, 8.10, 8.12–8.15, 8.20, 9.2, 9.5, 9.8–9.10, and 9.12 based on illustrations by Khalida Lockheed.

Figure 5.14 courtesy of Tektronix, Inc.

Figure 6.4 based on an illustration by Sherwood Anderson and Luis A. Camargo.

Figures 8.5, 8.8, and 8.9 based on illustrations by Dick Rauh, Suk-Il Hong, and Khalida Lockheed.

Figure 8.6 based on an illustration by Suk-Il Hong and Khalida Lockheed.

Figure 8.21 courtesy of Manhattan Transfer; U.S. Tennis Open. Creative Director: Micha Riss, 3D animation and compositing: Paul Lipsy, Software: Softimage 3D, Softimage particle, Softimage eddie.

Figure 8.22 courtesy of Andreas Minas.

Figure 8.28, *Steamy Teacup*, © 1991 David S. Ebert.

Figures 8.29 and 14.18 courtesy of Bill Denahy-Visual Effects Supervisor, Scott Gordon and Paul Lipsky- 3D Animators, and Erik Day and Dave Larson- Junior 3D Animators.

Figure 9.1 based on an illustration by Dick Rauh, Suk-Il Hong, and Khalida Lockheed, after Eli Levinson.

Figures 9.3 and 9.4 based on illustrations by Dick Rauh, Suk-Il Hong, and Khalida Lockheed, after Roy Madsen.

Figure 9.6 based on an illustration by Dick Rauh, Khalida Lockheed, and Luis A. Camargo.

Figures 9.7, 10.1, 10.2, 10.4, 10.7, 10.10, 10.13, 10.15–10.39, 11.1, 11.3–11.9, 11.12, 11.38, 11.40–11.42, 11.45, 11.47, 11.49–11.51, 12.24, 13.5, 13.10, 13.12, 14.1, 14.5, 14.14–14.17, 14.22, 14.24, and 14.25 based on illustrations by Helen Bayona.

Figures 10.6, 10.8, and 10.9 based on illustrations by Joanna Morrison and Gwen Sylvan.

Figures 11.2, 11.10, 11.19–11.23, 11.43, and 11.48 based on illustrations by Kathy Konkle.

Figure 11.11 based on an illustration by Kathy Konkle, Luis A. Camargo, and Helen Bayona.

Figure 11.14 based on an illustration by Raymond Stivala.

Figures 11.25–11.29 based on illustrations by Brenda Garcia.

Figure 11.34 based on an illustration by Luis A. Camargo after D.C. Tao.

Figures 11.35 and 11.37 based on illustrations by D.C. Tao.

Figure 11.44 based on an illustration by Kathy Konkle and Luis A. Camargo.

Figures 12.1, 12.4, 12.10–12.12, 12.14–12.19, and 12.21 based on illustrations by Dena Slothower.

Figure 12.3 courtesy of Nick Foster and Dimitris Metatexas.

Figures 12.6–12.9 based on illustrations by Matt Alexander.

Figure 12.25 "Artificial Fishes: Biomechanics, Locomotion, Perception, and Behavior." By Xiaoyuan Tu and Demetri Terzopoulus. Presented at the SIGGRAPH 94 conference. Image courtesy of Xiaoyuan Tu and Demetri Terzopoulus.

Figure 12.26 Image Source: "Automated Learning of Muscle-Actuated Locomotion through Control Abstraction." Reprinted, by permission, from the ACM, copyright 1995 Association for Computing Machinery. Illustration courtesy of R. Grzeszczuk and D. Terzopoulos.

Figures 13.1 and 13.2 courtesy of Mechanism Digital, Inc.

Figures 3.12(a), 13.3, 13.24, 15.1–15.7, 15.9–15.13, 15.16, and 15.17 courtesy of the Judson Rosebush Company.

Figure 13.17 courtesy of The Effects House.

Figures 13.21 and 13.23 based on illustrations by Dick Rauh, Suk-Il Hong, and Helen Bayona.

Figure 13.26 courtesy of Peter Litwinowicz, copyright 1993 Apple Computers, Inc.

Figure 14.2 courtesy of Pierre Jasmine, Luis A. Camargo, and Helen Bayona.

Figure 14.8 based on an illustration by Luis A. Camargo and Helen Bayona.

Figure 14.10 from Macromedia Director.

Figure 14.19, *Hand-drawn Spaces*, copyright 1998 Merce Cunningham, Paul Kaiser, and Shelley Eshkar.

Figures 14.20 and 14.21, *Ghostcatching*, copyright 1998 Bill T. Jones, Paul Kaiser, and Shelley Eshkar.

Figures 15.14, *Rainforest*, and 15.15, *Oil Rig*, designed by Cuscuma Multimedia, exhibit design by DMCD Inc., New York. For Oculus: Executive Producer: Angela Bowen; CG Supervisor: Bruce Gionet.

About the Authors

Lynn Pocock is an artist, and associate professor of fine arts and coordinator of computer graphics at the New York Institute of Technology, where she teaches courses in 3D modeling, computer animation, drawing, and 2D computer imaging. Under her guidance, students explore concepts and storytelling through digital media. Formerly, Pocock served on the faculty of Pratt Institute in the Department of Computer Graphics and Interactive Media, where she was the primary advisor within the area of interactive media; she also served as the department's acting chair.

Pocock's artwork has often taken the form of experimental computer animation, which has been exhibited worldwide including the New York Film and Video Expo, the London International Film Festival, and SIGGRAPH's Computer Animation Festival. Her recent work takes the form of digital monotypes that explore personal issues of self and memory. Her prints have been exhibited internationally, including the SIGGRAPH Art Gallery, WOMENTEK, the New York Digital Salon, and most recently, on the cover of *Leonardo*—the Journal of the International Society for Arts, Sciences, and Technology.

In the past, Pocock explored the connections between the visual arts and artificial intelligence. Her research resulted in the unique automatic generation of 2D images and animation and the corresponding paper can be found in *Leonardo*. Other scholarly writing can be found in the *Art Journal*.

Her professional activities include chairing the SIGGRAPH 97 Ongoings: Fine Arts Gallery, where she organized one of the most important annual exhibits of digital art in the world. The exhibition featured a body of work for thirteen artists from around the world, and after a one-week showing in Los Angeles, the exhibit traveled around the world for two years. Pocock also directed an interactive educational project for the IBM Latin American Headquarters. In this capacity, she directed a small team of experts in completing an animated interactive session that could be used by IBM Latin American employees for training in new business procedures. She has also served as a consultant to the U.S. Defense Mapping Agency, developing software systems that would drive digital mapping systems.

Pocock has been extremely active within the ACM SIGGRAPH animation community. She coproduced the SIGGRAPH 93 Small Animation Theaters and twice she served as a member of the Computer Animation Festival juries (1996 and 1999). As such, she has been recognized as a leader within the field of computer animation. She also served on other SIGGRAPH juries, including Sketches and Applications, Art Papers, and the Art Gallery juries. Pocock has also lectured extensively, including at the School of Visual Arts, Pratt Institute, the Noyse Museum, the Living Arts Center, Art & Science Collaborations, Inc. (ASCI), Brooklyn Arts Summit, and SIGGRAPH conferences. She has been very active within the New York city digital arts community, serving in such roles as panelist/juror for the first computer artist grant given by the New York Foundation for the Arts; Vice Chair of the ACM SIGGRAPH NYC Board of Directors; lecturer at the Women in Cyberspace event for local high school students; and Co-chair, ACM SIGGRAPH NYC Annual Conference.

Currently, Pocock is the Conference Chair of SIGGRAPH 2001 in Los Angeles. In this role, she serves as the leader of the most important computer graphics event in the world, closely overseeing a team of approximately thirty-five volunteers and contractors and ultimately being responsible for the work of several thousand people. The conference includes a technical session of Papers and Panels, an Art Gallery, Computer Animation Festival, Courses, Creative Applications Lab, Educators Program, Emerging Technologies Venue, GraphicsNet, International Resources, SIGGRAPH Online, Pathfinders, SIGGRAPH TV, Sketches and Applications, Student Volunteer Program, and the Studio. The conference hosts approximately 40,000 attendees.

Pocock holds a Bachelor of Arts degree in Mathematics and Art from Rutgers University, a Master of Science degree in Computer Science from the University of Maryland, and a Master of Fine Arts degree in Computer Art from the University of Massachusetts.

Judson Rosebush is a director and producer of multimedia products and computer animation, as well as an author, artist, and media theorist. He graduated from the College of Wooster in 1969 and received a doctorate from Syracuse University. He has worked in radio and television broadcasting, film and video production, sound, print, and hypermedia, including CD-ROM and the Internet.

He combines this experience in media production with an ability to articulate the role of media in the world and the impact of digital technologies on the future. A frequent lecturer and author, Rosebush has shared his insights with students, media professionals, and the art and business communities.

He created his first computer animations in 1970 and founded and ran Digital Effects Inc. (1978–1985), the first digital computer animation company in New York City. Television credits include directing over 1000 commercials and logos for major advertising agencies and networks worldwide; feature film credits include Walt Disney's *Tron.* In the early 1990s, he coauthored and directed television programs on volume visualization, HDTV, and the quest for virtual reality.

The Judson Rosebush Company, founded in 1986 and located in New York City, is a creative multimedia studio currently producing commercial and entertainment CD-ROM titles and Web sites. The company completed its first CD-ROM, Isaac Asimov's *The Ultimate Robot,* published by Byron Preiss Publications and distributed by Microsoft, in 1993. Rosebush then directed Gahan Wilson's *Haunted House* CD-ROM, published by Microsoft in 1994. Other titles include *Ocean Voyager,* in 1995, and *The War in Vietnam,* a joint venture between CBS News and *The New York Times,* distributed by Macmillan Digital in 1996. In 1996 Rosebush's company delivered *Look What I See,* a CD-ROM title devoted to teaching art appreciation to young people, produced in conjunction with the Metropolitan Museum of Art. In 1997 he directed a three-screen project for the Whitney Museum, *The American Century,* which showcased super-HDTV and was also released as a CD-ROM. Numerous business-to-business CD titles include work for CBS, Dunn & Bradstreet, NYNEX, and Mars, Inc.

The Judson Rosebush Company currently publishes, under the name of Wildside Press, a line of fine art CD-ROMs of classic steel engravings. Titles include *People and Portraits, Designs and Dropcaps, Arms and Armor, Animals,* and *Castles and Cathedrals.*

Rosebush is coauthor of *Computer Graphics for Designers and Artists,* originally published in 1986 by Van Nostrand Reinhold, with a second edition released in 1994, and of *Electronic Publishing on CD-ROM,* published by O'Reilly in 1996. He is the former editor of *Pixel Vision* magazine, author of the serialized *Pixel Handbook,* and a columnist for *CD-ROM Professional.* His most cited writings include "The Proceduralist Manifesto," a statement on computer art published in *Leonardo,* and he is also known for his extensive writings on computer graphics and new media. More popular credits include articles in the *Village Voice* and *Rolling Stone* magazine.

Rosebush has exhibited his computer-generated drawings and films in numerous museum shows, and the drawings have been reproduced in hundreds of magazines and books, prompting speaking engagements as a national ACM lecturer. He is skilled at computer programming and system design as well as graphic arts. He is a consultant for media technology companies in America, Europe, and Brazil, has assisted Hammond World Atlas in designing their digital mapping system, worked with the Oxberry Corporation to install the first digital motion picture scanners in New York and Beijing, and performed expert witness work in federal court.